The Awkward State of Utah

THE AWKWARD STATE OF UTAH

Coming of Age in the Nation, 1896–1945

Charles S. Peterson & Brian Q. Cannon

UTAH STATE HISTORICAL SOCIETY

THE UNIVERSITY OF UTAH PRESS

Salt Lake City

Copublished with the Utah State Historical Society

Utah Division of
State History

A DIVISION OF THE UTAH
DEPARTMENT OF HERITAGE & ARTS

The Defiance House Man colophon is a registered trademark
of the University of Utah Press. It is based on a four-foot-tall
Ancient Puebloan pictograph (late PIII) near Glen Canyon, Utah.

19 18 17 16 15   1 2 3 4 5

LIBRARY OF CONGRESS CATALOGING-IN-PUBLICATION DATA
Peterson, Charles S.
  The awkward state of Utah : coming of age in the nation, 1896-1945 /
Charles S. Peterson and Brian Q. Cannon.
     pages cm
  Includes bibliographical references and index.
  ISBN 978-1-60781-421-4 (pbk. : alk. paper)
  ISBN 978-1-60781-422-1 (ebook)
1. Utah—History—19th century. 2. Utah—Politics and government—19th century. 3. Utah—
Economic conditions—19th century. 4. Utah—History—20th century. 5. Utah—Politics and
government—20th century. 6. Utah—Economic conditions—20th century. I. Cannon, Brian Q.
II. Utah State Historical Society. III. Title.
  F826.A94 2015
  979.2ʼ02—dc23

                            2015015499

Printed and bound by Sheridan Books, Inc., Ann Arbor, Michigan.

CONTENTS

ILLUSTRATIONS

ACKNOWLEDGMENTS

It is often said that some of the best things in life take time. We hope this manuscript vindicates that claim. With the encouragement and support of the Utah State Historical Society through its Utah centennial history project, Chas began drafting chapters in 1994, and Brian joined him as a coauthor in 1998. We hoped to complete the project by mid-1999 and made good progress, but when other pressing commitments interfered we reluctantly set this project aside. Despite good intentions, the incomplete manuscript languished until 2011, when we at last returned to it. We carefully revised and abbreviated what we had written, updated our manuscript and notes to reflect recent scholarship, and wrote three new chapters. Finally, in 2012, we had a manuscript ready to submit to John Alley at the University of Utah Press. We are grateful that John expressed interest and confidence in our work, encouraging us to complete it and submit it for publication. We were fortunate to work with him. We express appreciation to Richard Sadler, who provided sage advice and feedback at critical stages. Stan Layton and Phil Notarianni carefully reviewed the manuscript and offered excellent suggestions that guided us through the final revision process. The Utah State Historical Society and Brad Westwood, director of the Utah Division of State History, enthusiastically supported publication of our work. Finally, we express appreciation to our families for their love and support.

INTRODUCTION

When Utah became a state on January 4, 1896, Thomas S. Seymour was nearly eighteen years old. The son of Mormon converts who had emigrated from the British Isles, Seymour had been born in a small home in Rockport, Summit County, the sixth of eleven children. Although the transcontinental railroad passed through Echo Junction, only a couple dozen miles north of Rockport, Seymour's daily life was little removed from the primitive living conditions characteristic of frontier settlements. "The only schooling we got was from father.... We would get snowed in, in the winter. It was so far away from school that we couldn't walk or ride the oxen in the bad weather," he recalled in 1972. Homes and public buildings were heated with woodstoves, and candles and coal oil lamps provided light after dark. The Seymours were too poor to buy a team of horses, and it took three days by ox team for the family to travel from Rockport to Salt Lake because the oxen were "as slow as coal tar."

Seymour's adult working life roughly coincided with Utah's first half century as a state, bookended by his call to serve a mission for the Church of Jesus Christ of Latter-day Saints (LDS) in Kansas in 1898 and his retirement from the restaurant business at the end of World War II in 1945. It was a momentous era of modernization, incorporation, and globalization for the state and its residents. Seymour's career reflected the impact of these momentous changes upon ordinary Utahns. In his twenties he tended horses and drove teams at a livery stable and then took a job driving a horse-drawn mail wagon between Kamas and Park City. Then in 1914 he parked his wagon in a shed and began delivering mail by truck. In 1924 Seymour moved to a tract home in Salt Lake City and began selling mass-produced electrical appliances. Commercial airline passenger flights in and out of Salt Lake began a year after Seymour moved there, and in 1931 he opened a café at the airport. Over the next fourteen years while operating the Salt Lake Airport Café, he met travelers from across the nation and from abroad. Once he climbed into the cockpit of a plane and with a bit of help piloted the aircraft over mountains and valleys where he had driven ox and horse teams. "He may be…the only man who has ever flown an airplane and driven oxen," journalist Denise Edwards speculated in 1972.[1]

Utahns of Seymour's generation witnessed profound changes in the fifty years between statehood and the end of World War II. They felt the reverberations of armed conflicts on distant continents, as Utah's geographic isolation was breached and Utah citizens traversed the globe to fight in the Spanish-American and Philippine-American conflicts and in two world wars. The seeds of what would later be called globalism were planted in this era. Lifestyles changed as even many farms and small communities received electrical service, telephones, and indoor plumbing. In a drawn-out confrontation, urban and industrial influences supplanted agrarian traditions, displacing people socially, draining the countryside of its population and vigor, and producing quite as critical a crisis in values and self-identification as had the Mormon question earlier. New mass media, including radio and film, enveloped Utahns in a nationwide culture of entertainment, news, and fashion. Educational opportunities expanded, and literacy improved as school attendance became compulsory; many of Seymour's generation did not finish the eighth grade, but high school attendance became the norm for their children and many enrolled in college.

In this volume we use historian Alan Trachtenberg's term *incorporation* to encapsulate many of the changes that occurred in the period of early statehood, Utah's sometimes awkward years of adolescence and maturation. The term encompasses the rise of national corporations, including railroads and smelters, and large-scale systems of production, distribution, and marketing as well as mass labor movements. But it also entails agricultural production for distant markets, Utahns' involvement in national political movements, and the socialization of each subset of the state's population, including Native Americans, Mormons, and immigrants within the democratic, corporate culture that became twentieth-century America.[2]

The legacy of incorporation was particularly pronounced in the mining sector. In 1896 copper, the mineral that would become Utah's leading export, had not yet been exploited on a large scale. Over the next half century, the Beehive State's low-grade ores, concentrated in the Oquirrh Range, were exploited thanks to new technology and heavy investment from outside the region. Mining and smelting built enormous fortunes, although much of the wealth flowed eastward into the pockets of absentee investors. Nevertheless, mining was good for the state's economy: it swelled the tax base and provided steady employment for a new professional class of salaried engineers and scientists. It also created relatively high-paying jobs for thousands of blue-collar workers in boom times. Unfortunately, miners also endured dangerous working conditions and a boom-and-bust economy with reduced wages and layoffs in bad times. The corporate, colonial economy of mining linked the state's fortunes to domestic and foreign markets and producers. The economic inequities in the mining sector radicalized some Utahns and led others to join unions and participate in strikes.

Agriculture also changed in response to processes of incorporation between statehood and World War II. The process of incorporation was fragmentary. Factory farms were rare, and while immense ranches such as Deseret Land and Livestock incorporated and built fortunes for their boards and shareholders, most Utah farms remained small operations. Although some village-oriented farmers resisted change, many small producers played the market as they transitioned from subsistence farming, which had been the backbone of the Mormon village system, to cash crops. Expensive, speculative reclamation projects in places such as the Bear River Valley, Delta, and Grass Valley; a network of agricultural experiment stations and farms; and new opportunities to sell farm products, including milk, wheat, sugar beets, and tomatoes, to corporate canneries, sugar factories, and condenseries with names such as Del Monte, Utah and Idaho Sugar, and Borden encouraged farmers to commercialize their operations. Small producers' incomes rose as they produced for the market, but some complained about the concentrated wealth and monopolistic practices of the corporations to whom they sold their goods. Moreover, tied as it was to national and even international markets, the demand for Utah products oscillated.

The federal government's investment in the economy, a key catalyst of Utah's incorporation, expanded enormously between statehood and World War II. Government policy and investment had significantly influenced Utah's economy in its territorial era, beginning with the construction of Camp Floyd in 1858 and extending to the Sherman Silver Purchase Act of 1890 that guaranteed a market for Utah's silver mines. But the government's investments in the territorial era were modest compared to what occurred between statehood and World War II. Federal largesse included land grants when Utah became a state and expensive, sophisticated water systems engineered by the Reclamation Service and its successor, the Bureau of Reclamation. In the 1910s Congress began to heavily subsidize highway construction. As national forests, national parks, and national monuments were designated, additional funds and jobs flowed to Utah. Starting with the massive Reconstruction Finance Corporation during Herbert Hoover's presidency and extending to a potpourri of government agencies known by their "alphabet-soup" acronyms during the administration of Franklin Roosevelt, federal dollars poured into Utah; the state ranked ninth in the nation in per capita investment by the federal government during the Depression. Then during World War II, unprecedented levels of investment created a mammoth steel plant in Utah Valley, a small-arms factory that became Salt Lake County's leading employer, a huge Japanese internment camp near Delta, ten defense installations, and a military hospital. By 1945 Utah was connected at the hip to the federal government, heavily dependent on federal investment.

Most Utahns anticipated in 1896 that statehood would ensure greater self-government and lessen federal oversight. Statehood did bring an end to federally appointed officials in the state's executive branch, and it expanded Utah's role and clout on Capitol Hill in Washington. But the amount and scope of federal oversight multiplied over the next half century. Both the executive and the legislative branches increasingly regulated economic activities, including mining, grazing, and timber harvesting on public lands. National concerns about big business and monopoly made Utah's mining and sugar industries the object of federal investigations and regulatory oversight. Beginning in the 1930s banks were subjected to federal oversight, and bank deposits were federally insured. Congress established minimum wages for workers and guaranteed their right to join unions and bargain collectively with their employers.

In the decades after 1896 Utah experienced an influx of thousands of southern and eastern European and Japanese immigrants, a key force in linking Utah to distant lands. Recruited to work in the state's mines and smelters, these immigrants took part in a dramatic intercontinental migration, impelled by American industrial growth and the poverty, insufficient land, and political instability in their homelands. Defenders of traditional America charged that these "new immigrants" were inferior, dangerous, and incapable of assimilating because they were largely non-Protestant, nationalistic, poorly educated, and dark complexioned. Their migration created islands of ethnic diversity, particularly in Salt Lake, Tooele, and Carbon Counties, drawing Utahns into national debates regarding 100 percent Americanism and immigration restriction and providing fertile ground for emerging class consciousness and an incipient labor movement. As they crisscrossed oceans, these migrants developed transnational identities along with social networks and economic linkages that spanned the globe.

In the first half century of statehood, networks and linkages that crossed traditional ethnoreligious divisions multiplied. Mormon leaders, who had used business and political connections to facilitate statehood, embraced corporate models and methods in the new century as the means of promoting the region's economic development. The LDS Church did not withdraw entirely from politics in the first fifty years of statehood, but the extensive involvement and fierce partisanship that had pitted Mormons against non-Mormons in territorial politics had dissipated by 1945, after tumultuous struggles. A new political organization representing the interests of Gentiles and lapsed Mormons, the American Party, complicated Utah politics from 1904 to 1910 and for a time controlled the governments of Ogden and Salt Lake. Overtones of Mormon-Gentile tension also animated a secretive political fraternity, the Order of Sevens, during the 1920s. But by the 1940s, inveterate political infighting between Mormons and Gentiles on the state level was largely outmoded; Utah elected non-Mormon governors with substantial support from Mormon voters in 1916, 1924, and 1928, and the Order of Sevens permanently collapsed in the late 1920s.

Having reached their nadir in the mid-1890s, Utah's Indian populations began to rise. Their incorporation within the national polity advanced in seesaw fashion, sometimes igniting forceful resistance: early in the new century the last gasp of militant resistance occurred in San Juan County, and hundreds of aggrieved Utes sought unsuccessfully to ally with the Sioux against the United States. Utah's Indians became US citizens by virtue of legislation, including the Indian Citizenship Act of 1924, and hundreds of them fought for the United States in the Second World War. Much of the Utes' land base was whittled away, as their reservation was subdivided under the federal policy of allotment. New reservations were created for the Paiutes and Goshutes, and the Navajo reservation's boundary was extended northward to the San Juan River in southeastern Utah. Federal Indian policy sought the assimilation of Indians into the Utah mainstream until the 1930s, when the government began encouraging Indians to revive traditions, increase their land base, and elect tribal governments.

By the time Utah celebrated its fiftieth anniversary, Thomas Seymour and his cohort ranked among the eldest 10 percent of the population. As the following chapters demonstrate, the changes stretching across their lifetimes had profoundly altered the Beehive State and its residents. Utah had become more heterogeneous, urbanized, and economically stratified, and the state's economic and social linkages to the nation and world had multiplied.

I

POLITICS AT THE TURN OF THE CENTURY

ERA OF GOOD FEELINGS

Just after noon on January 6, 1896, the government of the state of Utah convened for the first time. Coming after nearly a half century of conflict, it was a moment rich with portent, comparable for Utahns, in its symbolic meaning, to the signing of the Declaration of Independence. In a more immediate way it represented the promise of home rule and an escape from disruptive tensions in Utah society. To pay homage to that portent and give it life, Utah's first state officers and more than ten thousand citizens crowded into the Mormon Tabernacle in Salt Lake City.

The mood at the tabernacle, as elsewhere in the new state, was one of general satisfaction and immediate celebration but not of unrestrained optimism. For the moment, at least, most felt events had come to a significant juncture, that times past and future were joined in statehood and full national citizenship. People were grateful as Mormon president Wilford Woodruff's opening prayer was read and Methodist reverend Thomas C. Iliff offered the benediction. Many were also proud as their first state governor, native son Heber M. Wells, was sworn in and read a long inaugural address covering Utah's entire past and much of its future, including the tasks of self-government that began as he spoke.[1]

In all, citizens could hardly have gone about these first functions of statehood with more self-conscious decorum. Electrically lighted in the huge flag that spread across the tabernacle's ceiling, the forty-fifth star heralded the promise of statehood and a new century. The wintry shadow from the temple next door spoke of tensions unfinished and of hoped-for frameworks in religion, business, and politics. The cannonade echoing from Fort Douglas bore witness not merely of the federal presence, as in times past, but of union and the sisterhood of states.

This first meeting of statehood was an intensively managed event. Aimed at the future, it was a statement not fully representative of Utah, but orchestrated in hopes that self-identity and national image would be molded. The statehood ceremony was a high point in what event managers had been calling "the era of good feeling." Thoughts of the bitter acrimony and ongoing conflict that had characterized so much of Utah's territorial history were out of mind for the moment. Phrases such as "Star of the West," "Queen of the Rockies," and "Empire State of the…Mountains," hackneyed though they seem, reflected a boom-engendered optimism and a determined vision of glories to come.[2] Yet the tabernacle audience could not but have been keenly aware of contradictions and challenges inherent in the era's good feeling. Now, well over a hundred years later, we may be forgiven if we wonder at the juxtaposing of promise and new conflict reflected in the temple shadow, in the cannonade, and in the flag's new star.

THE BIPOLAR TERRITORY AND CORPORATE TRANSFORMATION

The road to statehood had been long and difficult. Although its walls may be exaggerated, a bipolar regime existed during the territorial period. People lived apart. Virtually every walk of life was invested with distance. Mormons had been expelled, threatened with extermination, massacred, and accused of heinous crimes and tyrannies. Gentiles had been affronted in their religion, impugned in their morality, isolated socially, and excluded politically, and at Mountain Meadows some had been massacred by Mormons. Newspapers gave the language of divisiveness printed form. The People's Party of the Mormons and the Liberal Party of the Gentiles gave politics a single issue and, America's "wall of separation" notwithstanding, carried religion directly into the functions of state.[3] Federal intervention was ongoing. As Mormon leader and former territorial delegate George Q. Cannon recognized in 1891, "a chasm" had pitted "class against class."[4]

Although all of Utah's statehood movements have rightly been viewed within the context of this religious and political split, the statehood movement of the 1890s was actually a great deal more. In an immediate and direct sense, it was the product of an economic boom in Utah and the West during the late 1880s and of a growing national determination to round out the sisterhood of states into a continental empire and to incorporate the natural resources of the West into the nation's burgeoning industrial and urban complex.[5] Statehood and the adjustments that followed were part of a larger national transformation then under way. Called the "Civil War for Incorporation" by historians Alan Trachtenberg and Richard Maxwell Brown, among others, it involved changes in American society quite as profound as, if less violent than, the economic and cultural disruptions confronted in the Civil War.[6] The corporate system "spread across the continent" between 1865 and 1920, affecting every phase of life. It tightened "systems of transport and communication," extended urban forms and the "market economy," and reshaped "the cultural perceptions" on which society rested. "New hierarchies of control" emerged along with new "forms and methods in industry and business." It was a "change so swift" that contemporaries were often "unable to fathom" its extent.[7]

At the center of this transformation was the corporation itself. Providing "capitalists with a more far-reaching instrument than earlier forms of ownership," corporations strengthened the alliance between business and politics, isolated businessmen from economic risk, established "virtually self-perpetuating boards of directors," and substituted new values and icons for those of agrarianism and rural community.[8] The directors of Mormondom in the turn-of-the-century decades made themselves at home in the disciplined and institutionally directed boardrooms of corporate America. More locally, association in commercial clubs, the Chamber of Commerce, professional societies, and other booster organizations increasingly allowed Mormons and Gentiles to work within the larger framework of change growing from the move to corporate culture. In this shifting climate Gentiles found new appeal in the politics of statehood, and Mormon leaders found conventional avenues in which they could exercise power.[9]

With a major economic boom in full course, the colonialism of the "distracted" territory began to yield to characteristics of statehood by 1890. Silver and lead mining prospered as never before. Smelters, railroads, and streetcar services were extended and improved. Commerce, livestock, real estate, agricultural markets, manufacturing, and cities all showed strength. An affluent elite began to call Utah home. A few, such as the Walker brothers, Thomas Kearns, Joseph Delamar, Enos Wall, John J. Daly, David Keith, John Judge, A. W. McCune, Jonathan Browning, and David Eccles, lived conspicuously. Building mansions, traveling abroad, and maintaining civic and educational philanthropies, they gave Utah an economic profile it had never enjoyed before.[10] The professions took hold: engineering, architecture, medicine, journalism, and publication began to join the law, the clergy, and public service as viable opportunities. Mormons were learning to "acquire property and take care of it."[11] Economic development broadened associations and expectations and introduced class divisions and competing ideological loyalties.

During the 1890s, more than ever before, Utahns questioned the "old regime" of the bipolar territory. Could Utah, and indeed the nation, afford a territory whose main business was division? To an increasing number of Utah Gentiles and American businessmen and politicians, the answer was no. In Washington increasingly tough legislation and court rulings jump-started statehood as they disfranchised polygamists and all Utah women, seized church property, and threatened to destroy the church as a temporal institution. Dissatisfaction with the old order was apparent among young Utahns, who sought education outside, organized Democratic clubs, worked for municipal change, and searched for a new social order. One of their number, Isaac Russell, characterized the "new generation" as "striving by every possible means to work away from the old issue [of polygamy]." They were interested in joining hands across religious lines to "pull together" in order to advance economic development, "welcome the tourist, to make him at home, to get him over certain old ideas."[12]

With the boom at high tide and Mormon women and polygamists excluded from the polls, the Liberals drove the terror of lost power deep in Mormon vitals in 1889 and 1890 when they mobilized the new workforce and dissenting Mormons to win municipal elections in Ogden and Salt Lake for the first time. To meet the mounting crisis, the church hierarchy worked within the context of its growing relationship with the business community. Agents were stationed in the power centers of the East. Lobbies curried favor with the railroad and sugar trusts. Special envoys approached high officials of both national parties who made it indelibly clear: polygamy had to go, and church influence in politics had to be modified. In exchange, as Mormon Democrat James H. Moyle recognized, church leaders gained access to the "environment of wealth," which "altered" their "point of view" and expectations.[13]

UNYIELDING PARTISANSHIP

The first steps in dismantling the old regime were quickly taken. The Manifesto ostensibly ending polygamous marrying was issued in the fall of 1890. Although tithing collections were interrupted and church finance was in disarray, Mormon leaders established, among other things, the sugar beet industry, a giant electric works in Ogden Canyon, the great Saltair amusement facility, and new saltworks on Great Salt Lake, and they pushed railroad schemes toward Los Angeles.[14] Division into national parties was achieved in 1892, with top Mormon leaders favoring a balance of church members in the two parties but working to deliver Republican votes to sustain their developing alliance with the corporate world. Young Utah Democrat Joseph L. Rawlins and Frank J. Cannon, Republican son of a Mormon counselor, represented the new order as territorial delegates.[15] Nationally, the drive for punitive legislation temporarily lost steam. Amnesty was granted to polygamists in 1892, and an enabling act endorsed statehood in 1894.

With the economic boom that had fanned the fires of union now banked by depression, the "era of good feeling" reached its high point in the Constitutional Convention of 1895. Made up of fifty-nine Republicans, forty-eight Democrats, seventy-nine Mormons, twenty-eight Gentiles—and presided over by reenfranchised but still polygamist Apostle John Henry Smith—the convention treated Utahns to the spectacle of Mormon hammering Mormon and Gentile baiting Gentile on such issues as women's suffrage, Prohibition, and protectionism. Ultimately, the state constitution not only ensured women's right to vote but also guaranteed religious freedom and bravely, but somewhat prematurely, prohibited polygamy and church interference in state functions.[16] As it was completed, Charles S. Varian, formerly a "relentless" foe of Mormons but by all odds the convention's "most active member," optimistically concluded that the constitution had buried "the dead past." It was, of course, too much to hope for, but, as Varian put it, they had indeed "fought the good fight."[17]

With constitution in hand and statehood a fact, Utahns of 1896 faced a half century in which the old and the new acted upon each other to form the state's character. In large measure this was worked out through political processes.

In the annals of the early state the politics of the 1896–1903 period stand out. Its politics were almost unbelievably volatile. The state was quick to pay heed to appealing regional issues and national figures and, more than many new states of the period, was subjected to national reform pressures. Tensions continued to arise from polygamy and church influence in politics. Partisanship was intense both within groups and between them. As longtime Democrat James Moyle put it, "More bitter and unyielding partisanship never developed anywhere." Moyle laid much of this to the Mormon tendency to "treat politics on the same principle as religion—truth vs. untruth, the one all right, the other all wrong."[18]

Political actors of the era included a remarkable set of politicians, if indeed not statesmen, and a fair number of the West's most striking entrepreneurs and church leaders. Some had been lured by the boom. Some had come by a process of political selection that because of the furor may have attracted men a cut above the ordinary carpetbag appointee. Others were homegrown, products of the extraordinary pressures of the same controversy. Important issues included start-up procedures, silver, polygamy, two-party politics, and the proper role of the church.

Suggesting just how fragile the Constitutional Convention accord was were tensions that asserted themselves in the special election of 1895, the first of a veritable explosion of elections necessary to start state government. In November citizens were to vote on the constitution, choose state executive officers for a five-year term, and elect legislators for a one-year term who would elect US senators.

Although there was much apprehension that something would still scuttle statehood, the constitution passed easily in a 31,305 to 7,687 vote. Republicans made the best of the "Cleveland panic" and of the uneasy truce between onetime Liberals such as A. L. Thomas, former territorial governor, and C. C. Goodwin of the *Salt Lake Tribune*, on the one hand, and top church leaders, including Apostles Joseph F. Smith and John Henry Smith, who were leading many Mormons into the Republican fold, on the other.

Republican candidates in 1895 included Utah-born Mormon banker Heber M. Wells as candidate for governor and a slate of lesser state officers. Gentile Clarence E. Allen was running for Congress, and Republican candidates for the one-year legislature looked expectantly toward their role as electors of Utah's first senators.

Headed by Orlando W. Powers, "peerless orator" who had led the Salt Lake Liberals to victory in 1890, the Democratic organization attracted many prominent Mormons, including Brigham H. Roberts, an independently inclined member of the church's Seventies Quorum, and maverick Apostle Moses Thatcher. Also much in evidence in the campaign of 1895 were suffrage workers Zina D. H. Young, widow of Brigham Young and president of the General Relief Society Board (1888–1901); Bathsheba W. Smith; Jane Snyder Richards; and Emily S. Richards.

Democrats bitterly denounced the church for controlling the election but continued to play for the Mormon vote. In September John T. Caine, former territorial delegate, was nominated for governor and Roberts for Congress, together with a heavily Mormon slate of state officers and legislators.[19] Democrats selected Thatcher and Joseph L. Rawlins as their US senatorial nominees.[20]

On Election Day the Republicans won across the board, and Utah moved on to its rendezvous with statehood. Not surprisingly, a pressing matter involved finance. With the former banker Wells's guidance, legislators passed statutes governing taxation and distribution of revenues and issued bonds to cover an indebtedness of two hundred thousand dollars carried forward from the territory. A state court system was provided, while the penitentiary, reform school, insane asylum, and school for the deaf, dumb, and blind, institutions that had been distributed in cities around the territory as a form of patronage, were formally brought under state auspices. Commissions, staffs, and budgets were authorized for each, as they were for the University of Utah and the Agricultural College. Statewide farmers' institutes were authorized for the Agricultural College, and steps were taken to accept a federal gift of sixty acres of the Fort Douglas reservation for a University of Utah campus. Rented quarters for state government were found in the newly completed City and County Building and at the "Industrial Home," a refuge for displaced polygamist women for which there had been little need. Governor Wells performed much of his official work in his private office at the State Bank of Utah.[21]

Reform legislation involved considerable, but conventional, public response. A controversial measure providing nonpartisan control of police and fire departments passed. An even more explosive proposal to regulate railroads failed when railroad interests warned that regulations would arrest construction and curtail economic development. A hotly contested act limiting the workday in underground mines and smelters to eight hours passed and was almost immediately upheld in the Supreme Court case of *Holden v. Hardy*.[22]

If the legislative work seemed routine, the first legislature's electoral function was not. By some untraced process it was understood that one senator would be Gentile and the other Mormon. The Democrats were out of the running, but there was no dearth of candidates. Prominently mentioned were the *Tribune*'s redoubtable editor, C. C. Goodwin; C. W. Bennett, a Liberal Republican and longtime Washington lobbyist; O. J. Saulsbury, a mining man and regular Republican who stood well with the Mormons; and Arthur Brown, a lawyer with large ambitions and limited integrity. In addition, there was Isaac Trumbo, a Californian with Mormon business and family ties who in expectation of political preference had lobbied tirelessly for statehood but whose pretensions now seemed unwarranted. The front-runner was Frank J. Cannon, the last territorial delegate to whom a majority of legislators were said to be pledged. Young Cannon had rendered signal service during the late 1880s and 1890s. Keeping his prospects in the air, however, was the possibility that his father, counselor in the First Presidency George Q. Cannon, would run. Rumors spread that President Wilford Woodruff felt it was God's will that the senior Cannon reassume his doubly anointed role as church leader and head of Utah's Washington delegation. The *Salt Lake Tribune* fumed, and Democrats looked on uneasily. Church leaders expressed various positions privately and sought to measure how stable legislative pledges were. It was a sensitive situation, but the younger Cannon was not swayed. A day or two before the filing deadline, the father finally bowed out, and the legislature (forty Mormons and twenty-three Gentiles) proceeded to elect Frank J. Cannon and Arthur Brown, who determined by lot that Cannon would have the four-year term and Brown the one-year term.[23]

Meantime, events moved toward a showdown for B. H. Roberts and Moses Thatcher, whose political independence was a matter of deep concern in their churchly councils. Roberts's case was long-standing and compounded by internal issues but proved the easier to resolve. He was brilliant, versatile, independent, opinionated, and, once engaged, unwavering in principle and unflinching in combat. He had extended Mormon theology enough to invite close scrutiny, and on one or two points outright opposition, among his church superiors but had maintained close working relations with them and had made relatively few concessions to the corporate world.

However, Roberts's penchant for partisanship and independence got him in deep trouble in 1894 and 1895. Paying no heed to the presidency's position, he had opposed the inclusion of women's suffrage in the constitution in a noisy fight that attracted nationwide attention and sharp female enmity. Similarly, as we have seen, he ignored "counsel" when the Democratic Party nominated him for Congress in September 1895. Early in 1896 church leaders, led by Joseph F. Smith of the First Presidency, moved to bring him in line. At his trial they threatened, pleaded, argued, and finally suspended his right to act officially, whereupon he signed a political manifesto and was readmitted in good standing.[24]

Thatcher had been at cross-purposes with church leaders even longer. In part this reflected a true liberal's appreciation for the individual vis-à-vis authority and community. Even before 1887 he had resisted further concentration of power in the hands of President John Taylor.[25] Thatcher was especially critical of the free political hand given Joseph F. Smith and John Henry Smith in delivering a Republican vote and saw efforts to restrict his own activities as invasions of "his rights as a citizen."[26]

Brought frequently to heel, Thatcher relapsed as often. No disciplinary action was taken until the April 1896 conference. Even then action seemed more general than specific when all of the church's general authorities were asked to sign what came to be known as the "Political Manifesto," which made it clear that for general authorities, church obligation superseded political duty but left the door ajar for them to accept political office when circumstance seemed to require.[27] Thatcher refused to sign the Political Manifesto, with the result that his name was left off the list presented for the conference's sustaining vote. It was a serious reprimand that placed Thatcher's ecclesiastical status in question, but it stopped short of resolving the controversy. He was still a political power to be reckoned with. The election of 1896 was at hand, and the prospects were good for Democrats.

THE ELECTION OF 1896 AND A FALSE DAWN

Just how good, Utah Democrats could not realize, but 1896 was their election year. In the short run they won from the "top to the bottom of their ticket."[28] William Jennings Bryan took about sixty-four thousand votes, or 82 percent of the total, compared to national winner William McKinley's 17 percent. In the congressional race William H. King launched Utah's most long-lived legislative career of the twentieth century when he carried 61 percent of the vote, reportedly causing Reed Smoot to quip that he did "not believe in sending a man to Congress who is all wind." Democratic judges won throughout the state, and in the legislature Democrats took more than 86 percent of the house seats and all senate seats except one carried by a Populist-fusionist.[29] Waiting in the wings for the legislative session in January

1897 were senatorial hopefuls such as Joseph Rawlins, H. P. Henderson, Orlando W. Powers, and the controversial Thatcher.

Nationally, the Democrats' campaign for free and unlimited coinage of silver was a key issue. Western in origin and nationalizing in influence, it dated back at least twenty years to the "Crime of '73," when coinage of silver dollars was dropped. Silver-producing mountain states prospered when production was stimulated by the Bland-Allison Act of 1878 and the Sherman Silver Purchase Act of 1890 but were hard hit by the 1893 repeal of the Sherman Silver Purchase Act by Congress and by the depression of the 1890s. In 1896 the gold standard and high tariff stance of the Republicans alienated silver and cheap money advocates, who gathered under Bryan's free-silver banner.[30]

If silver was dominant nationally, it was a contagion in Utah. Few questioned that its "magic appeal" would "stimulate mining," produce "a mild inflation," strengthen agriculture, and bring prosperity.[31] In addition, silver had a powerful symbolic meaning in silver-producing states, all of which were catapulted into unwanted prominence by its national attention.

Politically, women achieved a standard of involvement in the election of 1896 and the ensuing legislatures that would not be resumed for decades. Emmeline B. Wells, longtime feminist and editor, was continued as vice chairperson by the Republican Party. Along with Lucy A. Clark of Davis County, she ran unsuccessfully for the state senate, as did Martha Campbell of Salt Lake County and Mrs. F. E. Stewart of Utah County for the house. The Democrats sent four women to the national convention as alternate delegates. For state representatives they nominated and elected Eurithe LaBarthe of Salt Lake County and Sarah E. Anderson of Weber County. Also elected was Senator Martha Hughes Cannon, Salt Lake City physician and fourth wife of Angus M. Cannon, a Republican state senate candidate, who as president of the Salt Lake Stake had been one of the churchmen who objected to the role of Democratic women in 1895.

The domestic aspect of a contest in which Dr. Cannon got 11,413 votes to her husband's 8,742, along with her considerable achievement in the legislature and the added tension of a critical national election, has obscured 1896's importance as a false dawn of equality for Utah women.[32] Democratic candidate Aquila Nebeker, a Rich County rancher who beat Lucy Clark for a house seat, revealed a common bias when he complained that victory would reflect "no credit" and that defeat would make him a "laughing stock."[33] In the 1897 legislature Eurithe LaBarthe was associated with the so-called High Hat Law, making removal of head wear mandatory in public places and with a resolution requesting the United States to donate the "Industrial Home" to Utah for educational and benevolent purposes. Sarah Anderson, who had unsuccessfully argued in a court case that the state constitution gave women the right to vote in the election of 1895, left little mark on the 1897 legislature.[34]

Martha Hughes Cannon has become the best known of the women legislators of 1897. She had studied medicine at the University of Michigan, practiced privately in Salt Lake, taken advantage of time on the polygamous underground to visit European hospitals, established a training school for nurses, and played active roles in the national woman suffrage movement. In the 1897 legislature she introduced three bills: Senate Bill 31 to "Protect the Health of Women and Girl Employees"; SB 22, "Providing for Compulsory Education of Deaf, Dumb and Blind Children"; and SB 27, "Creating a State Board of Health." Cannon was shortly appointed to the resulting State Board of Health and in the 1899 legislature introduced SB 40, providing health regulations. Significantly, she voted her own mind in the senatorial elections of both years, casting her ballot for Moses Thatcher in 1897 in a vote that ran counter to her husband's wishes and in 1899 ignoring rumors of vote buying to support millionaire A. W. McCune throughout the 164 ballots of a futile electoral exercise.[35]

A colleague of Martha Cannon in 1899 was Democratic state senator Alice Merrill Horne. A graduate of the University of Utah, Horne had toured the art galleries of Europe and America and became one of Utah's greatest advocates of the arts. In the legislature of 1898 Horne introduced "the University Free Scholarship Bill" and supported other measures related to higher education and public health. However, she is best remembered for her bill establishing the Utah Arts Institute. Like Cannon, Horne was appointed to the State Board of Health by Governor Wells, who, in appointing the two Democratic women, was bound by no narrow partisanship.[36]

Interest in new voters extended to Salt Lake City's African Americans. In this case Republicans held their own.[37] A small population of blacks had come to Utah with the Mormons and the railroad and had been recently augmented by black regiments at Fort Douglas and Fort Duchesne. By the mid-1890s a community of sufficient complexity existed to give partisan division a voice in the *Broad Ax*, edited by Julius Taylor, a Democrat, and the *Utah Plain Dealer*, edited by Republican W. W. Taylor (no relation). Blacks also organized a variety of political and social clubs and called for a share in political patronage. They debated the merits of the two parties, and Julius Taylor extolled "the New Democracy." Most important, Salt Lake City Republicans nominated W. W. Taylor for the legislature and supported him in his campaign call to open public places to blacks. If the *Tribune* was less enthusiastic about Taylor's candidacy than some whites, it was nevertheless supportive. The Democratic *Herald*, on the other hand, printed racial cartoons. With 6,512 votes Taylor, like other Republicans, was defeated. In a less meaningful gesture, the victorious Democratic legislature designated blacks Julius Taylor as messenger to the senate and Henry Durham as sergeant at arms.[38]

Still pending after the general 1896 election were the senatorial elections and the Thatcher controversy. In mid-November Thatcher threw down the gauntlet when he told a *Tribune* writer he would be a candidate. The *Deseret News* insisted it was an assault on the "organic existence of the Church." Evidently agreeing, the Quorum of the Twelve dropped Thatcher from its ranks on November 19. During the next month he maneuvered through the mails for a public hearing. When it was not forthcoming, he released correspondence about his case to the newspapers. In addition, several broadsides were issued in December attacking and defending Thatcher. Rarely has an issue been more bitter or more fully aired.[39]

Thus informed, the legislature went through fifty-three ballots. Electioneering was intense, interest was high, and the City and County Building was thronged. Through most of the balloting, Thatcher led. Gentile H. P. Henderson, who was seen as the church candidate, was close behind. Toward the end Henderson's support shifted to Joseph L. Rawlins, giving him the necessary thirty-two votes. Although he was seriously ill throughout the entire controversy, Thatcher acted with dignity, expressing himself with restraint and with telling effect. "There is room" in Utah, he said, for "all societies and all organizations, but they must confine themselves within the proper limits. (Applause.) He who desires peace and prosperity for Utah will draw the line sharply between the rights of the citizens, the powers of the State and those of the church. (Applause.)"[40] Within a year Thatcher faced a church trial, recanted many of the charges he had made, and accepted the Political Manifesto but was not reseated in his quorum.

THE ROBERTS CASE AND A SPLENDID LITTLE WAR

In the years after 1897 the good feeling that carried the statehood movement decayed rapidly. In part this was due to the softening of the boom-engendered consensus that a harmonious economic climate was Utah's first order of business. In addition, certain symbols of goodwill had come and gone. Spent was the solidifying influence of the half-centennial celebration on July 24, 1897, which gave Utah an entry in the parade of expositions and fairs then much in vogue. The death of Wilford Woodruff the next year took a nonthreatening figure out of the picture. And then, too, as times changed, it became increasingly apparent that it had been overly optimistic to hope the division over political rule could simply be walked away from.

Less apparent but in the long run inseparable from political influence and its exercise was the fact that polygamy did not end in 1890. Challenged on what they took to be a divine imperative, Mormon leaders publicly closed the door on polygamy but privately left it ajar. Originally announcing the Manifesto in ambiguous language and circumstances, they were soon crowded into statements that gave it public status as God's revealed word and extended its meaning to terminate existing plural relationships (cohabitation) as well as prohibit future plural marriages. From the first, however, church leaders continued to cohabit with pre-Manifesto wives and families. They also secretly authorized and performed new polygamous marriages, erecting elaborate screens to hide them. Some also gave quiet voice to their faith that polygamy would be restored, implying that its restriction was little more than a temporary dodge. Confusion resulted among rank-and-file Mormons, who were less than sure what the signals called for. Mormon liberals were disappointed and discomfited, fundamentalists were determined, and most established polygamists cohabited to some degree. Some Gentiles apparently took closet polygamy to be a Mormon way of life that would pass with time. Others angrily reported it, including the members of the last Utah Commission. Officially, goodwill and the demands of economic development, statehood, and partisan politics overrode distrust until 1898.[41]

As the campaign of 1898 began, Utah Democrats had reason to hope that at least some of 1896's victories might be repeated. Silver still promised to offset the continuing depression as an issue, and Republicans appeared ready to split again. Democrats still had holdover strength in the legislature, and B. H. Roberts was willing to run again for Congress, this time with the permission if not the full blessing of his church colleagues. True, Roberts was the admitted husband of three wives (one married after 1890) and the father of recently born twins. On the other hand, relatively little had been said about his private life during earlier campaigns, and if Roberts had any inkling that the time of probation was passing, he was not deterred by it.[42]

Several of his church brethren and a good number of Democrats opposed his candidacy. Included among them were Cache County dissidents who considered that he had abandoned Thatcher in an unseemly fashion in 1896 and a Weber contingent beguiled by Frank Cannon's will-o'-the wisp posturing on silver. Chosen by the Republicans to face Roberts was Alma Eldredge, a Summit County Mormon who was hardly in Roberts's class.

In spite of Roberts's apparent advantages, his election was no cinch because of the swinging pendulum of public opinion concerning polygamy. At the nominating convention Martha Cannon and Ellen Jakeman, who believed Roberts had "domestic duties…enough to keep him…away from Congress," initiated a determined feminist opposition that before the campaign was through drew support from national suffragette Susan B. Anthony.[43] More threatening, for the moment at least, were well-publicized warnings from the Utah State Presbytery late in August that polygamy and hierarchical rule had not been abandoned and protests in October against Roberts's candidacy from the Presbyterian Synod and the Congregational Association.

Rising to these stimuli, and to promptings of its own, the *Tribune* launched a "furious and incessant campaign." Repeatedly, it charged that Roberts "owed a 'higher fealty'" to the church, that he was living in violation of the law, that he lacked knowledge and experience in government, that he opposed woman suffrage and the eight-hour workday, that his candidacy violated pledges made before statehood, and that his election would retard economic development.[44] As the election approached, Governor Wells joined the attack, lamenting that Roberts's "personal disabilities" obscured "every other issue." George Q. Cannon worried that Roberts's private life would become a "whip" against the church and seemingly did his best to ensure that it would when he announced that "any man who cohabits with his plural wives violates the law."[45]

Nevertheless, Roberts was elected in November 1898 and looked forward to claiming his seat in December 1899. Within weeks sectarian opposition in Utah crystallized in the Salt Lake City Ministerial Association. Leveling charges against Roberts, it invited "religious bodies all over the country . . . [to] protest" against seating him.[46] Under fire again, LDS leaders stoutly denied that the church had anything to do with Roberts's election.[47] Like Roberts and the Democratic Party, they learned much about national sentiment during the next year.

Immediately at hand was the Democrat-controlled senatorial election of early 1899. A bumbled affair from beginning to end, it "provided drama, excitement, suspense, weeks of florid oratory—everything," political scientist Jean Bickmore White has written, "except a new senator." On the surface, the task did not look complex. Democrats held forty-one seats, compared to sixteen for Republicans and six held by the Silver-fusionists pledged to Frank Cannon. Factions supported Democrats Orlando W. Powers, William H. King, and Alfred W. McCune. In addition, there were Republicans George Sutherland, Frank Cannon, John Henry Smith, and George Q. Cannon.[48] With the public again crowding the galleries and halls, this "warfare of the Toga" proceeded through 164 frustrating ballots.[49] Just as it seemed McCune would carry the day, he was accused of vote buying. Never proved, the charge halted proceedings and revealed that McCune had covered deficits at the *Salt Lake Herald* in a way that could not stand the scrutiny of the situation. Score? One failed Senate election, among several during this period that contributed to the Seventeenth Amendment, providing for direct election of senators in 1913.[50] It was also evidence of how low statehood's grandiose dreams of position in the sisterhood of states had fallen, proof that the church's control was far from absolute, and a staggering blow to Utah Democrats.

The Spanish-American War coincided with these developments. The difficulties between Spain and Cuba, together with burgeoning imperialism, drew Utahns' attention to national issues quite as surely as silver had done two years earlier. Utah's congressional delegation was among the most hawkish in Washington, DC, and at home citizens responded avidly to the growing sentiment for war. Newspapers were filled with jingoism and were frequently impatient with the McKinley administration's restraint.

Few were more stirred than the Mormons. As historian D. Michael Quinn has shown, they fundamentally changed how they regarded war as hostilities approached.[51] With a Bible-like ambivalence, they had traditionally yearned for the earthly kingdom (Zion) as a refuge from strife but simultaneously had often been militant in temperament. Religious interest rather than patriotism had generally shaped their views. In 1898 this ambivalence flared briefly before settling into wholehearted support of war and expansion. Quinn traces the dramatic decline in pacifist sentiments among church leaders between March and May. The question crystallized at the April conference. Several, including George Q. Cannon and Apostle Brigham Young Jr., emphasized Zion as a place of refuge and the church's obligation to advance peace. Cannon, however, returned to the question of war later in the conference. Sketching a dual obligation to state and church, he stretched Mormon teachings about America as the promised land to encompass a national mission to extend the principles and institutions of liberty worldwide.[52] As Milton L. Merrill has observed, "patriotism" was becoming a "religious principle."[53]

Apostle Young might have accepted Cannon's speech and in time even mirrored it, but conditions around him were more than he could countenance. The black Twenty-Fourth Infantry departed Fort Douglas to fanfare on April 20, waved off by upwards of 20,000 enthusiastic citizens.[54] On April 21 war was declared. On the twenty-third McKinley called for 125,000 volunteers and late in May for 75,000 more. Willard Young and Richard W. Young, brother and nephew to Brigham Jr. as well as West Point men, and the bellicose *Deseret News* editor, John Q. Cannon, rushed to recruit cavalry and artillery units. Worse yet, Apostle Young's sons fairly breathed fire. Three enlisted within days. A fourth, too young to enlist by himself, badgered his father for permission. For girls "real brass army buttons" became the "decoration of the day," the "craze" reaching such heights, according to one observer, that "at the depot," as volunteers entrained, "otherwise modest girls scrambled...to cut the buttons from the clothes of entire strangers." The "button fiends" were so unsparing that some soldiers were off to war with pinned-up pants.[55]

In a tabernacle speech before the Salt Lake Stake on Sunday, April 25, Young rashly stepped before the rush. Let Mormon boys devote "the means they make" to the war effort, he said. "Loafers" aplenty could be found "to go be killed." Around town on Monday he was commended and condemned for his pacifist position. To one who accosted him most vigorously, he exploded: the "war spirit" was "anti Christ," and "those who encourage" it and "do not repent...will go to hell." On Tuesday he, his brother, and his nephew met with Wilford Woodruff, who scolded him for defying the government and, to his chagrin, instructed "Willard and Richard to go on receiving volunteers." An official statement "advising the saints to volunteer" soon followed. Young bowed to authority, but three youthful relatives died in "the splendid little war."[56]

With visions of mission and glory, Utah's young men enlisted. Quotas were set at 425 men, but after appeals for larger authorizations and considerable maneuvering, about 800 were accepted. National Guardsmen were enrolled first. Under Governor Wells's directive, recruiters canvassed the state. Volunteers assembled at a tent facility called Camp Kent on the lower part of Fort Douglas. There they were organized in cavalry and light artillery outfits, officered by local men appointed by Wells.[57]

The volunteers set off for war in a surprisingly short time. For most it was garrison duty in the Southeast, at San Francisco, or in one of several national parks. There they suffered from malaria, typhoid, boredom, and, perhaps most of all, unrealized glory. Two artillery companies, however, were assigned to the Philippines. There they saw action against both the Spanish and Aguinaldo's insurgents. They quickly tired of killing and being killed. Tensions arose among them just as quickly, and boyish dreams seemed increasingly difficult to sustain. Petitions for early release were rejected, but by August 1899 they were home. Wiser and less filled with idealism, they still had a sufficient sense of destiny to immediately produce at least two books extolling their exploits.[58]

With the war winding down, B. H. Roberts presented himself to be seated in the House of Representatives in December 1899. In the thirteen months since his election, awakening antipolygamy sentiment had become a virulent national passion. A nationwide reform network with strong sectarian and feminist elements, including the National Congress of Mothers, the National Council for Women, the American Female Guardian Society, the League for Social Service, and the National Anti-Polygamy League, gathered seven million names on petitions demanding Roberts's exclusion. Encased in American flags and piled before the Speaker's desk, they bespoke citizen power that few in Washington dared ignore.

Newspapers and journals had a heyday. In Salt Lake City the *Tribune* sharpened what Milton Merrill called its "policy of imprecation." Taking the lead nationally, Hearst's *New York Evening Journal* serialized Arthur Conan Doyle's anti-Mormon "A Study in Scarlet." Much of the outpouring was fluff. The offerings of one or two, like New York journalist Eugene Young's "Revival of the Mormon Problem" in the *North American Review*, were well informed and moderate in tone, if firm in their determination that polygamy and church dictation had to go.[59]

Utahns did their part to unseat Roberts. Charles Mostyn Owen, a civil engineer with the Denver and Rio Grande Railroad who had worked quietly gathering unimpeachable evidence on new marriages and cohabitation; Dr. William M. Paden, a Utah Presbyterian; and Methodist Thomas C. Iliff stirred anti-Roberts sentiment. Arguing that Mormonism violated the four cornerstones of American society (the true God, separate church and state, education without priestcraft, and the monogamous home), Iliff's lecture hit hard enough that the church assigned damage-control speakers to follow his course.[60]

The Roberts case moved immediately to committee. With Theodore Schroeder carrying the case for the prosecution and Roberts acting for himself, hearings proceeded throughout January 1900. Discussion turned mainly on four issues of the law and the relation of Roberts's conduct to those issues. First, did polygamist disfranchisement under the Edmunds Act apply to states? Second, were explicit provisions that amnesty depended on future compliance with the law diminished by the fact that the law had not been enforced? Third, did the Enabling Act and subsequent oaths before the Utah Commission restore the political rights of polygamists? Fourth, did the "compact between the United States and Utah" bar cohabitation as well as new polygamist marriages? Ongoing discussion of a constitutional amendment barring polygamy and church influence made it clear that the agitation looked beyond Roberts to the church at large. Throughout the hearings Roberts comported himself with skill and dignity but to no avail. The committee's majority report recommended that he not be seated. A minority recommended that he be seated and then ejected. With the monster petition and public agitation still very much before it, Congress voted overwhelmingly to exclude him.[61]

In Utah Mormons greatly feared an antipolygamy amendment would be passed in the wake of the hearings. Before 1900 was over a deal was reportedly struck with the national Republican Party secretary, Perry Heath, to deliver Utah for the Republicans in exchange for a guarantee that the amendment would be scuttled.[62] City patronage played further into Gentile hands. Church president Lorenzo Snow firmly denied that "the church was seeking to re-establish polygamy," and the search for suitable senatorial candidates among general authorities who were practicing polygamists was abandoned. Governor Wells reaffirmed that no more polygamists would be sent to Congress and called on all Utahns to get the "Utah problem" out of "our newspapers, our pulpits and our platforms," publicizing instead the state's "illimitable" resources and "unsurpassed" climate.[63] In token submission polygamists were retired from some public positions, including postmasters in Provo and Logan, Agricultural College president Joseph Tanner, and board member Marriner Merrill. For a good portion of 1900 the state was represented only by Senator Joseph Rawlins. Turning his attention to the new problems of a Pacific empire, Rawlins failed to provide the leadership Utah Democrats desperately needed.[64]

THE NEW GENERATION

If Utah Democrats were short on leadership, promising prospects were in good supply among Republicans. Indeed, in 1900 it became clear that a new generation of business-oriented politicians had taken over. Among the leaders were four young Republicans. Over the long haul Reed Smoot, senator for thirty years, and George Sutherland, congressman, senator, and US Supreme Court justice, stood at the top, but in the turn-of-the-century years mining millionaire Thomas Kearns and the popular Heber M. Wells often seemed to have the upper hand. All four were under forty and possessed strong egos, ambition, organizational talent, the capacity for self-promotion, and political support.[65]

Politically, the four boasted a variety of assets. Polygamy was, of course, no problem for Kearns and Sutherland, Wells was unyielding in opposition, and Smoot was untainted personally and looking for a way out for Utah. Sutherland had been a leader in the legislature, where he put himself forward for senator without acquiring serious political liabilities. Kearns had been at the Constitutional Convention, maintained touch with labor, enjoyed important connections with national Republicans, and possessed a ready supply of money. Banker Wells had demonstrated almost flawless form as governor in the maelstrom of the years just past. Smoot was a business prodigy and active in party politics. Perhaps his best qualifications were a penchant for regularity and the timeliness of his advance to the apostleship in April 1900 just as death, and the Roberts case, cleared the decks of old-guard polygamist aspirants.[66] Together with a distinguished cast of fellow workers and behind-the-throne powers, the four of them, Smoot, Sutherland, Wells, and Kearns, made for a time of excitement as the "Mormon Problem" fought itself to a kind of conclusion by 1908.

Rarely has more been up for grabs. With the single-handed representation of Senator Rawlins in Washington, the need to rebuild appeared critical. After Pennsylvania's governor tried to appoint political boss Matt Quay to a vacant senatorial chair, prospects that Governor Wells could claim the empty Utah senatorship for himself placed him at the center of a circle of intense political preening. His ability to call a special election to fill the empty congressional chair also enhanced his power. Republican interest in both positions was high.

Wells's secretary of state, James Hammond, looked more and more like the Republican candidate for Roberts's seat. In a midwinter 1900 arrangement that gave Hammond visibility, Wells made an extended trip east, leaving Hammond as acting governor with full authority to appoint new officers to positions vacated at the Agricultural College when polygamists were forced out.[67]

Speculation ran rampant by the time Wells returned. Names frequently mentioned for the Senate included Wells, Kearns, and Sutherland, as well as Utah Supreme Court justices James A. Miner and George M. Bartch. Smoot's name too began to appear but in a minor key that gave way for the moment, when his appointment to the Quorum of the Twelve Apostles was announced early in April 1900. But in the short run the governor's maneuvers came to naught. Hammond ran for Congress but was no match for Democratic judge William King, who lined up a whirlwind tour by William Jennings Bryan and campaigned convincingly on his own behalf.[68]

But these were momentary reverses. In the general election of 1900 Wells continued to advocate business growth and easily beat Democrat loyalist James H. Moyle to win another term. In a quick reversal Congressman King was defeated by George Sutherland and filled only the remnant of the Roberts term in Congress.

Developments in the Smoot and Kearns camps were even more dramatic. Timed almost as part of the campaign, Kearns met late in the summer with Senator W. A. Clark, a Montana millionaire, and R. C. Kerens, Republican National Committeeman from Missouri, to organize the Los Angeles and Salt Lake Railroad Company. Sometimes called the "Hot Air Road," it included the takeover of a church road to Saltair and a board position for Smoot in the new company. It is generally held that President Lorenzo Snow agreed to support Kearns for the Senate in a move related to both the railroad and a previous bargain with the Republican National Committee to deliver a Republican congressional delegation. As the senatorial election of 1901 approached, the unpolished Kearns campaigned widely in support of Republican legislators. In the process he repeated Wells's call for development, denounced Bryanism, and endorsed Pacific expansion and an Isthmian canal. He won plaudits from workingmen and disdain from party regulars when he referred to Alaska as an island and Filipinos as "Filyponies."[69]

Smoot ached to be a candidate for the Senate. Yet during the fall of 1900, Lorenzo Snow apparently directed Smoot to yield in favor of Kearns. Soon afterward President McKinley reportedly advised him that his candidacy would injure Utah and the church. Before December was over Smoot was supporting Kearns's 1901 candidacy with the understanding that Kearns would return the favor in 1903. After conversing with Lorenzo Snow on January 3, Smoot's fellow apostle Anthon H. Lund wrote, "In regard to a senator Kearns is thought to be the man who can do us the most good, but what a man to send east! It will be a bitter pill for many to swallow."[70]

This accomplished, everything seemed shipshape. The Republican majority caucused on Friday, January 18, as the candidates hustled off for a weekend of last-minute arm-twisting. On Saturday word of Kearns's support from the church broke in the *Tribune*. Opponents of Kearns accused "the Church of having bargained the senatorship for favors on the polygamy question," as wrote Anthon Lund in his diary. Kearns denied it. Snow was unavailable. Although the very atmosphere reverberated, Kearns was elected to a four-year term in the Senate and by the end of the month was off for Washington, having seeded a field of distrust among Gentiles that soon yielded support for Smoot and, in time, a different kind of political division for Utah.[71]

In 1901 and 1902 neither man was idle. With the same boldness that had made his mining fortunes, Kearns plunged ahead. He temporarily cemented relations with Theodore Roosevelt and initiated pork-barrel legislation and patronage that offended Congressman Sutherland. At home Kearns struggled to balance his Gentile support with his Smoot-church partnership, pushed the Salt Lake Railroad, and completed his South Temple mansion. Suggesting he hoped Smoot could be dropped from the equation, he quietly purchased the *Salt Lake Tribune*. In a move that some thought implied Republican National Committeeman Perry Heath was his candidate for Utah's other senator, Kearns brought him to Utah as publisher and general manager of his newspaper. It was an impressive beginning.

THE SMOOT HEARINGS

Soon, however, things took a turn in Smoot's favor. On October 10, 1901, Lorenzo Snow died, breaking the essential link in the chain that secured Kearns's Mormon alliance. His replacement, Joseph F. Smith, was less susceptible to Kearns's blandishments and gave his undeviating support to Smoot.[72] Of equal significance, Congressman Sutherland, who had crossed swords with Kearns on patronage issues, differed sharply with him over tariff policy and became increasingly interested in his senatorial seat. This finally outweighed Sutherland's reluctance to see an apostle in the Senate. Ignoring his distaste at sometimes being referred to as Smoot's "puppet," he threw his support to Smoot, who had been a boyhood friend and, as Sutherland recalled, had at one time joined the Liberal Party along with "a great number of younger Mormons," thinking to rid the "Church of its peculiar institution."[73] Wells also had misgivings about Smoot's apostle-senator linkage but with two years remaining in his term was in no position to cut him off by running himself. In frequent contact with Kearns, Smoot worked to keep their agreement alive but at the same time engineered the appointment of a set of loyal followers to federal offices. Called the "federal bunch," these men became "the nucleus of the 'Smoot machine.'" Important among them were Mormons James Clove of Provo, E. H. Callister and James J. Anderson of Salt Lake City, Joseph Howell of Cache County, and William Spry of Tooele County. With the possible exception of Spry, these men gave themselves to Smoot with "a loyalty which did not distinguish" between the man and the church. Equally important was the non-Mormon mining man and Smoot confidant C. E. Loose of Provo.[74]

For Republican insiders the election of 1902–3 was one of controversy leading to crisis. Misgivings about Apostle Smoot's candidacy were widespread. Reform groups opposing theocracy began to reassemble as the campaign progressed and press opposition fired up. Speaking through Kearns, Theodore Roosevelt called for Smoot to withdraw as a candidate. Led by William King, Samuel Thurman, and state chairman

James H. Moyle, the Democrats could by no means be written off. Yet Smoot persisted and ultimately prevailed. Paramount elements in his election were his party workers (the federal bunch), President Joseph F. Smith, and the anti-Kearns followers of George Sutherland, whom Smoot agreed to support for the senate.

Apostle Smoot's election provoked a full-scale national reform movement. Backed by a protest group of citizens, the Salt Lake City Ministerial Association was among the first to blow the whistle. Nationwide, Protestant and women's groups ("the storm bureau," according to the *Salt Lake Herald*) rallied quickly, spurring a senatorial investigation that dragged on until 1907.[75] The storm center was the Senate Committee on Privileges and Elections, which was chaired by Julius C. Burrows of Michigan. Antipolygamy sleuth Charles Mostyn Owen dusted off his files from the Roberts case, and former congressman R. W. Taylor was chief counsel for the prosecution. The investigation became a searching examination of polygamy and the role of the Mormon Church in politics in spite of efforts by Smoot and his attorneys, Waldemar Van Cott and A. S. Worthington, to keep the focus on Smoot, a squeaky-clean monogamist. In Utah Smoot had E. H. Callister, C. E. Loose, and other machine members work to sell him to non-Mormon Republicans who, with Kearns in opposition, were the swing element in party politics. In Washington Smoot played the role of junior senator with a sure instinct for submissiveness and regularity that won grudging respect in the Senate and vocal support from Roosevelt that was frequently all that stood between him and defeat. Behind the entire proceedings loomed disfranchisement for all Mormons.

Held at several different periods between 1903 and 1907, the Smoot hearings aired the Mormon problem thoroughly.[76] Evidence mounted that post-Manifesto polygamist marriages had been common and that cohabitation was an everyday reality. To the conviction of everyone except inner-circle Mormons, who knew how precarious their political power really was, the church was represented as being in outright control in Utah and Idaho. Walking a tightrope between committee members, reformers, Gentile Utah, and the church, Smoot was a telling witness on his own behalf. Other church leaders, including President Joseph F. Smith and Apostles Francis M. Lyman and John Henry Smith, were less effective. Indeed, President Smith shocked and angered the country when he almost defiantly admitted to ongoing plural living and to eleven post-Manifesto sons and daughters. Also damaging were his denials of church political activities and feigned ignorance about post-Manifesto plural marriages.

In hopes it would be taken as evidence of good faith, President Smith issued the Second Manifesto in 1904, declaring again that polygamy was ended. This time the church took firm steps to enforce stated policy. Some questioned the church's sincerity when two apostles, John W. Taylor and Mathias F. Cowley, who had been active in perpetuating polygamy, eluded subpoenas to testify at the hearings and

Smith apparently acquiesced. Smoot secretly declared his readiness to resign if Smith felt it would serve the church. Short of this, he reported, Washington friends saw church discipline against Taylor and Cowley as necessary precursors to seating him and sidetracking a disenfranchising amendment. After much soul-searching, the two recreant apostles were dropped from their quorum, as peace offerings and, according to some, as sacrifices to Smoot's inordinate ambition.

The Senate committee was not mollified. Its majority report held against Smoot, but the Senate voted in his favor after hearing concluding speeches by many of its prominent members, including a bitter anti-Mormon oration from Thomas Kearns and a persuasive statement that polygamy was truly receding from Utah's junior senator, George Sutherland. Although the anti-Mormon crusade flared from time to time in the popular press, it never became a major national issue again, and in Utah the Mormon question focused increasingly on Salt Lake City.

The first eight years of statehood revealed how tenuous the display of good feelings and comity at the statehood celebration had been. The religious tensions that had inflamed territorial politics quickly resurfaced, as Utahns sought the optimal Gentile-Mormon balance in elected office. Polygamy and theocracy cast a pall over the election of prominent Mormons to high offices. As a counterpoint to their religious divisions, Utahns' support of the Spanish-American War demonstrated their patriotism and jingoism and symbolized their incorporation within the American Republic. Although it did not signify political equality, women's electoral and legislative participation enriched and complicated the political process. Most important, as a harbinger of the future, a new generation of political leaders keenly attuned to the corporate worlds of banking and business emerged, represented by Reed Smoot, George Sutherland, Thomas Kearns, and Heber M. Wells.

2

POLITICS IN THE PROGRESSIVE ERA

THE AMERICAN PARTY

As the Smoot case moved toward its tortured close, the focus of political conflict shifted to Salt Lake City and to a new non-Mormon political party. This development began in March 1904 when Salt Lake City Gentiles responded angrily to evidence emerging in the Smoot hearings that polygamous marriages were still being performed. Perhaps even more irritating to them was testimony from top Mormons justifying "plural living" on the grounds that taking care of existing families had been tacitly condoned by "Utah law enforcement officers" and the "general populace."[1] Convinced that neither the Manifesto of 1890 nor terms making amnesty contingent on submission to antipolygamy laws had been complied with, disillusioned reformers and politicos protested. In addition to the Salt Lake Ministerial Association, leaders of the initial protest included attorney Parley L. Williams and a variety of businessmen and city officials. They reasoned that Mormon domination was facilitated by the division of Gentiles between the two national parties and concluded that a reunion of all Gentiles within a single party was the most promising solution. They aspired to control Salt Lake City first, then the county, other cities, and ultimately the state.

After several meetings in March 1904, the movement lapsed, only to rise again in September. Over the summer the interests of Thomas Kearns and the Salt Lake

City protest converged, as Smoot, his federal bunch, and Joseph F. Smith became increasingly hostile toward Kearns. To Smoot's distress Governor Wells was friendly to Kearns, if not actually in his camp. As convention time rolled around in September 1904, the Salt Lake protest got under way seriously. A series of organizational meetings was held. Organizers named the movement the American Party, focused its opposition on Mormon leaders, condemned "apostolic power" and Mormon control of education, and demanded that pledges to abandon polygamy and cohabitation be honored. When the Smoot machine took control during the conventions, Kearns allied with the Americans. Former senator Frank J. Cannon, now in bitter opposition to the church, soon became editor of the Kearns-owned *Tribune*. With its essential elements in place, the American Party nominated a slate of candidates for state and Salt Lake County offices, supported the Republican cause nationally, and, with Cannon's invective aimed directly at Smoot, turned to a bruising fight.

Smoot and his supporters were badly frightened and ran a determined and ultimately victorious campaign. Agreeing with his lieutenant E. H. Callister that it "will never do to have a governor who is not your friend," Smoot opposed Wells's bid for a third term and waffled back and forth from Callister to businessman John C. Cutler, finally designating the latter as the machine candidate for governor in 1904.[2] In one of Utah's most rugged conventions, the Smoot machine carried Cutler over Wells, who in anger returned to banking but was later supported for a federal appointment by Smoot. Cache Valley's Joseph Howell was reelected to Congress, and a Republican legislature was elected that chose Sutherland as senator in January.

The Americans won no offices in the state election of 1904, but their showing made it clear they were a force to be reckoned with in Salt Lake City. In the December city school board election they drew first blood, electing Joseph Oberndorfer from the municipal Fifth Ward. With Kearns's newspaper opening a blistering path before them in the years that followed, the Americans continued to win city school board and municipal elections. Plans to extend the party's influence to the county and then the state never materialized, although the county became a major field of contest. American mayoral candidate for Salt Lake City Ezra Thompson beat very respectable Republican and Democratic candidates in 1905, and a majority of the city council belonged to the third party. When Thompson retired suddenly in the midst of a police scandal in 1907, businessman John S. Bransford was appointed to fill his term. Bransford was elected in his own right in the city elections of 1907, 1909, and 1911 notwithstanding budget overruns, various scandals, and the determined effort of the nonpartisan, nonsectarian Civic Improvement League to consolidate city and county government and advance the commission form of government that finally displaced the American administration after 1911.[3]

THE EFFORT TO GO STATEWIDE

While Salt Lake City was their power base, the American Party and the Kearns press seized upon a number of state issues in their bid for wider power. Of particular importance was the opening of the Uintah and Ouray Reservations to mining and homesteading. Due in some measure to the efforts of early senators Frank Cannon, Arthur Brown, and Joseph Rawlins, mining law had been modified by 1898 to provide long-term leases (ten years) in the Uinta Basin Indian territory and otherwise make reservations more available for white exploitation.[4]

During Kearns's term as senator (1901–4), the reservation issue continued to gather steam. September 1905 was set as a final date for placing the reservation's twelve to fifteen hundred Indians on individually owned allotments and opening upwards of a million acres to homesteaders from which a much smaller acreage of arable land was to be high-graded for individual Indians. As senior senator, Smoot was closely connected with the mechanics of the opening, as was Utah's land commissioner, William Richards. A land office at Vernal handled the actual entries, while Provo, Price, and Grand Junction, Colorado, were designated as registration towns. Interest was fevered in Utah and throughout the West. Nationally, the Country Life and Back to the Land movements were in full swing, creating a backdrop of moral support for the continuing takeover of Native American lands.

Wasatch Stake president William Smart issued what came to be known as the "reservation circular" to other Mormon stake presidents and bishops. In it, as the *Tribune* pointed out, he came close to issuing a church "call" for Mormon homesteaders and explained that he and his counselors were identifying the best land and developing connections in the land office to facilitate Mormon settlement. Thinking to do Smart's circular one better, Brigham City's stake president, Oleen Stohl, had it published, giving the *Tribune* a made-to-order opportunity to cry church-state interference.[5]

Thousands of would-be homesteaders gathered at the land offices in Provo, Price, and Grand Junction. As the drawing, applications, and site selection proceeded, the *Tribune* lobbed journalistic shells at Joseph F. Smith, Reed Smoot, and William Smart, accusing them of land fraud and conspiracy. The *Tribune*'s flaming headlines conveyed the essence of the attack. Typical was the yield for July 17, 1905: "Thwart Plans of Hierarchy," "Don't Permit the Theft of the Uintah Reserve," and "Church Scheme Has Been Revealed in Letter of the Wasatch Stake Presidency." August 2 was nearly as productive: "Word Is Obeyed to the Letter," "Hierarchy's Instructions to the Saints to Rendezvous at Provo Are Fulfilled," and "Eight Out of Every Ten Registered [Are] Mormons."

In Salt Lake City, civic groups, church organizations, the American Party, and its women's auxiliary joined the outcry. Under the direction of Mrs. A. V. Taylor,

American Party women worked to expose the inequities of the land drawing.[6] The furor notwithstanding, the drawings were finally completed, and some sixteen hundred homestead entries were initiated. Mormons and other homesteaders found no agricultural mecca, and the *Tribune*'s campaign failed to make the American Party a state force, but another bite had been taken out of Ute resources.

THE STOCKADE

A sensational chapter of American Party governance involved vice. Like other cities, Salt Lake was beset with gambling, drunkenness, and prostitution. An episode developed in connection with the latter that helped weaken the Americans and contributed to reforms that enabled the state to play down divisive conflict between local groups. This was the so-called stockade plan to concentrate and regulate prostitution.

For decades a downtown red-light district had existed on Commercial Street, later renamed Regent Street, between Main and State and First and Second South Streets. After the turn of the century, prostitution spread to other areas downtown. In addition to perhaps 100 women who worked in established houses of prostitution, as many as 300 plied their trade elsewhere in the city. City ordinances prohibited prostitution, but public and official sentiment appears to have been divided between those who called for rigid enforcement and eradication and those who, feeling that eradication was impossible, looked for ways to minimize prostitution's evils and, in some cases, to derive revenues from it.

Between 1908 and 1911 a fair number of American Party administrators and law enforcement officials were clearly in the latter camp. Police monitored the Commercial Street houses early in the American Party administration. A system of fines that approximated licensing existed. According to the *Deseret News*, about 135 prostitutes paid a ten-dollar monthly fine in the late summer of 1908. Police worked somewhat to contain prostitution and to clear the streets of streetwalkers and pimps.[7] In the eyes of some, prostitutes were unduly maligned. Western writer Frank Robertson fondly recalled the charity of Commercial Street girls during the period when he often passed through Salt Lake while moving as a "social derelict" from mining camp to construction job to shearing shed. Registered at the Salvation Army's Volunteers of America employment bureau on Commercial Street, he often passed the girls, who came to know him, "[calling] out cheerfully, 'Hey Slim, you had anything to eat today?'" Robertson did not need their charity but declared, "If I'd had to panhandle I would have started with the girls. Outside of Major and Mrs. [Tom] Mackey [who ran the Volunteers of America hall] ... they were the only ones who cared. ... I was a Mormon, and Salt Lake City was the headquarters of Mormonism, but not once did it occur to me to look up any of the authorities.... I knew instinctively that all I would have got was a lecture on thrift."[8]

Police chief Tom Pitt made the first official reference to the idea of a stockade as a solution to the city's growing embarrassment. In his annual report for 1907 Pitt described the stockade as a means of removing vice from the city center. Although Pitt later withdrew his support, a movement to implement the stockade quickly ensued. A corporation called the Citizens Investment Company was franchised under state law and during the summer of 1908 bought west-side property and initiated construction that totaled about a half-million dollars. Front person for the operation was Dora B. Topham, otherwise known as Belle London, a notorious madam from Ogden, who reportedly held 90 percent of the stock in the undertaking.[9] Backing it, apparently with general approval of the entire city council, which was dominated by members of the American Party, were Mayor John Bransford, who as a private investor built a boardinghouse for off-duty prostitutes across the street, and council members Lewis D. Martin, an architect who drew up plans for the installation, and Martin E. Mulvey, "a rotund and jovial" Commercial Street saloon keeper.[10]

Construction proceeded quietly until mid-September. At that time more than four hundred unserved warrants issued by the city attorney drew Sheriff Frank Emery's attention, and he initiated a series of raids against Commercial Street houses and streetwalkers. At about the same time, the stockade's imposing walls and unfinished cribs also attracted attention. Newspapers finally got the story, and major articles appeared with background information on the Citizens Investment Company and details about the stockade. The *Deseret News*, the *Intermountain Republican*, and the *Salt Lake Herald* immediately protested. The *Tribune* and the *Telegram* hesitantly supported the American administration until December and then lashed out at the stockade policy.[11]

Salt Lake ministers vocally condemned the stockade, especially as prostitutes moved into the new facility in December. Antipolygamy reformer and Presbyterian W. M. Paden denounced police protection, as well as the system's supporters. Silver-tongued Congregationalist Elmer I. Goshen lamented the fact that the "social evil" seemed beyond suppression. Reverend P. A. Simpkin characterized the system as "a brutal scheme of cattle-pen segregation" and the stockade as a "leper-spot," urging parishioners to protest to the city administration and, failing in that, to petition the county. Worst of all, Simpkin objected, was "planting...the forbidden thing on the skirts of the great workingman's district." Mormon leaders indirectly opposed the stockade through the *Deseret News*.[12]

The stockade issue inevitably figured in the campaign of 1908. However, the opposition found it difficult to take full advantage of prostitution's potential as an issue. The extent of city administrators' involvement was unclear during the campaign, and aside from city officials American Party leaders repeatedly condemned the stockade idea. Beyond that the stockade question was a city issue, and 1908 was a general election in which no city officers were up for reelection. Supported by *Goodwin's Weekly* and *Truth*, as well as the *Tribune* and the *Telegram*, the Americans continued to whale away at Mormon leaders and Smoot. The *Intermountain Republican* replied in kind, focusing on Kearns. The Democratic *Herald* let both the Republicans and the Americans have it. Without bringing its guns to bear on Bransford, the *Deseret News* condemned the stockade and the American Party but otherwise let others carry 1908's noisy campaign.

It truly was a wild election. At the American Party convention Frank J. Cannon demanded "prison or exile" for the "band of twenty-six" Mormon general authorities. The American Party denied any connection with the stockade and ran a full slate of Salt Lake County and state candidates. In a ploy to draw votes from both parties, they tinkered with a dual ballot, tying their county and state tickets to both the Republican and the Democratic presidential candidates.[13]

Republicans listened with delight as Sutherland described the Americans as "more a sickness" than a party.[14] The "cold and naïve" incumbent Republican governor, John Cutler, had run the state effectively for the previous four years, but being "unfortunate enough to believe that the people of" Utah "elected him," he had paid too little "attention to the crowd who had made him." As E. H. Callister put it, Cutler appeared not to "know the game." Smoot agreed that Cutler mismanaged his policies and appointments, so they cost the machine more votes than they gained.[15]

In the end, the Republican machine jettisoned the unfortunate Cutler, nominated Smoot lieutenant William Spry for governor, ran Cache Valley's durable Joseph Howell again for Congress, and fielded a full slate of state and county candidates. At low ebb Democrats nominated Samuel W. Stewart for the supreme court, Lyman R. Martineau for Congress, and after a futile attempt to entice the popular mining millionaire Jesse Knight to stand for governor substituted his son Will J. Knight.

Republicans scored an overwhelming victory in November. Smoot won a second term when the legislature met in January 1909, and Howell rejoined Smoot and Sutherland in the Washington delegation. Spry, who for the moment worked well with the Smoot machine and was popular among non-Mormons and Mormons alike, bolstered the party at home. The Americans won nowhere, not even in the December school board election, except for the redoubtable Joseph Oberndorfer of the municipal Fifth Ward who was unopposed.

For the American Party more severe blows soon followed. The elections over, city administrators publicly announced plans in December to move the prostitutes from Commercial Street to the stockade and promised to provide close police supervision. Almost immediately, a squabble flared. Police chief Tom Pitt withdrew his support, refusing to oversee the removal of the prostitutes or to police them once moved, so Mayor Bransford replaced him with Sam Barlow. Bransford now acknowledged that the stockade had been his idea and argued that it would be "one of the best regulated districts" in the country.[16] City attorney J. J. Dininny stated his intention to block the mayor's plan, and other leaders in the American movement stood in opposition. Even the *Tribune* editorialized that Bransford's course ran counter to the law. But the mayor persisted, and Salt Lake City's prostitutes moved to the stockade.

For three more years and two additional elections, the Americans figured prominently in city politics. Mormon and polygamy issues were now supplemented by watershed problems and the stockade question. Newspapers shamelessly "traded name calling, criminal charges and sarcastic comments."[17] As a nonsectarian and nonpartisan force, the Civic Improvement League and other reform groups called for the adoption of a commission form of government and organized the Citizen's Party movement of 1909. Efficiency and honesty in government were continuing issues, as scandal and financial difficulty dogged American administrations.

Never particularly popular within the party, Bransford exacerbated internal factions and weakened external support for the party through his actions. Factions withdrew from the party. Reform-minded friends like Reverend Paden continued to harp on the matter of vice and the stockade. Repeated reports of police protection, together with Belle London's conviction for forcibly holding sixteen-year-old Dogney Lofstrom Gray as a prostitute in the stockade, disheartened other supporters, many of whom breathed with relief when the stockade closed late in 1911.[18] Ringing down the end for the American Party was the legislature's passage of a commission government act for first- and second-class cities in 1911 in an effort to reform the system that had contributed to the excesses of the American administrations.

PROHIBITION: BACKGROUND

Over the first two decades of the twentieth century, the reform impulse ran strong nationwide. Progressive reformers stressed democracy and distrusted special interests, power brokers, and political machines. With its opposition to political corruption, call for economic efficiency, and advocacy of the commission form of government, the Civic Improvement League reflected the reformist impulse, as did various insurgencies, including women's suffrage, direct election of senators, and conservation.

Progressive reform on the state level began in earnest during Spry's two terms as governor (1909–17). Within the nation Utah was in the forefront of states regulating women's and children's employment and wages and adopting the eight-hour day for men working in the mines but fell far behind in political reforms such as direct election of senators and the initiative, referendum, and recall. In 1909 the legislature established a board to prevent the sale of contaminated food. In 1911 the legislature prohibited night work by children and limited the workweek of children in factories to fifty-four hours, excepting farmwork and domestic service. That same year women's employment was limited to nine hours a day, and in 1913 the state established a minimum wage for women, albeit a very low one. Also in 1913 the legislature established a state banking department.[19]

Among the reform movements in the years after 1908, Prohibition was particularly controversial and divisive. From early in the nineteenth century alcohol had repeatedly attracted reformers' attention. As the Progressive movement took hold, temperance became a key issue throughout the country. While it reached its climax with ratification of the Eighteenth Amendment in 1919, the temperance struggle played out largely on the state and city levels. For many years the Republican Party, which was often in power, but not by comfortable margins, took local option as the best liquor policy, letting states and municipalities decide who was wet or dry.

Utah had all the markings of a dry state but was nevertheless sharply divided over Prohibition. From the first Mormons had recognized their "Word of Wisdom's" proscriptions against alcohol as part of their religion. But for many Latter-day Saints, abstention was honored more in the breach than in practice. Dixie wine was legendary, consumed mostly in state, although some was doubtless exported to eastern Nevada mining camps. Other pioneer localities, remote and lost to social amenities, were noted for excessive drinking as well. With the boom of the 1880s and early 1890s, burgeoning cities, sheep camps, cow towns, and construction jobs all invited free and easy indulgence. Yet as polygamy waned, abstemiousness became increasingly the hallmark of Mormon peculiarity, and the Word of Wisdom was stressed. By 1894 some proposed writing a temperance clause into the state constitution. And as the temperance movement picked up momentum nationally, few issues possessed greater appeal to Mormons.[20]

Yet Utahns viewed temperance from a variety of positions. For some it was a threat to Utah's small but profitable brewing and liquor distribution industries and a signal that the Mormon determination to govern the state was entering a new phase. To others it was a heaven-sent opportunity to bring the problems of moral decay onto the political stage. To the Republican Party's beleaguered coalition of Mormons and moderate Gentiles, it posed almost impossible challenges. Would "prohibitory legislation" be taken as proof that "at the first opportunity," Apostle Smoot's party had enacted "the Word of Wisdom into law"? Would voters "wonder" what new "'blue law' Smoot would bring forth next from the *Doctrine and Covenants*?"[21]

An interesting case involved the 1903 "Drunk Bill" or "Booze Bill" introduced by Simon Bamberger, who with two other popular Democrats had survived the overwhelming Republican landslide in 1902. Progressive in outlook, the Drunk Bill called for treatment of alcoholics at county expense. Bamberger argued that drunkenness was a "social disease and therefore a social responsibility." Benefits to society, he thought, would far exceed costs. The bill was widely opposed as "socialistic." Some denounced Bamberger as a dangerous radical. At this distance it seems in keeping with the Progressive bent later apparent in Bamberger's politics. Opposition to the Booze Bill centered more among urban legislators than among rural ones. Whatever the event, Democrat Bamberger took the defeat of his bill in good stead, letting a native flare for fellowship and witty antics (he hid the Speaker's gavel so it would be safe for the Democratic majority he was predicting for the next legislature) add to the esteem in which he was held.[22]

PROHIBITION, 1908

The temperance debate warmed up early in 1908. Few had yet recognized the question's explosive character, and not all knew the line of their best interest. In Washington national Republicans prudently chose to favor local option and a waiting game. In Utah Smoot-machine functionary and devout Mormon E. H. Callister, manager of the *Intermountain Republican*, ran a daily feature on the front page "whipping up" Prohibition.[23] In March Rev. W. M. Paden of the First Presbyterian Church declared that Mormons held the key to Prohibition in Utah. If they ever went after temperance aggressively, he promised, Protestants would help them where Mormons were not in the majority.[24] Church leaders responded cautiously. Many leaders discussed abstinence, some zeroed in on saloons and rejoiced that the spirit of temperance "bids fair to become universal," and others spoke of the economic costs of intemperance. Church president Joseph F. Smith asserted that church leaders were in complete harmony with the temperance movement and urged its support. But he called also for "local option and temperance" rather than outright Prohibition and made it clear that the church wanted "nothing drastic, nothing...illiberal or oppressive."[25]

Whether Smith wanted anything drastic or not, his rhetoric caused an angry outburst. Predictably, the *Tribune*'s explosion was extreme. In tying temperance to the Word of Wisdom, Mormon leaders showed themselves to be "a bunch of hypocrites"; they had fostered looseness from the first, and their "drugstore" at ZCMI was the foremost liquor outlet. Few would be duped by such "false pretenders."[26] A more compelling protest came from Ogden's Fred Kiesel. A Democrat and millionaire liquor distributor, Kiesel complained to Reed Smoot that the *Intermountain Republican* had been stirring up the Prohibition issue. In soft words that did little to obscure the steel of his intent, he advised the senator, "for your party," that to embrace Prohibition would be a personal as well as a political blunder that would cause the American Party to once again "break out." To avoid such "evils," Kiesel suggested that "your party should not commit itself" to outright Prohibition, "until they do so nationally, but rather recommend a waiting attitude.... All we ask of you then is to keep down the present agitation in Utah and await developments."[27]

As he must have known, Kiesel's was a big order. Nevertheless, the approach spelled out by Kiesel became the policy of the Smoot machine and the Utah Republican Party. Supported by business interests both in and out of the church, and by the national party and with President Joseph F. Smith as silent partner, Smoot undertook to hold the temperance movement in check: for the next eight years he extolled "the virtues of temperance" and local option whenever Prohibition was mentioned. Mortally afraid of the American Party and the explosive hostility of anti-Mormonism nationally, Smith gave frequent lip service to Mormon involvement in Prohibition but at critical times dampened the fervor of his followers. It helped keep the shaky accord between Gentile and Mormon alive but made a near-lethal weapon of Prohibition.[28]

Smoot's tightrope walk was not easy, though. When in 1908 Governor John C. Cutler announced his candidacy for reelection and later made the fatal mistake of speaking out for Prohibition,[29] Smoot dumped him as the party candidate in favor of William Spry, who well understood the utility of wooing Gentile support and the need to sidetrack Prohibition.[30] Another pillar in the senator's local-option faction was Cache County's Joseph Howell, who was again nominated for Congress, bringing an undeviating loyalty to Smoot and the Republican Party along with a northern Utah team of his own, headed by Logan newspaperman Herschel Bullen.[31]

As the election approached, questions about the church's position sharpened when Apostle Heber J. Grant introduced a resolution at the October conference calling for Mormons to use their influence to have "such laws enacted...as may be necessary to close saloons, [and] otherwise decrease the sale of liquor."[32] With Taft running for president, a new candidate for governor, the steadfast Howell for Congress, a "no change" platform as far as liquor regulation was concerned, and (one suspects) an adequate campaign fund, the Republicans swept into office, including legislators pledged to reelect Smoot. For the moment, at least, Prohibition seemed under control. But if there was a lull, it was the quiet before a storm.[33]

Early in January 1909 as the legislature met, the storm broke when the Cannon Bill, "a stringent state-wide prohibition measure," was introduced in the House. Smoot's "no change" temperance policy came under heavy fire even as he was being reelected by the Republican legislature. Newspapers flayed him. Exposés portrayed him as a conspirator of diabolical cunning who first stirred up the liquor interests, let them buy him off, and, betraying principle, party, and voters, diverted the movement. Friends "denounced him" scathingly or "in sorrow." Fellow apostles "called him to repentance" or "castigated him in terms...reserved for Tom Kearns and Frank Cannon."[34] The most savage attacks came from A. S. Reiser, Nephi

Morris, and others styling themselves as "Prohibition Republicans" whose invective reflected Prohibition's divisive potential.[35]

Smoot took refuge, as was often his wont in times of stress, in Washington, DC, far from the madding crowd. At home E. H. Callister, James Anderson, James Clove, C. E. Loose, and others of the federal bunch took a much worse beating, as they held legislators in line one day and lost them the next. All but overwhelmed by seventy-five thousand signatures demanding statewide Prohibition, they faced a crack corps of Anti-Saloon League workers unconditionally committed to statewide Prohibition and headed by Charles W. Nibley (the "Richelieu of the church," James Clove dubbed him during the storm's fury), Heber Grant, and Protestant coworkers like Rev. Louis Fuller. Agonizing in the realization that in the worst of eventualities he was expected to veto Prohibition, William Spry told old friends that if "fanaticism" continued to mount, "burning at the stake would be in order in six months."[36]

In their correspondence to each other Smoot and his workers marveled that other Mormons failed to appreciate what to them was plain: a moratorium had to be called on the fight for Prohibition. Gentiles in Washington and Utah took the church's "October resolution" and the blitz that followed to be a clear case of "church domination of state."[37]

With the legislature under way, Smoot and his local managers made separate appeals to Joseph F. Smith in the forepart of February. Smith's response bolstered them all for the long haul. "Political operations," he wrote, "had crashed headlong into... moral fervor." The church itself was not in the fight. Church members were. At this point they could not be called off. On the other hand, Smith was by no means willing to "sacrifice" Smoot. Be patient and hold the line, he pleaded.[38]

The Cannon Bill was defeated in the state senate. Smoot supporters Henry Gardner and Carl Badger, respectively president of the senate and Smoot's former secretary, drafted bills setting up strictly regulated local option. In the last days of the legislature the Badger Bill made it through both houses, apparently to the surprise of Smoot, Spry, and other "no change" advocates. To the delight of the Utah and national brewery interests, Spry vetoed it on March 23 after the legislature had adjourned. Spry explained that laws giving local authorities the same power already existed, making the tougher Badger Bill unnecessary, but he evidently saw his veto as a concession to the liquor interests.[39]

PROHIBITION: LULL IN THE STORM

In 1910 the Prohibition issue was relatively quiet, as Mormon activists were reined in by LDS Church leaders. Heber J. Grant complained of being "muzzled," and Salt Lake Stake president Nephi Morris, an outspoken Smoot critic and avid prohibitionist, was silenced by general authorities.[40] As a result of local-option elections,

Provo and several smaller cities and rural counties went dry. Reformers worked with town boards and county commissions to shut down saloons and restrict liquor sales in drugstores. At the state conventions both parties wrote temperance planks, the Democrats endorsing outright Prohibition and the Republicans pledging enforced local option.

With the Republicans in control, a retooled local-option law was passed early in 1911, providing for local-option elections the following June in every incorporated town and city. On June 27 in the state at large, the drys won 39,766 to 31,477, but it was a hollow victory. Salt Lake City and Ogden voters rejected Prohibition, the former by a 14,008 to 9,327 vote. Without these two cities, no pretense could be made that Utah was dry. The election reportedly closed 101 of the state's 336 saloons. Of the remaining 235, 141 were in Salt Lake, 32 in Ogden, and 62 scattered in twenty-one camps and towns.[41]

In a sermon that suggests how deeply his ambivalence ran, Joseph F. Smith addressed the liquor question in October 1911. Describing the corporate arrangements under which the church's Hotel Utah was built and operated, he acknowledged that its amenities included a bar but blamed his listeners, who, he said, had not voted it dry during the local-option election. He argued it was better for travelers "who want to 'wet up'" to see the "beauties of Zion" from the vantage of the Hotel Utah than to have to "see everything that is not beautiful" from other watering spots.[42]

Smith's speech was widely seen as a strike against Prohibition. It indicates the extent to which the corporate values then transforming America, including the booster mentality and the profit motive, had seeped into the very heart of the church.[43] Indeed, the issues at hand may have cut as deeply into the Utah cultural milieu as had the Manifesto and the development of two-party politics.

The Prohibition movement met few great tests in 1912, but other developments continued to distance the dominant church from progressivism. Nationally, Theodore Roosevelt and the "Bull Moosers" bolted from the Republican Party, Woodrow Wilson brought new hope to the Democrats, and a three-way presidential race developed between President Taft, Wilson, and Roosevelt. Happily echoing B. H. Roberts's angry charge that Republicans had made Utah the most "boss-ridden, trust bound," and subservient "state of the Union," Democrats wrote a platform that embraced Wilson and a wide range of Progressive measures, including Prohibition, but nominated the slow-footed John Tolton for governor.[44]

The Smoot-dominated core of the Republican Party stood fast in all this. Boasting that "there are no half-breeds" among them (an allusion to Roosevelt's third-party attempt at the White House), they along with Joseph F. Smith backed Taft, rejected progressivism "lock stock and barrel," stayed with protectionist economic policies and local option, and concurred with President Smith that the constitution ought to be defended from the "fads" of progressivism, paramount among which were proposals for "direct government."[45] Picking up on the constitutional theme at the LDS conference, other church leaders happily condemned progressivism by "implication and name." James E. Talmage claimed that of all dangerous counterfeits, none was worse than the "spurious brands of liberty and freedom" that were "being offered on every hand." Counselor Charles W. Penrose inveighed against the "multitudes" assuming functions delegated to representatives by the constitution and warned listeners not to tear out its "vitals."[46]

Nevertheless, Progressives made inroads into the Smoot machine. C. E. Loose, Smoot's business associate and longtime party worker, and William Glasmann, Ogden mayor and publisher of the *Evening Examiner*, defected to Roosevelt. Even worse were insurgents such as former senate president Stephen H. Love and the prohibitionist Nephi L. Morris, who ran, respectively, for Congress and governor on the Progressive Party ticket. A full-scale feud was also under way between Smoot's Utah party manager, E. H. Callister, and Governor Spry, who was building an independent power base more successfully than Cutler had done earlier.

Securing 37.7 percent of the vote, Taft carried Utah by 5 percentage points over Wilson.[47] Socialist Eugene V. Debs took 8 percent of the Utah presidential vote, and the Progressives ran well. But the Republicans retained control of the legislature and reelected Congressman Howell. They laid special significance to Spry's easy defeat of John Tolton, heartening themselves with the idea that it was a mandate for local option and a defeat for Prohibition.[48]

In 1914 Prohibition seemed at first glance far from the minds of Utah voters. The European outbreak of World War I, Wilson's mounting personal popularity, and Latin American and Mexican crises were much in the news. At home the Democrats needed to identify a center of gravity for a party badly divided between silver-tongued orators such as B. H. Roberts, perennial candidates William King and James H. Moyle, and "sugar daddies" Simon Bamberger, Samuel Newhouse, Jesse Knight, and A. W. McCune. Republicans were distracted by the Spry-Callister feud and needed to woo Prohibition Progressives like Nephi Morris and the Bull Moose followers of Ed Loose and William Glasmann from the "heresy" of 1912. Smoot faced the attractive Democrat James H. Moyle in a first-ever direct senatorial election. This challenge he met with a "great man" campaign, emphasizing his national reputation and association with top national Republicans. His pitch had a telling impact on Mormon voters. Prohibitionist leader John M. Whitaker grudgingly excused Smoot's local-option stand with the diary notation that the senator "is now reckoned the most competent legislator and powerful Chairman of Washington."[49]

PROHIBITION, 1916

Nevertheless, wets and drys moved toward a shoot-out. National developments loosened the restraints on the back of the local-option policy that had so long guided Utah's Washington delegation. The Kenyon-Runyon Act of 1913 sought to regulate interstate commerce difficulties growing from the effort to stop the flow of liquor from wet to dry states. Locally, temperance-minded Mormons and Gentiles cooperated more easily.

John M. Whitaker, a capable commoner who had married a daughter of church president John Taylor, played a key role in this cooperation after he became president of the Utah Federation of Prohibition and Betterment Leagues.[50] Soon before this new period of activity began, Whitaker was invited to a temperance meeting on March 24, 1914. To his surprise he found it was a "meeting of Salt Lake Ministers," including Presbyterian reverend Frank Leonard, Methodist Episcopal reverend D. E. Carter, and a number of "Christian Endeaverers and Temperance workers." A Mrs. Oxhurst was chair, and Whitaker ended up speaking on how they could organize to "bring on national prohibition." He soon saw that people he had earlier taken to be enemies were friendly. The Anti-Saloon League of Salt Lake County was reorganized, and Lady Holder of the Women's Christian Temperance Union talked about Utah conditions and helped modernize the Anti-Saloon League organization. By mid-June Whitaker had a nonsectarian lecture series going in support of a local-option election in Murray. Speakers included Protestants H. W. Rehard, G. F. Goodwin, E. C. Mork, and H. L. Paige and Mormons E. S. Sheets, Joseph F. Merrill, and himself, who often worked together. By common consent both the meetings and the lectures "never allowed religion to be discussed. Only the one cause—prohibition."[51]

On October 3 the Federation of Prohibition and Betterment Leagues was in place. Consisting initially of twenty-one different organizations, the federation was nonsectarian and "without political bias." It sought to establish county organizations, promote national Prohibition, and pass statewide Prohibition laws in 1915. Although such prominent prohibitionists as Richard R. Lyman, George H. Brimhall, and Orson H. Hewlett raised some opposition, a resolution passed calling for pledged legislators and for a bill that would become state law only when ratified by a majority of voters. Whitaker was elected president; George Startup, an outspoken Provo candy manufacturer, as vice president; and Provo's Rev. Philip King as general secretary.[52]

During the rest of October the federation was active. By October 12 candidates for the legislature had been circularized, a preliminary list of approved candidates drafted, and interviews scheduled. On the seventeenth Michael J. Fanning, a national leader from Philadelphia, spent the day with Whitaker. On the twenty-second Whitaker met with Reed Smoot, explaining that the federation would not support unpledged candidates. Smoot declared he was "as much in favor of Prohibition as" Whitaker and wanted only to see "this cursed enemy to mankind abolished." He explained that he had "discussed the matter for months in all its phases" with national Republican leaders and that he had felt he "was doing what the people of Utah wanted" when he pledged himself to support local option again. The two men parted amicably, Whitaker still convinced of Smoot's greatness, but uncompromising in his own commitment to "bone-dry" Prohibition.[53]

In January the legislature entered into a process even more frenzied than the hectic session of 1909. The Prohibition federation's draft bill was given to Senator John H. Wootton and known by his name. In February Prohibition Republican Nephi L. Morris asked Smoot to support the Wootton Bill; Smoot replied that he could accept the "purpose" of the bill, but it would have to be amended to "be fairer in its administration."[54] Smoot man James H. Anderson pushed a local-option bill instead, and another faction "wanted no law at all." While the bills were in process, league representatives toured the entire state, "met ministers and…lectured in their churches." Among other things Whitaker addressed the question of absolute Prohibition and sacramental wine with Catholic father W. K. Ryan, who "said promptly—You can't do that, You might as well do away with the Catholic Church." Explaining that "the church must have it [wine] at all costs," Father Ryan emphatically concluded that Catholics wanted "regulation and not prohibition." Wanting even less in the way of regulation than the Catholic Church were Utah's new immigrants, to whom Prohibition made no sense at all. As Helen Papanikolas has written, liquor was "traditionally part of their ceremonial and communal festivities of their cultures." A Greek-language publication, *To Fos* (The light), touted the health benefits of moderate alcohol consumption: "By a large majority doctors consider alcoholic beverages useful for therapy." But opponents came in aplenty from other quarters as well, "moving every power known" to influence the legislators. In the midst of this Spry kept his own counsel, convincing the avid Whitaker, at least, that he would sign the Wootton Bill.[55]

But the opposition had other ideas; local-option interests and the liquor industry joined forces and persuaded legislators to back down on campaign promises. Prohibition organizations retreated to local option. Mormon leaders were marshaled to whip defaulting legislators back into line, and state government divided against itself, with Spry trying desperately to keep his options open, while state attorney general Albert R. Barnes lobbied tirelessly for Prohibition and as a last desperate measure prepared impeachment action against senate president L. Mont Ferry when in an effort to derail the Wootton Bill he adjourned the senate.

The Prohibition federation pushed on "with…blind" and uncompromising "fury."[56] Of seventy amendments offered, only four were written into the bill. Opponents of the Wooten Bill held that it would impede industrial development, reduce the number of tourists, impose Mormon morals upon the entire state, and, most objectionable of all, "destroy property value without compensation."[57] At the end, representatives of both groups stayed on the governor's trail, "pleading, begging, threatening and cajoling." As Whitaker wrote, "What...bitterness...[and] hate surged throughout the capitol, [the] City, and the state." Provo's fractious prohibitionist George Startup came in for special pressure. According to one report, liquor men set fire to his candy factory, paraded around his home breaking beer bottles, and entered his house in an apparent attempt on his life.[58]

On March 6 the Wootton Bill passed both houses and was rushed to the governor late in the day. Tempers were running high: a public shouting match ensued between three prohibitionist senators—Wootton, William Seegmiller, and Orlando Bradley—and Governor Spry, whom they tracked to the Hotel Utah after hours to deliver the bill. Following this unseemly outburst, a "dry-territory" bill was hurriedly pushed along in the last hours of the legislature as an alternative to statewide Prohibition. The bill set up severe penalties for shipping alcohol from wet to dry localities. The dry-territory bill passed and was left in the governor's hands at adjournment, along with the Wootton Bill. Some charged that the dry-territory bill was an attempt to "influence the governor to veto [the Wootton] bill" or ease pressure on him. Whether this was the case or not, Spry vetoed the Wootton Bill and signed the other, making "dry territory absolutely dry."[59]

Before long rumors reached Whitaker that Spry had vetoed the Wootton Bill on directions from Joseph F. Smith. This word came with the force of a bombshell. On March 18 the "Flying Squadron," Prohibition shock troopers, belatedly arrived on the Utah scene. One of them commented as he was introduced to Whitaker by Presbyterian reverend George E. Davis, league vice president, that he was "greatly disappointed" to learn that "the President of your church told the Governor it was his wish that he VETO your bill." Thunderstruck, Whitaker denied the charge and felt he had repaired the "damage" before the VIPs left town.[60]

But the end was not yet. Senator William Seegmiller broke another bombshell in the *Kane County News*, his own paper edited by J. A. Borlase, an "ultra modern" newspaperman from Salt Lake City.[61] Seegmiller and the two other stake presidents in the senate, Uintah County's Don Colton and Wayne County's Joseph Eckersley, had been summoned to Spry's office, where he allegedly told them that he loved Joseph F. Smith and the church above all other things. Smith "could see very plainly," Spry reported, that "anti-Mormon persecution would be repeated" if Prohibition passed. It could be "stopped" only if the governor vetoed the bill and thereby destroyed his chances for reelection, offering "himself as a sacrifice." Spry claimed that Smith desired the three stake presidents to "sustain" his veto and defend him "to your people." Still angry from the Hotel Utah incident, Seegmiller regarded Spry's story as a shoddy fabrication.

Apostle Anthon Lund's diary makes it clear, though, that there was at least a measure of truth in Spry's account. Spry approached Smith, stating that he "feared that the Prohibition Bill would bring much trouble upon the church" because more than one hundred non-Mormons had threatened to bring back the American Party if it passed. When Lund and fellow apostle Charles Penrose advised Spry to sign the bill anyway to "kill the saloons," Smith said he "felt that he did not like to expose the Church to any danger" associated with the American Party. Smith therefore "promised the Governor that if he should see any of the Senators he should tell them that he had studied the matter and has his reasons for vetoing the bill."[62]

Seegmiller's story hit the Salt Lake papers at the April conference. Colton and Eckersley disagreed with Seegmiller on fine points but did not deny the "substance" of his charge.[63] At conference Apostle Joseph Fielding Smith, son of the president, vehemently denounced "whisperings" that the "authorities of the Church...do not want prohibition." The father, however, still seemed to equivocate. "Wherever prohibition can be effected," he told conference goers, "I believe in it...[and] will...use...every opportunity or power within my reach for prohibition, in wisdom, and not in unwisdom."[64]

Historian Bruce Dyer's study of this issue acknowledges that Smith sometimes shifted from outright Prohibition to local option and that his support for the latter peaked in 1909 and 1915, when the intensity between opposing factions was highest. Dyer concludes that Smith did indeed fear that "direct Mormon entrance into the controversy" would reopen anti-Mormon agitation.[65] Whitaker's experience during the rest of 1915 and 1916 seems to substantiate this view. Asked by church leaders to carry on in his role as front man for the movement, Whitaker found many Mormons prohibitionists were reluctant to continue the fight unless Joseph F. Smith clarified his position.[66]

PROHIBITION: PROGRESSIVE REFORM

Clarification came soon enough and in ways that some have thought added up to a revolution in Utah politics. After sizing up the force behind the strict Prohibition drive during his November 1914 reelection, Reed Smoot tried to recapture the initiative by tentatively outlining a Prohibition policy that would allow beer to be manufactured and exported and give other liquor interests time to dispose of their property. When approached for their reaction, members of the Mormon First Presidency were apprehensive that "drastic action" would reawaken the American Party. However, Smoot's contacts in the liquor industry, including Ogden's Gus Becker and Salt Lake's J. N. Eldredge, thought Smoot's plan "was the best that could be done." Local-option elections further dried Utah during 1915, and the process of organizing for the fight continued, with Smoot and the Republicans hoping they could still salvage the day by abandoning their obstructionist position.

By January 1, 1916, three factions plagued the Republicans. Heading one element was Governor Spry, who in eight years in the governor's chair had developed a loyal following. Another group, loosely composed of prohibitionist Republicans, reformist younger men, and Progressive insurgents, was typified by Nephi L. Morris. An avid Prohibition campaigner and Progressive Party candidate for governor in 1912, Morris's taste for insurgency once led E. H. Callister to refer to him as "a pocket edition B. H. Roberts, with many traits of Frank Cannon" thrown in, but the party struggled to accommodate Morris and the "new dealers," as the reform wing of the party was called.[67]

In the third faction were the regular party followers of Reed Smoot who still exerted some unifying influence but were weakening as Smoot's capacity to stem the tide of reform diminished. Senator Sutherland was facing reelection, as was six-term congressman Joseph Howell. Both were uneasy. Sutherland rightly sensed his seat was in jeopardy, to either Spry or to Democratic aspirants William King or Simon Bamberger. Howell saw mounting evidence that his constituents regarded his long tenure as an impediment to direct democracy and as a bastion of support for the special interests and without much fuss recognized he might be the first to go.

In February Smoot invited Spry, reformed Bull Mooser C. E. Loose, and church representative Bishop Charles W. Nibley to Washington for a top-level Republican conference with Sutherland (by now Utah's junior senator), Howell, and himself. Spry failed to show up, leading the others to suspect he would try to seize control of the party in his own interest. E. H. Callister had often been invited to such confabs before, but with his feud with Spry running high, and a feeling growing in the Washington delegation that he might be more easily sacrificed than Spry, he was left at home. Plans were laid to downgrade Callister to a federal appointment and offer his position as manager of Smoot's *Herald Republican* to Spry in an attempt to divert his attention from Sutherland's seat and dissuade him from running for a third gubernatorial term in view of his long tenure and unpopular stand on Prohibition. Smoot had advised Spry that if he was "nominated he could not be elected on account of his Prohibition position and the third term question."[68] Unable yet to stomach Nephi Morris's Progressive heresy and without a candidate for governor, the meeting broke up.

Not surprisingly, word of this restoration effort was soon out. To many it proved that change was necessary. For a time Spry kept his own peace about whether he would run for a third term or for the Senate. He finally settled on a third term after Kearns and Wells lent support. Still convinced that Spry could not win, Smoot regulars first supported unknown E. E. Jenkins, but as he failed to develop momentum they fell in behind the more dynamic Morris—a major concession to progressivism.

Returning to Utah late in the campaign, Smoot found a divided and dispirited party. Trying to turn the tide, he called for unity, fought for Morris, and bolstered Sutherland in what proved to be a failing contest with William King.

Democrats sensed that 1916 was their year and approached the election in high hopes. Yet initially, they were nearly as divided as the Republicans. James H. Moyle and other state committee people were at each other's throats, and both Simon Bamberger and William King had a yen for Sutherland's seat that bid fair to split the party. Bamberger, a mining and interurban railroad executive, got off the pad early, "jumping on the prohibition bandwagon" in May 1915 and declaring late in the year that he was available for nomination to the Senate. To get some hold on national questions related to Utah, Bamberger made a grand tour east in 1916 that continued to sugar-rich Cuba. Apparently convinced he could not support Wilson's low tariff on sugar and recognizing that his withdrawal would tend to unify the Utah party, he announced his intent to withdraw from the Senate race.

King's name stayed before the public as a potential candidate, but he waited to formally announce until July. Looking more and more interested in Progressive issues and showing a real affinity for attracting votes, Bamberger announced his candidacy for governor on August 10. A day or two later he was followed by Alfred W. McCune, a Mormon railroad and mining tycoon from Nephi.[69] The Utah Progressive Party parted sadly with Nephi Morris when he opted for the Republicans and instead worked out a mutual ticket with the Democrats, including Congressman James H. Mays, who had been elected in 1914.

In addition to a strong state ticket, the Democrats had a winning presidential candidate in Woodrow Wilson. Utah had begun to reflect some of the West's general enthusiasm for Wilson in 1914, and by 1916 the slogan "He kept us out of war" was as heartfelt in the Beehive State as anywhere. As Sutherland ruefully put it shortly after the election, a "peace craze swept Utah last Tuesday as the silver craze swept it twenty years ago."[70] In addition to the peace issue was Wilson's success in "uniting progressives, including many former opponents," behind a consistent set of policies.[71]

For related reasons many Utahns likewise sympathized with Wilson's restrained treatment of the Mexican crisis. Giving them a direct stake in it were the Mormon colonies in Mexico and a National Guard detachment stationed on the Mexican border during the summer of 1916, which fortuitously returned without having fought just before the election. Democratic apostle and former Mexican mission president Anthony W. Ivins was especially vocal in his support of Wilson's peaceful resolution of a crisis that many thought should be met with force. By contrast to Republican candidate Charles Evans Hughes, a great jurist who proved to be a poor campaigner, Wilson's appeal in Utah was enhanced even further. Even his tariff policy, which undeniably hurt wool, silver, lead, and sugar, and the repeated

Republican warnings that hard times were imminent failed to divert voters more afraid of war than of depression.[72]

Republicans never had a stormier convention than in 1916 or Democrats a more congenial one. In the one exception, Republicans quickly nominated Sutherland for a third term. Spry fought for the gubernatorial nomination down to the wire, finally accepting Smoot's version of Prohibition and even agreeing to go down quietly if he were defeated. In the end, Nephi Morris won the nomination by half of one vote. Joseph Howell was dumped for First District congressman in favor of Timothy Hoyt, the Ogden Forest Service solicitor and a political novice. Newcomer Charles Mabey was nominated for Second District congressman. For Republicans it was a tough day. The wreckage of the Smoot machine lay all around. Because he faced no election, its central figure was personally unscathed. But smarting yet from blows taken earlier were Tom Kearns, Heber Wells, John Cutler, and poor Ed Callister. Now it was Spry's turn and Joseph Howell's. At the November 1916 election, it would be Sutherland's.

The Republican platform, too, smacked of defeat. In keeping with the Progressive sentiment engulfing Utah, it belatedly called for a public utilities commission, workmen's compensation, and voluntary association for workers. Beyond these issues it was more hawkish on foreign affairs and made a call for statewide Prohibition that quieted but few memories of the party's long local-option bottleneck.[73]

The Democrats' convention nominated William King for the Senate. In nominating Simon Bamberger they achieved something akin to statesmanship. In public address he was affable, intelligent, and convincing rather than an able orator. In the walk of life he was a friend maker, deft in wit and long in memory. As a businessman he was a builder. He saw the elements of production, put them together, made them pay, and moved on, leaving established systems to others. He was experienced in the legislature and in problems of public education, as well as a frequent source of funds. In the name of party harmony he had stepped aside for King. He had seen Prohibition coming and adjusted his business and his thinking to conform. As a Jew, a non-Mormon, and a Democrat, there was no precedent for his election, but his connections with the threatening past were few.

All this was turned to asset in a brilliant nomination address by B. H. Roberts, last of the great orators who had so enthralled Utah Democrats over the years. The Republicans had nominated a factional candidate, Roberts told the convention. Democrats could pick up votes by nominating a candidate who appealed to all classes. Bamberger was such a candidate. Moreover, he represented an opportunity to break with Utah's "unwritten law" (Roberts also branded it as "absurd" and "un-American") that demanded that governors be Mormon, one senator be "Gentile" and the other "Mormon," and tickets be balanced along Utah's cultural fault line.[74]

Prohibition featured largely in the campaign. As political scientist Kenneth G. Stauffer has written, "Morris would seem to have been the natural favorite," given his long-standing support for Prohibition, but Bamberger "came out well" on the issue, spoke clearly, and let his action in closing down the saloon at his Lagoon resort speak for him. Morris muddled statements on Prohibition and never escaped the fallout from his defection from the Republican Party in 1912.[75] Sutherland, who after some show of Progressive sympathy earlier was swinging back in the direction of the conservative economic thought that became his hallmark, was branded a "reactionary," a "tool of the interests," and, worse, an "associate of Smoot," the "'self-appointed dictator'" who no longer delivered the vote.[76]

It was a hard-fought and expensive campaign to which outside speakers contributed significantly. Republican visitors included presidential candidate Charles Evans Hughes, vice presidential nominee Charles W. Fairbanks, and Senators Warren G. Harding of Ohio and William E. Borah of Idaho. William Jennings Bryan and several senators represented the Democrats, and a team of Progressives toured on behalf of Wilson. As a modest show of good intention, the Democrats involved women and young people in their campaign.[77]

Democrats scored an overwhelming victory. Wilson carried every county with 84,501 votes, or 58.9 percent of the total. William King carried all but one county, receiving 81,057 votes, or 56.9 percent, and Bamberger carried all but five, with 78,502 votes, or 55.6 percent. Democratic candidates for Congress did nearly as well as did state and county officers. The legislature was composed of fifty-eight Democrats and five Republicans. After three decades of near-total denial, the Democrats were in at last.

It was a good deal more than a changing of the guard. The nation and the Rocky Mountain region were firmly Democrat. The Utah Republican Party was in disarray. The Smoot machine was a total wreckage. The influence of the apostle–senator–church president team that had so often worked its will was vastly reduced. Not merely was the way open to Prohibition, but the very floodgates of Republican conservatism were down. At last the way to Progressive reform so long barricaded by the Smoot machine stood open. To many, then and since, it seemed a veritable overthrow.[78]

Even the accepted wisdom that senatorial posts were the most prized plums of politics had changed since the early days of Thomas Kearns and Reed Smoot. In 1917 Smoot continued to work his wonders with tariff schedules and Senate committees, but his role, like the arrival of William King to the Senate and James Mays and Milton Welling to the House of Representatives, was largely unnoticed in Utah. The real field of action was in the new state capitol in Salt Lake City, where what was probably the most liberal Utah state legislature of the twentieth century met. As K. G. Stauffer points out, "Utah had adopted little progressive legislation by

1916." The state had been one of four to reject the Sixteenth Amendment (allowing Congress to levy an income tax without apportioning it among the states) to the
United States Constitution and the only one to reject the Seventeenth (providing for
the direct election of senators).[79] It was time to put Progressive reform in place, to
make changes long needed, and to enact the platform upon which the Democrats
had run.

A Prohibition bill was one of the first things the legislature addressed when it
met in January 1917. Richard W. Young Jr. introduced the bill, which was maneuvered quickly through both houses. Governor Bamberger slowed its progress when
he called for a special enforcing commission and threatened a veto. The legislature
resisted and, given the subject at stake, the governor yielded. But it all seemed anticlimactic; indeed, most of the questions at stake had already been answered in the
previous election. Smoot's objections had been dropped and his machine swept
away. Party platforms were united in their call for Prohibition. The nation was moving quickly toward a constitutional amendment and nationwide Prohibition. On
August 1, 1917, the state's "dry-as-a-bone" Prohibition law went into effect. To guarantee that "such legislation may not be repealed," the legislature also prepared a Prohibition amendment to the state constitution, which was duly ratified by the voters
in 1918. Gone were the elaborate restraints that had kept the Mormon-Gentile truce
in place and postponed Progressive reforms.

The legislature then moved on to the larger task of enacting a plethora of Progressive measures. A public utilities commission, an issue that had been unsuccessfully addressed from the time of the first state legislature, was finally established. An
industrial commission to administer the provisions of the Workmen's Compensation Act was established in response to pressure from labor unions and the Socialist Party. A new corrupt-practices law limited candidate expenditures, prohibited
the issuance of free travel passes, and regulated lobbying practices. Belatedly, Utah
enacted the initiative and referendum, permitting voters directly to pass and repeal
laws. The legislature also passed an anti-injunction act, guaranteeing workers'
right to organize and picket and restricting the courts' ability to issue injunctions
against strikers. Lawmakers revised laws pertaining to employment of children,
taxes, inheritance, auditing of state funds, and elections. The term of office for
Utah Supreme Court justices was increased from six to ten years and the number
of judges from three to five; longtime Democratic stalwarts Samuel R. Thurman
and Valentine Gideon were appointed by Governor Bamberger to the court at once.
Thurman was the first Mormon ever appointed to the state supreme court, and his
appointment reflected improved relations between Mormons and Gentiles.[80]

In 1918 death and the off-year election consolidated the Progressive gains of
1916. That year former US senator Thomas Kearns and church president Joseph F.
Smith died within a short time of each other. The revolution initiated by the Smoot

machine's collapse and the Democratic victory came full term symbolically in the demise of these two old adversaries and in the adjustments in the Mormon Church and the Gentile organ the *Salt Lake Tribune* that resulted from their passing. Both men came out of an earlier era. More than any others, they symbolized the divisions that split Utah during early statehood, although they both had lately modified their opposition. Heber J. Grant succeeded Smith as Mormonism's prophet and devoted much effort over the next twenty-seven years to "healing old sores and pushing 'the irrepressible conflict' into the past." In this enterprise he had the equally dedicated collaboration of those in control of the *Tribune*, the traditional voice of the opposition. O. N. Malmquist, longtime *Tribune* reporter and historian, rightly wrote in 1971 that "viewed from the vantage point of more than a half-century, 1918 emerges as the year in which policies of conciliation cautiously inaugurated by both sides of the old conflict in 1911 were confirmed and permanently established." As he put it, "There had been 'springtimes' of accommodation on prior occasions," but they had always been "followed by relapses." The significance of 1918 "depended upon their permanence."[81]

The off-year elections in 1918 consolidated the Democrats' hold upon Utah. At stake in that election were two congressional seats, three supreme court judgeships, three constitutional amendments, the legislature, and a variety of county and municipal offices. World War I was winding down. Both parties supported the war, and by common agreement partisan activities were at a minimum. Party conventions were not held until late, and a liberty-bond drive and the influenza epidemic interrupted campaigning. Schools were closed, church meetings canceled, and business houses emptied. As the *Tribune* quipped, the campaign was for all practical purposes "meetingless, speechless, and stumpless."[82]

Fewer than 45 percent of the voters turned out for the election. Nationally, the Democrats lost control of the Senate, but Utah lagged behind the national trend and voted solidly Democratic. After the election no Republican was seated in the state senate, and thirty-seven of forty-seven members of the house were Democrats. Congressman Milton H. Welling defeated Republican industrialist William H. Wattis of Ogden for the first congressional seat, and Progressive-Democrat James H. Mays routed former governor William J. Spry, signaling how far the mighty had fallen. Perhaps most significant, the victory of the three Democratic supreme court candidates guaranteed a court sympathetic to reform legislation well into the 1920s.[83]

GLOBAL TILT: UTAHNS AND THE GREAT WAR

Utah's legislature and governor embraced Progressive reform at home in 1916–18, just in time for Utahns to join the First World War, America's Progressive crusade to spread democracy abroad. Like the Spanish-American and Philippine-American wars, World War I took Utahns to distant lands. More than 200 Serbs and a small number of Greeks left Utah and crossed the Atlantic to fight in the Greek, Serbian, and French Armies. Wilhelm Kessler, a German immigrant serving an LDS mission in Europe when the war broke out, enlisted in the German Army in 1914. Close to 21,000 Utahns served in the US military during the war. Hundreds serving in the Utah National Guard when America entered the war were swept into the Fortieth Division of the US Army by a presidential proclamation in midsummer. Others responded to the inducements of recruiters and volunteered. The majority of men in the military (about two-thirds nationwide and nearly 60 percent in Utah) were drafted. The regional draft board in Salt Lake ruled in August 1917 that married men with children should be passed over for conscription, so most draftees were young single or recently married men. Civic-minded citizens who were too old to serve themselves worked to persuade Utah boys to either enlist or register for the draft. For instance, in Roosevelt community leader Reuben S. Collett spearheaded a gala recruitment rally at the library with a dance, refreshments, and patriotic speeches. Local girls bestowed occasional kisses and colored ribbons on each of the men who enlisted or registered.[84]

Many immigrants were initially reluctant to join the US military. As historian Helen Papanikolas sympathetically explains, they were "fearful that they would be taken into the army where they did not understand the language and where they could be killed and all hope of fulfilling traditional duties to their families would die with them. They did not rush to volunteer." Many Greeks also feared that Greece might lose territory in the war and did not want to betray their homeland. Many requested exemption from the draft as aliens. Ultimately, 2,073 immigrants residing in Utah served in the American military. The largest subsets were Italians (385) and Greeks (349). Seventy-five Germans and 49 Swiss immigrants served. Elizabeth Hofer, a Swiss native living in Washington County, described the dilemma the war posed for many immigrant families when she wrote, "Now our sons here must use weapons against their own relatives. That is, for me, very terrible."[85]

Utah's guardsmen trained at Camp Kearny in California, while draftees from the Beehive State trained at Fort Lewis in Washington. Most who trained at Fort Lewis were assigned to the Ninety-First Division of the American Expeditionary Force (AEF), dubbed the "Wild West" because of its heavy concentration of westerners. Utahns were so heavily represented in the division's 362nd Infantry Regiment that soldiers commonly called it "a Utah regiment."[86]

Partly because of personality conflicts between General John Pershing, commander of the AEF, and Frederick Strong, commander of the Fortieth Division, Pershing designated the Fortieth a depot division, which relegated the unit to Stateside duty for months. Not until June 1918 were 389 members of the 145th Field Artillery, a Utah unit, shipped overseas as replacements to serve in other divisions already in Europe. The rest of the Utah doughboys in the 145th finally disembarked for Europe in August, where they trained for weeks using French .75mm guns; the former guardsmen had just received orders to participate in an assault on Metz when Germany surrendered. Private Ralph Duvall of Midway groused, "At De Souge they made us like it, We began to drill some more, But it wasn't any use at all, for soon they stopped the war. Now all we want to know is, what the Hell we soldiered for?"[87]

Utah draftees and enlistees, along with the rest of the AEF, made their primary contribution to Germany's defeat in the Meuse-Argonne offensive, a costly campaign stretching over forty-seven days during which more American soldiers died than in any other battle in American history. Nearly half of the 362nd Regiment, composed mostly of Utahns, perished as they toiled to take a landscape that machine gunner Gus Faust of Fillmore described as "checkered with machine gun nests, camouflaged, and in every possible way, cunningly concealed." Both sides deployed poisonous gas, adding to the risks on the battlefield. Utahn Lamar Deming described the "nightmare" of advancing with his unit over terrain on the Verdun front that had been cleared of Germans by an advance party of US Marines two hours previously under heavy fire. "The fields were covered with dead," he wrote, and the corpses of the ill-fated advance party "were still warm and still dripping blood." Their first night out Deming and his comrades camped in "little holes" they had dug. A storm of German shells shook the camp through the night, killing several horses. One shell exploded twelve feet from where Deming slept, creating a six-foot crater. When the war ended in November, 219 Utahns had died of battlefield injuries, while an additional 864 were wounded; 446 more had succumbed to disease or accident.[88]

At least 37 Utah women served overseas as noncombatant nurses with the Army Nurse Corps and Navy Nurse Corps, while even more served Stateside at military bases and training camps. Sometimes working on surgical teams in makeshift quarters such as hospital tents, they labored feverishly to save the lives and limbs of wounded or gassed soldiers. Mabel Bettilyon wrote her mother, "So many people are anxious for German souvenirs, but...seeing our men wounded and dying is all I want that refers to Germany." A few female Utahns, including Maud Fitch of Eureka, drove ambulances as representatives of private philanthropic enterprises, while other women staffed Salvation Army or Red Cross canteens.[89]

On the home front the State Council of Defense, organized by Governor Bamberger and chaired by L. H. Farnsworth, promoted patriotism and preparedness. Twenty-eight subcommittees were organized covering all facets of preparedness, including propaganda, fund-raising, Americanizing immigrants, recruiting soldiers, sanitation, conserving food and fuel, boosting industrial production, and preventing sabotage. Parallel defense councils at the county level complemented the statewide organizations. One of the state council's first tasks involved boosting agricultural production to ensure adequate food for the troops. The council boosted food production by procuring 1.25 million pounds of additional seed and persuading farmers to plant it, using their crops as collateral to ensure loan repayment. Members also worked with Forest Service personnel to ensure that ranges were stocked to their maximum livestock carrying capacity. One subcommittee promoted the "Gospel of the Clean Plate" and encouraged Utahns to consume "less wheat, meat, milk, fats, sugar and fuel [and eat] more fruit, vegetables, foods that are not suitable to be sent to camps." Another responded to a request from the War Department by producing detailed maps of the state showing topography, utility lines, roads, trails, and bridges. Hundreds of teenage boys were recruited and registered in the Boys Working Reserve for work on farms, particularly in thinning sugar beets, picking apples, and harvesting potatoes.[90]

Generally, the committee's actions were prudent. In the matter of loyalty, though, an alarmist mentality drove preparedness efforts to unwarranted excesses. When Farnsworth attended a coordinating conference in Washington, DC, he heard Secretary of the Navy Josephus Daniels advocate "full Americanization," meaning that "not only will every American be mobilized for war, but we will put the fear of God into the hearts of those who live among us and fatten on us, but are not Americans." Farnsworth returned to Salt Lake, alarmed at the large number of German-language newspapers and German-speaking parochial schools and at the political power of German immigrants and their children. Fearful of German sabotage and worried that German speakers were susceptible to German propaganda, he persuaded the state council to pass a resolution urging schools across the state to discontinue German-language instruction. Although some school administrators believed there was "not the slightest relation between the teaching of the Teutonic language in the classroom and the successful waging of the big war," they complied. German-speaking churches and the German-language press also came under fire. Utah's German newspaper, the *Beobachter*, managed to stay in print throughout the war, despite allegations of disloyalty, but a German Lutheran church in Ogden closed due to anti-German pressure.[91]

Perhaps reflecting the Progressive commitment to efficiency and hypercoordination, the governor appointed the Committee on Women's Work in the World War, chaired by Mrs. W. N. Williams, to encourage and coordinate women's support of the war by acting as a liaison between the state and women's clubs, sororities, and other women's organizations. The committee encouraged women to form chapters of the Red Cross and to knit socks, sweaters, and shoulder wraps for soldiers. Under the leadership of Janette Hyde, the Committee on Food Supply and Conservation encouraged home gardening and canning by sponsoring contests. Another subcommittee led by Charlotte Stewart hosted parties and dinners for soldiers in transit, while yet another, led by Mrs. F. E. Morris, identified job vacancies in factories and other businesses and recruited women to fill them. In June 1918 the Committee on Women's Work supported and circulated a resolution calling for nationwide Prohibition as a means of reducing grain consumption.[92]

Seizing the opportunity to be patriotic and make money at the same time, entrepreneurs established new industrial and mining operations, nurturing ties between corporations and the federal government. These included a new sugar factory in Brigham City, a potash plant in Piute County, an antimony mine in Garfield County, and an ozokerite mine in Wasatch County. Meanwhile, existing coal mines expanded production, and new coal mines opened.[93]

Public and private universities also supported the war effort by training soldiers. The State Agricultural College in Logan was designated a training center for the Army Air Corps. At Brigham Young University (BYU), a unit of the Student Army Training Corps operated. Organized by the War Department, the corps trained soldiers in vital skills for the war effort, including carpentry, blacksmithing, and auto mechanics.[94]

War's end was the cause for immense celebration at home, even though some Utah soldiers who had been preparing for battle in Europe were disappointed to have missed the chance for heroic combat. In Salt Lake so many celebrants thronged the streets "from early day to late night" that a planned parade had to be called off because it could not proceed. Revelers danced for hours on Main Street to the music of three bands. "Victory confetti" thrown from the tops of high-rise buildings downtown blanketed the streets, the kaiser was hung in effigy, and "a screaming multitude laughing and gay" engaged in "a riotous revel" that one reporter characterized as "a merger of the wildest New Year's Eve demonstration when John Barleycorn wielded the scepter, with the biggest Labor Day and Fourth of July manifestations." One resident of Wasatch County recalled, "The town simply went wild. Every place of business closed up; people were parading up and down the street, getting their horse and buggy and riding like mad.... I went riding up and down the street, yelling at the top of my voice."[95]

Soldiers returned home to households and communities under quarantine due to the deadliest influenza pandemic of the century, the product of an H1N1 virus that provoked a severe immune system response. When combined with bacterial coinfections such as pneumonia, the virus often proved fatal. In the United States and in Utah, one-fifth of the population battled the virus, and more than 600,000 died. Many cases were never reported to the state public health authorities, but the Utah Health Department cataloged 91,799 cases between 1918 and 1920 with 2,915 deaths, or a death rate of nearly 3.2 percent. Among the state's Native Americans, death rates from the disease were much higher: 16 percent. Many Native Americans lived in remote areas and lacked access to medical care. Navajos commonly abandoned their hogans after a death occurred there for cultural reasons, and their consequent exposure to the elements in the winter likely weakened their ability to resist the disease.[96]

Although the first outbreak of the deadly viral infection in the United States had occurred in Fort Riley, Kansas, in March 1918, the first reported cases in Utah occurred during a deadly nationwide comeback of the disease that commenced in September and October 1918, only weeks before the war's end. On October 10 Dr. T. B. Beatty, Utah's state health officer, banned all public meetings, including church services, and urged school officials to cancel classes until the epidemic subsided. The quarantine was temporarily lifted for celebrations of the Armistice ending the war on November 11, but then reimposed. Although the Utah Board of Health opposed any parades or public celebrations of the return of the Utah National Guard early in January, city officials and Governor Bamberger vetoed their recommendation and permitted the troops to parade through Ogden, when the troops arrived by train on January 15, and in Logan, where they were housed for a week before demobilization was completed. No welcoming banquets were held, but Governor Bamberger, LDS Church president Heber J. Grant, and Brigadier General Richard W. Young took off their protective respiratory masks to address the troops in a public meeting.[97]

DISSENT IN A RIGHT-WING STATE

Progressivism was no monolithic or one-dimensional phenomenon. It expressed itself in almost every phase of life. Education, science, race and class relations, religion, and business as well as country living and urban growth were all more or less reordered and restructured by it. Although its fulcrum was in the middle class, including college-trained professionals, its reformist influence animated the broader political spectrum. The Democratic and Republican Parties as well as all third-party movements responded to its promptings. Involving change, it was closely tied to dissent and reform.

Responding to many of the problems arising from industrialization, urbanization, and incorporation that concerned the Progressives, the Socialists fielded candidates in Utah elections throughout the Progressive Era. First organized in Utah in 1901, they exerted the greatest influence between 1901 and 1912. They reached their apogee in 1911 when thirty-three Socialist candidates were elected to municipal office in ten communities. All told, they elected close to one hundred candidates to office in nineteen communities and were represented in the state legislature. In 1912 Socialist presidential candidate Eugene Debs polled 8 percent of the vote. The party enjoyed a symbiotic relationship with the labor movement and drew upon a "wide cross section of people" and "a strong working class base," according to historian

John McCormick. They "tended to be radicals in theory" but focused upon public ownership of utilities such as gas and water in practice. Never attracting many supporters after 1912, their appeal was weakened further by the Progressive programs enacted in 1917 and called for in the Democratic platform of 1918. But hurting them worse was their opposition to American involvement in World War I. They were also tarred by the brush of the Russian Revolution and fear of all things radical. In 1918 they were strongly condemned in Utah and received less than 1 percent of the vote.

William Spry's well-known opposition to radical labor reflected the attitude of most Utahns toward Socialists and other radical groups. In a 1917 speech he is said to have cautioned that internal disorder was "perhaps more dangerous than the Germans." Warming to his denunciations, he went on to say that "a few executions" would serve as "a remedy for the traitor evil." *Goodwin's Weekly* concurred and, on the grounds that the "Bolsheviki" would "be our greatest internal menace after the war," thought Spry's election to Congress would be therapeutic.[98]

But for all this, reform and dissent attracted some supporters, perhaps because of frustration or a sense of powerlessness or anger at how little they governed their own lives. A case study in the relationships of frustrations and the nature of Utah radicalism was Parley P. Christensen, sometime Republican, unremitting dissenter, and Farmer-Labor Party candidate for president in 1920. Born in Cache Valley to a onetime Mormon family, he was educated there and at the University of Deseret before getting his law degree at Cornell in 1897. Handsome and charismatic, he was a gifted speaker, shallow intellectually, politically motivated, a consistent reformer, willing to play both ends against the middle to win a point, and driven by an active ego and a taste for public acclaim.

After returning to Utah and setting up practice in Salt Lake City, Christensen displayed an insatiable appetite for political discussion and immediately became active in the Republican Party. As a lawyer he showed a special interest in labor's cause, handling cases for Park City miners and construction tradesmen from Salt Lake City that earned him the lasting enmity of Thomas Kearns and Salt Lake City building contractors. He served as Salt Lake County attorney for two terms, working with antimachine Republicans but maintaining his distance from the American Party.

After losing his reelection bid in 1906, Christensen repeatedly tried for the Republican nomination for Congress. In the process he took every opportunity to define a reform point of view and challenged the Smoot machine's popular Joseph Howell, who regarded him more as a nuisance than a serious contender.[99] As a rule he drew more votes in outlying mining and railroading counties than along the Wasatch Front, where he was better known. Favorite political themes included anti-bossism, miners' rights, direct primaries, the initiative and referendum, as well as the Bull Moose insurgency. Tending increasingly to radicalism, he remained a Progressive Republican until 1919, when he could probably be termed a Labor Party socialist.[100]

Christensen's capacity to be his own worst enemy showed at the height of his Utah success. In 1914 he helped draft a strong Progressive platform promoting equal distribution of "the rewards of industry," good roads, full enfranchisement of women, quality education, and a referendum on statewide Prohibition. Along with fellow Salt Lake Progressive Lily C. Wolstenholme, he was elected to the Utah House of Representatives by a good margin. After a fusionist combination bid fair to elect him Speaker, a turn of events led to his defeat, whereupon he bolted from the legislature, returning only after about a week of sulking and then to the derision of many of his colleagues and the press.[101]

While Progressive reforms met the need of more moderate insurgents such as C. E. Loose and William Glasmann locally and Teddy Roosevelt nationally in 1918–19, radicals in both the political and the labor fields viewed the disparity between haves and have-nots with mounting alarm. Many left-leaning Progressives like Christensen were convinced it was time to organize a national labor party that corresponded with leftist labor's interest in an independent party. Reflecting his increasing radicalism, Christensen took cases about this time for the Industrial Workers of the World (IWW), the Culinary Alliance, and the Amalgamated Association of Streetcar and Electric Railway Engineers in Salt Lake City. He also affiliated with the Newswriters' Union and, notably, was connected with the national Committee of Forty-Eight, a moderate and intellectually inclined socialist group.

In 1919 Christensen found himself in Chicago, where the limelight finally fell upon him. By now middle-aged but still with a flair for striking dress and self-presentation, he rose in the course of two days from an unknown to chairman at the Committee of Forty-Eight convention. There he steered delegates past an ugly impasse. When they adjourned to the Labor Party convention, he was again called to preside. When Robert M. La Follette refused to accept their nomination, Christensen was nominated on the second ballot, primarily by Labor Party delegates, as many of the less radical and eastern Forty-Eighters bolted. Thus, in one of Utah's greatest Cinderella stories, Parley Christensen became the presidential candidate of a party that soon styled itself the Farmer-Labor Party.

His candidacy was greeted with derision in Utah and with little attention nationally. He campaigned without an effective plan yet logged more than thirty-six thousand miles and invoked many radical agrarian and labor themes, denounced American foreign policy as the tool of international bankers, and portrayed the Farmer-Labor Party as a "100 percent American effort to restore to the people the right to govern themselves."[102] Although the *New York Times* predicted he would carry nine states, he actually polled about 250,000 votes. Running best in South

Dakota, Washington, and Montana, he garnered only 4,475 Utah votes, or 3 percent of the total.[103] As John Sillito shows, Christensen concluded after a long engagement with the conventional two-party structure that success "would require new political parties and a realignment of the American political structure."[104]

Christensen's career, born of his experiences in Utah, shows how varied the state's political scene was in the Progressive Era. Despite business and religious conservatism, the Smoot machine's dominance, and the slow pace of Progressive reform in many regards, the Beehive State's mines and railroad camps nurtured discontent and even radical calls for reform.

The general tenor of the state, though, was conservative and suspicious of most strains of Progressive reform until late in 1916, when they elected Woodrow Wilson, Simon Bamberger, and a Progressive Democratic legislature. The fragile coexistence of non-Mormon and Mormon in these awkward adolescent years of statehood and the constant threat of a return to the American Party induced key Mormon leaders, including Joseph F. Smith and Reed Smoot, to maintain their distance from statewide Prohibition. As the following chapters show, Mormon and Gentile elites instead found common ground in corporate values and a quest for commercial prosperity.

3

AGRICULTURE IN THE NEW STATE

NEW SETTLEMENT

As statehood dawned in 1896, the self-sufficient and subsistence farming that had undergirded the Mormon economic system was giving way to commercial or cash-crop agriculture. Commercial farming entailed changes in the crops that were raised, the method and purpose of raising them, and the way Utahns involved themselves in the agricultural movements of the era. Cash-crop farming incorporated many of Utah's natural resources within the nation's burgeoning industrial complex. Utah's best land had long since been claimed, but the profit motive spurred new land claims and settlement more strongly than ever. The myth of turning desert into blossom was widely accepted, and the speculative impulse ran strong—it was time to grow.

Under this regimen land entry and settlement developed as at no other time in the state's history. During the 1890s total land in farms increased almost four-fold, from 1.3 million acres to 4.1 million, far outstripping development in the hey-day of Brigham Young's best colonizing efforts. Improved farmland nearly doubled, and irrigated land increased by 132 percent. After a lull during the first decade of the new century, land entry surged again between 1909 and 1918, when settlers took up "575,000 new acres each year," mostly in remote desert country. Farms increased from 21,700 in 1910 to 25,700 in 1920. Mormon farmers threw off any lingering qualms arising from Brigham Young's injunctions against profiteering on land and became speculators, taking advantage of their own improvements as well as unearned increments. During the first decade of the century, the average value of farmland reportedly increased from $9.75 to $29.28 per acre. Estimates rarely placed arable land above 5 percent of the state's total, but by 1920 more than 9.6 percent of its total area had been claimed for agriculture.[1]

The efforts of women homesteaders, among others, illustrated the strength of land settlement during the 1890s and the early decades of the new century. As historian Jill Thorley Warnick has shown, females represented a significant proportion of those who filed and proved up on homesteads in the Cedar City (12.9 percent), Logan (12.5 percent), and Monticello (9.9 percent) areas. Tract books show three women filing in the Cedar City area in the 1880s, forty-six in the 1890s, twelve from 1901 to 1910, and fifteen between 1911 and 1915. In the Logan area twenty-five filed in the 1890s, eight during the next decade, and twenty-one in the teen years. Monticello showed no women filing until the second decade of the new century, when they filed fifty-six claims.[2]

Utah's homesteaders responded to a number of national developments; the "Country Life" and "Back to the Land" movements, with Theodore Roosevelt's avid support, did much to refocus national attention on the family farm. Together with the growing science of dryland farming and the Progressive enthusiasm for putting land resources in the hands of actual homemakers, the Country Life movement prompted Congress to pass the Enlarged Homestead Act in 1909 and the Stock Raising Homestead Act in 1916 in hopes that arid agriculture's "highly specialized" methods would transform marginal lands into productive American homes.[3] Also encouraging movement onto desert lands were the Carey Land Act of 1894 and the Newlands Act of 1902, which put the federal government in the reclamation business and created the Reclamation Service. The Dawes Severalty Act of 1887, which allotted individual farms to Indians and diverted remaining reservation lands to white settlement, also facilitated land settlement.[4] The first decades of statehood were also a time of great conventions, including the irrigation and dryland congresses, which issued an outpouring of periodical literature, promotional books, and technical publications proclaiming the virtues of unclaimed lands.[5]

Utah's scientists and engineers were well received by the irrigation and dryland farm movement and played important roles in promoting western agriculture generally. Senator Reed Smoot helped frame the new land policy of desert expansion. The LDS Church continued to promote land settlement, preaching it from the pulpit and assigning its best men to head up colonization efforts. The State Bureau of Immigration and State Land Board published reports advertising land-settlement opportunities.[6]

Utah investors saw land as a special arena, commercial clubs flourished, and chest-thumping rural newspapers did what they could to advance the cause.

Capitalists from the Midwest and California showed a lively interest in Utah land schemes, and established railroad corporations worked to advance agriculture along their lines. New roads mounted especially vigorous land promotions. Along with land developers, well-educated, fast-talking land agents such as University of Utah–trained engineer William L. Woolf bought, groomed, and resold farms; showed prospective customers planned towns and market roads; promoted alkali flats; and blithely promised water.[7] Developers and manufacturers maintained experimental farms that played the same role.[8] New canneries, creameries, flour mills, sugar factories, and woolen mills lured would-be settlers with promises of ready markets and handsome prices for farm products.

Thus motivated, both men and women moved onto Utah's marginal lands. Most of the new settlers came from within the state itself, but many also gathered from other regions, including the Midwest. Even an occasional immigrant group arrived to take up ill-starred communal holdings, as did a Hungarian colony on the slope of southeastern Utah's La Sal Mountains and a party of Russians near Kelton in Box Elder County. Leaving a much clearer mark were Jewish immigrants from Austria and Russia who in 1911–12 came by way of New York and Philadelphia to Clarion in central Utah. Led by Benjamin Brown, who went on to establish the Intermountain Farmers' Association, they were part of an international back-to-the-soil movement that drew Utah into its orbit. Clarion was situated on a state reclamation project at the end of the long and newly constructed state-operated canal that was supposed to carry water from Piute Reservoir. The Jewish families who together took some six thousand acres were hardworking and determined but inexperienced. Moreover, they lacked sufficient capital to survive drought and irrigation-system failures. Most of the Jewish colonists left in defeat by 1915.[9]

As settlements proceeded on leftover lands, the story varied only in the detail and background of settlers. In the Uinta Basin, upwards of a million acres were taken from the Ute Indians and in 1905 opened to homesteading and sale. At filing offices in Provo, Price, and Grand Junction, Colorado, more than thirty-seven thousand prospective settlers gathered in tent cities, waiting for lots to be drawn.[10] A land office was established in Vernal. Approximately sixteen hundred homestead families were shortly located on the bench-and-hollow slopes of the Uinta Mountains. A good many lived in close proximity to Ute allottees, in keeping with the assimilationist philosophy of early-twentieth-century Indian policy.

The Bureau of Indian Affairs (BIA) launched the $625,000 Uintah Irrigation Project to provide water for Indian farmers and to sell water to white settlers. Work on the project enabled many white homesteaders to survive until their farms produced but provided little support for the Uinta Basin's hard-pressed Native Americans, who utterly opposed allotment and the assimilation that it implied. As farm settlement proceeded, Uintah County's population rose from sixty-four hundred in 1905 to twelve thousand in 1907, and Duchesne County was created. Some intermixing of Indians and whites distinguished the cultural landscape from earlier Mormon villages as well as from the ranching country in neighboring Wyoming and Colorado. Settlement proved to be more a matter of individual response than big promotion. No railroad passed through to attract developers and capitalists. With the Uintah Irrigation Project under way, heavily capitalized state and private water projects did not materialize. Settlers organized new towns, named them for presidents, established unheeded newspapers, and stood by as delivery dates for water were postponed, drought tightened, and debt deepened. Mining wizard Jesse Knight moved to rescue homesteaders of the Blue Bench District north of Duchesne. One reverse precipitating another, he built a faulty canyon-side flume, took over failing farms on debts, but failed to make the Blue Bench pay.[11]

In southwestern Utah Cedar City banker Lehi Jones and several Salt Lake City developers pinned their hopes on the vast Escalante Desert. There, the New Castle Project built a hotel in the midst of dust and sagebrush, bought two Cadillacs to whisk salesmen and prospective buyers around the country, broke new ground with steam tractors, and scoured the country for wood to fire their boilers. The company built a dam and tunnel in neighboring Grass Valley, used Japanese workers to divert Pine Valley Creek through the "Jap Ditch," and for a short time brought water from the Colorado Plateau to the Great Basin before drought and developing leaks defeated it.[12]

In Millard and Beaver Counties, Carey Land Act promotions and water projects attracted settlers to what the State Land Board optimistically advertised as irrigated farms. Delta was the focus of much of this promotion. By dint of much sacrifice, the Sevier River Bridge Dam was raised to hold more than 225,000 acre-feet of water. Work was done primarily by area farmers. A succession of Utah companies, including the National Savings and Trust Company in Salt Lake whose directors included Heber J. Grant and William S. McCornick, Oasis Land and Irrigation, Delta Land and Water, Sevier River Land and Water, and Deseret Irrigation, put up money for irrigation structures, hoping to sell water to the settlers at a profit. Successive waves of settlers faced drought, floods, and alkali's creeping takeover. Drainage systems were overbuilt or ineffective, and unceasing court battles defended water rights. Alfalfa seed, which grew well, provided a cash crop, and somehow the community grew.[13]

Coinciding with new irrigation projects was a major movement onto dryland homesteads. In all, approximately five thousand drylanders proved up on "about a million and a quarter acres of submarginal" land in the western deserts of Box Elder, Tooele, Utah, Juab, Beaver, and Iron Counties during the century's second decade. Encouraged by wet years, wartime demands, and good prices, settlers

aimed to grow wheat. At Grouse Creek, Park Valley, Yost, Dugway, Faust, and Vernon, and in the miles between, the hopeful families located. They were joined by
corporate opportunists such as Charles and Justin Skidmore's Rush Valley Farming Company, whose directors included Utah's future governor Henry H. Blood
and prominent Logan businessman Lee Thatcher. The company employed workers around the clock in 1907–8 to break more than ten thousand acres of desert soil
with horse-drawn plows and a steam-powered tractor and sow winter wheat.[14]

In San Juan County big things were expected from dry farming, too. Numerous homestead districts took shape after 1915, as settlers gathered from the maturing
communities of Utah and from the Mormon colonies in Mexico. The "out east" districts along the Colorado border east of Monticello were part of the dry-farm boom.
One town site was surveyed on the south slope of the La Sal Mountains near the
headquarters of the sprawling La Sal Livestock Company. A school was built and a
Mormon ward established to serve some four hundred people who farmed by mixing dry-farm techniques with seasonal irrigation from high-water runoff. The area
shortly became "an island of hardcore poverty." Homesteaders ate what they raised,
lived in mud-roofed cabins, tended their "limp fields," and trapped, freighted, or
worked for the company or at copper mines and oil rigs. A season of good rains
quickly passed, and settlers ran up bills at the company store. In the end, most La
Sal dry farmers sold out to the company or simply walked away.[15]

Dry farmers were influenced by experimental arid farms established by John A.
Widtsoe, director of the Agricultural College's experiment station and a national
leader in the arid-farm movement. He tested its possibilities, demonstrated its
methods, preached its virtues with religious fervor, and founded arid-farm companies and districts.[16]

Widtsoe protégés included Dan Perkins and Will Brooks, who spent the summer working at his huge arid farm in Juab County's Dog Valley. Later, Brooks and
Perkins ran the San Juan County experimental farm, bought three thousand acres
of state land, and took out enlarged homesteads. During 1909 they cleared land,
built fences, and started farming. For much-needed cash, Brooks taught school and
clerked in trading posts. Perkins's wife died of typhoid, and Brooks lay at death's
door. The shock barely slowed the partners. Indeed, it was a time of great promise.
But things changed quickly. Brooks took a wife who had no taste for the new frontier, and by mid-1912 they pulled out. With the boom still under way, he sold his
interests for eight thousand dollars, a princely sum in dry-farm circles. Most were
less fortunate, struggling on for years and giving up in the hard times after World
War I. Not all dryland farmers failed, but as Craig Torbenson has noted, "For nearly
every success story...there was a story of failure." As historical geographer Marshall Bowen concludes, on "submarginal lands of the Great Basin" dryland farmers

"experienced an almost inevitable sequence of crop failure, land destruction and human despair."[17]

ORCHARD BOOM

In Utah's central valleys one of the earliest agricultural promotions involved fruit culture. California groves attracted favorable attention, as did the fruit industry in Colorado and Washington. However, with thousands of aging town orchards, Utahns of the 1890s faced not only a "mass of ill-kept, abused fruit trees" but a blight and pest infestation that threatened to destroy all vestiges of fruit production. After "much agitation" mandatory spraying laws were passed in 1893 and again in 1895 and 1897. To put teeth in the fruit laws, the State Horticultural Board was created, the forerunner of what would become the State Department of Agriculture and Food in 1921, and county inspectors appointed.[18]

By 1898 the Wasatch Front counties were cleaning up infected orchards. They inspected nurseries, enforced the spray law, and burned 16,000 infected trees. Salt Lake County inspector J. P. Sorensen supervised the "disinfection" of 100,000 trees. In Sanpete and Sevier Counties, where orchards varied from a "dozen to one thousand trees," the campaign made good progress. Juab County orchardists, however, resisted until "prosecution under the law" forced compliance.[19]

By 1900 fruit was being hailed as a Utah bonanza. Great irrigation projects were built on its prospects.[20] Counties gave their support. Orchard associations were organized, delegations were sent to fruit-bearing regions, and new orchards were planted. In 1909 Frank Barber, founder of the Hurricane Nursery Company and vice president of the town's commercial club, organized a fruit festival to promote fruit farming. It was reported that the Bear River Irrigation Company had started more than 100,000 trees in Box Elder County and that the Mount Nebo Company had planted 15,000 in Juab County.[21] Fruit growers and investors in Weber County organized the Ben Lomond Orchard Company in 1912 and purchased a canner from Edwin G. McGriff in North Ogden to can fruit. Cache County, which sold $3,204 worth of fruit in 1890, marketed fruit valued at $65,432 and $200,000, respectively, in 1910 and 1920. Simultaneously, it saw a succession of promotions at the westside communities of Trenton and Cornish based primarily upon the area's prospects for orchards. Speculative planting continued until 1912, when more than forty-three thousand acres were in orchards. Then as trees came into production, the bottom fell out of the market, and frost and drought proved to be formidable foes. Shipped fruit either suffered in transit or reached glutted markets. Entire trainloads were dumped, and hard-pressed growers were billed for the "dumping besides the cost of" production, packing, and transportation. Sobered, orchard men pulled out as many as 140,000 trees per year, reducing orchards to twenty-nine thousand acres by 1916.[22]

DAIRYING

Developments in dairying were more successful. Original pioneers brought live-stock from the Midwest and traded for more "states cows" from Oregon Trail trav-elers. Devon and Durham breeds—multipurpose animals useful for beef and draft as well as milk—dominated bloodlines. For decades dairying was little more than an adjunct of family life and fitted more in the context of the pooled livestock herd than as an independent industry. Milk was sold or exchanged locally. Surpluses were manufactured into cheese and butter, sometimes as home enterprises but increasingly at summer dairies in the mountains operated by women and children, as families responded to new markets, found homestead opportunities, and sought climatic relief and escape from summer diseases.

Although it is difficult to gauge the magnitude of this business, there were hun-dreds of mountain dairies. Butter may have brought 25 cents a pound but often as little as 8 or 9 cents. The 1890 census reported 45,982 milk cows in the territory, with the largest numbers in Cache, Salt Lake, Kane, Sevier, and Utah Counties, and reported production of more than 8 million gallons of milk, 1.8 million pounds of butter, and more than 163,000 pounds of cheese in 1889.[23]

Before 1890 year-round milking for manufacturing purposes was little known. The summer operation took advantage of spring calving, lush feed, and heavy lac-tation that rarely lasted beyond September 1. While their men farmed or worked sheep, dozens of Cedar City women and children fanned out each summer at dair-ies along the edge of Cedar Mountain and in the High Plateaus beyond. They made thousands of cheeses, salted down tons of butter for winter markets, and established grazing rights and homestead claims. Apostle Brigham Young Jr. organized a cattle operation on San Juan County's remote Elk Ridge that included an extensive sum-mer dairy.

Hundreds of town families plied a summer trade in butter and cheese. Near present Granger in Salt Lake County, Mary Alice Lambert churned a few pounds of butter each week that she carefully cooled with dampened, fresh-cut grass or alfalfa as she made her way to the "city" markets. In the North Point sloughs not far from the present Salt Lake Airport, the parents of Harry Lunn homesteaded and milked cows. Each summer his mother churned 75 or more pounds of butter weekly that was marketed for a premium 25 cents a pound at the New York Cash Store and the posh Knutsford Hotel. Buyers told a neighboring Swedish lady, "We just can't use your butter anymore.... [W]e seen pieces of flies" in it. She retorted, "I know bet-ter.... I spent hours a pickin' them flies out."[24]

A few dairies were relatively large undertakings. Brigham City's mountain dairy, for example, milked 650 rented cows near Collinston. Managed by Christen Hansen and his wife, it employed more than twenty milkmaids and a similar number of adults and boys. The Hyrum United Order milked 350 cows above Hardware Ranch in Blacksmith Fork Canyon, but in the mid-1890s it passed into the capable hands of Andrew Israelsen, who ran it with his family in the summer.

The turn-of-the-century years were marked by the importation of cows, year-round milking, and herd improvement. The earliest purebred bulls dated to the mid-1870s, but it was not until after 1910 that breeding programs established recognizable concentrations of purebred Holsteins in Cache Valley and of Jerseys and Guernseys on the Wasatch Front. In 1915 Holstein producers in northern Utah initiated the Richmond Black and White Days that provided competitive impetus for Cache Valley in supplying purebred breeding stock and high-producing heifers. The Babcock butterfat test, an inexpensive technological breakthrough, enabled manufacturers to pay according to fat content by the late 1890s and by 1911 made milk production testing possible. Beginning in Denmark with spectacular success, production testing spread to the Midwest by 1910. Dairymen in Cache Valley experimented with it in the years just prior to World War I, but it was not seriously applied in Utah until the 1930s.[25]

About 1890 what were probably the first year-round creameries were established by Lorenzo Hansen and Samuel McMurtie at Wellsville and Paradise in the south end of Cache Valley and by Marriner W. Merrill and his family at Richmond. Each of them found that local milkers were initially reluctant to commit themselves to production by contract, but in time sustained production caught on and additional creameries were built and established plants enlarged, nurturing corporate ties between farmers and processors.[26] To begin with, creameries encountered serious transportation problems. Short-haul railroad rates were sufficiently high that the Pacific Express Company, which charged "$1 per hundred pounds for shipping butter from Logan and Wellsville to Salt Lake City," had the carrying business tied up. Thinking it could be done for sixty cents a hundredweight, Lorenzo Hansen approached Pacific Express. When his overtures were rejected, he bought "eight head of wild mules" and set up his own freight business. After two years Pacific Express met Hansen's terms, informing him to get "them damned mules off the road."[27]

Within a few years milk plants were established throughout the state, reaching a high of 125 plants in 1904. Many were shoestring operations depending on anticipated rather than established milk production. A few, like one near Moroni that milked 147 cows, maintained large herds as their chief source of milk. The most ambitious were three condenseries built in Cache Valley after 1902 that forged links between local and outside capital and markets. Opening at about forty thousand gallons a day in capacity, they increased rapidly to as much as two hundred thousand gallons a day as outside interests established the Sego plant at Richmond and Borden Company bought the Lorenzo Hansen plant in Logan, making Cache Valley one of the significant evaporated-milk centers of the West.[28]

By 1914, 94 creameries had failed or sold out to larger operators, leaving 36 working plants in sixteen counties. A number of factors contributed to consolidation. Competition forced railroad rates down. The farm separator, which quickly separated cream from milk, came into general use, making distance from market a minor consideration. Also contributing were better prices from the condenseries and big plants such as the Elgin and Nelson's Creameries in Salt Lake City. Probably the most important factor in the falling plant numbers was the growing market for milk in Salt Lake City, Ogden, and the mining districts.[29]

In the century's first decade milk was still delivered in the Salt Lake market by the dipper full. Ten-gallon cans were cooled to about fifty-eight degrees in streams or springs, insulated with wet burlap and ice chips, and often hauled to as many as 150 customers per delivery wagon. By good management some operators claimed they could keep milk as cool as sixty degrees through the course of a summer day's deliveries.[30]

Fluid milk also sold well at coal and other mining camps. With strong seasonal rhythms and varying work opportunities, the coal industry apparently distracted many farmers, and Carbon County agriculture generally did not flourish.[31] Yet the railroads and mines created a milk market of considerable importance. In Price the Carbon and Modern Dairies were distributors, buying bulk milk from farmers along the Price River between Helper and Wellington and south to Miller Creek. At Spring Glen the Fazzios operated the Blue Hill Dairy.

Statewide, dairying grew slowly until about 1920. Dairying lacked the political clout of the sheep industry and the centralized corporate structure of sugar beets, but as demonstrated in 1910 when it yielded two million dollars it was an important contributor to the agricultural economy. Promoted by purebred breeders, major condenseries, creameries, and the Agricultural College, Cache and the Wasatch Front counties developed concentrations of well-bred animals, good dairies, and paying businesses. Testing, selective breeding, and feeding programs that gave priority to milk cows instead of horses led to increased production.[32]

In many ways Cache County was Utah's preeminent dairy county. The largest mountain dairies ran there. Intelligently designed and well-maintained barns gave it a landscape of bucolic prosperity. Several of the earliest creameries operated there, the state's only condenseries were established there, and the Agricultural College found it an easy industry to advance in the context of its US Department of Agriculture (USDA) family farm–oriented programs. In addition, Cache County dominated the dairy industry in income in all phases but the fluid milk market, whose large but fragmented business centered in Salt Lake and Weber Counties.[33]

SUGAR BEETS

The self-sufficiency of Utah's agricultural past merged with the new commercialism and the world of incorporation with especially important repercussions in the sugar beet industry. Initiated by leading Mormons, the sugar industry was an effort to stabilize established agriculture while at the same time embracing industrial and corporate America. Like dairying and dry farming, it employed new scientific systems of production and produced for markets outside Utah. But more than either, it was affected by the era's great questions regarding monopoly. Utah's sugar industry was quickly taken over by the sugar trust, and its local directors perpetuated and extended the paternalism arising from their church positions. Friction and enmity often divided farmer and factory, and management's first interest almost always seemed to be the factory. On the other hand, as historian Leonard Arrington observes, the company and its factories represented "an organic center" around which "the agricultural life" of the beet-producing family farms coalesced.[34]

On September 4, 1889, the Utah Sugar Company (USC) was incorporated by Mormon businessmen. It came at a time when federal legislation and increasing Gentile numbers threatened Mormon control. As Joseph F. Smith later recalled, it was hoped the sugar industry would "give employment to our people," thus in a modest way recapturing the initiative. By 1891 the company had selected Lehi as the site of its factory, and in a fortunate choice Lehi bishop Thomas R. Cutler was appointed general manager. E. H. Dyer, a specialist in beet-sugar factory construction, built a four-hundred-thousand-dollar plant, and 556 farmers grew eighteen hundred acres of beets that were successfully refined.

Yet Utah Sugar was not off to an easy start. Manufacturers worked to perfect the refining process, farm families struggled to raise beets profitably, and church leaders turned every expedient, both in and out of the church, to keep the project afloat financially during the panic of the 1890s and pushed discouraged farmers not to abandon their beet fields. The Lehi operation did not show a profit until 1897. As prospects picked up, slicing stations were built at Springville, Spanish Fork, and Payson, and a gravity-flow pipe carried beet juice twenty miles to Lehi. It was a challenging time, as the Lehi team experimented and learned at every phase of production.[35]

Drawing on a Lehi-trained cadre, Utah sugar beet production spread quickly. In response to interest among Weber County farmers, David Eccles and other financiers built a plant at Ogden in 1898. When Cache Valley farmers demonstrated beets did well there, Eccles headed a group that built a Logan plant in 1900 and shortly consolidated the two under the name of Amalgamated Sugar Company. Meanwhile, Utah Sugar Company's interest turned to the Bear River Valley as a region with unrealized potential. In a classic example of the difficulties private finance encountered in reclamation, corporate efforts to develop Bear River irrigation had bogged down into ever-deepening troubles, as a succession of local, national, and international promotions and engineering and organizational maneuvers failed. When Bear River beet experiments succeeded, the Utah Sugar Company was able to break the legal and financial impasse in 1901. With its church connection and promise of a cash crop, it provided "the right catalyst for the valley's development."[36]

In a wonder of water, land, markets, and homemakers, the most stable and lasting agricultural development of the era took place, enabling Box Elder County to rank with Cache as one of the state's premier farm counties. Utah Sugar soon extended the east-side canal as far south as Brigham City, established a power plant in it, and persuaded the Oregon Short Line Railroad to build a branch to what became Garland. Pushing hard, E. H. Dyer completed the Garland factory for the 1903 campaign. By 1906 eighty-four thousand tons of beets were grown, and 207,000 one-hundred-pound bags of sugar were produced. In the midst of the Bear River Valley takeover, Utah Sugar reorganized as the Utah Sugar Company, which was recapitalized at six million dollars. Japanese and Sikhs from India were recruited to labor in the beet fields or to grow beets as sharecroppers. Some saved enough money to lease or purchase farmland. By 1909 there were close to 1,025 Japanese workers in the beet fields of northern Utah as well as about 150 Sikhs.[37]

About the same time, the American Sugar Refining Company interested itself in the beet-sugar industry, which by 1901 numbered "thirty-one separate concerns." Under Henry Havemeyer's leadership, ASRC approached the Utah Sugar Company, which in 1902 went along with a merger proposal that gave ASRC a half interest in the company. In what at this distance seems like a remarkable, if not indeed an impossible, deal, ASRC agreed to participate in USC expansion at the rate of 50 percent and apparently guaranteed that the local management would stay in control, but at the same time it defined operating regions for Utah, Idaho, and Colorado sugar interests.[38]

A period of gratifying growth followed. A development program was launched in Idaho, and in 1907 two Idaho properties merged with the Utah Sugar Company to become the Utah-Idaho Sugar Company. With an authorized capital of thirteen million dollars, the new corporation, like the one it replaced, was headed by Joseph F. Smith and managed by the canny Thomas R. Cutler. With the exception of William S. McCornick, dean of Salt Lake City bankers, its heavy local stockholders were Mormon. By 1920 Amalgamated Sugar, whose stockholders included Thomas Dee, W. A. Wattis, H. H. Rolapp, M. S. Browning, and token Gentile Fred Kiesel, as well as the David Eccles family, had developed overlapping ties with Utah-Idaho Sugar, and both companies had built and taken over other factories in response to local pressures. Not surprisingly, market conditions were especially important. Perhaps most important was the rise of sugar prices during World War I and the destruction of the European beet-sugar industry, which seemed to signal a prolonged period of favorable markets.[39]

With its west side developing and the strongest farm economy in Utah, Cache County was particularly bullish on sugar factories in the World War I years. Almost immediately after the Eccles interests had constructed the Logan factory in 1900, Charles W. Nibley, onetime Eccles partner and rising church leader, led in building a plant at Lewiston. Eccles acquired a substantial interest in it, and in 1904 it came under the Amalgamated Sugar umbrella.

In 1914 Nibley, now presiding bishop of the LDS Church, masterminded a movement for the church to purchase the Sugar Trust's interest in Amalgamated Sugar. When the deal fell through, Nibley himself purchased a major interest in ASRC. At this point Logan's J. A. Hendrickson, aspiring knitting king, proposed that a new factory be built at Smithfield, which was countered by Amalgamated's announcement of plans to build in the same vicinity. Hendrickson then launched an effort to move Jesse Knight's Raymond, Alberta, factory to Cache County's west side, which resulted in a quick profit for himself, a resumption of control by the Knights, and reconstruction at Cornish under the direction of Ernest R. Woolley, an Eccles-backed mining broker, who turned it over to Amalgamated Sugar Company.[40]

With the Oneida Canal Company project to bring thirty-three thousand acres of prime Cache Valley land under irrigation in chronic jeopardy, Amalgamated Sugar undertook to bail it out in 1916, projecting yet another beet district and mill along the Utah-Idaho border. Oneida land values increased dramatically, some rising from five dollars per acre to two hundred dollars, but the bailout proved more difficult than Amalgamated anticipated. Although it ultimately finished the canal, it backed out on the factory, which, with farmers clamoring for the payoff, was initiated at Whitney, a few miles into Idaho, by the Pingree-Idaho Sugar Company, whose interest was later purchased by Ernest Woolley and, in turn, by a Washington State investor who placed it in production in 1922.[41]

Statewide, factory development proceeded at a frenzied pace during the World War I years. In part this was a response to high prices, but also to some degree it was a protest against the established companies. In 1917 West Cache Sugar Company built at Cornish and Amalgamated Sugar at Amalga. In addition, the Great Basin Sugar Company, with Joseph Delamar, noted plunger in desert mines, at its head, built the Delta factory, which locals hailed as the world's largest, and after years of fruitless negotiation with Utah-Idaho Sugar the Peoples Sugar Company built a plant at Moroni in Sanpete Valley. Baited with prospects of a factory and a railroad through Salina Canyon, Carbon and Emery County farmers signed up to grow some seventy-five hundred acres of beets. When Utah-Idaho Sugar backed off, Castle Valley farmers offered to help Colorado's Holly Sugar build a plant in eastern Utah, but had to settle for shipping beets to Holly's Grand Junction plant. In 1918 the Gunnison Valley Sugar Company built the Centerfield plant to serve northern Sevier, and the Springville-Mapleton Company constructed a plant at Springville, with Jesse Knight "supplying the principal capital."[42]

Influenced by the Country Life movement, farmers of the era thought in terms of equity and the good life. They bought on time, educated their youngsters, and overextended themselves for land, improvements, and equipment. Economic slow-downs in the mid-1890s, in 1903, and in 1907 reduced the cash flow and complicated country life. In this context their quest for cash crops and commercial markets was unrelenting.

In an effort to cope with the new forces of corporate society, they experimented almost feverishly with a variety of cash crops, including wheat, milk, peas, toma-toes, various fruits, and especially sugar beets. We glimpse the role of beet sugar in the economy of the family farm in the writings of Mapleton farmer William Tew. Like many farm families, Tew cultivated several scattered plots due to inheritance practices and the broken character of the terrain. He had his home place, a south farm, and a north farm, and he ran his father's farm, too.[43] Over the years he not only experimented with every cash crop that came along, but also manipulated his plantings between the four places, as he tried to anticipate markets, moisture condi-tions, frost patterns, insect infestations, and distances. As the basis of his livestock operation, hay was largely consumed on the farm but sometimes entered the cash flow directly when Tew sold it in Springville or Provo. The Tews staffed their farm, although neighbor youngsters helped with the beets and picked fruit.[44]

Diffidence toward Utah-Idaho Sugar reverberates through the pages of Tew's journal. He was a Republican, bishop of his LDS ward, and a sometime town coun-cilman. As agent for the sugar company he communicated contract information, distributed seed, and sampled beets for their sugar and water content, from which the company fine-tuned payment and "ordered" the schedule by which digging pro-ceeded. Tew angered neighbors in his rigid adherence to sampling standards but was himself irritated at the way autocratic orders were handed down.

Schemes for slicing stations or factories at Springville or Spanish Fork always found a ready ear with him. When a California promoter proposed a local factory and a flat-rate base of five dollars per ton for the farmer and four dollars for the company and an even division of any additional proceeds, he was all ears. As the relationship between Tew and Utah-Idaho Sugar broke down, he turned increas-ingly to fruit, tomatoes, and chickens. Although he was a devoted Mormon and doubtless aware of the church's recurring calls for farmers to support the company, he gradually got out of the beet business and toward the end of his life was not friendly to it.[45]

If Tew was sometimes diffident, others went much further, tending to see the sugar company as villainous and oppressive. As Matthew Godfrey has written, the Utah-Idaho Sugar Company, "in the name of profitability, attempted to destroy competitors and to enact policies that would keep it afloat in the cutthroat world of sugar." One who saw the sugar company as oppressive was Wellington farmer Ray Branch, who masterminded Carbon County's shift to Holly Sugar and served as a Holly field man. Another was Elisha Warner, Spanish Fork's "country printer." Raised in a home without a mother, he had worked hard, scrimped, labored at Tintic mines, and bummed through southern Utah and Nevada as part of the itinerant workforce. Warner worked his way up in Spanish Fork's print shop, spent his life as publisher of its local paper, and commented on the sugar industry in his memoirs.[46]

To Warner, it seemed sugar beets were the only cash crop for farm families in turn-of-the-century Spanish Fork. "How did we live on the $380 that our seven acre plot netted each year?" he asked. Wood came "charge free" except for the work. His family had two cows and a few hens. They grew cane, and Moses Beckstead, who also lived in Spanish Fork, processed it for molasses. Clothes were worn forever, one prizewinner wearing the same suit for twenty-eight years. Other crops could not be turned into cash. Wheat was deposited at the mills but withdrawn only as flour. Fruit was peddled, but most people had trees. Stores bought eggs and butter but paid in trade.

As cash became increasingly necessary, the "sugar company held the whip hand and they used their power to keep the growers always in a docile mood" and in "virtual serfdom." Warner's portrait of the sugar trust was only partly accurate. Sugar's development was indeed a key factor in the state's economy. Probably the farm community's lot was significantly better than it would have been without sugar beets. Yet on contemplating the stories of William Tew and Spanish Fork's "country printer," one cannot escape the sense that the sugar companies exploited Utah growers and built corporate fortunes upon their backs.

CATTLE

The grazing industry was central to Utah's agricultural economy in the decades following statehood. Fewer animals and more people were involved in Utah's ranching industry than in those of other western states. Two identifiable parts constituted the industry by 1896. The oldest was the farm-grazing culture of the core villages that ran north to south through the center of the state.[47]

In bloodlines the village cattle industry long tended to the multiple-purpose Durham, Devon, and Shorthorn breeds, or "states cows," although some cattle of Hispanic derivation were undoubtedly included. Village cattle husbandry was part of the general farming pattern that evolved in Mormon country, with almost every farmstead owning a few cattle. In its institutions village husbandry partook strongly of the Mormon doctrines of stewardship and community. Town pools and the growth of the kingdom were often more important than profits or personal empires. However, in its land ethic it was far more the product of pressing need and short-term gain than it was of the sustained yield that wise stewardship would seem to imply. The public domain was essential to its development, but its village base and town pools gave a distinct twist to the common range, customary rights, and cooperative roundup that characterized western cattle ranching generally.[48]

After 1880 the frontier cattle ranch was superimposed on the village system but did not supplant it, giving Utah a second and far more characteristic form of cattle industry, cattle ranching. Livestock numbers had grown slowly in Utah until about 1880, when both internal and external conditions acted to produce a sharp increase. This upswing began first in cattle, which numbered about 200,000 head in 1885. This number grew to 356,621 by 1895. Thereafter, with sheep coming on aggressively and with the adverse effect of the panic of the mid-1890s, cattle barely held their own until 1905. Stimulated by Forest Service policy that partially offset the advantages sheep had gained, cattle surged again to 412,334 in 1910 and with another stimulus from World War I reached a high of 505,000 in 1920, the heyday of the cowboy in the state.[49]

The two modes of ranching that existed in Utah in 1900 were geographically split. In the central valleys the village pattern predominated. More than ten thousand farmers ran a few range cattle, shifting them from public domain to national forest, to private pasture, and to village field or feedlot, according to season and need.[50]

By contrast the outlying corners of the state were ranching country, and competition between the village and ranch cattle cultures was apparent. In San Juan County the first small ranches were bought up or taken over in the 1880s by corporate outfits, including the Pittsburg Company at La Sal, the English-based Carlisle Ranch near Monticello, the L. C. or Lacy Company at Verdure, and the Texas-owned ELKs on Elk Ridge. Headed by Lemuel H. Redd, the Bluff Pool shifted from village agriculture to cattle to meet this onslaught, then quickly to sheep, and, seizing the initiative, to migratory ranging into Colorado. At first the pool barely hung on. Then, helped by A. J. Scorup's determined stand in the rugged and arid canyon land west and north of the Abajo Mountains, it forced the ELKs and the Lacys to withdraw. It then looked on and accommodated as the Pittsburg people sold to Cunningham and Carpenter, who with the Carlisles turned to sheep themselves.

Both finally sold out to a Mormon consortium in 1911 and 1914 after the virgin forage had been harvested.[51]

At Indian Creek the Scorup Summerville Company ran in rock mazes, toughed out an unbelievably cold winter in 1919, and ran 8,000 cattle on the La Sal Forest under one of the nation's largest permits. At the La Sal Ranch L. H. Redd's son Charles gradually assumed full control of what became Redd Ranches. The "Company," as it was locally known, enlarged its operations and expanded into blue-chip investments to meet future exigencies. Homesteaders and small operators lived adjacent to and ran on common public domain ranges with the company. Some, including George Washington Johnson and his descendants, got on well, working for the company as well as themselves during several generations. Others left the town of La Sal in bitterness, feeling the company had run them out, or stayed on, making a near feud a way of life. A few, according to local tradition, burned company barns and haystacks.[52]

Establishing claim to grazing resources on the public domain early in the twentieth century was often difficult. An interesting 1906 case involved Joe Biddlecomb, who had been crowding his way onto an established grazing district with a herd of cows, some of which he had apparently mavericked. He was warned in an almost sympathetic way by a delegation of cattlemen with recognized claims that there was no room there for him or for his questionable methods of building a herd. Desperate for land, Biddlecomb and his wife, Millie, drove their stock to the inaccessible but still unclaimed Robbers Roost country, north of the Henry Mountains. By making cattle management more than profits or comfort their objective, they established a successful ranch operated exclusively on the public domain.[53]

Also moving north was Preston Nutter, who from 1886 to 1892 ran cattle in the deserts and Book Cliffs north of the Colorado River, among other things making good contacts with Uintah Agency officials. Agreeing to hold no other interests or cattle in Utah, Nutter joined New York investors late in 1893 in the Strawberry Cattle Company, pulled strings in Washington more effectively than others, and won a five-year lease to 645,000 acres of reservation land in Strawberry Valley at seventy-one hundred dollars a year on which he was authorized to graze 16,000 cattle.[54]

Contending for Strawberry grasslands during Nutter's lease, and prior to it, was an association of hard-fighting stockmen from Heber. After a one-year extension, at the end of his lease Nutter lost out to the Heber pool in 1898, which paid twelve thousand dollars per annum for their lease. Forest grazing examiner Albert Potter, who visited Strawberry Valley in 1902, reported that the Heber stockmen were "managing" things "as though they intend to continue in the stock business permanently." Other observers, however, blamed them for grazing the reservation into the ground with 150,000 to 200,000 sheep. As New York financial backing and leases and markets at the Uintah Agency and Fort Duchesne played out, Nutter turned his attention to national markets after 1902. He married the gracious and gifted Katharine Denton, a Uinta Basin homesteader of 1905; bought the Brock Ranch in Nine Mile Canyon along the road between Price and the Uinta Basin for his headquarters; and divided up to 25,000 head of cattle between Nine Mile and the Arizona Strip.[55]

At Brown's Hole, where Utah, Colorado, and Wyoming meet, a backwash of small ranchers congregated. Like Biddlecomb, their ethic countenanced a certain amount of rustling, especially if it preyed upon big outfits such as the Boston-financed Middlesex Land and Cattle Company and Colorado-based Ora Haley and the Two Bar "cattle empire" that were pressing into Brown's Hole ranges. The small ranchers first checked the oncoming cattle with rustling and sheep and then turned with increasing sympathy to Wild Bunch outlaws when what was apparently a hired killer assassinated two of the small ranchers.[56]

Problems were a little different in Utah's northwest corner, but developments there were also marred with tension, as contending grazing systems faced off. Already hard hit by a bad winter, the huge Bar M or Promontory Stock Company, heir to Central Pacific grant lands, suffered a monumental but hardly surprising reversal when Judge Charles Zane rejected its appeal for an injunction closing public entry to 350,000 acres of public lands checkerboarded within its 36-by-40-square-mile ranch, thus leaving the entire operation open to serious management problems. Fencing was impossible. Sheepmen overran it. Squatters settled on odd-numbered sections, sometimes isolating one part of the ranch from another and precipitating squatter-stockman tensions. In time it was sold to the Promontory-Curlew Land Company, a Cache Valley land and sugar company consortium.[57]

To the south a succession of cattle ranchers enlivened economic developments but left no very clear record. Among them were Texas cattlemen turned mining moguls Samuel and William McIntyre and the Whitmore brothers—James and George—of Nephi, Price, and Sunnyside. Rounding out a partial listing were Wilford Day of Parowan, Cedar City sheepmen Lehi Jones and David Bulloch, the Orderville companies, and the Mohave Cattle Company, led by Anthony W. Ivins. Most interesting but in many ways the most enigmatic of all was B. F. Saunders, a stock buyer and rancher whose home was in California but who headed the Grand Canyon Land and Cattle Company and bought and sold thousands of cattle and vast sheep herds between Flagstaff and Salt Lake City.[58]

In the 1890s Anthony W. Ivins, the Atkins family, and a good many others from St. George ran cattle on the west end of the Arizona Strip. Rights to the country and to the springs that made ranching there possible were apparently held only by customary use. Into what had sometimes been an intense and occasionally mean-spirited but brotherly competition rode the redoubtable Preston Nutter in 1893, amply backed by Salt Lake City banker William McCornick. Strawberry Valley lease in hand, he purchased 5,000 cattle around Kingman, Arizona, during the late summer and, hoping to make Strawberry Valley before winter, crossed the Colorado River near Scanlon Ferry below the worst of the Grand Canyon and headed on through the western edge of the strip. Time played out before Nutter's cattle got to the railroad in Iron County, and he turned back, wintering near St. George and along his trail through the Arizona Strip, despite the opposition of other ranchers, including B. F. Saunders and Anthony Ivins, who warned him away from their springs. By springtime he recognized the situation's potential and, acquiring "preferred Indian scrip" in Washington, DC, "at a premium price," posted springs, deputized Texas cowboys, and held the water holes against their former claimants. Within a few years he defused the potential for a range war by acquiring the operations of Ivins, Saunders, and a host of smaller ranchers to become the controlling factor in the strip's west end. In time survivors lost their anger, worked cattle on common grazing districts with him, and were pleased when their sons found employment with him. But it was a clear case of the ranching frontier overwhelming Utah's village-based cattle operations.[59]

In summary, cattle graziers and cowboys played an important part in the early statehood period. Comparatively, Utah's cattle industry was small. Yet there were giants in the field, mythic heroes, and points of economic and cultural significance. A native two-level cattle industry evolved as village and ranch systems were juxtaposed. With tens of thousands of village farmers running cattle, a widespread cowboy ethos took form that may well run as deeply as it does in Wyoming, Montana, or Idaho, where the range industry has been much more important economically. Successful cattlemen took their position as bankers and businessmen in a wide variety of industries. Some also played important political roles, but they lacked the organization and political clout that sheepmen applied to their interests.

Early in the twentieth century, meatpacking plants were established near stockyards adjacent to the railroad in Ogden as a corollary to the livestock industry. In 1906 the Ogden Packing and Provision Company was organized by eight local investors led by F. E. Schlagater. Subsequently, the company erected a slaughterhouse and marketed meat products. In 1909 it advertised that it was "the only U.S. inspected packing plant in the city." The company became the largest meat packer in Ogden and was reorganized as the American Packing and Provisioning Company in 1924. That year it and the Fox-Keller Dressed Meat Company slaughtered 18,000 cattle, 70,000 hogs, and 10,000 sheep.[60]

SHEEP

Utahns were slow to recognize the potential of sheep as a range industry. Consequently, their increase was small until the 1880s, when sheep grazing began to emerge in earnest. The census count for 1870 showed 59,672 head and 233,121 in 1880. By 1885 they numbered about 1 million head. Increasing rapidly for a decade and a half thereafter, they tallied 1.5 million in 1890 and 3,818,000 in 1900. Forest Service regulations and drought reduced sheep numbers to about 2.4 million by 1905, a number that held relatively steady for twenty years.[61]

With their numbers at an all-time high, sheep were crowding cattle from many Utah ranges in 1900. The state's "crossroads" location had some bearing on this, and herds numbering in the hundreds of thousands trailed from neighboring states. Also contributing was the fact that desert ranges—primarily the vast West Desert in the Great Basin and the East Desert on the Colorado Plateau—could sustain more animals than Utah's mountain ranges. Utahns held grazing rights only by customary usage and water control. In the absence of regulatory mechanisms, Utahns stocked winter ranges to maximum capacity and heavily overstocked summer ranges.[62]

Long past their pioneer period, certain Wasatch Front towns played an important role in the sheep industry. With more young people than farm opportunities and with favorable access to range, such places became sheep towns through which the seasonal migrations moved. Draper at the south end of Salt Lake Valley is an example. Of its 257 employed people, 39 worked with sheep. Seventeen were young men who each gave his father's household as his place of residence but listed sheepherding as his occupation. Other sheep towns included Paradise, Brigham City, North Ogden, Woods Cross (home of the Deseret Land and Livestock Company), Taylorsville, Lehi, Heber, Spanish Fork, Nephi, Cedar City, and many Sanpete towns.[63]

Typical of those who became sheepmen was Lehi's Andrew Peterson. Son of immigrants and without means to get into farming, he herded on shares to build a small flock. Staying close to home, he ran sheep in American Fork Canyon and Cedar Valley, took his younger brothers out of school to herd, and for a time did well. E. J. Jeremy, who controlled land in East Canyon, operated on a grander scale. With boys hired from Salt Lake County, he made properties along the Jordan River the axis for a sheep operation numbering about 10,000 head. He wintered on the West Desert, trailed his sheep from the Vernon area with upwards of 300,000 others, sheared and lambed near Grantsville, and in a comedy of dust, grazed lawns, sheep manure, and frayed nerves made an all-day trek through Salt Lake City. A ten-day race to the head of the Duchesne River ensued, with sheepmen competing to maintain grazing advantages.[64]

One of Utah's biggest sheep operations was the Deseret Live Stock Company (DLSC). It was incorporated at Woods Cross in 1891 by Davis County sheep owners, including about thirty women. Major players included the families of John Moss, Stearns Hatch, and James and Alice Moyle. As initially organized it consisted of nine thousand shares of capital stock worth ten dollars per share, 28,830 sheep constituting the lion's portion. It ran on the public domain and owned about a quarter of a million acres of private range and meadowland purchased early at very attractive prices from the Union Pacific Railroad (UP) and the State Land Board. By 1917 DLSC had acquired Iosepa, a defunct Hawaiian colony, from the Mormon Church and several other large West Desert ranches, including the giant Niponset. It had also picked up a large number of smaller holdings through purchase and dummy entrymen. Amounting to more than eight hundred thousand acres, public and private, most of DLSC's land was in Rich, Morgan, and Summit Counties, but upwards of thirty thousand deeded acres were in the neighborhood of Skull Valley, located to facilitate the control of water that made several hundred thousand acres of West Desert winter range usable. Ranches and stores at Woods Cross, Wasatch, and Iosepa were used mostly to facilitate sheep management, although for years it was assumed that the store turned about 10 percent of the company's profits.[65]

The Deseret Live Stock Company made money from the first. Building its herds to a maximum number of 80,000, it made seasonal drives to and from desert and mountain ranges during its first decade and a half. To save their ewes and get better lamb growth, its managers began to ship by rail from Tooele in 1904. Like other sheepmen, DLSC marketed both lambs and wool. In time it ran a horse herd of some 400 head to meet its needs, acquired cattle ranches, and by the 1930s had 3,000 head of cattle. Investors and directors often lived in Davis and Salt Lake Counties except for summers. Managers, foremen, and stock workers lived on the ranches and at the sheep camps. Topflight foremen were "riders," who, knowing the operation like the back of their hand, patrolled it on horseback in watch of irregularities. Up to seventy-five regular workers were employed throughout the year, with many more during shearing, lambing, haying, and other busy times.

Especially important in the development of Utah's sheep industry were purebred breeders. At the forefront were W. S. Hansen of Brigham City and three Mount Pleasant neighbors, J. K. Madsen, John H. Seely, and David Candland, who as a key member of the State Land Board was in a good spot to help the sheep industry. Under their astute leadership the Rambouillet became the dominant breed in Utah and perhaps the entire West. The Mount Pleasant trio and Hansen dominated fairs and expositions throughout the entire West and as a merchandising technique developed world-famous ram sales in Salt Lake City. In a globetrotting endeavor that signified the international dimensions of the new agricultural order, Seely searched Europe and the eastern United States in search of foundation Rambouillet bloodlines and later supplied Japan and Russia with foundation stock. The Forest Service looked to him for grazing expertise, borrowing his "principal employee," W. C. Clos, "an encyclopedia on range management," to help formulate grazing policy after 1905. Like his sheep, Seely's farms, ranges, and other livestock were models of country living at its best.[66]

As the number of sheep in the state rose, several new woolen mills were erected in Cache Valley early in the twentieth century, including the Fonnesbeck Knitting Company, the Union Knitting Mills, and the Logan Knitting Factory. These firms competed with the Cache Knitting Works and the Hyrum Woolen Mills that had been established in 1890 and 1892. Southward in Utah County Jesse Knight purchased the Provo Woolen Mills and renamed it Knight Woolen Mills. The mills developed marketing divisions, including agents who sold woolen goods door to door.[67]

Far more than cattle graziers, sheepmen organized to protect their interests and actively engaged in state politics. Under the able leadership of Charles Crane of Kanosh, the Territorial Wool Growers' Association in 1892 lobbied aggressively against a "Seven Mile Limit" law, making it illegal to graze or hold livestock in the watersheds of established communities. Most sheepmen, like Crane, who was a perennial candidate for governor in the early years of statehood, were Republicans, and the association and its successor organizations worked unflaggingly over the years for protective legislation and made good use of connections with wool manufacturer and senator Reed Smoot. They praised their contribution to the state's economy, moved onto community herd grounds with little respect for tradition, grazed recklessly, and stood foursquare against the establishment of national forests and the successive cuts imposed on sheepmen by the forests. The Wool Growers' Association also represented sheepmen in negotiations with Boston and St. Louis commission houses and occasionally handled labor relations with shearers, many of whom resented and distrusted the great sheepmen. The lonely sheepherder, by contrast, seemed to have little sense for class discrimination or collective bargaining.

Inevitably, discord between factions flared in regions where farm settlement and ranching interests coincided or where the sheep and cattle industries competed for resources. Conflicts mainly played out in the courts and in crimes against property. A few people, such as Joe Biddlecomb, were forced off from ranges, and occasionally a cattleman, sheepman, or homesteader was murdered in the backcountry.

As World War I ended, Utah's agricultural industry had just experienced a decade of unparalleled prosperity. As war engulfed Europe and devastated farmers on the other side of the world, Utah's farmers had prospered as never before, evidence of their integration within the global economy. Large amounts of land had come into cultivation. Utah's sugar beet industry had expanded across the state, wedding the fortunes of Utah farmers to decisions made in corporate offices and boardrooms in Salt Lake and New York. New creameries operated by corporations like Borden and Sego, canneries owned by Utah investors and the California Packing Corporation (Del Monte), meatpacking plants, woolen mills, and flour mills such as the Layton Milling and Elevator Company dotted the state, urging farmers and ranchers to expand production. Farm-implement companies had multiplied. Utah's farmers and ranchers looked for continued growth and prosperity.

Yet it is clear in retrospect that agriculture was overextended.[68] The homestead myth coupled with the arid-farm boom and speculative promotion had carried too many people onto marginal lands or lands lacking in water. Debt was heavy and overgrazing was widespread. More social tension beset the sugar industry than its industrialists and churchmen recognized, and the buoyant Progressive mind-set was ebbing. A period of relative drought lay in store. The stage was set for major social dislocations as agriculture slipped into a profound postwar recession.

4

INDUSTRIAL DEVELOPMENT IN THE PROGRESSIVE ERA

DANIEL JACKLING, MINING TITAN

For many years a statue of mining titan Daniel Jackling has graced the state capitol building in Salt Lake City. Jackling is an appropriate symbol for Utah in the early statehood era. He was an industrialist, chemical engineer, and organizer. Seeing opportunity in Utah's low-quality ores and in the evolving technology and changing markets of his times, he applied himself to their exploitation. The state was enriched by his effort, yet his focus on corporate success and profits depended heavily upon and contributed to forces far beyond Utah. Callous in his relations with labor, ruthless in competition, calculating in his application of science, and fortunate in his quest for financial support, Jackling was subject to Utah only as the place of his endeavor. Yet he was lionized by dominant elements in the state who admired the outreach he made famous. In many respects Jackling's Utah career epitomizes the romance and the rambunctious vitality of the state's early economy, its progressive and ingenious application of technology, and its capacity to reward the chosen few. Equally, however, it reflects the low quality of Utah resources, the state's dependence on outside forces, its limited social and gender conscience, and its abuse of the environment.

Jackling dealt with an emergent economy during the first decades of the century. As historians Leonard Arrington and Thomas Alexander point out, in the turn-of-the-century years vestiges of the self-sufficient Mormon commonwealth and the "individualistic economy of the early miners and traders" were evolving into a "partially unified and specialized economy based on commercial agriculture, mining, and smelting."[1] Not unlike third world countries of a later era, Utah's economy was extractive and exploitative, and its business psyche was intensely boosterish and often defensive. The emerging infrastructure for such an economy included railroads, mining camps, processing works, generating plants, and new reclamation projects. Utah's economy depended upon technological and corporate developments and was highly vulnerable to outside forces, including protective legislation, war, and national panic. The new economy attracted male workers from the immigrant ships then docking at America's ports and from the roustabout West. At the same time, the new economy affected longtime residents, alternately curtailing and expanding the possibilities of some as it facilitated entry into the professions, education, or business.

Utah's economy was sufficiently active to create momentum and produce millionaires. It both broadened and deepened loyalties to the state, enriched and enlarged Salt Lake City and Ogden, and made large areas around them tributary.[2]

POPULATION

Utah's population grew more rapidly than the mountain region at large until 1870. Thereafter, the region's population grew more rapidly than Utah's except during the hard years of the 1890s, when both regions grew at about the same rate. One factor slowing Utah's growth was out-migration, which outpaced in-migration.[3]

The percentage of Mormons in the population reached a longtime nadir in the 1890s. The quasi-public Perpetual Emigration Fund no longer functioned to bring Mormons to Utah, and church leaders, appalled at the spectacle of thousands unemployed during the panic of the mid-1890s, discouraged the ingathering of Mormons. One study pegs Mormon population at no more than 56.1 percent of Utah's total in 1890. In this environment the non-Mormon Liberal Party was victorious in both Salt Lake and Ogden elections. From the 1890s onward, Utah experienced intermittent infusions of industrial workers as boom periods, and new mines attracted itinerant workers and migrant labor from southeastern Europe and Asia. By the early 1930s, metal mining counties ran about 50 percent non-Mormon, Salt Lake County was 52.3 percent, and in coal mining Carbon County, non-Mormons accounted for 72.6 percent of the total. Elsewhere, the population varied from 56.6 percent Mormon in Weber County to 92.4 percent in Kane.[4]

Utah's population moved increasingly toward commercial and industrial centers. In 1870 only 15,981 people, or 18.4 percent of the territory, lived in Salt Lake,

Ogden, and Provo. By 1920, 48 percent of all Utahns lived in cities of more than 2,500. Salt Lake City's population had reached 118,110, Ogden's 32,804, and Provo's 10,303.[5] Herein lay the elements of industrial growth: a growing urban home market and a labor force split between largely skilled home guards who were inclined to break strikes and migratory unskilled labor.

THE ROLE OF CITIES

In the first quarter century of statehood Salt Lake City and Ogden emerged increasingly as commercial and industrial centers with far-flung hinterlands. Both had Chambers of Commerce and commercial clubs that worked to shift interest from cultural divisiveness to economic development.

Salt Lake had been Utah's religious and political center from the first. However, railroad development kept Ogden in the picture. Agricultural connections and mining in Montana and Idaho strengthened Logan to a degree but worked most directly in Ogden's favor. The Eccles, Wattis, and Browning families also gave Ogden strength in north- and west-reaching lumber, sugar, and heavy construction interests. Although Provo benefited from its proximity to the Tintic mining district, Salt Lake City clearly dominated mining and smelting. Feeding directly into it were populations and businesses emanating from the two Cottonwood districts, Park City, Bingham, Tooele, Stockton, Camp Floyd, and Tintic. Mining entrepreneurs built elegant homes along South Temple Street, had business blocks on Main Street, owned newspapers, and participated lustily in politics, which helped make Salt Lake a major outpost of federal authority and governmental administration.

Also tributary to Salt Lake but at greater distance were southern Utah's varied but scattered mining districts and eastern Nevada's rich mining country. By 1896 the Salt Lake Mining Exchange had formalized commerce in mining properties and stock.[6] Salt Lake Hardware, Scott-Strevell Hardware (after 1902 Strevell-Paterson), Consolidated Wagon, Silver Brothers Iron Works, Sherman Engineering, F. C. Richmond Machinery, Electrical Engineering & Construction, Patrick J. Moran Construction, and a variety of other foundries, wholesale firms, and equipment and supply houses competed bravely with out-of-state firms for the mines' business.

TINTIC: "ALL-AROUND DISTRICT"

Overall, Utah mining ran about fifth among the western states. Never a dominant regional force, Utah's mines worked mineral resources that were modest in size and low in quality. By the turn of the century in most major mining districts, including Mercur, Bingham, Frisco, and Park City, the individual mines of earlier days had been consolidated into great enterprises. Smelters and a wide variety of other reduction works sprang up, with entrepreneurs competing for economic advantage and experimenting to turn failure to success.

Sometimes called "the All-Around District," Tintic, where consolidation was less pronounced, was at once the least spectacular and the most typical of the great mining districts. With fewer ties to corporate America, the Tintic mines were developed with "very little outside capital," Utah writer and mineralogist Don Maguire reported in 1898. The Tintic was a workaday producer of lead and silver, laced lightly with copper, and tantalized by showings of gold. Production at Tintic followed seesaw patterns that kept the district alive in slow times and made it a heavy payer in good times.[7] Its operators worked ore deposits too modest to attract great infusions of finance and too conventional in makeup to invite striking metallurgical innovations. Of twenty-six Utah mines paying dividends in the boom year of 1916, ten were in the Tintic district. However, dividends from Tintic mines were modest, varying from $300,000 at Jesse Knight's Iron Blossom to lows of $10,000 at the Lower Mammoth and the Eureka Hill companies. Altogether they paid dividends amounting to $707,138, or only 5 percent of the state's total. Tintic mines dotted the north end of Juab County and lapped into Utah County. Accessible to relatively low-budget operations, the district attracted many operators. Surrounded by a cluster of mines, Eureka was a well-developed business center by 1900, and camps came and went with the tides of fortune at Homansville, Diamond, Mammoth, Robinson, Silver City, Knightville, and Dividend.

Tintic's development may be divided into four periods. A pioneer stage extended from the 1870s to about 1890, followed by a developmental era in the early 1890s. Mature mining operations extended from 1896 to the early 1920s. An extended recessional punctuated by moments of glory then ensued.

Despite its prosaic character, Tintic had its share of outstanding figures and episodes. Its earliest developers included the Texas ranching brothers Samuel and William McIntyre and John Beck of Lehi, who launched the great Bullion Beck mine at Eureka.[8]

Tintic helped build the fortunes of the Bamberger family, mine management wizard and later governor George Dern, Reed Smoot, and C. E. Loose. With prospects for the shoestring operator until well into the twentieth century, Tintic also enriched Emil J. Raddatz. Establishing the Tintic Standard Mining Company in 1907, Raddatz operated on "jawbone," store credit, and Standard's nearly worthless stock before striking ore in 1916. By 1918 an outpouring of wealth enriched stockholders, and his company town was happily renamed Dividend.[9]

Provoan Jesse Knight arrived on the Tintic stage in 1896, having mortgaged his ranch in Payson for $12,000, ostensibly on the hunch or spiritual intuition that great treasure awaited him there. Uncle Jesse built a one-room shack with his son Will and began prospecting with two other hired men. Jesse mucked the ore and hauled it out of the tunnel in a wheelbarrow, while Will and the two hired men worked in shifts around the clock, blasting the rock with a single-jack hammer. When they at last struck a rich vein, Will recalled, his father loaded up his wheelbarrow with rock, pushed it out of the mine, "dumped it on a small platform and said, 'I have done the last day's work that I ever expect to do where I take another man's job from him. I expect to give employment and make labor from now on for other people.'" A man of the people who closed his mines on Sundays and paid relatively high wages, he was popular, even revered, gifted by instinct, sound of judgment, and persistent. Uncle Jesse was most of all lucky. Investing his personal fortune recklessly, he vertically integrated his operations in ramshackle fashion to combat centrally controlled railroads and smelters. Knight opened mines, built smelters, dug drainage tunnels, operated model mining camps, developed seven electrical power plants, and maintained good relations with working men. Uncle Jesse's personal luck held to the last. Shortly after he sold his Humbug Mine to Simon Bamberger, the mine began to play out; Bamberger reportedly quipped that Uncle Jesse "might not have had a revelation when he found the mine, but he surely had one when he sold it." While Tintic flourished, he flourished. He died in 1921 before he fully realized the difficulties of that year's collapse.[10]

Admirable though it may have been, Knight's approach was outmoded in its integration, scope, and organization by the 1910s. By 1912 the Utah Power & Light Company (UP&L) was moving aggressively against independent competitors like Knight. His railroad sought to deliver ore and supplies to his Silver City smelter (1909–10) but became superfluous when the smelter folded in the face of difficulties. Eleven smelters, many of them small operations like Knight's, had worked Utah ores in 1907 and twenty-eight had in 1890, but faced by court action, lawsuits over pollution, financial reverses, and technological difficulties, they "dropped out of existence...one by one." In 1916 only four remained—all giant operations owned and manipulated by the combinations.[11]

A number of indexes suggest Tintic's relative position among the state's mining districts. In 1920 Bingham was easily the first producer, its average "output being about double" that of second-place Tintic. Park City was a close third, its production being greater than all remaining districts combined. In terms of individual metals, Tintic "produced more gold than any other district," and in silver it was a close second to Park City.[12] From 1870 total dividends for the entire district were $15 million, or barely more than the cumulative payouts by Park City's famous Ontario Mine ($14.7 million) and the Silver King Coalition ($14.5 million). The $19.6 million dividend payments by the Utah Copper Company in 1916 alone give further dimension to Tintic's role. On the other hand, Tintic accounted for half (6,681,644 ounces) of the 13,455,597 ounces of silver mined statewide in 1918, compared to 2,572,586 and 2,056,005 mined, respectively, by Park City and Bingham. Some 167 million pounds of lead were produced the same year, about 80 million of them in the Bingham district, with Tintic and Park City districts coming in at 30.6 million and 24.3 million pounds, respectively.[13]

Working within the limits of its means but never overcoming these liabilities, Tintic epitomized the state. By contrast Park City rose above Utah's general limitations by merit of extensive and deep-running deposits of high-grade silver and lead.

PARK CITY: BANNER MINING DISTRICT

To many, Park City was Utah's banner district. External investment capital was critical to its development. Located on the east summit of the Wasatch Range, thirty-five miles from Salt Lake City, it opened about 1869. During the next fifty years Park City ranked with the foremost camps of the West. Its first great strike was on the rich Ontario Ridge. The claim was purchased in 1872 and developed by San Francisco capitalists, including mining magnate George Hearst, under the able direction of Hearst's fellow Californian and mine manager Robert C. Chambers. By 1876 the Ontario Mine was producing $14,000 a week and the entire camp $20,000. Word of rich strikes in Park City attracted wealthy investors from Grand Island, Michigan, beginning in 1873, among them Edward and William Mont Ferry.[14]

Park City operators engaged in deep mining. They ran hundreds of miles of exploration and drainage tunnels, shipped high-grade ores directly for smelting, and built mills to concentrate ores of lesser richness on-site. Although still productive, the Ontario Mine ceased to dominate Park City by 1902, as the Mayflower and Silver King mines flourished. Such Park City miners as John Daly, John Judge, James Ivers, Edward and Mont Ferry, John Bransford, and R. C. Chambers molded the physical and social character of Salt Lake City.

Probably the greatest partnership in Utah mining, that of David Keith and Thomas Kearns of the Silver King mine, came to the fore after statehood. Keith, who had worked his way up the ladder in Virginia City from common miner to mine foreman, was brought to Utah by his friends Hearst and Chambers to install and operate huge pumps in the Ontario Mine. In Park City he met Thomas Kearns, an Irish immigrant, who hired him as a mucker at the Ontario and later as a contractor at the Woodside Mine. After Kearns discovered a vein of silver while tunneling in 1889, he formed a partnership with Keith and leased land adjacent to the Woodside. Within a few months they struck pay dirt, and in 1892 they purchased adjacent claims and incorporated the Silver King Mining Company at $3 million, using their own wealth, earned from their mining ventures in Utah as well as investment capital from fellow Utahns John Judge, Albion Emery, W. H. Dodge, and Windsor V. Rice along with David D. Erwin of Michigan. Keith was astute, dignified, deliberate, and private, a stabilizing influence. The impetuous Kearns is said to have charged his staid partner with such hesitation that "if he rushed into" a "three-holer... out-house," he would be unable "to make up his mind" until too late.[15]

Kearns and Keith extended their interests aggressively, steadily acquiring new properties and pushing underground boundaries to the point that they were often in court. Their labor relations were generally good: a 1911 strike led to a three-shift, eight-hour-day policy in outside operations, but in 1919–20 tensions due to wage scales and a prolonged strike marred relations.[16] The Silver King and its successors assumed a position at the head of high-paying properties. By 1911 it challenged the Ontario's long-held position as Park City's richest payer. At that time the district had produced a "grand total exceeding $400,000,000." Of this the Silver King contributed $30 million and paid $12,522,000 in dividends. The Ontario produced $40 million and paid dividends of $14,962,500.[17]

MERCUR: "JOHANNESBURG OF AMERICA"

In the turn-of-the-century years Mercur, some forty miles southwest of Salt Lake City, near the south end of the Oquirrhs, was equally showy. Previously known as Lewiston, a silver camp, Mercur took on new life in 1883 when its finely pulverized gold was detected.[18] A branch railroad was extended to Mercur from the Salt Lake & Western Branch, which the Union Pacific was building from Lehi to Eureka. Nebraska investors headed by John Dern and E. H. Airis, wealthy farmers from the Cornhusker State, established the Mercur Gold Mining and Milling Company in 1890. Often called "buncoed" farmers, the Dern group built a mill that tried unsuccessfully to extract large amounts of gold from ore by adapting conventional processes. Learning of Denver experiments with the newly discovered McArthur-Forrest cyanide process, Mercur Mining shipped a carload of ore to Denver for processing. When "about 80 percent" of the gold was successfully extracted, Mercur Mining adapted its mill to the process. In a second striking innovation made necessary by the first, it contracted with Lucien L. Nunn of Colorado's Telluride Power Company to run high-voltage lines thirty-two miles from a hydroelectric plant on the Provo River.[19]

Soon a half-dozen or more companies built mills in the district. Joseph Delamar, a Dutch immigrant based in New York who had made a fortune in shipping and western mining, erected the foremost mill, the state-of-the-art Brickyard–Golden Gate Mill, by 1898. In 1899 Delamar and Mercur Gold merged, creating the Consolidated Mercur Gold Mines Company, the moving force at Mercur. Sometimes called "the Johannesburg of America," Mercur became a town of twenty-three hundred inhabitants, burned down, rebuilt, produced $19 million worth of gold, paid $3,881,323 in dividends, and closed down again in 1913.[20]

BINGHAM COPPER: FROM WASTE TO GAIN

Utah's greatest mining story involved the Bingham Copper Mine. All but replete with magic wands, it made coaches of pumpkins and gave the scullery maid of mining states an hour at the ball. Copper's emergence as a central factor in the Industrial Revolution and as the most important element in the economy of early statehood epitomized the spirit of the times. Its developers applied industrial initiative, open-pit mining, cutting-edge technology, and big concentrations of capital to the near-worthless porphyry ores of Bingham Canyon to produce fabulous wealth. To many it seemed they made something out of nothing, thus validating the conviction that technology, management, and capital would solve mankind's problems.

Bingham Copper Mine introduced mining methods that spread worldwide. It doubled Salt Lake County's tax base and paid dividends that amounted to 38 percent of gross receipts to perhaps twenty-five hundred holders of Utah Copper stock. To early statehood it was what pioneering and irrigation had been to the Mormon commonwealth, although it gave a miserly cut to labor, filled Salt Lake Valley with pollutants, and scarred the land.

Bingham's great heroes were engineers and practical miners grown wealthy. First among them were Daniel Jackling, Samuel Newhouse, Enos Wall, Joseph Delamar, and Meyer and Daniel Guggenheim, who entered a game of chance in which there were a score of losses and won big.

Few fitted the gambler's mold more fully than Wall. With a high roller's instinct for the unlikely, Wall was the first to recognize the potential of Bingham copper. Trained to watch for the unexpected at southern Utah's Silver Reef, where he helped discover the anomaly of silver in sandstone, he began prospecting Bingham's abandoned claims in 1887. Gradually, he accumulated a group of claims where minute scatterings of copper were mixed at random with nonpaying materials at 1 to 2 percent ratio (20 to 40 pounds per ton), along with even smaller traces of gold, silver, lead, and zinc. For more than a decade, Wall promoted "a laughing stock" that many called "Wall rock." When copper picked up, he struggled unsuccessfully to control it and became the inveterate enemy of the new leaders.[21]

Among the earliest of these was Samuel Newhouse, a onetime attorney in Pennsylvania who had profited from mining investments in Colorado. A brilliant performer with good connections in the East and London, Newhouse stumbled onto the copper scene in 1898 at Bingham's Highland Boy, a worked-out silver mine. With English capitalists he formed the Utah Consolidated Gold Mines, Ltd. Finding both gold and sulfide copper ores, Newhouse and his partner, Thomas Weir from Leadville, Colorado, completed a 250-ton-per-day copper smelter early in 1899 and sold the entire package to Standard Oil buyers William Rockefeller and Henry H. Rogers, reportedly for $12 million. In the meantime, Weir had located sixty-five additional Bingham claims encompassing 350 acres high in the canyon. Basing his sales pitch on estimates that the property encompassed 290 million tons of ore, bearing "1 to 2 percent copper," Newhouse overcame widespread skepticism regarding low-grade ore and again attracted British capitalists, this time forming the Boston Consolidated Mining Company. Rich in both sulfide and porphyry ores, the Boston Consolidated placated stockholders with meager dividends from deep sulfide diggings while it worked desperately to put porphyry's open-pit procedures together on a paying scale. Finally, in 1903 it turned a profit of $127,245 and in 1905 entered into a contract with American Smelting and Refining Company, a processing combine with a huge smelter at Garfield at the north end of the Oquirrh Range. The next year Boston Consolidated built its own 300-ton mill in the same neighborhood and initiated Utah's first open-pit mine.[22]

Boston Consolidated's smelter was part of an established smelting industry that led Utahns to refer to Salt Lake City as the nation's smelting capital. Early smelting had centered primarily in the Murray and Midvale areas, south in Salt Lake Valley. As operations shifted from oxide ores and charcoal furnaces to sulfide ores fired by coal and coke, air quality deteriorated. Pollution became even worse, as plants of the size necessary to refine porphyry coppers were built.

Trees and grass as well as crops and animals in Salt Lake County began to be blighted throughout large "smokebelts" as a result of a series of rain- and windstorms in the summer of 1903. Hoping to avert a disastrous face-off between Utah's two greatest industries, John A. Widtsoe of the Agricultural College issued a report later that year that granted the obvious injury to farmers but advised defensive measures short of legal action. Disgusted farmers turned to litigation in 1905. In the far-reaching case of *James Godfrey et al., v. American Smelting and Refining Company, et al.*, federal district court judge John A. Marshall ruled against five corporate smelters in the Murray-Midvale area. The Highland Boy Mill; the American Smelting and Refining Company; the Utah Consolidated Smelting Company; the United States Smelting, Refining, and Mining Company (USSRMC); and the Bingham Copper and Gold Mining Company were ordered to control pollutants or cease operations. All closed their doors except for the American Smelting and Refining Company's sulfide plant, which met the standard and continued operating at Midvale. New smelting operations were built by the smelter trusts at Magna, Garfield, and Tooele, shifting smoke patterns to the valley's west side, easing the problem of pollutants, and for most purposes ending the day of locally controlled smelters.[23]

A final, and as it proved main, line of copper development grew from efforts to interest Joseph Delamar in Enos Wall's Bingham holdings. Delamar was noted for his bold takeovers, but in the case of copper he was a cautious buyer. In the late 1890s his engineers made repeated estimates of Bingham's prospects. Momentarily encouraged, Delamar placed Wall's holdings under options, which he allowed to lapse. Finally, Daniel Jackling, a brilliant young mining engineer who had managed Delamar's Mercur plant and who possessed good connections in Colorado, produced a careful analysis for production-line mining that featured Wall's porphyry ores, a smelter at Garfield, open-pit mining, and mass processing. Figuring ores at more than 37 million tons with 2 percent copper as well as reclaimable amounts of gold, silver, lead, and zinc, he projected monthly profits of $90,000.

To Jackling it seemed an unparalleled opportunity. Delamar, however, was unmoved and only reluctantly bought a quarter interest in Wall's property for $50,000, taking an unexercised option on three-quarters of what remained at $350,000. Jackling and other examining consultants independently sought finance elsewhere. Among others they approached General Electric, Tharisis Sulphur and Copper Company, and Montana "copper kings" Marcus Daly and W. A. Clark. Agreeing with the *Engineering and Mining Journal* that the more porphyry ore a company had, the "poorer it" was, they refused to buy. Ultimately, Jackling and his associate Robert Gemmell were able to persuade Charles M. MacNeill and Spencer Penrose, owners of the United States Reduction and Refining Company in Colorado, with whom they had previously worked, to invest. They organized Utah Copper Company, built a pilot mill at Copperton, and started a 300-ton mill at Garfield. In the crucial stroke of the entire venture, the Jackling team finally in 1904 got into the deep pockets of Meyer and Daniel Guggenheim, millionaire smelting magnates in Philadelphia who controlled the monopolistic American Smelting and Refining Company.[24]

Bitter competition followed. With its mining property down canyon from Boston Consolidated's, Utah Copper was forced to temporarily de-emphasize open-pit mining in favor of underground tunnels. Nevertheless, with ample funding from the Guggenheims, Utah Copper survived the panic of 1907 and developed railroad connections, heavy earth-moving procedures, and superior smelting techniques. Boston Consolidated and Utah Copper continued to jockey for position in the years after 1907. In what Wall charged were crooked accounts, Utah Copper showed strong income, while Boston Consolidated's exasperated stockholders kept Newhouse under pressure. In 1910 Utah Copper finally took over Boston Consolidated in a complicated deal that included another giant Guggenheim copper property, Nevada Consolidated at Ely.[25]

Utah Copper paid dividends throughout the period. The mills at Magna and Garfield were enlarged, ultimately processing 55,000 tons per day. Extraction procedures kept apace. Estimates of available ore went from the hundreds of thousands to the hundreds of millions of tons.[26]

By World War I John D. Rockefeller could well call Utah Copper's giant excavation "the greatest industrial sight in the world."[27] More important, it was also Utah's greatest business and its heaviest taxpayer. It employed some forty-six hundred miners and other workers, many of them immigrants. By 1920 the mine had treated 88,339,523 tons of ore and produced 1,546,115,992 pounds of copper.[28]

THE POWER OF THE ROAD

Railroads were vital to Utah's mining industry. Legions of Utahns swarmed to build the transcontinental lines; the Oregon Short Line; the Denver and Rio Grande (D&RG); the Santa Fe; the San Pedro, Los Angeles, and Salt Lake; and the Western Pacific. Ogden and Salt Lake and perhaps a dozen smaller towns, including Utah County's Springville and Juab's Nephi, emerged as construction company centers. Numerous construction dynasties grew, including the giant Utah Construction Company's Wattis family; David Eccles, a northern Utahn with a Midas touch; the Juab County, Salt Lake, and Pacific Northwest's Alfred McCune; the Bambergers, ubiquitous mine and interurban road developers; and the father-son team of Albert J. and Walter C. Orem.

By 1915 the State Board of Immigration listed twenty-six Utah railroads with about 2,225 miles of main track and 655 of branch line. The largest, the Denver and Rio Grande, had 763 miles of main track and 236 of branch line, reaching Marysvale, Park City, Tintic, Bingham Canyon, and Ogden, the coveted "gateway" to the West Coast.[29] Over the years the big railroads took over the local lines, carved the state into fiefdoms, monopolized the coal industry, and controlled freight rates.[30]

KING COAL

Coal mining became a vital Utah industry in the years surrounding statehood. The relative, if not the real, economic position of coal may be seen in the assessed valuations resulting from revised tax laws in 1918. The Salt Lake County mines, including Utah Copper, were assessed at $61.3 million, or slightly more than 62 percent of the state mining total. Carbon County's coal mines followed, with $17.25 million, or about 18 percent of the total, while mines in the rest of the state accounted for the other 20 percent.[31]

No event affected coal mining more directly than the 1883 arrival of the Rio Grande Western (RGW), the D&RG's western extension. Organized by William Jackson Palmer in 1870, the D&RG was financed with investment capital from England and Pennsylvania, including funds from Palmer's mentor, J. Edgar Thompson, the head of the Pennsylvania Railroad and one of America's most successful businessmen of the nineteenth century. By 1883 Palmer was "the largest coal mine operator in the Mountain West." Taking over a narrow-gauge road between Springville and Pleasant Valley, 120 miles southeast of Salt Lake City, the RGW operated at least two coal subsidiaries, the Pleasant Valley Coal Company and the

Utah Fuel Company, to exploit vast coal deposits in the Book Cliffs and Wasatch Plateau of eastern Utah as well as excellent coking coal at Sunnyside. By 1900 the RGW had cornered much of the West's exploding smelter market with Sunnyside coke and supplied its own smelter in Pueblo, Colorado. With company towns at Clear Creek, Scofield, Castle Gate, and Sunnyside and with newly created Carbon County (1894) a company fiefdom, the RGW had achieved a tight hammerlock on Utah energy. By manipulation of its rail services and smelter connections it held the Union Pacific and the San Pedro, Los Angeles, and Salt Lake roads at bay; hauled about 90 percent of Utah's coal and "all of its coke"; and until 1906 stifled competition generally.[32]

Pursuant to this the Rio Grande Western also monopolized promising coal prospects. Like railroads elsewhere, its coal mining subsidiaries fraudulently bought federal grant lands with known coal prospects at grazing-land rates through the State Land Board, employing "dummy" entrymen and key employees as filing agents, including Jefferson Tidwell and his sons, hardscrabble farmers at Wellington. Company locators included Robert Forrester, a Utah Fuel geologist and one-time territorial mine inspector, and Charles Mostyn Owen, source of damning polygamy data in the Roberts and Smoot investigations. Competing prospectors such as youthful Arthur Sweet were fired on, their claims jumped, and their workers strong-armed.[33]

Word of fraud in Utah's coalfields attracted adverse attention. Under the administration of Theodore Roosevelt, federal investigations were initiated. Disappointed at the scale of fraud—little more than thirty thousand acres had been filed on—federal prosecutors nevertheless brought indictments against the RGW subsidiaries and "other dubious land acquisitions." Utah Fuel refused to capitulate, and in 1909 a hand-slapping settlement was negotiated.[34]

Two important developments emerged from the Utah coal lands suits. First, when restored to entry, coal land withdrawn during court procedures came back on the market at vastly elevated values. Asking prices escalated from $10 to $90 an acre. In 1912 a forty-acre tract commanded a high price of $145 an acre, or a total of $5,800, and in 1918 a Utah consortium paid $130,000, or $200 per acre, for Carbon County coal lands. "As one editorial lamented, 'the chances for a poor man to own a coal mine'" had passed.[35]

Second, a new class of independent entrepreneurs broke on to the scene following the federal probe. Independent Coal and Coke Company led the pack. Picking up a speculative development of Salt Lake attorney Frederick Sweet and his younger brother Arthur, Salt Lake hardware men Charles N. Strevell and James H. Paterson backed by Chicago money incorporated the ICCC in 1906. Working the mine vigorously, they founded the company town of Kenilworth and built a spur four miles to the D&RG at Helper. The ICCC soon employed more than two hundred men.[36]

Other independents soon followed Strevell's example. Robert A. Kirker pushed interests at his Anthracite and Castle Valley coal mines in Carbon County and opened new mines in southwestern Utah. The Federal Coal Company, Crystal Coal Company, and Consolidated Fuel all incorporated during 1907. Improving upon their Independent Coal and Coke sale, the Sweet brothers joined Albert J. and Walter C. Orem, a metals mining and interurban railroad team who had ties to Boston capitalists, to open the Utah Consolidated Company's Hiawatha and Black Hawk mines. They also joined the Castle Valley Coal Company at Mohrland in building the Southern Utah Railroad, connecting to the Denver and Rio Grande in Price. In a setup so shot through with nepotism as to lead one to believe the Sweets had been working for the syndicate all the time, the Hiawatha, Black Hawk, and Mohrland operations were sold as a package to the "nationally recognized giant" holding company the United States Smelting, Refining, and Mining Company, based in Boston. Headed by W. J. Sharp, onetime general manager of Utah Fuel, USSRMC renamed its purchase the United States Fuel Company.[37]

At relative peace with the Union Pacific but otherwise unhumbled, the D&RG gave its subsidiaries first call on coal cars and kept freight rates high. The independents fought back, turning to the courts, the Interstate Commerce Commission, and in time Utah's Public Utilities Commission. Thoughts of building competing railroad lines also ran wild. In its Sweets deal United States Fuel acquired the Southern Utah Railroad's twenty-one miles of track. To round out the company's access to trunk lines, W. J. Sharp planned and promoted the $5 million Utah Coal road from the Carbon-Emery county line ninety miles northwest across the Wasatch Plateau to a Provo connection with Southern California and the Northwest via the San Pedro, Los Angeles, and Salt Lake line and the Western Pacific. With even grander vision, Independent Coal and Coke's Strevell seemed determined to expand the tiny Kenilworth and Helper spur to a looping giant from Salt Lake City south to Kenilworth and then northeast via Nine Mile Canyon through the Uinta Basin's gilsonite fields to a transcontinental connection with the Moffat road in Colorado. Elsewhere, promoters talked and surveyors explored, but few miles of road were actually built.[38]

The D&RG's yoke remained heavy, but the independent coal companies persisted. Developments at Spring Canyon were suggestive of their growth. Among the first developers was Jesse Knight, who in 1912 used profits from his Tintic mines to establish the Spring Canyon Coal mine, four miles west of Helper. Locating the bone-dry company town of Storrs, he built a railroad spur to access it. Knight soon had 200 men at work and with his legendary luck finessed his way through the quagmire of land rulings that bogged down many of his colleagues. Never far from promotional propositions, the Sweets bought property above Knight, incorporated the Standard Coal Company, extended Knight's railroad, and built a state-of-the-art tipple. In maneuvers that led directly to the district court, Standard manager

Leon Rains appropriated water and land he had supposedly purchased for Sweet and with L. R. Wattis established Carbon Fuel on adjacent land.[39]

Inevitably, the D&RG's control diminished. It still dominated the all-important transportation question and had a corner on coke at Sunnyside, whose 726 ovens processed 424,294 tons by 1916. Otherwise, Utah Fuel split eastern Utah coal production evenly with the independents. In 1916, for example, 1,757,577 tons of coal were produced by Utah Fuel's six mines, compared to 1,855,208 tons by the ten largest independents. Manpower too was evenly divided, with 1,816 men working for the company and 1,895 for the independents.[40]

The split between independents and Utah Fuel extended to Carbon County politics, which had been a tight Utah Fuel satrapy. Protest voices called for an "independent ticket" as early as 1910. Inspired partly by blatant corruption in local government, Carbon County socialists organized formally for the first time in 1912. Progressives posed sufficient threat to be barred from campaigning in company halls. Two Progressive candidates for the county commission squeaked by at the polls along with a Democratic sheriff, in what was otherwise a sweep for company-supporting Republicans. The two Progressive commissioners challenged Utah Fuel directly when they held that the Magnolia Trading Company, the saloon-owning arm of Utah Fuel, "would no longer be the sole liquor vendor" in the company camps. The ins and the outs jousted throughout 1913 and 1914. They broadened political involvement and crowded the worst corruption out but otherwise did more to reduce Utah Fuel's political power than to vote progressivism in.[41]

During World War I demand and prices for coal soared. Latuda, Wattis, Peerless, and other new camps opened. In car distribution and freight rate schedules, the D&RG catered shamelessly to its subsidiaries. Distribution broke down, a serious coal shortage developed, and citizens suffered from a lack of fuel. Appeals, hearings, and court cases blossomed.

By mid-August 1917 something like monopoly was imposed upon them by the newly organized Federal Fuel Administration. W. W. Armstrong, Salt Lake City banker and onetime associate of mine operator Leon Rains, was appointed regional FFA head and sought desperately to rationalize the mayhem that the wartime coal industry had become. Distribution more than production or price was the Gordian knot. Coal cars were allotted, quotas were established, and with the nationalization of railroads traffic was regulated. Before routines took shape came the Armistice, November 11, 1918, followed in 1921 by economic collapse.[42]

In the decades following statehood, Utah's coal industry had contributed significantly to the development of a regional railroad system. The coal industry had produced in eastern Utah a distinct economy that both sustained the larger economy and stood somewhat apart, less directly tributary to Salt Lake City and more fully satellite to Colorado than perhaps any other part of Utah.

GILSONITE AND OIL

Out-of-state forces patently controlled Uintah County's gilsonite industry. First recognized as a valuable resource in the early 1880s, gilsonite deposits laced across the remote eastern end of the Uinta Basin in unlikely vertical seams. A natural asphalt, gilsonite was marketed for lacquer, electrical insulation, and waterproofing. The industry was fanned into life by eastern asphalt interests and the local promotions of cowboy marshal Sam Gilson (hence the name), D&RG surveyor Bert Seaboldt, and Park City millionaire R. C. Chambers. During the late 1880s and 1890s, two to three hundred tons of gilsonite were freighted annually to the Price railhead, and access was worked out to gilsonite deposits, most of which were on the Uintah and Uncompahgre Indian reservations. Indians were the primary losers in the deal.[43]

Local capitalists, including Jesse Knight, Thomas Kearns, and Reed Smoot, lobbied to open the reservation, but by the time it was opened to mining in 1903 they had completely lost control to the Gilson Asphaltum Company, a subsidiary of a Philadelphia trust owned primarily by A. L. Barber.[44]

Under the able western leadership of C. O. Baxter, the Barber trust moved aggressively in 1903. In a rare concession to Utah interests, it hired the Utah Construction Company to build the narrow-gauge Uintah Railway, a wholly owned subsidiary. Extending fifty-three miles from Mack, on the D&RG line west of Grand Junction, the railroad twisted over the 8,422-foot elevation of Baxter Pass on the Book Cliffs to the Dragon mine between the Green River and the Colorado border. By the end of 1904 the Uintah Railway was in service, and a toll road for wagons snaked sixty miles to Vernal and Fort Duchesne.[45]

In the decades that followed, the Barber trust held the country tributary. It mined most of the gilsonite, charged competitors and other Uinta Basin businesses high freight rates, and repeatedly defended its rates before the Interstate Commerce Commission. Hauling up to thirty-five thousand tons of gilsonite each year, for which America's growing road systems and varnish and lacquer industries guaranteed good markets, the Utah operation made a tidy enterprise for General Asphalt. Its railway also carried most of the Uinta Basin's freight, mail, and visitors, and its Wagon Road Company managed one of Utah's few toll roads. Many of the two hundred men who worked for the Barber trust mines and railroad were Utahns, but the company was nevertheless absentee owned.[46]

External developments also influenced a series of "embryonic oil boomlets." Reports of oil and tar seeps dated back to pioneer times. Claims to first drillings dated to 1891 and 1892 and were attributed in the Green River district to Simon Bamberger and on the San Juan to E. L. Goodridge, indefatigable oil prospector, or to Melvin Dempsy, a Cherokee Indian.[47]

Stimulated by "the splendid success" of the California fields, Utah promoters plunged into a noisy but short-lived survey of the state's oil prospects in 1901. Along with industrial periodicals, Utah's daily and weekly newspapers seized every rumor as grist for the promotional mill. With Perry Heath, onetime Republican Party national chairman and publisher of the *Salt Lake Tribune*, leading the way, Utah capitalists expectantly formed the Salt Lake Oil Exchange. A surefire procedure to leach oil from sand and shale was proudly announced, and in 1902 an oil congress was called for Price. Then the boomlet collapsed. Precious little oil was found, and no capital was attracted.[48]

Thereafter, the oil fields "were neglected but not forgotten" until 1907, when Utahns entered another period of excitement. By May the Pittsburg–Salt Lake Oil Company had seven operating wells and a refinery twenty miles east of Evanston. In the months that followed, the contagion spread. There was talk of oil on the San Rafael, at Green River, and at Rozelle in Box Elder County. New finds were lauded at Escalante and Enterprise, on the Sinbad in Emery County, and in Juab County, where the Salt Lake Route hoped to produce oil for its own engines. Two new focal points in 1907 that had been ignored in 1901 were the Virgin and San Juan Rivers.[49]

Closely connected with the latter was E. L. Goodridge. Floating down the San Juan in 1879, he came on "oil seepages" long known to prospectors a few miles below where Bluff City would be settled the next spring. He is said to have returned in 1883 and 1892. Backed by A. C. Ellis of Salt Lake City, Goodridge failed to find oil in 1901 but "brought in a gusher at Mexican Hat in 1908." A rush of modest proportions ensued. Promoters and capitalists looked toward Denver more often than Salt Lake, and a few, like the London and San Juan Oil company, even looked abroad.[50]

An announcement in 1907 that the Salt Lake Route would use only oil-burning locomotives gave the Virgin River field added impetus. The pioneer well struck oil in the North Creek drainage two miles north of Virgin in July, at a depth of 566 feet. It was deepened to 610 feet without increasing the quantity of oil, which rose within 300 feet of the surface. Several hundred barrels of oil were pumped before a flood washed over it. North Creek property worth "twenty-five or fifty cents per acre" in May sold "for ten to twenty dollars" in August. Californians led the assault. Active locals included George Middleton, a Salt Lake physician recently of Cedar City, who netted a paper gain of $12,500 on land he optioned to a California buyer.[51]

By October 15 southern Utah was full of developers. Oil rigs reportedly crowded the roads, and a few even began drilling. The "Badger Brothers" shipped a few barrels of oil to Salt Lake City where it was tested and samples forwarded to the Fairbanks, Morse Engine Company of Chicago and the Point Richmond Standard Oil plant in California. As one Salt Laker put it, "Like Rip Van Winkle, the southern counties" had "awakened."[52]

During 1908 and 1909 the boom continued at an abating rate. On the San Juan, Goodridge #1 was "pronounced" to be "an eight hundred–barrel well," but actually produced far less before its uncased walls caved in. In doing assessment work

Goodridge struck oil elsewhere in the vicinity of Mexican Hat, while a Mr. Brice of Ogden and the Galloway brothers from Colorado brought in producing wells at some distance. At the Virgin River field the excitement continued into 1908 but apparently played out quickly thereafter. Local promoters, including Cedar City banker Lehi Jones, San Juan rancher Lemuel H. Redd, and Green River booster Bert Silliman, continued to speculate in oil.[53]

Various factors explain the boom's demise. Most important, paying oil was not found. A fortunate few drilled and capped promising wells, but far more simply walked away, leaving open holes. Secondary deterrents included the "money panic of 1907" and the isolation of the Virgin and the San Juan fields, both of which were approximately one hundred miles from rail service. A final factor was a temporary oil-leasing controversy. Recognizing the inadequacy of existing legislation, President Taft "temporarily" withdrew some three million acres of public petroleum lands from entry in Utah, Wyoming, California, and Oregon.[54] As the leasing problem was resolved in the mid-1910s, exploration picked up. The Dixie Oil Company bought many of the defunct Virgin wells in 1917 and by 1919 was processing enough to meet "local demand." And a high-grade paraffin-based oil was encountered in Millard County. The Mt. Vernon Company operated near Hanksville in Wayne County. But oil was all hype and no production, a false hope that pointed conclusively to the disadvantages of low-grade resources and to the determined optimism of the Progressive mind.[55]

PUBLIC UTILITIES AND SERVICE AGENCIES

Growing from and serving the state's basic agricultural and mining industries were other industrial developments, including electricity, streetcars, and banking. Electricity was a testing ground for corporate mechanisms, local and absentee finance, and Mormon-Gentile adjustment at the business level. As a Utah industry electricity grew out of four market characteristics and three natural conditions. Marketplace influences included domestic needs, industrial demand, public illumination and transportation, and the availability of local and foreign capital. Equally influential in giving form to the electrical industry were the concurrent abundance of coal and waterpower for generation and the availability of natural gas as a competitive form of urban energy.[56]

The first tentative steps were taken to utilize electricity for municipal lighting in Salt Lake in 1881. Limited lighting service was initiated to downtown businesses and private homes.

On August 8, 1889, the Salt Lake City Railroad Company ran Utah's first electric streetcar and soon had eight cars operating on nine miles of track out of a makeshift powerhouse on Second East Street. The next year three new streetcar companies challenged the SLCRR. Two small east-side routes were easily controlled, but the west-side Salt Lake Rapid Transit Company engaged in a bitter decadelong battle with the SLCRR during which franchised areas were invaded, competing tracks torn up, and armed standoffs experienced. In 1895 SLCRR owner A. W. McCune led out in organizing the subsidiary Utah Power Company, which built a power plant in Big Cottonwood Canyon to supply the system's streetcars and furnished power to smelters in Murray and Sandy.[57]

In 1897 the Union Light and Power Company (ULPC), a local combine, made an initial bid to consolidate this snarl of municipal and corporate companies. Burdened with debt, its leaders reorganized, establishing the Utah Light and Power Company in 1899. With bonded debt drastically reduced and interest payments down from $270,000 annually to $120,000, ULPC kept division somewhat at bay and showed a profit. To reduce competition and increase efficiency in Salt Lake City's streetcar business, the Consolidated Railway & Power Company was organized in 1901, merging the city's four competing street railways and SLCRR's power-producing subsidiary, the Utah Power Company.

In a final effort to streamline the Salt Lake railway system and the electric business in Salt Lake and Ogden, the Utah Light and Railway Company organized in 1904.[58] Operated by a consortium of church and business interests for two years, it was taken over in 1906 by New York's E. H. Harriman of the Union Pacific Company who renamed it the Utah Light and Traction Company. Harriman was most intent on the streetcar business but upgraded and built additional power plants, put in new rolling stock and other equipment, built new power lines, and modernized both divisions of the system.[59] In a 1914 reorganization the electric utility was separated from the street railway business entirely and leased to the Utah Power & Light Company.[60] That year Salt Lake Traction hauled 38 million passengers more than "5.25 million passenger car miles" and with the base fare at 5 cents collected gross revenues of $1,482,143. By 1920 fares had risen from 5 cents to 6, and the 34.7 million passengers hit an all-time high, as did gross receipts at $2,069,483.[61]

Without complications from urban transit and without sufficient population to invite outside capital, municipalities elsewhere quickly developed power-generating systems of their own. Most of these were small, independent efforts depending on poorly conceived plants for steam or hydrogeneration. Prompted by the same local instincts that had complicated efforts in Salt Lake City and Ogden, most moved independently. Unusual in their joint effort were Lehi, American Fork, and Pleasant Grove. Helped by Logan electrical developer Christian Garff, the three towns organized the Utah County Light and Power Company in 1899. The company erected a power plant near the mouth of American Fork Canyon, traded streetlight services for rights-of-way in the three towns, and by the next spring provided service as regularly as drought, ice flows, and breakdowns permitted.[62]

In southern Utah progress was equally difficult. In Cedar City talk of an electrical system began at least as early as 1900. In 1906 the Cedar City Light and Power Company was organized. The next year a site was chosen a few miles up Cedar Canyon, a dynamo ordered and installed, and a diversion dam and delivery ditch built that failed to carry water. A steam tractor was pulled in to provide interim power, and by dint of constant attention a "sundown until 11:30 p.m." schedule was maintained, with two afternoons weekly for washing and ironing. The open ditch was replaced by redwood pipe in 1910. With its problems still unsolved in 1919, the Cedar Electric Company was taken over by the Dixie Power Company, which became a Utah Power & Light affiliate about 1930.[63]

Meantime, L. L. Nunn, a Colorado lawyer, entered the Utah electricity scene. He built a plant on the Provo River in 1897 and ran a first-of-its-kind line carrying forty-four thousand volts the thirty-two miles to Mercur. He shortly organized the Telluride Power Company and within a few years had plants at Battle Creek in Utah County, near Richfield on the Sevier River, in Logan Canyon, at Grace and Oneida on the Bear River in southern Idaho, and at the Jordan Narrows. With these plants and a larger interconnected system utilizing Bear Lake's water, Nunn sold dependable power directly to many of the mines and smelters and to retail companies.[64]

Second only to the Telluride system in meeting industrial needs were the seven hydroelectric stations of the redoubtable Jesse Knight in Summit, Wasatch, Salt Lake, Utah, and Juab Counties.

In 1912 the Utah Power & Light Company was organized. An agent of the Electric Bond and Share Company of New York, it was set up for the express purpose of consolidating power companies in Utah, southern Idaho, and western Colorado. It immediately purchased Telluride Power, including its Colorado and Idaho properties. After some resistance Knight Consolidated Electric yielded in 1914, as did some 130 smaller companies. The service area thus established extended from Rexburg, Idaho, to Richfield, Utah, and from Ouray, Colorado, to Tooele County. Connecting and extending its predecessors' systems, Utah Power & Light Company created a powerful network.[65] Generally efficient, it was hard-fisted in its competitive methods, a fact that Provo and Logan municipal power operations learned to their rue.[66]

BANKING

Banks expedited enterprises of every kind. By 1920 there were 134 in the state.[67] Not surprisingly, the Wasatch Front dominated in banking. The first banks began in the 1870s and 1880s and thereafter centered in Salt Lake and Weber Counties, with Utah and Cache Counties playing supporting roles. Nevertheless, by 1918 every county except for Daggett, Piute, and Wayne had at least 1 bank. Salt Lake County boasted 25 banks. Deposits provide a striking index to the Wasatch Front's control over money. Total deposits in all banks amounted to $105,938,090. Salt Lake City institutions held $52,958,000 (49.99 percent), Ogden banks $17,128,000 (16.17 percent), Logan banks $4,868,500 (4.6 percent), and Provo banks $3,053,000 (2.88 percent). The four cities accounted for 73.64 percent of all deposits.[68]

Banks were recognized as necessary institutions and bankers as community leaders. They were prominent politically in the first generation of statehood, bearing out the close relationship between business and government that most of them assumed was proper. Both bankers before they were governors, Heber M. Wells and John C. Cutler remained close to the industry during their stints in the statehouse and returned to banking thereafter. Also suggesting the closeness of banking and politics was William Spry's appointment as president of the Farmers & Stockgrowers Bank of Salt Lake City during his second gubernatorial term. Similarly, Senator Reed Smoot headed the Provo Commercial and Savings Bank for many years.[69]

Directorships were widely spread and interlocking. Presidents appear to have been appointed both for titular reasons and because they were men of ability and influence. Of the latter sort was David Eccles, who served as president for a number of northern Utah banks and sat on the boards of many others.[70] Only a little less influential was Eccles's close associate M. S. Browning, who presided over several Ogden and northern Utah banks during the 1910s. American Fork's James Chipman presided simultaneously over banks in American Fork, Pleasant Grove, Lehi, and Midvale, several of which were served by his sons as cashiers. Also sitting as president for several banks were James Pingree and W. W. Armstrong, who served as food and fuel administrator in Wilson's wartime government. Mormon Church presidents Joseph F. Smith and Heber J. Grant also headed several banks, including Zion's Savings Bank and Trust Company and the Utah State National Bank.

Dean of Utah bankers was William S. McCornick. President of one of Salt Lake City's greatest banks, he also presided over smaller banks in the hinterlands. He was also an expediter: at critical points he pushed the porphyry coppers; the San Pedro, Los Angeles, and Salt Lake Railroad; and similar projects, and for years he served as chairman of the Utah Agricultural College board of trustees.

As McCornick was to the state, bankers of lesser wealth were to their localities. In Cedar City an enterprising group of stock growers and professionals set out to capture some of the action for southwestern Utah by establishing the Bank of Southern Utah (BSU) in 1904. Main movers were Nathan T. Porter, new principal of the Branch Normal School, and Mormon leaders and stockmen Uriah T. and Lehi W. Jones, who between them presided over the bank until the 1930s. BSU grew slowly. Increasing its capital stock from $25,000 to $40,000 in 1906 and to $75,000 before 1918, it stimulated business and paid dividends from 10 to 15 percent. Impressed, another group headed by J. W. Imlay, William R. Palmer, and M. J. Macfarlane organized the Iron Commercial and Savings Bank in 1917. The BSU and the

IC&S both did well, showing respective assets of $697,964 and $284,636 by 1920. As it became apparent that the younger institution could offer real competition, BSU acted on merger overtures made earlier and absorbed IC&S, seating Palmer and Macfarlane on its board.[71]

By 1920 Utah's industrial landscape was dominated by mining. Lead, silver, gold, copper, coal, and gilsonite mines generated jobs, tax revenue, and personal wealth. Utah produced 23 percent of the nation's silver, 14 percent of its lead, 10 percent of its copper, 4 percent of its gold, and 1 percent of its bituminous coal. The band along the east and west flanks of the Oquirrh Mountains was the largest smelting district in North America.[72]

The mines and railroads enjoyed a symbiotic relationship. Meanwhile, demand in the mines and smelters was a crucial impetus for the establishment of power plants and an electrical grid. Mines, smelters, railroads, and power plants incorporated Utah within a nationwide capitalist system of production and exchange. Investors in Boston, Michigan, New York, Philadelphia, Colorado, and London took a lively interest in the mineral wealth of the Beehive State, underwriting the infrastructure and equipment necessary to extract and refine ore. The fortunes of the mines rose and fell with federal policy, national consumption, and the vagaries of the stock market. Mining enriched copper and silver kings such as Samuel Newhouse and Thomas Kearns who made Utah their home, but much of the wealth empowered out-of-state investors, some of them industrial titans and monopolists such as the Rockefellers and Guggenheims. Utahns joined their fellow Americans in debating the merits of an urban-industrial order that enriched the nation but magnified the economic disparity between capitalists and workers and between the centers of corporate finance on the East Coast and their investment frontiers in the interior, including the Beehive State.

5

THE FORMATION OF THE WAGEWORKERS' FRONTIER

THE INCORPORATION OF AN INDUSTRIAL WORKFORCE

Between statehood and 1920 Utah, like the South during the Gilded Age, became a "loyal 'satellite'" of northeastern capital and "bulwark" to the industrial order by furnishing raw materials for it. Large-scale reclamation and arid agriculture were introduced, the sugar industry established, mining and smelting industrialized, coal fields opened, railroad mileage redoubled and improved, an electrical system established, and, perhaps most gratifying of all, a vast industrial spectacle established at Bingham Canyon's open copper pit.[1]

For many Utahns, the era seemed an almost sublime reaffirmation of the inevitability of progress from the simple to the complex and from the useless to the productive. Industrial growth recapitulated the American miracle, defined in terms of productivity, profit, and state-sanctioned private property.

According to this vision, the machine was benefactor to the human race, the factory system the proper heir to domestic manufactory. But for the working man, industrialization often translated into permanent dependency. The Civil War had been fought in part to free labor, and, as historian Eric Foner has written, at the time of the war workers defined a "successful laborer" as "one who achieved self-employment, and owned his own capital—a business, farm or shop."[2]

With industrialization in the decades following the Civil War, the prospects for skilled craftsmen diminished. Industrial workers had little need for traditional skills; at best workers in the factories became operators and tenders of machines. Muckers, rail layers, and stoop workers were required in large, easily manipulated numbers. Lifelong dependency became an enduring possibility. The day of the permanent wageworker had arrived. With it came the need for a controlled labor pool and the consequent demand for new immigrants. And with it also came labor discord.

Industrialization, incorporation, and the displacement of skilled labor occurred nationwide, and perhaps for that reason Utah historians have devoted less attention to these matters than to the era of religious conflict that preceded it. The convergence of the "new industry" and the "new immigration" came late and with less violence than in some quarters. Yet in critical ways the first decades of statehood belonged to capital and to labor; a struggle for the soul of the state unfolded as the corporate system met the human dimensions of production and as corporate mines, smelters, railroads, and other businesses sought to socialize and incorporate workers within the new order.

In 1896 native sons constituted a goodly portion of Utah's labor force. Products of the Mormon gathering or spin-offs from frontier resource booms, they expected upward mobility or at least security and respect from the crafts and building trades that were making Salt Lake and Ogden modern cities. Other workers in the state had come in troubled pulses from distant homelands.

While these new immigrants saw America and Utah as a land of opportunity, many also saw themselves as sojourners. Most had known want in its rawest forms, and many had experienced deep social and political upheaval. Some had worked in Europe's industrial regions and had more than a passing acquaintance with radical economic and political thought. More, however, knew only regional and national influences and wanted initially to make money and then return home. Native patriotisms and ethnic allegiances fairly burned in the veins of some. Many hoped Utah and the surrounding regions held a quick fix, not a new life. Well over one-third did return to their homelands, carrying part of Utah with them in the form of new outlooks, lifeways, and social networks. But others remained, developing a hybrid, transnational identity—the product of daily life in Utah combined with ethnic foodways, celebrations, organizations, letter writing, and international travel. In a pattern that would recur repeatedly over the next century, the influx of so many immigrants alarmed old-stock residents, who feared the immigrants would take their jobs, depress wages, and undermine the state's culture, language, and social order. Inevitably, these immigrants changed the course of Utah history, among other things contributing to a rich labor tradition and making Utah more cosmopolitan and culturally diverse.

THE UTAH WORKER: BACKGROUND

Although Utah unionism had its first stirrings in 1854 with the formation of a social organization of printers and typesetters, the Deseret Typographical Association, the boom of the late 1880s and early 1890s brought a large influx of workingmen and introduced industrial unionism, a potent reaction to the corporate order. By 1890 central organizations for both the crafts and the building trades had been formed in Salt Lake City. Ogden too was well on its way toward union organization. The influence of the American Federation of Labor (AFL) and Samuel Gompers's "unionism plain and simple" became increasingly apparent among them.[3] The craft-conscious leaders of the Federated Trades began to draw a line between themselves and unskilled workers that in time made them predominantly a federation of skilled workers. The streetcar men's union was disbanded. Thereafter, the Western Federation of Miners (WFM), a militant union of hardrock miners founded in 1893 and based in the Intermountain West and a "radical bloc," became increasingly the "driving force" behind the state's "unskilled workingmen."[4]

The Utah Federated Trades and Labor Council lobbied successfully for protective laws. Article 16 of the Utah Constitution provided the basis for the Board of Labor, Conciliation, and Arbitration; an eight-hour workday on "public-works"; health and safety regulations for factories, smelters, and mines; and procedures governing recovery of damages for injuries resulting in death. The constitution also provided the basis for laws prohibiting underground work by women and children under fourteen, employment of convicts outside prison grounds, political or commercial control of employees, and exchange of blacklists. The first state legislature made beginning efforts to enact most of these reforms, including the office of coal mine inspector and a mine safety package.[5]

The late 1890s appears now to have been a time when an increasing number of wage-earning Utahns began to class themselves against the corporate order and among the disinherited. Others, clinging to the American dream, continued to see themselves as share takers in its gifts. During the depression of the 1890s, the labor movement had virtually ceased to exist, but after 1896 it came back quickly among urban craft and trade workers. The defunct Federated Trades was replaced by the Utah Federation of Labor, and September 7, 1896, was celebrated as the first "state labor day."

During the 1890s Utah miners moved modestly to the left. Eureka miners initiated the trend when they pulled out of the Federated Trades in 1893 in favor of the WFM. In 1896 Park City's miners organized Local No. 43 of the WFM. Still tending to particular skills rather than industry-wide causes, Local No. 43 admitted only underground workers and refused to accept unskilled mill workers or outside crews.[6]

When the WFM met in 1898 in Salt Lake City for its sixth convention, it made reorganization its main order of business. The Western Labor Union was voted into existence on May 9, and a constitution was accepted that put it in head-to-head competition with the American Federation of Labor in the West, with the purpose of bringing "all...skilled and unskilled workers" together. By 1900 four Utah miners' unions were affiliated with the WFM, and the cooks and waiters', cigar makers', carpenters', and bricklayers' unions were affiliated with the Western Labor Union, bringing its "total membership [to] about ten thousand." Radicalism was afoot, but the appeal of the gentler federationism was apparent in the four thousand persons from twenty-three unions at the Federation of Utah Labor's picnic at Lagoon on Labor Day.[7]

While the revival of urban unionism in Salt Lake and Ogden was almost complete by 1900, organized labor was far from an established force statewide. Agricultural labor was totally unorganized. Only a sprinkling of Texas cowboys, New Mexican herders, and traveling shearers joined the itinerant workers who were beginning to follow the state's industries.[8] Grain harvesters and workers at canning and sugar factories came typically from farm families engaged in crop production, while haying crews were made up of vacationing city youngsters.[9]

Coal miners too were not unionized in 1900. A subcommittee of the US Industrial Commission in 1899 attributed this to contented workers. According to its observations, employers rarely forced workers to live in company boardinghouses, trade at company stores, or pay medical assessments. Reflecting what coal operators had let them see, the committee members concluded that a "great number of employees with families and homes" considered "themselves practically a part of these great mines."[10]

This affinity between labor and capital had its limits. Still, the subcommittee's observations were not entirely off the mark in a rather complex labor profile. The work experiences of William Gilbert Gould and Patrick J. Moran illustrate how older relationships and opportunities to advance within work-related communities muted frictions between English-speaking workers and management while isolating Utah's unskilled immigrant wageworkers.

THROUGH THE EYES OF A D&RG ENGINEER

D&RG engineer and raconteur William Gilbert Gould was "born to" an impoverished family of Welsh "coal miners and ironmongers" who migrated to Utah about 1890. As a "boyhood preoccupation" and a lifetime commitment, he "followed the railroad." To Gould it seemed a life of near heroes, high adventure, and great romance—a culture separate from and far above all others.[11] By 1914 Utah railroads employed a total of 4,987 men. Of these 1,341 were operating crews, a skilled elite, at the head of which stood the engineers; 1,312 were shopmen, among whom were also many skilled workers; 1,563 were track workers, unskilled section gangs, and their foremen; and 771 worked switches and whistle-stops along the way.[12]

Gould, like many of his peers, grew up within this system but portrayed the struggles of his section-boss father and lodge-keeping mother as steps of progress rather than sacrifice. Born to street, shop, and road rather than to church or school, Gould advanced from Jackson fork dump boy to newsboys' unionist to quality-control lab assistant at the Salt Lake Cement Works. From there he moved to young dandy at the original Salt Palace's bicycle track, D&RG supply-shop flunky, beginner on delivery trains around Salt Lake's "Horn," apprentice and full-fledged fireman, and, finally, mountain division engineer, all by the time he was twenty-seven. For the D&RG he fired and ran Park City ice trains, worked Ogden passenger and freight engines, ran the Copper Belt and Magna stretches of the Bingham branch, worked summer and winter on the Tintic extension, labored occasionally on the Sanpete branch, and pulled assignments on various hill, bridge, and helper crews. He also ran the mainline engines that labored up Price and Spanish Fork Canyons. From about the age of thirty, he was a ranking engineer on the Utah Railway Company's line from Hiawatha to Martin and on to Salt Lake City over tracks shared with the D&RG. On the Utah Railway his career soon peaked, but life was still filled with satisfactions. By World War I Gould knew the Rio Grande road through Utah's mountain division by heart. Its stations, passing switches, bridges, and cuts, as well as the idiosyncrasies and modifications of its grade, were his second nature.

Gould remembered his common labor roots but recognized many onetime workingmen in company management. He knew roundhouse crews, station staff, beanery waitresses, and passing-switch operators, including a hermit widow and her two daughters who maintained a lonely vigil at a derail switch below Soldier Summit. But the heart of his society were the fifteen hundred brakemen, conductors, firemen, and engineers from whom the five-man train crews were constituted. They frequented the same saloons, boardinghouses, and railroad neighborhoods and belonged to the brotherhoods of their appropriate unions. Traditions of tragic accidents and near-tragic escapes bound them. Scores who were killed or maimed were Gould's acquaintances. In one tragic engine crash near Soldier Summit in 1915, Gould's close friends and mentors Art Campbell and Dutch Schafer were killed. By the time Gould arrived on the scene, a "heavy stench" hung in the air, and Gould glimpsed "a foot sticking out of the piled up wreckage...and other little reminders of lives snuffed out." Words could not convey his anguish; he reflected, "How feeble is the effort to convey the real feelings that come over a person when he hears news like that concerning men that he has known so intimately."[13]

Hierarchical aspects were strong in this society. Experience, seniority, rank, and internal discipline played important roles. Near the top were examining inspectors, traveling engineers, train masters, and master mechanics—autocrats who controlled their lesser brethren. From their ranks rose division superintendents and other second-flight managers.[14]

This was a society in which northern Europeans and Yankees dominated. Among Gould's close associates, only two were clearly not of northern European or Yankee stock. Gould does not describe a tension- or conflict-free system of labor. However, labor relations do appear to have been both more humane and limited by the romance and myth within which the railroads operated and by the mechanisms of skill and seniority through which upward mobility flowed.

PATRICK J. MORAN: APPRENTICE, UNION MAN, CONTRACTOR

The experiences of Patrick J. Moran, head of one of Salt Lake City's foremost turn-of-the-century construction firms, illustrate the blurring of class identity in a society where some laborers did rise meteorically. Born in 1864 to Irish parents, Moran began work at the age of seven in England when his father died, flushing game for shooters, herding geese, and after a year or two mining coal. When he was fourteen he stowed away for America on the steamship *Carmania*. The ship's master steamfitter put him to work and wrote a note commending him to a master fitter in Cincinnati under whom Moran apprenticed. With industry burgeoning, Moran became a journeyman steamfitter, troubleshooting in New England and for the Union Pacific Company and for Richard Crane, head of Chicago's Northwestern Manufacturing Company.

Twenty-three years old and still very much a grease-and-work-clothes mechanic, Moran was dispatched to Salt Lake City in the early fall of 1887 to solve problems in recently installed heating systems. With a team of local fitters he was able to right the problem before snow flew and entered a partnership with J. W. Farrell, "owner of Salt Lake City's best and largest plumbing company." Delighted, Crane made him a representative for Northwestern Manufacturing Company fittings and equipment and in time established plants in Salt Lake City himself. Moran took up modest quarters in a downtown hotel, joined a variety of clubs, courted politicians and the wealthy but made friends at every level, and avoided the Mormon conflict. In 1889 he set up his own company, selling supplies and taking contracts. He also became president of the first plumbers' union in the Mountain West.[15]

Moran was elected to the Territorial Council in 1891. In the legislature, he promoted worker legislation, including safety and eight-hour-day bills and labor-day legislation. Later he was elected to the city council, where his overlapping interests were apparent in his support of an eight-hour-day ordinance and construction of the City and County Building as a public works project. With the financial aid of Irish mining men, Moran got the big company he needed off the ground by 1900 and in time owned equipment worth two million dollars and employed some fifteen hundred men.

He undertook many of Salt Lake City's greatest railroad projects, including a major contract on the Lucin Cutoff, a causeway across the Great Salt Lake; street and sidewalk paving; the great aqueduct from Big Cottonwood to Parley's Canyon; the basement and grounds for the state capitol building; and numerous schools.

It is unclear whether Moran was able to sustain good relations with his employees as his outfit grew, but it seems unlikely. But Moran's career shows that near the turn of the century, traditional influences, including the rags-to-riches myth, and blurred distinctions between workingmen and management encouraged a sense of community between Utah's trade and craft unions and its businesses.

THE WAGEWORKERS' FRONTIER

As Utah industrialized it became part of what historian Carlos Schwantes has called the wageworkers' frontier. The Utah wageworkers' frontier was largely English speaking until 1900. Even thereafter, English-speaking wageworkers were the largest component in most Utah labor forces. Their work was seasonal and highly mobile, if not actually migratory. Winters were toughed out in enforced idleness or, for the lucky, in coal mines, where work accelerated during cold months. Most wageworkers were young. Considering wage work a stopgap, many counted on upward mobility within the labor force or planned to "settle down" in farming, store keeping, freighting, or some other form of commerce. Too few availed themselves of insurance or even membership in unions or fraternal orders to help in the event of death or injury. Not unusual was John MacNeil, who was killed in an accident at Park City's Daly West mine in 1903, leaving his children orphaned and with no benefits. On the other hand, Martin Powers, who was killed in the same accident, belonged "to the order of Workmen," which guaranteed burial benefits and two thousand dollars for his family.[16] Vulnerable, dependent, and often discontented, English-speaking wageworkers were given to nativism and hostility as competing groups entered the wageworkers' pool.

CHINESE: FIRST ON A NEW FRONTIER

From the "joining of the rails" in 1869 Chinese were a noticeable but diminishing factor in Utah's workforce and ethnic mix. According to a passing reference in the 1942 *Utah Guide*, 5,000 Chinese were "left behind" after the rails were joined. The 1870 Census identified only 445 Chinese residents, though. Working as section hands on the Central Pacific and busying themselves otherwise, they made Box Elder County Utah's center of Chinese population for many years. Long after the initial building period, railroads continued to attract Chinese. In addition to section work, they found their way into the bottom tiers of the service sectors at track towns and terminals. For example, the 1900 Census for Helper listed 4 Chinese, 3 of whom were domestic help at the D&RG Hotel.[17] Chinese were part of the scene too at Silver Reef, Mercur, Bingham, and other mining camps but rarely in sufficient numbers to threaten other workers. By statehood there were well-established Chinese "microcommunities" along Twenty-Fifth Street in Ogden, at Plum Alley in downtown Salt Lake City, and at Park City, where they gathered in an area "back of Main Street." The 1890 Census showed 500 Chinese in the three cities and more than 800 in the state. With the Chinese exclusion act barring immigration after 1882, statewide numbers fell to 572 in 1900, 371 in 1910, and 342 by 1920.[18]

A few Chinese such as Wong Sing, the famous Fort Duchesne trader, scattered elsewhere throughout the state. Nearly all of the Chinese were men—William Louie, who grew up in Ogden in the 1920s and 1930s as the son of Chinese immigrants, could recall "only three Chinese families among two hundred men" there—and most expected to return to China. They maintained connections with San Francisco's Chinatown and with the old country, utilizing the Bing Kung Tong, a fraternal society, which rendered economic, legal, job-finding, and communications services. Nativism, which had run high in California, dogged Utah's Chinese. Biases widely held among other workingmen appear to have been at the root of this, but management's interest in keeping the workforce divided joined the press in keeping anti-Chinese nativism alive. As late as 1942 half-joking passages in the *Utah Guide* still conveyed nativist sentiments. If they stayed in their place, the Chinese were tolerated, even appreciated for the diversity they brought to the urban centers and the human kindness they often exhibited, as well as for the work they did. In Ogden consumers appreciated the Chinese, while laborers resented them. In 1885 the *Ogden Herald* and the Knights of Labor in Ogden organized a boycott of Chinese vegetable vendors, hoping thereby to drive the Chinese from the city, but vegetable sales to sympathetic customers actually increased. Hard-rock mining was generally off-limits to the Chinese. When they took jobs that others wanted, persecution could be direct and violent, as at Wyoming's Rock Springs and in the oft-referenced instance when "white workers" allegedly deported Chinese from Carbon County's coal fields in a free-rolling boxcar. One former miner, Howard Stevens of Mapleton, recalled, "They went out on strike and the company brought in a lot of Chinamen to work. Do you know what those old miners did? They loaded them in a boxcar and turned it loose down the track. I never did hear what happened to that, but I guess it scared those old Chinamen out and they never did come back. (laughter) They got rid of them."[19]

FINNS, COAL, AND MOUNTING TENSION

In the late 1890s people of other ethnic backgrounds began to enter the wageworkers' frontier. Among the first were Finns. Although they hailed from northern Europe and were Lutheran, Utah's first Finns stood apart, much more a distinct ethnic group than other Scandinavians. Some spoke Swedish, but Finns generally were held in low esteem by their Scandinavian neighbors, and those who came to Utah carried the burden of adverse homeland biases.

Utah's Finns came largely from the west-central coastal regions of the country. They were part of nearly 400,000 migrants who relocated between 1864 and 1927 due to "population pressure, Russification policies, and the industrialization of agriculture." Young men came first. Women and families followed. At Eureka "nuclear Finnish families were abundant, as were boarders and lodgers." Some households consisted of as many as 25 people.[20] Finnish enclaves developed at Bingham, Eureka, and Park City as well as in Carbon County, particularly at Clear Creek and Scofield. In the coal fields their tendency to cluster was taken as evidence of their standoffishness but was encouraged by company policy.[21] A crude index to their situation may be garnered from State Bureau of Immigration data, showing that Utah's Finnish population had more than doubled from 734 in 1900 to 1,535 in 1910. Of that number in 1910, 595 were children born in America since 1900. Such a substantial natural increase suggests a fair number of families by 1910.[22]

Finns had rarely been miners in the old country but adapted well. Their settlements were marked by sauna baths, Finn halls, boardinghouses, and Finnish neighbors. Hardworking and competitive, they met with considerable hostility. In the early 1890s Cornish miners at Bingham struck rather than work with Finns, and as the century closed others charged them with greed and carelessness.[23] In addition to social ostracism, Utah Finns paid dearly for the opportunities the new land gave them in the Winter Quarters mine disaster of 1900.

LIMITS OF SYMPATHY: THE WINTER QUARTERS MINE DISASTER

On May 1, 1900, 63 Finns, 4 Italians, and 133 English-speaking miners were killed in an explosion at the Winter Quarters coal mine, some 110 miles southeast of Salt Lake City. Utah's worst industrial accident and at the time the worst in the West, the Winter Quarters calamity brought Utahns face-to-face with the industrial age. The awful price paid by the miners themselves, the numbing losses sustained by their families, and the limits of aid provisions left a lasting shadow over the state's labor and ethnic development.

In 1900 the Pleasant Valley Coal Company, a mining subsidiary owned by the largest coal mine operator in the West, was in the midst of aggressive expansion.

PVC opened new mines during 1899 at Winter Quarters No. 4; at Clear Creek, a few miles up the canyon; and at Sunnyside, about 40 miles farther east by automobile.[24]

Producing about 90 percent of Utah's coal, the Pleasant Valley Company featured largely in the state's rise from a panic low of 172,958 tons in 1895 to 878,122 in 1899. Holding a virtual monopoly in eastern Utah until after 1906, its output surged in 1900 to 1,085,374 tons—nearly 88 percent of the state's output. Employment followed much the same pattern. Rising from 574 workers in 1898, PVC employed 1,328 men in 1900; by contrast, only 176 were employed by all the rest of Utah's coal producers.[25]

This quick advance had been accompanied by some warnings. In 1890 a coal-dust explosion at the Castle Gate mine killed 3 miners and led to the installation of an electrical system to ignite dynamite shots after crews had gone home. Thereafter, coal dust at Castle Gate was regarded as highly volatile, but by dampening it the mine was considered workable. Nevertheless, on March 22, 1900, as new production schedules were implemented, a dust explosion ripped through the entire Castle Gate mine after the routine evening shots. Workmen were out of the mine and no casualties occurred, but vast damage was sustained and production was delayed.[26]

Following its March 1900 explosion, the Castle Gate mine was quickly brought back into production. Company officers thanked their lucky stars for the special shooting procedures and hurried to bring the new pit at Winter Quarters and new mines at Clear Creek and Sunnyside into full production. If the coal dust at Winter Quarters No. 4 lacked the properties that had always convinced workers and management alike that Winter Quarters Mines No. 1, 2, and 3 were virtually explosion proof, no one noticed. Production was at high tempo as a crew of about 110 men entered No. 4 the morning of May 1, along with a crew of perhaps 200 who went into connecting No. 1. At approximately ten thirty an explosion occurred deep in No. 4. Feeding on disturbed coal dust, it reverberated throughout the entire mine, sweeping everything before it, including a driver who is said to have been hurled some eight hundred feet out of the mine's portal. "After damp" (carbon monoxide) produced by the explosion swept through the tunnels, infiltrating large areas of the No. 1 mine, but dust in the older mine did not ignite.[27]

The first limited rescue teams entered the mine at once. Within hours general manager W. G. Sharp and state mine inspector Gomer Thomas arrived from Salt Lake City, joining Winter Quarters superintendent T. J. Parmley, No. 1 mine foreman Andrew Hood, and Clear Creek superintendent W. D. Williams to direct retrieval efforts. It was soon apparent that many miners had died, and a medical team from Salt Lake City busied themselves with families of the deceased. Almost to the last man, miners in No. 4 were killed. The dead in No. 1 were victims of the after damp, lying as it caught them, but outwardly unmarred. Recovery crews labored heroically. More than a hundred volunteers came from the Clear Creek, Castle Gate, and Sunnyside mines. "Divided into parties, then into shifts," they "reinforced the handful of [surviving] home miners."[28] Working to save friends or relatives, many entered harm's way, and several lost their lives. The general record of the disaster is singularly devoid of immigrant names other than those of the unfortunate Finns.

Only 2 Finns were credited with active participation in the recovery effort.[29] It seems that ethnic tension was high in the camp: the paucity of Finn rescuers was widely associated with the idea that Finns triggered the entire catastrophe by caching powder in the mine or by greed and carelessness (miners were paid by weight, and Finns were said to cut corners). Although he had to abandon the theory later, mine inspector Thomas initially laid responsibility on Isaac Macki, one of the Finnish victims, whose poorly detonated shot allegedly ignited the stored powder, which company advocates of the inert coal-dust theory held would have been necessary to ignite the dust in an otherwise safe mine.

More objective accounts commiserated with the unfortunate Finns, who proportionately suffered more than any other group. J. W. Dilley, the disaster's historian, cites speculations that Finnish reluctance to help retrieve their countrymen may have rested upon cultural superstitions. Although there is no explicit evidence, perhaps Finns feared for their lives in the chaos of a situation that would take them outside their protective groups.[30] The earlier expulsion of Chinese miners from Pleasant Valley by Anglo-Americans conveyed a clear message. It seems possible it was not lost on the Finns.

In Utah and in the nation beyond, the reports issuing from Scofield on May 1 were jumbled but horrifying. From a telegram early in the day Mormon leader Seymour B. Young was first led to believe "25 men were killed," but by evening he knew of "further horrors." By morning he seemingly accepted newspaper accounts that 300 had died. "Most of them," he concluded, *"are our people."* At Mapleton farmer William Tew recorded, "416 Men were Killed." A *Los Angeles Herald* writer made a case against management and minorities. "Monopolists," he complained, controlled the coal industry and in the East were replacing "intelligent, civilized... American labor" with the "offscourings of Europe." Then as if to see a silver lining, he concluded that conditions in Utah were "not quite so pronounced, and the long list of the butchered... indicates that many Americans were employed."[31]

As bodies were recovered, the count of victims firmed up at 200 dead, 113 widows, 306 fatherless children, 12 "full orphans and 91 dependent parents."[32] Under close direction by company officers, bodies were identified and readied for shipment or for burial. In the process some interesting social profiles emerged. The victims had been residents of a closely knit workplace. While Scofield was technically not a company town, Pleasant Valley Coal's presence was pervasive, leaving workers to fight for control of their lives at home as well as on the job. About 115 of the dead regarded Scofield as home or at least were buried there. Of these 63 were Finns and were interred by a Finnish Lutheran pastor from Rock Springs in rocky graves dug by local and Provo volunteers directed by company surveyor G. W. Snow.

Only 4 of the dead can be identified as Italians. Services for them were held in Salt Lake City with Rev. Father Keenan of the Catholic church officiating. In attendance "150 strong" were the Società Italiana Christofaro Columbo along with Helds Band and "about twenty" relatives and friends from the coal and railroad camps. Salt Lake City Italians, including a brother of one of the deceased, picked up the tab. Otherwise, most victims were Anglos. Many had migrated from Wales, England, or Scotland and had experience in mines in the old country. The 60 or so English speakers buried at Scofield were interred under the auspices of Mormon authorities George Teasdale, Heber Grant, Reed Smoot, and Seymour Young. Eleven of the dead hailed from Coalville and were buried there. The number of the dead who were members of extended families was striking. Among the hardest hit was Ogden's Hunter clan, which lost 10 men. Only three months in America, aged Finns Abe Luoma and his wife lost 6 sons and 3 grandsons. The widow of Alexander Wilson, whose first child was only three days old, buried a total of 13 relatives. Tragedy visited often in threes. Among them were the Miller brothers of Springville, the Wilsons of Coalville, American Fork's Padfields, and father-and-son threesomes from Richfield and Springville.[33]

No unions existed at the time in Scofield, but the fraternal societies were important. The International Order of Oddfellows (Lodge No. 32) and Knights of Pythias (Rathbone Lodge No. 9) were well organized in Scofield, as elsewhere in Utah. Nineteen victims belonged to Lodge No. 32, and 3 others were members of other IOOF lodges. Fifteen were Knights of Pythias, 4 of whom "were members of the endowment rank of the order," 3 carrying insurance for $1,000 and one for $500. The orders announced their intent to bury dead members.

Fraternity and service were at the heart of the Scofield societies, but much of labor's instinct for organization and caring for its own was there as well. Possibly the fraternal societies had been encouraged by management as a substitute for unions. For the moment, at least, they represented an attempt to reach beyond the division between Mormon and anti-Mormon and the growing class disparities. A case in point was William Parmley, dead foreman of the ill-fated crew. He was an Odd Fellow, Knight of Pythias, and Mason; a blood brother of the mine superintendent and Mormon bishop; and a fraternal brother to laborers, businessmen, teachers, and county officials.[34]

Utahns responded with an outpouring of sympathy. The facts were bad enough, but distribution of the dead to fifteen localities, multiple funerals, and long burial processions carried the tragedy across the state. First came volunteers, then trainloads of flowers, then relief in kind, then cash donations. The Pleasant Valley Company moved publicly to help survivors, evidencing both compassion and responsibility. Bills at the company store were written off; the paymaster went from house to house, paying a month's wages. Ultimately, the company "donated" $500 to "the family of each of the men killed," or a total of $100,000.[35]

As private interests moved to set up relief drives, the governor called for a state-wide campaign. Through gifts from in state and out and various promotions, an additional $116,289.81 came in. On the assumption that getting aid in a lump sum rather than receiving it incrementally in a monthly pension would enable dependents to become self-supporting, plans were made to pay by the following schedule: to each widow over fifty $720, to each widow under fifty $576, to each boy over fourteen and each girl over fifteen $108, to each full orphan under fourteen $432, and (maybe most interesting of all in our post–welfare state era) to fully dependent single parents $720, to fully dependent aged couples $1,080, for partially dependent single parents $540, and for partially dependent aged couples $900.[36]

It was little enough, but in light of the tiny pensions veterans of Indian wars were lining up to collect it does not seem like an insignificant effort. On the other hand, suggestions that recipients might use the payments to homestead, set up boardinghouses, or improve family gardens make it clear that public welfare was in its incipiency.

Its contracts in hand, Pleasant Valley Coal rushed to put the Winter Quarters mines back in production. On May 25, twenty-four days after the explosion, the mine inspector cleared both pits for work. On the twenty-eighth full production was resumed in No. 1, and No. 4 soon followed. The company replaced the dead workers and during the year hired new men in record numbers. Many were single.[37] Company officials, coroner's juries, the grand jury, the state mine inspector, and the governor all concurred: "Responsibility or blame...could be attached to no one." Other than the culpability of coal dust, even the cause was never fixed. For all, except the sorrowing families, business as usual was resumed.

ITALIANS AND THE WORKFORCE

More than a thousand Italians lived in the state by 1900.[38] At that time most of them were from northern Italy and had felt the nationalistic flames of *Il Risorgimento* and the clamp of poverty that drove many Italians to work expeditions in Europe and South America. As America industrialized, they came increasingly to the United States. A few came to Utah as Mormon converts as early as 1870, but the first wageworkers came much later, perhaps following the Denver & Rio Grande Railroad into the state. Once in Utah they worked in the mines and railroads, suffered serious discrimination, played important roles in social and labor conflict, and spread in the business and professional community.

By 1880, 35 of them were in Bingham, where they were "called 'Short Towns' because of their stocky builds."[39] In 1900, 170 Italians were enumerated in Salt Lake

TABLE 5.1. Population of foreign birth or parentage, 1900–1910

Nationality	1900 Foreign Born	1910 Foreign Born	Second Generation 1910	Total
Austrian-Serbian	272	2,085	785	2,870
Finnish	734	1,012	523	1,535
Greek	3	4,039	23	4,062
Italian	1,062	3,117	1,111	4,228
Japanese	417	2,119	N/A	2,119

Compiled from the 13th Census of the United States Taken in the Year 1910: Abstract of the Census, 206–9.

County, of whom 102 lived in the city, where they worked for the railroads and owned a variety of small businesses. The Tintic district in Juab County and Stockton, Ophir, and Mercur, all in Tooele County, drew Italians during this period, and some found employment in Ogden. Enough lived at Mercur to justify construction of a Catholic church in 1904, and many were "dispersed among the rest of the population." Utah Copper's opening at Bingham and the establishment of giant smelters resulted in Italian communities there and at Murray, Magna, and Garfield.[40]

Italians were imported by the eastern Utah coal mines at an early time and constituted a significant portion of the pre-1900 population, but the record is sparse. By 1900 Castle Gate boasted two hundred coke ovens, and as Sunnyside coal's superior coking qualities became known, nearly a thousand ovens were constructed. Hard and dangerous work, coking was assigned to Italians. Many of the workers in the coking operations, like Rosario Fazzio, commuted periodically between Italy and Utah. Fazzio's daughter Filomena recalled, "My dad used to migrate. He migrated four or five times. He'd come here and go to work, then he'd go back, stay a year, come back, and go back again." By 1903, when mounting labor tensions made ethnicity relevant, Italians were the largest group in the coal fields. Of 2,076 miners employed by the Pleasant Valley Coal and Utah Fuel Companies, 848 were Italian. The 742 who spoke English made up the next largest group. Castle Gate, where 356 Italians were employed, was called "an Italian mine," but Sunnyside with 246 Italians also had a substantial Italian community, as did Clear Creek with 172 and Winter Quarters with 74.[41]

At least 9,800 immigrants (Finnish, Italian, Japanese, Austrian-Serbian, and Greek) entered the state between 1900 and 1910. In terms of national origin Italians were the largest group, Greeks were a close second, Austrians (including Serbs) ran third, Japanese fourth, and the Finns last.[42]

As had been the case at Winter Quarters, growth in the coal industry had serious social repercussions. In the years after 1900 production increased annually, and the Utah Fuel Company was organized as a new D&RG subsidiary to handle the growing business of the Castle Gate and Sunnyside mines. Those mines soon outproduced the Winter Quarters and Clear Creek end of the business, which remained under the auspices of Pleasant Valley Coal. The advent of independent operators, beginning in 1906, marked another major upsurge in coal output. With the new independent mines coming into full production, eastern Utah's coal and coke output topped three million tons in 1912. Each advance made new demands on manpower, which the companies met through recruiting drives and contract agents who delivered new workers, often in ethnic gangs.

With more than twenty coal mines in production, it was the heyday of the company town. Like other miners, Italians lived in company houses and boarding facilities; used company-generated electricity; shopped at the company store; participated in the company benefits package; went to the company doctor; drank at the Magnolia Trading Company, the "saloon owning wing" of the Utah Fuel Company; and submitted to a good deal of harassment from the "company bulls" who cleared the streets at night, helped distribute pay, and bullied miners if patronage at the company store sagged. Workers were segregated by national background, the best jobs and pay going to Americans. People were housed by income, nationality, skin color, language, and, to some extent, marital status. Miners moved frequently in response to market fluctuations, the seasonality of coal sales, high accident levels, labor disputes, and opportunities to enter the professions and business. Immigrant miners often resisted company paternalism. Added to darkness of complexion and cultural differences, this made them special "targets" for intimidation and discrimination.[43]

Helper was Carbon County's ethnic center and labor stronghold as well as the D&RG's division point. A giant "57," advertising Heinz foods and painted on a neighboring cliff, was said to number the town's ethnic groups, but more careful counts suggest between sixteen and twenty different groups.[44] Whatever the count, it seems clear Helper's ethnic mix ran ahead of Carbon County's general heterogeneity.[45]

Helper also emerged as a primary place of business. By 1903 the four Italians who "maintained businesses" there had launched a process that led to a total of twenty-two Italian business establishments by 1923, one of which was the Helper State Bank, founded and presided over by Joseph Barboglio, avid labor leader.[46] Some Italians moved also into the professions after they and their families worked untold hours in the coke ovens to finance advanced education.

Rifts divided Utah's Italians. Most significant was the line between northern Italians, who accounted for most of the early immigration, and the southern Italians, who arrived later, often from peasant backgrounds. Internally, this rift ran deep, leading in extreme cases to accusation of "black hand" terrorism, but giving way to larger commonalities during strikes or in the face of outside discrimination. Italians were avid joiners, organizing a long list of fraternal societies, including the northern Italian Stella d'America (founded at Castle Gate in 1898) and its southern Italian counterpart, Società Fratellanza di Mutuo Succorso, Principe DiNapoli, Loggia No. 77. They took a first step toward unionization by blacklisting members who served as strikebreakers.

THE STRIKE OF 1901

To say that the shock of the Winter Quarters disaster and the rapid hiring that followed deeply changed labor relations understates the situation. Within a few months the workforce was greatly enlarged and its cultural context altered forever, as the English-speaking core gave way to new ethnic majorities. In perhaps the most statesmanlike address to come out of the disaster of 1900, Catholic bishop Lawrence Scanlon had called for Utah to recognize the sacrifice coal miners were making "at the shrine of capital" and pleaded for management to "soften its heart" and treat miners "more justly, considerately and kindly." But justice and kindness were not in the cards.[47]

In January 1901, while memories of the explosion were still raw, change led to confrontation at the beleaguered Winter Quarters mine. A committee of workers demanded a pay increase of "fifteen cents on the ton or the 3,200 lbs" for miners, a "proportionate advance" for "day-labor," and control of weighing procedures, which miners claimed were blatantly dishonest. When general manager Sharp flatly rejected their demands except for limited concessions in weighing practices, miners voted to strike by a margin of 132 to 113.

Following this split vote, they closed the mine and opened campaigns to extend the strike and gain public support. Midnight marches complete with two bands and the Scofield school drum corps won a slowdown at nearby Clear Creek but fell short of the hoped-for strike. Requests for organizers from the United Mine Workers of America (UMWA) produced no help. In friendly but almost pointless gestures, the Utah Federation of Labor called its members to boycott Pleasant Valley coal and made relief donations that netted only $64.25. Mormon and Catholic leaders advised their people to "keep out of strikes," and the company fired strikers and threatened to shut down the Winter Quarters and Clear Creek operations "indefinitely."[48]

Efforts to bring Castle Gate and Sunnyside workers into the strike ended in special frustration. Denied use of the railroads, 125 strikers struggled thirty miles through the snow to Castle Gate, where mine officers excluded them from meeting halls, chased them from the warmth of coke ovens, and threatened Castle Gate workers with "instant dismissal" if they fed, housed, or showed sympathy to the strikers. Friendly but thoroughly cowed, Italians at Castle Gate gave no immediate support but quietly blacklisted scabs from their fraternal associations.[49]

Under intense pressure from the company, facing a "barrage of antistrike sentiment," and still unsupported by miners elsewhere, the Winter Quarter strikers gave up late in February and tried to negotiate a return to work. In a punitive peace the company "denied employment" to many and paid reduced wages to the rest. It also forced them to sign an "ironclad," or yellow-dog, contract, swearing they were not union members and that "they would not join" unions in the future.[50]

THE STRIKE OF 1903–4

In 1903 the coal fields erupted again, this time in widespread and bitter discord. Unions throughout America had enjoyed a number of successes and were making special advances in the Mountain West, where both the WFM and the United Mine Workers of America mounted organizing campaigns. As the winter of 1903 approached, Colorado coal mines were embroiled in a violent struggle, and miners and union organizers moved freely to and from the Utah coal fields. On November 9 about 200 miners laid down their tools at Sunnyside. Echoing 1901 laborers, strikers demanded pay increases, honest weighing procedures, fair prices at company stores, and the eight-hour workday, but differed sharply on the right-to-organize issue and recognition of the UMWA. The confrontation spread quickly. Organizers were soon on the scene, and between 1,300 and 1,400 Carbon County miners joined the union. Asserting their entitlement to strike and retain their jobs, strikers took up arms, intimidated nonstrikers and scabs, and brawled with company guards and company-controlled county officials. Production slowed in all the mines but stopped only in the Italian-dominated Castle Gate mine.[51]

For many months the UMWA lent moral and economic support. A strike fund was established, tents were provided for displaced families, and camps formed with colorful names such as Unionville, Strike Town, and Mitchellville, the latter to honor UMWA president John Mitchell. Among the organizers assigned to Utah were a self-pronounced "radical socialist" Italian exile named Charles DeMolli and Mother Mary Jones, a nationally known widow who helped organize the rabble-rousing Industrial Workers of the World in 1905. Recognizing the negative impact of violence upon public support, DeMolli denounced violence and worked to discipline the strike.

D&RG subsidiary Utah Fuel offered a modest pay increase and made a few other work-related concessions, but it rejected outright the move to unionization.

It increased its guard force to 120 men, met intimidation with intimidation, and responded to production slowdowns with dismissals, evictions, arrests, injunctions, and court proceedings. Although workers at the Sunnyside mine dropped from 775 to a low of 33, Utah Fuel kept the mine open by recruiting desperately for strike-breakers among off-season Mormon farmers. It appealed to their prejudices in a well-publicized promise from Sunnyside superintendent Joseph R. Sharp to hire native-born miners in the future rather than foreign crews.[52] In its approach to the public, Utah Fuel played up antiforeign and class-warfare fears and law-and-order issues.[53] It insisted that Utah coal miners had no real complaints and that the strike was the work of Italian anarchists, called only to advance the cause of Colorado strikers and organizers.

Carbon County sheriff Hyrum Wilcox and a citizen alliance joined coal company officials in calling for National Guard intervention. After preliminary investigations by mine inspector Gomer Thomas and General John Q. Cannon, Governor Wells dispatched nearly 300 members of the guard on November 24 to Sunnyside, Castle Gate, and Scofield. They were welcomed by the company and to some degree by the strikers and helped make a number of key arrests, including the charismatic DeMolli. The presence of the guard had a quieting effect, but militiamen quickly became bored and chafed about their own salaries. Winter, Christmas in camp, and infestation with lice made matters worse. Citizens, too, wondered about costs and the justice of using state force to suppress wage earners.

By January 25 the guard was home. Reflecting a thoughtful point of view, Sergeant J. L. Ewing, editor of the *Nephi Record*, wrote that strikers were "quite as law abiding as" were "the emissaries of the coal trust" and quite as much in need of protection as were company employees and property. If the strikers were "a lot of anarchists," as the company claimed, "the trust" had "imported" them and gotten what it deserved. "Militiamen," Ewing concluded, "are in sympathy with the strikers, and when they arrived in the coal camps the very reverse was true."[54]

Tension continued to mount, as the two sides remained split over the questions of unionization and recognition. Italian consul Dr. Giuseppe Cuneo put in a brief appearance late in November. After he met first with company and public officials and only then with Italian committees, his statement took a law-and-order spin that did little to modify the strong antiforeign tenor of public opinion. Strikers hoped a thaw was in the offing early in December when the company announced it would accept applications for men to reopen the Castle Gate mine but were disappointed when the company made it clear that strikers would be accepted only if they abjured all union connection.

A cruel eviction of union members left hundreds homeless during the winter of 1903–4, but for the most part it proceeded without violence, as evictees moved into tents and carried on with the strike. A key exception involved 225 strikers who owned homes on company ground. Involved was a question of property rights, the fundamental principle upon which the company position stood. To sidestep the issue, G. W. Kramer, Utah Fuel general manager, and union attorney W. H. King, future US senator, worked out an agreement by the terms of which appraisers set the value of houses, and strikers left their homes immediately but retained the right to sell or move them until October 31, 1904. All but a group of Castle Gate Italians signed the agreement, which proved largely to be a dead letter, as only in "three or four instances was restitution ever made." Houses valued at more than four-fifths of the appraised total "were confiscated."[55]

During 1904 company recruiting continued, primarily among Mormons, whose leaders with vested interests in big business supported the company and openly counseled members to take jobs. Strikers agreed with Thomas Phelps's lament that Mormons were raised "scabs from the cradle," and deep anti-Mormon animosities were engendered among Utah Italians and other new minorities.[56] In February DeMolli returned and was quickly arrested, along with Joseph Barboglio, treasurer of the Sunnyside local of the UMWA, and other union leaders.

Mother Mary Jones, who was seen variously as a "Joan of Arc" or a "vulgar, heartless, vicious creature," came from the Colorado coal fields in April and in a mix of the comic and the tragic shared the general suffering of the Carbon County Italians. One hundred twenty Italians were seized in the excitement of their attempt to protect Mother Jones, who proceeded to a joint conference of the Utah Federation of Labor and the WFM, where with other socialists she fended off a drive to affiliate with the moderate AFL.[57]

The Italian strikers were held for weeks in an exposed bull pen at Price. Even when incarcerated the strikers maintained their militancy, as they insisted on cooking traditional food, spaghetti, in coffee cans. Finally, twenty-two were tried on various charges. As costs mounted, eleven were sentenced and the remainder turned loose. Eventually, John Mitchell and the United Mine Workers of America began to cut their Utah losses. After a final installment of seven thousand dollars to buy strikers one-way tickets, aid was stopped and organizers departed. Many who hung on agreed with an Italian striker named Marchiori that the UMWA was "putrid and corrupt." Some doubtlessly concurred with John Macketa of the Scofield local, who charged that John Mitchell "had been a traitor against us." He promised support "for three years" but "sold himself to the company."[58]

"The remaining strikers, most of whom were Italians," left Utah's coal mines. Most left the state. Some found railroad and smelting work, and some entered businesses and the professions. A handful found land along the Price River and as far distant as Mapleton, where they ran successful truck and fruit farms.[59]

The strike itself was characterized more by intransigence and ill will than by violence and bloodletting. Yet its consequences were considerable. The hostility of

Mormons and other established Americans grew toward foreign strikers. Utah Fuel was unyielding in its antiunion policy. With about two-thirds of the total workforce signing with the UMWA, the seeds of unionism were sown, yet in a cutting irony the unwavering support of "foreign strikers" that nourished the seeding diminished the public support necessary for unions to take root.[60]

By the end of 1904 much of the earlier sympathy between worker and master had passed. Long periods of labor quiescence lay in the future, but the years before the New Deal were not good times for Utah labor or the state's minorities. In the short run, Italians and Finns paid the primary costs for the strike of 1903–4. In 1903 the Pleasant Valley Coal and Utah Fuel companies employed a total 2,076 miners, of whom 848 were Italians and 254 were Finns. In 1905 the total workforce was down to 1,720 as the company regrouped. More important, only 171 Italians were employed, for a net reduction of 677, while 157 Finns were still employed, for a loss of 97. Admittedly, Italians were often the third-largest nationality (after Americans and Greeks) in reckonings of the labor force, and, it is also true, the irrepressible Frank Bonacci furthered the cause of labor immensely in the decades to come, but after the blows of 1903–4 Italians never stood at labor's forefront in quite the same way.

Joseph R. Sharp's voluble pitch to the Mormons came to little, as Mormons, who were determined to be neither "hewers of wood nor drawers of water for heathen Egypt," quickly proved to be an unsure labor supply for the coal mines. Mine operators turned increasingly to Greek, South Slav, and Japanese workers. Austrians or South Slavs gained 28 workers, from 232 in 1903 to 260 in 1905. Appearing for the first time on Utah coal company rolls in 1905, Greeks and Japanese accounted for 111 and 46 workers, respectively.[61]

6

THE TORTUROUS MATURATION OF AN INDUSTRIAL WORKFORCE

GREEKS IN UTAH

In many ways the Greeks stood at the center of ethnic and wageworker developments in the decades after 1904. They were among the last new immigrants to flock
to Utah, but for twenty years after 1904 Greeks were near the flash point of ethnic
and labor tension in the state.[1]

Many Greeks, including most who came to Utah, looked to America initially
as a voluntary exile rather than a new home. For millennia Greece had been a "bat-
tleground," as historian Helen Zeese Papanikolas has explained. Ongoing invasion
by the Turks had turned the Greeks into fierce resistance fighters. Passed over while
great movements changed the world, Greek learning declined and illiteracy spread,
yet national sentiment remained at white heat. With no industry, and dependent
on a single export crop, currants for the French wine industry, the Greek economy collapsed completely after 1898 when bad harvests were followed by total crop
failure in 1907, turning general poverty to "acute suffering." "[The villagers] didn't
have anything. Let me tell you, they was living a pretty bad life," recalled Peter Condas, who left a hardscrabble farm in Greece when he was nineteen. Unable to meet
the costs of ironclad dowry customs and other fundamental needs, families faced

destruction. Encouraged by their government, "170,000 young men entered the United States" between 1901 and 1910. Most planned to go home within five years, after having made enough money to provide for themselves and dowries for their sisters. Thus, while they worked in America, they maintained strong affective and economic ties to their overseas kin.[2]

Greeks began arriving in Utah about 1900. Their numbers increased fairly steadily until 1912, after which immigration slowed sharply as World War I began. Immigration resurged as the war ended and then all but stopped, as anti-immigration legislation went into effect in the 1920s. By 1910 4,062 Greeks were enumerated, of whom only 23 were American born. No more than 10 were women.[3] No Greeks were included in the Pleasant Valley Coal Company's work roster of 1903, but with the expulsion of the Italians their influx to the coal mines ensued. In 1912 1,245 Greeks worked in the coal mines and more than 3,000 elsewhere.[4]

With no "technical knowledge," they became part of the wageworker pool upon which railroad, smelting, and mining corporations relied. Recruited initially in the coffeehouses and ports of Greece, they were processed through the labor marts of Chicago, Omaha, Denver, Butte, Salt Lake City, and Pocatello, which teemed with men in a saturated labor market. Alienated in the full sense, the Greek sojourners rode the rails from one low-paying job to another. "The working man didn't have nothing. And if you didn't like it, there was always three or four hundred people outside wanting your job.... It was rough times. Life was cheap," recalled Greek miner Peter Condas. "There were times [at the Bingham] they killed two or three people in twenty-four hours because there was no protection. The banks were 145 feet high; and when the steam shovels loaded the dirt, rocks came down on people working at the bottom—just knocked them down."[5] Greek workers bached, lived in boardinghouses, frequented coffeehouses that gave their lives some coherence, toughed out sickness and unemployment, and sustained and exploited each other. In keeping with their tradition, they sometimes showed both individual and group capacity for militant action that guided their approach to labor relations more than class consciousness or ideological radicalism.

Cumulatively, they sent millions of dollars home, enough to provide partial relief to families and even to be felt in the national economy. Their remittances were tangible evidence of transnational identities and a nascent global economy in which resources in the form of labor and dollars crisscrossed the ocean, linking Utah and Europe. Confronted with contempt, Greek immigrants "retreated into a fiery nationalism." Forty percent are said to have returned to Greece. The rest prolonged their exile and, in time, became American citizens.[6]

Gifted with lingual skills, ambition, and good luck, a few struck up fortuitous relationships with management. Becoming labor contractors, they acquired both wealth and power. Others, like Bingham's Levantis brothers, ran coffeehouses and Greek-town stores that became labor halls and outposts of home. Naturalized American Nicholas P. Stathakos found means to establish the Bank of Athens in Salt Lake City and built a conspicuous South Temple Street home.[7]

After 1910 women and families came, as men reconciled themselves to a longer sojourn. By this time, some of the men were approaching middle age, having labored for years to provide dowries for their sisters. A few girls who immigrated as intended wives for the men came more or less by themselves or under improvised chaperonage. A few men apparently brought wives with them, and some took Italian, Yugoslavian, and German brides. A handful, including Peter Jounakis of Carbon County, ignored almost impenetrable cultural barriers and married Utah girls.[8]

For the women it was a process fraught with trauma and risk. Most were younger than the men they married and better educated. In a few cases, deception complicated negotiations, as aging men sent photographs of themselves when they were young or even substituted pictures of better-looking men. The agony of relocation and match making was almost unbearable for the few who came unbetrothed. Nevertheless, the advent of women and families placed some limits on the far-ranging mobility of earlier times. Some, like the John Diamanti household, said to be Carbon County's first resident Greek family, added to the stabilizing influences of the coffeehouses and stores. Although Utah's first Orthodox church may have predated the first woman, families enhanced the role of the church, and a succession of priests was assigned to Utah—reputed among them to be the Siberia of clerical service. Marriages were solemnized, holidays kept, the traditions and language of homeland and orthodoxy taught. Greek Orthodox churches were consecrated, first in Salt Lake City in 1905 and then in Price in 1916, giving Utah some claim as a center of Greek orthodoxy and culture in the mountain states.[9]

In the years before 1912 the forces that drew the Greeks into the center ring of Utah labor relations began to converge. Held in contempt by English-speaking Utahns and with few connections outside their own community, they demonstrated a remarkable penchant for group action and a capacity to take advantage of work opportunities over a region stretching from Chicago to Los Angeles and from Morenci, Arizona, to Butte, Montana. They followed railroad construction as it tied the West together and met the demands of new industry when Utah Copper opened Bingham Canyon.[10] They replaced Italians in the Utah coalfields after the strike of 1903–4 and manned the independent companies that tripled production after 1906.

In no small part their lives were governed by padrones, labor agents who under contract with corporations delivered work crews, taking a twenty- to fifty-dollar cut for "a single temporary job" and a fee of a dollar or so per month for job protection thereafter. Prominent Utah labor agents included Edward Daigoro Hashimoto and Moses Paggi, who marshaled Japanese, Korean, and Italian workers. But most powerful and best known was Leonidas Skliris, "Czar of the Greeks." Operating out

of the Hotel Utah, Skliris imported men from the old country and across America
to fill contracts with Utah Copper and other companies in the mountain states. In
constant touch with workers, management, and a staff of underlings, his operation
was an intermediary level of exploitation. Initially, the padrones were accepted as
a given of life. By 1908, however, Skliris stirred enough animosity that his Carbon
County subagent, George Demeter, was killed by Steve Flemetis at Winter Quarters.
During frictions that ensued, Gregorios Pologeorgis shot and nearly killed Skliris in
Salt Lake City. As class cleavages grew, "bad" padrones were compared to the "hated
Turk." Skliris generated special anger when he bought the Panhellenic store in Bing-
ham and, as an added exaction, forced Greek workers to pay inflated prices.[11]

BINGHAM STRIKE OF 1912

With new mines and great smelters, Carbon and Salt Lake Counties were points
of festering labor discord.[12] In the Bingham Canyon mines in 1911, immigration
inspector V. V. Viles reported 1,210 Greek workers among 3,129 "aliens" in a total
workforce of approximately 4,600.[13] Italians followed with 634 men, Austrians with
564, and Japanese with 254. Internal divisions among the Greeks, including the lines
between the volatile Cretans and the mainlanders, did not keep them from acting in
unison on many issues. Shared interests with the Japanese, Italians, and South Slavs
also led to joint action, but internal tensions, on the one hand, and defensiveness,
on the other, neutralized the Americanizing influence of the well-established Western Federation of Miners local, led by radically inclined Americans.[14]

As the proportion of Greeks employed in the coalfields increased, tensions
grew there. On February 2, 1911, Greeks struck at Kenilworth's Independent Coal
and Coke mine, charging the company with favoring Americans and cheating at
the scales. After preliminary talks during which 15 Greeks were discharged, strikers retired to the surrounding hills, fired on offices and homes, and killed Thomas
Jackson, company guard, reportedly as he led a charge to displace them. Years later
Jackson's eldest son, George, recalled that his father had played a mediator's role,
relaying laborers' complaints about the crooked scales to the management. Assured
scales were accurate, he temporarily convinced the complaining workers. When
they learned differently, they struck. Still convinced he could effect a peaceable settlement, Jackson was killed in the attempt. The following morning Jackson's two
brothers took their Boer War rifles and, pushing into range in a line of coal cars,
engaged the strikers in a shoot-out in which a Greek was killed.

Several strike leaders were arrested, and others escaped. Greek unrest grew
amid mounting public hostility and demands for reductions in the number of
Greeks employed. The coal companies defended Greek hirings on the grounds that
a "divide and conquer" policy was working. Acquiescing, Greek business leaders,

men whose interests were influenced by class ties, toured Carbon County, quieting the workers and public ill will to the point that no reapportionment was made and some strikers were rehired.[15]

Meanwhile, labor relations deteriorated at Bingham Canyon. There, according to historian Gunther Peck, Greek workers defined an approach to collective action based on "vital connections between ethnicity, race, and class." In an August 1908 act of cooperation that surprised even some of their countrymen, 300 Greek workers had struck at the Utah Copper smelter, demanding that wages reduced during the panic of 1907 be restored. Rather than push them into an alliance with the "old radicals" of the WFM local, Utah Copper met their demands.[16] Still distrusting the American-led union but looking for a way to break labor agent Leonidas Skliris's oppressive hold, 50 of them wrote Governor William Spry in 1911. When he failed to respond, they wrote again, this time over the signatures of 500 workers, demanding that Skliris be dumped, that the company hire directly, and that they be given liberty to patronize whatever store they chose.

In an effort to turn Greek solidarity to union advantage, E. G. Locke, secretary of Bingham's WFM local, sent a letter to the Turkish ambassador (who still represented the island of Crete), calling for an investigation of Skliris's "villainy," a copy of which went to Spry. Reflecting incipient class differences among the Greeks, Skliris's banker Nicholas Stathakos denounced Locke's letter as an unwarranted intervention in Greek affairs. Without strengthening the workers' relationship to the union, the incident fed Greek hatred of Skliris and reflected an incipient Americanization of class relations among the Greeks.[17]

American Smelting and Refining Company's use of 800 Cretans from Bingham Canyon and Helper as strikebreakers in a controversy over wages and union recognition at their Murray smelter in May 1912 further roiled the waters. Violence and property damage flared as the strikebreakers took over. An attempt was made on the smelter superintendent's life, and Governor Spry talked of bringing in the National Guard. However, by the end of June the strike was broken. Greeks functioned as submissive tools of the company in this altercation, but emerged more convinced than ever that Skliris worked against them.[18]

In the fall of 1912 Greek and other foreign workers did an about-face and began to join the Western Federation of Miners as Bingham Canyon moved toward a showdown. Union information was translated into Greek, and "agitators" worked the streets and the meeting places of Bingham, talking both union and grievances. WFM membership exploded from 250 in June to 2,500 in October. Militant and cohesive, the new members challenged the control of the "American-born radicals" who headed the organization, pressing for an immediate strike. Reflecting ambivalence between the union's "radical constitution and its organizing strategy," as well as a treasury exhausted by earlier strikes, Charles Moyer, moderate national president, rushed to Bingham to avert or at least control the strike. However, on September 17 1,000 foreign workers "voted a walk-out" that ultimately extended to the whole canyon and "4,800 men," including many Americans.[19]

Reaction to the strike varied. Moyer struggled to discipline it. Advocating non-violence, union recognition, and a pay hike, he called for further negotiations. Greek and Austrian workers "bought arms in quantity," demonstrated wildly, took fortified positions on the canyon side, and initiated armed picket activity. With coffeehouse keeper John Levantis calling many of the shots, "getting Skliris fired" remained the first order of business for the Greeks. One of the most unflinching antiunion outfits in the West, Utah Copper denied that the "padrone system" and other grievances existed, defended Skliris, refused to negotiate with the union, and built a force of 250 armed guards commanded by the violence-prone Axel Steele. Governor Spry considered martial law; met with the company officials, Moyer, Greek Orthodox father Vasilios Lambridos, and banker N. P. Stathakos; and in an appeal for order visited Bingham.[20]

Press response varied. The *New York Call* saw "an American working class," finally uniting, "across" the lines of nationalism, ethnicity, and skill. Local papers focused on "racial tensions," skin color, and nativist issues. The *Deseret News* reported that "3500 aliens" were arrayed against "the 'white' element." The *Herald Republican* condemned foreigners living in "powder-box houses" who sent $580,000 to Europe and contributed little to Utah. Allegedly, only 30 percent of the payroll remained in Bingham Canyon.[21]

The spirit of the strike shifted considerably after September 20. Greek determination to make Skliris's firing the main issue was aired, endorsed by Austrian and Italian workers through a Scottish spokesman and accepted by Charles Moyer, who thus won Greek support for his disciplined strike policy. The success of the fused "immigrant and union demands was dramatically evident just one week" later, when Skliris resigned, fulfilling the essential objective of most of the foreign strikers. Still denying that Greek strikers were "committed to unionism and the abolition of the padrone system," Skliris was undoubtedly among those who at this point joined N. P. Stathakos in forming a chapter of the Panhellenic Union with the objective of helping Greeks become "desirable citizens." As Gunther Peck points out, this organization reflected "an upwardly mobile, middle-class type of Americanization" in opposition to the WFM's working-class approach embraced by Bingham's Greek workers.[22]

As the strike continued, the WFM successfully called a sympathy strike among the 3,000 men employed by Nevada Consolidated Copper at McGill, Nevada, a sister Guggenheim mine. However, the giant combine continued to meet its commitments with other copper mines in New Mexico and Arizona. In what many hoped would be a period of easing tensions, 2 Greek strikers were killed in spasmodic outbursts, and perhaps a dozen men were wounded. No one was ever called to account for the casualties. A number of strike leaders were also arrested, including John Levantis, Yanco Terzich (an Austrian member of the WFM local's board of directors), and local secretary E. G. Locke. "Whites" left the canyon in large numbers, along with Japanese, who had honored the walkout but had been denied union membership by the union's ban on Oriental members. In the days that followed, strikebreakers, many of them newly arrived Mexicans, infiltrated the canyon, despite unarmed pickets who tried to block them. By late October they numbered upwards of 5,000, and the mines were back in business.[23]

The Bingham strike of 1912 had important repercussions. Not only did one of Utah's great workplaces remain unorganized, but public sentiment became increasingly antilabor and nativist. To most Utahns, militant action had become an even more frightening prospect as a result of the strike. For the Greeks, there was good news and bad. Skliris was gone, and the padrone system with its exploitation of immigrant workers was called into the open. On the other hand, the role of mainland Greek strikebreakers in forcing the hand of the Cretan strikers drove a wedge of anger into the Greek community. Already sensitive that mainlanders made too little of enosis, or Greek union, Cretans let their anger ripen into a schism that lasted well into the 1920s.[24] Skliris no longer harassed the Greeks, but other contractors continued to supply labor for Utah industry.[25]

The outbreak of the Balkan War that same fall adversely affected the strikers' interests. On October 1 the Greek government called all male subjects, including those in Utah, between ages eighteen and thirty to active duty. Possibly put off by the fact that the ubiquitous Skliris directed the Utah repatriation movement, few Bingham Greeks left immediately. However, within a year or so, as copper was declared contraband, markets failed, and unemployment spread, many Utah Greeks responded to the call of repatriation. In 1913 811 Greeks left the state "to assist their countrymen in their fight against the Turks." The following year, as the economy rebounded, the number of repatriates was 453. South Slavs and Italians also left Utah for war-related reasons in those same years. Arriving Greeks stating a Utah destination, many of whom may have been making their second trip to America, numbered 1,280 for the two years, or 16 more than the 1,264 who left.[26]

MEXICAN IMMIGRATION

Spanish-speaking cowboys and sheepherders had come to southeastern Utah as migrant workers in the 1880s and 1890s. Eventually, some of these New Mexican laborers brought their families northward; by 1910 they occupied small ethnic neighborhoods around Monticello at Spring Creek, Carlisle, and La Vega and worked at major stock outfits like the La Sal Livestock Company. A few, such as

Ramon González, came to homestead. Fleeing the instability of the Mexican Revolution, hundreds of Mexicans, primarily single males, traveled the migratory labor circuit and wound up in Utah during the 1910s. Some found work in sugar beet farming communities such as Garland, Delta, and Spanish Fork, especially during World War I. In the 1920s Jeff Pino, a Mexicano, and N. J. González operated labor-recruiting businesses in Salt Lake, furnishing agricultural workers for the sugar beet industry. One of those workers, Rafael Torres, described the difficulty of stoop labor. "You get awful tired. Especially when you cultivate beets. See, you…bend over all day. It wasn't easy." Others worked in Hispanic gangs as tracklayers and maintenance workers for the Union Pacific and Denver and Rio Grande Western Railroads, earning rock-bottom wages for arduous labor. "Being a laborer on the track gang entailed hauling ten- to twenty-foot rails and pulling out old ties and replacing them with new ones. Each worker had to replace eight ties a day, which usually wore out two picks a day," explained John Florez, whose father worked on a track gang for "most of his life.… In the winter, he had to be out there at all times because the tracks were always breaking down and the switches were constantly freezing and had to be cleaned. It was nothing for his boss to stop by in the middle of the night and tell him to get out and work."[27]

Hundreds of Mexicans and Mexican Americans came to Utah as recruited strikebreakers during the Bingham strike of 1912, while others were recruited for the coal mines. Utah Copper Company records identify 330 who arrived from Old Mexico and Arizona during the strike; historian Jorge Iber estimates that "several thousand" may have worked as strikebreakers. Most of these workers came without family. Those listed on the company rosters worked an average of only forty-three days. One Mexican who landed in Bingham during the strike, Rafael Lopez, became a folk hero of sorts; in 1913 after he shot one Juan Valdez, he gave dozens of deputies the slip and disappeared into the maze of tunnels that laced Bingham Canyon. Especially during the 1920s Spanish speakers replaced southeastern Europeans and Japanese in the lowest-paying jobs in the mines, such as laying track. Eventually, the men were joined by family members from south of the border. By 1930 there were nearly 4,000 Mexicans in Utah, more than 1,000 of whom were children. In a society that classified immigrants on a racial hierarchy of "whiteness," Hispanics ranked below southern Europeans. Jose Palacios, who came to work in Carbon County's mines in 1924, recalled that the American-born, Italian, and Greek miners "were always given the better opportunities to make better money, to make a better living. We didn't have the opportunities." In Bingham workers periodically circulated petitions calling for the ouster of Mexicans.[28]

During the 1920s a Hispanic community coalesced on Salt Lake's west side. The Guadalupe mission provided religious rites, arts and crafts classes, a summer school, a Boy Scout troop, movies, and Americanization classes for Hispanics as well as Italians, Syrians, and Armenians. Six sisters and a succession of four priests from Mexico were assigned to the mission in the late 1920s. They established a Spanish school, taught music lessons, established an afternoon kindergarten and a summer school, and taught religion and communion classes.[29]

THE IWW, DEEP CREEK, AND SOLDIER SUMMIT

Although Americans linked foreigners to class warfare and revolution, the most radical elements in the permanent labor pool were English-speaking Euro-Americans. Victims of the transformation then under way from frontier opportunity to corporate enterprise, they were reduced from capitalists on the make to migratory workers dispossessed of the American dream. Outraged, class conscious, violent, and migratory, left-leaning individuals moved through the West, giving every union a militant branch and touching every job with potential radicalism.

Seeking to harness this chaos, radicals of every stripe organized one of the nation's most controversial and revolutionary unions, the Industrial Workers of the World (Wobblies), in 1905 in Chicago. Among the organizers of the IWW were Eugene Debs, perennial Socialist presidential candidate; Daniel DeLeon, Social Labor Party leader; and T. J. Hagerty, "anarcho-syndicalist" and maverick priest. Also prominent were WFM leaders W. J. "Big Bill" Haywood and Charles Moyer, who hoped to unite all workers under the umbrella of "dual unionism." Women IWW leaders included the fiery and profane Mother Mary Jones and syndicalist Lucy Parsons. Ultimately, Haywood and other direct-action radicals carried the day over moderates like Moyer. To advance their advocacy of class warfare, violence, and one big union, western IWWs employed general strikes and the "free-speech" form of street agitation.[30]

In the years after 1912 Salt Lake City IWW organizers Samuel Scarlett and M. Dezettel led out with street meetings at Liberty Park, at Second South and Commercial Street in Salt Lake, and at Twenty-Fifth Street and various parks in Ogden. In addition to local talent, an impressive list of imported agitators passed through, including Haywood, who drew a big 1911 Labor Day crowd. Characteristic free-speech fare included denunciations of the flag; blasts at the "twin traitors" of mainline unionism, Gompers and Mitchell; and calls for class struggle and overthrow of the government. Wobblies were especially quick to denounce the "scab-wages" ($1.50 per day) offered by local "make-work projects" during the financial crisis of the European war's first year and called on workers to "let no law stand" in the way of what they had coming.[31]

The 1913 IWW's Soldier Summit strike against the giant Utah Construction Company elicited the same unyielding antiunionism found in Utah's copper and coal industries. Utah Construction doctor Joseph Peck's account of the company's

1916 Deep Creek Railroad contract from Wendover to Gold Hill along the state's western border places the Utah Construction workforce situation in perspective as a preface to a discussion of the Soldier Summit strike.[32]

The Deep Creek outfit was put together from odds and ends. Preliminary surveys had been run by novice engineers from the Gold Hill mining company. A half-dozen work camps were located along the seventy-five miles of winter-muddied desert between Wendover and Gold Hill. The company's "tar-paper nobility" included the superintendent, the chief engineer, and a handful of bosses, all of whom were under the direction and occasional visits of Utah Construction general manager A. H. Christensen. Peck counted himself number six in this hierarchy and like others at his level merited an eight-by-ten-foot tar-paper shack and a five-foot cubicle at headquarters. Even more symbolic of his status was the dilapidated jitney by which he kept in touch with injuries and the $1,000 per month income the chief surgeon told him to expect, which curried class suspicion among men who averaged "$2 per day." Status consciousness was encouraged among the crews, which descended in a rigid hierarchy from the lordly train crew through a succession of powder monkeys; teamsters; plow men; scraper men; rail, tie, and hammer crews; and muckers, all of whom bivouacked in tents or decrepit railroad cars. They ate in "circus"-sized mess tents presided over by cooks who were lords in their own domain and manned by "kitchen swampers," the job's lowliest "vassals." Mules were picketed in long lines at each camp. A mud-besmeared work engine brought three cars to the end of the track each day, loaded with ties and rails, where about a mile of track was laid.

For the crew Deep Creek was the end of the line. The two doctors before Peck had been fired for alcoholism. The thirty-year-old Peck, who had interned at St. Mark's Hospital in Salt Lake, had reached the limits of his emotional and economic resources in central Utah's Gunnison, where no one knew they needed his services. The chief engineer was a far-gone alcoholic whose precarious hold on "the wagon" was quite literally his last chance. Wendover's prostitutes were jaded and worn, at the end of trying careers. Peck came to understand their frequent suicide attempts as the last form of protest open to them more than as attempts to end it all.

Hiring was an ongoing process. By an arrangement with police, drunk tanks at Salt Lake City and Sacramento were disgorged regularly into the company's custody. The practice was open, everyone apparently accepting its coercive aspects. If the shanghaied men chose not to work, they could catch the next freight out. If, like the chief engineer, they wanted to dry out or grubstake themselves, they stayed. If they survived the stiff examination for chronic ailments and contagious diseases by which the doctor earned his princely commission, and submitted to the dehydrating therapy he prescribed and the cooks administered, a beginning slot on the crew was ensured. In this way Peck and the cooks were labor agents, facing in some degree the moral incongruities that turned Greek workers against "good padrones."

The drunk tanks yielded a cross-section of the "floater's" West. Some had worked at St. Rupert's Island in British Columbia, some in Chile; some were educated; and some were overbearing ideologues. "It was a good place," Peck conceded, to learn of "wild ideologies," but labor relations for the Deep Creek crews were regulated more by the country's winter remoteness, by the inertia that came with living on the drunk tank's cusp, and, perhaps, by sentiments Peck attributed to one old-timer. "Envy and opposition," not "classless society and equal division of wealth," made the world go 'round.[33]

On another Utah Construction job the IWW struck on June 10, 1913, at Soldier Summit on the D&RG, ninety miles south of Salt Lake City. It was a summer job, perhaps with "drunk tank" crews in lower profile than off-season coal miners. To many the strike seemed to be an extension of a violent, ongoing United Mine Workers effort to organize Colorado's coalfields. Early in June IWW organizers arrived in construction camps. In a feat of mobilization that suggests either heavy prior infiltration or men with grievances that predisposed them to follow the Wobbly lead, 1,500 of the job's 2,000 workers laid down their tools. The IWW quickly presented demands for a twenty-five-cent pay increase, a workday reduced from ten to nine hours, elimination of the dollar-a-month hospital fee (the backbone of Dr. Peck's hope that he might make up to one thousand dollars a month on the Deep Creek job), payment in cash rather than discountable checks, and baths, bunks, and bedding.

General manager A. H. Christensen refused to read the demands, charging they were not drawn up by company workers. W. H. Wattis, president of Utah Construction and one of the wealthiest and most powerful men in Utah, denigrated the IWW as "tramps" who had stirred up "laborers who love excitement better than work." Denying the conditions on which some of the demands rested and rejecting the rest, he called in 50 strikebreakers under the leadership of the hard-nosed Utah Copper Company enforcer, Axel Steele, and predicted an early end to the strike. Wobbly leaders spoke in moderate language and cautioned against violence, but among the workers "pick handle" persuasion was exerted. Rumors that strikers had seized the dynamite supply, on the one hand, and a posted notice that the cavalry was en route from Fort Douglas, on the other, caused a good deal of unrest, and many workers pulled out, not wanting either to strike or to be called scabs. Axel Steele's "deputies" rounded up 128 men at Tucker and shipped them off toward Provo, stopping at other camps, where deputies fired over the heads of strikers who refused to board. At Provo 8 Wobbly leaders, including tough-talking F. J. Morgan, were sentenced to up to seventy-five days for breaking the peace. Only a few made their way back to the job.[34]

Wattis had predicted the strike would soon end, and so it proved. Little more was heard from the IWW in the construction camps. However, the struggle moved into the streets of Salt Lake City and into its labor halls and newspapers, where in the climate of ill will generated by the strike, the "free-speech" campaign became increasingly shrill. Freed from the Provo jail, F. J. Morgan was badly battered at a street rally by Axel Steele's "deputies" in an attack that turned to riot and gunplay, injuring 6 men. Morgan was charged with intent to commit murder, but no charges were leveled against Steele. Free-speech meetings continued during the fall, attracting visits from IWW general secretary Haywood and British IWW Tom Mann. Anti-IWW sentiment continued to mount.[35]

"JOE HILL WILL NEVER DIE"

About the time of the Morgan-Steele altercation, Joseph Hillstrom, or Joe Hill, a Swedish-born IWW ballad writer and bottom-rung organizer who sometimes called himself a "West Coast wharf rat," arrived in Utah, setting in motion one of the most sensational and bitterly contested murder trials in American labor history. Hill worked at Park City during the fall of 1913, lost his job, and returned to Murray, where, with longtime Swedish friend Otto Applequist, he was boarding when the new year began. Hill played the piano well, and in addition to writing ballads that couched IWW principles in direct work-related language, he was popular in intimate groups but had taken no part in the IWW meetings.

On the evening of January 10, 1914, two masked men entered an Eighth South and West Temple grocery in the Salt Lake workingmen's district. After shouting something like "We have got you now," they shot proprietor John G. Morrison and his seventeen-year-old son, Arling, killing both. Arling had returned the fire, and a younger son, Merlin, observed that the taller of the two assailants was hit, favoring his upper body as he fled. The elder Morrison was a former policeman and had experienced two earlier shooting incidents at the store in which "he [had] wounded his attackers, giving... [survivors] motive to return and conclude their violent business with him."

Late that evening Joe Hill appeared at the door of Socialist doctor Frank M. McHugh, who patched up a serious chest wound received, according to Hill, in a fight with his lover's husband. McHugh noticed Hill was armed but did not immediately report the incident. Three days later a Murray policeman picked Hill up, shooting him in the hand in the process. Hill was charged and tried for Morrison's murder before Judge Morris L. Ritchie of the Utah Third District Court. In addition to botched police work, the Joe Hill trial was characterized by the prosecution's failure to establish a motive and by its dependence upon circumstantial evidence, resting mostly on the gunshot wound and Hill's general appearance. Also inviting debate were the uncorroborated lovers-quarrel story, which was the only explanation Hill ever made, and mounting sensationalism when Hill's connection with the IWW produced allegations of ideologically charged injustice and of antilabor conspiracy on the part of Mormon hierarchs and copper barons.[36]

The case proceeded with escalating tension until November 19, 1915, when Hill was executed. There were courtroom pyrotechnics; international press coverage; a death sentence on July 8, 1914; appeals, Utah Supreme Court, and Board of Pardons hearings; eleventh-hour execution stays; prison ballads; and well-publicized cell-side correspondence and interviews. IWW and liberal-radical support came from many quarters—locally from Salt Lake Wobbly secretary Ed Rowan and Socialist University of Utah professor Virginia Snow Stephens, daughter of former Mormon church president Lorenzo Snow. The showy women's organizer for the IWW Elizabeth Gurley Flynn, Big Bill Haywood, and thousands of concerned citizens became involved. Among the most influential advocates of clemency were Samuel Gompers, Woodrow Wilson, and the Swedish minister to the United States. Hill denounced his accusers and the system that backed them but maintained a mix of gallantry and composure that ironically rested on faith in the legal system.

To Wobblies the trial and execution amounted to a "judicial murder," a hate-inspired legal railroading, and a capitalist conspiracy. Given their frame of mind, evidence was close at hand. First, the properly licensed Wobbly orator F. J. Morgan had been jailed for attempted murder. His assailant, company guard Axel Steele, though clearly initiating the attack, was never charged. Then as Joe Hill awaited the firing squad, the case of police major H. P. Myton made it seem even more clear that justice was differentiated. On October 30 Myton had an angry confrontation with Wobbly free speecher R. J. Horton. Going for his gun, he returned and shot Horton down. Myton was initially charged with first-degree murder, which was reduced to manslaughter and then involuntary manslaughter. He was finally "acquitted by the jury after three hours' deliberation" in the friendly Third District Court, where he had served for years as bailiff. To the IWW it was par for the course.[37]

Tension broke especially on Governor Spry. A link between Mormon and corporate Utah, Spry mirrored the bunker mentality of the state's economic and official establishment. He abhorred threats against authority and property and spoke earnestly and honestly of justice. He called for new evidence and, like many others, pleaded with Hill to defend himself. But standing behind the narrow procedural soundness of the case and Hill's undeniably quixotic failure to substantiate his lovers-quarrel alibi, Spry concluded finally that "burden of proof" doctrines had been fulfilled. Thus convinced, he fended off reexamination of a case in which motive had never been proved and in which, some have continued to think, doubt was not extinguished by the weak circumstantial evidence connecting Hill to the Morrison murders.[38] By his death Hill became an American legend, "the martyred troubadour of labor." He remains a legend today.[39]

XENOPHOBIA AND AMERICANIZATION

As America was drawn into World War I, nativism rose to new heights. By that time immigration had altered the composition of many neighborhoods. In Salt Lake the district bordered by South Temple, Pioneer Park, Main Street, and Fifth West was a polyglot hive of activity. John Lund, who came of age in that era, remembered that "signs in mysterious foreign languages covered windows and doors.... Strong odors of liquor, spices, and sweat covered the neighborhood." The new immigration touched even agricultural districts of the state. In the Pleasant View precinct, an agricultural district north of Provo with 129 households, one could find a dozen immigrant families from Syria, Finland, and Italy, most of whom operated fruit and general farms. All immigrant groups appeared suspect to many native-born Utahns in a climate of world war and Communist revolution.[40]

With their own preoccupations and little appreciation for American idealism, Utah Greeks during the war were subjected to antiforeign persecution second only to Germans. Greek consul G. A. Papailion organized "the Greek colony" for the war effort, and Greeks wisely contributed to benefit drives, purchase of war bonds, and "get out the coal rallies." However, they had difficulty sharing the state's whole-hearted endorsement of Woodrow Wilson's moralistic, mission-oriented approach to the conflict. Most of all, they contemplated military service with reluctance as the war began. Sustained by group cohesiveness, they feared the social isolation individuals would face in the military services. Many also feared that the fortunes of war would adversely affect Greece's national interests. With some justification they felt that draft quotas were high and that aliens should not be subject to conscription. Offsetting such inhibiting considerations was the fact that citizenship was granted as a perquisite of successful military service; later in the war large numbers of Utah Greeks went into the service. Out of a nationwide population of 310,000 Greeks, nearly 60,000, or 19 percent, served in the war. It seems reasonable that a comparable percentage of Utah Greeks served.[41]

In spite of Greek war efforts, hostility mounted. The persistence of "Greek nationalism" was "incomprehensible" to some Utahns. Press coverage was intensely unfavorable, and incidents involving Prohibition and race relations were played up. The killing of Bruce Dempsey, brother of boxer Jack Dempsey, by a Greek at the Saltair depot in Salt Lake City in June 1917 triggered a lynch threat that showed good prospects of getting out of hand until Greek nationals gathered and threatened to meet violence with violence. Similarly, a Price outburst involving dating between a Greek boy and an American girl cooled off only when Greeks and Italians met lynch threats with a show of force.[42] Elsewhere, personal antagonisms had near-tragic consequences for individual Greeks. In Salt Lake City Antonio Berris, who froze his feet "beat[ing] his way, from Cheyenne," was rescued from the street by a kindly restaurant owner but refused admission to both the county hospital or the "emergency hospital" and was finally given a cot in the jail for the night.[43]

Part of this issue was the pace at which foreign nationals embraced naturalization. Although most of Utah's 50,732 unnaturalized residents in 1920 were of northern European birth, factors including skin color, language, religion, and ethnic differences brought prejudice to bear directly upon aliens from southeastern Europe and the Orient. Also subject to prejudice and maltreatment were Utah's 3,589 alien Germans, some of whom were ambivalent about their status and many of whom were subject to suspicion. German efforts to be red-blooded Americans sometimes took tragic turns, as in the murder of German-born forest ranger Rudolph Mellenthin, who was killed in 1917 by a Mexican American deserter, himself part of a maligned minority.[44]

The American Legion's patriotic campaigns gave a special stir to anti-immigrant sentiment. Softening its negative impact to some extent were Greek, Italian, and Serb legionnaires who met allegations that "oil and water...foreigners and Americans...don't mix" with angry rejoinders that they too had fought for the United States. Nevertheless, the war and its aftermath left injuries that lasted until World War II.[45]

Alongside heightened tensions among new immigrants during the war were the hatred and violence that characterized relations in the "Third War Prison" at Fort Douglas between April 1917 and April 1920.[46] Although guaranteed by international law, the civil and human rights of some 1,500 enemy aliens and radicals (mostly Germans and Austrians with a Wobbly bent) were swept aside by wartime xenophobia and prison conflict partly of their own making. Clearly a product of the war, the Third War Prison debacle nevertheless had much in common with Utah's tradition of troubled labor and ethnic relations. Practically, it was a confrontation between three forces: an opinionated and combative prison population; an administrative search for balance between victory, discipline, and justice; and public opinion molded largely by a nationalistic and "sensational" press.

The Third War Prison consisted of fifty buildings enclosed by barbed wire and divided to facilitate internee and discipline categories. It was staffed by about 150 soldiers and guards under military commanders, notably Colonel George Byram and Major Emory West. Unyielding disciplinarians, these men and their subordinates were roundly hated by internees, who appealed to every tribunal possible in a flood of correspondence and fiercely resisted prison administration. An "important spokesman" for the prisoners was Dr. William Beer, a well-known Salt Lake City physician who ran the hospital but whose potential for ameliorating discord was sharply limited by a staff that was often accused of sadistic mistreatment of patients.[47] The Utah press wholeheartedly bought into the wartime hysteria. According to historians R. K. Cunningham Jr. and J. A. Nagler, the press badly distorted Byram and West's administration, drawing mainly from the same divisions and spirit that characterized Utah's ethnic and labor confrontations.[48]

Statistics give this situation dimension. About 8.5 million of America's population of 92 million were of German or Austrian stock, of whom 2.25 million were targeted for surveillance as enemy aliens. The process was of such magnitude that it invited the involvement of various protective leagues and, to a degree, of the entire non-German population. While fear of spies and saboteurs became a virtual hysteria, only 6,300 were actually interned. Fifteen hundred of them from around the West were sent to Fort Douglas. A handful of specifically named individuals were Germans of aristocratic background. A small number were identified as being educated or sometimes even as intellectuals. The majority, however, seem to have been radicals who were considered security risks and disloyal. Advocates of anti-American sentiments, they were often referred to as Wobblies. In 1918 a move to intern 85 women failed to gain support. If there were none from Utah, as secondary sources seem to suggest, the impact on Utah's 25,000 German Americans (of whom perhaps 10,000 were foreign born) was devastating. They were progressively forced to reject their initial sympathy for the "fatherland" and then all things German, and finally they were brought face-to-face with the anti-German hostilities generated by the press accounts of the arriving prisoners and lurid accounts of the Third War Prison's long agony.[49]

Prisoners fell into two groups. The "Internees' Committee," or "Protesters," the overwhelming majority, were well organized and composed mainly of anti-American radicals with a marked disposition for activism. In spite of their radical penchant, they were led by a count's son, the successful Seattle businessman Alvo von Alvensleben. In opposition, a much smaller group of pro-Americans included most of the better-educated individuals but lacked the tightness of purpose and organization displayed by the larger group. Whatever their disposition, they spent much time appealing their cases to the US attorney general, the Justice Department, or the Swiss Legation, which represented German interests in wartime America. In this activity von Alvensleben appears to have been among the group's genuine leaders. However, within the compound his group spent much time in general resistance, antagonizing authorities, and digging and hiding a Keystone Cops network of tunnels. There were several shootings. Two men fled in an early escape, and 17 later left through a major tunnel, of whom all but 5 made good on their escape. Informants were carefully cultivated by the administration and group divisions encouraged. Rocks were thrown, bombs and hand weapons manufactured, parades held, mock names assigned to the streets and facilities, and a demeaning exchange of expletives engaged with guards.

The intern program, thus launched, proved difficult to end. Complicating the process were difficulties of repatriation and deportation and a ruling that parole back into the American mainstream required an awaiting job. In addition, paranoia shifted from German militarism to communism, which seemed to accommodate the interned radicals. Negative opinion in Utah was doubtless reflected in anti-German legislation favored by Senators William King and Reed Smoot, who in March 1919 viewed the internees as "criminals of the worst kind." Accepting Byrum's embittered opinion that all but "about twenty ought to be deported," Smoot wired the attorney general, urging him to reverse an order to parole all 200. However, by April 1920, as the prison was phased out, 412 had been paroled, 271 repatriated, and only 7 deported. A product of war? Certainly. But it was also an accentuation of sentiments long apparent in Utah's ethnic and labor relations.[50]

Shortly after the war ended, the *Deseret News* editorialized in favor of efforts to make Utah's immigrants 100 percent American, noting that "many thousands of residents in our state are at the present time not sufficiently acquainted with American ideals and customs." Under these circumstances, the *News* opined, "it is hoped that…the people of Utah will demand that all residents of the state shall become Americans both legally and in their ideals." To that end, the legislature passed a law in 1919 appropriating a paltry twenty thousand dollars to school districts for Americanization night schools and requiring all foreigners between the ages of sixteen and forty-five who lacked a fifth grade knowledge of English to attend. Those who failed to attend could be charged with a misdemeanor and fined up to twenty-five dollars. Utah's legislature drew up its compulsory Americanization program in response to a National Education Association (NEA) initiative to "educate for citizenship."[51]

At first glimpse, the Americanization program had great appeal. It enjoyed immigrant governor Simon Bamberger's enthusiastic support and passed both houses with slight opposition. In Price Catholic priest Alfredo F. Giovannoni joined with other prominent Italian residents, including attorney Henry Ruggeri, in forming an Italian Americanization Club in 1920 to promote English-language literacy and to prepare immigrants to pass naturalization tests. Promoted in a statewide advertising blitz, the program won the overwhelming endorsement of various business, church, and professional groups and was hailed by the NEA's national convention, which met in Utah in 1920, as the tide of the future. But mortal flaws soon surfaced in the program.[52]

First, it implied an enumeration of aliens and a determination of how many were subject to the law. English reading proficiency to the fifth grade level was the primary rule. No one knew how many people were involved or, beyond the public media, how to contact them, nor was a really satisfactory census ever achieved, except in Ogden, where door-to-door canvasses were conducted.[53]

In the first year of the law's operation, Americanization classes were held in seven school districts in Cache, Weber, Tooele, Salt Lake, and Carbon Counties. In a performance that suggests that Carbon County's aliens initially took the Americanization program seriously, 381 enrolled in 1921–22, approximately doubling percentages in the more dispersed populations of runners-up Salt Lake and Weber Counties. Pushed by energetic initial publicity, statewide enrollments had totaled 2,016 in 1919–20. No records survive for 1920–21, but enrollments declined from

1,628 in 1921–22 to 699, 415, and 341 progressively for the next three school years, after which the program was abandoned.

Stylian Staes, Greek vice-consul, worked hard to make the compulsory education classes go. Japanese attended the night classes dutifully, as did "a few Greeks, Italians, and Slavs," but most Greeks went "straight to the coffeehouses after work." "They're afraid they can't do it," Staes told a friend. Besides, the classes meant little to men who still counted on going home.[54] Ultimately, nearly all districts "arrest[ed] aliens and...[took] them into court before attendance could be secured."[55]

In addition to the diffidence they felt at being singled out as a problem group, aliens sensed the state's loss of interest in the program as the war's high idealism gave way to the cynical materialism of the 1920s. C. C. Woodward of the Carbon District wrote that it was loss of resolve, not need, that had changed. There were still as "many children" who could not "speak English" as before. "Americanization classes" had decreased, "not because there is no further need...but due to the laxity in the enforcement of the Americanization law." In closing the program down, the state superintendent of public instruction rightly condemned it. Its "compulsory feature [was] obnoxious to the foreign people," it interfered with attitudes necessary "to learning," it "was expensive and uninviting to communities with large foreign populations," and employers supported or opposed it according to narrow corporate needs.[56]

A RISING MIDDLE CLASS

Meantime, many of the new immigrants left "labor's ranks" for various business and professional opportunities, demonstrating that upward mobility was a genuine possibility on the wageworkers' frontier. As old country obligations were met, Greeks and others followed the example of Bingham's Levantis brothers, establishing coffeehouses, restaurants, and stores. After years as a foreman of migratory railroad crews, George Zeese attempted unsuccessfully to homestead and keep store in Idaho. Moving to Carbon County, Zeese opened a coffeehouse in the new camp of Cameron. After that venture folded, Zeese moved to Helper, where his next coffeehouse was busy far into the night. In time he traded again and in partnership with N. S. Malouf ran a combination store and pool hall with an attached room where mine managers played cards. With old friends Stylian Staes, now "Greek vice-consul," and Angelo Raekos, Zeese won an unprecedented $235,000 contract to bring Helper's water line twenty-five miles down Price Canyon. They eased through various labor tensions, lost time when war-short materials were delayed, and netted half as much as they had calculated, and Zeese suffered a fire in his Helper pool hall. Nevertheless, he opened a restaurant and the "Bank Cigar Store" in succession, became a bank director, and within a few years moved to Salt Lake City, establishing a chain of eleven grocery stores, including one in Helper.

Other Greeks became successful sheepmen. Originally, they met the needs of their countrymen, supplying lamb for families, boardinghouses, and Greek stores in small sideline operations. In time some broadened from this single product specialty into ewe herds and wool operations. As it was to thousands of others, the public domain was a key to their success. Although they focused mainly in Carbon County, with a smaller contingent in southern Salt Lake County, they spread from winter ranges on the San Rafael desert and summer ranges on the Range Creek–Book Cliff elevations into the Uinta Basin and even into Colorado.[57]

WAR'S END, PERSISTING TENSIONS, AND THE STRIKE OF 1922

During the labor-scarce war years something of a truce existed between labor and management. Strikes were few, but the war years were tumultuous for Utah miners. Cowed by the Federal Labor Mediation and Conciliation Board, a wartime "watchdog of anti-union practices," Utah management showed some evidence of a thaw, yet yielded little ground to unions.[58]

With the war's end things heated up again. By 1919 the country had begun to drop into a postwar recession, and general strikes in Seattle and Winnipeg and riots in New York and Cleveland provided a context for "the Red Scare." "Domestic Communist parties" were organized, and nativist attitudes surged again. In Utah newspapers including the *Salt Lake Tribune*, *Deseret News*, and *Ogden Standard Examiner* formed a chapter of the National Association of City Editors to promote Americanism by deriding Bolshevism and radicalism in print. The so-called Red Flag and Sabotage bills were made law during the winter and spring of 1919. The Red Flag Bill prohibited the "disloyal display of the red flag or any other emblem of anarchy." The Sabotage Bill made it a felony to advocate, teach, or suggest syndicalism or sabotage. The bills targeted the IWW and the newly organized Workers', Soldiers', and Sailors' Council, which endorsed the Russian Socialist Republic and, Wobbly-like, set out to unite the laboring class and seize control of politics and industry. In a dramatic bid for support, the WSSC offered every Utah union a seat on its council.[59]

Called for May Day under the direction of the WSSC, a nationwide mass meeting devoted to "class struggle" produced thirty-six mail bombs. Three were intended for Senators Reed Smoot and William H. King and Salt Lake attorney Frank Nebbeker, who, as assistant attorney general of the United States, had "successfully prosecuted a hundred members of the IWW" for violating the Espionage Act of 1917. In some sections of the land, the May Day event led to riots and strikes, but in Utah, where the bombs were not learned of until May 2, the grand demonstration passed off quietly. Later, as news of the incidents spread, deep anti-Bolshevism churned.

On May 6 Park City miners struck, demanding a six-hour day, a $5.50 daily wage, and no discrimination against union members. The strike was taken over by radicals who called out pump men at the fabulous old Ontario Mine, flooding miles of underground works. With the mine owners and public opinion infuriated at this disregard for property, the strike was called off on June 21, its demands unmet. A Salt Lake cooks' and waiters' strike escalated overnight from a specific grievance to a major test of strength over the open-shop issue between organized labor and the Associated Industries, an alliance of business and civic leaders. Management won the contest when Utah's peaceful picketing law was repealed that fall.[60]

Meantime, a nationwide strike of union mines was called in the coalfields for November 1, 1919, as the UMWA demanded that wages negotiated in September 1917 be increased. Although still nonunion, Utah coal mines were in turmoil. After the wartime thaw, organizers had returned to the state in 1918, and eight UMWA locals with some two thousand members were organized in the face of determined opposition. Strikes over local issues had been called at American Fuel's Sego mine in Grand County and at Knight Investment's Spring Canyon operation. At Hiawatha the United States Fuel Company fired and evicted ten men with large families because of union affiliation. Among them was Frank Bonacci, union strategist and chief critic of Colorado UMWA District No. 15 and its Utah representative John McLennan, but Utah coal miners failed to find effective local leadership.

Expecting trouble as the nationwide strike approached, Utah operators called in two hundred federal troops. Already closing production down in support of their own grievances, Utah miners reluctantly bowed to last-minute instructions to stay on the job from John L. Lewis, who felt the state's partially organized and poorly led movement would be jeopardized by the November 1919 strike. As it turned out, much of the organizing work of the year before was undone by the operators' victory, along with the postwar "retreat" of the Federal Labor Mediation and Conciliation Board and the internal struggle between Bonacci and other Utah insurgents and District No. 15 representatives. In an effort to salvage something from the debacle, Utah was switched to Wyoming's District No. 22 on July 21, 1921, which with the postwar depression set the stage for the strike of 1922.[61]

Because local grievances and union recognition were underlying issues, there was no letup in the Utah coalfield situation. At the same time, Utah, like the West generally, was propelled by the national struggle that was taking form as workers sought to protect other interests. Under the direction of Martin Cahill, president of District No. 22; James Morgan, secretary-treasurer; and organizer William Houston, the revival of the Utah UMWA locals was rapid. Frank's relative Vito Bonacci, who assisted with the organization effort, "talked to the miners and told them it'll be better if we joined the union because we'd get better wages and be treated more like white people.... Them days the coal miners were treated like slaves." Still unsure of their strength, John L. Lewis did not include Utah in the April 1, 1922, strike that idled 650,000 coal miners nationwide.

However, when Utah operators announced a 30 percent wage cut for the same day, miners in the north end of Carbon County walked out. Within a month 70 percent of the workforce was idled. Action varied according to local conditions, with Spring Canyon and Scofield miners showing greater intensity than Castle Gate, Sunnyside, and the United States Coal Company workers at Hiawatha and Mohrland. Strikers armed themselves and picketed to keep replacement labor out. Both miners and the companies applied intimidation and force. With an eye to men who were still working and to strikebreakers, operators made nominal concessions in the form of lowered rent and reduced prices on powder and fuel, and they temporarily indicated there would be no discrimination for union membership. County government was heavily infiltrated by company men, including the county commissioners who were employed by three independent mines. Guard ranks were strengthened and deputized but commanded by the companies. Spies were employed, evictions aggressively applied, competing merchants crowded from company camps, and the strike branded as the work of radical and disloyal foreigners.[62]

In mid-April District No. 22 leaders offered a four-point settlement. They offered to resume work at the reduced pay with future rates to be fixed according to Wyoming wages, demanded the right to organize, and insisted upon hiring policies that did not discriminate against union men. The mine owners gave the package no consideration. Tension escalated late in April when a company guard, Sam Dorrity, and two picketers were shot in Scofield. The Associated Operators stepped up their campaign to have the National Guard sent in, but investigators offered conflicting reports about the extent and causes of disorder. Governor Charles R. Mabey pushed county officials to enforce the law and refused to intervene. Strikers who were forced from company houses moved into nearby tent colonies. Pickets and guards patrolled the public roads and railroads to discourage strikebreakers, on the one hand, and fend off property damage and intimidation, on the other.

On May 14 Deputy Lorenzo H. Young shot and killed John Tenas near Helper. In the process Young received a wound that witnesses agreed was self-inflicted. They insisted Tenas had been unarmed. In a defiant protest and show of solidarity, hundreds of Greeks demonstrated as Tenas was buried, making racial and national issues more than ever the crux of the strike. Carbon County's company-controlled press stepped up the "Race War" campaign, while the county commissioners "requested five hundred rifles, ten machine guns, and ten thousand rounds of ammunition." After an incognito visit Mabey offered a five-point peace plan between operators, union leaders, and county officials that would disarm aliens, discharge mine guards, return command of deputies to the sheriff, stop intimidation on both sides, and allow every man to work. No one in the strike zone was satisfied, conflict increased, and picketing of strikebreakers became more effective.

On June 14 another major encounter took place. In an effort to stop picket action or get the National Guard called in, company officials ran a well-armed locomotive pulling a carload of strikebreakers through Jacob's Switch, west of Helper, where picketers had previously turned back strikebreakers. In heavy fire company guard A. P. Webb was killed. Company men H. E. Lewis and W. R. Abbott and striker Andreas Zulakis were wounded. That afternoon Governor Mabey proclaimed martial law and ordered in the National Guard. Masked riflemen seized unfortunate Greeks during the night at Standardville and along the Spring Canyon road and threatened to kill them before ultimately releasing them. On the morning of the fifteenth, the National Guard unloaded at Helper, herded three hundred tent-dwelling strikers into a vacant lot, explained what martial law meant, searched them, collected forty-five weapons, and arrested twenty men, apparently all of them Greeks. H. E. Lewis, one of the wounded company men, claimed he had seen the twenty men from the train at the Jacob's Switch shooting.[63]

With attachments at Helper and Scofield, the guard soon took up routine patrol functions. On June 17 they emptied pool halls and coffeehouses of 150 patrons, designated by the *Deseret News* as "loafers," marched them to a school yard, searched them for weapons—only "two or three were found"—and detained them until witnesses could look them over to identify any who had been present in the canyon that day. Initially, the guard kept strikebreakers out as well as deprived strikers of both force and persuasion by disarming them and denying rights of assembly and free speech. "They took *everything* we had.... The militia even took our knives. So we had to break [bread] with our hands," recalled Vito Bonacci. The use of the guard to keep strikebreakers out was greeted with appreciation by the strikers and by a storm of protest from the operators. It was soon rescinded, making the guard seem, as Samuel King, UMWA lawyer said, "a weapon...to safeguard the operators" and "destroy organized labor."[64]

The strike ended in August. Nationally, the UMWA and the coal companies restored wages to the prestrike level. In Utah the Associated Operators restored "the wage scale in effect before the 30 percent reduction in April," promising to reward men who had worked during the entire strike by making the wage adjustment retroactive to April 1, 1922. Utah Fuel Company kept this commitment, but many independent producers did not. Arguing that the wage increase required it, the Operators Association upped coal prices. Governor Mabey suspected "illegal combination in restraint of trade," a grand jury was called, and indictments were found against the operators.[65]

AFTERMATH AND A VACUUM OF LEADERSHIP

It was as near to victory as Utah coal workers had ever come. Yet on the underlying issue of union recognition, the Associated Operators still remained unmoved. The UMWA maintained a narrow interest in the Utah coal mines, among other things coming up with some $140,000 for the defense of thirteen Greeks charged with murder in the June 14 killing of A. P. Webb. On the assumption that public hostility would abate, attorney Samuel King was able to set up separate trials and, after the first two, succeeded in getting a change of venue out of Carbon County, with the result that sentences were successively lighter. With the repeated testimony for the prosecution looking more contrived with each repetition, all charges were dropped against eight of the accused, and in 1926 "paroles were granted" to the others.

The "restored pay scale was short-lived." Pay was reduced in 1925, 1928, and 1931, and for most miners work was irregular and limited.[66] Over the decade unionism in the coal mines and in Utah industry generally succumbed to the Associated Industries movement and the "American Plan," or company union and open shop, until organized labor dwindled away almost completely.

Thus, as the 1922 strike ended, Utah's coal and metalworkers remained unorganized, despite the best quarter of a century the industries ever enjoyed. Silver and lead had sustained themselves. Copper had burgeoned. Utah coal had grown from the tight monopoly of the D&RG's Pleasant Valley Company mines to the competition of twelve or fifteen large independent companies, among which the United States Fuel Company had even "entered the field" as both "producer and carrier," loosening, if indeed not breaking, the D&RG's stranglehold on transportation. Coal production had mounted from lows of 450,000 tons annually to a 1920 high of 6 million tons. The workforce had grown from fewer than six hundred men to all-time highs of approximately forty-five hundred in 1920 and 1921. By playing nationalities off against each other, running company towns, controlling county politics, and most of all holding firm against organization, coal operators had suppressed every impulse toward unionization. They had defeated every attempt to raise an effective local leadership, although promising leaders sometimes appeared, including Charles DeMolli in the 1903–4 strike, Martin Cahill and James Morgan in 1921–22, and Charles Moyer in the Bingham strike of 1912. But DeMolli was chased off by Governor Heber M. Wells.[67]

With its dual ties to political federalism and the function of craft or trade, the American Federation of Labor and its Utah affiliates came much nearer to a stable statewide structure for miners. The name of Frank Bonacci stands virtually alone as one who tried in a lasting way to tie grassroots needs to a miner's organization in such a way as to give it coherence and staying power. During years when it was not only a thankless task but also dangerous, he kept unionism alive in the coalfields, finally ending up as a long-term state representative and hero second only to Franklin D. Roosevelt among Utah coal miners.

DISASTER

Adding to the difficulty of the mining industry's effort to organize effectively was its high mortality rate. Running from 8 to 20 deaths in each industry per year, smelting, hard-rock mining, and coal mining all took heavy tolls, in addition to great disasters like the Winter Quarters explosion of 1900. In coal mining, which exceeded other industries in accidental deaths, Utah averaged 5.44 deaths per million tons of coal each year between 1914 and 1920, or a total of 179 men. Operators and state officials regarded the loss as regrettable but acceptable.[68]

Until 1917 Utah had no effective system to compensate injured workers or survivors of those who died. In 1917 lawmakers spelled out terms of workmen's compensation and established the State Industrial Commission to administer relief. Employers were required to carry accident insurance. In cases of death or total disability, dependent survivors were to be paid up to $16 per week for a maximum of 312 weeks. The merits of each case were considered individually by the Industrial Commission and awards made accordingly. The Utah law applied to foreign nationals as well as Americans. Lump payments were sent to dependents of several Greek fatalities in Greece, and passage to Europe was paid for wives and children, with cash amounts running as high as $1,000. In at least one case, homeland dependents of a Greek fatality were awarded the full $4,992, in return boat fare and monthly payments in Greece, for a widow and three children.[69] Yet as time would tell, provisions were still woefully inadequate.

On March 8, 1924, the Castle Gate mine suffered another great explosion. This time a full crew was caught inside: 171 men were killed, and another died in the recovery process. The problem in 1924 was not accelerated production, as it had been in the nonfatal March 22, 1900, Castle Gate explosion or the Winter Quarters "terror"; more likely, slowdown in production neutralized safeguards that usually controlled the mine's highly volatile dust and known capacity for explosive gas. Routines had long since been established. Sprinkling was carried to the mine's farthest recesses to dampen and lay the dust. Dynamite was fired electrically at night when crews were home. Vigilant in all mines, fire bosses at Castle Gate were doubly so. The morning practice was to quickly load out the coal that had been shot the night before and then turn to dust control and other precautions. The system worked best when the mine worked at full capacity and worst when idle days interrupted the precautionary routine. In 1924 coal orders were off, giving dust time to accumulate and letting sprinkling schedules lapse, and March 8 was the first eight-hour shift of the month.[70]

Money was short, so kindly foremen had posted the names of a disproportionate number of family men for the shift. New carbide lamps had been received but not yet charged. Crewmen entered the mine at 6:30 a.m., wearing their old flame lamps for the last time. An hour later two explosions alerted the town. Every man underground was dead, some killed by the first blast, others in the second, probably triggered when they sought to relight their lamps. Family members raced to the mine. By the time Pete Condas arrived, "women were standing by the entrance screaming, yelling, hollering, crying." The force of the explosion had blown out "dirt, timber tracks, coal and everything else," depositing it "hundreds of feet from the mine entrance." Crack rescue teams assembled from Utah's eastern coalfields. Recovery of the bodies took nine days. Sustained by the awkward oxygen apparatus of the time, rescue crews sorted through the wreckage and carnage. When the miners' bodies were brought to the surface, many were blackened with poisonous gas, and some were decapitated. Many corpses were so badly mutilated that it was difficult to identify them. Bodies were identified sometimes by a sock or a shoe, and more often by Dave Jones, former chief clerk at Castle Gate brought back from Colorado because he knew the victims well, including his own father and a brother-in-law. Once a body had been identified, the victim's name was posted on a bulletin board in the Knights of Pythias Hall, which served as a temporary morgue.[71]

Anguished families milled in the streets and mourned at home. Saline Hardee Fraser, a teenager at the time, later recalled, "Downtown was chaos. Everybody was running every which way, everybody had different stories, people were crying, some were really screaming." As stock was taken, it was apparent that 50 Greeks had been killed, 45 Americans including 2 blacks, 32 Englishmen and Scots, 25 Italians, 12 Welshmen, 4 Japanese, and 3 Austrians. Services for the Greek dead were held in the Assumption Hellenic Orthodox Church in Price, where most of them were buried. Others were buried at Iron County's Kanarraville and at several Sanpete and Emery County towns as well as at Salt Lake City, Spanish Fork, Helper, Nephi, and Heber. Only 1 man was buried outside Utah, contrasted to 9 in the Scofield tragedy, suggesting that interstate movement on the wageworkers' frontier was slowing.[72]

If there was evidence of the passing frontier in the places people were buried, there was even more striking evidence that significant social corners had been rounded in the assistance provided to disaster victims. Poverty was still widespread and options for widows and orphans were few, but society shouldered responsibility it had shirked earlier and expected more from management. Dependents of the dead miners numbered 415, "including 114 wives, 239 children [of whom 180 were under ten]...25 unborn children, and 37" others. Governor Mabey immediately appointed a "Relief Committee" that classified the financial situation of 94 widows and other adults as poor and 9 as fair. Of 151 adult dependents, 143 "were without income and did not own their residences." One owned a small house; another was a schoolteacher. As historian Kent Powell points out, the committee's report gave striking confirmation to the "precarious financial circumstances under which most Utah coal miners lived." Few owned homes, and with their only income "earned mining," they were often deeply in debt and had little savings or insurance.[73]

To these people the importance of the state workmen's compensation law can hardly be overstated. Under the terms of the law, any company that was self-insured, such as Utah Fuel Company, had to come up with the funds to compensate the victims and their families—in this case about $750,000. Death benefits provided up to $5,000 spread over six years, in addition to funeral expenses. An additional $130,000 was raised by private donation. The volunteer Relief Committee administered this fund through Annie D. Palmer, a paid welfare worker who supervised its distribution until payments ended in 1936, by which time "sixty-one widows had remarried and eleven had died."[74]

Utah Fuel rushed to put the mine back in production at an estimated cost of $250,000, manning it from a backlog of desperate, idle coal miners. Coal operators and state officials, who had been so comfortable with the status quo as to appoint a coal mine inspector from within the industry's inner circle, were deeply shaken. They called on the legislature to fund more inspectors, to limit the size of explosive charges, to require that all shots be fired electrically while workers were absent, and to require that all flame lamps be replaced. Mandatory rock dusting (powdered stone) and rigorous sprinkling and dust-removal regulations were also required. Mercifully, disaster on the magnitude of Castle Gate did not recur, but lesser tragedies still spotted the record.[75]

Routine and legal responsibility had everywhere been apparent during the course of the Castle Gate disaster. Grief, loss, mourning, and distress had also been in evidence locally. Seemingly absent was the statewide upwelling of horror that accompanied the Winter Quarters explosion a quarter century before. Perhaps perception had been dulled by world war and revolution. Or perhaps the same hatred and chauvinism that animated the Ku Klux Klan in the 1920s dampened sympathy for immigrant miners.

THE KU KLUX KLAN AND THE BEEHIVE STATE

The second Invisible Empire of the Ku Klux Klan got its start nationally about 1915 and, with wartime hatred and postwar fears stirring it, reached its apogee in the first half of the 1920s. Trafficking in nativism, racism, and anti-Catholicism, as well as secrecy, ritualism, and vigilantism, it presented itself as an agent of social regulation and defender of traditional Americanism against the forces of modernism. As a Utah phenomenon the Klan was neither strong nor threatening to the institutional superstructure of the state, nor did concern over it supplant the "endemic animosities between Mormons and non-Mormons," but it heightened already rampant forces of xenophobia and bigotry and played on tensions long aggravated by labor discord and increasing secularization and cultural heterogeneity. Its area of highest impact corresponded most closely with the industrialized and urbanized Wasatch Front and its coal mine extensions in eastern Utah.[76]

The Klan's Utah course moved on two more or less independent thrusts. The earliest manifestation of interest was a largely homegrown movement in Salt Lake

City and Ogden between 1921 and 1923. In Salt Lake County the Klan announced its presence during April 1921 in a striking hooded appearance at the Sandy burial of Gordon Stuart, a lawman slain in the line of duty. It made charitable contributions in his name as well as to other civic causes. However, it achieved only modest success in recruiting efforts and then faded from sight.

Lacking fuller records, historian Larry Gerlach depends on Klansman Charlie Kelly's detailed diary to understand its initial lack of appeal. Gerlach finds Kelly to have been irreligious, cynical, virulently anti-Mormon, a maverick, and "in dire financial straits," any of which might throw light on why Kelly joined the Klan and why it failed to hold him. Economic factors were apparently Kelly's "overriding motive," and his loss of interest lay in the Klan's failure to bolster his income, as well as in his "uncompromising individualism" and his lack of sympathy for the Klan's "militant Protestantism" and its support of Prohibition.[77] Working among individualists like Kelly and facing strong opposition from the press, major political figures, and the Catholic and Mormon Churches, the early Salt Lake movement soon faded.

The early movement featured more dramatically in Ogden, where masked men paid a dramatic visit to Pastor Lemuel Garrison's First Baptist Church in April 1923. A close encounter followed. In a series of ringing sermons Garrison portrayed Klankraft as "a patriotic, Christian crusade," condoned its vigilantism, and called for more Klaverns (local chapters). He characterized Christ as the "Klansman's criterion character" and denounced the Catholic Church, the Knights of Columbus, and parochial schools. Among those who reacted were the Right Reverend Joseph S. Glass, bishop of the Catholic Diocese of Salt Lake; former district court judge James A. Howell; county attorney David J. Wilson; Samuel G. Dye, president of the LDS Ogden Stake; the Women's Christian Temperance Union; and the *Standard Examiner*, whose publisher, A. L. Glassmann, proved to be an unwavering enemy. Although the Ogden Klan was checked somewhat by this wave of opposition, it possessed enough political power to defeat Mayor Frank Francis in his 1923 bid for reelection.[78]

During 1924 the Klan initiated the second phase of its Utah career by setting a regional organizing campaign in motion. At the head of this effort were recruiter William M. Cortner of Ohio and a brilliant lecturer named John C. Polly, a dentist from Washington, DC. Entering Utah from Pocatello, they paused briefly in Logan, where hostility from the American Legion, "usually a hotbed of recruits," denunciations from the local press, and a quickly enacted antimask ordinance stripping Klansmen of their anonymity sent the organization team on its way. In Box Elder and Davis Counties, "rurality and 'Mormonness'" stymied the Klan.[79]

In Ogden the tide shifted. In disrepute Pastor Garrison was fighting unsuccessfully to retain his congregation, while the Reverend Charles C. Wilson of the First Congregational Church was launching a full attack, showing the difference between the creeds of Christ and the Klan in a series of sermons. Head of the Ogden movement at this point was H. B. Sawyer, who joined Cortner in chartering the Klan as a Utah corporation. Lighting crosses, holding meetings, and demonstrating, the Klan made front-page news when Catholic contractor and Klan foe W. Earl Roche drove his car headlong into a ceremonial gathering. Three shots were fired through his windshield, and he avoided running over several Klansmen only by evasive maneuvers. In the aftermath Dr. Polly delivered a nativist harangue to a crowd of five hundred, arguing that "foreigners" committed "90 percent" of America's crime and called on all good Americans to demand that immigrants give up "their native manner[s]" and "live and work as we do." After Ogden passed antimask laws, forcing the Klan underground, Polly and Cortner continued on to Salt Lake County.[80]

At Magna, one of Utah's most ethnically diverse towns, Klan campaigners quickly found leaders among businessmen and rank and filers among the town's skilled laborers. "One of them was a Mormon bishop and [an]other was a businessman in Magna," recalled Sid Matz. New immigrants, particularly Greeks and Italians, were roundly hated, and economic antagonisms were double-barreled. English-speaking workers felt the new immigrants menaced their job security, and native businessmen were threatened by Greek and Italian "hotels, butcher shops, coffeehouses, coal yards, restaurants, automobile dealerships, and pool halls [that] began to outnumber" their own. Accepting the "debauched foreigners" stereotype, many natives also agreed the new immigrants whored, drank, gambled, and brawled.

Perhaps most of all, natives feared relations between the young men who made up most of the new immigrant ranks and English-speaking girls. The September 15, 1924, elopement of Andrew Dallas, a young Greek pool hall owner, and Nell Maddy, a Mormon, gave form to this fear. In combination with Polly's recruiting efforts, the Dallas-Maddy marriage caused "a sudden explosion of bigotry." The newlyweds received threats. "Crosses burned on the hillsides" and in Maddy's parents' yard. Crudely sketched skulls and crossbones on the windows of his pool hall warned Dallas. Klan officers drove through town in full regalia, and nocturnal phalanxes "wended" ghostlike along the streets. Immigrant communities were badly frightened, but the fury quickly spent itself. As Gerlach points out, "Greek and Italian residents were too numerous and too influential to permit the polarization of the community along ethnic lines." In addition, townspeople knew each other too well, causing the delicate balance of secrecy and publicity on which Klan operations fed to break down.[81]

At Bingham Canyon the organizers found another "ethnic babel" of some eleven thousand residents among whom aliens outnumbered citizens at least two to one. Crosses burned on the canyon's promontories and at dance halls where ethnic mixing sometimes happened. A Greek pool hall and two "notorious speakeasy brothels...the Canyon Resort (Greek) and the California Hotel (Italian)" were wrecked. In response, Klan meetings were broken up by gunfire and a prominent Klansman beaten. Although there were men who fitted the Klan mold in goodly number, the heterogeneity of the canyon's population made "overt cultural toleration a necessity," and again a quick explosion of intimidation and wreckage was followed by a rapid decline in Klan activity and influence.

At the Klan forefront in Bingham were Russell G. Frazier, a West Virginia Mason, company doctor, Colorado River white-water man, and Antarctica explorer; Arthur LeRoy Inglesby, a Canadian Shriner and Mason, dentist, Capitol Reef promoter, and graduate of Northwestern University; and Thomas LeRoy Porter, Mason, newspaperman, and Kansan. They resembled most known Klansmen in Utah in having been born out of state. Catholic members were rare and new immigrants almost unheard of. Mormons and Jack Mormons belonged in inverted proportion to their general population. In Utah it appears that most Klansmen were mature, sober, serious members of the community. "Some were incurable fraternalists seeking yet another bond of brotherhood" or "fragile egos seeking a sense of identity" or a "sense of superiority denigrating immigrants, Jews, and blacks." A "distinct minority" were "faddists, hoodlums, thrill-seekers, psychological cripples, and swindlers." Many were "motivated by the sincere desire to defend and disseminate traditional middle-class WASP religious and political values."[82]

The recruiters soon moved on from Bingham. Leaving Utah County for a glib charlatan named Milfred Y. Yant to bilk, they proceeded to Carbon County, going public on September 30, 1924. Although the county's population was comparable in numbers and ethnicity to Bingham Canyon's, there was a scope or dimension to Carbon County Klankraft not found at Bingham. In many ways the Klan's Carbon County stand climaxed the statewide effort. For one thing, it involved a hotly contested election in which the Klan tipped the scales against popular county attorney Henry Ruggeri, Italian husband of Clara Kimball, member of a prominent Mormon family.[83] It also involved the takeover of Helper's city government and police force when newly elected mayor Glenroy Ballinger appointed police chief "Iron Mike Brennan," a lapsed Catholic and known Klan recruiter. "Nativism was the driving force behind" the Klan, and "public morality was its wellspring," not only at Helper, as Gerlach points out, but also at Price, where the movement took even stronger hold, and in coal camps throughout the county.[84]

With the election at hand, Dr. Polly lectured at the Price City Hall on November 3. "Claiming a national membership" of millions and a "'vast army'" in every community, he depicted a rapidly growing Klan rising above "the vilification of unpatriotic classes, [and]...those who hold allegiance to foreign" potentates. Klansmen he described as "native born, white Protestant, Christian freem[e]n" and their detractors as bootleggers, dope peddlers, and "hyphenates."

Pyrotechnics and nocturnal activity characterized the Carbon County Klan. Fiery crosses signaled events and targeted "offenders." In defiance Catholic immigrants burned fiery circles, suggesting that the Klan would come to naught and driving most Klan activity into the anonymity of darkness. Drawing upon the Mediterranean custom of wearing amulets for protection from the evil eye, immigrant children wore amulets during the daytime and slept with them under their pillows at night. The Klan movement grew through the end of 1924, maintained itself into the summer of 1925, but quickly fell apart after the dynamiting of the Klan's outdoor ceremonial site up neighboring Gordon Creek.[85]

In a Salt Lake attempt to recapture momentum, Klan recruiters staged a dramatic initiation ceremony in the spring of 1925. On April 6, shortly after the conclusion of the LDS Church's general conference, Klan members lit several large crosses atop Ensign Peak, north of the Capitol Building. On the plain below members erected two altars as the staging ground for the induction rituals of perhaps hundreds of new members.[86]

Not a Klan undertaking but reflecting badly on it was the lynching of Robert Marshall, a Castle Gate black miner accused of murdering Deputy Sheriff J. Milton Burns, a Klansman, east of Price on June 18, 1925. Burns was shot five times and mutilated, and circumstantial evidence pointed to Marshall as the killer. After a sheriff's posse apprehended Marshall, he was taken to the county courthouse and then abandoned to the devices of an angry mob composed of men, women, and children who hanged him from a cottonwood. When a posse arrived on the scene and cut down Marshall, he was still alive. Four men wrapped the rope around his neck and hanged him a second time. The men were arrested, along with seven other accomplices, several of whom belonged to the Klan, and charged with first-degree murder, but a grand jury could not identify any witnesses who would implicate the men, so they were released.[87]

Beset nationwide with scandals involving embezzlement, flight, arrest, and rape, the Klan rapidly fell apart by January 1926. In comparison with many states, its Utah campaign had been a failure. It faced unyielding opposition from the Catholic and Mormon Churches and from the overwhelming majority of the state's newspapers. The rural counties proved to be generally beyond its reach, and it never found a formula that enabled it to sustain its attack on the ethnic enclaves. With the heavy influences arrayed against it, Utah's Klandom was less characterized by violence, outlawry, and raiding than in many states. Yet it played upon bigotry, xenophobia, and middle-class fears to leave a legacy of covert hostility and discrimination that complicated the overt adjustments of the late 1920s and 1930s, as immigrant groups and wageworkers continued to search for solutions. Contributing to this process in particular ways were the South Slavs and the Carbon County strikes of 1933.

SOUTH SLAVS

Referred to as Austrian and Yugoslavian in turn-of-the-century Census materials and more pejoratively as Bohunks in the vernacular of the day, the "South Slavs" played a somewhat less important role in labor disputes than the Greeks and Italians until the 1933 Carbon County strike, when they were clearly among the most militant unionists. Therefore, they are discussed here.[88]

Divided along old country lines into Croat and Slovene (Roman Catholic) and Serbian (Greek Orthodox) subdivisions, the first South Slavs appeared in Utah's coal-producing Southeast by the late 1890s in itinerant, youthful, all-male groups. Census data showing 758 native-born children in 1910 suggest that Utah's Croat and Slovene community included an appreciable number of women. In this they resembled their Italian contemporaries. The presence of Slavic women may have also been due to the fact that many Slavic men had lived for some time in the Midwest and Colorado before moving to Utah. Helper drew many South Slavs, as did Midvale and Highland Boy. Serbs came a few years later and perhaps, like their Greek coreligionists, brought fewer women initially. Unlike the Greeks and Italians, South Slavs rarely came as contract labor.

Historian Joseph Stipanovich raises questions about the accuracy of the Census. Citing Croatian immigrant scholar George Prpic's figure of 7,000 Croatians in Utah, he worked with lodge books and oral sources to arrive at a rough count of 10,000 South Slavs by the midtwenties.[89]

At Midvale, between Murray and Sandy, South Slavs worked mainly at the American Smelting and Refining Company (ASARCO) smelter. Many came as young men, some as second-generation wageworkers, and they lived in dispersed South Slav homes and private boardinghouses. Sometimes housing up to 40 lodgers who ate and slept in shifts, Midvale's boardinghouses practically enslaved women, who often ran them single-handedly. Together with godparents, saloons, lodges, and holidays, these boardinghouses were primary institutions of adaptation. Migration and industrial labor weakened family bonds; letter-bride relationships were shaky; divorce was difficult, especially for Serbs; prostitution existed, yet adultery was frowned upon; and education was seen as a means of making America work for the second generation. In a woman-short, accident-prone situation, widows who wanted to remarry had many options. At least one woman went through five mining husbands. Croat and Slovene religious needs were met by the existing Roman Catholic Church. Serbs built their own church, brought in a Serbian Orthodox priest, and then fired him. Orthodoxy maintained Serb identity and helped Roman Catholic Croats and Slovenes focus their own identity. Generally, however, the South Slav experience in Midvale was remarkable for its lack of "cultural disorientation," as the institutions that developed there eased the South Slavs into American life.[90]

Life in the Serbian-Croatian community of Highland Boy at the head of Bingham Canyon was less tranquil but in some ways more productive. Growing with the copper industry, Highland Boy's population rose from about 150 in 1900 to 1,000 in 1910 and 2,000 in 1920. After 1908 more than half were Serbs and Croats. In the early years old-country tensions divided Serbs and Croats into "guerrilla" factions, and vendettas and blood feuds entailed a heavy loss of life. This "leisure time" turbulence began to abate after a fire in 1908 "leveled" most of the "Serbo-Croatian" dwelling area.

Joe Melich, storekeeper, ideologue, and leader extraordinaire, facilitated healing. Without challenging company authority, Melich kept the attention of South Slavs focused on political events in the strife-torn Balkans and defused Highland Boy's bombastic character by exporting 200 of its young men to the Serbian army. The 15 who went to the US Army helped ameliorate southern Salt Lake County nativism. In the post–World War I era, separate but friendly, if not equal, Serbian and Croatian lodges were built along with four saloons (added to three earlier drinking spots), four new boardinghouses, six restaurants, and a variety of other businesses. Traditionally hostile toward government, skeptical of Progressive idealism (especially Prohibition and global crusades), and lacking a highly developed sense of civic duty, Highland Boy's South Slavic community nevertheless produced in Melich a leader of international stature.[91]

At Helper South Slavs associated with Carbon County's "rudimentary union movement" in 1903–4 but suffered less visibly from the strike than did Italians. By 1914 500 of them worked at the Utah Fuel camps and many others for the independent coal companies and in Carbon County businesses. Following World War I, sizable numbers of South Slavs continued to migrate to Carbon County.

Discrimination against South Slavs by old-stock Utah Mormons was apparently more active and distressing in Carbon County, where by 1930 Latter-day Saints accounted for only 27.42 percent of the population, than it was in Salt Lake County, which was nearly half Mormon.[92] One intriguing possibility is that not only did Klan activity reach its apex in Carbon County, but it left a legacy of what Larry Gerlach refers to as "covert" bigotry and xenophobia that continued to tear at the county's social innards in spite of the "overt" reconciliations demanded by the numerical strength of the new immigrants and their movement into the middle class.[93]

END OF AN ERA: THE STRIKE OF 1933

Unionism was at low ebb throughout the entire decade following the strike of 1922. In part this resulted from the aggressive, proactive stance of management, which attempted to undercut unions' appeal by treating workers relatively well, sponsoring in-house unions, pushing leisure activities and semipro sports, maintaining their own organization (the Utah Associated Industries), and untiringly promoting public sympathy for their point of view. T. A. Stroup, superintendent of the Clear Creek coal mine, reflected the paternalism common to managers of the 1920s when he maintained that "80 to 90 percent" of the "working population" was "subnormal" and incapable of "clear thinking or self direction."[94] The open shop, which amounted to nonunion workplaces, was particularly effective, as Utah craft and trade organizations diminished in number and size. Mine Mill and Smelter unions had never been strong but deteriorated further until only the Eureka Local No. 151 remained by the late 1920s. In the surviving unions Communists and other radicals tried to "bore from within" until the worsening times of the Depression enabled them to move more openly into politics. As a result, a modest renaissance of dual or industrial unionism led by radicals formed united front groups with revolutionary goals. In 1928 after John L. Lewis forced leftist elements out of the UMWA, they organized the Communist-influenced National Miners Union (NMU), which played an important part in Utah's 1933 strike.

Throughout the 1920s coal operators also kept up direct pressure. They hired spies and tracked the affairs of known activists, fired strikers, employed "yellow-dog" contracts, and continued to push the open shop. Particularly effective were spies from the Globe Inspection Company, who lived and worked among coal miners and under coded names reported on the efforts of UMWA District No. 22 organizers, including Frank Bonacci, a district employee. The determined Bonacci bought a car to travel from one mine to another on union business and at one point struck a major coup when he showed the film *The Growth of American Labor* at a rented movie house in Helper with good effect. District No. 22 tried unsuccessfully to mount an organization drive in 1926 and 1927. To protest wage cuts, reduced hours, and compulsory kickbacks, occasional wildcat strikes were called and in some cases met with momentary successes, but in general the twenties were extremely hard times for unions in Utah's coal mines.[95]

Among the rare defenders of labor in Utah was the Catholic Church. One spokesman was Monsignor (later Bishop) Duane G. Hunt, whose views reflected the "doctrines of 'social justice' contained in two papal encyclicals" issued later by Pius XI. Declaring that it was "imperative that workmen receive living wages," Monsignor Hunt defended the right of workers to organize and to employ boycotts, slowdowns, and closed shops to achieve "just" objectives. "The good to be derived," he continued, "very often outweighs the unavoidable and incidental harm, the loss of profit to employers, temporary harm to business and the rise in the cost of living to the consumers." Workers appreciated Hunt's "fearless and outspoken stand," but little came of it in the short run.[96]

With Franklin D. Roosevelt in office and the New Deal taking form, Section 7a of the National Industrial Recovery Act (NIRA), enacted in 1933, guaranteed the right of labor to organize and take collective action, thus revolutionizing labor's situation in many industries. At long last the rules of play had changed; labor's day had finally arrived in Utah's coalfields. Even so, unionization was a difficult transition. It altered the political complexion in Carbon County and made an enduring hero of Franklin D. Roosevelt.

In 1933 conditions were ripe for change. The United Mine Workers had struggled to establish themselves for several decades, and a skeleton force had survived through the 1920s. Nationally, few labor leaders embraced the NIRA more enthusiastically than John L. Lewis. Hailing it as the most significant blow for "freedom" since the Emancipation Proclamation, Lewis immediately set in motion a "vigorous organizing campaign" that soon completely organized the bituminous coal industry. Other forces for change included widespread unrest in the Carbon County mines and a threat from the radical National Miners Union, which since its 1928 break with the UMWA had worked to mold all workers—skilled and unskilled, craftsmen and industrial workers, ethnics or Yankees—into a force that could overthrow capitalism.[97]

Led by Utah radicals Charles Weatherbee, Jack Hall, and Tony Bonacci (no relation to Frank) and national organizers Paul Crouch and Charles Guynn, the NMU had beaten even canny old John L. Lewis to the punch, laying the groundwork for an organizing campaign in Carbon County during the winter of 1932–33. Well received by Helper mayor Frank R. Porter and with headquarters in Spring Glen, a Helper suburb, the NMU opened formal operations in May 1933. Offering an action program, a newspaper (the *Carbon County Miner*), social and athletic activities, and women's and youth auxiliaries, the union saw membership grow to one thousand by June 28 and fifteen hundred by July 4.[98] Membership was strongest at Spring Glen and Helper and in the mines tributary to them in Gordon Creek and Spring Canyon, immediately to the west. The Slavs were quick to join. Slavic men and women alike embraced the NMU's message of revolution and overthrow and, with only a few holdouts, supported the strike without reservation. Italians too joined in large numbers.

Getting off to a slower start, the United Mine Workers established headquarters in mid-June at Price. Under the able leadership of national organizer Nicholas Fontecchio and local stalwart Frank Bonacci, the UMWA soon had seventeen locals in the Scofield, Hiawatha, and Sunnyside districts. It was seen as the lesser evil by local and state government, the press, and organizations like the American Legion, as well as many of the mine operators.[99]

The Carbon County upheaval of 1933 was unprecedented in many ways. Although some operators struggled to play the two unions off against each other, the UMWA was quickly paired with the business and political establishment, and the NMU was cast in the role of revolutionary spoiler, as all unions had been in earlier years. In the competition for workers each union accused the other of intimidation, threats, and injury. The NMU billed UMWA members as strikebreakers, pawns of management, and thugs; the UMWA called the NMU a Communist outfit. To ease the onus of anti-Americanism, NMU leaders played up local concerns, but most of its organizers were likely Communists, as were a fair number of its members.[100]

In a war of words and agitation the NMU clearly had the best of it. In addition to three brilliant speakers in Guynn, Crouch, and Weatherbee, they had access to Helper's streets and parks, a membership keen to disrupt, and a responsive, sharp-witted little press. Perhaps most important of all, the NMU involved its women to an unprecedented extent. Belle Taub, International Labor Defense leader, worked in Carbon County during the NMU's organizational phase and stirred broader aware-ness of the miners' cause later. Fully the equal of their husbands in fervor and skills were Rae Guynn, a gifted speaker and publicist who aroused audiences and focused issues in the *Carbon County Miner*, and Sylvia Crouch, strategist and coach in strike techniques who molded the wives and daughters of the strikers into an awesome force. Most important of all were the local women who used pepper in nonlethal but effective chemical warfare, marched at the front of demonstrations, heckled in the most contemptuous and bawdy language, and applied diversionary tactics.[101]

Early in July interunion competition and discord crescendoed. Price mayor Rolla West, an American Legionnaire, ardent nationalist, and carpenter and join-ers unionist, barred the NMU from the July 4 ceremonies. This magnified tensions between the two unions. Then the NMU announced a general strike for Labor Day. Not content to wait, the local at Mutual struck on August 2, calling for work and pay concessions and union recognition. When the operators made concessions, other Spring Canyon and Gordon Creek locals struck, bringing the two unions into head-to-head confrontation as the UMWA refused to honor the strikes and the NMU mounted armed pickets, blocking access to several of the mines and the roads approaching them. Mines throughout the county closed.

As calls for intervention poured in, Governor Henry Blood called a meet-ing. Deciding in favor of local action, Blood went over Sheriff Marion Bliss's head, appointing Rolla West chief of an ad hoc deputy force. West recruited more than one hundred World War I veterans, with men drawn from each mine. Most were UMWA members and understood they would enforce peace. Simultaneously, Blood assigned a crack highway patrol unit to keep roads open and two National Guard riot squads to cooperate with West.[102]

West's forces broke the NMU's hold on Gordon Creek and Spring Canyon. On August 26 West and the main force of deputies came up the road and assaulted Consumers, a Gordon Creek stronghold, while smaller detachments approached along the ridges. Joe Bono led the Consumers deputies within the camp. In one of the great incidents of any labor confrontation, David Parmley, Consumers' superin-tendent, eluded the armed pickets but was pursued by "6 big Austrian women" who disarmed him, threw him down, and in an expression of utter contempt, as Parmley related, "peed on me." In a different kind of encounter, a belligerent Mormon bishop knocked down three young NMU sympathizers. As evening approached the invaders finally took Consumers, dispersed the "200" strikers, and left Joe Bono and "his Consumers detachment" in charge. Two days later deputies launched a three-pronged invasion on Spring Canyon. Although West was beaten about the head and shoulders by a purse-wielding Italian baker, and women and children from Helper led a determined counterattack with pepper spray, the use of tear gas and a lot of strong-arm tactics by West and his forces paid off handsomely. Routing 600 NMU supporters, they took 210 prisoners, including 130 aliens, and locked them all in a bull pen in Price.

Later raids invaded Helper, the NMU citadel, where leaders Charles Guynn and Charles Weatherbee were seized. With Paul Crouch, who had been arrested earlier, they were soon out on five thousand dollars' bail, much to the disgust of West's deputies. Guynn and Weatherbee were soon taken again. The general strike planned for Labor Day did not come off, but in one last act of defiance 400 NMU members supported by many women and children marched on the county courthouse in Price on September 11, demanding that Guynn and Weatherbee be freed. Turned back by tear gas and high-pressure water, the strikers retreated to Helper.

At this point protests poured in "from many quarters." In a mass meeting at Salt Lake City's First Congregational Church on September 14, 1933, an audience of 600 listened to coal miners' testimony and expressed their ire. Among the most vocal were Mormon general authority B. H. Roberts, radical state legislator Warwick C. Lamoreaux, International Labor Defense representative Belle Taub, and Farm and Labor League representative Murray E. King. The 210 prisoners were released. Ultimately, only 7 were tried, including Crouch, Guynn, and Weatherbee.[103]

While the Carbon County strike was at its apex, the Western State coal operators met in Salt Lake City, drawing up operating codes in keeping with NIRA provisions. Included were minimum wage and maximum hour codes and guarantees covering the right to organize and bargain collectively. On November 8, 1933, UMWA District No. 22 representatives signed a contract with officials of the Utah Coal Producers and Operators Association subscribing to the same principles. Columbia Steel's coal mining subsidiary refused to sign the agreements until Roosevelt forced the steel industry to grant coal miners in "captive" coal mines the same guarantees enjoyed by other miners. Men discharged at Columbia over union issues were rehired, and the UMWA was accepted in the Utah coalfields. "The last vestiges of the NMU were absorbed" when Charles Guynn and 50 former members of the NMU at the Maple Creek mine joined the UMWA. As Frank Bonacci summed it up, the man and the union that had "played Hell" in Utah for the "past 18 months" were tamed at last.[104]

The events of 1933 were the last of Utah's hard-fought free-for-all strikes. After three decades, a nonunion industry had been unionized. Confronted by the radicalism of the National Miners Union, management and the state quietly accepted the United Mine Workers of America as the lesser of two evils. The UMWA had worked almost as an extension of management during the strike. Later, as the National Labor Relations Board regulated labor relations and the Congress of Industrial Organizations came into being, the UMWA influenced coal mining policy in numerous ways.

Unionization changed the political character of Carbon County, too. Controlled by the D&RG and the mining bosses, the county had been solidly Republican until 1933; thereafter, it was solidly Democratic. As John W. Davis, who worked at Spring Canyon Mines recalled, in the years after 1900 Winter Quarters superintendent T. J. Parmley lined miners up "prior to each election and" told "them to vote Republican or lose their jobs." In one election there were said to be only seven Democratic votes cast in Scofield. The next day Parmley admitted he did not know who cast the votes but chose seven likely candidates, fired them, and ran them out of camp. After the revolution of 1933, Carbon County returned heavy Democratic majorities in election after election, as an operator-controlled Republican county became a worker's Democratic county.[105]

The day of silenced, unvoiced workers and disfranchised new immigrants had passed. The strike by which that voice had been found was no less hardhanded than earlier strikes, but backed by national legislation and changing attitudes toward labor, the outcome was radically different. Memories of abuse rankled among the Slavs and other former members of the NMU, as they did among other new immigrants, but a significant forward step had at last been taken. As in the early Mormon adjustments, it had been forced by the federal government after hard-fought contests with major mining and railroad corporations. For immigrants, unionization was an important step that together with education, business connection, the passage of time, and World War II finally began to give them a place in the state.

7

AT THE WHIPLASH END OF PLURALISM
Indians in the New State

NEGLECT AND DEPENDENCY

When statehood dawned the era of Indian wars had been replaced by government policies that sought to incorporate American Indians within the American mainstream through assimilation, individual land allotment, and education for citizenship.[1] White pressure and federal organization had resulted in the division of Utah's Indians into five tribal groups: the Southern Paiutes, the Goshutes, the Northwestern Shoshones, the Northern Utes, and the San Juan Navajos. Although the major Indian reservations had taken form, agriculture and mining interests called for further reductions. The end result was often neglect, land seizure, dependency, and marginal existence for Native Americans. Even well-intentioned reforms after 1925 set new rounds of suffering in motion. For none was this truer than for the Paiutes.

PAIUTES

At the time of contact Utah Paiutes comprised several dozen small, closely related bands. With their population spread over much of southern Utah, the Paiutes' identities depended more on the block of natural resources they exploited than upon prominent leaders. Some Paiute groups were more closely related to the Utes than others; all traveled extensively between groups. As they colonized southern Utah, Mormons settled well-watered sites where the Paiutes had headquartered. By the time of statehood the Paiute population had dwindled drastically.[2]

Although population estimates are undependable, some general ideas about tribal size may be formed. Zion National Park historian Angus M. Woodbury refers to pioneer reports that 1,000 Paiutes lived "along the Virgin River in the [18]50s and 60s." Careful reading of pioneer sources suggests Paiute populations consisted of fewer than 2,000 persons even in the mid-1850s, and perhaps substantially less. In a count that ethnohistorian Ronald Holt holds to be suspect, John Wesley Powell found only 528 Paiutes in Utah in 1873, in a total Indian population of 1,474. Whatever the facts, disease, starvation, and attrition due to reservation life and conflict with other tribes continued to reduce the size of the several Paiute groups before population began to inch up by 1930.[3]

During territorial times Paiutes consistently resisted governmental pressure to remove to the Utes' Uintah Reservation. Instead, they remained near their ancestral grounds, often residing in the neighborhood of Mormon communities, which asserted paternalistic control over them but lacked the means or the will to provide many economic and educational opportunities. Many Paiutes were traditional horticulturalists, especially along riverbanks. Modern agricultural instruction began early and continued into the first decades of the twentieth century with indifferent success and with a growing tendency for Mormons to turn Indian policy over to the federal government and to other religious groups. For example, in Washington County Mormon-sponsored Indian farms, of which there had been at least five in the late 1880s, had been reduced to the single Shivwits reserve west of St. George in 1891, which was given official reservation status in 1903. Enlarged to 26,880 acres by presidential proclamation in 1916, it thereafter increasingly became the preserve of Protestant missionaries.[4] For many years even the role of Indian farmer was assigned to William McClure and his wife, dedicated Presbyterian laypeople from Erie, Pennsylvania.[5]

By 1900 Utah Paiutes had been reduced to six communities. These were located at the Shivwits Reservation; at Cedar City; at Indian Peaks, west of Beaver; at Kanosh and Koosharem in Millard and Garfield Counties; and in San Juan County, east of the Colorado River. Other closely related Paiutes lived at Moccasin, just across the border on the Arizona Strip, and at Moapa and Las Vegas in Nevada. With the exception of the Cedar City colony, each of these ultimately had reservation status. However, the Bureau of Indian Affairs paid scant attention to the southern Utah Paiutes.[6]

In 1917 an Indian agency was finally established. Dr. Edgar A. Farrow was stationed at Moccasin on the Kaibab Reservation, "a 12 by 18 mile" piece that had been set aside in 1907 for about one hundred Kaibab Paiutes, and also had responsibilities in Utah. Cattle were issued to the Kaibabs, and in 1930 Farrow thought their prospects compared favorably to the white residents of the area. A decade later the BIA tried to combine the scattered Paiute groups into a single agency headquartered in

Cedar City. There for a few years many Paiutes received treatments for trachoma, tuberculosis, flu, and childhood maladies.[7]

The more volatile San Juan Paiutes received small agricultural holdings. Interacting heavily with reticent Ute Mountain and Southern Utes and off-reservation Northern Navajos, the San Juan Paiutes first foraged between the Henry Mountains, Navajo Mountain, and the San Juan River and then were given undifferentiated access with the far-ranging Western Navajos to the so-called Paiute Strip. Left largely to Mormon and stockmen's promptings, Paiutes ranging north of the San Juan River eked out a meager existence by traditional gathering and a combination of day labor, beggary, petty theft, and stock rustling. From the perspective of many of the whites, an Indian named Posey was the ringleader of the rustlers and raiders. San Juan Mormons' patience wore increasingly thin, as materialism supplanted the original missionaries' altruism. The Mormons unsuccessfully petitioned the commissioner of Indian affairs to remove the Indians and thereby "relieve the good people of the County of the burden of being preyed upon by a reckless bunch of Indians."[8]

Tensions boiled over in the Posey War, aptly relabeled by historian Robert McPherson "the last white uprising." After two Ute boys known to the whites as Joe Bishop's Little Boy and Sanup's Boy were arrested by the sheriff for raiding a sheep camp, they were brought to trial. During a court recess prior to sentencing, the Indians attempted to escape. When the sheriff raised his gun to fire at them, Joe Bishop's Little Boy grabbed the gun and fired back, wounding the sheriff's horse before escaping. A Mormon posse under the sheriff's direction rounded up about forty Indians living nearby and placed them under armed guard in the schoolhouse and then fanned out, looking for the two escapees, Posey, and any other Indians at large. George Hurst, a resident of Blanding, recalled decades later that the sheriff ordered the posse to "shoot everything that looks like an Indian." The deputies spotted Posey and three or four of his comrades a few miles south of Blanding in an old cabin, but they were too well armed to capture. The next day a member of the posse spotted Posey near Comb Ridge and fired at him, mortally wounding him. When Joe Bishop pursued a member of the posse up a side draw, the deputy fired in self-defense, killing Bishop. Several additional Indians, including Sanup's Boy, surrendered and were placed under armed guard. The captives were confined in two hastily built hogans ringed by a high barbed-wire fence in the center of town. The shooting was over. Indian agent E. E. McKean arrived from Ignacio, Colorado; took charge of the children in the stockade; and sent them to a boarding school in Towaoc, Colorado.

In the aftermath of this incident, most San Juan whites favored moving the Paiutes to a distant reservation where they could be controlled, but a significant minority favored locating them in a canyon south of the Abajo Mountains. Bolstered by guarantees made by General Hugh L. Scott that traditional rights to the

South Abajos would be respected, the Cottonwood–Allen Canyon tract was withdrawn from the La Sal National Forest, where the Indians received personal allotments. By 1940, however, they obtained additional lands on White Mesa, eleven miles south of Blanding.[9]

In western Utah a few thousand acres were designated between 1910 and 1920 as Paiute reserves. The Indian Peaks Reservation was located in excellent pine nut country west of Beaver. Migration to Cedar City combined with disease depleted the Indian Peaks population by the late 1920s. The Kanosh group secured land in the south end of the Pahvant Valley, and the Koosharems, who had originally been known as the "Fish Lake Utes," obtained a few homesteads in the upper Sevier Valley between Greenwich and Koosharem.[10]

As aboriginal lifeways became more impossible and as Paiutes depended more on ranch and farmwork, lease revenues, begging, and domestic service, they became an underpaid and underemployed labor pool. Sale of buckskin crafts and pine nuts along with scavenging and occasional government annuities kept some alive but provided opportunity for no one.

Before the New Deal era, both the BIA and the state's Mormon majority agreed Indians had to be instructed in the way of individual farming and private landholding and led away from tribal collectivism. Mormons generally controlled the effort to bring about some kind of assimilation and make independent farmers of the Paiutes, while the BIA focused its energy on a modest school effort. A few Paiute children were taken to distant boarding schools, and a handful of San Juan Paiute children went to the Tuba City Boarding School in Arizona.

More important educational efforts were made at Shivwits, where a day school began in 1898, directed by the dedicated Laura Work, and at Moccasin, where for more than thirty years a day school operated. Work's efforts led in 1903 to the establishment of the Panguitch Boarding School, where about thirty boys and girls enrolled annually until 1909, when the day school at Shivwits reopened.[11] Ironically, as the Indian New Deal came into force in the 1930s with its efforts to revive tribalism and Indian collectivism, more Indian young people apparently began to attend white schools.[12]

Paiutes made concessions to the overwhelming force of the oncoming whites in matters of religion, as they did in other aspects of their lives. While for some Christian conversion was undoubtedly wholehearted, for others the outcome involved concessions that made life possible. The early Mormon period generated mass baptisms, some with gifts, which it was said led Indians to offer themselves for subsequent baptisms and new gifts, or, as time went on, to show up with equal enthusiasm to Presbyterian and Mormon celebrations. Traveling evangelists sometimes held revivals with good effect. For example, in 1907 James Hayes, a regionally noted Nez Perce preacher, ran an eleven-day revival at the Shivwits Presbyterian church, which was named for him.[13]

Death rates were high among turn-of-the-century Paiutes. Indigenous practices promoting hygiene were no longer possible, and whites did little to extend such modest improvements as southern Utah's villages were able to develop to the Indian encampments. Infant mortality was especially grievous, and Paiute children living close to the Mormon villages were particularly vulnerable to childhood diseases. Influenza struck Paiutes heavily, as it did the entire population. Late in his life Ralph Thompson, a former Kanosh resident, recalled the devastation the flu wrought in the Kanosh Indian community during 1918 and 1919.[14]

While many whites paid little heed to this ongoing tragedy, some doctors apparently bolstered their income and invested considerable time in their Indian practice. Among physicians who made some contribution at St. George were Israel Ivins, a Mormon, and Joseph Walker, a Presbyterian. Edgar A. Farrow, Paiute and consolidated Paiute-Goshute agent from 1927 into the 1930s, recalled that his administration was devoted more to medical services than any other aspect of Indian care. In addition to Native medicine men, a few Indians raised in white homes helped ease Indian suffering. David Lemmon, a white-raised Ute who married a white woman, became a noted faith healer.[15]

Although interaction between whites and Indians was largely limited to work situations and some church contact, Indian funerals in which both Indians and whites participated were sometimes held in Mormon wards. At the Moccasin funeral of nine-year-old Victor Tom, Paiutes and whites spoke, sang, and prayed. Speaker Tony Tillohash, who had been raised in a white home and educated at Carlisle, touched on the profound as well as the beautiful when he said, "I know that there are two bodies here before us, the body of a person and the body of a rose. The Rose had roots, the person had a soul. The Rose has lost its roots and the Body has lost its soul and has, we say, died."[16]

GOSHUTES

The Goshutes, or Western Shoshones, had made their aboriginal homeland in a vast rectangle extending from Utah Lake and the south shores of the Great Salt Lake to well into Nevada. A treaty signed in 1863 promised cash payments for concessions made to whites but still permitted the Goshutes to range across some 5.9 million acres of America's most searing desert. John Wesley Powell and other officials argued they should be attached to the Uintah Reservation for economy's sake. When the Goshutes refused, they were in large measure neglected by the government and left to fend for themselves.[17] By statehood Deep Creek Goshutes had lived through a Mormon mission period during which many were baptized, some were instructed at a Mormon day school, and a few had dabbled in landownership and agriculture. Others had located at Skull Valley, where they interacted with ranchers and other settlers, including the

Hawaiian colony at Iosepa, a few miles to the north. The Goshutes found the barest means of survival by adapting their desert gathering modes to itinerant wage work. Only a few whites, though, such as William Lee, worked closely with them. Unlike the Paiutes, they did not settle in colonies adjacent to Mormon villages.[18]

After the turn of the century the federal government gradually awarded specific resources to the Goshutes. Water rights were acquired at Deep Creek. Skull Valley Indians Tabby and Shiprus as well as Don Dougan, a Deep Creek Goshute, proved up on homesteads filed during 1883. In 1911 Lorenzo Creel investigated the situation on behalf of the BIA and recommended that the government step up efforts on behalf of the destitute tribe. While it ran counter to the government's emphasis on assimilation, Creel's recommendation led to the creation of the Scattered Bands in Utah Agency and the movement toward Goshute reservations. In 1914 33,688 acres from the public domain were set aside as the Deep Creek Goshute Reservation. To this were added 66,155 acres in Nevada in 1938, and nearly 9,000 additional acres were purchased under the Indian Reorganization Act, bringing the total on the reservation to 108,000 acres, 38,000 of which were in Utah.[19]

In 1912 the Skull Valley reservation was created by executive order, and in 1919 it was enlarged to encompass some 17,000 acres. Wood-frame houses and a small school were built, and an Indian farmer was assigned. Similar provisions were made at Deep Creek. Joseph H. Peck, company doctor at a nearby mine, operated a "well baby" clinic at Deep Creek in response to eastern reformers. He kept up a friendly competition with medicine man and chief Annies Tommy, "the Howler," who treated ailments with chants, herbs, and skillful use of taboos. Peck came away with grudging respect for both the medicine man's practice and the child-rearing habits of the Goshute women, which sometimes threatened infant lives but seemed to Peck well adapted to raising up a race able to face life in the West Desert. Within five years the Scattered Bands Agency was abolished due to the small number of constituents. The Skull Valley school and farm program were eliminated, ostensibly so that the bureau could concentrate its efforts upon the larger Deep Creek Reservation. Some of the Skull Valley band did relocate at Deep Creek, but by 1936 thirty-nine Goshutes still resided at Skull Valley.[20]

Goshute activists of the teens and 1920s were anxious to preserve traditional claims to a much larger homeland than the specific reservations that were established. They also sought to recoup unfulfilled cash awards promised by the treaty of 1863. In pursuit of these interests, Willie Ottogary, a Box Elder County Shoshone; Harry Dixon, a Nevada Goshute; and other Goshute leaders made several trips to Washington between 1915 and 1924. BIA administrators regarded Ottogary and Dixon as troublemakers rather than as serious threats to the regional peace.

A brief upheaval among Deep Creek Goshutes in 1917 and 1918 involved World War I. With American entry into the war, the Selective Service Act required all male residents (including Indian citizens) between the ages of twenty-one and forty-five to register. Indian agents across the country were instructed to register reservation Indians but were told at the same time that noncitizen Indians were exempt from the draft. The citizenship status of many Goshutes was murky. An appreciable number of Indians had become US citizens during the preceding quarter century by homesteading on the public domain, by living "separate and apart from any tribe," and by adopting "the habits of civilized life."[21]

Beginning at Fort Hall and working its way south and west, the draft question had generated a good deal of heat by the time registration commenced at Deep Creek late in 1917. Agent Amos R. Frank, a longtime BIA professional, had little love for the Goshutes generally and less for leaders who complicated his job. Resistance was centered in the local headman-shaman Annies Tommy and the ubiquitous Willie Ottogary. A second-generation Mormon who had inherited part of his father's homestead in northern Utah's Box Elder County, Ottogary was eligible for the registration and by submitting to the draft personally would have admitted citizenship by reason of his homestead and by an anomalous relationship to the tribe.

As resistance to Frank's effort to register the Goshutes crescendoed, the Deep Creek eligibles disappeared, ostensibly on a sheep-shearing expedition. A bellicose liquor-control deputy, G. J. Knapp, was disarmed when he undertook to arrest Tommy and Ottogary. Withdrawing to Gold Hill, Knapp telegraphed news of an uprising, seized Indians who attempted to wire their own version of the situation, and stirred up events. Ultimately, a force of soldiers from Fort Douglas traveled to Gold Hill by train and motored the remaining thirty miles in subzero weather by private cars lined up by a reluctant Dr. Peck. Peck claimed the pursuit ended in a drinking spree in which soldiers and captured Goshutes, for the moment ready to register, celebrated a truce. Annies Tommy and one or two others from Deep Creek were jailed, as was Ottogary. As the excitement subsided, charges were dropped against all parties.[22]

Late in 1940 the Confederated Tribes of Goshute Reservations adopted a constitution for the governance of the Goshute reservations under the Indian Reorganization Act. Although the Skull Valley band chose not to organize under the constitution, the Deep Creek Goshutes approved it and proceeded to form a five-member tribal council to govern affairs on their reservation.[23]

THE "WASHAKIE LETTERS" AND THE NORTHERN SHOSHONES

Historically, the Northern Shoshones occupied lands lying east and north of the Great Salt Lake. Many were slaughtered just north of the Utah-Idaho border in Cache Valley in 1863. Most of the survivors eventually removed to reservations in Idaho and Wyoming. A handful remained in northern Utah, though, and converted to Mormonism. An Indian town and LDS ward were established at Washakie in Box Elder County, as was a collective church farm under the leadership of George Washington Hill, George M. Ward, and his son George M. Ward Jr.[24]

Washakie was the most successful of several Indian communities established by the Mormon Church as a missionary effort and alternative to the federal government's assimilation program. Between 1906 and 1929 more than five hundred letters by Willie Ottogary chronicling life in Washakie were published in northern Utah newspapers. These letters offer a richly textured portrait of early-twentieth-century life in a Utah Indian community. Washakie inhabitants traveled regularly by horse and train, and later by car, throughout Shoshone country—northern Utah, southern Idaho, and western Wyoming—to attend family affairs, Sun and Bear Dances, rodeos, and Indian social and religious events, as well as to conduct business. Wild West shows, baseball, horse racing, prizefighting, and movies attracted them to neighboring white towns and to the more distant Shoshone and Ute centers. Frequent Friday-night dances took place at the church in Washakie. Holiday festivities and recreational events in nearby communities were popular, and it was a rare fair, Peach Day celebration, horse race, or circus that did not draw a contingent of Washakie participants and spectators.[25]

Washakie boys played baseball regularly. Although the Fort Hall "Industrial School" team drubbed them fifty-five to ten, they won some engagements with white competitors. Ottogary's sons, Chester (Kickapoo Dan) and General Custer (Custer was his real name), boxed professionally in northern Utah towns and Salt Lake City during the late 1920s. The two boys drew good crowds and made a little money, but suffered frequent injuries, poverty, cultural isolation, and racism.[26]

Washakie provided a rich variety of hunting, trapping, and gathering opportunities.[27] These activities remained part of the community's annual routine and were pursued more or less as need required. Agriculturally, the Bear River country constituted one of the great oases of the West, and with the sugar industry well established Washakie Indians raised beets as well as wheat. Beets also provided field work and shipping jobs for Indians who had no access to farmland of their own.

Steered by Mormon planners, at least fourteen Box Elder Shoshones had taken out independent homesteads in addition to the collective church farm. Although by the 1910s the original homesteads were being subdivided among descendants (Ottogary's own place was shared with two siblings), land alienation moved at a slower pace than in some areas, and leasing to whites was not as common as it was on the Northern Ute reservations.[28] Indian water rights were mediocre, but their land was in a region where successful dry farming was practiced. Although inadequate water and a disposition to turn crops to cash as quickly as possible led to hay shortages in all but the mildest winters, Box Elder Shoshones owned horses for driving and racing as well as draft purposes. Shearing crews worked for local sheepmen and less often in western Box Elder County and Wyoming. Otherwise, Box Elder Shoshones were not engaged in animal husbandry. After a show of reticence at first sight, they embraced automobiles and by the midteens sported many secondhand Fords, Overlands, and Willies and an occasional new car.

The tempo of the traditional gathering cycle guided the Shoshones' activities. Spring work began with anticipation and relief. Crops were put in, work gangs formed, and wage work was taken. Some Washakies worked land that they leased from others locally or at Fort Hall. Then the summer round of travel, visiting, and politicking began. Hay and wheat were harvested in season. Berry, root, and pine-nut picking came next, and as fall unfolded Washakie home guards returned to harvest their own crops and work in Cache and Bear River beet fields and to man the beet dumps. By December 15 work details and traveling parties were home, and the annual work cycle drew to a close. Washakie was a winter camp. There people waited out the cold of January and February as they eyed diminishing hay supplies nervously and as disease and malnutrition took their toll. This winter shutdown was punctuated with the day school, church activities, rabbit hunting, leather crafts, and holidays.

Until the hard winter of 1921–22 Ottogary made no reference to annuities from the Shoshone agency. In that year of postwar depression many sold out to whites. In answer to "begging," a few hundred pounds of flour, a little sugar, and some wheat seed were made available.

Children were educated in a variety of venues. Washakie's day school was apparently not supported by the federal government until after 1925, when the Indian Service built a schoolhouse and helped fund schooling, as the white school district had apparently done earlier. Ottogary's own children attended the Elwood District School. His oldest son, Chester, graduated and to Ottogary's pride was the first Indian to attend high school. Charlie Broom, apparently an older product of the Washakie school, taught at the Deep Creek day school in 1912.[29]

For Ottogary public life was important. He was an active churchman. He spoke occasionally at Washakie and elsewhere, attended the Logan LDS temple, and filled a short-term mission in Nevada, where by his report ninety-six people awaited baptism. He frequently visited with editors, businessmen, and political figures and was always amazed at the technology of white society. Although it is a near constant of Ottogary's writing, anger is always subdued. Injury and injustice were dealt with as matters of fact.

Ottogary played his most important role in connection with Indian lands. He was occasionally called a chief and is said to have negotiated as one in Washington. Ottogary lacked the stature of a Washakie or the ego of a Pocatello, earlier Shoshone leaders, yet he was driven to improve the access to land of younger Shoshones and worked tirelessly to alleviate poverty and secure justice. These themes—land, relief, justice—ran through his columns, although his style was to quietly report, not to indict or persuade.

In addition to his Washington trips, Ottogary traveled in the East and visited key Indian centers in Kansas and Oklahoma, where agitation over Indian issues ran high. His columns report almost constant contact with prominent Indians in the three major Shoshone subdivisions and among northern Utah whites. They also suggest a conversance with the issues that Native Americans of his era were facing. Among other things, he was clearly aware of the interconnectedness of individual landownership, Indian citizenship, the draft, and taxation. During his earlier years as a reporter, he called frequently for land to be allotted individually among young Indians, but as the scandals associated with Republican secretary of the interior Albert Fall and the Merriam Report of 1928 raised questions about allotments and assimilation as civilizing forces, Ottogary talked more about a Box Elder County reservation for northern Utah Indians and of cash settlements from the Treaty of 1863. In the months before his death in 1929, he communicated with Congressman Don B. Colton and Senator William King on these subjects.[30]

Unfortunately, Willie Ottogary's window on Washakie affairs ended shortly before the Indian New Deal of the 1930s was initiated. The Depression affected the farm dimension of Washakie's cash-dependent economy in terms of both sales for their own products and work opportunities. Washakie held together in some measure into the 1940s, when wartime opportunities led to major migration to white towns and cities as work became available.[31]

THE UTES: AT THE CENTER OF THE STORM

The dominant element in Utah's Native American story as statehood began were the Northern Utes, composed of three major bands: the Uintahs, tribesmen pushed from central and western Utah by white conquest, and the White River and Uncompahgre Utes, who had been forcibly removed from western Colorado. The angry and defiant White River Utes had been placed with the more conciliatory Uintahs on the Uintah Reservation, which extended north into the Uinta Mountains, south into the basin's desert badlands, and east and west along the Strawberry, Duchesne, and Uinta Rivers. They belittled Uintah efforts to get along with the agency and voiced their conviction that in dealing with whites, trouble produced better dividends than cooperation. The Uncompahgres were placed on a new, austere reservation extending south through the deserts east of the Green River. They were dismayed and devastated at the trade-off from Colorado mountains to the arid wastes of their reservation.[32]

Bureaucrats in the Indian Service advocated assimilation and agrarian civilization, but, as ever, federal policies resulted in Indian removal and land loss. An agency, a subagency, and boarding schools were located at Whiterocks and Ouray.[33]

Reduced in number by 1882 to some twenty-eight hundred on about four million acres of reservation land, the Northern Utes were caught in the maelstrom of forces that were remaking Utah and the nation. Indeed, a multiple-front assault on Ute property and culture was under way that kept them at the heart of the state's lamentable Indian history. The avid search for new mineral treasure drew both local promoters and eastern trusts to the Uinta Basin as gilsonite's usefulness was demonstrated. Prospectors, engineers, and men of high finance overran the reservations, crowded the halls of Congress, and curried favor with Native Americans and Indian agencies as a new bonanza seemed to hinge on Indian lands.

As early as 1888 more than seven thousand acres had been withdrawn from the southeastern end of the Uintah Reservation. The resulting "strip" became not only the center of the gilsonite industry but also a pesthole of violence and Indian degradation and an outfitting grounds for further trespass. As the industry developed, the entire Uncompahgre Reservation was opened to mineral entry in 1898, precipitating a mining rush and a badly handled effort to find farmable lands to assign to individual Indians. In the end, a few Uncompahgres were crowded onto Uintah Reservation allotments, and many were deprived of a homeland.[34]

About the same time, a whole congeries of agricultural developments emerged that constituted an unstoppable challenge to Northern Ute lands and water resources. As noted earlier, Utah's livestock and ranching industries exploded in the years after 1885. Stockmen moved their animals out of Utah's central valleys, among other places invading Indian lands in the eastern part of the state. With a small tribal cattle industry and perhaps twelve thousand horses, the Utes objected strenuously. Detesting the unmarketable ponies, and fearing the collectivism and nomadism inherent in herding, as well as desperate for cash, the agency overrode them. Leases were let on the western end of the reservation, first to the Strawberry Valley Cattle Company, organized by Preston Nutter, and then to Heber Valley stockmen, and increasingly to sheepmen. By 1905 the Utes were "receiving between $25,000 and $50,000 annually in 'grass money.'"[35] Grover Cleveland delivered a serious blow to Northern Ute land interests in 1897 when he withdrew approximately one million acres from the Uintah Reservation to create the Uinta Forest Reserve.[36]

Through the entire period, pressure built to allot land to Indian individuals and open the reservation to white homesteading. According to procedures worked out under the General Allotment Act of 1887 (the Dawes Act), up to a quarter section was to be distributed to each Indian head of household and lesser acreages to other family members. Behind these provisions lay the idea that allotments would become the basis of private property, individualized interests, sedentary habits, and a self-sustaining farm society. Allotted lands would be held in trust by the Indian Bureau for twenty-five years. Together with modest-size community grazing grounds, the allotments would constitute the entire Indian landholding. Remaining reservation lands were then to be returned to the public domain and opened for private entry by whites, who as neighbors would become mentors in the arts of civilization.[37]

Under the terms of the Dawes Act, a majority of a tribe's male adults had to agree to the allotment process and the concomitant loss of reservation lands. This loss of Indian lands was rarely accomplished without objections and various commissions appointed to "sell" the reluctant tribes on the idea. Few Indians were more determined in their rejection of allotments and farming than the Utes. Insisting they needed every foot of land, and fearing Mormon neighbors particularly, they repeatedly refused to vote for allotments. For five or six years after 1898 the Utes' passive resistance seemed to stall proceedings, as white authorities surveyed the reservations and worked out blueprints for the Strawberry reclamation project. With white demands for land mounting, an amendment to the Indian Appropriation Act of 1903 gave the secretary of the interior authority to impose allotments and reduce tribal landholdings without Indian approval. Agent C. G. Hall hastily issued 1,365 allotments amounting to 103,265 acres during the summer of 1905. Many of the Utes, however, continued to ignore farmwork, creating acute water-rights problems when white homesteads were intermixed with Ute holdings on the newly defined reservation.[38]

Utes continued to resist allotment in various forms. Forty-two demanded non-agricultural allotments. Others refused to farm. The White Rivers took the most direct action. During allotment twenty-five of them headed for South Dakota but were quickly returned. Less than a year later nearly four hundred led by White River headmen Appah and Red Cap headed for the Black Hills again. Hoping to find freedom among the Sioux, they were received without enthusiasm and toughed out a year or two, working part-time for the railroad before returning "under guard and little honored."[39]

White assaults on Ute agricultural lands and water continued. The reservation was opened to white homesteading in 1905. The Strawberry reclamation project to divert Uinta Basin water to Utah County farms got under way the same year when Theodore Roosevelt withdrew some 200,000 acres from the reservation for reservoir purposes. Not understanding the subtleties of water law, the Utes were especially vulnerable with relation to it. Utah water policy was firmly based upon beneficial-use doctrines. Earlier attempts to tap unused water flowing from the reservation's Strawberry Valley for the Heber area had demonstrated that transmontane diversions were technically possible and that water rising on the reservation was feebly held, if at all, by the Utes.[40] As BIA officials W. H. Code and C. G. Hall had allotted land during the summer of 1905, they made it clear that the land allotments were useless without water rights. Complicating the issue further was the Ute determination not to farm, the primary standard of beneficial use.

Two crucial steps relating to water followed the BIA's rushed effort to get Indians onto farms in 1905. First, the $650,000 Uintah Irrigation Project, covering some 80,000 acres of Indian allotments, was initiated in 1906.[41] Second, a program was patched together leasing allotted Indian lands to white farmers and selling unallotted lands to them to secure their aid in bringing water to Indian allotments. Struggling for cash to help them meet the costs of homesteading, whites profited most from UIP construction, doing the lion's share of the work for pay. In the process they acquired flow rights in Indian canals and other direct benefits to their own water systems. Interpretations of *Winters v. U.S.* (1908) fixed Ute claims at the date the reservation was created; thus, Indian water rights predated white filings. However, maintaining those claims depended upon "beneficial use" of the water for farming. By 1914 "Utes held 6,147 improved acres and leased another 7,113 acres. This left 68,147 allotted acres (84 percent) idle" and ignored water rights that whites valued at the price of blood. Recognizing that both water rights and unused allotted lands were increasingly at risk, Ute superintendent A. H. Kneale lowered prices on leases and sales and mounted a vigorous publicity campaign. Consequently, by 1917 1,764 leases, "totaling fifty-four thousand allotted acres," had been let and "nearly twenty thousand allotted acres sold" or dickered for.[42] Through Kneale's strategy, "the Indian Irrigation Service" perfected water rights by 1921 on "77,195 allotted acres—23,108" of which were owned by whites and most of the rest of which were under white leases. All told, the Uintah Irrigation Project brought 80,306 acres under cultivation at staggering costs to the Utes, who had to reimburse the government for about "double the original $600,000 appropriation." In large measure it was a federal gift to whites "who bought Ute allotments or used their canals." But without the irrigation project, Ute lands would have been worthless for farming, making a mockery of claims that allotment made Ute households economically self-sustaining.[43]

Difficulties notwithstanding, the 1912–28 era marked the high point of Uintah-Ouray agriculture. In 1909 only 78 Uintahs were said to inhabit and work their farms, along with 8 Uncompahgres and 16 White Rivers. Horse herds, which contributed more to prestige than income, remained large. In 1920, though, 217 of the 275 able adult males on the reservation "owned cultivated fields averaging 41 acres." District farmers were appointed who worked closely with them. Leasing of these lands to white farmers remained high, but in the latter year Utes still "controlled 15,243 irrigated acres and leased another 28,819 acres to area farmers." Indian farms were scattered along the river bottoms, and many raised "gardens, vegetables," and watermelons. Ranching also flourished. Horse herds held their own, and cattle and sheep increased from 3,500 and 2,554 in 1911 to 6,663 and 6,400, respectively, in 1922, as a few Uintah and Uncompahgre ranchers prospered and a grazing association was organized. Alfalfa seed did exceptionally well until the late twenties, after which drought and disease reduced production and sales.[44]

Despite agricultural progress, the Ute population continued to decline. A 1909 census showed a population of only 1,208 Northern Utes—443 Uintahs, 469 Uncompahgres, and 296 White Rivers. Indians often refused to send their children to the boarding schools, and when they did the death rate from white diseases terrified them. The downward trend in numbers continued until 1930, when it bottomed out at 917.[45]

Native religions emerged during this period. Many Northern Utes, like other Utah Indians, had "adopted the outward trappings of Christianity—becoming nominal Mormons, Episcopalians, or both." They also recognized Native medicine men, maintained an interest in the traditional Bear Dance, and "experimented with the Sun Dance and Peyote religions."[46] The Uintahs first began sponsoring Sun Dances in 1890, importing the dance from the Wind River Shoshones. According to anthropologist Joseph Jorgensen, the Utes sought "redemptive" influences in the Sun Dance, hoping it would lead to better health, help them cope with change, and allow them to reject white evils—all to the end that individual and societal integrity and identity could be maintained.

Sun Dances were held annually around Whiterocks during the 1890s and spread from there to the Ute Mountain and Southern Ute bands. Each of the three reservation groups traveled the trail along the tortuous rim of Desolation Canyon and crossed the Roan Cliffs and the Green and Colorado Rivers to attend the other's Sun Dances.[47]

Dances were held in a "corral" fashioned with a forked center pole made of cottonwood. From it extended twelve peeled lodgepole pines thirty feet in length, making a circumference of perhaps sixty feet around which leaned a wall of branches cut in full leaf. An opening on the east side faced directly into the rising sun. Around the walls were "stalls" for dancers. As many as three hundred dancers were said to have participated in the 1911 event. After 1906 spectators were apparently tolerated for a price, and many whites observed the seventy-two-hour ritual, which was accompanied by drums and occasional singing. Rest stops were permitted, but dancers refrained from sleeping, eating, or drinking. Minutes before sunrise dancers walked to the eastern opening and as the sun rose gazed steadily at it, scooping in its rays and symbolically cleansing their bodies with them. On the final day men fell frequently, signifying they were receiving visions as well as far gone in fatigue.[48] Strong with cultural meaning, the Sun Dance aroused heavy opposition. It was banned in 1913, but when social worker John Collier became Indian commissioner in 1933 both the Native American Church (the Peyote Way) and the Sun Dance were permitted as legitimate Indian religions.

Peyote worship apparently came to the Utes from the Dakotas. Some authorities estimate that this occurred with the return of the White Rivers in 1908, but others attribute the arrival to a Sioux missionary in 1914 who gladly turned a profit by selling hallucinogenic peyote buttons. Most students of peyotism in Utah agree that it began with the Uintah band and spread to the Goshutes, Paiutes, Southern and Ute Mountain Utes, and the San Juan Navajos. It was transmitted through intermarriage, bilingualism, and contacts made in the Indian Civilian Conservation Corps.

Christianized Utes both joined the movement and opposed it, as did the BIA and Utah whites. By 1919 more than 550 Northern Utes are said to have embraced the Peyote Way—more than half the total tribe. After a thorough consideration of earlier studies and oral accounts, David F. Aberle and Omer C. Stewart concluded in 1957 that while not "triumphant" during the 1917–31 period, "the cult" was far from inactive. Looking at the Navajos as well, they concluded it was "vigorous" and "dominant" by 1940. Like the Sun Dance, the Peyote Way included Native American and Christian features and looked to the curing of psychological and physical ills and the stabilizing of Indian society.[49]

In order to promote assimilation, Albert Kneale, reservation superintendent from 1915 to 1925, encouraged Ute parents to withdraw their children from the boarding school at Whiterocks and enroll them instead in local public schools. "If I can put these Indian children into the public schools among white boys and girls and let them fight and learn that twenty-five cents is a quarter of a dollar, by the end of six years I can abolish the Indian agency altogether, for the Indian population will be gradually assimilated in the affairs of the communities, and the Indians will be able to take care of themselves," he optimistically forecast in 1925. But Anglos and Utes resisted Kneale's plan; one schoolteacher refused to teach Indians in her class, and the school district defended her. At another school parents blocked the registration of Ute children on the grounds that they posed a health hazard. Ute parents who enrolled their children in the public schools often kept their sons and daughters at home. Not until 1935, when the Ute agency made its tuition payments to school districts contingent upon students' attendance rather than merely their enrollment, did attendance rise. By the mid-1930s close to 100 Utes attended public schools in the basin regularly. But racism and antagonism remained palpable in the public schools.[50]

Although the Depression made proportionately less difference to Utes than to whites, Utes suffered grievously. By 1936 they cultivated only 58 percent of "their predepression" acreage, crops dropped to "50 percent of the 1926–1931 state average," and sheep replaced cattle as more intensive grazers. Problems incident to the mechanization of agriculture, transportation, collapsing markets, and the general decline of rural Utah affected them adversely. Together with a succession of cash settlements for earlier land losses that began in 1911, the receipts of which tended to increase dependency among the Uintah-Ouray Utes, farm contraction and continued leasing tended to place them at the periphery of society. An economically marginal people, they were anything but in control of their own destiny as the New Deal was launched.[51]

For the Northern Utes, the Indian New Deal was a mixed bag. The agrarianism that had been pushed upon Indians for four decades was dropped from Commissioner John Collier's program, and a tribal land base was reestablished. The Uintah-Ouray Business Committee was able to buy back some three hundred thousand dollars' worth of land from whites within the Uncompahgre Grazing Reserve. In 1941 217,000 acres "of opened and unsold lands within the reservation" were returned by the secretary of the interior, and finally, in 1948, the Hill Creek Extension was restored, bringing some 726,000 acres of the nearly 2 million acres of the former Uncompahgre Reservation back under partial Indian control. The Indian New Deal permitted tribes to organize politically and draft constitutions. Full-blooded Utes found the white political models of the Indian Reorganization Act bewildering and frustrating. Mixed bloods and a few Uncompahgre ranchers surged to the fore, arousing resentment that culminated in action cutting mixed bloods from the tribe.[52]

It had been a hectic half century. As historian David Lewis observes, the Northern Utes had "searched for a balance between self and group, needs and wants," as they had been "pushed and pulled" from collectivism to individualism and back again to collectivism. When they "finally ventured into market production," their efforts were "swept away" by the Depression's collapse. "Full incorporation and dependency followed in 1937," when they "accepted the Indian Reorganization Act and an economy based on per-capita income from claims cases, leases, and natural resource royalties."[53] Subject to many of the same forces were the Northern Navajos.

NAVAJOS IN UTAH

By 1896 the overall Navajo population, which had been reduced by the Long Walk to Fort Sumner, had increased to about twenty thousand, nearly half of whom competed with whites for off-reservation grazing.[54]

An industrious people, Navajos early in the twentieth century tended subsistence farms and ran sheep, which were owned and managed by both women and men. Sheep gave the Navajo economy two marketable products (wool and lambs), which they, and the ubiquitous Navajo traders, improved upon through weaving, a traditional craft plied by the women. Navajos also had a fair number of cattle and thousands of horses, which had great noncommercial value in Navajo society. In times of stress they continued to hunt and gather. Men joined work crews for railroad construction, commercial agriculture, and forestry. On the whole, the Navajo people followed their herds and available water. Moving from one camp—a hogan, corrals, and water hole—to another, they left multiple sets of facilities unoccupied for much of every year and, when conditions demanded, abandoned improvements for longer periods.

Enlarged again and again, the sixteen million acres of the Navajo Reservation spread through northeast Arizona, northwest New Mexico, and an isolated and rugged stretch south of the San Juan River in Utah in 1896. Yet given its physical characteristics and the character of the Navajos, it was never large enough. Encouraged by agents and traders, and following ancient custom, Navajo herdsmen pressed north onto the public domain in San Juan County, where they were welcomed by traders and Protestant missionaries, but met head-on by Mormon stockmen who harbored a special sympathy for Indians but were determined to bar the Navajos from the public domain. Other factors working against Navajo penetration north of the river included Ute and Paiute claims; the Indian agency's desire to concentrate Indian populations for education, health care, and economic development; and the assimilationist-agrarian predilections that guided Indian policy. Meanwhile, the Navajos' pastoral instincts, their growing population, the BIA's determined defense of Navajos' range rights on the public domain, and competition between Protestants and the Mormons encouraged or promoted migration to the north. So did the fact that white interests were defended by so few people. The number of white residents in the vast San Juan County was minuscule: 204 in 1880; 365 in 1890, as compared to "200–300 Navajos"; and 1,023 in 1900, compared to 2,000 Indians reported by agent William T. Shelton in 1906.[55]

The first officially recognized Navajo homesteads were established on the public domain north of the San Juan River during the late 1880s, and seven trading posts were opened along its north banks. As agent S. S. Patterson reported in 1887, traders anxious to be free of agency restraints and open new resources sought to "persuade and invite the Indians to trade with them, at the same time telling them that they have as much right to locate upon the lands of the public domain as white men." The extent of Navajo trade is hard to estimate, but in good times it flourished, with as many as 950 Navajos trading at the Bluff Co-op in 1908, for example.[56]

The panic of 1893–94 and a decadelong drought all but stopped the Navajo movement north of the river. All of the trading posts but one closed by 1895.[57] Once the economy picked up, Navajos returned to the public domain, particularly at Aneth, where McElmo Creek ran into the river.

By 1898 Methodist missionaries Howard R. Antes and his wife opened the Navajo Faith Mission there. Antes quickly became a vocal advocate of Navajo rights to the public domain.[58] Especially galling was an attempt on the part of San Juan County (Mormons) to "license" or tax Navajo sheep that ran on the public domain.[59] When the agency approved the tax, Antes issued grazing passes to help Navajos resist white efforts to expel them from the public domain, claiming official authority.[60]

Several remarkable white women entered the Northern Navajo service at this time, including Harriet M. Peabody, a five-year Aneth veteran who advocated that "these self supporting Indians" be given individual allotments on the public domain as a means of protecting established Navajo claims.[61]

In 1904 Howard Antes went directly to President Roosevelt with a request that the triangle between the mouth of Montezuma Creek, the Colorado border, and the point where the San Juan enters Utah near the Four Corners be added to the reservation. When this request reached Shiprock, a newly appointed Indian agent, William T. Shelton, took the first of many trips to the lower river, where he found some "250 Navajos" around Aneth. They were, he judged, a "barbarous people," hopelessly lacking in morality but for all that deserving of attention by merit of improvements they had built there. Finding no white improvements in the triangle that became the Aneth Extension except three traders along the river and the Antes mission, he immediately endorsed Antes's request. On May 15, 1905, the Aneth–Montezuma Creek area was set apart by executive order for Navajo use. In 1933 the Aneth Extension–Paiute Strip area was added.[62]

Shelton then moved to further rout the forces of "ignorance and superstition." He pushed road development and advocated schooling, both for its civilizing effect and as a kind of punitive measure against nonconforming parents. Aneth and Bluff seemed to be possible school sites, and the Bluff Mormons and missionary Antes began to tout the virtues of their respective properties. Shelton estimated two thousand Indians, "mostly Navajos, lived in the area" and that with the exception of Bluff, "all the public land north of the San Juan...was occupied by" them. To encourage herd development, he limited sheep sales to wethers and aged ewes and located three new dipping vats north of the river in 1906. Hoping to facilitate schools, he also worked to induce the Navajos to settle more permanently in one place. Dispatching agency farmers and matrons and various headmen to announce his programs, he also activated a six-man Indian police force. All of this was infused with Shelton's reformism. Alcohol, gambling, polygamy, rape, firearms, and opposition to his programs were on the straitlaced agent's hit list.[63]

Shelton's most serious challenge came from an enigmatic Navajo called Ba'álílee, or "the One with Supernatural Power." An Aneth resident of remarkable attainments, Ba'álílee was known as a healer, as a sorcerer, and, shortly, as Shelton's opponent. About thirty resisters rallied to his camp, where they became a threat to Shelton and the agency. After it became apparent that no Utah Navajo dared serve in his police force and that his representatives would be either scorned or hexed, Shelton himself visited Ba'álílee in 1907. Although Shelton temporarily isolated Ba'álílee from his supporters, the medicine man resisted more fiercely, so Shelton requested a show of military force. Once the army was in the area, it decided to seize Ba'álílee and his most belligerent supporters. In the process two young Navajos were killed.[64]

Without benefit of court action, Ba'álílee and nine others were imprisoned for two years at Fort Huachuca, Arizona. Before they left the reservation, the offenders told Navajo dignitaries their hearts had changed. According to Captain Harry Williard, the "prisoners, one and all, advised the other Indians" to turn in their arms, "dip their sheep...send their children to school...[and] attend to their flocks and farms." They also urged them to "stop raping...[and] selling girls,...having several wives,...introducing whiskey,...making bad medicine,...gambling,...[and] lying."[65]

Although the response was mixed, most Indians accepted the spirit of the prisoners' farewell. Jim Joe reported in a letter that Navajos near the Rincon, perhaps a hundred families by this time, and in Monument Valley were "all feeling good" about Ba'álílee. It was even "all right" that one of the two boys killed was from Joe's camp; he had been warned but "had no ear" and got what he deserved. In a spirit of conciliation Joe concluded he would "work on the road." In a move to quiet any "remaining unrest," Shelton issued wagons at Aneth "in exchange for labor."[66]

Less inclined to conciliation was Howard Antes. By this time badly inflamed against Shelton for not buying his Aneth improvements, the missionary turned his pen on the agent's handling of the Ba'álílee affair. Among other things, he charged that the prisoners' dependents were destitute. Shelton went again in April 1908 to Aneth, where he was reassured as to their well-being by traders, agency personnel, and wealthy sheepmen. In spite of a forced apology following an investigation of his charges by General Hugh Scott, Antes maneuvered Shelton into buying his Aneth improvements for twelve hundred dollars.[67]

In the years that followed, Navajo numbers continued to increase, according to "reservation censuses," mounting from "17,204 people in 1890, to 21,009 in 1900, and 38,787 in 1930." The Paiute Strip, which had swung back and forth from public domain to Indian homeland according to the variables of economic interests, became a permanent part of the Navajo Reservation in 1933 after a spirited appeal in 1929 by twenty-one-year-old Sherman Institute graduate and Monument Valley "spokesperson" Elsi Holiday and other sympathizers. Perhaps more important was that the Mormon cattlemen promised not to use Monument Valley as a winter range as long as the Navajos would give up their filed allotments north of the San Juan River, except for the Aneth Extension. The Navajos would stay south of the San Juan River for both grazing and settling purposes.[68]

Utah Navajos were drawn reluctantly into the federal and tribal administrative apparatus. The 1903 establishment of the Shiprock agency had been a first step. In the midteens Navajos were further subdivided into six subagencies, with both the Western and the Shiprock agencies extending into Utah. In 1923 a tribal business council competent to sign for petroleum and other resource exploitation was organized, first in a twelve-man version and later as a seventy-person body. In 1927 chapter houses were inaugurated to address local economic problems, distribute rations, and arrange loans. One hundred chapters had been set up by 1933 on the entire reservation, although few chapter houses were found in outlying districts such as Utah.[69]

On the Navajo Reservation, Commissioner John Collier's Indian New Deal and the Soil Conservation Service instituted stock reduction, a conservation measure taken to reduce the approximately one million sheep units foraging on the reservation by about half. In Utah Navajos ran sheep between Four Corners and the Rincon, on both sides of the river, farther north up McElmo Creek on the Aneth Extension, and along Montezuma Creek on the public domain, as well as on McCracken and White Mesas. Extending from Monument Valley and elsewhere south of the San Juan, sheep also ranged onto the Paiute Strip.

By the 1930s the ranges were badly overstocked, and water was in short supply. The Indian Irrigation Service (IIS) had been developing water holes for a quarter of a century, and many grazing areas not accessible early had been opened and seriously overgrazed. Complicating all of this was a region-wide drought that culminated in the devastating year of 1934. Desperate, Navajos hunted new range and supplemented the water-development efforts of the IIS, digging wells, clearing springs, and erecting dams. With brush barriers they turned mesas, rims, and box canyons into management facilities that better utilized water.[70]

Tribal leaders reluctantly accepted Collier's call for sheep reduction with the assurance that they would receive new public domain lands in New Mexico, Arizona, and Utah into which they could continue to expand. When the promised trade-off failed to materialize, they blamed Collier for both the failure and the loss of wealth incurred through sheep reduction. The number of sheep and goats on Navajo lands in southeastern Utah fell from more than sixty-three thousand in 1930 to thirty-six thousand in 1934. Partly in retaliation, Navajos voted to reject the Indian Reorganization Act championed by Collier with its provisions for self-government. Instead, their six subagencies were combined into a single administrative headquarters at Window Rock, consolidating services under a tribal code that was revised in 1938 under Collier, the archenemy.[71]

Governmental services continued to lie largely beyond the reach of Utah Navajos, as they had always done. Navajo children were refused admission to the public school at Bluff and perhaps elsewhere, and Navajos were hardly more welcome at white hospitals. The most convenient of the reservation hospitals was in faraway Shiprock, and to many reservation hospitals seemed places of infection more than houses of healing. In keeping with Collier's emphasis on Native culture, fifty-one new day schools were built, bringing the total on the entire reservation to fifty-seven by 1940. But the day schools were poorly equipped, insufficiently staffed, and lacking in road and water systems. Only the Navajo Mountain day school and a boarding school at Aneth were in Utah. Father H. B. Liebler finally brought a day school and minimal medical benefits to Bluff Navajos in the mid-1940s at St. Christopher's Mission.[72]

The changes of the era had been profound for the Navajos. Herd reduction had been effected with socioeconomic consequences only somewhat less traumatic than the Long Walk itself. Traditional farming, gathering, and raiding activities were ended, as was herding for many who needed it most. More critical yet, expansion, the way of Navajos since time immemorial, was ended. The elements of Navajo self-reliance were drastically misshapen.[73] Yet population growth continued.

For all Utah Indians, statehood had brought continuing defeat, dependency, and marginal existence at what might be called the whiplash end of American pluralism, although Navajos did manage to extend their land base in Utah in 1905. Sporadic federal campaigns to incorporate Utah's Indians within the mainstream generally failed. By 1940 Utes remained at the mercy of whites who leased their lands and ran stock around them, continuing victims of adjustments that acknowledged earlier injustice but did little to prepare them for life in the midcentury West. Paiutes and Goshutes were impoverished in their tiny southern and western Utah enclaves. Shoshones at Washakie managed to hold on to some land until they scattered to wartime jobs in the 1940s. At that point, tribal arrangements among the Eastern, Northwestern, and Western Shoshones defined community away from Box Elder County.

8

CHANGING FEDERALISM

The Outdoors and Its Management

SANCTUARY: "LANDSCAPE OF HOPE"

Mixing pleasure and business, Brigham Young and a party of Mormon dignitaries made a tour of southern Utah in 1864 that climaxed at the "Towers of the Rio Virgen" in what became Zion National Park. Transfixed by the juxtaposition of splendor and desolation, Young paused to describe the canyon as the ultimate retreat from hostile forces, and so it was viewed—hence the name "Little Zion." The name signified a profound attachment to place that for the earliest Utahns reached far beyond the dictates of economic advantage or political abstraction.[1] Later, Zion Canyon attracted interests beyond Mormondom and became a retreat of a different kind, making it a new kind of mecca. To it came visitors seeking moral and emotional sanctuary. Their quest reflected a nationwide shift in attitude, a shift that caused a reversal in public land policies from selling the public domain to preserving and protecting it.

Coinciding with the first half century of statehood, this transition precipitated some of Utah's most painful adjustments. For decades preceding 1896, the "great frontier" worldwide had been distributed to corporate and private interests with reckless abandon. Like Zion Canyon, much of Utah had sharply limited prospects

as private property, a condition that for decades kept most of the land in the territory under very loose federal oversight. This situation maximized local use, whether
by Mormons, miners, or railroads.[2] In the 1890s the expectation that the flow of
land to local control would continue seemed fully validated. Statehood's Enabling
Act appeared to give Utah well over one-eighth of its fifty-two-million-acre landmass as grants-in-aid. Moreover, the Carey Act of 1894 offered arid states up to one
million acres to promote irrigated settlement. Similarly, the Reclamation Act of
1902 augured well for passing a landed patrimony to settlers. Nevertheless, the federal government incorporated valuable timbered lands in forest reserves in the late
1890s on the theory that a "wider public good would be served by retaining title in
the government." Once established, national forests were administered under what
many Utahns regarded as dangerously paternalistic regulations. Then in the 1930s
the entire remaining public domain was closed to settlement. Taken together, the
closing of the public domain and federal regulation of activities thereon considerably reduced the self-rule Utahns expected to enjoy after statehood. As a later state
official put it, with most "of its land in federal ownership," and national interest in
Utah as a scenic and recreational destination emerging, Utah fell "a country mile
[short] of having sovereign authority equal to the Original States."[3]

"THIS PLACE IS MINE"

Although early Mormons were moved more by Old Testament imagery than
romanticism (much less a wilderness ethic), their appreciation for Utah's mountains and deserts grew quickly after their arrival. The desert's threat to human life
often blinded pioneers, but involvement with nature became progressively broader
as mastery over the desert increased. By the time of statehood, a wide variety of outdoor interests flourished.[4]

Near the forefront of the growing national affinity for the natural were Salt Lake
City–based artists and publicists who mixed aesthetic interests with sense of place.
Among these was H. L. A. Culmer, an English-born landscape artist and journalist
who decried the ravages of sheep grazing, guided landscapists Albert Bierstadt and
Thomas Moran on a sightseeing tour of the Wasatch Mountains, and gave feminine
names to many Wasatch lakes. Culmer toured widely in the state, promoted irrigation projects on the Green and San Rafael Rivers, and publicized the canyonlands
with some of Utah's finest landscape paintings.[5]

Even nearer the spirit of the state's emerging naturalism was English-born
artist-poet Alfred Lambourne. Immigrating in the mid-1860s, Lambourne had visited the "Towers of the Virgen" by 1870. In the following years he reveled in high
country, popularized the Wasatch and Uinta Mountains in hundreds of local articles, and wrote more than a dozen books, all personally illustrated. His sense of

place was given classic dimension in *Our Inland Sea* (1909), which recounted his experience as a homesteader on the Great Salt Lake's Gunnison Island. "That is best," he reminisced, "that lieth nearest." "Without title or deed...a place becomes a part of us...it is ours...we own it...absorb it...have our lives shaped by it" and stamp it "with our individuality." Speaking of Gunnison Island, Lambourne concluded: "THIS PLACE IS MINE!"[6]

Yet sense of place was widely shared. It showed up among homesteaders and ranchers as well as town and city dwellers, in the music of Tabernacle Choir conductor Evan Stephens, and in the benefactions of industrialists such as copper magnate Enos Wall and Park City millionaire Edwin Holmes.

It also surfaced in the work of scientists and engineers, some of whom had accompanied John Wesley Powell and the other great surveyors in their Utah visits of the 1870s. Plant taxonomy was passionately pursued by both women and men. Jane Carrington, daughter of a Mormon assistant to Howard Stansbury, collected "59 species in the basin of the Great Salt Lake." Ellen Powell Thompson, Powell's sister, is credited with prime southern Utah collections, as was F. M. Bishop, Powell expedition scientist who later taught at the University of Deseret. Collecting also were Kane County rancher A. L. Siler, cactus expert for the Wheeler Survey, and Edward Palmer of the Smithsonian Institution and Peabody Museum.[7]

Indeed, the golden age of Utah plant taxonomy may have been the 1890s. In 1892 and again in 1895 Alice Eastwood of Denver shocked southern Utah with prolonged Grand and San Juan County tours in the sole company of cowboy archaeologist Albert Wetherill. She remained interested in Utah through her final trip in 1941 at the age of eighty-two.[8] As a Utah collector, Eastwood was excelled only by Marcus Jones, a self-promoting University of Utah professor. Captivated by the state's outdoors, Jones unflaggingly publicized problems related to grazing, watershed management, meteorology, petroleum booms, and coal claims. Although new plant identifications diminished after 1900, contributions continued in the twentieth century by Professors J. H. Linford and A. O. Garrett, an underappreciated University of Utah botanist. Better known was the university's Walter P. Cottam, who after 1920 led the way in shifting attention from taxonomy to plant ecology. Bold in denunciation, Cottam's work, including *Is Utah Sahara Bound?* (1947) and *Our Renewable Wild Lands* (1961), retained much of the Progressive Era's faith in science.[9]

The study of birds led others to the field. The "dean of Utah's field ornithologists," C. W. Lockerbie, improved a boyhood interest that began along the Jordan River, where he robbed nests, created an egg collection, counted flight patterns, gunned down "bad birds," and bought thousands of ducks from local shooters for Salt Lake's west-side markets. Clarence Cottam and Walter Cottam's introduction to the biological sciences grew from a 1907 meeting with unnamed ornithologists classifying birds on their St. George farm. First reproving the boys sharply when Walter killed a bird, the ornithologists instructed them in the merits of scientific study. With help from Vasco Tanner at Dixie College and later Brigham Young University, Clarence rose in the US Biological Survey (later the Fish and Wildlife Service) to play a major role in the fight against pesticides.

At the University of Utah geologists James E. Talmage and F. J. Pack often led geology field trips. After 1920 widely heralded summer schools were instituted at the Utah State Agricultural College and at BYU's Aspen Grove. There the loved and gentle conservationist J. H. Paul drew a following that would later give his writing on floods and watershed rehabilitation instant authority.[10]

Antiquarians and archeologists nurtured an interest in natural history while leaving conflicting marks on southern Utah. At least from William Huntington's 1854 discovery of Hovenweep's spectacular towers, the Four Corners country was recognized for its rich prehistoric remains. Abetted by the work of Powell and Henry Gannet, W. H. Holmes, and William H. Jackson of the Hayden survey, interest in prehistory grew, while Mormon railroader and sometime general authority John W. Young launched the Deseret Museum, which included Indian collections.

Accompanying this development was an awakened interest in southeastern Utah's stupendous canyonlands. Locals such as prospector Cass Hite, slickrock rancher A. J. Scorup, and guide-caretaker Zeke Johnson promoted White Canyon's Natural Bridges. From his ferry across the Colorado, Hite visited the bridges as early as 1883, as did Scorup and other cowboys by the mid-1890s. In 1903 Scorup guided mine promoter H. J. Long to the bridges, and in 1905, after the story of their visit appeared in *Century Magazine*, Scorup also led the Salt Lake Commercial Club's White Canyon expedition. Promoted by club president Edwin Holmes, the party consisted of Culmer; Holmes's son Carlton; S. T. Whitaker, director of Utah exhibits at various world fairs; and Bluff's Frank Adams, an experienced pot-digger.

In 1906 Congress passed the National Antiquities Act. The next year Byron Cummings of the University of Utah mapped White Canyon. On the basis of those maps Theodore Roosevelt established the Natural Bridges National Monument in April 1908. As custodian of the monument, Blanding raconteur Zeke Johnson emerged as perhaps the foremost Utah guide, taking generations of photographers, journalists, and promoters into the canyonlands. Among them were advocates of a vast national park encompassing Monument Valley, Navajo Mountain, Rainbow Bridge, the lower canyon of the San Juan, and Glen Canyon on the Colorado. As forces built, they undertook the Rainbow Bridge–Monument Valley Expedition, which they hoped would move Congress to establish a giant park.[11]

Cowboy antiquarians were important to archaeology. These included Bluff City Mormons C. L. Christensen, A. J. Scorup, and Frank Adams, as well as Bluff's token Gentile Charles Goodman. More important were Colorado-based Charles McLoyd and C. C. Graham and the five Wetherill brothers, especially Richard (nicknamed Anasazi by the Navajos); Alfred, who guided botanist Alice Eastwood; and, John, a Navajo trader at Oljato in Utah's Monument Valley. During the late 1880s the Wetherills discovered Cliff Palace and dozens of other Mesa Verde ruins. In time they scattered through the Four Corners, responding to the Navajo trade, San Juan gold, oil, freight, and tourism, as well as ranching.

But cliff dwellings remained their passion. They searched the entire San Juan Basin for ruins. Defying Indians' opposition to grave digging, they lacked formal learning, institutional backing, or legislative sanction. But for upwards of a quarter century curators, professors, speculators, publicists, and government officials enlisted their aid. Artifacts poured from their diggings, lecture tours flourished, and scores of museums were stocked. Especially productive were Utah digs at Grand Gulch, White Canyon, Montezuma Canyon, and Alkali Ridge. In the successive burial and material layers of these excavations, Richard Wetherill, Charles McLoyd, and C. C. Graham, who had worked Grand Gulch before him, found evidence of cultural progression from Basketmaker beginnings to classic pueblo builders. Many trained scientists, including the University of Utah's Henry Montgomery, scoffed at their claims for stratigraphic progression.[12]

But the time of the cowboy antiquarian was passing, and the National Antiquities Act began to restrict pot-digging. Richard Wetherill was killed by a Navajo at Chaco Canyon in 1910 amid racial, economic, and bureaucratic tensions. Alfred increasingly felt the sting of alienation as professionalism closed the door on pioneer diggers, and canyonlands specialists John and Louisa Wetherill moved from Oljato to Kayenta, Arizona.[13]

No one did more to stimulate Utah's interest in the Four Corners than Byron Cummings. To arouse interest in the state's "great natural wonders and beauties" and its "ancient people," Cummings initiated a summer field program in 1907. Subsidized by mining millionaire Enos Wall and functioning under the auspices of the Archeological Institute of America, Cummings mapped the Natural Bridges and collected for the university's museum of natural history. In 1908 he joined Harvard's A. V. Kidder in a dig at Alkali Ridge southeast of Monticello. At summer's end he heard exciting rumors from Navajos of a monster arch in the slickrock labyrinth between Navajo Mountain and the Colorado River. Guided by John Wetherhill, Cummings devoted the next summer to exploring the great northern Arizona sites that became the Navajo National Monument. With W. D. Douglass of the General Land Office (GLO), he "discovered" Utah's Rainbow Bridge, which immediately attracted nationwide interest.[14]

Well-connected sojourners also made their way to the Four Corners region to explore it for themselves. Frederick Dellanbaugh, advantaged New Yorker and Powell expedition boatman and topographer, long presided as "poet laureate" of canyonlands adventure. John Riis, son of social commentator Jacob Riis and protégé of Teddy Roosevelt, traveled to the La Sal National Forest. In *Ranger Trails* (1937), he gloried in the primitive. Prompted by a barrage of *National Geographic* articles, Robert Aird and John Newell, son of US Reclamation Service director Arthur Newell, hiked 320 miles from Blanding to the Natural Bridges and then back via Monument Valley to prehistoric sites near the Colorado border in 1923. As Aird noted, it was a junket in which "untamed ruggedness and...extreme nature" roused "primal impulse[s]." In contrast to their short flirtation, Everett Ruess, a boyish but "sensitive and intuitive" privileged Californian, wandered the Four Corners from 1931 until his disappearance southeast of Escalante late in 1934. A "vagabond for beauty," Ruess's haunting refrain is a commentary on how the landscape shapes people and gives form to legend.[15]

Cummings's relative and student Neil Judd often checked prehistoric sites in southern Utah and the Arizona Strip and conducted exploratory digs at Beaver, Kanab, and Paragonah. Guided by Navajo Cauz-zus-see, Judd led the 1923 expedition to the Rainbow Bridge and the stone jungle around the mouth of the San Juan.[16]

Less romantic yet still by no means pragmatic was Earl Douglass, excavator at the Uinta Basin's dinosaur quarry. A foremost mammalian paleontologist, Douglass let a side excursion into Jurassic fossils become a lasting contribution to Utah when in 1909 he located the steeply tipped geological phenomenon that became one of the world's most productive dinosaur quarries. Bringing his wife and extended family, Douglass hired locals including John T. Kay and his sons Jay and LeRoy to work the quarry, homesteaded the site to fend off poachers, and supported a Carnegie Museum effort that won national monument status for the quarry in 1915. Only aborning, the Park Service set no regulations for Dinosaur Monument, and the museum "mined" the site, warehoused original fossils, and wholesaled plaster casts to museums around the world. Advocating an on-site exhibit, Douglass was stymied by the Carnegie Museum but encouraged by locals who looked on the museum and the Park Service as consummate grave robbers.

In 1923 the Carnegie Museum, to which Douglass had shipped more than six hundred thousand pounds of materials, closed its quarry. Busy with other schemes, the Park Service still showed little interest. Congressman Don Colton of Vernal introduced a bill to fund operations that got nowhere. For the rest of the 1920s, as historian Mark Harvey writes, the Park Service "virtually abandoned Dinosaur National Monument." Somehow the Smithsonian Institution and the University of Utah kept Douglass busy for a year, and in September a "dinosaur caravan," consisting of twelve wagons, made a well-publicized trip to the university, where Douglass prepared the fossils for mounting. John Kay was soon hired at the university and his son LeRoy by the Carnegie Museum. The geology "professorship" Douglass anticipated fell through, perhaps, as writer Wallace Stegner asserted, because the LDS Church did not approve of Douglass. Douglass lost his homestead to unpaid taxes and eked out a meager living as a consultant in Salt Lake City, where he died in 1931. Seven years later the monument was enlarged to "include scenic canyons of the Green and Yampa rivers." At Vernal the Field House of Natural History was established in the 1940s and directed by Ernie Untermann and Billie Untermann.[17]

CONSERVATION: THE FOREST SERVICE

At the same time that interest in the state's flora, fauna, and natural history was growing, a public conservation movement was blossoming. Enthusiasm for conservation drew strength from major national and regional forces. Yet conditions in Utah made for a distinctive experience in the conservation of its forestlands and watersheds.

Rooted in artist George Catlin's vision of a "nation's park," the impulse to reserve certain lands in the public interest had seen Yosemite become a state park and Yellowstone the first national park by 1872. With incipient Progressive ideas of reform and regulation, the perception that the frontier was closing, and the growing recognition that prodigious waste of the nation's forests could not continue indefinitely, preservation developed a utilitarian turn by 1891 when the far-reaching Forest Reserve Act was passed. Under its terms in the 1890s, Presidents Harrison, Cleveland, and McKinley (two Republicans and a Democrat) created forest reserves by withdrawing some forty-six million acres of the public domain from homesteading and other forms of private entry. As it further developed under Theodore Roosevelt and forester Gifford Pinchot, conservation came to stand for the "greatest good for the greatest number," as prescribed "by the scientific and responsible few." It focused on regulated utilitarian development and commodity production, sustained management of natural resources to prevent waste, and federal retention of key resources.[18]

Utah was caught on the cusp of this change in the 1890s as it came under the paternalistic supervision of federal agencies, including the Forest Service, the Park Service, and the Grazing Service. As Utah forests and rangelands were incorporated within a system of federal ownership and management, the no-holds-barred access to resource development that most Utahns looked on as the great patrimony of statehood and their chief means of achieving equality in the sisterhood of states was lost. Some championed and others opposed the federal agencies. Conflict was bitter throughout the early decades of statehood, as the pioneer culture of wilderness conquest gave way before the centralizing national pressure for conservation.[19]

With nearly 70 percent of the land federally owned, questions about land use penetrated virtually all walks of life. Utah leaders were committed utilitarians; economic growth through private ownership and development of land resources seemed essential. Few had responded more directly to wilderness sanctuary than the Mormons, among whom principles of stewardship and progress made for responsible use of farms and water. Yet the Mormon approach to natural resources was overlaid with fierce protection of individual and local interests and complicated further by belief in an imminent apocalypse that perhaps diverted some from the long-range implications of resource abuse.[20]

Overlapping and absorbing Mormon utilitarianism was the developmental ethos of corporate and political Utah, which operated on the assumption that high environmental costs were inherent in the effort to make Utah's low-grade natural endowment competitive. Nevertheless, a sense of environmental responsibility was not entirely lacking, and to some Utah's austere environment made waste seem especially abhorrent. To these people, regulation seemed inevitable. Its extent, who applied it, and how it could be turned to advantage were harder to define.

Some Utahns took preservation seriously when Presidents Harrison and Cleveland established forest reserves. Indeed, by 1896 a forestry association was supported by Governor Wells and headed by prominent business and professional people, including G. W. Snow, surveyor general at the Salt Lake branch of the General Land Office. Probably included also were J. W. Sanborn, Samuel Fortier, and G. L. Swendsen of the Agricultural College.[21]

The movement was likely orchestrated by Washington: G. W. Snow of the federal Land Office began surveying Uinta Mountain watersheds in July 1895. Aided by architect Richard Kletting and A. F. Doremus, he drew maps and drafted plans for three reserves bracketing the "headwaters of...the Bear, the Weber, the Provo, and the Duchesne." Others worked quietly to educate the public about the "wanton destruction" of Utah's watersheds and advocated "parking," or planting trees. After the state legislature drafted a "timber reserve" petition, Republican congressman C. E. Allen presented it to the secretary of the interior. When Cleveland included the Uinta Reserve in his February 1897 forest withdrawal, some viewed it as an "answer to" Utah demands, not as a dangerous extension of federal power. With the proreserve forces mobilized, the protest from Utah's delegation at the size of the Uinta withdrawal—about a million acres—was far less vociferous than in neighbor states.[22]

Changing its tack, the second state legislature memorialized Congress for a state park near Fish Lake in Sevier and Wayne Counties. The state park idea fell flat, but after a second memorial the president established the Fishlake Reserve by executive proclamation in 1898. Federal officials ignored demands that the reserve be managed by Utahns and that the door be left open for returning the land to the public domain or transferring it to the state. Making the best of this refusal, Wells concluded that since the "state [could]...use...the property," it was perhaps best that the federal government would pay for its management.[23]

The Department of the Interior withdrew a vast central Utah region as national forest on December 1, 1900. Justified as an effort to protect "the water supply of certain cities and towns," it did not inhibit grazing other than in the "Forks of Manti Canyon," where all grazing was stopped and flood controls were erected. Extending 150 miles south, the reserve aroused immediate opposition and was revoked within a year, leading to premature optimism about the efficacy of local resistance.[24]

As a drought cycle climaxed in July 1902, Albert F. Potter, a former Arizona sheepman and Land Office grazing chief, initiated a five-month examination of rangeland from Cache Valley to the Arizona border. Potter found evidence of natural and human problems everywhere.[25] Animals were poor, range was depleted, forests had been overcut for ties, and erosion was common. Dairies and ranches had been crowded off the mountains by sheep, and, ironically, Manti and other central Utah towns were simultaneously threatened by drought and floods. Potter found that most towns favored regulation of grazing, and some even welcomed the prospect of federal control. Only Levan in Juab County seemed neutral. Beaver and Parowan strongly opposed regulation. Most sheepmen opposed federal controls, but a few big flock masters like Thomas Smart and John H. Seely recognized that ranges were overstocked and saw the need.[26]

Numerous small reserves and several larger ones followed almost immediately. Among the smaller were the Salt Lake, Payson, Grantsville, and Vernon Reserves. Larger reserves included the Wasatch, Cache, and Manti. Drawn up to reflect watersheds, most included major untimbered areas, which aroused suspicion about conservationists' greed. Towns and village-based farmer-cattlemen whose local ranges were threatened by large-scale commercial sheep grazing remained strong in their support; in Sanpete, Emery, and Carbon Counties, townspeople and farmers crusaded for the Manti Reserve and once it was established pushed foresters to reduce sheep grazing from some 800,000 animals in 1903 to about 125,000 in 1940.[27] By 1903 Utah's forest reserves encompassed 4 million acres. Over the next five years forests like the Ashley in northeastern Utah, the Dixie in the Southwest, and the La Sal in the Southeast were added, bringing the total acreage to about 7.5 million. Thereafter, forests were consolidated and boundaries adjusted, but little new land was added until the 1930s, when the government purchased scattered pieces to control flooding, erosion, and fires.

Although the prospect of large reserves was threatening, initial fears were low, in part because the General Land Office was slow to establish its administrative apparatus for forest management. GLO surveyors staked out the initial boundaries, and a single agent set up office at Coalville. During the first five years, a few other appointments were made and traveling inspectors worked the public lands, but interference was minimal. However, the Land Office had laid an administrative foundation by 1905 with the appointment of forest supervisors such as W. C. Clos and the legalistic A. W. Jensen.[28]

That year the Division of Forestry, headed by Gifford Pinchot, was transferred from the Interior Department to the Department of Agriculture, redoubling the utilitarian bent of conservation, and the name was changed to the Forest Service. By 1908 District 4, later Region 4, was located in Ogden, and local forests and ranger districts became directly responsible for grazing, watershed, and timber management. Chosen from Utah and the West, foresters shared the values of the farmer-stockman, village, and timber constituencies "with whom they" worked and, like them, discounted "aesthetic, cultural, and recreational concerns." As Thomas Alexander has noted, foresters' values were "a combination of individualist spirit and progressive ethos." Esprit de corps was strong, sense of rightness sure, and commitment to mission almost religious.[29]

Foresters found the intensively used Utah forests to be a challenge. Thousands of farm- and village-based stockmen depended upon grazing permits, giving some Utah forests more permittees than entire neighboring states.[30]

In the quest for limited grazing privileges, bitter battles ensued. In the counties around the Manti Forest, big sheepmen cried foul play and pulled every string to circumvent grazing restrictions. Cattlemen and farmers, who were nearly synonymous, made alliances with townspeople interested in good watersheds. Claiming they represented 90 percent of the forest's users, they argued for heavier cuts on big users, permit redistribution to themselves, and further protection of select watersheds. These collisions were seemingly as bitter as the Mormon controversy of the late 1880s or modern environmental clashes. The lines of hostility and hatred between operators and officials could hardly have been keener.

Early foresters favored the village-based Utah graziers, with sweeping social and environmental consequences. Basing grazing privileges on the doctrines of "commensurate property" and "prior use," the Forest Service immediately eliminated the tramp sheepmen who had no property adjacent to the forest. To accommodate town-based farmers who needed grazing permits for a few animals, foresters also sharply limited the number of animals any permittee could run. Consequently, marginal operators multiplied, while large owners and livestock corporations—the only class with enough at stake to be interested in environmental protection—dwindled. As the Enlarged and the Livestock Homestead Acts (1909 and 1916) took effect, public lands adjacent to the forests passed into private hands, adding more farmers-graziers who needed permits and diminishing the supply of public land open for spring and fall grazing. Displaced alien sheepmen struggled to offset cuts on forest grazing by invading the deserts for year-round grazing, thus complicating the management problems of foresters. Meanwhile, elk and deer populations on national forests skyrocketed between 1919 and 1930. The exacerbated grazing problems created new interest groups as the State Fish and Game Department and sports clubs developed. In the face of these pressures, ranges continued to deteriorate, especially during the prolonged drought of 1930–34.[31]

By contrast with grazing land management, the management of timber in Utah seemed limited in scope, good-spirited, and routine. According to a 1930 USDA report, only "about five million acres" were timbered in the state. Under even the best management, the state's forests could produce only half the 188 million board feet used annually in the state. In practice, "only about 37.5 million board feet" were cut each year.[32]

As a result of heavy usage in the pioneer era by settlers and railroads, by 1902 old-growth timber on accessible watersheds had been fully harvested—at Alta grazing surveyor Albert Potter found no stick big enough to kill a snake.[33]

Although Potter turned up some promising new growth, timber stands were spotty, inferior, and remote. During the early decades silviculture was based on European precedent and imposed practices that did little for Utah's marginal stands. Within a few years foresters adjusted management ideas and in 1908 launched an ambitious, decadelong reconnaissance to ascertain the real character of the state's forest. On the Manti timber reconnaissance proceeded during the summers of 1910–12 and on the La Sal in 1911. The La Sal's twelve-man crew mapped 246,000 acres, estimated timber at 180 million board feet, and treated such questions as species, soil, elevations, fire, insects, and relationship to forage.[34] Backed by such information, Region 4 administrators began by the 1920s to produce timber management plans that aimed at reforestation and sustained yield, community development, and income.[35]

Timber operators played some role in the process. Utah milling had generally been the business of small, seasonal outfits. Access to timber was a problem, and timber drives on the streams of Cache and Summit Counties and on the north slope of the Uinta Mountains continued for years after statehood; in the eastern part of the state, T. W. Branson regularly floated rafts of lumber from Castle Valley to Moab until 1908. Mills were usually portable and powered by steam.[36] On the La Sal Forest, which was typical, most of the sawmills that operated before 1940 were one-man enterprises or partnerships that catered to occasional buyers, local retailers, and projects such as the construction of Moab's Colorado River bridge in 1911. At the highest they produced little more than a half-million feet of lumber annually. As a timber surveyor summarized, it was a wasteful business, "without profit either to exploiters or to the forest."[37]

Where commercial markets existed, Utah forests fared a little better. With coal mines and new railroads rimming its east boundary and with fire-killed timber, the Manti Forest exploited the need for props and ties. For a few years its "timber sale receipts were greater than any forest in Region 4." This continued until 1919, when the Uinta Forest "broke up the Manti prop business by selling green Douglas fir and lodge pole props for about half" price.[38]

Covered with lodgepole pines on its north slope, the Uinta Range played an important part in the Union Pacific Railroad's tie market and the related mining-prop business. Flumes were built in the nineteenth century, and several streams were developed for driving logs. After 1912 the Standard Timber Company, a UP affiliate, took a nine-year contract for more than 9 million hewn ties from the Mill Creek Fork of Bear River. Employing up to 180 people, of whom 125 were Scandinavian, and local tie hacks, Standard set up a commissary and winter camps and with Forest Service help straightened, cribbed, and refurbished Mill Creek and the Bear River with apparent indifference to environmental costs. Hacks averaged 20 ties per day, which were banked along the creek. During the two months of high water, the same crews ran 200,000 to 700,000 ties down the Bear to Evanston.[39]

Forest Service efforts to rationalize timber management were reflected in sustained-yield plans that rangers devised. Paul A. Grossenbach, for example, wrote a long-term management plan in 1942 for the Bear Lake Working Circle, a two-state area of 201,052 acres. Basing calculations on a growth cycle of 150 years and cutting cycles of 50 years, he laid out objectives to: cut for "continuous yield," harvest mature timber, work toward even-aged cuts, coordinate timber harvest and demand, reduce disease and insect damage, encourage reproduction, and replant. Optimum annual sales were projected at 2,260,000 board feet. As it turned out, harvests from the Bear Lake Circle between 1939 and 1948 closely approximated Grossenback's estimates, suggesting that in the state's best forests, sustained yield was working. In the state at large, though, environmental objectives slipped out of focus during the Depression and war years, as commodity production was prioritized over conservation.[40]

Although timber and grazing remained the primary focus of the national forests in the years prior to World War II, some Utahns valued the forests for their recreational potential and the income that might generate. In 1923 the Salt Lake Chamber of Commerce encouraged Utahns to explore the state's national forests. The chamber sponsored an illustrated lecture by J. E. Broaddus highlighting the rugged scenery and splendid recreational opportunities available in the Wasatch and Uinta Mountains. Broaddus criticized most Utahns for failing to appreciate the income potential of Utah's scenery and encouraged them to enter the tourist industry. The number of beautiful, private sites for camping in the Granddaddy Lakes area of the Uintas alone could accommodate every family in New York City, he said.[41]

GRANT LANDS AND STATES' RIGHTS

Conservation interests led not only to regulations on national forestlands but also placed limitations on the state's disposal of its grant lands and resources. Especially important was the school land grant under the Enabling Act, which granted sections two, sixteen, thirty-two, and thirty-six in each of Utah's townships, or one-ninth of the state's total land area, to the state. Utah's officials and congressional delegation contended that "absolute title should vest in the State, irrespective of the character of the lands involved" as of the Enabling Act's 1894 date. The State Land Board's objective was to get the land in the hands of "the largest possible number of citizens." The Land Board encouraged buyers to "designate the land they want[ed] to purchase" and then proposed to get it for them just "as the government does in disposing of the public domain." In this effort the state and the buyers of prospective state lands were often frustrated by conservation interests. State interpretations notwithstanding, grants were construed to exclude lands known to contain minerals at the time of the grant and, increasingly, to entail only surface rights, leaving mineral, coal, petroleum, and waterpower rights under federal control. To subvert such developments, various loopholes were employed, including an ambiguous 1873 coal law under which coal lands were often claimed as agricultural lands or by dummy claimants and convoluted corporate entities. Federal efforts to combat fraud of this kind led to a quarter century of bitterly contested court cases, among other things placing state grant lands in limbo and clouding or reversing title on much state land that had already been transferred to private ownership.[42]

Further enlarging federal control over land that early state officers had assumed would pass unvexed to state and private ownership was the General Leasing Act of 1920. Sponsored by Reed Smoot, the leasing act opened resources to development and paid 45 percent of the proceeds to the state but retained federal ownership and control. Rulings that state grant lands were actually transmitted only when the land in question had been surveyed complicated the flow of even uncontested lands into state and private hands. As late as 1923 nearly two million acres, or approximately "one-third" of the total school grant lands, were still in abeyance for that reason alone. Even worse for the state was the fact that for years, virtually "all the lands selected" by the state had been "sold before they" were actually conveyed "to the State," making for a welter of contested rights.

Lieu-land provisions, which ostensibly offered comparable lands in exchange for disqualified sections, also worked to the state's detriment. While this was fair in theory, Utah's long period of settlement, various federal reservations, and the sheer quantity of seemingly worthless desert made it almost certain inferior lands had to be accepted in lieu-lands transactions. Coupled with policies reserving mineral, petroleum, and hydroelectric resources and attendant leasing regulations, the lieu-lands rulings threatened development, diminished taxable property, and subjected the state to stifling controls.[43]

Under these conditions Utah governors became increasingly less enamored with federal conservation policies and opposed some of them vigorously. Especially galling were the multiplying withdrawals and reserves and the consequent clouding and even cancellation of already perfected titles. Although Governor William Spry (1908–16) worked untiringly to open Zion National Park and Governor George

Dern (1924–32) played a key role in passing Utah's leasing law in 1919, they loudly advocated states' rights in land matters, taking leading positions among the western public land states that all faced numerous restrictions to their development. Applying well-developed constitutional arguments, they held that the public domain had from earliest times been "held in trust" by the federal government, waiting only until states were established to convey it to the people. Late in his administration, however, in somewhat of an about-face, Dern rejected Herbert Hoover's proposal to cede public lands minus mineral rights to the states.

NATIONAL PARKS

Yet Utah officials did not consistently oppose all conservation. Nor was the fight for conservation a simple matter of states' rights versus federal power. Indeed, both state and federal officials played both sides of the field when expediency required. Described as a "business oriented conservationist" by historian Thomas G. Alexander, Senator Reed Smoot played dual roles, acting as the grazier and land developer's advocate, on the one hand, and, on the other, special friend to conservation in Washington. William Spry, who in his second administration (1912–16) worked out a regionally acclaimed states' rights argument, later found himself in opposition to states' rights when he was appointed commissioner of the General Land Office in 1921.[44] Utah officials operated in a complex situation where automobiles tested the strength of rail systems and the Park Service and the Forest Service jockeyed for predominance. All of them worked to mold the era's affinity for "scenic nationalism," tourism, and pure preservation into natural resource programs that would serve public needs and advance their own agendas.[45]

By 1910 preservationists were widely dissatisfied with the utilitarian conservation of the Forest Service and had begun to define their own federal program. Congress had created twelve national parks. Most of the parks met high scenic and scientific standards but not all. In 1906 Roosevelt had thrown a fillip to preservation with his support of the National Antiquities Act.

As we have seen, archaeology and monumental scenery drew wide attention to Utah and resulted in the creation of Rainbow Bridges National Monument in 1908. In spite of wide enthusiasm for a vast park embracing Monument Valley, the Natural and Rainbow Bridges, and Glen Canyon in southeastern Utah, natural conditions and regional development favored southwestern Utah as the locus for parks until well after World War II.

Park fervor was especially strong for Zion Canyon, which had long attracted the passerby. Don Bernardo Miera, mapmaker for the Dominguez-Escalante expedition in 1776, represented the Virgin's upstream reaches as pyramids rising from plateau bases, a form not used elsewhere in his map.[46] In words that evoke the same imagery, the recorder of the first Mormon exploration of the region (1849–50) described "vast mountains, one rising above another" in view of their route. In the spring of 1852 J. C. L. Smith and a party from Parowan found their way into the East Fork of the Virgin's narrowing canyon west of Mount Carmel, where they inscribed their names in a cave. Another exploration six years later led by Jesse N. Smith scrambled along the bottom of the East Fork of the Virgin and its south rim; marveled at "Pilot House peak, which stands in the junction of the north and south [the East Fork] branches of the Rio Virgin"; and observed the upstream course of the North Fork, for "miles among the perpendicular cliffs."[47]

Settlement began on the Upper Virgin in 1861. Utah sightseers were visiting the area by 1864, and artists came shortly after. With an unfailing eye for the dramatic, John Wesley Powell made the trek down the East Fork and explored the North Fork in 1872, calling them the Parunuweap and the Mukuntuweap Rivers, Indian names. Clarence Dutton and artist W. H. Holmes visited the Virgin River canyons in 1880 when the latter's superb *Smithsonian Butte—Valley of the Virgen* was painted. Together with glowing verbal descriptions in Dutton's *Tertiary History of the Grand Canyon District*, Holmes's artwork tied Zion Canyon to the emerging national taste for monumental scenery. Then came the 1903 return of Frederick S. Dellenbaugh, whose *Scribner's Magazine* article revealed Zion Canyon to the nation and whose Zion paintings highlighted the Utah exhibit at the St. Louis World's Fair in 1904.[48]

In the years that followed, Governors Wells and Cutler continued to push Utah exhibits at expositions across the country. Yet there is no direct evidence that Utah as yet sought to join the growing list of states for which Congress was creating national parks.

Opportunity for recognition came in 1908. In response to petitions from homesteaders, Smoot machine governor John C. Cutler applied to the Land Office for a survey of the Rio Virgin headwaters. In an era when requests for surveys often languished on the commissioner's desk for years, deputy US surveyor Leo A. Snow, a St. George resident and University of Utah engineering graduate, was assigned to the job immediately and was in the field by September. His crew included three young men who later proved themselves as conservationists: naturalist Angus M. Woodbury, environmental ecologist Walter Cottam, and physician and parks promoter M. J. Macfarlane. Snow's survey included a report on the North Fork's singular beauty and a laconic recommendation that it be "set apart...as a national park." On July 31, 1909, President Taft signed a proclamation creating Mukuntuweap National Monument, consisting of 15,840 acres, barely encompassing Zion Canyon's North Fork main stem.[49]

After this show of activity, things moved slowly. No custodian was assigned to the monument, but "two or three times" a year Land Office officials checked with David Hirschi, the genial bishop of Rockville, and reported their observations. In

1914 G. E. Hair found the monument "in excellent condition." Exaggerating, he reported that it was accessed by good state highways and "traversed by a long established," well-kept county road. A handful of visitors from across the country lauded the monument's beauty, and some three hundred Utahns found their way to it between July 1, 1912, and October 1, 1913. Fuel gathering tidied the canyon floor, but undergrowth existed to the extent, according to another report, that it would profit from a good pruning. Hair, however, concluded, "There are no improvements necessary... [and] no... [reason] for the Government to expend any money."[50]

The good-roads movement helped to bring the canyon within reach of additional prospective visitors. In concert with the Smoot machine, Governor Spry connected tourism with Zion's development and became its enthusiastic sponsor. For decades the Great White Throne, perhaps the canyon's grandest spectacle, was known as "El Gobernador" in his honor. Encouraged by Cedar City architect Randall Jones, Spry appointed a "committee to travel over the west and study tourist centers." Convinced "all they needed were roads and accommodations to make south-Utah a scenic mecca," the Jones committee launched a "gigantic push" that Spry and his successors endorsed. Spry pushed the Salt Lake to Grand Canyon road and the Arrowhead Trail over routes that later became US 91 and I-15.[51]

In 1910 existing national parks were independently administered, often by poorly qualified political appointees. Most of them were under the loose supervision of the Department of the Interior. Badly needed were a sense of mission and people "who could devote their working careers" to promoting national parks and monuments.

Wilson's secretary of the interior Franklin K. Lane undertook this challenge. A pragmatic Californian who saw parks more in terms of scenery and recreation than absolute preservation, Lane chose as park administrators fellow Californians Stephen T. Mather, well-connected promoter who had created a national market and a personal fortune selling Twenty Mule Team Borax, and youthful legislative assistant Horace Albright. Advocates of the possible, Mather and Albright directed the national park movement for two decades, selling it to the nation and moving it away from the absolutist and elitist stance of John Muir and other purists toward a recreation-oriented but "easy on the land" posture. Mather and Albright glorified America, played to and drew support from the growing consumer culture of the era, and promoted roads, intensive visitation, and park facilities on the assumption that they would leave natural wonders intact for future generations. With long-range implications for the character of federalism, they also laid the groundwork for out-of-state constituencies that influenced the utilization of Utah resources.

With help from preservationists and park-conscious congressmen, including Smoot, who had been working to establish a "parks bureau" since 1910, the National Parks Act was passed in 1916. It created the Park Service and specified that the "fundamental purpose" of national parks was to conserve scenery, natural and historic objects, and wildlife and "provide for the enjoyment of the same in such manner and by such means as will leave them unimpaired for the enjoyment of future generations." Smoot's "growing prestige" in the movement was reflected in his selection as keynote speaker at the nationwide parks conference the next year. Sounding every inch a nationalist, he declared he did not "want to see any of the natural resources taken from" the nation's parks or their beauty marred. By contrast, an appropriation putting them in "condition that they can be enjoyed by the people of the United States [would be] the best money Congress could spend."[52]

With the Mukuntuweap National Monument at its heart, the "Grand Canyon District" was an immediate beneficiary of these developments. Through Douglas White, head of its industrial relations division, the Union Pacific, whose West Yellowstone spur was showing a profit, claimed "this marvelous scenic area" as a "tributary territory" and promised to see it was "given its proper place." Envisioning the Mukuntuweap as a centerpiece for the district, White began calling it Zion National Park (an easier name to pronounce), toured its main canyon with railroad and business VIPs, explored the Kolob wilderness and commended it as an extension, and cranked out articles and news releases. Smoot secured an appropriation of fifteen thousand dollars for road development in Zion Canyon. Beyond Zion Canyon a lonely track proceeded south and east to the Kaibab Forest and the North Rim. In time the track became a road connecting back to Bryce Canyon and Cedar Breaks, both in national forests, before dropping from the High Plateaus to Cedar City and grinding 35 miles northwest to the whistle-stop town of Lund. In all it was 483 miles—a dusty, misshapen loop that gave context to the southern Utah parks.[53]

Pushed by Smoot, railroad officials, and Cedar City interests, Horace Albright of the Park Service finally made it to Lund, and across 100 miles of "perfectly terrible roads," to look at Zion in September 1917. Charmed by its gentle people, Albright was won over by its scenic and scientific worth and convinced it made an essential link in the chain of national parks being forged. Undeterred by park superintendent Mather's initial lack of enthusiasm, or by immigrant governor Simon Bamberger's determination to "build no more roads to rocks," Albright spearheaded the successful campaign to upgrade Mukuntuweap National Monument. In 1918 the monument was enlarged to 76,800 acres and its name changed to Zion National Monument by presidential proclamation, and in 1919 it was upgraded to national park status by an act of Congress.

In 1919 the state legislature passed a memorial asking Congress to designate Bryce Canyon as a national monument. The following year Ruby and Minnie Syrett, local homesteaders and ranchers, built a small guesthouse to accommodate tourists, and in 1924–25 the Union Pacific financed an imposing two-story lodge at the monument. With the state showing no enthusiasm for Bryce Canyon as a state park, which Mather favored, and amid sharp interagency sparring with the Forest Service, Bryce became a national park only "after the Union Pacific...deeded [over] their holdings" there in 1928.

A sharp encounter over whether Cedar Breaks could be better run by the recreational approach of the Park Service or the multiple-purpose management of the Forest Service culminated in a Park Service victory. In 1933 it too became a national monument, thus completing the loop from the railroad to Zion, the North Rim, Bryce, and Cedar Breaks that Albright and the railroad had advocated. As the auto age became more important, the southern Utah parks became part of an even more extensive regionalism when newer national monuments at Hovenweap (1923), the Arches (1929), and Capitol Reef (1937) joined the Natural Bridges (1908), Rainbow Bridge (1910), and Dinosaur (1915) in forming the grand circle of Colorado Plateau parks and monuments that tied the Four Corner states together. Only Timpanogos Cave (1922) in Utah County lay outside the plateau.[54]

The tasks of attracting visitors and building an administrative organization remained. Initially, Zion Park was little known outside of Utah. Of the 3,692 registered visitors in 1920, all but 486 lived in Utah. Major celebrations were staged when Zion was dedicated in June 1920 and on the occasion of President Harding's June 27, 1923, visit: after careful planning by Reed Smoot and weeks of unpaid work by two hundred southern Utah volunteers to settle "hub deep dust," the president and his wife rode the first passenger train on the Lund-to–Cedar City spur and motored to the park. There they spent an hour or two with VIPs and upwards of a thousand enthusiastic citizens, including a Scout troop that had hiked in from Orderville during the night. Thereafter, masters of public relations Mather and Albright took advantage of every occasion—"show-me" tours, dedications, tunnel drives, or remembering old-timers—to boost Utah's wonderland.[55]

Even before the park was dedicated, the effort to sell it as a national playground and to take care of visitors began. On its face this was much more a matter of corporate management and promotion of industrial tourism than of protecting natural resources.[56] From Yellowstone the UP brought W. W. Wylie, whose immaculately kept tent camps and good food (called the "Wylie Way") were favorably known. Against the railroad titan, Cedar City brothers Gronway and Chauncey Parry maneuvered to retain control of bus tours. The effort to package the scenery of southern Utah and northern Arizona met many problems. Bridges had to be constructed, highways built over new grades, inept contractors worked with, and the so-called Seven Percent system, by which Federal road subsidies were provided, applied.

Claiming an interest "second only to that of the nation and the state," the Union Pacific Railroad made an all-out effort to attract visitors in 1923. The wholly owned subsidiary Utah Parks Company (UPC), a holding company, was organized that year. It bought the Wylie interests and purchased "40 eleven passenger auto-stages." With these the UPC took over the Zion, Bryce, and Cedar Breaks traffic and contracted with the Parrys to handle the distant North Rim run. That spring the railroad built the Cedar City spur, where train and bus stations, garages, and other supporting buildings soon rose on land donated by the city. The UPC also took over the partially constructed El Escalante, a pretentious Main Street hotel designed by Randall Jones. While gratifying wealthy travelers, the Escalante always operated at a heavy loss. Yielding to Mather's sense that a grand hotel was inappropriate in Zion's cramped canyon, the UPC planned a lodge and cabins to accommodate 184 guests along with forty-six cabins at Bryce. Rounding out its package, the UP launched a nationwide advertising blitz costing one hundred thousand dollars for the 1925 tourist season.[57]

Railroad officials also stepped up pressure for road improvement, although it was beginning to object to auto tourists. Roads and bridges in the park were subject to repeated washouts, and in 1923 and 1942 major landslides occurred, requiring almost constant roadwork as well as extensive management of the river. From at least 1920 when Governor Bamberger dispatched Randall Jones to a park-to-park highway conference, Utah worked aggressively to integrate its roads with regional systems. In an attempt to promote sightseeing in the park, the Utah State Automobile Association relabeled the highway connecting Salt Lake City with St. George, formerly known as the Arrowhead Trail, the Zion Park Highway on state maps. Work continued on Highways 89 and 91, much of the latter being oiled by 1941, connecting south to Las Vegas, the Boulder Dam, and Los Angeles. The Forest Service and local counties joined to bring "approach" roads up to successively advancing standards.[58]

Road development climaxed in 1928–30 with the construction of the Zion–Mount Carmel highway, a huge boon to local residents in need of work. A spectacular mile-long tunnel with six galleries was built through the canyon walls inside the park. A high-profile dedication brought the glad-handing Albright, seventeen governors, church leaders, and hundreds of others to hear Utah governor Dern declare "every American" held "a share" in the Utah parks and invite each of them to "inspect your property." Involving comparable engineering and a hundred miles of marvelous red rock scenery was Arizona's construction of the Marble Canyon Bridge and improvement of Highway 89's dusty approach to the North Rim, opening the Utah parks to South Rim traffic and the burgeoning transcontinental flow along Highway 66.[59]

The Utah Parks Company quickly built a genial staff of summer workers, which soon reached a maximum of seven hundred. Like semipro ball teams, many of them were recruited as performers and were remembered as saxophone players or vocalists in a sentimental entertainment world as yet uninvaded by glitz. For

some, including local historian A. K. Larson of Washington County who remembered "play downs" between marching bands, it was part of an abiding love affair
with the red-rock country and the national parks idea. For others, the UPC afforded
an opportunity to grow with the country, as did Henry Scholzen, who came to cook
and stayed to marry and launch a poultry enterprise that fed the parks and a delivery service that grew into a multimillion-dollar construction supply house.[60]

In response to these efforts, visitation increased modestly. Zion's visits jumped
from 8,400 in 1924 to 16,817 in 1925 and from 33,383 in 1929 to 55,186 in the first year
after the tunnel's completion. Not surprisingly, the Depression resulted in diminishing attendance in 1931–33, but healthy growth in each of the decade's remaining
years reflected the mounting popularity of the national playgrounds idea and southern Utah's improved accessibility. Before attendance plummeted to about 75,000 as
America went to war, visitors reached an all-time high of 190,016 at Zion in 1941
and 341,627 with Bryce and Cedar Breaks thrown in.

Although the Park Service was satisfied with these visitation rates, the railroad
was disappointed, especially as most traveled to the park in private automobiles; its
share of the passenger traffic was rarely higher than 5 percent and diminished to less
than 2 percent during the 1930s. Nevertheless, the Union Pacific viewed southern
Utah as a developing region, maintained its physical plant, and offered occasional
gifts to enhance the parks. As World War II ended the railroad agreed reluctantly
to continue the Utah Parks Company after an independent study by UPC manager W. S. Rogers showed a modest profit for every year since 1930 on all concessions except the El Escalante Hotel.[61]

With national park status had come the need for field officers. In early 1917
Freeborn Gifford of Springdale was suggested as the first custodian, but before the
year was over Albright followed Bishop Hirschi's recommendation and appointed
Walter Ruesch, also of Springdale, who became acting superintendent and, later,
longtime chief ranger. A bit uncouth, Ruesch was replaced in 1925 by Eviend T.
Scoyen, the first professional superintendent, in an effort to present a more sophisticated image to visitors.

As professionals came they addressed management problems and concerns
relating to plant life and the park's geological integrity. An immediate problem was
overgrazing on "about 100 miles" of private and public ranges that constituted the
North Fork's "upper watershed," from which increasingly large floods were discharged into the park. In 1929, for example, the river did "big damage," washing out
the West Rim trails, cutting away sections of land at the campground and lodge, and
filling the main road with slides. As park superintendent Scoyen wrote, "Unless a
person has seen one of these floods it is quite impossible...to form a conception of
what actually takes place. The water is loaded with silt. Boulders weighing tons are
rolled around in the river bed. Trees that a hundred men could not lift are carried

along like straws. Banks...melt like sugar, and any obstruction in the river channel is swept away." "Sixty-one consecutive" days of rain led Scoyen to fear that the whole upper watershed had "started to slide" and that the canyon would be filled.

In an attempt to avoid this fate, the park managed the river intensively, especially during the 1930s, when the Civilian Conservation Corps (CCC) and other relief programs undertook major environmental engineering. Yet projects that sought to treat the problem at its origin failed because of growing tension between the park and local residents. For example, a CCC project was abandoned at Blue Springs high on the North Fork when a Cedar City physician who had worked with Albright to establish the park refused to jeopardize grazing by permitting one hundred CCC boys to camp at the spring.[62]

Recreational activities for early park visitors were limited to sightseeing, hikes, horseback riding, nature lectures, and wading short distances up the narrows. Sports in the usual meaning were not encouraged. Except for occasional deer and cougar reduction programs, all hunting was forbidden. Floods scoured fish and their habitat from the canyons, and proposals for fishing ponds and stream stocking were inconsistent with nature.[63]

In the mid-1930s a sunset Easter pageant, "Southern Utah's World Famed Outdoor Spectacle," was inaugurated. Written and directed by Grant Redford of the Branch Agricultural College, it was a joint effort of the park, the colleges in St. George and Cedar City, and the communities. Initially drawing perhaps two thousand spectators, it grew in popularity until nine thousand reportedly spent the day and night in the park in 1940. Church concern about secularizing Easter and the park's recognition that the pageant had become a management monster led to its discontinuation, but for many Utahns the tradition of Easter in Zion continued.[64]

Positioned somewhere between frowned-upon sport and darling of nature lovers was mountain climbing. The first park employees became mountaineers as they identified and improved trails. In addition, a few men in Springdale occasionally climbed for fun, including the Crawford brothers, who in 1904 climbed to a flying buttress "on the side of Bridge mountain" at the southeast corner of the park. Attempts to repeat the feat failed until December 1929, when in bold headlines the *Salt Lake Tribune* hailed the "Intrepid Climbers" who after a "Quarter of a Century" overcame "Thrills and Difficulties" to reach it again. The account was more prosaic: Scoyen and two rangers discovered a crack by which they scaled sheer cliffs that had turned others back. Plans for a trail were abandoned, probably because a band of mountain sheep, discovered at the foot of the arch, took precedence. Nevertheless, a rope was tied in the "chimney," and climbers, including two Springdale women, occasionally visited the site.[65]

By 1925 many visitors were spending several days in the park, and the adventuresome sometimes abandoned trails in favor of sheer cliffs. Some of the UPC's employees also became climbers. "Mount Zion," directly in front of the lodge, was a favorite challenge, leading at least one veranda sitter to wonder how the "young and inexperienced" climbers escaped "serious accident." Cathedral Mountain was also relatively safe and popular. But the Great White Throne defeated all comers for years.

In 1927 W. H. W. Evans, a young Canadian living in California, tried the Great White Throne's north face unsuccessfully, as others had done. Then, without informing anyone, he scaled the Throne's even more defiant south front on June 27. That night he lighted fires seen from the auto camp, but fell as he descended the next morning and was the object of a full-press search on the twenty-eighth and twenty-ninth. Park employees, including Walter Ruesch, A. M. Woodbury, and Barney Gifford, all experienced hikers, undertook climbs beyond their interest otherwise. Late on the twenty-ninth Evans was found at the bottom of a seventy-degree slickrock descent, battered and dehydrated but alive. Improvising a stretcher, they got him to doctors on the East Rim trail and to the lodge by eleven thirty. When he left for home on July 11, his body was healed, but he could not remember the fall.

Superintendent Scoyen, who at heart wished "no one would ever" climb the Great White Throne, had "no doubt" that Evans reached "the summit of our greatest mountain." But full conquest of the great tower, that is, a successful trip to the top and back, was still apparently four years in the future. In 1931 Ronald C. Orcutt successfully made the round-trip. His glory was short-lived; he died on the much lesser Cathedral Mountain a few days later, perpetuating the pall associated with attempts on Zion's crown jewel.

Meantime, cliff-related mishaps continued. Albin Brooksby, a school official from Orderville, was killed in a freak accident on April 12, 1930. In July Eugene Cafferata of St. Louis met his death in a thoughtless nighttime incident. Much later, in August 1946, UPC cook Roger Clubb of Stillwater, Oklahoma, was rescued with much risk to park employees, some thought from the very ledge where Evans had fallen. Disgusted with the "selfishness" that led lone climbers to seek "empty glory" no "sane person would...attempt," Zion officials apparently did little to promote climbing as part of the nature ethic. But they also apparently made little effort to restrict climbing.

Early rescue squads took ropes only as afterthoughts, made no use of drills or pitons, and were extremely reluctant to undertake cliffs too big to mount with a cut tree or a thrown rope. The early accounts do not mention rappelling. Nevertheless, by 1946 ropes, drilling, and pitons had become part of rescue procedures. Perhaps the detachment of mountain troops that occupied a defunct CCC camp at Zion during World War II influenced the change.[66]

In Zion Park's early years the park administrators' most complex challenge was balancing local interests with preservationist values and the park's national ownership and constituency. There is little evidence of sympathy for pure preservation in Utah; tourism and development were the primary interests. As we have seen, park administrators worked closely with Reed Smoot, southern Utah residents, and the railroad and were clearly dependent upon them. They were equally dependent upon the development of roads and tourist accommodations. Their most crucial constituents were the visitors themselves, a nationwide constituency in which had been fostered not only aesthetic and scientific appreciation but a patriotic and moral attachment to the park and its environs that both broadened and deepened the workings of federalism. As the "national park idea" took hold, an out-of-state sense of place, or absentee factor, that had not existed before came to bear on the affairs of southern Utah.[67]

Although often ill at ease with local inhabitants, early park administrators lived closely with them. Rather than pushing to enlarge the park to include adjoining areas of "great scenic magnificence," they generally deferred to established communities, private interests, and vested grazing rights. Compromise of protectionist principle was an everyday reality.[68]

Yet administrators believed strongly that "lands should be put to the use for which they are best adapted." Fighting for what they believed in, they sometimes laid the seeds of local tension, as in their campaign to extend the southern boundary of the park. A critical part of the effort was the Springdale approach: about six hundred acres of private land, early cottages, and dilapidated outbuildings in the mouth of the canyon. Old-line Mormon owners were not inclined "to hold up the government," but felt they were not at liberty to abandon the church mission to colonize; they sold their property only after the church assented. The ground was fairly appraised, but the individual selling price was a mere pittance; a gift of twenty thousand dollars donated by the Union Pacific constituted the bulk of the purchase fund. Some quickly began to feel they had sold their birthright for a mess of pottage, which with the Union Pacific's monopoly on concessions and the flow of visitors contributed to a sense that they had been disinherited.[69]

To offset this disenchantment, park administrators linked preservation with increased tourist income. None of them did this more effectively than the youthful Scoyen, a protégé of Horace Albright, who had worked at Yellowstone and the Grand Canyon before coming to Zion as superintendent. In 1931 Scoyen spelled out to the Associated Civic Clubs of Southern Utah how Park Service preservation went beyond the sustained yield of the Forest Service, to the protection of "forests...shrubs, flowers, grass, streams, waterfalls, mountains, and...wildlife" for all time.

Preservation could "benefit...residents of southern Utah" by making national parks the "main objects which attract tourists." Aware that many southern Utahns regarded parks and tourists as outsiders, he turned to a discussion of income directly related to park travel.

The Park Service continued to traffic in tourism to bolster its relations with Utah. A major 1943 position paper argued that parks were a "non-diminishing economic resource." It pointed out that population between 1920 and 1940 in the park-area counties had grown by 30 percent in contrast to a statewide growth rate of 22 percent. From total statewide income of $127 million in 1941, tourist income was calculated at $10,675,906—35 percent of which was derived from the four park-area counties. The point was clear. The Park Service was in the tourist business and catered to it—at some expense to preservation.[70]

Early field administrators in Utah were offended when the service came under attack for developing roads and trails. Among the most vocal objectors was the *Saturday Evening Post*, which in 1927 published an essay by George Vanderbilt Caesar. Describing parks as "wilderness tableaux to be but lightly touched," Caesar denounced the roads, which, with the "jostling jazzing hordes" that used them, spelled doom "to anyone with taste." Condemning the Park Service and "commercial interests who regard" parks only as "magnets to draw the maximum tourist trade," Caesar concluded, "There is only one practical method of preserving a wilderness area for the use which nature intended—roads must be kept out."

Scoyen fired off a letter, taking issue with virtually all Caesar's points, including the charge that the service was thoughtlessly invading wilderness and that "tin can tourist[s]" had no capacity for appreciation. Explaining that he had no quarrel with those who sought the backcountry, Scoyen asked if the fact that "some do not choose to worship in a crowd" was reason to exclude "the crowd." The editor of the *Post* stood his ground; parks should not be "gridironed by...roads."[71]

As the 1930s and 1940s advanced, Caesar's point of view grew in the service itself. Among other things, wilderness and wildlife featured much more directly. Reflecting the ongoing dialectic was a sharp rebuke from Secretary of the Interior Hubert Work in 1925, directing nature guide A. M. Woodbury to "cut out demonstrating and explaining snakes to visitors" because it scared them off.

Changes in Forest Service policy also affected the Park Service. After maintaining for two decades that scenery and recreation were "altogether outside" its "province" and regarding visitors as a nuisance if not an outright "menace," the Forest Service began to adopt visitor-friendly programs after 1920 that the Park Service in turn took to be a direct challenge. Long-term summer home-site leases were issued, scores of sensitively situated campgrounds and a growing number of well-conceived educational sites were developed, and hunting and fishing were enthusiastically encouraged. Following the lead of Arthur Carhart and Aldo Leopold, the Forest Service became increasingly aware of wilderness and established the "High Uinta's Primitive Area," in 1931. Utahns and a growing national clientele flocked to the area contributing appreciably to forest visitation that approached 1.4 million by 1940.

The Forest Service challenge and long-term interests clearly influenced new concerns about the impact of trails and roads in Zion National Park. A case in point involved park superintendent P. P. Patraw's proposal to extend a "footpath" deeper into the Narrows. Reflecting wilderness interests, national parks director A. B. Cammerer likened the extension to desecrating the "Holy of Holies." Again, when Patraw wrote to assistant director H. C. Bryant in 1933 concerning a proposed interagency cougar hunt, Bryant replied, "My feeling is that we are reducing national parks to the same status as national forests...if we...modify the number of any...animal....The outstanding feature of park administration...is that all animal life is" protected.[72]

In a related spirit, the mission of parks to "serve the people of the entire nation" took increasing precedence over work with the "neighborhood and state" constituencies so necessary earlier. Recognized in terms of "sanctuary, scientific, and primitive values," remote areas came in for new attention. Always permitted in backcountry parts of the park, grazing fell from about 12,700 cattle in 1919 to 2,000 in 1941. These cuts were likely insufficient to reverse habitat degradation and certainly did not satisfy national and regional administrators, whose feet preservationists held to the fire, but locally they marked the Park Service as public enemy number one.[73]

THE TYRANNY OF CHANGE

All told, the decade before 1940 was a time of transition in public lands administration, and for representatives of the old order it was a time of deep trouble. President Herbert Hoover appointed a Public Lands Commission in 1929 chaired by James R. Garfield, former secretary of the interior. Representing Utah was William Peterson of the Utah Agricultural College. Acting on the commission's recommendation, Hoover offered to transfer surface ownership of the public domain to the states while keeping mineral and oil rights under federal control. In this as in much else, Hoover's timing was unfortunate. Retreat from the land had replaced the homestead boom, a grim agricultural depression was in process, and a bitter fight over eastern Utah coal lands was just ending. Few Utahns were interested in the exhausted surface lands. After polling prominent livestock men who agreed action was necessary but were loath for the state to take over the worn-out land, Governor George Dern referred to the proposed gift as a "squeezed lemon" and another "tribute" to be levied "upon the states." In even more caustic terms, he complained, "Comes now the Government...offering us [a] large white elephant." Mark Anderson, Provo mayor and former range manager, "opposed all suggestions to transfer...public domain lands, to the several states," on the simple grounds that "local interests" would be "better served by the federal government." Dern convened a meeting of western governors from the public lands states to discuss the proposal. In his address to the governors, Dern pointed out the difficulty of economically administering lands that were valuable chiefly for grazing and called upon the federal government to cede mineral rights to the states. Utah received huge federal subsidies for reclamation and highway construction as a result of federal ownership of more than half of its land, and it could lose those subsidies if it assumed control of the land. Largely as a result of the organized opposition of western governors under Dern's leadership, the Hoover initiative failed. Indeed, as Stanford Layton has observed, Dern became "something of a star witness" before the House Committee on Public Lands as it conducted hearings on the matter in 1931.[74]

Now under intensive use for more than three-quarters of a century, Utah's public domain was a shambles. Marginal to begin with, it was overgrazed, eroded, and in recession, as perhaps five thousand dry-farm and homestead families abandoned winter-wheat fields to weeds and exotic brush in the state's five northwestern counties alone. By 1934 nearly 32 million of Utah's 52,597,760 acres, or 61 percent, were judged to be severely eroded. Included were seven grazing counties, mostly on the Colorado Plateau, where 89 percent or more of the land was severely impacted. Carbon, Emery, Grand, and Kane Counties showed "erosion to the extent of almost 100 per cent." Studies of the East and West Deserts suggested that half to two-thirds of the plant life was dead and that the remaining crowns that often stood "two to six inches above the soil surface" indicated periods of plant injury extending back at least ten years, making it clear that some damage occurred prior to the drought of the early 1930s. Where plant life survived, noxious and ephemeral grasses, shrubs, and forbs had replaced superior native varieties.[75]

Driven to the wall, Utah stockmen joined the movement favoring federal management of the public domain. Among them was Vernal's Congressman Don Colton, who assumed an active role in public lands legislation. Out of this dilemma, which reflected a broader national crisis, came the Taylor Grazing Act of 1934, placing 142 million acres of public land outside the national forests in grazing districts throughout the West and closing most of the remaining public lands to homestead entry. Frequently called a relief measure rather than a law aimed at protecting resources, the act set up the Grazing Division in the Department of the Interior. The division became the Grazing Service in 1941 and the Bureau of Land Management in 1946. In the grazing districts that were created as a result of the law, private interests were protected by advisory committees composed of local stockmen.[76]

Early in the 1930s federal land agencies were invited to make "want lists" involving expanded boundaries and programs. The Forest Service and the State Department of Fish and Game proposed that more than 2,255,000 acres, mainly in the foothills below the forests, be absorbed by the Forest Service for wintering game. A Washington County pilot project failed, and interest in big-game additions lapsed. Other want lists included land for flood and fire rehabilitation. In Summit County the Wasatch Forest proposed and acquired 106,000 acres for timber and fire protection.[77]

Simultaneously, talk of additions to the national parks and monuments picked up. This was driven largely by the Park Service and outside interests, but in some Utah localities business and civic organizations had been working for years to stimulate tourism through park extensions or new parks. In 1930 the Associated Civic Clubs of Southern Utah organized to promote "publicity... [of] scenic and commercial resources." In the towns of Iron, Wayne, and Grand Counties, agitation focused on Kolob Canyon, Capitol Reef, and a canyonlands area extending down the Colorado River from the Arches near Moab to Arizona, referred to as the Escalante National Monument.

The Park Service directed Zion superintendent Scoyen in 1930 to examine Kolob Canyon, a superlative area south of Cedar City. Scoyen soon recommended that although it included about 12,000 acres of private land, an area of 49,000 acres ought to be considered as an addition to Zion National Park. The Kolob extension took on new vigor when the Taylor Grazing Act raised the need to round out Park Service programs. Kolob was targeted again, along with Capitol Reef and the Yampa and Escalante extensions, aggregating 5.3 million acres, the Utah portion of which was grazed by more than 232,000 sheep and 33,500 cattle.[78]

The Park Service proposals presented stockmen with a particularly difficult dilemma. Fearing further contractions in their business, they were threatened by the idea of preservation, hostile toward parks generally, and specifically opposed to new and enlarged national monuments. Colorado stockmen directly involved in the Dinosaur's Yampa extension finally yielded. Southeastern Utah stockmen first won grazing concessions and then helped defeat the Escalante Monument proposal.

During this period park officials left no stone unturned to curry support with the state and major economic groups. Unlike earlier governors who had openly supported national parks, George Dern (1924–32) and Henry Blood (1932–40) were slow to back the great park-enlargement drive. At Zion Park Scoyen warned his successor that Dern was an ardent states' righter. Calling the political climate unsettled rather than hostile, the Park Service held "hearings" to inform stockmen and if possible to get their endorsement before opposition coalesced behind them.

After successful sessions at Craig, Colorado, and at Price, Utah, the Kolob hearing convened at Zion National Park on June 16, 1936. Included were J. Q. Peterson, regional director of the Grazing Division; D. M. Madsen, Park Service wildlife inspector; and about seventy-five ranchers and businessmen. During an all-day discussion, civic clubs gave low-key support to the parks, and stockmen spoke bitterly of injustice. Ranchers in the counties adjacent to Zion Park were convinced that as small as park acreage was, the limited grazing cutbacks implemented in the park had been a significant factor in the decline of the livestock industry. But they admitted few would be ruined by the Kolob proposition. At length they reluctantly agreed to the withdrawal of 37,312 acres of public land and 11,318 privately owned acres for a national monument.[79]

Included in the package was a controversial grazing arrangement licensing 15,650 sheep and goats and 327 cattle, but at the same time closing part of the proposed monument to livestock immediately and phasing the rest out at the end of the lives of the current users and their heirs. Because the Park Service planned to phase out grazing privileges entirely, ranchers were not permitted to transfer their grazing rights to others. This provision drastically reduced the value of the private property to which the grazing right was attached. To ease the shock, the negotiators spoke confidently of a "million dollar" road from US 91 "through the Kolob Canyons...to Utah Route 15," near Zion National Park, a promise apparently forgotten.[80]

By this time old Bishop Hirschi, closely allied to the stockmen as state senator and president of the State Bank of Hurricane, had abandoned his propark stance. When his understanding was confirmed that grazing rights on the extension would not be salable and that there would be no compensation for the consequent reduction in value, he summed up the loss some of them faced as a "distinct detriment and damage to a man's estate." To the extent that total property and income potentials were reduced, Kolob's graziers were victims of new preservationist values and the government's abandonment of the open-land policy so important to the conquest of the West. While understanding trade-offs between the general welfare and the grazing industry, Hirschi expressed deep suspicion of any move to privilege someone else's interest over those of lifelong residents. Signaling the utter futility of their cause, he asked the government men, "What we will do and where we will go?"

The "people of this section," Hirschi recalled, "cooperated 100% with" Zion's establishment, but its benefits went "largely to" corporate interests such as the Utah Parks Company and the railroad. Even the "automobile dealers and gas and oil stores" got only a pittance, trafficking as they did in goods "manufactured in" distant places. Prophetically, he feared "encroachments" would be ongoing. In the parlance of modern historian Hal Rothman, Hirschi was feeling the sting of industrial tourism, which had become a "devil's bargain" for locals.[81]

Economic concerns were doubtless paramount to all ranchers, but some, including those gathered at the lodge that June day, sensed the diminishing role played by residency and occupation in the way America distributed the rights and perquisites of federalism. In the management of the state's public lands, questions of property, equity, morality, and the balance of power between the state and the nation would long remain profoundly important in Utah. It is difficult to escape the sense that the rights of Americans generally to national playgrounds and of environmentalists to perpetual wilderness were achieved at uncompensated costs to stockmen in the interwar years. On the other hand, it is undeniable that abuse of the public domain had to be remediated.

AWAKENING ENVIRONMENTALISM

For a time it almost seemed as if the economic and environmental crisis that led to the Taylor Grazing Act's closing of the public domain would carry Utah for conservation. After all, southern Utah ranchers acquiesced, however grudgingly, to the expansion of Zion Park with its attendant reduction in grazing rights. But as war unfolded and prosperity returned in the 1940s, it was apparent that there was still much to contend for in the state's out-of-doors. Outdoor interests continued to grow, especially in the urban centers. Nevertheless, Utah remained overwhelmingly utilitarian in its views about natural resources. Very little evidence of activist organization existed prior to the war's end in 1945. But overtones of environmentalism were beginning to stir.

Fish and game continued to attract new supporters, as Utah's wildlife management produced hunter success. Often mercurial, wildlife enthusiasts made constituencies that could be manipulated to the advantage of conservation but had minds of their own about doe hunts, game-herd reduction, tolerance of predators, and other management issues. With urban populations mounting due to wartime development, access to the Uinta Mountains for hiking, fishing, and hunting also escalated, leading to head-on collisions between constituencies. With recreation-oriented foresters such as supervisor F. C. Koziol of the Wasatch Forest carrying the ball, recreation increasingly won out over stockmen, who were limited numerically but sometimes well organized locally. Judging "heavy grazing" to be incompatible "with every recreation use," foresters like Koziol moved toward "complete eliminations" in several areas of the Uinta and Wasatch Ranges. Stockmen protested, but "pressure from the other side of the public use was such that we really had no choice but to go ahead." Complete areas were closed to grazing and "set aside for recreation."

Skiing, too, developed as an outdoor interest in the 1930s, as a rope tow was built by the Wasatch Mountain Club at Brighton in 1936 and a chair lift was built at Alta in 1938. The Works Progress Administration (WPA, renamed the Work Projects Administration in 1939) also built ski trails and ski-jump takeoffs at Park City. Influenced by Averill Harriman, who had promoted the Sun Valley Resort, Region 4 forester R. H. Rutledge assigned F. C. Koziol to become the region's winter-sports specialist. A backslapping outdoors enthusiast with a flair for tourism and Chamber of Commerce promotion, Koziol pioneered ski resorts in Idaho and Wyoming in the late 1930s and joined Ogden skiers in exploring Snow Basin's prospects.

Fortunate in Snow Basin's proximity and its "slopes and...snow conditions," Ogden ski advocates had a resort well under way when the war broke out. Having established a "good foundation for the expansion of winter sports," Koziol moved to the Wasatch Forest in Salt Lake City in 1943 as supervisor. Backed by regional forester Chet Olson and aided by wartime shortages that placed a premium on nearby canyons, he orchestrated an explosion of recreational use that focused upon what in the years immediately after the war became Utah's ski industry. With men like Koziol at the helm, the Utah forests increasingly favored recreation and other urban needs over more traditional uses.[82]

All told, the Utah environment between statehood and 1945 was made to serve the needs of in-state residents, the state itself, and the nation. Under the recognition that the resource waste of conquest could no longer be tolerated and that the arid regions were physically incapable of sustaining competitive exploitation, the institutions of resource management were extensively overhauled. Indeed, the full scale of conservation came to apply: utilitarianism in the Forest Service, the Fish and Wildlife Service, and the Bureau of Land Management and preservation for aesthetic and future uses, which in 1945 were still essentially monopolized by the National Park Service.

But the processes of conservation had been by no means merely a federal effort. With both urban and rural societies, with strong commitments to the pioneer's attachment to irrigation, and with a robust cowboy tradition growing from the fact that 70 percent of the state's thirty-five thousand farms ran range cattle in the 1930s, Utah society cut across many of the great national myths and interests. To a significant degree, the state tended to be divided against itself in matters of natural resource policy. Depending on their interest, Utahns had rejected or embraced federal programs, as a fluid set of natural, economic, social, and political conditions led them to group and regroup.

The degree of local control over land that Utahns hoped to achieve upon statehood never materialized. Federalism defined itself differently in Utah than it had in Virginia, Massachusetts, or Florida. Constitutions and laws notwithstanding, the sovereignty of statehood was a functioning myth that strengthened the federal Union but was compromised by the tripartite national, corporate, and local adjustments of the era.

As the first half century of statehood ended, the basic commitment to utilitarian conservation still persisted. Postwar prosperity and urbanization would call forth a resurgence of interest in preservation and outdoor recreation. The underlying values and issues that had shaped resource developments through 1945 would persist, but in the postwar era preservationist views would gain broader support.

9

WATER FOR AN ARID STATE

WATER WOES

In the spring of 1922, floodwaters ravaged Utah. Flooding in the Salt Lake Valley was more severe than at any time since the pioneers' arrival. Creeks and rivers along the Wasatch Front overflowed their banks, many streets were lined with sandbags and hay bales to prevent floodwaters from inundating basements, and some homes could be reached only by rafts. In the Uinta Basin, two essential bridges over the Strawberry River collapsed, cutting off communities from each other. Midstate, the Sevier River rose twenty-two inches in ten days, cresting at its highest point since the area had been settled and washing out bridges, flooding farm fields, and wreaking havoc. The irony was that by the end of the summer, water would be in short supply. The *Deseret News* editorialized in favor of new reservoirs to store spring runoff: "The time must come when the flood waters will not be allowed to go to waste."[1]

In the second-driest state in the nation there were few years like 1922. But nearly every year for a few weeks in the spring, runoff exceeded water needs. Moreover, great rivers with daredevil rapids carrying runoff from the Rocky Mountains in Wyoming, Colorado, New Mexico, and Utah coursed through the sparsely settled Uinta Basin and Colorado Plateau. The Green and Colorado Rivers were untamed, dangerous, and undeniably exhilarating for the few who managed to run them successfully. What if those rivers could be harnessed for transportation or irrigation? The paucity of precipitation during the summer months combined with the diminished flow of most creeks and rivers after the spring snowmelt subsided induced residents of the Beehive State to look to elaborate schemes for water storage, including interbasin diversions, for solutions. Pressed by a horde of water-related problems, Utah entered the age of modern, professionally designed water storage and conveyance systems during the first half century of statehood, financed by the state and federal governments as well as corporate investment.

ILLUSIVE EDEN: IRRIGATION

Propelled by economic interest and caught up in the idealistic will to subjugate the desert that characterized the irrigation movement, Utah irrigators dreamed of Eden but experienced bitter competition, deep-running controversy, and overexpansion in the first few decades after 1890. It was often said Mormon pioneers made the desert blossom as a rose, and indeed they were singularly successful irrigators in the 1850s and 1860s. Modifying riparian doctrines guaranteeing community rights along streams, rather than rejecting them outright as long claimed, pioneer irrigation was notable for its cooperative character, its utility, its investment of real control over water rights in local users, and its equitable combination of public ownership, beneficial use, and prior appropriation to distribute risk and benefit. Pioneer irrigation works were simple. Mostly, they consisted of diversion dams and local canals constructed, owned, and managed to supply cooperating irrigators with water at cost. By 1900 upwards of one thousand of these "mutual associations" existed, with scores of them herring-boned along accessible streams, while larger distant waters were still undeveloped.[2] Central church leaders had dominated water development in each colony's first years, but as they turned their attention to new colonies, local irrigators controlled their own systems. Operating under the overlapping authority of county courts, the local companies became the primary keepers for the values and habits of shared risks, fractional stream division, and dispute resolution by means of mediation.[3]

Local companies continued to serve when efforts to enlarge the scope of irrigation projects by means of quasi-public irrigation districts failed after 1865. Similarly, the mutual companies softened the flaws of what irrigation historian George Thomas termed the "retrograde" Act of 1880. That statute made water a salable commodity, freed from the land and public controls. Even the state constitution deferred to the unwritten provisions of the mutual companies, guaranteeing vested rights in water, but otherwise leaving fundamental control in the hands of irrigators.[4]

Recognizing that Utah's irrigation infrastructure and water laws had fallen seriously behind those of neighboring states, Governor Heber M. Wells called repeatedly for revisions to regain leadership, but encountered grassroots insistence upon local control. In 1903, however, a useful water law began to take form. Revised in 1919, it did service through World War II. Based on the principle of public ownership of water, it centered authority in the state engineer, who was directed to issue and record water and reservoir rights, measure stream flow, and appoint river commissioners. Later, irrigation and drainage district laws were passed to facilitate bonding and taxing procedures required by costly projects. The Enabling Act's Reservoir Grant and the Carey Land Grant conferred major responsibilities for water upon the State Land Board, thereby limiting the state engineer's control, while the federal Reclamation Act of 1902 gave rise to the Arid Lands Reclamation Fund Commission.[5]

All of these developments shifted oversight from private and local entities to public agencies. A landmark undertaking that convinced many Utahns that corporations were poorly equipped to handle reclamation was the giant Bear River project. Planned by Elwood Mead and Samuel Fortier, perhaps the nation's foremost irrigation engineers, and financed by investors in St. Louis and across the Atlantic in Glasgow, New Castle, and Birmingham, it was plagued with difficulties and reorganizations but foundered ultimately because landholders were slow to buy or rent water. In 1903 the Utah-Idaho Sugar Company purchased the waterworks, which had cost more than $1.25 million to build, for $300,000.[6]

A classic reenactment of pioneer cooperation in water development was the Hurricane Canal Company in Utah's Dixie. Launched in 1893, its canyon-bottom diversion dam and cliff-hanging canal were hand hewn by farmers from farther up the Virgin River who had only "sweat" to invest. During the eleven winters of construction, a Desert Land Act filing requiring that irrigation be initiated within four years lapsed, leaving the company landless. A quick loan of $5,000 from the Mormon Church and a timely state land selection rescued their land at the last moment. Although "thirty to forty" stockholders quit, town lots and some 2,000 acres of farmland were distributed to fifty-eight families by 1910. Secure from drought and floods and toughened by the long project, they prospered, an affirmation of pioneer ways.[7]

In the Weber River Basin "old customs" also prevailed, but water had always rolled unneeded to the Great Salt Lake. For decades no one asserted wide control. Each ditch officer became "a law unto himself, manipulating" his own headgates and often "assisting in the management of others." When the crisis of drought and overappropriation did strike, solutions came easily for a time. The farmer-dominated Davis and Weber Counties Canal Company built the East Canyon Dam in 1899, impounding water for late-summer use. The dam paid for itself the first year, and the DWCCC added to it in 1900 and 1902. In 1916 the company built a much larger dam. In the midst of this good fortune, state regulation, stream measurement, and consolidation movements threatened to take away water control. The

Weber Basin irrigators resisted, mediating disputes when possible and going to law when necessary.[8]

By contrast, conditions on the overworked Sevier River forced innovation. Situated at the end of the stream, the Deseret Irrigation Company (DIC) composed of Mormon water users had some of the earliest water rights, but in the turn-of-the-century years no water reached its ditches during growing seasons. Seeking to force upstream users to honor the seniority of their rights, the "Higgins Decree" of 1901 placed all lower Sevier water rights on a "common priority," prorated shortages, and gave a commissioner the formidable task of enforcement. Aware that even in those dry times 55,000 acre-feet of unallotted winter water escaped into the Sevier desert sands, DIC president Jacob Hawley filed on 1,700 cubic-second feet of winter flow and a reservoir site at the Sevier River Bridge, now the Yuba Dam, in August 1902. With no harvest, DIC farmers went to work immediately, taking stock for pay. Planning to store water for dry cycles and not just seasonal variations, they built big, aided by the best engineers available: former state engineer A. F. Doremus and University of Utah professor Richard R. Lyman.

For-profit companies also acquired interests in the Sevier Bridge Dam: the Melville Irrigation Company, headed by the president of the Delta State Bank; the Sevier River Land & Water Company, headed by W. S. McCornick, Utah's foremost banker; and the Nevada-based and Chicago-financed Oasis Land and Water Company. After two diversion dams built by the Oasis Company as part of a Carey Act project washed out and forced the company into bankruptcy, the Delta Land & Water Company (DL&WC), organized by investors Walter J. Moody of Chicago and George A. Snow and Henry B. Prout of Salt Lake, took over the Oasis Company's debts and its 43,000-acre Carey Act land grant. By 1912 the Sevier Bridge Dam rose to a height of 80 feet and held 104,000 acre-feet of water. As building continued, it reached maximum storage of 235,962 acre-feet, making it the second-largest reservoir in the state. At the same time, the companies built canals and supporting reservoirs and promoted various speculative land projects in West Millard County. They also undertook the state's most demanding drainage project, applying the best that technology and the law had to offer.[9] Generations of settlers came and went, first trusting and hopeful, then water starved, victimized by alkali, financially broken, and unable to repay their mortgages to the Delta Company.[10]

The Delta Land & Water Company also undertook several Beaver County projects. In 1911 the DL&WC picked up the pieces of several earlier speculations, including promising land tracts and the Beaver County Irrigation Company's water rights and dams at Rocky Ford and Minersville. In the first year or so, they sold some 5,000 acres to Utahns and closed deals with more than seventy Californians, who reportedly walked away from their improvements during a brief financial downturn in 1915. DL&WC officers responded by seeking out trouble spots and rewriting mortgages to make for "permanent success and peace of mind." They struggled to improve water delivery and offered settlers options, including day labor on company farms and contract hay farming (a form of tenantry) as well as selling cleared land with prebuilt farm homes. Few Utahns rose to the bait, and the company recruited in Montana and California, threatening darkly to hire "Bulgarians" if local farmers were not forthcoming. The DL&WC began to fail in 1918 and had to sacrifice its Beaver County property late in 1919 to settle a judgment of $1,048,620.[11]

As an alternative to privately financed development, the state plunged into reclamation. Under the mandate of the Enabling Act's reservoir grant, the Land Board idealistically undertook two reservoir projects and financed several others. Built to hold 13,000 acre-feet of water where two earlier dams had failed, the Hatchtown Dam broke in May 1914. Recruited settlers, mostly from Missouri, were stranded on 6,700 waterless acres near Panguitch. Those who had made payments and improvements were compensated, and the state wrote off $329,185 in expenditures.

Completed in 1909 to a capacity of 93,000 acre-feet, the Land Board's Paiute Dam cost $1,297,068. It was potentially the second-largest impoundment on the Sevier, but possessing only secondary rights, it rarely filled. Equally unsound, its forty-five-mile canal suffered from washouts, evaporation, and seepage. From its early failure to deliver full water rights to the Jewish back-to-the-landers at Clarion, the state canal was undependable. In the aftermath of Clarion's collapse, the state talked of extending the canal to Juab County but glumly turned two-thirds of the system over to the Piute Reservoir and Irrigation Company for $671,405 on which all interest was later excused. Due to drought and depression, only $125,828 was paid by 1930. Six years later 175 of the project's 250 farmers had left, and others were bankrupt.[12]

As chief financier of the Mammoth Dam and a key lender for the Scofield (or Horseley) Dam, the Land Board suffered additional reverses. In 1917 the Mammoth Dam broke, flooding mining towns and severely damaging railroads in Carbon County. In 1928 the Scofield Dam nearly failed, giving added evidence of the difficulties of reclamation. In May as floodwaters piled up behind the dam, exceeding its 60,000 acre-foot capacity by more than 15 percent, a watchman spotted a leak near the base of the dam, caused by loose fill and a beaver tunnel at the base. Residents of communities below the dam at Colton, Rolapp, Hale, and Kyone fled their homes, carrying their possessions and driving their livestock to higher ground. About 150 volunteers from the communities converged on the dam and began dumping boulders and debris into the hole at the base of the dam, which had widened to 90 feet. Complaining that he could not leave his post because the phone was ringing off the hook, the telephone operator in Colton remained in his office after everyone else had fled the town. "I expect to be drowned here on the job," he told one caller. Eventually, a special train arrived from Price, bringing additional men, shovels, and cement bags. By evening there were more than 500 on the job. A railroad steam shovel also arrived and dumped huge quantities of earth into the hole. Within a day the hole had been successfully plugged with more than eighty thousand bags of sand. Disillusioned by events near Scofield, the Land Board thereafter used low-interest farm loans as a safer form of subsidy and joined the Water Storage Commission in promoting federal reclamation.[13]

Irrigation districts also disappointed many. Established in 1909 and improved over the years, irrigation district laws allowed irrigators to organize, issue bonds, and levy taxes, processes that gave them public powers but also produced widespread loss of land for unpaid taxes during the 1920s and 1930s. Typical in its problems, but with interesting ties to big business, was Duchesne County's Blue Bench District. When its bonds did not sell, mining philanthropist Jesse Knight accepted them as payment for an impossible hillside canal that he agreed to build. Over time water problems persisted, and Knight took over the Blue Bench's 9,000 acres as ruined farmers defaulted and departed. Until the Depression Knight's heirs paid interest on the bonds, which he had given to BYU. Supported by top Mormons, the Knights made a strong but unsuccessful bid for a federal takeover of the project.[14]

Meanwhile, hard times and technical difficulties began to prepare even standoffish Davis County farmers to appraise federal assistance more favorably. In 1920 the Bonneville District was organized in Bountiful and Centerville to pump Jordan River water to five thousand acres of fertile truck farms. Surplus Utah Lake water was allocated, and bonds amounting to $725,000 were peddled to the Anglo California Bank, which erroneously assumed the LDS Church backed them. In time the system brought murky, weed seed–impregnated water to the farms. With Utah Power & Light charging a heavy fee to power the pumps, farmers were unable to pay when the bottom fell out of Salt Lake City's lucrative farmers market after World War I. Paying for power and evading interest payments, the district jousted with the Anglo Bank and sought relief from the Utah Supreme Court, which ruled that only land actually irrigated was subject to takeover for debt. As the economy hit rock bottom in 1931, the district persuaded the bank to accept a 20 percent payment on an indebtedness grown to $1,121,460. Even so, Bonneville users were badly dissatisfied with private finance and ready to embrace federal reclamation by the 1940s.[15]

FEDERAL RECLAMATION

After somewhat equivocal beginnings, federal reclamation eventually gained the ascendancy over private and state control. Utah's Arid Land Reclamation Fund Commission had been created in 1903, shortly after Congress passed the Newlands Reclamation Act, to represent Utah's interests in the new movement. Headed by state engineer A. F. Doremus and assisted by lawyer F. S. Richards, the commission immediately negotiated for federally funded projects with US Reclamation Service commissioner F. H. Newell.[16]

Doremus proposed a federally funded "comprehensive" scheme, the "Bear Lake Duchesne project." His politically and technically complex plan proposed to bring the entire flow of the Bear, Weber, and Provo Rivers into play, using Utah and Bear Lakes as reservoirs. By diverting much of the Duchesne River's flow, appropriating the Blackfoot River from Idaho, and siphoning a lesser amount from the Weber into the Provo drainage, the project would triple northern Utah's water supply.

Amid initial optimism federal engineers pushed ahead with surveys. Richards worked with solicitors to define the legal ramifications of "reclamation" in a developed area, and Doremus and others tried fruitlessly to line up more than ten thousand irrigators who, according to federal regulations, needed to unite in a single region-wide association if Doremus's grand design was to proceed.

Troubles soon surfaced. Engineers determined that broad-surfaced, shallow, and soft-bottomed Utah Lake could not be improved as a reservoir. Diversions from the Duchesne's tributaries were too costly. Interstate tensions were rife in Wyoming and Idaho. But most important were problems with the Weber River water users themselves, who distrusted scientific government help and flatly refused to sign rights over to a regional association.

Spanish Fork's water companies were more progressive. Recognizing that scientific management was a great time saver, they initially favored consolidation. In 1905 they embraced the radically downsized, federally financed Strawberry Project.[17]

Dwarfed by projects in Arizona and elsewhere, Strawberry was still a substantial beginning. It involved transferring Colorado Plateau water to southern Utah County, which was shifting from small grains to beets, orchards, and alfalfa, all of which required late-summer water. In one of the master exchanges of Doremus's career, the Strawberry water users accepted project water in place of storage rights to Spanish Fork River, thus letting the stream's off-season and high water run into Utah Lake, where Salt Lakers had storage rights. The Strawberry Project consisted of a dam 75 feet high and a lesser dike, a transbasin tunnel 19,500 feet long, miles of canal, and three small hydroelectric plants that supplied power to project towns and helped pay construction loans. The project cost $3,499,734 and impounded 283,000 acre-feet of water. Serving 2,817 full-time farmers by 1923 and providing supplementary water to 47,460 acres on established farms and water to 23,465 acres of new farmland, it stimulated strong rural growth in southern Utah County.[18]

Yet Strawberry users were far from content. Bitter disputes arose between new and established farmers over how existing rights were to be distributed and about payment formulas on canals. This led for a time to separate water users' associations and more important to major tensions between the Reclamation Service and farmers over payments. As happened on projects everywhere, loan payments were extended from ten years to twenty in 1914, but even this grace period proved insufficient in the face of the agricultural depression of the 1920s. By 1923 only 11.4 percent of the construction cost had been repaid. After extensive investigations in 1924 by a blue-ribbon federal fact-finding commission whose members included John A. Widtsoe, the payment schedule was again extended. The Water Users' Association would not make its final payment on construction costs until December 1974.[19]

During the 1920s and 1930s the federal government funded additional reclamation projects in Utah. The most ambitious of these were the Echo and Ogden River Projects. First proposed as part of a private undertaking in 1904, Echo Dam on the Weber River came under serious consideration in 1922, this time as a federal project. The government proceeded with field examinations during the next two years. By 1926 fifty-nine irrigation companies and various other water users from six counties had united as the Weber River Water Users' Association, pledging to sponsor the Echo Project and buy 80 percent of its expected 74,000 acre-feet of water. Construction of the earth-fill dam began late in 1927. When completed in 1931, it included supplementary water for 90,000 acres in Morgan, Davis, and Weber Counties. The savings from water stored in the dam enabled the bureau to divert some water from the Weber River into the Provo River, thereby delivering increased water to Utah Valley.[20]

Investigations were also conducted in the early 1920s for developing the Ogden River. Several sites were proposed, but disputes involving the upper and lower river valleys derailed the project until worsening economic conditions and drought in the early 1930s retracked it. To sponsor the undertaking, the Ogden River Water Users' Association was organized in 1933. Showing the mounting complexity of water interests, sixteen irrigation companies, four municipalities, and conservation districts in Box Elder County and Ogden subscribed for water in the project. With guarantees of cooperation in place, the Bureau of Reclamation let contracts to Utah Construction Company of Ogden and Morrison Knudsen of Boise for a job complicated by fifty-one wells supplying Ogden's culinary water located in the bottom of the proposed reservoir. The project was completed in 1937, including the 44,170 acre-foot reservoir, canals, and delivery systems.[21]

The Utah Water Storage Commission and the Bureau of Reclamation initiated several other projects during the 1930s, including the Hyrum and Newton Projects in Cache County and the Moon Lake Project in Duchesne and Uintah Counties. Construction also began on the Provo River Project in 1938. Consisting of the 235-foot-high earth-fill Deer Creek Dam and various power and delivery systems, the Provo Project impounded 152,600 acre-feet of water for irrigation, municipal and industrial use, and power production. Completed in 1951 at a cost of $37,855,000, repayment was prorated over seventy-five years.[22]

These federally funded projects represented a coming of age in Utah water development and established a precedent for reliance upon federal investment and engineering expertise that would persist through the twentieth century. In 1896 the pioneer values that had dominated water development for a half century prevailed. Although they reflected much that was good about Utah, the old ways in the long run retarded development. The corporate entrepreneurs who invaded the Bear River valley in the 1890s offered a different model of development. Notwithstanding the widely accepted conclusion that private capital failed as an instrument of water development, Utah remained a field for speculative water development in places like Delta. The federal largesse of the turn-of-the-century years—the Enabling Act's Reservoir Grant, the Carey Land Act, and the Reclamation Act—chipped away at local control and cooperative development, as did Progressive reformers who sought to update and formalize water law. By 1945 the federal government had firmly established itself as the fulcrum for water development in Utah.

"ROMANCE OF THE RIVER"

At the same time that Utahns were diverting and damming rivers for irrigation, others looked to the state's largest rivers for transportation, gold, or adventure. The river trips of John Wesley Powell with their heroic and tragic dimensions formed the foundation of a rich lore surrounding the Colorado River and its tributaries. The romance began to build again after Robert B. Stanton's 1889–90 "Colorado River Survey" for a water-level railroad.[23]

Gold and oil rushes contributed to the river legend. After abandoning the idea of a water-level route, Stanton established the ill-starred Hoskaninni Company in the late 1890s to dredge Glen Canyon's finely pulverized gold. Hauled in by wagons and assembled on the river, a giant dredge failed to extract gold and soon became a rusted ruin. Similarly, the San Juan River placer equipment of the Zahn brothers and Charles H. Spencer was hauled overland, as perhaps were three Green River dredges.[24]

Scattered and remote, ferries and crossings featured in the myth. Made dangerous by quicksand and floods, the San Juan River had a suspension bridge at Mexican Hat, major Indian fords at Aneth and Bluff, and unnumbered lesser crossings. On the Grand (name changed to the Colorado in 1921) River, ferries operated at Hall's Crossing in Glen Canyon and at Hite, Moab, Cisco, and Dewey. On the Green ferries operated at Green River, Desolation Canyon, near Myton, at Jensen, and at Brown's Park, where ferryman John Garvie was murdered and his body set adrift in 1909. Riverside hermits included the "goat man" at the Moab bridge; Amos Hill, the "Red Canyon Hermit high on the Green"; and Pat Lynch of "Pat's Hole" (Echo Park).[25]

Ranchers feared the rivers. Among the few who boated was Hod Ruple of Island Park. In the 1920s he bought a surplus US Geological Survey (USGS) boat to facilitate a cattle operation that spanned the Green River. In 1911 cattlemen told Desolation Canyon promoters Ellsworth and Emery Kolb that the canyons of the Green were impassable. Remembering the drowning of their father and two ranchers in the wild country north of Green River, Utah, they feared the river and kept life jackets for unavoidable crossings.[26]

By the mid-1890s the town of Green River had definite navigation aspirations. In part this grew from placer mining in Glen Canyon and in part from interest in water connections with Moab. In December 1901 Green River's F. H. Summeril brought his steamboat, the *Undine*, to Moab and dickered to run a "line of boats" between the two towns at a 25 percent cut in freight costs. In the high waters of May, however, the *Undine* turned over eight miles upstream and came "rolling sideways" to the Moab ferry. In 1905 E. T. Wolverton, a rancher at "Riverside," twenty-five miles below Green River, built the steamboat *City of Moab* whose maiden voyage was turned back by a mud slide. A bit later H. E. Blake and others built the *Ida B* and the *Utah* in another abortive effort to connect with Moab. Wolverton maintained this interest and by 1911 had a fleet of boats.[27]

By the 1890s a fraternity of white-water men began to coalesce in the region's consciousness. Finding a common identity in river experiences, keepers of the myth bickered about past feats, boat design, and relative importance, and they promoted the river as a link to a romantic past. An essential figure was Nathaniel (Than) Galloway, a Vernal trapper and solitary boatman, whose feats extended from the headwaters of the Green to Mexico and included advances in boat design and navigation. Aspiring river runners sought out Galloway, promoted trips in his company, and copied his flat-bottomed, sharply raked boats and his stern-first shooting of rapids. Julius F. Stone improved on Galloway's design and introduced industrial fabrication of boats. In an unprecedented 1909 run, Stone and Galloway brought two new boats through the entire white-water district between Wyoming and Needles "without an upset." Sons Parley and John inherited his flair for trapping and rough water but fell short in the evolving myth.[28]

Albert (Bert) Loper emerged with a clear place in the tradition. Loper made numerous boat and raft trips over long portions of the San Juan during the years he prospected there. When the San Juan gold boom played out, he remained near the center of river activity, living at Bluff, Hite, and Green River. In a 1907 experiment with all-steel boats, Loper along with C. S. Russell and E. R. Monnette failed to make it to Needles after pausing at Hite for repairs. A few years later Loper and Russell tried again but had to hike out when the latter sank their boat in Cataract Canyon. By 1921 and 1922 Loper was head boatman for the USGS surveys of the San Juan and the Upper Green. In 1923 he led a Grand Canyon expedition. Loper carried his river love affair into the 1940s, suffering a heart attack as he ran Marble Canyon.[29]

Also active in government surveys were Ellsworth and Emery Kolb, who took a step toward modern river expeditions when they tried to assert proprietary rights to still and motion photography on the river in 1911. Ellsworth's *Through the Grand Canyon* was a valedictory for themselves as much as romance and promotion. Therein, Ellsworth told of an unlikely encounter with Charles Smith below the confluence of the Green and the Grand. Blind in one eye, clean shaven, and dressed in a "neat whipcord suit…light shoes and a carefully tied tie," Smith had all the markings of a dude yet was a man of "indomitable nerve." He was trapping in a dilapidated Galloway boat and knew nothing about Cataract Canyon's dangers but was unperturbed by the news. Smith successfully negotiated Cataract that year and made a trip in company with Galloway but did not survive a 1913 trip.[30]

After World War I mounting interest in utilizing the Colorado River led to intensive commercial and official surveys. Crews from the Reclamation Service, Utah Power & Light, and California power companies swarmed over the entire Colorado Basin. As early as 1911 the Kolbs had seen three official engineering parties. Elsewhere, private engineers worked the watersheds, seeking to turn a dollar.[31]

During the 1920s the first commercial tours were initiated. One of the earliest tour men, Kanab's David Rust, had been involved in North Rim and canyon-bottom developments as early as 1902. Rust favored the benign waters of Glen Canyon, where he began comfortable tours in 1923. In 1926 he hosted Governor George H. Dern, as questions over apportioning the river's water among the states sharpened. Rust's business flourished, and in 1929–30 he hired Emery Kolb and Bert Loper as assistant boatmen. After a Depression hiatus, Rust reopened his Glen Canyon run in 1938, but his tours fell short of the rough-water exhilaration then evolving.[32]

Building contractor Robert (Bus) Hatch and his Vernal associates blundered into boating accidentally. Fishing enthusiasts, they found that seining on the Green River vastly enhanced their catch but required a rowboat. From this beginning their rough-water interests evolved through a succession of poorly conceived homemade boats, bad advice from Parley Galloway, and hilarious but near-fatal experiences in Ladore and Red Canyons. By 1932 they had designed and built Galloway-type crafts—the first two whimsically named the *What Next* and *Don't Know*. In 1933 they undertook an expedition that got as far as Lees Ferry. Continuing the next year, they became the eleventh party ever to tackle the Grand Canyon and the ninth to succeed. In 1940 Hatch made his Vernal home and equipment a northern Utah base of operations. Thereafter, many white-water celebrities put in at Hatch's. Large-scale commercial outfitting awaited the availability of inflatable rafts in 1947, which brought together rough water and passengers in paying numbers.[33]

DIVIDING THE WATERS: COLORADO RIVER COMPACT

Notwithstanding river romance, placer speculations, and some 300,000 acres irrigated on the Colorado Plateau, few Utahns thought about the Colorado River as a water source until after World War I. During the next fifteen years the river entered Utah's awareness with a bang, opening a new chapter in the state's incorporation within the federal system and forcing it to confront regional imperatives and competing demands for water. In an agonizing rush to define and defend previously neglected interests and rights to the Colorado River, Utah found its lot cast inextricably with six other Colorado Basin states and Mexico. As the state muddled its way into high-stakes regional resource competition, it lined up with slow-developing upper-basin states (Colorado, Wyoming, and New Mexico) in muted opposition to the lower-basin states (fast-developing California, slow-developing but grasping and tenacious Arizona, and Nevada, which asked for little but won more real substance at Hoover Dam than in the Las Vegas bonanza). Throughout the Colorado River controversy, Utahns feared that federal interference would deprive them of resources belonging to the state.[34]

In the contest among states for control of the Colorado, California had the advantage of prior appropriation because Imperial Valley irrigators had laid early claim to the river. In addition, Southern California's relentless growth required domestic and industrial water and electrical power. Southern California with all the means of wealth, political power, and public relations found ready allies in the Bureau of Reclamation and in Congress, where a variety of Colorado River acts were considered. Predictably, response to California elsewhere along the Colorado River was defensive, as residents sought "to guard against threats to their water supply."[35]

Utah entered the Colorado River conflict when Governor Simon Bamberger of Utah helped establish the League of the Southwest in 1917. A booster group, the league advocated a sixty-million-dollar basin-wide project to reclaim 4 million arid acres, 800,000 of them in Utah. Bamberger called meetings throughout Utah and appointed a prestigious committee composed of W. R. Wallace, soon-to-be Utah water czar; William Spry; and Anthony W. Ivins to direct the state's activities.

When the Land Settlement Congress for Soldiers, Sailors, and Marines met in Salt Lake City in 1919 to promote settlement of veterans on public lands, harmony prevailed among the Colorado River states. The lower-basin states even endorsed a resolution calling for water to be developed on the river's "upper reaches" first and continue "progressively downward."[36]

However, the upper basin lost whatever advantage the "upper reaches" resolution may have conferred at the league's next meeting. To a large extent, it appears, Bamberger dropped the ball. The bureau presented a plan for great dams at Ouray on the Green River and Dewey on the Grand, both in Utah. Bamberger, who planned to extend a railroad eastward through the Uinta Basin to a connection with the Moffat line in western Colorado, spoke vigorously against the Ouray dam. He may well have articulated Utah's prevailing sentiment, but he also represented his own interests. Claiming that the Ouray proposal would flood 250,000 acres and several towns, as well as "prevent the construction of a much needed railroad," he killed whatever prospect this project held for "early development."[37]

Thereafter, momentum built for a dam at Boulder Canyon, a deep defile between Arizona and Nevada, and for the new All-American Canal from the Colorado River to the Imperial Valley. In the upper-basin states, apprehensions soared that their own rights would slip away. Delph Carpenter, a brilliant Colorado lawyer, proposed that the Colorado River question be settled by interstate compact. Put off by a California proposal to leave distribution of water rights to the Bureau of Reclamation, Utah supported the compact as its only hope to reduce California's reach.[38]

In a victory for state action, the Colorado River Commission with representatives from each state in the basin, including state engineer R. W. Caldwell from Utah, was appointed to draft a compact apportioning the river. At a January 1922 meeting, contending positions were aired. Each state except Nevada "claimed an amount great enough to offset" their worst fears. Demands exceeded Reclamation director Arthur P. Davis's optimistic stream-flow estimates by 75 percent.[39]

Hearings followed in the various states during March and April. Not surprisingly, new problems surfaced, including interbasin transfers, the role of the newly created Federal Power Commission, urban needs, and Arizona's plan for a high-line canal to convey Colorado River water to Phoenix and Tucson. The hearings also added to the tension about the benefits prior appropriation would give California. The appearance of the Fall-Davis report, as the bureau's Boulder Dam plan was known, and fear that Congress might allocate the water unilaterally spurred Caldwell and Carpenter to skirt the thorny problem of individual state demands and propose a single division of the Colorado River's water between the upper basin, where almost all of it originated, and the lower basin, through which much of it ran. Carpenter's plan was refined, dividing the larger basin at Lees Ferry in Arizona and guaranteeing each division 7.5 million acre-feet of water annually. To no avail, Caldwell prudently argued that 6 million acre-feet of water for each of the divisions was all the Colorado's long-term run-off could sustain. After an acrimonious November 1922 conference near Santa Fe, the Colorado River Compact based upon Carpenter's plan was signed by all delegates.[40]

Back home, Caldwell prematurely reported that Utah's interests had been secured. For the "first time," he wrote, "the rule of priority" had been "set aside." California would no longer be able to "initiate a right by [the] mere storage of water." With Utah leading the way, the upper-basin state legislatures quickly ratified the compact, as did Congress. California signified its satisfaction but burdened ratification with unacceptable reservations, essentially making it contingent upon construction of a high dam in Boulder Canyon. The compact left Arizona no guarantee for its substantial but long-range demands, so the Grand Canyon State refused to ratify, preserving its right to assert ownership of water reserved for the upper states.[41]

Colorado River rights remained unsettled for more than two decades. Republican governor Charles Mabey attended several of the 1922 hearings and supported Caldwell but otherwise appears not to have pushed hard for resolutions. When it became clear that Arizona would not ratify, a "six-state" pact was proposed as better than no guarantee at all. Some Utah Republicans, including Senator Smoot and Congressman Elmer Leatherwood, were convinced that guarantees under any six-state pact were meaningless. They feared that letting the compact take effect without Arizona's approval would strengthen federal control of the river.[42]

During the long compact fight, Governor George Dern became one of the most articulate advocates in the West for state control of land and water. Appearing widely, he spoke with goodwill toward California and Arizona but resisted the Swing-Johnson, or Boulder Canyon, Bill that asserted federal ownership of the river and provided for federal construction of Boulder Dam and the All-American Canal for California's benefit. Dern reasoned that in the absence of a compact ratified by all states, the bill's assertion of federal ownership of the river would deprive the upper-basin states of their claims to water in the river. He insisted that "snow and rains that" fell "in Utah" were gifts of nature not to be handed over to downstream interests. In 1927 Utah's overwhelmingly Republican legislature with Dern's cautious support reversed its earlier approval of the six-state pact. Moreover, in an act of independence reminiscent of Arizona, Utah lawmakers tried to block construction of a dam on the river without state approval by asserting that the Colorado was a navigable stream and that therefore under federal law the riverbanks and bed belonged to the states through which it flowed rather than the federal government. The Supreme Court would uphold the state's claim to the riverbed and banks in 1931.[43]

In response to concerns regarding states' entitlement to water, the Swing-Johnson Bill was amended to acknowledge the claims of the upper-basin states and Arizona to Colorado River water. Under the amended bill, the lower-basin states together were allotted an average of 7.5 million acre-feet of water annually. Democratic senator William King supported the amended version, while Smoot and Leatherwood still opposed it. The amended Boulder Canyon Project Act finally passed Congress in December 1928, contingent upon approval by seven states, or, after six months, by six states. Five states soon signed. Arizona remained adamantly opposed. Still badly divided, Utah gave its assent after Dern endorsed the bill, and on June 25, 1929, the Boulder Dam Act took effect. The law limited California's "sovereignty" over the Colorado River to 4.4 million of the lower-basin states' 7.5 million acre-feet and appropriated $250,000 for investigations of potential reclamation sites in Utah as well as similar investigations in the other upper-basin states.[44]

Construction of Boulder Dam followed during the early 1930s. The Utah Construction Company as part of the so-called Six Companies general contractor involved itself in this giant regional undertaking.[45] Otherwise, Boulder Dam (later

Hoover Dam) was anticlimactic in Utah. The upper-basin states did not apportion their share of the Colorado among themselves until after World War II, in 1946.

FLOODS, DROUGHT, AND WATER MANAGEMENT

The floods of 1922 were exceptional in their extent, but on a smaller scale spring runoff or flash floods from thunderstorms plagued sections of Utah almost every year. Each summer mudflows and grinding rocks occurred throughout southern Utah following summer storms. Heavily overgrazed, Kanab Creek and the percolating brooks of Mountain Meadows cut microcanyons by the late 1880s. Before 1890 floods visited Manti with devastation and epidemic and in the twenty years that followed wasted Ephraim, Mount Pleasant, and the Emery County towns. In sparsely settled Wayne County, ten towns were badly flooded between 1918 and 1938. Cash losses along the Fremont River, rightly called the Dirty Devil, were estimated at $2,990,000, and an uncalculated human drain ensued as families left. Unleashed by what was quite likely the state's most severe overgrazing, floods scooped "fifty major gullies...within a thirty miles radius from Price" by the 1920s. Not untypical was Gordon Creek, which changed from a meandering brook to a canyon one hundred feet deep and four hundred feet wide.

In Grand County, where L. L. Taylor maintained a careful flood count, conditions were perhaps even worse. The collapse of the Valley City dam between Moab and Thompson on July 1, 1910, became Flood No. 1. No. 2 swept off the La Sal Mountains through Pack Creek before the month was over, and in 1911 storms played havoc from Cane Spring, ten miles south, to Courthouse Wash, fifteen miles north. And so the devastation was recorded, one flood in 1918; two in 1919; two in 1923; three in 1925; one each in '27, '29, and '30; and by 1936 six more as overgrazing intensified. It can hardly be wondered that townspeople rallied in support any time a ranger cut grazing permits or that town and country were divided almost street by street and house by house. Slowly, government agencies took action to curtail damage. In 1922 in response to flood hazards in the mountains east of Nephi, the US Bureau of Agricultural Engineering teamed up with the state experiment station and the Extension Service to build a check dam across Salt Creek to capture rocks and debris.[46]

But what must be wondered at is that somehow many along the Wasatch Front and in the seats of Utah power remained almost oblivious to grazing-induced flooding for decades. Suggestive of this was state engineer George Bacon's response to a National Flood Control Congress inquiry in February 1930. Bacon did acknowledge that there were "one or two localities where flash summer floods have done sufficient damage" to require control works to channel them to safer grounds and catch debris. But, Bacon concluded, costs were not large, and prospects for "future demand" for flood control were small.

Even before Bacon wrote, however, events had begun to demand attention along the Wasatch Front. Killing at least eight people and inflicting millions of dollars in damages, the floods of the 1920s and 1930s represented a crisis to Utah's main population centers and for the Forest Service.[47]

In August 1923 a wall of mud poured from Willard Canyon in Box Elder County. Homes, farms, orchards, crops, and the city's power system were severely damaged, and two women died in their homes. Simultaneously, a "rolling mass of boulders, mud and timbers" thirteen feet high hurtled through Cottonwood Grove in Farmington Canyon, a few miles to the south, killing four Boy Scouts and a newlywed couple. Neighboring canyons, including one above Centerville, suffered a similar fate.[48] Almost immediately, F. S. Baker from the Intermountain Forest and Range Experiment Station and J. H. Paul, a professor of natural science at the University of Utah, associated the floods with torrential rains at high elevations on overgrazed, tramped-out, and burned-over watersheds of no more than three thousand acres extent at the heads of Willard and Farmington Canyons. Convinced that revegetation would be the only lasting insurance, Baker and Paul urged the communities to buy the land and launch seeding programs. Only Centerville undertook a revegetation project at this time. The town acquired and replanted the tiny flood-source slopes near the crest line of its canyon, providing what proved to be permanent flood relief. Willard and Farmington opted for a necessary but inadequate system of control works. Under the direction of L. M. Winsor, a county agent and railroad engineer, and with support from the state highway commission, the railroads, and local governments, a complex of dams, dikes, and settling basins was constructed on the Willard and Farmington floodplains.[49]

However, Utahns ignored rehabilitation of the critical upper reaches until after 1930, when cloudbursts struck again. Especially severe in the Farmington canyons, the 1930 mudflows propelled boulders of as much as two hundred tons, engulfing much property and burying roads and railroads. Together with mudflows and gully cuttings, the floating of gigantic boulders gave undeniable evidence that comparable floods had not occurred in the twenty-five thousand years since Lake Bonneville. Satisfied that rainfall of equal severity had occurred both within memory and throughout geological times without causing mud-rock floods, both scientists and the public recognized overgrazing, timbering, and fires on the summit slopes as the causative factors.

With its attention finally focused, the legislature gave the State Land Board wide authority pertaining to flood prevention on state lands, including the power to purchase threatened property. In the same spirit, Governor Dern appointed a flood-control commission of foresters, scientists, bankers, and stockmen headed by Sylvester Q. Cannon, former Salt Lake City engineer and presiding bishop of the LDS Church. After examining the flood sources, the commission returned a comprehensive plan calling for the removal of critical areas from private ownership, complete prohibition of grazing, construction of terraces along the entire drainage, fire control, and revegetation.[50]

Two conditions favored aggressive action. In stark contrast to the century's first two decades, private, state-owned, and county-owned land, most of it erosion stricken, was a drag on the market and available for protective applications. Finance, normally the major difficulty, began to be available from frightened private and municipal sources and then, in regular infusions, from federal relief programs.

Missed by the floods of 1930, Willard and points north took "false security" from Winsor's control works and failed to join the rehabilitation effort at this time. Davis and Weber Counties, however, moved at once.

Rehabilitation was initiated in 1932 using Reconstruction Finance Corporation funds, but the major effort began the next year with Civilian Conservation Corps manpower. In key undertakings high-elevation flood zones were contour trenched, reseeded, and replanted under Forest Service direction. Although the restoration of natural ground cover was still far from complete, major cloudbursts in 1936 and 1945 produced no runoff from treated areas, while heavy mudflows descended from adjacent untreated lands. Reed Bailey, the Intermountain Experiment Station flood specialist who headed the project, won international fame for pioneering high-elevation erosion and flood control.[51]

When floods again struck Box Elder and Cache Counties in 1936, forty homes were destroyed at Willard, its cemetery was wrecked, and farms and orchards were severely damaged. Finally aroused, the town condemned holdings of seven private owners at the head of the rock funnel through which floods flushed and sought the aid of the Cache National Forest, which supervised intensive rehabilitation from a CCC camp at the head of nearby Perry Canyon. In the fall of 1936, crews cut a six-mile road into the rugged Willard drainage from the back side, erected timber supports in the canyon slopes, and began reseeding and conifer planting. Interrupted by waist-deep November snows, CCC crews walked out six miles and then returned to complete the worst tract in bitter cold. Work continued until 1940, and the next year 1,807 acres were deeded to Cache Forest by Willard City.[52]

Meanwhile, other critical watersheds were also rehabilitated. The privately owned Wheeler Basin, a key part of Ogden's water system, was badly overgrazed, cluttered with dead animals, and siphoning silt into the system through worn-out pipes. Working closely with civic clubs and the city, the basin was purchased and incorporated into the forest by 1939. On a larger scale were movements to take over Cache and Box Elder Counties' Wellsville Mountain drainages after 1937 floods. Forest supervisor A. G. Nord and Robert Stewart, Box Elder County agent, founded the Wellsville Mountain Area Project Corporation to raise money for land purchases. By 1939 large acreages, including the 1,100-acre J. K. Spires ranch, had been annexed. Contour terracing followed with great success.[53]

Conservation also proceeded in the 1930s in areas of severe wind erosion. Among them were abandoned dry-farm areas in San Juan, Millard, and Box Elders Counties and a small but "menacing blow area" at the defunct fruit-orchard town of Mosida, west of Utah Lake. A dust bowl enveloped nearly 100,000 acres near Grantsville. "Promiscuous overgrazing, and attempted dry farming" had stripped the valley of its ground cover as the drought of the 1930s set the stage for a literal blowout. "A pall of dust" imperiled drivers on windy days by 1929, and in December 1934 an unprecedented three-day blackout caused accidents on the US highway and complicated life in Grantsville. Dust blackouts were a regular feature of the next year. "Formerly depressed road ruts" stood more than a foot above ground level. "Blow holes," several hundred acres in extent, caused by "swirling winds, reached fifteen foot depths," and jackrabbits and prairie dogs reportedly abandoned the country.

Agricultural College experts urged locals to buy the land and take control. Instead, after some negotiation, the Soil Conservation Service established a demonstration area on the worst 32,000 thousand acres, fenced it tightly, removed all livestock, and planted hardy perennials. By late 1937 the wind still blew, but the dust had stopped and the SCS opened part of the plot to a handful of sheep. When rains brought new growth, two or three thousand sheep were pastured the winter of 1938–39 and nearly twice as many by 1940–41.[54]

In addition to wind and water erosion, dust storms, and floods, Utahns in the 1930s struggled with drought. Utah and Salt Lake Valleys received some drought relief when 28,000 acre-feet of "new" water was squeezed from Utah Lake in 1933 by lowering the outlet and, in 1934, 112,000 acre-feet more by means of the newly installed Pelican Point pumps, which left "little more than a mud puddle" at Utah Lake.

The rich northern Utah and southern Idaho farming districts that drew water from the Bear River and Bear Lake faced a more immediate crisis. Prior rights to Bear River water had been acquired by the Utah-Idaho Sugar Company in 1902 when it bought the defunct Bear River Valley Canal project in Box Elder County. Subsequent arrangements had been made with Utah Power & Light to regulate stream flow and to supply stored water from Bear Lake in connection with UP&L's plants at Cutler Dam west of Logan; at Grace and Soda Springs, Idaho; and at the north end of Bear Lake. The corporate partnership in water storage and delivery worked smoothly, and by 1928 Utah-Idaho Sugar sold some two thousand Bear River valley farmers water, delivered by UP&L, whose control over irrigation had increased as a growing number of canal companies bought Bear Lake water or power to pump from the Bear River.

According to UP&L, the lake received an average of 187,248 acre-feet of water from the river each year by the early 1920s, as compared to 114,140 from other streams, for a total average intake of 301,388 acre-feet. This exceeded the 273,395 acre-feet taken out annually. By 1928, however, increased demand and diminishing rainfall forced the power company to dredge outlets and draw the lake down below its natural level. Upswings in precipitation provided relief in some years, but the tightening drought persisted, reaching a climax in 1934. With the lake at an all-time low, there was virtually no snowpack or spring runoff.

Farmers all along the river went about crop preparation until May 2. Then, suddenly, the power company announced that it could deliver only the Bear River valley sugar beet growers' (the Utah-Idaho Sugar's) prior-rights water. Water and power would be unavailable for others. The outcry was loud. On May 7 250 irrigators along with company and state officials crowded the capitol at the invitation of Governor Henry H. Blood. UP&L reported the lake was at the 5,909-foot level—13.5 feet below normal. The company's dragline was operating twenty-four hours a day, deepening the outlets, but power and pumps could barely keep abreast of the minimum needs of the Utah-Idaho Sugar beet growers. Irrigation companies testified that without water, Cache Valley's dairy industry faced total collapse and that its beef and sugar beet industries faced severe injury.

UP&L quickly agreed to make power generation secondary to irrigation needs. With the exception of Utah-Idaho Sugar, the irrigators voted unanimously to forgo established water rights in favor of an emergency share-and-share-alike distribution. That afternoon Blood appointed a committee headed by Logan banker F. P. Champ and including representatives from the power, sugar, and irrigation companies; the state engineers; William Peterson of the Utah Agricultural College; and E. J. Baird, Idaho Bear River commissioner. Also represented were the Bear Lake citizens who were furious about the heavy drawdown from the lake.[55]

The committee went to work that evening. Dealing with hard facts, they hoped to get water to 160,000 acres. Figuring on a maximum of 220,000 available acre-feet, they aimed at 1.5 acre-feet per acre of land high along the river and a little more than 2.2 acre-feet in the Bear River valley, reducing Utah-Idaho Sugar's share from 190,000 to 115,000 acre-feet. By May 12 the pumps were running. Bear Lake residents initially threatened to stop the continued downdraft by whatever means. However, they finally condoned pumping to the 5,904-foot level with the understanding that no request for further drawdowns would be forthcoming in 1935. George D. Clyde, later governor of Utah, was appointed "conservator" and, with E. J. Baird from Idaho, worked to police water consumption. At summer's end Clyde credited the emergency measures with generating $3,149,811 in income for Utah farmers and $683,095 for Idaho growers.[56]

To resolve water shortages along the Bear River, some Utahns proposed transferring water a hundred miles from the head of the Green River to the Bear River. With Bear Lake residents hotly opposed to drawing down the lake and with the drought unabated, such a prospect appealed to many Utahns. It was hoped water could be impounded at Daniel, Wyoming, and a viaduct run a hundred miles to the Bear River west of Kemmerer, with supplementary water for 275,000 acres and water for 70,000 new acres in the three states. Utah and Idaho officials joined a

UP&L tour of the reservoir site, and veteran USGS surveyor of the Green River Ralf Wooley made preliminary studies.[57]

Officials from Utah were enthusiastic. Idaho officials were dubious but supportive to the point of ignoring strong pressure to solve Bear Lake's problems otherwise. Wyoming's representatives signed favorable petitions but faced stiff opposition at home. The three governors discussed the topic in Salt Lake City in October 1935, initiated feasibility studies, and sent a petition to Franklin D. Roosevelt. After spring storms in 1935 ended the crisis, corporate interest in tapping the Bear River remained high until 1937 but then subsided as broader considerations turned attention elsewhere.[58]

In a day of mounting federal intervention, the Bear River crisis was a notable example of interstate cooperation involving private, state, and corporate sectors. It is also a reminder that Utah's richest river valley was developed in the main by corporate enterprise rather than government action. Moreover, for Utahns at the time, the Bear River drought confirmed that despite the sophisticated and expensive irrigation works constructed in the state in the first third of the century, the desert had not been subdued; the state remained vulnerable to water shortages—a fact that would give rise late in the 1930s to the roots of what would become the Central Utah Project.

Late in the Depression decade Leland W. Kimball, engineer of the Salt Lake Metropolitan Water District, pushed what was called the Colorado River and Great Basin Plan. Elaborating concepts that dated back to the Strawberry Project, Kimball called for several dams on the Green River. Keyed to a huge impoundment at Echo Park, the proposed system involved what were later deemed to be prohibitively costly pumping operations, a 230-mile aqueduct across the toe of the Uintas to a vastly enlarged Strawberry Reservoir, and north extensions to Salt Lake and Tooele Valleys and south as far as Kanosh in Millard County. The Colorado River and Great Basin (later the Central Utah) Project was estimated at prewar costs of $400 million, and some two million acres of Utah land were classified in anticipation of its development. Simultaneously far-reaching and to many disconcerting, Bureau of Reclamation surveys were under way for projects along the north slope of the Uintas, on the main trunk of the Green at Flaming Gorge Canyon, Swallow Canyon, Split Mountain, Minnie Maud Creek, Rock Creek, and at Rattlesnake, a few miles upstream from the confluence of the Price and Green Rivers. Investigations were also under way on the Colorado for dams at Dewey, Dark Canyon, and Glen Canyon, as well as on affluents of the two rivers throughout the state. Portents of change, these investigations would lead in the second half of the century to the creation by the federal government of mammoth dams on the Green and Colorado at Flaming Gorge and Glen Canyon and the crown jewel of the Central Utah Project, Jordanelle Reservoir, on the Provo.[59]

Parade celebrating Utah's statehood, 1896. Note the forty-fifth star atop the brightly festooned ZCMI building. Courtesy of Brigham Young University.

A crowd in Springville awaits a Rio Grande Western train carrying Spanish-American War veterans, ca. 1899. The "splendid little war" offered residents of the new state an opportunity to demonstrate their patriotism. At the same time, the conflict, along with the resultant Philippine-American War, acquainted Utahns with Spain's far-flung colonial possessions. Photograph by George Edward Anderson. Courtesy of L. Tom Perry Special Collections, Harold B. Lee Library, Brigham Young University.

Red Cross volunteers with baskets of food ready to serve World War I veterans disembarking from the trains at the Logan Oregon Short Line Railroad Depot, January 1919. Note the flu masks worn by the volunteers. Both the war and the flu epidemic were transnational developments that profoundly affected Utahns. Courtesy of Special Collections and Archives, Merrill-Cazier Library, Utah State University.

A young family in front of their frame shack on their dry-farm tract in Blue Creek, a settlement in Box Elder County near Snowville in 1911. Commercial wheat production on dryland farms linked the fortunes of farmers like this family to national market demand in sharp contrast to the subsistence farming of the pioneer era. Courtesy of Utah State Historical Society.

Utah Sugar Company's Lehi Sugar Factory, the first beet-sugar factory in the mountain states, was photographed by Harry Shipler in 1905. The factory's reflection in a placid spring-fed millpond beguilingly suggests a harmony between nature and industry. Sugar beets became an important cash crop for Utah farmers, linking their fortunes to decisions made in corporate boardrooms, tariff policies devised in Congress, and Progressive trust-busting. Courtesy of Utah State Historical Society.

A steam shovel loading ore onto a freight car in the Utah Copper Company's Bingham pit. Note the train tracks and trestles ringing the mine in concentric circles. Mines and smelters were powerful agents of Utah's incorporation, attracting out-of-state investment capital, immigrant workers, and labor organizers. Mining generated economic growth, jobs, and environmental disruption. Photograph by Shipler Commercial Photographers, January 16, 1909. Courtesy of Utah State Historical Society.

Mining magnate Daniel Jackling hosted this banquet in the Hotel Utah for seventeen guests from the East, including John D. Ryan, the powerful president of the Amalgamated Copper Mining Company, and thirty-two locals on May 1, 1912. The profits of mining and smelting flowed eastward into the pockets of well-heeled investors but also bank-rolled the mansions and social whirls of Salt Lake's nouveau riche. Courtesy of Utah State Historical Society.

Workers' housing and privies clung to the sides of the Bingham Canyon mine, separated from each other by railroad tracks and retaining walls. Courtesy of Utah State Historical Society.

Immigrants who came to Utah formed transnational communities that spanned the globe. For this photograph taken ca. 1912, Greek immigrants posed in their best attire as if to assure relatives overseas of their prosperity, manliness, and friendship. Symbolically, they hold pistols and bottles of expensive liquor, while sprigs of basil, a token of friendship, adorn their vests and lapels. Courtesy of Utah State Historical Society.

The grieving family of Levi Jones surrounds his coffin following his death in the catastrophic Winter Quarters mine explosion in 1900. Mining disasters and industrial accidents raised pressing questions about corporate obligations to workers and their families. Photograph by George Edward Anderson. Courtesy of Utah State Historical Society.

Police attempting to force members of the National Miners Union from Price's Main Street during a march on September 11, 1933. A struggle for the soul of the state unfolded as the corporate system met the human dimensions of production. Photo by J. Bracken Lee. Courtesy of Multimedia Archives, Special Collections, J. Willard Marriott Library, University of Utah.

Shoshone laborers from Washakie planting "mother beets" at a Utah-Idaho Sugar Company farm in Garland in 1903. To an extent Shoshones embraced the new corporate order, as they creatively melded traditional activities such as hunting, gathering, and trapping with agricultural wage labor and farming. Photograph by Alma W. Compton. Courtesy of Special Collections and Archives, Merrill-Cazier Library, Utah State University.

Governor Charles R. Mabey warily eyes renegade leaders Poke and Posey (whose left arm is the only part visible in this photo), in June 1921 following the jail break of two Ute boys suspected of killing a calf. Speaking through an interpreter, Mabey warned them that the raiding must end. Two years later, after another round of thefts, Posey was mortally wounded in a firefight with deputies. Through various means many of Utah's American Indians resisted incorporation within a social and economic order that served white interests. Courtesy of Utah State Historical Society.

Students and instructors in BYU's 1922 Alpine Summer School studying the geology of Mount Timpanogos. Sense of place and an emerging naturalism surfaced in the work of geologists, botanists, ornithologists, artists, and recreationists. Courtesy of Utah State Historical Society.

Canyoneering enthusiasts George Stone and Russell Frazier atop Rainbow Bridge in 1938. Intense interest in southeastern Utah's stupendous canyonlands galvanized an unsuccessful campaign in the 1930s to create a vast national park encompassing Rainbow Bridge, Monument Valley, Navajo Mountain, and Glen Canyon. Photograph by Charles Kelly. Courtesy of Utah State Historical Society.

Members of Norman Nevills's 1938 Colorado River expedition. *Right to left*: Nevills, Elzada Clover, Lois Jotter, and an unidentified man. Enterprising river-running enthusiasts commodified the romance of the river. Courtesy of Utah State Historical Society.

Tourists and bus drivers pose in 1938 in Zion National Park. Zion Canyon attracted visitors seeking recreation, aesthetic contemplation, and emotional renewal. Their quest reflected a nationwide shift in attitudes that privileged preserving public lands over selling them. Photograph by Charles Ford. Courtesy of Sherratt Library, Southern Utah University.

Flood damage near the mouth of Willard Canyon in 1923. An avalanche of mud from the canyon's overgrazed slopes damaged homes and farms. Two women trapped in their houses died. One of the greatest challenges to Utah's planners and engineers involved water control. Photograph by Compton's Studio. Courtesy of Special Collections and Archives, Merrill-Cazier Library, Utah State University.

The federally financed seventy-seven-mile Strawberry High Line Canal and distribution system, photographed here shortly after its completion in 1916, provided farmers in southern Utah Valley with a dependable supply of water diverted from the Uinta Basin. Utah turned to elaborate engineering schemes designed and funded by the federal government to offset its hot, dry summers. Photograph by George Edward Anderson. Courtesy of L. Tom Perry Special Collections, Harold B. Lee Library, Brigham Young University.

These Slavic miners celebrated Prohibition in Carbon County by flouting the law in 1924. The decade's most intense culture war, Prohibition exposed deep social and moral rifts within the Beehive State. Courtesy of Multimedia Archives, Special Collections, J. Willard Marriott Library, University of Utah.

Jovial students posed for this photograph en route to Salt Lake City on the Orem inter-urban train in the 1920s. Sporting the latest fashions in dress and grooming and flocking to mass commercial entertainments from ball games to motion pictures, Utah's young people enthusiastically pursued incorporation within American mass culture. Courtesy of University Archives, L. Tom Perry Special Collections, Harold B. Lee Library, Brigham Young University.

Three children of a miner posed in front of their home in the company town of Consumers in March 1936. Dependent upon erratic work in an era of declining consumer demand, the state's miners suffered intensely during the Depression. Photograph by Dorothea Lange. Courtesy of Prints and Photographs Division, Library of Congress.

Weber College students displaying their tuition payments. Utahns resourcefully coped with shortages of cash during the Great Depression by reducing expenses and by exchanging goods for services. Courtesy of Archives Department, Stewart Library, Weber State University.

Relief laborers employed by the Civilian Conservation Corps constructing a lookout at the new Cedar Breaks National Monument. Many workers on CCC crews in the Beehive State hailed from New York and New Jersey. Despite their initial reservations about unruly single men and boys descending upon their communities, most Utahns became staunch fans of the CCC boys and their conservation projects. New Deal agencies such as the CCC exerted a profound nationalizing influence. Photograph by J. L. Crawford. Courtesy of Sherratt Library, Southern Utah University.

A Works Progress Administration paving project at the corner of Center Street and University Avenue in Provo was well under way when an unknown photographer captured the scene in 1939. The federal government's assumption of responsibility for citizens' economic welfare was controversial. Critics charged that the acronym *WPA* more appropriately stood for "We Piddle Around." Some WPA laborers countered that it was the hardest work they had ever done. Courtesy of Provo City Library.

A Danish immigrant in Widtsoe, Utah, clutches her first Old Age Assistance check in 1936. Although Denmark was a pioneering pension country much admired by the framers of Social Security, this Danish Mormon convert's downcast gaze may reflect the opprobrium attached to government assistance in Mormon discourse. Photograph by Dorothea Lange. Courtesy of Prints and Photographs Division, Library of Congress.

Shoppers in the LDS Church Welfare Program's general store in Salt Lake City. The Depression marked a critical juncture in the process of incorporation. Church leaders sought to reenthrone economic models based upon local control and self-sufficiency. The finality with which Utahns embraced centralized authority and federal largesse marked the true end of pioneer-era ideals and aspirations. Courtesy of Utah State Historical Society.

A Navajo code talker in the South Pacific in November 1943. The Second World War functioned as a powerful agent of social, cultural, and political incorporation for the code talkers and many other soldiers. Courtesy of Utah State Historical Society.

Employees of the General Motors Group posed for this photograph as part of an August 1942 war-savings-bond drive. Along with Americans elsewhere, Utahns often failed to meet the goals or quotas for bond purchases set by the government, but they nevertheless invested millions in war bonds. Photograph by Shipler Commercial Photographers. Courtesy of Utah State Historical Society.

Newly arrived residents of the Central Utah War Relocation Center in Topaz gather their belongings from stacks alongside tar-paper barracks. Although most internees at Topaz left Utah following their release from the camp, some chose to remain. By 1950 the number of residents of Japanese descent in Utah stood at 3,060, an increase of nearly 1,200 over the 1940 population. Courtesy of Topaz Museum.

10

UTAH IN THE 1920S

UNEVEN PROSPERITY

In the public imagination, the 1920s and prosperity are tightly linked—and for good reason. Real wages increased over the decade, and Americans enjoyed a consumer society lubricated by abundant credit, mass-produced automobiles, electrical appliances, and generous advertising budgets. Indeed, this was the decade in which advertising executive and author Bruce Barton published his best-selling *The Man Nobody Knows*, a depiction of Jesus Christ as "the founder of modern business."[1]

The decade's vaunted prosperity was unevenly shared, favoring investors, business executives, and professionals over the working class. The urban-industrial order rose to new heights, as cities flourished while the rural hinterlands languished, with some exceptions. In the Beehive State low prices dogged farmers and coal miners throughout the twenties, although the price of copper, the state's key mineral, soared in the second half of the decade. The fact that the state's major smelters, its largest mine, and many of its agricultural industries were controlled by out-of-state investors—a legacy of incorporation—meant that much of the wealth generated by those industries flowed out of state, too. As long as wages were adequate and credit was available, Utahns in the cities enthusiastically built and furnished homes and bought new mass-produced appliances and automobiles, ignoring the fact that their lifestyles and the state's economic growth came at the price of economic self-sufficiency, interest payments, and dividend checks to outside investors.

AGAINST GREAT ODDS: THE AGRICULTURAL ECONOMY

Agriculture, the state's leading employer, was hit hard by the postwar recession. The state's farmers had never as a class been very prosperous; most of the larger operations had minimal irrigation water. The bulk of the state's farmers worked smallholdings that had been established in the course of Mormon colonization. Intensively cropped and with a substantial and dependable water supply, such farms could be highly productive. But water, the inclination to farm intensively, and markets were often lacking. In his study of Ephraim, sociologist Lowry Nelson found that most families farmed fewer than fifty acres of irrigable land and possessed only a modicum of water. In a rural community where the birthrate was high, young people had little hope of acquiring a farm of their own. A growing landless minority lived in town and hired out as day laborers on road crews, on farms, or in the mines.[2]

The postwar recession of 1920–22 made matters worse for those who hoped to earn a living by farming. Demand for Utah's products had surged during the war as the government purchased foodstuffs and other products for the war effort and as the conflict disrupted European agriculture. After the Armistice production in Europe resumed, and governments around the globe stopped buying commodities for their troops. The prices of farm products fell into a tailspin beginning in 1920. Wheat, which had sold for $3.40 a bushel in 1919, sold for $0.98 in the fall of 1921. The value of Utah's largest cash crop, sugar beets, plunged from $12.03 a ton in 1920 to $5.47 the following year. The next year brought more of the same. As Leonard Arrington has written, "havoc and ruin" resulted. Although Utah-Idaho Sugar had been debt free at the war's outset, the firm had nothing like the capital needed to buy the harvest at contracted prices, nor could it borrow from any of the usual sources. In desperation the LDS Church came forward with $3 million, and in what was probably the biggest bailout to that time Congress extended the life of the War Finance Corporation, authorizing millions for faltering agricultural industries. Through the "agency of Senator Reed Smoot and [church] President [Heber J.] Grant," a loan of $9.5 million was made to Utah-Idaho Sugar immediately and during the next two or three years several million dollars more. As part of the deal the bullish C. W. Nibley was replaced as Utah-Idaho manager by Ogden construction executive W. A. Wattis.[3]

Facing substantial losses of their own in income, farmers defaulted on the high-interest mortgages they had entered during the war, causing many rural banks to fail and credit to dry up. In the western portion of the Uinta Basin, the Bank of Duchesne closed in 1921, followed the next year by Myton State Bank. Creditors in charge of liquidating the banks' assets found few buyers, because "all of the real estate loan companies ha[d] withdrawn" from the region.[4]

Although the agricultural recession eased slightly after 1923, the economic outlook in rural Utah remained discouraging. Farm income rose modestly from $57 million in 1924 to nearly $65 million in 1925 but then fell to roughly $62 million in 1926 and $61 million the next year. E. G. Peterson, president of the State Agricultural College, lamented in 1927, "Agriculture is the only member of our national economic family which is not thriving as it should."[5]

The profits of sugar beet growers were further confounded in the 1920s by an extensive outbreak of curly-top blight, a viral disease that ravaged beet fields and thereby dulled beet sugar's competitive edge against sugar cane. During the 1910s curly top had plagued some localities in the Intermountain West and had wreaked havoc in Nampa, Idaho. As farmers coped with falling prices after World War I by abandoning dryland wheat fields, they created an ideal breeding environment for the virus's vector, the white fly. Curly top caused the leaves of young plants to wilt and the roots to shrivel and harden. Few areas of Utah escaped its ravages in the decade after the war. A sugar factory in Brigham City that processed 246,000 bags of sugar in 1923 processed less than one-fourth of that amount in 1924 because of the virus. In the state at large, sugar production fell by 40 percent between 1925 and 1926 due to curly top. As harvests plunged, sugar factories in many towns, including Lehi, Brigham City, Delta, Elsinore, Payson, and Moroni, closed. Some factories managed to remain open, and beet harvests rose modestly in 1927 and 1928. But the market for beet sugar remained disappointing: in 1929 Utahns planted only 40,104 acres of sugar beets compared to 93,359 in 1919. Even after blight-resistant varieties of beets were developed, farmers distrusted the crop.[6]

A struggling rural economy underscored the cultural as well as the economic decline of the countryside. As the farm economy languished, Utahns moved to the cities in record numbers, seeking educational and occupational opportunities. The out-migration adversely affected rural-community institutions from sports teams to dramatic associations. As Elmo Geary and Edward Geary observed with regard to Emery County, the population drain would eventually leave "the Emery County communities largely composed of the old and the very young, with a relatively small proportion of the population in the twenty- to forty-year-old range."[7]

Thousands more packed their bags and left for sunny Southern California. The Golden State had long been a favored vacation destination of Utahns, and its economy was more robust than the economies of the mountain states. LDS Church membership records offer a glimpse of the magnitude of the migration from Utah: at the end of World War I, only four hundred Mormons resided in Los Angeles, but by 1923 there were ten times that many, most of them natives of Utah and Idaho. In 1923 George W. McCune, an emigrant from Utah who owned an investment company and had recently been called as president of the church's new Los Angeles Stake, wrote that moving to the City of the Angels had "become a fad" among Mormons. McCune warned those contemplating a move not to "rush pell-mell to southern California." Many who had arrived without job offers now wished they had stayed in Utah. Despite his warnings, growth continued, and by 1927 more than eight thousand Mormons lived in Los Angeles.[8]

Despite the generally gloomy market for Utah's farm products, there were a few encouraging developments in the years following the war. One during the early 1920s involved alfalfa seed. Farmers and ranchers across the nation turned increasingly to alfalfa as a forage crop in the 1920s, and as luck would have it, climatic conditions in the Uinta Basin and Millard County were optimal for raising and harvesting alfalfa seed; Utah soon became a leading producer, due partly to the entrepreneurial efforts of N. L. Peterson and George H. Tingley, residents of Myton who persuaded farmers in the area to form the Uintah Basin Seed Growers Association and talked the J. G. Peppard Seed Company of Missouri into building a seed-processing facility there. By 1924 twelve hundred farmers were raising alfalfa seed in Duchesne and western Uintah Counties. Production peaked in 1926, when Utah produced nearly half of the nation's alfalfa seed. Production that year was valued at $3.2 million. But in the second half of the decade, this wonder crop suffered reverses from water shortages; infestations of lygus bugs, weevils, grasshoppers, and Chalcis flies; and competition from midwestern growers. By 1930 Utah was growing less than 4 percent of the nation's alfalfa seed.[9]

Unlike the euphoric but ephemeral alfalfa-seed boom, an increase in truck farming was more enduring and brought welcome cash to growers along the Wasatch Front. Utah's dominant truck crops during the twenties were tomatoes, peas, onions, and beans, with much of the production centered in Davis and Weber Counties, near many of the state's largest canneries. A specialty market also developed for Utah celery. The acreage Utahns devoted to tomatoes, peas, onions, and beans rose from 6,398 in 1919 to 17,493 a decade later. In 1929 the combined value of these four crops was nearly $1.8 million. In terms of crops their value was exceeded only by wheat ($4.3 million), sugar beets ($4.1 million), and hay ($2.4 million). Demand for truck crops depended partly upon canneries' ability to market canned vegetables and ketchup out of state. In some years such as 1925, demand was high and profits were solid; by contrast, in 1926 canneries were unable to sell their stock of goods because of high freight rates. When demand declined at the canneries, tomato farmers still managed to make some money by shipping green tomatoes on the rails to out-of-state markets, although shipping costs reduced their profits.[10]

Taking advantage of abundant water and sandy soil, farmers in Green River found a profitable crop in melons during the 1920s, after experimenting unsuccessfully with peach growing. One Green River concern alone shipped more than three hundred carloads of melons to market in some years, reaching markets as far away as New York. In the state at large, growers experimented with cantaloupe. The acreage devoted to the crop more than doubled, rising from 240 acres in 1919 to 599 in 1929.[11]

Nearly two-thirds of the state's farm income in the 1920s came from the sale of livestock and livestock products, but prices were disappointingly low. Each year beginning in 1922, Ogden hosted a livestock show, where ribbons were awarded for prize animals. In 1926 a new coliseum was erected to house the exhibition. Unfortunately, the animals exhibited were atypical; impacted by the close historical relation of dairying to the Mormon village-grazing industry, tens of thousands of Utah's half-million range cattle in the 1920s were of dairy breeds, making Utah's beef industry poorly bred. Although ranchers moved aggressively to upgrade their herds, the dairy strains slowed the advance of the industry generally. The number of beef cattle remained fairly constant over the first half of the decade and then dropped more than 20 percent between 1925 and 1930. As the numbers fell, beef prices inched upward in 1926 and 1927 and then rose more dramatically in 1928 and 1929, but even at that level they were unimpressive. Opportunities to make money by selling sheep or their wool were greater than in the cattle industry, particularly in the middle years of the decade, and this induced Utah ranchers to increase their sheep herds by nearly half between 1920 and 1930. In the spring of 1930, a quarter-million sheep were sheared in the southeastern portion of the state alone. Additionally, the number of chickens raised on farms in the Beehive State more than tripled over the decade; the bulk of revenue in the poultry industry came from the sale of eggs. Beginning in 1928, growers in Moroni developed a specialty in turkey raising.[12]

Dairy farming expanded considerably after a postwar sag in 1920–21: the number of milk cows rose from 66,724 in 1920 to 82,898 in 1925. A cream check was a welcome, regular boost to income, although the value of dairy products disappointed farmers who recalled the halcyon days of World War I. Dairy farmers in Weber and adjoining counties organized the Weber Central Dairy Association in 1924 as a means of marketing cooperatively in order to enhance their profits. Butter production in the state increased from about 3.5 million pounds in 1920 to more than 8.5 million in 1925, cheese grew from 849,000 pounds to 3,219,000, and condensed milk advanced 199 percent. Agents from major creameries such as Nelson-Ricks in Salt Lake City and Blackman-Griffin in Ogden bought milk from farmers in numerous towns. In Daggett County the Lucerne Creamery, formed by locals in 1923, shipped in dairy cows, sold them to ranchers on the installment plan, processed milk products, and marketed them from southern Wyoming to California. Milk was condensed and canned at plants in Cache County owned by the Utah Condensed Milk Company (purchased by Pet Milk in 1928), Borden, and Morning Milk, which opened a facility in Wellsville in 1923.[13]

MINING AND MANUFACTURING

Although more Utahns worked in agriculture than mining, the state's mines generated greater wealth than its farms and ranches during the twenties. Mineral products were processed on such a grand scale that Salt Lake and Tooele Counties constituted the leading smelting district for nonferrous metals on the continent. "By our smelts ye shall know us," quipped journalist Frank Eversoll.[14]

Among metals copper was the king in the Beehive State, and the Utah Copper Company was the unrivaled leader, generating three-fourths of the dividends of Utah mines. In the still of the night, the 3:00 a.m. blasts at the company's gigantic mine high in the Oquirrh Range could be heard miles away in Salt Lake City.[15]

Lead, a mineral used in paint, pipes, and bullets, was the second-most-remunerative metal mined in the state during the 1920s. Large lead-concentrating plants operated in Park City, Mercur, Tooele, Frisco, and American Fork Canyon. One of the largest lead and silver mines in the nation was the recently discovered Tintic Standard, near Eureka.[16]

The mining economy suffered, along with agriculture, from the postwar recession, although its recovery was much swifter. After peaking in 1917 at $29.3 million, mining-stock dividends tumbled to $11.2 million in 1919, largely because demand for copper collapsed. By the end of 1920 the recession had caught up with lead, zinc, silver, and gold producers, too, forcing mine owners to slash miners' daily wages by as much as $1. In 1921 the mining industry hit rock bottom, paying out only $4.3 million in dividends. The value of gold, silver, copper, lead, and zinc produced that year was down by three-fourths from its wartime pinnacle. Trading on the Salt Lake Stock and Mining Exchange was so sparse that one of the largest stock-brokerage firms closed its doors.[17]

Silver provided a small source of optimism in an otherwise bleak mining picture in 1922, when the total mining dividends were only $5.1 million. Its value was artificially boosted under the terms of the Pittman Silver Act of 1918, which provided for federal purchase of a limited amount of silver at $1 an ounce and coinage of that silver as a reserve to be held in the US Treasury. Western mines raced to cash in on the artificially high price of silver while it lasted. New silver-lead mine discoveries in the Frisco area west of Milford and the Park-Utah mine west of Keetley fueled a boomlet in 1922. At the end of that year, the silver and lead mines were operating full tilt; output in the Park City district was twice as high as it had been in 1921. When the director of the US Mint announced in 1923 that the silver reserves authorized by the Pittman Act had been attained, prices and demand plunged. By 1925 silver was selling for $0.65 an ounce.[18]

Despite the drop in silver prices, mining dividends were nearly twice as high in 1923 as the previous year, thanks to very high prices for lead and increased demand for copper. Utah Copper's earnings were seven times greater in 1923 than in the previous year. "The great intermountain empire that has struck rock-bottom on almost every product...has its worst behind it," the *Salt Lake Tribune* exulted. Dividends in 1924 held steady with the previous year and then rose in 1925 to $12.7 million. The year 1926 was a banner time for Utah's mines, with "remarkable" dividends of $15.1 million due to the "tremendous growth" of the zinc industry following the completion of flotation plants for separating zinc from lead. Demand for copper remained so high that Bingham Canyon's mines produced more copper in 1926 than ever before. In 1927 mine dividends rose slightly, to $15.5 million. The trade in mining stock was brisk, due partly to "sensational discoveries" in some mines in the Tintic district, which delivered a 13 percent return to investors. Lead and silver producers suffered from lagging demand and falling prices in 1928, but copper prices rose by 12 percent, hitting their highest level since World War I. King copper ensured that dividends from the state's mines rose that year to $18.3 million. Copper prices continued upward in 1929, as did mine output. Consequently, the state's mines paid out a record $38 million in 1929 ($32 million paid by Utah Copper alone); the *Salt Lake Tribune* reported that it was the best year in Utah Copper's history to that point. On balance, the prominence of copper in the Utah mining portfolio made the final years of the decade highly remunerative for the state's mining industry, despite reduced demand for other minerals such as lead and silver.[19]

Behind copper and lead, coal was the most valuable product of Utah's mines in the 1920s. Utah's coal mines employed between thirty-three and forty-five hundred men each year, although many worked only part of the year. Early in the decade the industry seemed immune to the postwar recession. Prices remained good, and employment was high in 1920 and early 1921, as shipments of Utah coal to the Pacific Coast continued. But as shipping from overseas coal mines to Pacific ports gradually resumed, a glut developed on the coastal market, driving down prices. Even though coal was cheaper than petroleum, railroads turned increasingly to oil as a fuel, reducing their yearly coal consumption by 110,000 tons. Although new mines opened in Carbon County in 1922 (the Columbia Mine near Sunnyside complete with a company town) to supply coal for a new steel plant being built near Provo and 1923 (mines in Gordon Creek Canyon at Consumers, National, and Sweets), the price of Utah coal fell steadily between 1921 and 1927, as did miners' wages. Average employment was about 19 percent lower in the second half of the decade than the first, and many miners worked only three or four days a week.[20]

Utahns avidly searched for petroleum deposits in the postwar decade. Soon after the war companies drilled unsuccessfully around the shores of the Great Salt Lake and on the Colorado Plateau. But on December 8, 1925, a large gusher of natural gas and oil erupted at the Frank Shafer No. 1 well alongside the Colorado River below Moab. The pressure of the gusher, estimated at sixteen hundred pounds per square inch, blew out the well casing. Experts estimated the well could yield anywhere from 350 and 1,000 barrels of oil per day. For months investors poured money into the well, desperately trying to seal it off from groundwater and regulate the flow of the liquid gold. After three years of trying, the company finally gave up and plugged the well in 1928.[21]

In a state heavily dependent upon income from mining, most Utahns regarded the smoke from coal-burning furnaces and stoves and the emissions from smelter smokestacks and automobiles as an acceptable trade-off for economic growth, jobs, efficiency, and cost-effective home heating. They possessed limited understanding of the health hazards of particulate pollution from smelters and coal-fired furnaces. Still, the adverse impact of smelter smoke upon vegetation was apparent. Moreover, the dense smoke that clogged northern valleys during fall and winter inversions was a "nuisance," and some feared it imperiled mental well-being and respiratory health. A nationwide study of air quality in 1919 in major cities showed Salt Lake to be the nation's fourth-smokiest city. Between September and December 1920, researchers tabulated twenty-six "dense smoke" days where visibility in the capital city was less than one thousand feet. In some years city residents could "not see the sun...for weeks," the *Tribune* reported. In light of these facts, city officials and the Chamber of Commerce teamed up in 1920 with smoke-abatement engineers from the US Bureau of Mines and the University of Utah to look for ways to reduce air pollution. They identified the largest industrial polluters in the valley, visited the factories, investigated production processes, and offered recommendations for reducing smoke. As a result, emissions from coal-burning trains and factories fell by 93 percent between 1919 and 1929. Seventy percent of the coal smoke in the air came from home heating systems, though, and that problem was harder to solve. Engineers established an office downtown where they educated home owners regarding ways to minimize the smoke that resulted from firing and operating coal furnaces and stoves. But this type of outreach was a piecemeal approach to a vast problem.[22]

In 1934 Utah native Bernard DeVoto pointed out that the region's heavy economic reliance upon large-scale corporate mining was harmful in other ways, too. DeVoto characterized the entire American West as "a plundered province." By this he meant that "the few alpine forests of the West were leveled, its minerals were mined and smelted, all its resources were drained off through the perfectly engineered gutters of a system designed to flow eastward." The interior West was essentially a colonial economy, producing raw materials for external investors and markets. Thus, the region's major industries were financed largely by external capital and devoted to processing the crops and minerals extracted from its soil and mountains.[23]

DeVoto's diagnosis closely fitted Utah's metals and milling industries. The state's leading smelters were controlled by wealthy New England and New York capitalists: the International Smelting and Refining Company was owned by the Rockefeller-dominated Anaconda Copper Mining Company, the American Smelting and Refining Company was controlled by the Guggenheim interests, and the United States Smelting, Refining, and Mining Company did the bidding of Boston investors. American capitalists in the twenties reserved the lion's share of corporate profits for themselves rather than increasing their workers' wages, so much of the wealth of Utah's smelters flowed out of the state and into the pockets of investors.[24]

Half a loaf seemed better than none at all, though. The mines and smelters contributed substantially to the local economy in taxes and wages. In 1924 Utah Copper's assessed property valuation exceeded the total value of assessed property in twenty-six of the state's twenty-nine counties; each year Salt Lake County collected more than eight hundred thousand dollars in property taxes from the company. Moreover, a cadre of managers in the mines earned handsome wages for their work. Among them was William O'Connor, who came to Utah in 1910 to work with ASARCO and was appointed general manager of its Utah operations in 1925. These newcomers rose to positions of prominence in the upper crust of society: O'Connor served as president of both the exclusive Alta club and the Alta Ski Association. Thousands of other Utahns owed their more modest monthly paychecks to these absentee-owned mining corporations. Indeed, in 1925 the smelters alone employed twenty-two hundred residents—more than any other manufacturing sector—and thousands more worked in the state's mines. ASARCO's copper smelter in Garfield at the northern tip of the Oquirrh Range with its four blast furnaces and seven reverberatories could engage up to fourteen hundred workers when operating at full capacity. It produced blister copper from ore-concentration mills at Magna and Arthur. ASARCO's Murray silver and lead smelter, nearly surrounded by "a mesa of black slag," had eight blast furnaces and could process two thousand tons of ore per day with the help of one thousand laborers. The United States Smelting, Refining, and Mining Company's silver-lead smelter in Midvale could likewise employ upwards of one thousand workers when operating at peak capacity, producing lead-silver bullion and white refined arsenic that was used in insecticides, fungicides, and other products. Over the mountains in Tooele, the International Smelting Company's plant could process twenty-five hundred tons of lead-silver and copper ore per day.[25]

Mining also spurred job growth in related industries such as steel and iron. In 1922 Columbia Steel Company of San Francisco purchased the coal mines of Utah Coal and Coke in Carbon County along with iron-ore deposits near Cedar City and announced it would construct a steel mill south of Provo. Anticipating that the factory would attract other steel mills and fabrication plants to the area, journalist Frank Eversoll predicted in 1922 that in five years, "the valley of Utah Lake and the Great Salt Lake will be flaming with gigantic flower pots—the sign and symbol of home riches and world ease." While Eversoll's prediction of a string of steel mills failed to materialize, Pacific States Cast Iron Pipe Company, a division of Alabama-based McWane Cast Iron Pipe Company, did establish a pipe foundry nearby in 1926. Together the two plants enriched out-of-state owners but also employed more than eight hundred workers.[26]

Locally owned foundries and companies specializing in mine machinery also developed because of the mines. Nathan Rosenblatt, an ingenious Russian immigrant to Utah by way of Denver, established three factories that manufactured mining machinery and structural steel. His companies employed hundreds in the Salt Lake Valley. On a smaller scale, the Christensen Machine Company, founded in Salt Lake in 1920 by Louis and Clyde Christensen, built ore samplers and flotation machines for mines as well as stokers for coal-fired furnaces.[27]

Utah's other leading industries, which processed agricultural products, also depended upon external investment capital, albeit to a lesser extent than the smelters. Canneries ranked second to smelters in the value of industrial goods produced in the state and also employed thousands of Utahns—particularly young women—seasonally. In 1925, an exceptionally good year for the industry, more than two thousand Utahns processed fruit, vegetables, and condensed milk in the state's thirty-plus canneries. Most of the canneries had started out as locally owned enterprises, and dozens remained under local control in the 1920s, including the Utah Canning Company, the Woods Cross Canning Company, the Kaysville Canning Company, and the Pleasant Grove Canning Company. The largest owner of canneries in the state, though, was the Utah Packing Corporation, a subsidiary of the giant California Packing (Del Monte) corporation.[28]

Other key agricultural industries were the state's seventeen sugar factories (many of them operated by the locally owned and interlocking Utah-Idaho Sugar and Amalgamated Sugar Corporations), which provided six hundred to one thousand jobs, and flour mills (two of the largest of which were located near Ogden and were owned by the California conglomerates Sperry Flour and Globe Milling). Dozens of smaller locally owned mills also processed Utah grains. Utah County had six mills, located in Lehi, Pleasant Grove, Provo, Springville, Payson, and Goshen in 1929. The state also had ten meatpacking plants in 1925, employing nearly four hundred workers. Ogden, a center of meatpacking, had slaughterhouses operated by Wilson Packing, the Ogden (Fox-Keller) Dressed Meat Company, and the Ogden Packing and Provision Company (renamed the American Packing and Provision Company in 1924). All were locally owned. By 1929 the Junction City had the largest livestock market west of Denver. Ogden's slaughterhouses employed more than two hundred workers and processed eighteen thousand cattle, seventy thousand hogs, and ten thousand sheep in 1929.[29]

Many of the state's ten woolen mills and knitting establishments were concentrated in the North, including the Utah Woolen Mills in Salt Lake County as well as Cache Knitting Works, Fonnesbeck Knitting Company, and Union Knitting Mills in Cache County. The workforce of Brigham City's Baron Woolen Mills, manufacturer of blankets, sweaters, scarves, and other clothing items, rose from six traveling salesmen and ten factory workers in 1923 to two hundred salesmen and about four dozen factory employees in 1928. That year the mill produced and sold goods valued at one million dollars.[30]

No one could guess that military installations, which would become the state's largest employers in later decades, held much economic promise. However, the US Army made a crucial decision in 1920 to build a storage site for ammunition on benchlands east of the Great Salt Lake in an effort to decentralize its stockpiles. Congress appropriated ninety-eight thousand dollars to buy the land. Over the next two years thirty-five magazines measuring 220 by 50 feet were constructed for storing the weapons at the new Ogden Arsenal. By 1925, convinced that war was unlikely in the near future, the government laid off most of the employees at the arsenal, classified the ammunition stored there as old and unnecessary, and stopped maintaining the facility. In 1929 thirty-one of the rusting and crumbling magazines blew down. But in the 1930s, as militarism abroad made conflict more likely, the government would refurbish the facility and establish other military installations nearby.[31]

Utah's economic outlook near the decade's end was mixed. The distances separating Utah from major urban markets, coupled with surpluses of farm products, continued to plague growers. Despite a generally weak agricultural economy, over the decade some farmers had managed to find markets for their truck crops or dairy products in the state's canneries and creameries, while others had enjoyed the alfalfa-seed boom before it faded. The coal industry languished, but hard-rock mining had returned handsome profits to investors, thanks to high copper prices in the second half of the decade. Absentee-owned smelters employed thousands of Utah workers. A nascent steel industry, along with locally owned foundries and manufacturers of machinery, provided additional jobs. Utahns also worked at a mixture of locally and nationally managed canneries, sugar factories, meatpacking plants, and woolen mills.

MODERNIZATION, CULTURAL INTEGRATION, AND THE LIMITS OF PROSPERITY

Signs of prosperity were most apparent in urban areas. In the first half of 1922 alone, more than six hundred homes were finished in Salt Lake County. The blocks south of Liberty Park were bisected by new streets during the 1910s and 1920s and lined with tract homes in subdivisions such as Highland Park and Gilmer Park. Kimball and Richards, Salt Lake builders, developed several new subdivisions between 2700 and 3300 South where buyers could obtain efficiently designed bungalows for one hundred dollars down and only thirty dollars a month. On the east bench, stately homes set back from tree-lined streets in the exclusive Bonneville on the Hill subdivision catered to the affluent. Home builders touted the advantages of suburban living, including fresh air, room for large families to work and play, and land for gardens and fruit trees. Prospective buyers in the Homefield subdivision near 2700 South could "raise your own vegetables" in the "deep black loam soil" of a large lot. They could spend their evenings golfing at the newly completed Nibley Park Course nearby, while the city was only a twenty- to twenty-five-minute commute. Those who preferred an urban lifestyle (or who could not afford a suburban lot) could rent an apartment in one of the scores of modern three-story apartment buildings that proliferated after World War I. Most were long, rectangular buildings with a single entrance to the building from the street and long corridors stretching down each floor. By 1931 Salt Lake had 180 multistory apartment buildings.[32]

Particularly in urban areas, retail and service establishments from mortuaries to movie theaters boomed during the twenties, as did investment companies and insurance agencies. Calvin Coolidge's aphorism "The business of America is business" applied well to urban Utah. In 1929 Utah's Commerce Department tallied 1,306 food stores; more than 600 general merchandise stores; 348 clothing stores; 230 dealers of cars, tires, or other automotive accessories; 554 gas stations; and 329 hardware stores. Not every business succeeded, but some who entered the retail trade in the twenties became Utah legends, including Maurice Warshaw, a Russian immigrant who came to Utah as a teenager, began selling vegetables door to door during World War I, and opened fruit stands in the 1920s. In 1928 he opened a market on Main Street in Salt Lake that became the foundation for a retail chain of supermarkets, Grand Central.[33]

The standard of living, as measured by access to modern conveniences, rose over the decade. Even in many farming districts, homes were wired for electricity by the 1920s. In Juab County, for instance, residents of Levan strung twenty-four miles of power line down Salt Creek Canyon and along the foothills in 1922, linking their homes and farms to a generator in Fountain Green. Northward, in Mona, residents received electric service in 1929. By 1930 more than 55 percent of Utah farm homes had electricity, the second-highest percentage in the nation, a fact attributable to the compact settlement pattern in many rural areas. Utahns' use of electricity rose by more than 80 percent between 1920 and 1929 as residents purchased new appliances, from refrigerators to washing machines.[34]

The premier appliance purchase for many families was a radio. By the end of the decade nearly half of the homes in the state had one. Opening the state's first radio broadcast, an announcer shouted, "Hello. Hello. Hello. This is KZN, KZN, the *Deseret News*, Salt Lake City, KZN calling." He promised that the station would "serve you daily with news bulletins, music, weather reports, and other data of interest." By the mid-1920s radio owners could hear broadcasts originating from across the nation, including music, talk shows, radio dramas, news, weather, and sportscasts. Salt Lake alone had six radio stations, and the state's major newspapers devoted a section each week to radio programming, technology, and equipment.[35]

Utahns purchased record numbers of automobiles during the 1920s. The inexpensive, monochrome Model T Ford was especially popular. The number of passenger cars registered in the state rose rapidly, from 38,016 in 1920 to 95,661 in 1929. Each February dealers displayed the latest models in a weeklong auto show at Salt Lake's Bonneville Pavilion on State Street and 900 South. In 1920 an estimated forty-six thousand attended.[36]

With increased automobile ownership came demands for road construction. The Federal Aid Road Act of 1916 and the Federal Aid Highway Act of 1921 appropriated money for highway construction. Both laws required matching money from the states, so the State Road Commission, created in 1909, petitioned the legislature for millions of dollars in bonds for road building. Soon more than a fourth of the state's tax revenue was being spent on roads. By the end of 1921 nearly three hundred miles of road had been built in Utah under this state-federal partnership at a total cost of $11.3 million. Under the State Road Commission's supervision, highways were typically paved in small stretches, with the most heavily traveled sections being improved first. In 1922, for instance, motorists could drive on newly paved concrete between Manti and Ephraim, but north and south of those points the highway was unpaved. Portions of transcontinental highways crossing the Beehive State were also paved in the 1920s, including the Lincoln Highway between Grantsville and Wendover and the Victory Highway between Vernal and Salt Lake.[37]

In the decade after World War I, Utah was also linked by air to the rest of the nation. In 1920 the Postal Service announced plans for an airmail route from Chicago to San Francisco. Much as they had done in the 1860s with the coming of the railroad, Salt Lake and Ogden vied with each other for an air station along the route. Salt Lake civic and business leaders won the bid by raising more than twenty thousand dollars to purchase 106 acres of boggy pasture south of the Great Salt Lake for a landing strip, airplane hangar, and other structures. The facilities were dedicated four days before Christmas in 1920 at a ceremony attended by Governor Bamberger, Salt Lake mayor Clarence Neslen, and heavyweight champion boxer Jack Dempsey. In 1925 Western Air Express, a Los Angeles–based company with an airmail contract, widened its operations to include passenger flights. Customers with ninety dollars could fly from Salt Lake to Los Angeles in eight hours. In 1928 LDS Church president Heber J. Grant permitted a directional sign for pilots and an arrow pointing to the airport to be painted on the convex roof of the Salt Lake Tabernacle. Also in 1928 Ogden entrepreneurs dedicated their own airfield, followed by Logan in 1929 and Provo and Payson in 1930.[38]

The automobile and airplane, along with the infrastructure that supported modern transit, connected urban Utahns to distant locales and strengthened the ties of incorporation within the national consumer culture. Even remote communities were affected. In the late 1920s Leo Munson, a grocer in Escalante, purchased a truck and began making regular trips to Salt Lake City for merchandise. Residents in remote communities like Escalante could now readily obtain mass-produced canned and packaged foods.[39]

Automobiles reduced travel times and made transportation more efficient, while electrical appliances enabled housewives to accomplish more work in the same amount of time. But there were also disadvantages to the new lifestyles. Per capita income in 1929 amounted to only 79 percent of the national average, a reflection not only of large family size but also of a colonial economy that siphoned profits out of state. Many of the new automobiles, appliances, and homes were purchased on credit. Orval Adams, vice president of the Utah State National Bank, cautioned that many consumers were overreaching themselves. "Installment buying in Utah is a matter of concern. Incomes of many workers are spent almost a year in advance for articles offered on credit," he warned at the end of 1928, a year when retail trade had grown by nearly 9 percent.[40]

Despite their efforts to prop up their living standards with credit, Utahns lived at a lower standard than the average American. A higher percentage of Utahns owned their homes than the national average, but their dwellings were relatively small and poorly appointed. The median number of rooms per home was only four, compared to five for the nation at large. Some families in remote farm regions lived in conditions not far removed from those of the nineteenth century. In Duchesne County only 4 percent of all homes had electricity. Some, including Anna and Frank Johnson, lived in tar-paper shacks made of one-inch boards. Other Utahns, such as Mary and Aussie Kimber, who had recently moved from a mining camp to a farm in Carbon County, lived in a dugout, "a big hole in the ground" with dirt walls and a log roof. Even in many of the state's urban areas, many homes lacked conveniences. In Ogden, the state's second-largest city, 8 percent of all dwellings in 1940 lacked an indoor flush toilet, bathtub, or shower. In Provo, the third-largest community, 16 percent lacked an indoor bathroom with running water. In the state at large, nearly one-third of all homes in 1940 had no functional bathroom, and barely half had a mechanical refrigerator. Only 37 percent boasted central heating, compared to roughly 49 percent of all homes in the nation, and in roughly two-thirds of all homes residents cooked on a coal or wood stove.[41]

POLITICS: CHARLES MABEY, GEORGE DERN, AND THE ORDER OF SEVENS

On August 26, 1920, Republicans selected Charles Mabey of Davis County as their gubernatorial nominee. A graduate of the University of Utah and a former schoolteacher and banker, Mabey spoke fluent German as a result of his LDS mission, had served in both the Spanish-American and First World Wars, and had cultivated contacts in state government as a representative in the state legislature from 1912 to 1916. Four days later Democrats chose Thomas N. Taylor, a Provo businessman and Mormon stake president. Mabey and the Republicans accused Democrats of having spent recklessly during Governor Bamberger's administration. Reflecting the conservative, probusiness climate sweeping the nation, they pledged to cut taxes and reduce government expenditures and debt by consolidating regulatory agencies with overlapping jurisdictions and eliminating duplication in services provided by the state's universities in Salt Lake and Logan. Mabey carried every county in the state on Election Day, as did the Republican candidates for the Senate (Smoot) and House (Colton and Leatherwood).[42]

As they debated where to cut government expenditures, the 1921 legislature factionalized along urban-rural lines. Rural lawmakers preferred to cut property taxes, which weighed heavily upon farmers, while urban legislators worried that they would have to raise other taxes and fees in order to offset the loss of property tax revenue. Ultimately, Mabey and the legislature delivered partly on their promises by creating the State Department of Finance and Purchase to streamline government operations and a board to reduce duplication between the state's two public universities. Budgets for education remained stable, but budgets for public welfare, highways, public safety, and public health were slashed. On balance the state spent 31 percent less in 1921 than in 1920—a remarkable feat. Many patronage positions were eliminated by "weed[ing] out the political garden of employees." Along with cutting expenditures, the legislature did cut some taxes, most notably levies on inherited wealth, but lawmakers raised college tuition, the property tax levy, motor vehicle registration fees, and other fees sufficiently to largely offset the tax cuts. After all was said and done, state spending still exceeded revenues by more than $1 million. Although the economic recession of 1920–22 played a role, the main contributor to the shortfall was a drop of more than $2.2 million in county and federal payments to the state for road construction and maintenance.[43]

In 1922 a commission appointed by Mabey to study state finances in order to avoid future shortfalls recommended a state income tax, an innovation that would require amending the state constitution. Remembering Mabey's campaign pledge to cut taxes, voters felt betrayed, and they defeated the proposed amendment at the polls by a margin of more than three to one. As a next-best option the legislature instituted taxes on gasoline and cigarettes in 1923 while cutting automobile registration fees. Mabey regarded the gasoline tax, along with federal subsidies, as essential for highway construction and maintenance. General administrative expenses were further slashed, as were appropriations for the State Department of Agriculture and Public Safety Services, but increases in spending for education largely offset those decreases. In 1922, 1923, and 1924 state revenues exceeded expenditures, and with some justification Mabey claimed credit for the improved fiscal situation.[44]

The 1923 legislature also appropriated matching funds to facilitate health care for mothers and children. Congress had passed the Sheppard-Towner Act in 1921, one of the few immediate Progressive gains of woman suffrage, in response to lobbying from the League of Women Voters. The law offered the states annual grants for preventative health care and education directed at mothers and infants, contingent upon the states matching the grants. Amy Brown Lyman, general secretary of the LDS Church Relief Society and a legislator in the Utah House, introduced an enabling bill in 1923 that passed unanimously. The church's General Relief Society presidency coordinated with state government agencies in organizing classes on health and hygiene and in setting up temporary clinics across the state for physical exams, immunizations, and consultations. Between 1925 and 1929 more than fifty thousand children received physical examinations at these clinics. Largely as a result of services provided under this act, infant mortality fell by 19 percent in the state between 1921 and 1928.[45]

Early in his administration Mabey reportedly aroused the ire of George Wilson, a government purchasing agent, and Wilson's cronies in the Order of Sevens, a semisecret political fraternity that sought to shape the outcome of Salt Lake County Republican elections through backroom deals, bribes, and favors. The order was composed of interlocking cells, each with seven members, who in turn recruited members of additional cells. Membership was by invitation only, and incoming recruits pledged to stand "all for one and one for all" and to keep the order's activities under wraps. Political scientists Dan Jones and Brad Hainsworth have identified likely charter members as Wilson (nicknamed Mr. Sevens), Ernest Bamberger, Salt Lake County Republican chair Charles Morris, Morris's law partner and Speaker of the Utah House Edward R. "Ned" Callister, Theodore Holman, and O. R. Dibblee. Alternately, historian Thomas Alexander identifies James H. Anderson and Edward H. Callister (Ned's father) as the organizers but indicates that by the 1920s, Wilson, Ed Callister, Ernest Bamberger, Ernest's brother Clarence Bamberger, and Clarence's father-in-law, George Odell, were the "principal leaders." Some historians have characterized the Sevens as anti-Mormon, and they did oppose some LDS candidates, but some of the charter members were Mormon. Most members regarded the Sevens as a Republican insiders' club. Some opponents branded it a machine, but it was unconventional in that its putative "boss," Wilson, inhabited a modest home and was never wealthy. The organization did promise position and power to those in its graces, though. Thus, when Wilson handed Mabey a list of his cronies for reappointment to positions in state agencies following Mabey's inauguration in 1921, he expected the governor to cooperate. When he refused, Mabey incurred the Sevens' wrath.[46]

The following year the Sevens used their Salt Lake County power base to shape electoral politics on the state level, portending an uphill battle for Mabey in the next gubernatorial race. At the 1922 Republican convention, Ernest Bamberger, reputedly a charter member of the Sevens as well as the scion of a wealthy Jewish mining family and the nephew of former governor Simon Bamberger, wrangled the Republican senatorial nomination from Ogden entrepreneur and corporate executive William Wattis. Instructing members how to vote, perhaps with some of Bamberger's immense fortune to grease the process, the Sevens delivered more than two hundred Salt Lake County delegate votes for Bamberger at the convention. One county chairman claimed he had been offered cash if he would vote for Bamberger; he assumed his five fellow delegates who had bolted to the Bamberger ticket at the last minute had been bought. "The matter was decided before the convention assembled," complained A. F. Doremus of Tooele County.[47]

Bamberger took on incumbent William H. King, who had survived challenges from W. W. Armstrong and W. R. Wallace in the Democratic convention. The chief policy-related distinction between the two involved the tariff: Bamberger endorsed a high protective tariff, while King opposed it. Bamberger spoke as a mining entrepreneur: "Do you want a tariff on wool, sugar, lead and other products of this state?" he asked an audience. "I believe that if anyone does not want protection for these basic industries of this state he should move out." King and fellow Democrats argued that the tariff benefited wealthy businessmen like Bamberger but forced consumers to pay higher prices for life's necessities. The Republicans championed organized wealth, King claimed, while he had worked indefatigably for the common man. The enormously popular William Jennings Bryan, whom Smoot derisively dubbed a "wandering Democratic gypsy," stumped the state on King's behalf. "There are two ideas of government," Bryan told an overflow audience in Provo. "There are those who believe that if you will only legislate to make the well-to-do prosperous, their prosperity will leak through on those below. The Democratic idea, however, has been that if you legislate to make the masses prosperous, their prosperity will find its way up through every class which rests upon them."[48]

Two weeks before the election, the Republican-leaning *Ogden Standard Examiner* linked Bamberger to the Sevens, Salt Lake County's "machine gang," and claimed the Sevens had bought the Republican nomination for their favored son. Bamberger denied the charges vehemently, but on Election Day King won by 561 votes and carried Weber County by 2,126 votes. It seems likely, as political scientist Brad Hainsworth has inferred, that the last-minute exposé of Bamberger clinched his defeat.[49]

Two years later when Mabey ran for reelection, the Sevens tried to block his renomination. As Mabey recalled, "The leaders [of the Sevens] and those who hold office in the City, County, and State and the organization as such" all opposed him.

Despite their opposition, he secured the nomination. In their convention the Democrats selected George Dern as their candidate. The son of German immigrants, Dern had been born and reared in Nebraska but had come west with his parents to the Mercur mines at age twenty-two in 1894. Moving upward in the ranks of mine management from bookkeeper to treasurer to assistant manager to general manager, he became well known in Utah business circles. In 1914 he ran successfully for the state senate and served there until 1922. A Progressive, he voted for workmen's compensation, the initiative, the referendum, and the Corrupt Practices Act, and he was endorsed by the venerable Wisconsin Progressive "Fighting" Bob La Follette.[50]

Mabey ran on his record of stringent economy. Dern and the Democrats accused Mabey of mindlessly slashing budgets and foolishly skimping on education and highway maintenance. They promised to be more prudent and "reduce government expenditures to the lowest possible limit compatible with a government honestly, efficiently, and economically conducted." Under Dern life would be "a little easier for the common man," the Democrats promised. Dern's campaign slogan, drafted by his nephew Ira Dern, was destined to become a classic in Utah political history: "Utah Needs a Dern Good Governor And I Don't Mean Mabey."[51]

Utah's Republican senator Reed Smoot and Republican congressmen Don Colton and Elmer Leatherwood all refused to campaign for Mabey, perhaps in response to pressure from the Sevens. Although Mabey carried most rural counties, he lost by huge margins in Carbon, Salt Lake, and Weber Counties, costing him the election. Mabey attributed his defeat to machine politics, a view shared by political scientist Brad Hainsworth, who studied the election. "The inescapable conclusion is the members of the Sevens organization had repudiated [Mabey] in favor of Dern," he observed. Noting that thousands more Utahns voted for Coolidge, the Republican candidate for president, than for Mabey, the *Deseret News* concluded, "Governor Mabey was defeated by members of his own party."[52]

While partisan factionalism and political vengeance may have contributed to Mabey's defeat, his opponent was undeniably an impressive candidate in his own right, and many Utahns voted for him on the basis of his business and legislative record. As the *Deseret News* observed following the election, "He is a splendid type of citizen, thoroughly acquainted with the affairs of government and will doubtless make a capable executive."[53]

Dern proved to be an exceptionally vigorous, effective governor. He served as chairman of the National Governors' Conference from 1928 to 1930. Dern's largest achievements involved negotiating with other states and the federal government rather than working with the Republican-controlled legislature in Utah. He complained in 1927 that he was a "lonesome Democrat completely surrounded by an overwhelmingly Republican legislature, which always has an eye on the political aspects of any question." Dern did not exaggerate; there were only six Democrats in the house and one in the senate in 1925, compared to forty-six Republicans in the house and nineteen in the senate. Throughout Dern's administration Republicans outnumbered Democrats in the legislature, although the numbers were more evenly split in 1929. On many occasions the lawmakers scuttled his recommendations.[54]

One of Dern's foremost accomplishments involved securing ownership of mineral rights on state school lands. Governor Mabey had initiated an abortive lawsuit to gain these rights. Dern chose to approach the issue through political organization. At a western governors' conference in 1926, Dern galvanized a successful drive to persuade Congress to pass the 1927 Jones Act, a law conferring mineral rights upon the states for state school lands.[55]

During his first term in office Dern promoted scenic tourism as an economic resource, including the designation of Bryce Canyon as a national park and construction of a highway through Zion Park to facilitate travel between Zion and Bryce Canyon. He also promoted new buildings at the state's universities and the State Mental Hospital as well as economy at the state prison. Dern lobbied the US Bureau of Mines to fund research at the University of Utah and encouraged the establishment of new agricultural experimental farms across the state. His open-door policy enabled common citizens to meet with him in his office.[56]

Midway through Dern's first term, Republicans swept the state in the 1926 elections. Representatives Colton and Leatherwood were reelected in what political scientist Dan Jones called "placid and dull" races. Smoot, running on his seniority, his apostleship, and his record of bringing a Federal Reserve Bank to Salt Lake as well as reservoirs and national parks, easily defeated Democrat Ashby Snow. After senate president Alonzo Irvine unfairly labeled Snow "Acquisitive Ashby," the beleaguered Democrat felt compelled to publicize his record of charitable giving in newspaper ads, a strategy that made him appear pompous.[57]

The year 1928 was again kind to incumbents. Dern adopted the clever slogan "One good term deserves another" and squared off against William Wattis, general manager of the Utah-Idaho Sugar Company and one of the founders of the Utah Construction Company. Both Smoot and his fellow LDS apostle and Republican David O. McKay endorsed Wattis, while Elders J. Golden Kimball and B. H. Roberts of the church's First Council of Seventy supported Dern. Aside from the protective tariff, an issue over which governors have no jurisdiction, the two candidates differed little in their pronouncements. Dern claimed noncontroversially that he stood for "economic efficiency, social justice, individual liberty, higher wages, elimination of waste, and a feeling of motherhood," the latter a reference to federally funded prenatal clinics. He claimed his record demonstrated his commitment to states' rights, intellectual freedom, religious tolerance, compassion for the mentally ill, and conservation. When an avalanche had struck Bingham Canyon and when floodwaters had threatened Carbon County, he had toured the areas and facilitated relief efforts. Wattis campaigned on his successful business record. Dern was reelected, as were Congressmen Leatherwood and Colton.[58]

The most explosive race of 1928 pitted Senator King against Ernest Bamberger of the Order of Sevens. In a year when Republicans were riding at high tide nationally, Bamberger's chances of unseating King seemed excellent, and he lavished his fortune on the race. Bamberger attacked King's voting record, including his well-known opposition to the Sheppard-Towner Act and his vote against a child labor law. For his part, King accused Bamberger of being an inexperienced puppet of Smoot. "It is bad enough that Senator Smoot has one vote in the Senate and I certainly don't want him to have two," he quipped. In late October the campaign focus veered from legislation and experience to ethics. On October 28 an open letter by prominent Salt Lake resident Joseph J. Cannon appeared as a paid advertisement in Salt Lake papers. Cannon derided Bamberger as an inarticulate political neophyte of "commonplace ability" who had outmaneuvered politician and statesman J. Reuben Clark in the Republican convention due to the machinations of the Sevens. "Men in whose integrity I have entire confidence, have told me they were offered money if they would vote at the State Convention at Ogden for Ernest Bamberger," he asserted. On November 2 the Republican state committee denied Cannon's charges of vote buying as "unfair, unwarranted and untrue." Friends, including Richard Madsen, Henry Rolapp, and Preston Nibley, vouched for Bamberger's honesty in advertisements appearing on November 4.[59]

That same day Mabey, still smarting from his political defeat in 1924, entered the fray, paying for space in the newspapers to print a denunciation of the Sevens signed by J. Reuben Clark. Dated October 31 and addressed to the Republican National Committee, Clark's telegram read, "Have always been and am now opposed to any and all secret political organizations whatever their name and however they are constituted." The next day a Republican ad tacitly acknowledged the existence of the Sevens but denied that Bamberger was a member. "Ernest Bamberger is not now, and never has been, a member of the Sevens and has never contributed a penny to their support." In another ad David A. Smith defended the integrity of convention proceedings. "All direct charges [against Bamberger] have been proven to be untrue....I was not bought, intimidated or coerced," he declared. The following day Smith retracted his general statements. "Evidence has been brought to me which convinces me that I was not justified," he admitted, in alleging that the charges against Bamberger were "untrue." In another ad on the following page, Mabey shared the incriminating evidence: a recent "notice for a meeting of the Sponsors of the Sevens" had listed the meeting place as "the office of Mr. Ernest Bamberger." There could be no other conclusion, Mabey maintained, than that Bamberger was "the beneficiary and motivating influence of the secret machine called the Sevens." On Election Day Bamberger carried seventeen of the state's twenty-nine counties but lost by a huge margin in Salt Lake County, the Sevens' fulcrum. The accusations of Mabey and Clark, which carried particular weight with many Mormon voters, had "split the Republican Party wide open," Judge Horace Beck believed, inducing many to cross party lines and vote for King. Whereas Bamberger had lost to King by barely six hundred votes in 1922, he lost by more than twenty thousand in 1928. The Sevens, along with Bamberger's political aspirations, were moribund. In time, though, Bamberger's reputation would revive. When he died in 1958, he was praised widely for his community service. The *Deseret News* eulogized him as a "philanthropist with a heart quite as large as his many successful enterprises."[60]

Apparently, Bamberger's alleged corruption tarred not only his own candidacy but that of many other members of his party. That year Democrats nearly regained control of the state house and senate, securing twenty-six of the fifty-five seats in the house and nine of the twenty seats in the senate.[61]

Midway through Dern's second term in the 1930 election, Republicans again did well. Republican representative Don Colton won handily over his opponent, Ogden mayor Frank Francis. Representative Leatherwood had died in office at the end of 1929. In the race to fill his seat, Republican Frederick C. Loofbourow, a district court judge in Salt Lake, defeated progressive University of Utah professor J. H. Paul. Paul would have likely won but for the candidacy of George N. Lawrence of the newly organized Liberty Party, which favored repeal of Prohibition; Lawrence drew 13.2 percent of the vote, compared to Paul's 42.4 percent and Loofbourow's 44.4 percent.[62]

In 1930 voters approved an amendment to the state constitution to permit a state income tax, a sign that the probusiness conservatism of the 1920s was waning as the economy worsened. Dern had worked with the legislature to create a bipartisan commission to study ways to make the state's tax structure, which relied heavily upon property taxes and thus discriminated against farmers, more equitable. Dern had identified tax reform as a key goal of his second term in office. Like the 1922 commission appointed by Mabey, the commission appointed under Dern recommended an amendment to the state constitution authorizing a direct income tax, including a tax on business income. The Republican Party, the *Salt Lake Tribune*, and the Utah Manufacturers Association opposed the amendment, which would tax intangible property such as investment income, arguing that it would discourage capitalists from moving to the Beehive State. Leading the opposition was senate president Hamilton Gardner. But the Democratic Party, the Utah Farm Bureau, and the Utah Education Association, which stood to benefit from income tax revenues that would be passed on to public schools, endorsed the measure, labeling its wealthy opponents "tax dodgers." Thus, educators and farmers regarded the 1930 amendment as a key victory. Following passage of the amendment, the legislature enacted a graduated personal income tax and an excise tax for corporations.[63]

Dern's second administration coincided with the state's descent into the depths of the Great Depression. He called upon the federal government to boost consumer buying power by purchasing and coining silver, a move that most economists opposed but one that would have benefited Utah's mine owners and workers. In an era when jobs were scarce, he ordered the State Road Commission to concentrate its construction efforts in the winter months when living expenses were greatest and work was scarcest in order to maximize the relief value of public employment. He also proclaimed May 8, 1932, as a statewide day of fasting and urged residents to donate the money or food they had saved thereby to charity. In 1931 Dern organized the State Advisory Council of Unemployment, chaired by Sylvester Cannon, to assist local governments in responding to unemployment and maximizing employment in the private sector and on public works projects. In 1933, following Dern's second term as governor, Franklin D. Roosevelt invited him to accept a position in his cabinet as secretary of war, the first Utahn to serve in a cabinet position.[64]

CULTURAL DEVELOPMENTS AND LEISURE

Public policies involving taxation, highway construction, and the tariff affected most Utah wageworkers and consumers. Yet for many residents of the Beehive State, key political questions of the era, such as those involving state versus federal control of the public lands or the water in the Colorado River, seemed abstract. Close to 40 percent of Utah adults of voting age failed to cast a ballot in the 1920 gubernatorial election. Moreover, nearly half of the state's residents were children or teenagers, many of whom lived their lives apart from the political questions of their era.

Cultural developments and trends shaped the lifestyles of a far broader cross-section of Utah's population in the 1920s, from children to senior citizens, in ways that were sometimes superficial and other times deeply resonant with their daily lives and values.

In 1920 Utah's 330,000 Mormons represented only .036 percent of the nation's 92 million inhabitants. By the workings of isolation and cultural relationships, this tiny minority was transformed into a staggering majority in the state itself. Although 130,000 Mormons were said to "have little interest" in the church, and "30 percent" were "under teen age," Mormons accounted for 73 percent of the state's 450,000 inhabitants and 90 percent of its churched population. About 20,400 were Roman Catholics. Close to 13,800 were Protestants. Protestant denominations broke down about as follows: Presbyterians 3,550, Methodists 3,220, Episcopalians 2,295, Congregationalists 2,295, Baptists 1,887, and Lutherans 609. Remaining were some 6,000 Utahns who made up the membership of Greek Orthodox, Hebrew, Salvation Army, Unitarian, and various smaller Pentecostal and Adventist churches. About 80,000 belonged to no church. Frustrated by this unchurched contingent,

Protestant clergymen sometimes inveighed against the "sleeping Gentiles" as "unawakened allies" or as "Godless Gentiles." Other churchmen justified them as part of a floating and overworked society or just as God-fearing people with no stomach for cultural conflict.[65]

Many Utahns were patriotic, and proud of it, during the 1920s, and they honored those who had served and given their lives in the war to end all wars. Chapters and women's auxiliaries of the newly created veterans' organization, the American Legion, along with the Gold Star Mothers, composed of women whose sons had perished in the war, and the Service Star Legion formed in many communities across the state to promote veterans' interests, patriotism, and civic improvement. In Nephi in 1925 the Service Star Legion completed an elaborate archway topped by a huge star with sixty-two red, white, and blue lights honoring local World War I veterans. In Beaver a chapter and women's auxiliary of the American Legion raised funds for a dance hall; sponsored social events; organized patriotic programs for Armistice Day, Memorial Day, Independence Day, and Washington's Birthday; and erected a monument on Main Street honoring those who served in the war. In Salt Lake mothers and wives of veterans raised funds for landscaping a tract called Memory Grove at the mouth of City Creek Canyon in honor of the 277 Salt Lakers who had died in the conflict. Similarly, in Provo a city block was set aside as a soldiers' memorial park. The beautifully landscaped setting contained a lily pond, graveled paths, and seventeen trees planted in honor of the same number of Provo boys who died in the war.[66]

Baseball, a popular sport in many Utah communities during the 1920s, occupied prodigious amounts of some Utahns' free time. From 1915 to 1925 thousands of fans crowded into Bonneville Baseball Park in Salt Lake to watch the Bees, a minor-league team affiliated with the Pacific Coast League. Although they were disappointed when team owner Bill Lane transferred the Bees to Southern California in 1926, they could still root for a semipro team that competed in the Utah-Idaho League between 1926 and 1929, playing in a new community ballpark on the corner of 1300 South and West Temple. Provo's semiprofessional ball club played at a diamond and one-thousand-seat grandstand built with donated labor and funds. The town had a difficult time filling the bleachers, though, especially for Wednesday- and Friday-afternoon games, when many residents were still at work, and for Sunday games, when church leaders discouraged attendance. Many communities fielded teams. In Cache Valley teams from Lewiston, Richmond, Logan, and Preston, Idaho, played on Saturday afternoons. In Carbon County mining companies recruited teams for their towns. As Philip Cederlof recalled, "All of the larger camps had teams. Competition and interest were keen. The superintendents and mine management went to great lengths to get good players. Both local and outside men were sought for their playing skills and could get a job anytime."[67]

High school sports nurtured community spirit and provided cherished entertainment. Evan Patterson recalled that in Beaver, "sports were the entertainment of the day," along with dancing. In 1927 the Minersville High basketball team, comprising all the junior and senior boys in the school, took the state title, earning the right to travel to the national high school tournament in Chicago by defeating BY High from Provo. The town turned out en masse to see the boys off at the train station. The Garfield High School hoopsters also traveled to Chicago after winning championship games in Richfield and Salt Lake. "I don't know of anything that ever happened in the schools of Panguitch that created as much excitement as this did," recalled one resident.[68]

Residents of the Beehive State spent time at the racetrack, too, especially between 1925 and 1927. Betting on horses had been outlawed by the legislature in 1913, but in 1925, by wide margins, the senate and house approved a pari-mutuel betting bill introduced by Charles Redd, a southeastern Utah legislator and rancher. The law established a state-appointed race commission to oversee betting on races at private tracks because placing bets through a bookie was still illegal. After each race the state would garner a portion of the proceeds as public revenue. The *Deseret News* favored the law on the somewhat dubious grounds that it would encourage livestock breeding and thereby provide better horses for the farm. What was more certain was that it would raise revenue for the state; during its first six months of operation, the law netted nearly $130,000 in state revenue. Unfortunately, the state's involvement in the racing business also bred corruption when racetrack owner William P. Kyne, a San Francisco speculator, hired members of the state racing commission to work at his track. An explosive allegation, never definitely proved, was that members of the commission had taken payments from Kyne in return for granting him the horse-racing concession at the state fair. Two years after it had supported pari-mutuel betting, the *Deseret News* reversed position. "Horse racing means gambling.... Every community that has had race meets reports an increase in vice and crime during and following the racing season," it editorialized. Redd did his best to make amends, introducing a new bill to abolish state-sponsored pari-mutuel betting. In mid-February legislators passed Redd's bill by wide margins. Despite the new law, though, bookies continued to take bets over the telephone and at gaming joints. In 1928 Salt Lake police raided eight clubs and stores where bookies operated. That same year the state deputy treasurer, David J. Pugh, was convicted of stealing $104,000 in state revenue and wagering much of the money on horses.[69]

Utahns also recreated at resorts such as Lagoon, Vivian Park, Geneva, Provonna Beach, and Saratoga. Particularly famous was Saltair, a 140-by-250-foot recreation pavilion and dance floor built out over the Great Salt Lake and capped by Moorish domes. The resort, which attracted close to five hundred thousand visitors in some years, boasted amusement rides, Utah's largest dance floor, and swimming facilities. A fifteen-mile railroad ran west from Salt Lake City to the resort. Common activities at resorts included swimming, baseball, concerts, beauty contests, and boxing and wrestling matches. In the evenings and on weekends Utahns also kicked up their heels at dance halls. Most resorts had them, but entrepreneurs opened separate dance halls elsewhere, too. For instance, halls were constructed in Carbon County in Price, Helper, and Wellington during the 1920s.[70]

Utahns enjoyed holiday parades and festivals such as Brigham City's Peach Days, too. The biggest summer holiday in Johns Valley, a farming district north of Bryce Canyon, was Pioneer Day, when families gathered in the mountains at Pine Lake for a dance, wrestling matches, horse racing, and footraces. An annual event in Beaver was the Deer Hunters' Dance, an all-night event where bootleg whiskey flowed freely the night before hunting season began. In eastern Utah the Uintah Basin Industrial Commission, organized by civic and church leaders, the Farm Bureau, and Ute leaders, established a popular community tradition of a fair, Chautauqua, and rodeo each August. In 1927 the three-day program included concert performances by the Fort Douglas military band, an outdoor theatrical performance staged by students from the University of Utah, and speeches by visiting dignitaries.[71]

From time to time, significant advances and red-letter events like the arrival of electricity or the paving of a town's thoroughfare called for special celebrations. In 1923, for instance, more than fifteen hundred residents of Salina and nearby communities pulled out all the stops to celebrate the paving of Main Street. Businesses were decorated, flags were draped across the street, bonfires were built to warm celebrants, and decorative lights were hung. After a dinner of barbecued beef, hot rolls, and coffee and a concert by the high school band, teenagers and adults repaired to dances in separate venues.[72]

Occasionally, elements of Utah's cultural past resurfaced, creating jarring elements on the modern landscape, throwbacks to the visionary, apocalyptic worldview that had attracted many of Utah's Mormon settlers in the previous century. The dissonance demonstrated how much had changed over the past few decades. In 1918 ten families gathered at West Tintic on land that Moses Gudmundson, a professor of violin and orchestra at Brigham Young University, was homesteading. As his daughter Emma recalled, her father "started feeling like the last days had begun" as a result of the influenza pandemic, "and he started the idea of getting a bunch to go off and live their religion the way they wanted." The group formed a communal order patterned after the United Order experiments of Brigham Young's era, sharing their resources and farming the land cooperatively. They became vegetarians, which created practical difficulties when rabbits ate the crops they planted. LDS authorities tolerated Gudmundson's eccentricities and established a branch at West Tintic, but after Gudmundson introduced the doctrine of "wife sacrifice," a twist on the historical practice of polygamy that involved wife swapping in order to help residents "overcome selfishness," LDS authorities excommunicated him and disbanded the branch.[73]

Notwithstanding its cultural throwbacks and peculiarities, Utah participated in national cultural trends as well as the glamour and thrills that characterized the Jazz Age. As was the case elsewhere, these developments, which particularly affected young singles, were most apparent in cities such as Ogden and Salt Lake and in college towns, including Provo, Logan, Cedar City, and Ephraim. In his study of Provo in the 1920s, historian Gary Kunz concluded, "Provo had jazz music at local halls where drunken couples danced close together. In addition Provo had titillating movies in the theaters, all night parties in private homes, bathing beauty contests, sports mania and soap series on the radio and in the newspaper."[74]

In 1925 the editor of the *Manti Messenger* printed an article, probably from a wire service, on immorality and the automobile, believing it would be relevant to Sanpete County readers: "The automobile, properly used, is one of the greatest of all instruments for pleasure as well as profit," the writer observed. However, "when misused it is the devil's own engine." The article warned of "the scandals of petting parties" in the backseats of automobiles, adding that "the highways...are now infested by the boldest acts that are shocking communities everywhere and...are breaking the hearts of fathers and mothers throughout the land."[75]

Guardians of traditional morals mobilized civic and legal resources to gauge the extent of this cultural onslaught. A 1922 report of the LDS Church's Social Advisory Committee derided the "absurd and sensual dress" and the "strange dancing and lurid music" that predominated at dances and parties in Mormon country. Law enforcement officials' reports corroborated their claims. In September 1921 Utah County deputy sheriff Otto Birk investigated a wild party at the Geneva resort near Utah Lake and reported, "Young girls of fourteen and fifteen were dancing the cheek to cheek, stopping frequently to kiss and embrace with men and boys. Before the evening was over, they were biting each other on the neck. There was liquor floating around, but liquor wasn't needed to intoxicate the girls and boys. The jazz music did that."[76]

Civic and religious leaders fought to reenthrone purity. To bolster traditional morals at the University of Utah, Bessie Jones, president of the Woman's League in Salt Lake, convened a meeting in 1922 to establish a women's court that would "prosecute" women for moral lapses, including dancing "the cheek to cheek" or liberally applying makeup in the fashion of Parisian "painted ladies." Brigham Young's daughter Susa Young Gates, a prominent writer and former editor of LDS women's magazines, preached against sexual indulgence in a bit of verse published in the widely circulated *Improvement Era* in 1929:

Be the parcel, not the wrapper; be a woman, not a flapper.
Stand up to your fate, for you can,

Just lift up your eyes, to the blue of the skies,
Be ready to marry a man!

L. John Nuttall III, dean of the College of Education at BYU, advised teachers of teenagers, "Let well-selected books and lessons, hikes, parties, and various entertainments, dramatics, community celebrations and fairs furnish [new experiences, new sensations, new excitements, new stimuli] rather than let youth find it alone in public dance halls, sensational motion pictures, automobile riding, and unusual 'thrillers' at resorts."[77]

To a large degree, reformers like Nuttall succeeded in implementing their vision of moral order. While Utah had its risqué dancing, petting parties, and bathing-beauty contests, young people also engaged in more conventional fun. Teens across the state regularly participated in violin and piano recitals and enjoyed high school ball games, dances, plays, comical skits, and readings such as "The Mysteries of Grandpa's False Teeth." Each winter the hiking club at the University of Utah sponsored a three-day outing at Pinecrest Inn, a lodge in Emigration Canyon. The outing was tame rather than a weekend fling of necking, petting, and dancing the cheek to cheek: the group skied; danced the fox-trot, waltz, and Virginia reel; sledded; bowled; and played pool and cards. Several married couples—primarily professors and their spouses—accompanied the club on their annual outing as chaperones.[78]

Despite the cheap amusements, new pleasures, and popular culture that gave the 1920s a reputation for frivolity, parties, and excess, the twenties also marked the apogee of coercive legislation regarding morals and private conduct. In this respect Utah followed national trends. Indeed, many of the legislative issues that seemed to matter most to Utahns involved private conduct and morals. Local officials in some communities adopted blue laws closing recreational enterprises on Sundays. In Provo the 1926 city council voted to close movie theaters on Sundays. Logan's city commission backed the owner of a new roller rink into the corner by banning Sunday skating.[79]

Nationwide the 1920s was the Prohibition decade, when it was illegal to manufacture or sell alcoholic beverages. The Beehive State's experiment with Prohibition began on August 1, 1917. At the time, because it was still legal to manufacture and sell liquor in Wyoming, it was relatively easy to flaunt the law. Many thirsty consumers beat a path to Evanston to stock up on liquor. After Summit County law enforcement officers established a checkpoint on the highway to inspect cars crossing into Utah from the Cowboy State, smugglers had to be more creative. According to local lore, a Park City mortician drove to Wyoming in a hearse and loaded a casket in the back with whiskey bottles in order to hoodwink unsuspecting deputies.[80]

After the Volstead Act took effect in 1920, Prohibition became the law nationwide. In Utah members of the Social Welfare League, derisively dubbed the "Purity Squad" by Salt Lake attorney and legislator Grant Macfarlane, vigilantly defended

Prohibition. Led by Milton Bennion, the dean of the University of Utah's School of Education, and Katherine Palm of the juvenile court system, the league examined problems related to health, education, recreation, and vice and lobbied officials to enforce liquor and tobacco laws. Its blue-ribbon membership included Ruth May Fox of the LDS Young Ladies Mutual Improvement Association, Methodist Episcopal reverend Frank W. Bross, Methodist reverend Stanley Curtis, Presbyterian reverend George E. Davies, Rabbi Adoph Steiner, and Amy Brown Lyman, founding director of the LDS Church Relief Society Social Service Department. The league influenced the outcome of county sheriff elections, demanded and received reports from law enforcement officials, galvanized official investigations, and precipitated ousters of lackadaisical deputies and officers.[81]

In some respects Prohibition worked: alcohol consumption in the nation fell by between a third and a half. Instances of public drunkenness, driving under the influence, physical abuse by drunken adults, and alcohol-related diseases fell. However, under Prohibition drinking became a glamorous, hip sign of sophisticated rebellion among young people. Bootleg liquor was ubiquitous at dance halls; the manager of the Geneva resort reported that it flowed freely at every dance held there in the summer of 1921. In 1923 parents and leaders of LDS youth in Utah Valley alleged that "the use of tobacco and intoxicants and profanity are increasing alarmingly among the minors of our local communities among both males and females."[82]

While advocates believed that tougher enforcement of the law would resolve the problems, Prohibition was difficult to enforce for several reasons. First, federal Prohibition agents were poorly paid and easily bought off. Second, many judges were "lenient" with violators. Salt Lake police chief Joseph Burbidge complained that judges typically fined violators and then allowed them thirty to sixty days to pay. Many never paid up, and the courts did not bother to track them down. "We have got jails and jails were built for the purpose of housing law violators," Burbidge complained. "Bootleggers must be given jail sentences to remedy the evils in the present system." A third reason that enforcement was difficult was because homemade liquor, or hooch, was easy to make and therefore abundant. Anyone could allow a mixture of grain or fruit, yeast, and sugar to ferment. Next the mixture was strained through a cloth into cooking pots and heated. Alcohol boils at a lower temperature than water. As the alcohol in the mixture reached the boiling point, it would rise as steam and pass through a hole in the top of the cooking pot and into a copper-tubing condenser. As it cooled the steam would condense into liquid droplets, flowing into an attached container. Following this basic process Utahns produced liquor in hundreds of stills set up in basements, barns, garages, warehouses, dugouts, washes, and ravines. As historians Jody Bailey and Robert McPherson have written, "Mormons and gentiles, miners and cowboys, farmers and businessmen, Mexicans and Navajos all trafficked in liquor."[83]

Despite the difficulties of enforcing the law, agents employed by the US Prohibition Bureau (housed initially in the Treasury Department), local law enforcement officials, and concerned citizens who were deputized by the governor scoured the state, looking for stills. In many places Prohibition offenses became the most common crimes. Grand County sheriff Dick Westwood spent more time tracking down bootleggers than any other criminals. On one occasion he and his deputies tracked bootleggers to their camp near Cisco. While the criminals snored, the deputies smashed their still, emptied most of their hooch after tasting it to be sure it was authentic, kept a couple of bottles as evidence, and then surrounded and arrested the bootleggers. On New Year's Eve in 1925, heavily armed officials in Salt Lake who were ready to "shoot to kill" busted what was purportedly "one of the largest liquor rings in the West." The ringleaders, Henry and Abe Wallace, had been shipping in liquor from Syracuse, New York, in large drums labeled linseed oil, diluting it in their two warehouses, adding whiskey and gin flavoring, and selling the liquor as genuine imported Scotch. During the eight months they had operated in Utah, the ring had cleared more than eighty thousand dollars, marketing their product across the intermountain region and supplying Salt Lake County with 90 percent of its bootleg liquor.[84]

Between 1923 and 1932 Prohibition agents discovered 448 distilleries, 702 stills, and forty-seven thousand gallons of alcohol. While some bootleggers and liquor dealers on the national level, including Al Capone and Joseph Kennedy, made fortunes in the alcohol trade, many Utah bootleggers were poor immigrants, like H. Yairo, a Japanese national living in Salt Lake County; James Papacostas, a Greek operator of a two-bit billiard hall in Thompson; and Bartolo Jaramillo, a struggling immigrant living in a shack in Monticello. Raids were often a mixture of tragicomedy, with inexperienced deputies, clumsy bootleggers, and (sometimes) innocent friends or relatives. In 1924 two plainclothes deputies entered a café on Salt Lake's west side owned by seventy-year-old Elizabeth Still, a fitting name for a Prohibition violator. Acting on a tip that a waiter at the restaurant was selling liquor on the sly, the duo sat at a table and asked him for a drink. When the unsuspecting waiter returned with a pint of whiskey, the deputies flashed their badges and the waiter fled. The commotion overwhelmed the elderly proprietor; she died of a heart attack while the deputies were scouring the establishment.[85]

Utah and thirteen other states outlawed cigarette sales and smoking as well as alcohol sales. Antismoking crusaders argued that smoking threatened the comfort and safety of nonsmokers, that it signified carelessness and lack of self-control, that smokers were more likely than others to abuse alcohol and drugs, and that smokers were less dependable and less efficient employees. A variety of pressure groups fought nationwide to suppress smoking, including the Women's Christian Temperance Union, the No-Tobacco League, and the Anti-Cigarette International League.

In Utah the LDS Church and the interdenominational Salt Lake Ministerial Association allied with these national groups. In 1921 the LDS Church's Correlation and Social Advisory Committee, chaired by Apostle Stephen L. Richards, "concentrate[d] its energies in an anti-tobacco campaign" that coincided with Senator Edward Southwick's introduction of an antitobacco bill in the legislature. The Southwick bill made it illegal to "sell cigarettes and cigarette papers; to advertise cigarettes and cigarette papers; to permit minors to smoke in certain places of business; [and] for any person to smoke in certain enclosed public places." The bill allowed tobacconists to advertise and market pipes, cigars, and chewing tobacco—seen as more dignified forms of smoking and symbols of power. Although business leaders, the Veterans of Foreign Wars, the Printers' Union, the *Salt Lake Tribune*, and the *Salt Lake Telegram* opposed the bill, it easily passed the senate, partly because of broad religious support. In the house a bare majority of the Manufactures and Commerce Committee, to which the bill was referred, drafted an alternate bill that banned tobacco advertising but permitted sales through licensed dealers, arguing that Southwick's bill would be "spineless" and unenforceable, like liquor Prohibition. In the end, the house passed the Southwick bill, and Governor Mabey signed it.[86]

After law enforcement personnel ignored the statute, the Salt Lake Ministerial Association and the LDS Church campaigned for candidates who pledged to enforce it. In 1922 Salt Lake County residents elected ardent Prohibitionist Benjamin R. Harries as sheriff. After his swearing in, Harries instructed his deputies to enforce the law. People smoking in restaurants and hotel lobbies were arrested, including on February 20 the former Republican senatorial candidate Ernest Bamberger; Edgar Newhouse, one of the wealthiest men in the state and director of the American Smelting and Refining Company; and A. N. McKay, general manager of the *Salt Lake Tribune*. Thanks to McKay, the arrest was soon national news, and Utah was lampooned. An article in the *New York Times* maintained, tongue in cheek, that "one enterprising member of the Legislature has announced that he may introduce a measure prohibiting the serving and eating of corn beef and cabbage in public dining rooms, inasmuch as it constitutes an element as obnoxious to some as tobacco fumes." Newhouse, along with other business and civic leaders, organized a repeal effort, reasoning, "If there is a law on our Statue Books that, when enforced, will prompt a man living in the Capital of the United States to wire his friend, 'Why don't you move to America' (meaning move out of Utah), it is a law that concerns all of us." Ominously, the organizing committee for a national convention slated to take place in Salt Lake threatened to move to a different venue, "unless you can assure us that our delegates will be permitted to smoke and will be immune from arrest."[87]

Utahns had been repeatedly ridiculed in the press in the nineteenth century, but by the 1920s they were more sensitive to mockery, a sign of their incorporation within the cultural life of the nation. Adverse publicity following the arrest of these influential residents and local pressure induced LDS Church leaders to support a watered-down measure instead. As the *Deseret News* explained, "The furor created when an attempt was made to enforce the law...did considerable damage to the state. The intensity of feeling aroused and the enmity created on the part of some gave rise to the necessity of seeking to formulate a plan by which the chief differences might be composed." The substitute bill, enacted in 1923, forbade all tobacco advertising, required merchants who sold tobacco to be licensed, forbade the sale of tobacco to minors, and required owners of restaurants and public facilities to post signs alerting prospective customers that smoking was permitted on the premises. The legislature also instituted a cigarette tax that year, which brought in $492,181 during its first five years of operation.[88]

As the brouhaha over cigarette prohibition showed, Utahns were hypersensitive about their national reputation. Thus, when an eminent native son incisively ridiculed his hometown and state in the national press only a couple of years after the cigarette debacle, accusing Utahns of being colorless and uncultured, he struck a raw nerve. In 1926 Ogden native and Northwestern University professor Bernard DeVoto, a 1920 Phi Beta Kappa graduate of Harvard, penned an irreverent portrait of his home state for literary critic H. L. Mencken's magazine *American Mercury*. DeVoto derided the "utter mediocrity" of Utah's cultural landscape. "No artist ever lived there ten minutes after he had the railroad fare out," he hyperbolically claimed. The Beehive State was no place for anyone with an "interest in social or intellectual or artistic life." A handful of residents possessed exceptional talent, DeVoto conceded, mentioning vocalists Margaret Romaine, Hazel Dawn, and Emma Lucy Gates. Other native sons and daughters such as the renowned and wealthy actress Maude Adams and sculptors Cyrus Dallin and Solon Borglum (and, he might have added, writers like himself) had left the state to pursue their careers, but they were Utahns only by accident of birth. Utahns were utterly bourgeois in their enthusiasm for electrical appliances, automobiles, modern homes, and golf courses. Thus, it was no surprise that the work of Donald Beauregard, a recently deceased, brilliant painter from Fillmore, was better known in Chicago, New York, and California than in his home state. At least life in Deseret in the nineteenth century had been interesting. Now the vituperative culture wars between Mormons and Gentiles had faded into a cross-cultural ethos of "amity and Rotary," undergirded by civic pride and devotion to capitalism. "How do people live in Utah?" DeVoto asked rhetorically. "They join the business-men's calisthenics class at the gymnasium. Or they buy Fords on the five-dollar-a-week basis. Or they yawn. Or they die."[89]

DeVoto's article elicited more than six hundred letters from irate readers, most of them unsigned. He was accused of being "a thief, a coward, a moral leper, a homosexual, a defaulter, an adulterer, a sensualist, and every other opprobrious and obscene term that the resentment of Utah could devise," DeVoto recalled. In response he backed down—a little—later admitting that he had been "irresponsible" in some of his charges.[90]

As historian David Lewis has demonstrated, though, there was much truth in DeVoto's overwrought rhetoric. The sharp divisions between Mormons and Gentiles had given way to a veneer of cross-cultural boosterism. And his claim of cultural mediocrity aptly fitted most Utah communities. Even Ogden, Utah's second-largest city and DeVoto's hometown, with a population of only 35,000, was too small to support a smorgasbord of fine arts and culture. Instead, Ogden's social and cultural events that were the talk of the town in the mid-1920s included a charity card party hosted by the Catholic Women's League, the annual policemen's ball, an "Old Home" party sponsored by the Ogden Camp of the Woodmen of the World, and a boxing tournament hosted by the American Legion. One of the most noteworthy annual events was a "Days of '49" ball each February to which hundreds of Elks Club members and "their ladies" repaired in gold rush–era costumes. Schools and churches in communities across the state sponsored plays, dramatic readings, and talent shows, but such events focused on developing confidence, nurturing amateur talent, and providing recreation and amusement rather than on refining artistic or aesthetic sensibilities.[91]

Although DeVoto accurately reported a paucity of high culture in most Utah communities, his characterization of Utah's cultural scene imperfectly reflected circumstances in Salt Lake City. Despite its population of only about 130,000, Salt Lake supported a relatively rich offering of music and art in the 1920s. Over the decade the Utah Federation of Music Clubs sponsored recitals and concerts, several of which featured the work of Utah composers such as Salt Lake violinist Arthur Pedersen. During the 1920s the Lucy Gates Grand Opera Company produced seven operas at the Salt Lake Theater, with Gates directing and singing the leading roles. German-born and Paris-trained organist Alexander Schreiner presented weekday concerts in the Salt Lake Tabernacle in 1926–27 and 1928–29 in between stints in Southern California. In addition to the Mormon Tabernacle Choir under the direction of Anthony C. Lund, several choral groups performed regularly, including the Salt Lake Oratorio Society, a company of more than 300 singers led by Berlin-trained musician B. Cecil Gates; the Swanee Singers, a men's group directed by high school music teachers J. Spencer Cornwall and Gerritt DeJong; a young women's Chaminade chorus directed by Lund; and a Mendelssohn male chorus directed by Cornwall. Many of these groups toured the state, giving concerts in numerous communities. On New Year's Day each year, the Oratorio Society performed Handel's *Messiah* in the Salt Lake Tabernacle. Salt Lake also boasted a community orchestra open to all performers. For a couple of years, the Salt Lake Symphony Orchestra directed by Charles Shepherd and funded by the Salt Lake Elks Club gave "high class performances" to small audiences of aficionados. Touring performers, including the Russian Symphony Choir, also visited Salt Lake and occasionally gave concerts in Provo, Logan, and Ogden. Additionally, high school and university students rehearsed and performed operas and plays.[92]

The indefatigable Alice Merrill Horne, founder of the Utah Art Institute and president of the Association for the Encouragement of Intermountain Art, ensured that Utah painters' work was regularly showcased over the decade in Salt Lake County, often at the Newhouse Hotel. Utahns who showed their work included James T. Harwood, Lee Greene Richards, Waldo Midgely, Lawrence Squires, Mary Teasdale, LeConte Stewart, Mabel Frazer, Corrine Adams, and Alfred Lambourne. Other prominent artists of the decade included John W. Clawson, Edwin Evans, and A. B. Wright.[93]

Although Salt Lake's cultural scene was more vibrant than DeVoto acknowledged, and although some business leaders financially supported artistic endeavors, DeVoto correctly charged that commercial values sometimes trumped artistic sensibilities. Tensions between artistic values and monetary considerations came to a symbolic head in the closure in 1928 of the Salt Lake Theater. Local actors and traveling professional stars had shared the stage during the nineteenth century. In the twentieth nearly all actors at the theater were guest artists from outside Utah, although local musicians associated with the Salt Lake Opera Company continued to perform there. By 1928 the theater had been struggling financially for a decade and was falling into disrepair. Salt Lakers apparently preferred to patronize the city's half-dozen movie theaters along with its vaudeville houses. As E. T. Hyde observed, live theater could "not survive the movie-talkies" with their "canned drama." The Salt Lake Dramatic Association's thirty-five stockholders under the direction of LDS Church president Heber J. Grant at last voted to sell the property to the Mountain States Telephone and Telegraph Company for two hundred thousand dollars. The company would raze the theater to make room for a tasteful Art Deco office building. "We cannot afford to go on having a loss of $100,000 capital and losing money in addition," Grant reasoned.[94]

After the *Salt Lake Tribune* broke the news of the sale, preservationists, represented eloquently by Fanny Woodruff, president of the Daughters of the Utah Pioneers, protested vigorously, although they seemed more concerned about the loss of an architectural jewel than the loss of a venue for drama. "This is the oldest theater in the United States and, like the splendid old buildings of New England, should be preserved. The Salt Lake theater is a monument to the culture and ideals of the western pioneer and should never be destroyed," Woodruff argued. Another preservationist acknowledged that the theater occupied "valuable" commercial real estate but reasoned that the same was true of "'Old South Church' in the heart of Boston" that had been lovingly maintained. Not all Salt Lakers agreed with the preservationists, though. One wrote that the telephone symbolized progress; it was "one of our most progressive modern conveniences," and an attractive office building for the phone company would be preferable to a "relic" when "we have a good many relics to make us remember the pioneers." Wrote another, "Let's get rid of the old Salt Lake theatre and every other ugly old structure which stands in the way of development just as soon as we can." A campaign to raise enough money to move the theater to a new location failed, perhaps a sign that DeVoto correctly judged many Utahns' disregard for the arts.[95]

In lieu of preserving the theater, a nostalgic committee slated a gala farewell performance for October 20. The spectacle featured orchestral accompaniment under the batons of Edward P. Kimball, B. Cecil Gates, and George Careless; the second act of Reginald DeKoven's *Robin Hood*, performed by the Salt Lake Opera Company; and the third act of Verdi's *La Traviata*, performed by the Lucy Gates Grand Opera Company.[96]

A crew began razing the building on November 5 and erected a wooden fence around the perimeter to protect spectators from harm. A witty theater lover scrawled a message on part of the fence: "Built by a prophet and torn down for profit!" President Heber J. Grant, who had saved the theater from destruction back in the 1890s by investing—and then losing—his own money in the venture, was infuriated by the insinuation that he was a money-grubbing foe of the arts. He protested, "After my losing over thirty thousand dollars, common courtesy would suggest those who know this not to criticize my action in finally selling the theatre."[97]

Before the telephone company was able to erect its planned office complex on the site, the Great Depression drained the company's coffers. In 1934 Myrtle Henderson visited the site and found only a gas station shaped like a large airplane, "a monument to modern progress and business!" Despite its inaccuracy, the story spread that the theater had been torn down to make way for the filling station.[98]

An alternate index of Utahns' priorities at the time was provided by a public opinion poll conducted by Robert Elliott, editor of the *Salt Lake Telegram*, in 1930. Elliott invited his readers to send their lists of the ten greatest living Utahns to the paper. In order to qualify as a Utahn, a nominee had to be either a native or a current resident. Two individuals who were frequently nominated, mining magnate Daniel Jackling and former heavyweight champion boxer Jack Dempsey, did not meet either qualification. The top vote getter in the poll was Senator and Mormon apostle Reed Smoot, followed by the Utah-born actress Maude Adams, who had taken Broadway by storm. Governor George Dern came in third, followed by LDS president Heber J. Grant, expatriate sculptor Cyrus Dallin, and Apostle Anthony W. Ivins. Politician and statesman J. Reuben Clark placed seventh in the contest, and Elmer I. Goshen, liberal minister of Salt Lake's Congregational Church, placed eighth. Rounding out the top ten were Republican senator William King and Democrat and University of Utah educator Elbert Thomas. The next ten (those between the eleventh and twentieth places) were the charismatic Mormon orator B. H.

Roberts, Mormon author and apostle James E. Talmage, inventors Nathaniel Baldwin and Harvey Fletcher, Supreme Court justice George Sutherland, musicians Emma Lucy Gates Bowen and Evan Stephens, University of Utah zoology professor Ralph Chamberlin, sculptor Mahonri Young, and cartoonist John Held Jr. On balance the poll suggested that Utahns—at least urban readers who responded to the poll—respected political success, religious leadership, and artistic achievement. Six of the top twenty were famous because of their artistic or musical achievements— the same number who were primarily known as religious leaders; only four were known mainly for political achievements and only two for their inventions or other commercial successes.[99]

Utahns shared unevenly in the reckless abandon and vaunted prosperity that supposedly characterized life in America during the Roaring Twenties. New homes, appliances, automobiles, and radios; an expanding network of highways and airports; a booming copper industry; and new factories such as Utah County's steel and pipe plants bespoke prosperity. But these developments coexisted uneasily with an intractable agricultural recession, a slump in coal prices, and the fact that much of the wealth generated in Utah flowed into the pockets of out-of-state investors. Petting parties, a baseball craze, amusement parks, dances, rough-and-tumble machine politics, and pari-mutuel betting imparted a carefree, even reckless, veneer to life, while a rich outpouring of high culture in Salt Lake City catered to more sophisticated tastes. But quiet, amateur entertainments predominated in most places, and Ernest Bamberger's political fortunes and the dreams of his cronies in the Order of Sevens went up in smoke in 1928. Meanwhile, blue laws and prohibition of cigarettes as well as alcohol nurtured the Beehive State's reputation as a puritanical cultural backwater. Indeed, a bundle of contradictory impulses and tendencies characterized the state in the 1920s.

When the bottom fell out of the US stock market in the fall of 1929, Utahns who had funds tied up on Wall Street suffered heavy losses on paper. But they were a tiny minority of the population. With a per capita income that year of $537 and considerable consumer debt, few households had the excess capital necessary to play the market. While the market collapse caused alarm, few at the time recognized they were on the brink of the greatest economic debacle of the century, a time that would profoundly reorient Utahns' worldview, their relationship to the federal government, and their priorities.[100]

11

HARD TIMES

Weathering the Great Depression

ECONOMIC COLLAPSE

Utah's economy declined modestly through 1930 and then fell into a tailspin over the next three years. By 1933 per capita income was only 55 percent of the 1929 level. As Utah's new governor, Henry Blood, observed in 1933, the state was confronted with "an unprecedented condition that we are not prepared through past experiences to meet." Forced back upon their own limited resources and ingenuity, Utahns would respond to the calamity by retrenching their expenditures and resorting to a bootstrap subsistence and barter economy reminiscent of the pioneer era, with its insular focus on self-sufficiency.[1]

Despite their resourcefulness and pluck, some families suffered immensely, including Henry and Louise Gim and their four children. After the Depression wiped out their restaurant and cattle ranch, the family moved to a cockroach-infested tenement in Salt Lake's small Chinese district, Plum Alley. Economic stress wore down Henry and Louise. When their oldest daughter, Helen, was thirteen, her father died of a heart attack, leaving his widow, who spoke no English, and the four children. "I had the distinct feeling I was going to have to be responsible....So at Christmastime I got a job at Kress's," Helen recalled. Two years later Helen's mother suffered a nervous breakdown, and Helen and her three siblings became wards of the state. Soon after she graduated from high school, Helen obtained custody of her younger siblings. She found a secretarial job and rented a place on Salt Lake's west side. "I felt tremendous tension," she recalled with considerable understatement. "I washed all the kids' clothes weekly....I remember there'd be times I was so tired from housework, I'd just see champagne bubbles. When you're really fatigued, prior to passing out, I guess, you see little bubbles."[2]

The indicators of economic distress were overwhelming. By 1933 35.8 percent of Utah's workforce was unemployed, compared to roughly one-quarter of the nation's population. Unemployment was particularly severe in urban areas. In Salt Lake's Southgate district the heads of 60 percent of all households lacked employment late in 1932; on the west side of Salt Lake, half were out of work. LDS Church welfare expenditures reflected the relative impact of unemployment in urban areas as well as the strong organizational apparatus of urban congregations: the six LDS stakes in Salt Lake City allotted $172,949 for welfare in 1931, while the four remaining stakes in rural areas of the valley spent only $13,279.[3]

Unemployment may have been harsher in the cities, but the agricultural sector, the state's largest employer, suffered devastating reverses. Gross farm income, which had already been low before the Depression began, plummeted from $68.7 million in 1929 to $29.5 million in 1932, a decline of 57 percent that slightly exceeded the national drop of 54 percent. Prices for farm products fell even below the level they had reached in the post–World War I recession. The price of wheat, which had plummeted from well over $3 a bushel in 1919 to between 65 and 98 cents in 1921, stood at 46 cents a bushel by 1931.[4]

The mining industry, a key source of export and tax revenue for the state, experienced even greater proportional reverses than did farmers. The value of Utah's total mineral production plunged 80 percent, from more than $115 million in 1929 to 22.6 million in 1932. By contrast, the value of mine output nationwide fell by 58 percent. Mines producing nonferrous minerals such as gold, silver, lead, copper, and zinc were especially hard hit, but coal mines struggled too, as the price of coal, which had been $2.53 per ton in 1928, fell to under $2 by 1934. Sunnyside, formerly the largest mine in Carbon County with a population of more than two thousand, lost four-fifths of its residents.[5]

Other sectors of the economy suffered, too. The value of manufactured goods in the state in 1933 was less than half of what it had been in 1929, and the number of employees in manufacturing had dropped by one-third. Of the 105 banks in Utah in 1929, 32, or nearly one-third, had closed their doors or been absorbed by other institutions by 1933, compared to the more sizable national reduction of 42 percent in the number of banks. Wholesale and retail trade suffered, also. Department store sales in the state for 1932 were 43 percent of what they had been in 1929. Increasing numbers of businesses also closed their doors: in 1932 206 businesses and industries failed, compared to 113 in 1929 and an average of 120 per year during the 1920s. This 82 percent jump in the number of commercial and industrial failures contrasted with a nationwide rise of only 39 percent.[6]

Measured by many key indicators, then, Utah's economic plight exceeded that of the nation at large by 1932–33. Its plight was similar to that of its neighbors in the Intermountain West. The disadvantages of the region's incorporation within the nation as a supplier of raw materials for distant markets weighed heavily. The Rocky Mountain states primarily produced bulky commodities such as crops, livestock, and minerals whose value dropped precipitously early in the thirties. Moreover, Utah and its neighboring states were far from the nation's major markets and manufacturing centers. The cost of shipping bulky goods to distant markets compounded the region's financial woes. In March 1933 nine hundred boxcar loads of Utah peas, cabbage, onions, and potatoes from the 1932 harvest had still not been shipped to market because of low prices and prohibitively high freight rates.[7]

Just as the Depression hit the nation unevenly, it afflicted some parts of the state more than others. Unemployment was especially high in the smelter districts of Tooele and Salt Lake Counties, the coal mines of Carbon County, and the metal mines of Salt Lake, Tooele, Utah, Juab, Wasatch, and Summit Counties. During the drought years of 1933 and 1934, Beaver, Duchesne, Emery, Garfield, and Utah Counties had both the highest relief rates in the state and the greatest per capita distribution of relief funds. By contrast, relief rates were lowest in those years in the far northern counties of Box Elder, Cache, and Morgan.[8]

NECESSITIES OF LIFE

Notwithstanding the severity of the Great Depression, Utahns generally possessed enough of life's necessities to get by. In 1930 half of the state's population lived in areas that met the Census Bureau's definition of rural places, and close to one-fourth of the workforce labored in agriculture. For most rural people food was quite readily available. As Frances Wilde, who grew up on a hardscrabble Utah County farm, recalled, "When you're living on a farm you always have enough to eat. You have vegetables and butter and milk and some meat." During the growing season even moderately healthy residents of urban areas, including the state's largest city, could walk to orchards, gardens, chicken coops, and farmers' fields, where they could beg or steal fruit, vegetables, eggs, or poultry if worse came to worst.[9]

Despite most Utahns' proximity to farms and gardens, some residents went hungry. In the cities lines formed outside soup kitchens, and in coal mining districts in the summer, when the demand for coal was low and many miners lacked work, "hunger was widespread." In Provo in 1932–33 more than 5 percent of schoolchildren received free school lunches. It seems likely that a similar percentage of the population at large struggled to feed themselves. Even in agricultural districts some unfortunate families lacked nutritious food; one Wayne County family sometimes ate only "bread with coffee over it" for dinner.[10]

To a much greater extent than food, clothing was scarce. As Lynn Sorensen, who lived in Murray during the 1930s, recalled, "We always had food on the table, but we had a minimum of clothing to wear." Some children, including Eugene Barber, a student at Salt Lake's Franklin Elementary School in the 1930s, attended school infrequently because he "just didn't have enough clothes." In Provo junior high students canvassed the community for clothing and offered it to needy families so that everyone could attend school. Even so, any Provo teenager "who had a warm winter coat somewhere near his own size was considered fortunate," recalled Madge Harris. Most of Harris's friends had "two or three different clothes for everyday and school, and one best dress."[11]

Clothes may have been in short supply, but nearly all Utahns had a roof over their heads throughout the decade. In 1930 nearly four in ten families in the state rented their homes. As the Depression deepened, some landlords slashed rental rates by nearly 50 percent in order to keep their properties occupied and generate at least some rental income. Even with reduced rates, many renters fell behind in their payments and pleaded with their landlords for clemency. Belle Berry, a Provo landlord, allowed one tenant to go three months without paying rent in 1932. When Henry and Rubie Nathaniel of Salt Lake "got so low we couldn't pay our rent," their landlord "didn't even come to collect it," although he also stopped repairing the place. When the leaky kitchen ceiling caved in, the Nathaniels tried in vain to patch it with cardboard. "I used to have to put on galoshes to cook," Rubie quipped. Other landlords arranged for tenants to work for them in lieu of paying the rent. Laurence Johns, a painter in Ogden, worked off his rent by painting apartment houses for his landlord.[12]

Some renters who fell behind on payments were evicted. In 1933 Hugh McMillian, a middle-aged coal miner with a large family, received a notice from the United States Fuel Company ordering him to vacate the company home he occupied because he had not paid rent for several months. "I have nine children and my baby is sick and they said if I wasn't out in three days they would have to come and throw us out in the street....I don't want anything for nothing and am perfectly willing to work to pay my rent and support my family but it is impossible to get work of any kind around here," he complained.[13]

Although some renters were thrown out of their homes, many found shelter with friends or family; a few wound up living in tents or automobiles or out on the street. In Salt Lake City several hundred families reportedly pitched tents on vacant lots. Others—principally adults who were passing through—sought shelter in freight cars, transient shelters, or public restrooms.[14]

Possessing some equity in their dwellings, home owners enjoyed greater security than renters. Nonetheless, they faced the possibility of losing their properties if they fell behind on tax payments. Those who had mortgaged their houses were especially vulnerable. At the outset of the Depression probably at least 40 percent of the urban homes in Utah were mortgaged, as was the case in the nation at large. Mortgages were most common in the state's larger communities. In 1932 bankers in Provo estimated that two-thirds of all homes there had been mortgaged, and in Salt Lake City by 1940 58 percent of all owner-occupied homes were mortgaged.[15]

Given the pervasiveness of unemployment and low income, it is not surprising that many Utah home and farm owners fell behind in their payments. The Federal Land Bank, the largest holder of farm mortgages in the state, reported in 1932 that 43 percent of its Utah customers were delinquent. By 1935 78 percent of the State Land Board's constituents were in arrears. Good data on urban mortgage delinquencies are not available for Utah, but a survey of twenty-two cities nationwide in 1934 showed a median delinquency rate of more than 38 percent, with the lowest rate more than 20 percent and the highest rate more than 60 percent; Utah rates were likely comparable.[16] Lenders in some cases foreclosed on delinquent home and farm owners. Pleas from farm owners facing foreclosure poured into the governor's office. Glen Gates pled: "My farm is being sold at sheriff's sale for interest. I have not the money to pay. I would like help." By mid-decade the State Land Board, a relatively indulgent lender that insisted that "in no case have foreclosures been instituted for the reason of interest or principal delinquencies alone," had repossessed 508 farms. By midway through the Depression, the Federal Land Bank had foreclosed on mortgages totaling $2,140,615, more than 40 percent of the bank's entire loan portfolio in Utah. In Millard County—where residents near Delta had bonded themselves heavily for elaborate drainage systems in more prosperous times—the Deseret Bank, the Federal Land Bank, other lending institutions, and real estate companies owned nearly one-third of the real property, largely as a result of foreclosures. Lenders foreclosed on urban home owners, too. Early in 1933, for instance, the Tracy Loan and Trust Company repossessed a duplex in Salt Lake, evicting home owner Lena Marie McDonald, a widow. McDonald had recently lost her job, and although she reportedly possessed a "large equity" in the dwelling, she had mortgaged the home for nearly $5,000 and had fallen behind in her payments. On the same day that McDonald lost her home, seven other pieces of property in the county were also repossessed.[17]

Home owners who fell behind in property taxes or payments to irrigation and drainage districts also risked losing their properties. Tax delinquency rates in rural Utah approached 40 percent by 1932, limiting counties' and school districts' ability to furnish services. Early in January 1933 three-fourths of Grand County's farmers and 70 percent of those in Duchesne County had fallen behind in their property taxes. Beginning in 1933 the legislature provided some relief for home owners by extending deadlines for payment of back taxes. Ultimately, lawmakers extended this tax relief period until May 1936. Shortly after the grace period expired, 430 pieces of property were auctioned in Uintah County alone. In the Delta area in 1936, the county had taken title to nearly two-thirds of the farms.[18]

Notwithstanding the threat of foreclosure, most Utahns held on to their homes. Moreover, some 17,500 families managed to move into brand-new homes over the decade. Thus, essentially the same percentage of Utah households owned their homes in 1940 as at the outset of the Depression.[19]

Regardless of their age or station in life, Utahns needed food, clothing, and shelter, and the Depression curbed access to these necessities. The Depression's impact varied widely, though, depending upon residents' age, sex, occupation, place of residence, personality, and ethnic or racial background.

UNEVEN BURDENS: THE EXPERIENCES OF CHILDREN AND YOUTH

For nearly half of the state's populace, the Depression coincided with their childhood and youth: in 1930 24 percent of the state's residents were under ten years old, and an additional 22 percent were teenagers. Over the next decade 115,000 more children would be born.[20]

The Depression did not weigh heavily upon the consciousness of most who were born during the 1930s, and its impact was likewise limited for those who had been infants or preschoolers when the Depression began. Barbara Rasmusson Carver typified many middle-class, nonfarm children in Utah during the 1930s. Born just days before the stock market crash in 1929, she spent her first ten years in Santaquin, Salt Lake, Provo, and Pocatello. In the space of two years the family moved three times as her father searched for work. Twice her family moved in with relatives in rural Santaquin. In Salt Lake City she and her family occupied a one-bedroom apartment on Third South with a covered porch that doubled as a summer bedroom. Their fare at mealtimes was simple. Dinner often consisted of noodles and a vegetable, although Barbara's mother usually offered her a cookie or pudding for dessert. Fancy meats such as turkey, roast, or ham were reserved for special occasions. Barbara's days were filled with school, chores, homework, and play. She played card games, spoons, and board games like Monopoly. Outside she and her friends played fox and geese, kick the can, jacks, and hopscotch; jumped rope; and roller-skated. In the evenings she and her brother listened to *Little Orphan Annie* and *Jack Armstrong* on the radio. Her older brother, who earned spending money from a paper route, would sometimes take her to see movies such as *Snow White and the Seven Dwarfs*.[21]

While many young Utahns during the 1930s like Barbara Rasmusson devoted much of their time to school, chores, and play, the financial and emotional pressures of their parents did affect them to an extent. Although she always had food to eat and clothes to wear, Barbara was old enough to know times were tough. She learned that food was precious: every morsel was either to be eaten or to be saved. She also learned that work was scarce when her father lost his job because his employer was losing money hand over fist. Despite her generally happy childhood, "there was a great feeling of walking on the edge" in her home because of the Depression, she recalled.

Other children were less fortunate than Rasmusson and lacked food or clothing. Eugene Barber and his brothers were so hungry that they stole a sack of potatoes. Spending money was scarce for many children. During their elementary school years, Daniel Maldonado, a child of Mexican immigrants, and his young friends on Salt Lake's west side learned not to ask their parents for money "because there wasn't any money around." To earn some change Daniel and his buddies picked up and marketed chunks of ice that fell from refrigerated cars as they were being loaded in the train yards in the neighborhood.[22]

Medical care was an unaffordable luxury in many households, and some children suffered as a result. When Mary Diamante of Bingham was nine years old, her kidney malfunctioned. Her bloated condition warranted hospitalization, but her parents "couldn't afford it." Instead, following doctors' instructions, they cared for her at home for three weeks, repeatedly wrapping her in sterilized blankets to force the water out through the sweat glands. Some families also made do without medicines for their children's ailments: drugstore sales were 23 percent lower in 1935 than they had been prior to the Depression, and the number of drugstore employees was down by nearly 9 percent.[23]

The Depression also affected children's educational experiences. Many public schools in the state closed early because of reduced tax revenues. Washington County's schools closed a month early in 1933. Two years later schools in Uintah County remained open only until April 5.[24]

To a much greater extent than their younger siblings, teenagers felt the Depression's sting. Some felt the stigma of poverty and inferior clothes. For fashion-conscious high school and college-age youth, wearing hand-me-downs or threadbare clothing was particularly embarrassing. BYU president Franklin S. Harris admonished students in 1932, "Don't let your wardrobe bother you too much," but threadbare clothes embarrassed many young people, such as Ora Gregerson, a farm girl from Mayfield; she turned down a date to her high school prom because she lacked the right kind of dress or the money to buy one. She was a good seamstress, but even fabric and a pattern for a dress cost more than her hard-pressed father could spare.[25]

The Depression also affected high school opportunities for some Utahns. Some rural school districts eliminated bus routes in order to reduce expenses. In order to continue their education, high school students from Hiawatha had to either find their own transportation or board with a family in Price after the county school board eliminated bus service. In 1940 34.5 percent of the state's young people in their twenties who had graduated from the eighth grade lacked a high school diploma. Their reasons for leaving varied, but some, including Jenean Amanetti of Lehi, quit school to help support the family. In 1940 approximately 11.5 percent of the state's youth between the ages of fourteen and nineteen were employed.[26]

Although most Utah teenagers in the 1930s graduated from high school, some relinquished hopes of a church mission or college education because their parents needed them to work instead. In the early 1930s the number of LDS missionaries fell to its lowest level of the twentieth century, with the exception of the World War II era. After her senior year in high school Marjorie Pay planned to enroll at the University of Utah, but when her father lost his job she went to work instead as a secretary at the Owens-Illinois Glass Company to help support the family. Other young Utahns who had set aside money for college in a savings bank lost their savings and had to forgo higher education. Still others changed their educational plans because a college degree no longer seemed to be worth the investment. Yukus (or Yuki) Inouye received a scholarship but decided instead to "branch out on my own" because he perceived that "during the Depression having a college degree didn't make it any easier to find a job."[27]

Despite the obstacles to higher education that the economic downturn created, a larger number of young Utahns managed to enroll in a university or college in the 1930s than in the previous decade. Indeed, the lack of employment opportunities for high school graduates—Sanpete County's extension agent counted 1,387 "unestablished" young people ages eighteen to thirty in 1939—coupled with ambitious recruiting initiatives by many schools and federally funded scholarships beginning in the mid-1930s made college appear feasible and desirable to many of the state's high school graduates. By 1940 more than half of the state's population ages twenty to twenty-nine had attended a college or trade school beyond high school, compared to only 12.7 percent of all Americans in their twenties. By contrast, the median years of schooling completed by those ages thirty to thirty-four in 1940 was 12, and the median for Utahns in their late thirties was 10.9.[28]

Every university in the state boasted a higher enrollment in 1939 than in 1929. Undergraduate enrollment at the University of Utah in 1939–49 stood at 4,286, up from 3,083 in 1929–30. This was an increase of more than 39 percent in a decade when the state's overall population rose by only about 8 percent. At the State Agricultural College in Logan, more than 3,000 students were enrolled in 1938–39, up from 1,836 five years earlier. And at BYU enrollment reached 2,894, up from 1,494 a decade earlier. Junior colleges in the state were also educating more students than ever as the decade ended.[29]

Most students attending college during the Depression walked an economic tightrope, uncertain whether they would be able to continue their education beyond the current term or semester. It was, recalled Wilford Lee, a BYU undergraduate early in the 1930s, "a real struggle for existence." The student newspaper at the University of Utah reported in 1932 that a "large number of students" were "having very serious difficulty in raising sufficient funds to continue their education." At Snow College in October 1932, 22 percent of the 190 students enrolled had been unable to pay any tuition, and an additional 29 percent had paid only a portion of it for that quarter.[30]

Struggling to make ends meet, some students from out of town hitchhiked when they went home, and many subsisted on a meager diet. At BYU in 1937 when students were earning twenty-five cents an hour and a hamburger or a loaf of bread cost a dime, 40 percent of the student body spent only three to six dollars a month on food.[31]

Universities, colleges, and affiliated social units trimmed extracurricular activities in the interest of economy. In 1933–34 the Weber College debate team participated in tournaments in Texas, Kansas, and California, but the next year the administration eliminated funding for trips. In 1934 over the vigorous objections of some students, the Intrafraternity Council at the University of Utah supported the university president by passing a resolution objecting to any coed "accepting flowers of any manner, shape or form for shoulder or vase for use at the Junior Prom, or in her room, or between the leaves of the family Bible or album, in or on the day of Saturday, February 24." Any who defied the injunction would be blacklisted as "unworthy of the attention of the University of Utah fraternity men."[32]

Early in the Depression most colleges allowed students to pay at least part of their tuition with farm products. Weber College accepted livestock, dairy products, eggs, and crops. BYU accepted gallon jugs of blackstrap molasses from Washington County students and arranged for one student to pay his tuition by delivering milk from the farm to the university cafeteria. University of Utah president George Thomas made similar arrangements and encouraged faculty who could accept farm products as partial compensation for their work "without disadvantage" to step forward.[33]

Local resources, including loans from generous businessmen and community leaders, enabled others to enroll in college. In Provo the Rotary Club established a revolving fund by collecting a dollar a month from each member. Students could borrow up to two thousand dollars at 5 percent interest. In Ogden the Lions Club administered a similar fund. E. G. Peterson, president of the State Agricultural College, personally loaned funds to some students so that they could register.[34]

On-campus jobs enabled others to stay in school. In 1931 a committee of students and faculty at the University of Utah successfully solicited money from the Chamber of Commerce and the mayor's office to "create make-work activities on the campus." Beginning in 1934, federal agencies such as the Federal Emergency Relief Administration and the National Youth Administration granted universities the funds to greatly expand on-campus employment opportunities. BYU obtained federal grants to employ two to four hundred students on grounds and custodial crews and in cafeterias, laboratories, and classrooms. By 1935 roughly seven hundred students chosen on the basis of need and scholastic merit at the University of Utah were working on similar types of projects. Officials at the State Agricultural College managed to garner sufficient federal funds to employ close to two thousand students in the mid-1930s.[35]

On campuses across the state, parties, activities, and sporting events were curtailed but not abandoned entirely during the Depression. BYU celebrated its first homecoming festivities in 1930, and as the second homecoming approached in 1931, the student newspaper editorialized, "We can't let the Depression…make us irritable and unsocial." The editor maintained, "It really is possible to enjoy parties for little cost, if restraint, brains and cooperation are employed." By 1936 two-thirds of the BYU student body participated in at least one club. At Weber College in 1935–36 the Women's Athletic Association, led by Helen Parmley, organized intramural basketball, swimming, archery, and squash tournaments.[36]

Notwithstanding carefree diversions, the economic crisis weighed heavily on the minds of mature students and spawned profound cynicism. Gordon B. Hinckley, who studied at the University of Utah from 1928 to 1932, recalled, "It was a time of terrible discouragement, and it was felt strongly on campus." The American dream seemed shattered, and platitudes about hard work, divine Providence, and the superiority of democratic institutions seemed outmoded to many students. Graduates like Bernie Rose, who finished his law degree at the University of Utah in 1934, learned firsthand that "there was no way to practice and no way to open an office" because of the economy.[37]

BREADWINNERS: AN UNEVEN PLAYING FIELD

While close to half of the state's population were children or adolescents when the Depression struck and therefore spent much of the Depression decade in school, adults in the workforce bore the brunt of the state's economic debacle. Nearly 17 percent of Utah's population in 1930 were in their twenties, 13 percent were thirtysomethings, 11 percent were in their forties, 7 percent were in their fifties, 4 percent were in their sixties, and slightly more than 2 percent were seventy or older (a marked contrast to Utah's sizable senior citizen contingent later in the century). Most who in 1930 were in their twenties and thirties and some who were in their forties would have time to rehabilitate themselves economically following the Depression. Those who were at the apex of their careers and salaries possessed the greatest reserves for weathering hard times. On the other hand, for many in that group who might lose jobs, life savings, or other possessions, the prospects of economic recovery—even if they lived well beyond the end of the decade—were less promising. As Helen

Bunnell, a young woman who began married life during the 1930s, put it, her parents' generation "had a lot more to lose" than she did.[38]

The Depression's effects for working adults hinged partly upon their occupation and place of residence. More Utahns worked in agriculture than in any other sector in 1930. Many farmers had suffered greatly in the post–World War I recession and had only partially recovered when the Great Depression plunged them into another downward spiral. Average farm income early in the 1930s was less than half what it had been in the darkest year of the postwar recession. For some Utah farmers, the Great Depression was less shocking than the postwar recession because they had less far to fall. "We were poor to begin with so it didn't matter," recalled Frances Simons Wilde of Salem. Her parents, Ezra and Effie Simons, had already lost a home through foreclosure during the postwar shakeout, and nothing as devastating as that loss beset them in the thirties.[39]

For other farm families the thirties were an unparalleled nightmare because rock-bottom prices combined with unprecedented drought. Between 1930 and 1934 the Wasatch Front experienced the first, third, and sixth driest years of the twentieth century. Although more irrigation water was available in other years, the region received "well below average precipitation" during the entire decade.[40]

For the entire state 1934 brought to a climax the worst drought farmers had experienced since 1856: precipitation for the state was only 35 percent of normal. To make matters worse, precipitation during the previous years had also been abnormally low, so small reservoirs contained no holdover water, and even the largest ones contained only a little from the previous year. Cash income statewide from farm crops fell to $8.8 million in 1934, its lowest level in the Depression. San Juan County's wheat crop was nearly entirely ruined, and Utah's average sugar beet harvest per acre was only about half what it had been in 1929.[41]

Not only drought but falling farm prices beset Utah's farmers during the 1930s. Cash income from crops in 1932 was less than half what it had been in 1929. Similarly, cash receipts from livestock, dairy products, and eggs declined at comparable levels. Utah's sheepmen were particularly hard hit: their income from the sale of wool, lambs, and sheep in 1932 was one-fourth the size of the 1929 level. Those who had borrowed heavily at high interest rates prior to the Depression were trapped by falling prices. Alta Albrecht, who worked in a Wayne County bank, recalled the plight of one sheepman: "He'd borrowed money from the bank to buy lambs to feed. He worked hard...to feed these lambs and when he sold them he brought every cent that he got out of it to pay off his loan...and he lacked twenty-five cents of having enough. I remember him putting his hand in his pocket—his overalls were rags—and got a quarter out. And that was his whole year's work." Fred and Loreen Wahlquist, a farm couple in the Uinta Basin, suffered a similar fate: they had purchased a farm for $2,800 and invested more in a dairy herd during the 1920s. "The first year our cows did fine and we had high hopes for the future. Then prices started a steady decline," Loreen recalled. In 1930 five of their cows died after eating grasshopper poison. The following year a farmer offered to buy their "five best cows for $70 each." They calculated the sale "would leave us with scarcely any cream check but still with a debt of over $3,500 so we turned it down. It was a big mistake as prices dropped so low we got practically no return from the cows and we couldn't sell them at any price." In 1935, with no feed for their cows because of the drought, they sold them "for sixteen dollars a head."[42]

Although they had little money, farmers generally were able to feed themselves. Farm laborers faced seasonal unemployment as they always had, but among urban and industrial workers unemployment was far higher and its consequences far more severe. Workers in Utah's mines and smelters were especially hard hit; the number of employees in the state's metal mines fell by 65 percent between 1929 and 1932, while employment in smelters and furnaces dropped by 63 percent and employment in coal mines plummeted by more than 47 percent. Employment in food-processing industries such as canneries, sugar factories, and flour mills fell by one-third. Unskilled workers in the state's industries were two and a half times as likely as skilled industrial workers to lose their jobs. Professionals and government employees enjoyed much greater job security than either skilled or unskilled laborers. In 1930 unemployment rates were six times as high for skilled workers in industry as for professionals or public servants.[43]

Among those fortunate enough to retain their jobs, workers in some sectors experienced more drastic wage cuts than did those in others. Nationwide, wages for full-time construction workers fell 48 percent between 1929 and 1933. Those employed full-time in manufacturing experienced a 30 percent wage reduction, which was largely offset by a drop of 25 percent in retail prices. Meanwhile, full-time federal civilian employees earned only 13 percent less in 1933 than they had earned in 1929. As a result of these differences, socioeconomic class distinctions took on new wrinkles.[44]

In the state's coal mines total production fell by more than 53 percent between 1929 and 1934. Consequently, hourly wages fell, and 19 percent of the state's coal miners were laid off. Many companies resorted to rotational employment to keep as many workers as possible doing something. The average number of days worked per year fell from 211 in 1929 to 171 in 1934. In Hiawatha miners were worse off—they were lucky to work 1 day in 7, earning twenty-two dollars a month—too little to feed and clothe a family. One resident of Hiawatha recalled that she "never had cash, not even two cents" for a stamp. Social workers classified unemployed or severely underemployed households in communities where there were few alternative sources of work as "stranded populations." A survey completed in March 1934 identified 2,068 stranded households, and most of them were in Utah's mining and smelting districts. Roughly 70 percent of the households had been unemployed for at least twelve months since February 1929, and 14 percent had been out of work for four years. For these families, "a comfortable living and adequate salaries ha[d] been replaced with suffering and broken morale."[45]

Even as their income fell, some Utahns were able to maintain an enviable standard of living because of the large cushion of discretionary income they enjoyed. Floyd Hatch, a surgeon at LDS Hospital and one of the owners of the Intermountain Clinic in Salt Lake, was unable to collect payments from some clients. Nevertheless, the unpaid bills were a relatively minor hardship because his income was so substantial to begin with. He and his wife, Donnette, and their four children lived sumptuously in a seventeen-room home near the University of Utah. The couple took breakfast on a sunporch in the summer and ate their dinner in an elegantly appointed formal dining room. The downturn in income did not prevent the Hatches from hiring domestic help or taking family vacations. At least twice a month the couple hosted dinner parties to which they invited the "the moneyed people" of the city. Their housekeeper recalled, "[Mrs. Hatch] had all these big, gold-rimmed plates, under plates and all this crystal and everything. She had a lot of luncheons, [too]. For lunch she would have a hollowed out tomato with crab salad.... She had beautiful china."[46]

Many professionals, prominent businessmen, and insurance agents lived well, too. Within a block of the Hatches' home in their affluent Salt Lake neighborhood lived owners and managers of prominent mining, real estate, smelting, and manufacturing companies as well as school administrators, a dentist, and a physician.[47]

Women's unemployment rates in the 1930s were lower than those of men, largely because their occupations were more insulated from the downturn than male-dominated sectors like construction and mining. Nearly 70 percent of the state's working women were employed in wholesale and retail occupations such as clerking and sales, professional work such as teaching and nursing, or providing personal services such as domestic work, laundry, and dry cleaning. Nevertheless women's salaries during the Depression were abysmal. In 1930–31 the average female elementary school teacher earned less than half of what the average male high school teacher made. In the mid-1930s female office workers earned between thirty and sixty dollars a month, domestic servants earned as little as twenty-four dollars a month, while full-time machine operators at knitting factories earned about twenty-nine dollars a month.[48]

On such meager salaries single mothers struggled mightily to provide for their children. Jo Petersen Salmon, a single mother of three living in Salt Lake City, could not earn enough to feed, clothe, and house her family. When she finally moved in with her parents in Sanpete County, her youngest child was "nearly starved to death." Rubie Nathaniel, who worked as a freight elevator operator at a Salt Lake hotel, had her salary cut from fifty to thirty-five dollars a month. Ten dollars of her salary went to pay a woman to watch her children while she was at work. "It was so hard to feed my kids," she recalled.[49]

GETTING BY: COPING STRATEGIES

Utahns who were affected to some degree by the Depression employed a variety of strategies in order to increase their income, reduce their expenditures, or obtain unaffordable commodities through barter or home production. Less heralded than the massive public works projects undertaken by state and federal governments to put people to work during the 1930s, these commonsense strategies were in fact more central to the economic well-being of most Utah families. As they relied upon locally available resources in order to survive, Utahns retreated to a degree from incorporation within the national economy. The focus upon individual industry and initiative, retrenchment in expenditures, and local production and exchange closely resembled the self-sufficient economic outlook Brigham Young had advocated in the pioneer era.

Utahns coped with the Depression by spending less. Some moved to cheaper apartments or homes or temporarily moved in with relatives. Frances and Bill Wilde compensated by moving from an eighteen-dollar apartment to a ten-dollar one. Twice during the Depression Alden and Catherine Rasmusson moved in with relatives to save money. Likewise, Alvornia Thompson, his wife, and their three children moved in with his parents-in-law in Ogden after he lost his job in a sugar factory.[50]

By replacing more expensive meats and fine produce with cheaper fare, others trimmed their expenditures. After his father died in 1931, future governor Calvin Rampton's family "economized on food. I never ate so many beans in my life.... Mother bought a gunnysack full of Mexican brown beans, and I don't know how many meals they made—hundreds, I guess. Every other night we seemed to alternate between beans and another dish...called four-in-one. Four-in-one was a macaroni, tomato, beef, and cheese concoction that was quite good. We did the best we could that winter to conserve."[51]

With minimal hardship some Utahns settled for secondhand furniture or makeshift tables, chairs, and beds, although many married couples somehow scraped together funds for a new sofa or bedroom set. Furniture store sales in Utah fell by 47 percent between 1929 and 1935, and the number of furniture store employees dropped 39 percent. After Donaciano Gomez lost his job with the railroad, his daughter Pancha recalls, he "couldn't afford chairs or beds," so he made benches for the family to sit on instead. According to Barney Flanagan, a labor inspector who visited the homes of hundreds of workers on welfare, "homes without furniture...were common. Beds consisting of blankets—sometimes a mattress—on the floor were not uncommon, and in more than one home the old-time wooden orange crate served as a chair and table."[52]

Residents also conserved money by cutting back on utilities. Cora and Karl Seely, like all electrical customers in Castle Dale, paid a minimum of one dollar each month for electrical service. Cora monitored the electric meter closely, and once they had used a dollar's worth of power, she pulled the breaker for the rest of the month. The Seelys were not alone; in 1933 Utahns used 45 percent less electricity than they had in 1929. Utahns also reduced expenses by eliminating telephone service: the number of working telephones statewide fell by nearly 18 percent between 1930 and 1933.[53]

Some residents of the state scavenged for fuel in order to heat their homes more economically. In Provo, recalled Madge Harris, "Men with sacks or boxes made daily treks to areas beside the railroad tracks," searching for coal that fell or was thrown from passing freight cars. Frequently during the winter of 1937, Joe Girot, a coal miner in Rolapp, and his wife, Jenean, walked along the railroad tracks, looking for coal. "Coal wasn't very high. It was cheap. Yet it was high for us. We just determined that what little he made was gonna go a long way and it did," Jenean recalled.[54]

One strategy for saving money that few Utahns adopted was deferring marriage. Young, love-struck Utahns such as June Grow and "Hod" Van Fleet, who met on the dance floor at Lagoon early in the thirties, tied the knot despite bleak economic prospects. The percentage of young Utahns in their twenties who were married had been rising for decades, and the trend even accelerated during the thirties. In 1940 51 percent of the state's young men in their twenties were married, compared with 46 percent of the same age group in 1930 and 45 percent in 1920. Similarly, 69.4 percent of Utah women in their twenties were married in 1940, compared to 66.1 percent in 1930 and 66.3 percent in 1920.[55]

Some newlyweds lived on next to nothing, though. In 1939 Sanpete County's extension agent identified 364 unestablished young couples in the county. One couple, Afton and Astrid Larsen of Ephraim, lived with Afton's father for several months so they could save on rent and groceries. Another young couple in Sanpete, Francis and Ora Petersen, married on New Year's Day in 1938 and moved into a two-room cabin next to the big house where Francis's parents lived. The newlyweds slept in the kitchen, while Francis's recently divorced sister and her three children occupied the bedroom. The cabin had a droplight but no appliances or conveniences. Conditions were primitive, but no more so than what their parents had known. Ora had been born in a two-room log cabin, and Francis had grown up sleeping with his ten siblings in a large, unfinished attic.[56]

Although many young couples defied the Depression, married during the 1930s, and lived on a shoestring, they did endeavor to minimize the financial responsibilities of married life by limiting family size. The refined birth ratio, or number of children under ten per one hundred women of childbearing age, dropped by nearly 16 percent between 1930 and 1940. Thus, in the long run many couples who married during the Depression wound up with smaller families.[57]

In addition to reducing expenses and creatively boosting their income, Utahns maximized available resources by producing, recycling, and bartering as opposed to buying. Many raised and preserved their own food. Alta Albrecht and her neighbors in Wayne County "all raised gardens" and bottled vegetables and fruit. Lula Liechty of Springville harvested enough produce to feed her family of nine during the summer months and canned an additional twelve hundred quarts of fruit and vegetables on her woodstove for the winter. Even many city dwellers in apartment buildings planted gardens. Officials in Salt Lake City permitted and encouraged residents to till vacant lots and made irrigation water available to them.[58]

Hoping to at least grow enough food to feed their families, some city people moved to the countryside. For most this back-to-the-land movement was short-lived, and it was offset by a larger migration from the countryside to the cities.[59]

Along with farming many Utahns kept enough chickens and cows to supply themselves with fresh eggs and milk. In Widtsoe, a farm village in Garfield County, "most everybody had a few chickens and a milk cow," recalled Ileen Reynolds. On larger lots in the state's cities and towns people kept animals, too: Karl and Evangeline Sachs, residents of Utah's sixth-largest community, South Salt Lake, had a large chicken coop as well as a garden on their one-acre suburban lot. On a much smaller lot east of Liberty Park in Salt Lake, Joe and Eunice McGinnis kept chickens, too.[60]

In addition to gardening and caring for cows and chickens, many Utahns further bolstered food supplies by hunting, fishing, and gathering wild plants. Zeke "Junior" Johnson of San Juan County reportedly raised his family on "buckskin," Omar and Helen Bunnell depended heavily upon their "annual supply of venison," and Reed and Ileen Reynolds "ate quite a lot of deer." On the west side of the Salt Lake Valley, near Bingham, Mary Kannes Diamante and her father would "gather dandelion greens and wild asparagus, cook them at home with a little oil and lemon and bread, and that would be our meal for the day." Late in the summer the Bagnall family in Sanpete County gathered and bottled wild plums.[61]

Friends and relatives also shared small surpluses with one another, ensuring that nothing would be wasted. Dora Ellis gave her recently married daughter, Helen, some chickens and corn to can. Catherine Rasmusson had two children of her own to feed, but she would sometimes buy groceries for her sister and brother-in-law who had even less money and six children to feed. Rubie Nathaniel, a member of Salt Lake's African Methodist Episcopal Church, struggling to feed three children on a meager salary, often received food from her pastor. "I thank God my minister was there," she reflected.[62]

By patching and mending old clothing, Utahns also maximized available resources. Helen Bunnell "sewed and made over, turned collars and put hems up and down, relined coats, and patched sheets." Patched clothing was commonplace, remembered Madge Harris, "the most common area being the elbows of suits, coats, and sweaters. Pants were patched in the seat and were worn this way to church when necessary. Many replaced worn soles in their shoes with cardboard or a piece of saddle leather." By renovating old clothing and doing without, Utahns were able to reduce their outlay for clothing, although the savings hurt clothing merchants. Nine percent of the state's clothes stores in 1929 were gone by 1935, and the number of salesclerks in clothing stores was down by 17 percent.[63]

As money became scarce, Utahns also maximized their economic resources by exchanging goods or services that they could provide for commodities or services that they desired. Some merchants, including the owners of the Piggly Wiggly in Logan, permitted customers to pay for store goods with eggs, milk, or other farm products. In Grand County utility companies likewise allowed customers to pay their bills with farm commodities. Belle Berry of Provo used milk to pay a man for painting her home and heated her home with coal that she had bought with dairy products. Some desperate people even bartered their bodies for fuel or food. On more than one occasion John Crus, a service station owner in Salt Lake, was approached by women "offering to go to bed with me for five gallons of gas."[64]

Utahns also searched for ways to augment their income. Although work was scarce, some managed to moonlight at a second job. As they had traditionally done, farmers and their families took seasonal work in sugar factories, canneries, or mines to earn cash. Likewise, some coal miners worked on farms during the summer. After mines and factories placed their employees on rotational, part-time employment, second jobs became almost essential. When Utah Copper reduced Anastasio Kannes to half-time, he "scrounge[d] what he could as a part-time plumber and carpenter" to try to make up the difference, his daughter recalled. Janet Rampton, a widow with a family to support, worked during the day at a motel and went door to door selling cosmetics and corsets in the evenings. Her sons, Byron and Cal, added to the family's income by staffing the front desk at the motel in the evenings and operating a nearby service station they had leased.[65]

Seeking better wages, many Utah workers joined unions. Prior to 1933, most workers avoided unions, partly because of restrictive and repressive employer practices. In 1933 Congress passed the National Industrial Recovery Act (NIRA), guaranteeing workers the right to bargain collectively. Under the New Deal's protective umbrella, union membership in Utah rose sixfold between November 1933 and February 1935. After the Supreme Court ruled in May 1935 that portions of NIRA were unconstitutional, Congress shored up workers' right to unionize by passing the Wagner Act, and union membership continued to grow, peaking in 1937.[66]

Some self-employed people who could choose their own hours attempted to augment their income by working harder and longer. Bill Wilde, a service station owner, "made a living…by working sixteen hours a day seven days a week." Yuki Inouye, a young man with a lot of stamina, made good money—one hundred dollars a week—by farming on his own and trucking produce to mining camps in Nevada. "I was a workaholic….I'd work sixteen to eighteen hours days then," he recalled.[67]

In order to earn enough money to support their families, some husbands temporarily took work far from home. When he lost his job at a drugstore, Alden Rasmusson became a traveling salesman. Leaving home on Monday morning, he would travel throughout northern Utah, selling tobacco and novelties. Henry Nathaniel of Salt Lake took work as a Pullman porter and had to be gone from home for a month and a half at a time. "The Depression frightened me. I was scared because Henry was gone so much…. Oh, it was an awful time," his wife, Rubie, recalled. Lengthy separation kept the bills paid but also wore on the nerves of Joe and Eunice McGinnis. When Joe lost his job as a mechanic at R. J. Fry Motor Company in Provo, he purchased two race horses and traveled the racing circuit around the western United States and Canada. Eunice remained in their rented home in Provo with their two small children. "It was awfully hard for both of us to be separated so much. We got so lonesome for each other," Eunice recalled. After three years of frequent separations, Joe sold the horses and the couple moved to Salt Lake, where he tried his hand at selling cars and raising sugar beets on a rented city lot.[68]

Some entire households left the state in search of money. Stella Pappas recalled, "We moved constantly, from Mutual to Rains, to Hiawatha, to Colorado, Wyoming and back to Utah. Every rumor of work and we moved." Utah experienced a net outward migration between 1930 and 1940, as nearly ninety-two thousand more people left the state than moved into it. The hemorrhage was greatest from rural regions. Most went to California and the mountain states.[69]

Although Utahns of all classes departed, minorities were the most likely to move. In 1930 more than four thousand Mexican immigrants had lived in Utah. By the decade's end, barely one thousand remained. Likewise, more than half of Utah's Japanese population left for California or Japan during the thirties.[70]

Well-educated Utahns were more likely to leave than those with less schooling. After he graduated with a bachelor degree from the University of Utah, Quayle Cannon moved to Washington, DC, where economic and educational opportunities were greater. After obtaining a teaching certificate, Fay Allred of Provo traveled east with a friend to look for work. The duo met in Washington and married in 1936. Like Cannon and Allred, 64.5 percent of the men and women ages twenty-five to thirty-four who left Utah between 1935 and 1940 possessed at least a high school education, compared to 53 percent of their peers who stayed in state.[71]

Moonlighting, working hard, and leaving home for jobs elsewhere were only some of the ways Utahns boosted their income. Farm women had long augmented the cash flow in rural households by selling eggs and dairy products, a trend that continued during the 1930s. Similarly, some urban women kept a few cows on town lots and supplemented their husbands' income by making and selling butter.[72]

Some women took jobs outside the home to augment or replace their husbands' earnings. Nationally, women as a proportion of the workforce inched upward, from 21.9 percent in 1930 to 24.6 percent in 1940. In Utah the percentage of women in the workforce was smaller to begin with, and it rose more modestly, from 17 percent in 1930 to 18.7 percent in 1940. Although most of the state's secretaries and stenographers, nurses, public school teachers, domestic workers, telephone operators, bookkeepers, cashiers, and machine operators in textile and garment factories were women, most of them were single. Nationwide, married women composed 28.9 percent of female workers in 1930 and 35.9 percent in 1940. In Utah a smaller percentage of working women were married: 23.9 percent in 1930 and 30 percent in 1940. Employers generally preferred to hire married men with families or single women. "Jobs were scarce and if you were married you'd just better not even ask for a job.... The men got the work," recalled Frances Wilde, who married in 1932. Even many who had jobs prior to their marriage were fired after they tied the knot. Maurine Campbell, for instance, had to relinquish her stenographer's job in 1937 after she wed. Likewise, when Gwen Jensen returned from her honeymoon, she learned that she had been replaced on the job by a single woman because her boss did not want "married women working for us." Many school districts continued a long-standing policy of replacing female teachers who married.[73]

Thousands of married women did find work, though. Beth Nelson of Logan sought work because of her husband's sporadic employment. In 1937 she was finally hired at $8.64 a week to operate a hemming machine for Cache Knitting Works. Nina Moore of Salt Lake City supplemented her husband's earnings as a mechanic by selling cookies door to door. She earned $13 a week, as well as all the broken cookies she cared to take home, for her efforts. Later she earned money as a door-to-door saleswoman selling forced-air furnaces. When a customer bought one, she received not only a commission but also the right to haul away and burn any coal that the customer no longer needed.[74]

Some teenagers and even a few children entered the workforce to boost their family's income. Frances Simons and her sister supplemented their widowed mother's meager earnings by working at the Del Monte canning factory in Spanish Fork, sorting peas for 13 cents an hour or snipping beans for 9 cents a peck. In Ephraim June Doke Crane and her sisters cleaned, sold tickets, and made popcorn at the movie theater in order to bring extra money into the family. While a large number of young people may have worked intermittently for wages to supplement their parents' income during the Depression, the number of teens with regular jobs may have actually decreased over the Depression decade, as competition for jobs intensified. The 1940 Census indicated that only 8.9 percent of the state's young men and 4 percent of the state's young women ages fourteen to seventeen were in the labor force, roughly half the percentage of young men (18.6) and young women (7.6) nationwide who were similarly involved. By contrast, in 1930 15.5 percent of the state's young men and 5.6 percent of the state's young women had been gainfully employed.[75]

Dissatisfied with the fruits of honest labor, some Utahns turned to illicit activities to boost their income. Early in the 1930s when moonshine whiskey was in high demand, some enterprising residents such as sheepman John Diamanti made money on the side by manufacturing and selling liquor. In smoke-filled back rooms, bookies processed bets on horse races. Ted Speros, a young man working as a busboy in a Salt Lake restaurant who occasionally wagered on a horse race, knew people who would "gamble up to five thousand dollars at a time." In 1938 Salt Lake investigators identified three lotteries, three bookies, seven poker games, and two dice games operating in the city.[76]

To supplement their income, others stole commodities or money. On Salt Lake's west side, remembered John Florez, "a lot of thievery [was] going on" because of residents' destitution. Petty thievery in order to obtain unaffordable necessities was relatively common. John Mills Whitaker, manager of the LDS Church's Deseret Employment Bureau, knew of court cases involving "good men that have been faithful all their lives [who] became so desperate from seeing their children hungry they walked into the stores and took a loaf of bread, a sack of flour."[77]

A few Utahns graduated from petty theft to full-blown burglary. In Salt Lake in 1931, 1,397 automobiles were stolen. In Emery County burglars stole much of the inventory of a dress shop in Green River and of the Peacock Cash Store in Orangeville and raided the safe of the post office in Huntington in 1932. After these crimes merchants in Castle Dale and Huntington hired a night watchman to patrol their properties. In the state at large, the annual robbery rate peaked in 1933, at eighty per one hundred thousand residents. By 1939 it had fallen to fifty.[78]

Whether it meant working long hours, raising and preserving much of their food, scavenging for coal, or economizing in other ways, hard-pressed Utahns devoted much time and energy to negotiating their economic challenges. Still, most Utahns found time for some recreation and entertainment. For some, such activities may have been particularly therapeutic, diverting attention from intractable economic challenges.

WELCOME DIVERSIONS

Informal socials, a long-standing tradition in the countryside, were common in rural Utah during the Depression. "People would get together and surprise each other at their doors with song and games," recalled Joe Bagnall of Sanpete County.

In some Garfield County towns, people traveled from home to home on winter holidays, visiting, caroling, and sharing baked goods. In Lila Gentry's community in the Uinta Basin, "the whole neighborhood would come to one place or another" for ice cream socials.[79]

The silver screen proffered another welcome diversion. Six in 10 Americans saw at least one film a week during the thirties, a decade in which five thousand films were produced. Utah in 1939 had 118 movie theaters, and Utahns spent two and a half times as much money at the movies as at all other places of amusement combined. Even more popular than the film industry was radio entertainment. The number of American households with a radio more than doubled over the 1930s. By 1940 92 percent of the households in the state boasted one. Utahns enjoyed radio programs like *Easy Aces*, *Amos and Andy*, and soap operas—the sappy serials sponsored by detergent makers.[80]

After the repeal of Prohibition in 1933, drinking establishments reappeared as legitimate places of entertainment. They were particularly common in working-class districts and mining towns. By 1937 Salt Lake had forty-four bars, Ogden had thirteen, and Provo and Logan each had one. Watering holes abounded in smaller mining and smelting communities: Price had nine beer parlors, as did Magna, and Helper had four, excluding its five private clubs. With liquor flowing freely, Stan Diamanti recalls, "On Saturday nights, Helper was like Mecca." Business was brisk elsewhere, too. Price's bars reported an average of 159 customers daily in each bar. Bars varied from high-class establishments such as the Rendezvous in the Hotel Utah to more casual places like Chick's Wonder Bar and the Eagle Tavern. Eldon Dorman, a coal-camp physician working for the Blue Blaze Coal Company in the Gordon Creek area, once performed an emergency operation atop a pool table following a fight in one of the state's rougher saloons, a beer joint in Sweets with "several inches of sawdust" on the floor, "hiding the blood and gore of previous Saturday nights."[81]

Utahns in search of a good time during the Depression also patronized billiard halls and pool parlors, bowling alleys, skating rinks, and commercially owned swimming pools, as well as municipal pools and parks. Thanks to New Deal relief laborers who built roads into the mountains and developed picnicking facilities, fireplaces, and amphitheaters in the canyons, a weekend or evening outing in the mountains became more feasible. Utahns also recreated at resorts such as Lagoon, with its dance floor, picnic grounds, and swimming pool. In 1930 the *Sho-Boat*, a ninety-foot double-decker yacht complete with a dance floor, began operations on Utah Lake, taking passengers on pleasure excursions on Sunday afternoons.[82]

School and community sports events provided another source of welcome recreation and entertainment, as they had done in previous eras. Sanpete County's baseball league consisting of teams from most towns and from CCC camps organized games on summer evenings. Similar leagues existed in many counties. Some towns also sponsored basketball teams. The Eastern Utah Basketball League, consisting of six teams from towns in Carbon and Emery Counties, complemented the high school basketball schedule for several years.[83]

For many Utahns, and particularly young men and women, dancing remained one of the most popular recreational activities. Popular dances included the Charleston, drag, and black bottom. Thirty-four commercial dance halls such as Rainbow Gardens in Helper, Dodge Springs in St. George, Park-Ro-She in Springville, and the Rosalie in Wellington were in business in 1939, but dances were also held in many schools, lodges, church buildings, and open-air pavilions. In Spanish Fork and Heber hardwood dance floors were built atop springs to give dancers an extra bounce in their step. Stiff breezes that whipped up the skirts of dancers added to the excitement at open-air pavilions. Parents and religious leaders fretted to no avail about the "low type patrons and low standard music," heavy drinking, reckless dancing, and loose morals at dance halls, where young men arrived in "gangs" and young women walked to and from the dances alone. But dancing was not confined to the younger generation. In Johns Valley during the winter months, adults and teenagers stoked potbellied stoves in the schoolhouse on Friday evenings and danced the night away, while the younger children slept on piles of coats spread out on the margins of the dance floor.[84]

Inexpensive dramatic and vaudeville presentations at lodges, schools, and church amusement halls provided another common diversion, particularly in the wintertime. Utahns could also take in summer band concerts in a park. In 1936 the Utah Music Project was organized, and in 1940 the Utah Symphony, an outgrowth of the project, held its first concert in the University of Utah's Kingsbury Hall.[85]

Recreation might divert people's attention temporarily from their economic woes, but it was least affordable for the poorest Utahns, who needed it most. A domestic servant earning six dollars a week would be hard-pressed to afford fifty cents for bus fare and twenty-five cents for a movie ticket on her half day off every week. Likewise, Utahns who could not pay their rent or buy clothes for their children could ill afford to take the family out for hamburgers and ice cream. Even radio, the democratic entertainment of the airwaves, was beyond the reach of the most indigent Utahns. A 1934 survey of more than two thousand desperately poor households found that 62 percent lacked a working radio.[86]

CHARITY AND RELIEF

For many of these poorest residents, the pioneer values of individual initiative and hard work, economizing, and maximizing family resources were insufficient. Far from looking for entertainment, some concentrated on begging in order to survive. At their home in South Provo, a half mile from the railroad tracks, Lowry and

Florence Nelson "began to have people knocking at our kitchen door very often asking for something to eat" who were "not traditional tramps, but people newly in want." Others in the state's cities secured meals at a soup kitchen.[87]

A larger number of destitute Utahns shunned panhandling or door-to-door begging but turned to government, churches, fraternal organizations, and charities for aid. In the hardest-hit communities, more than half of the residents applied for charitable assistance or welfare at one time or another during the Depression. At least half of Smithfield's residents received church or government relief in the summer of 1932. In Payson half of the population applied for government aid in 1933. Thirty percent of Uintah County's residents in July 1935, 71 percent of Duchesne County's inhabitants in June 1934, and 70 percent of those in Escalante in 1935 received public assistance, and others in the same locales were receiving help from church and civic groups.[88]

Attitudes of needy Utahns toward public assistance varied. Some desperately needy people held out as long as they could. Conversely, others regarded relief as an entitlement and banded together to press government and religious leaders for help. Illustrative of this latter trend, "gangs" of unemployed transients and local people who felt "ag[g]rieved for being laid off from plants and firms no longer able to hire them" showed up at John M. Whitaker's office in the Deseret Employment Bureau, "demand[ing] food and work." Similarly, on January 30, 1931, fifteen hundred protesters organized by the Communist Party marched on the state capitol under the banner "Organize or Starve" and demanded unemployment insurance. Two years later in Provo, five hundred unemployed people staged a "Utah County United Front Hunger March," culminating in a meeting with county commissioners, where they demanded unemployment insurance, welfare payments to the elderly, and cash relief payments. The following month hundreds of protesters stormed the steps of the Salt Lake City and County Building, chanting "Get the papers," and "virtually carried" Sheriff Heber G. Taylor around the building to prevent him from auctioning foreclosed property.[89]

Prior to the summer of 1932, local governments, community organizations, and churches provided piecemeal assistance to the poor. County and city governments were the most important players. Utah County in 1932 spent $63,685 on relief, and Provo, the county seat, spent an additional $8,114 for charity and work-relief projects. By contrast, the combined efforts of twelve religious, fraternal, and community service organizations in Provo netted less than $7,000 in assistance. Through its Relief Society and the charitable contributions of congregants, the LDS Church in 1932 offered $4,683 to needy Provoans. The St. Mary's Guild of the Episcopal church furnished clothing for two families, the Lutheran congregation assisted one household, the Ladies' Aid Society of the Congregational Church fed and clothed three families, the Catholic Women's League furnished cash for needy church members, and the Dorcas Society of the Seventh-Day Adventist Church made clothing and quilts and canned food for the needy. The Woodmen of the World, Odd Fellows, American Legion and Women's Auxiliary, Elks Club, Kiwanis Club, and Masonic Lodge collectively supplied more than $1,200 for relief.[90]

Much of the assistance furnished by local governments, churches, and clubs early in the Depression was doled out to recipients, but some local governments and community organizations organized work-relief projects and distributed benefits in return for labor performed. In Castle Dale, for instance, the American Legion arranged to pay unemployed men to trim trees. In Logan the Chamber of Commerce and county commission organized public works projects and raised funds to pay relief laborers by arranging for business and municipal employees to contribute 2 percent of their salary to a relief fund. Provo's mayor instituted a similar fund late in 1931.[91]

Alongside local organizations, the Red Cross played an important role in relief initiatives early in the 1930s, distributing surplus government flour, crushed wheat for livestock, and cotton goods to residents beginning in the fall of 1931.[92]

Social workers criticized the duplication and lack of coordination among welfare initiatives in most communities. In Salt Lake City the most extensive and best-coordinated relief efforts in the state evolved. The Community Chest, which had been established in 1926, coordinated the activities of most private social service and relief agencies in the city. During the winters of 1931–32 and 1932–33, the Community Chest, in tandem with Salt Lake County and the LDS Church, operated a warehouse where donated coal, food, and clothes were disbursed. Needy residents could approach the Community Chest, the County Charity Department, or an LDS bishop or Relief Society president to secure an order for goods from the warehouse.[93]

Next to county and municipal governments, the most prominent player on the relief scene in Utah early in the 1930s was the LDS Church. Across the state local bishops and Relief Society presidents disbursed locally contributed commodities to members of their congregations. In some places beyond the Salt Lake Valley, including Cache County, relief efforts were coordinated through a network of storehouses for distributing food and clothing early in the Depression. LDS relief efforts were best developed, though, in Salt Lake City, partly because of the extensive unemployment there but largely because the church's central offices were there. In 1930 Salt Lake City church units disbursed 46 percent of the entire amount spent in the general church and its ward organizations on welfare. The church's Deseret Employment Bureau in Salt Lake registered eighteen hundred people and found jobs for twelve hundred of them during the first nine months of 1930. That fall the bureau canvassed Salt Lake County, "contacting every firm, business house, manufacturing concern, professional and the great industries and private and public interests and contractors" in an effort to identify possible jobs for the unemployed.[94]

The most imaginative and ambitious initiatives in welfare by LDS wards and stakes also took place in Salt Lake. In Sugar House the Granite Stake encouraged working members to hire the unemployed to perform odd jobs, such as weeding gardens, shoveling snow, or pruning trees. The stake took orders for firewood and then put unemployed members to work cutting the wood. Local farmers donated food to the stake, which stored it in a warehouse and distributed it to needy members. The stake also facilitated sharecropping arrangements that would benefit jobless members and farmers who needed laborers but could not afford to pay them. In a stake sewing shop, garments were made and repaired. Other stakes adopted similar strategies. In 1932, for instance, the Pioneer Stake arranged for unemployed residents to farm forty acres of vacant land in the city. Garden vegetables were canned, and sugar beets were sold to pay the workers for their labor. Other members of the stake harvested onions under sharecropping arrangements, sorted and bagged the produce, and drove it to market in California in borrowed trucks.[95]

By 1932, despite the efforts of local governments and ambitious initiatives of community organizations, fraternities, and churches, the state's economy continued to worsen, and unemployment rose sharply. Try as they might, local governments, charities, and private citizens fell short of fully meeting the needs of the poor. Similar economic problems were swamping local and private relief efforts across the nation, and many were calling upon the federal government to mobilize its vast financial resources to ameliorate the economic distress. It was time, they contended, to cash in on the benefits of national association and incorporation. Responding to loud clamor for relief, Congress in the summer of 1932 authorized the Reconstruction Finance Corporation, a recently created federal lending agency, to grant funds to state and local governments for unemployment relief projects. President Herbert Hoover, who recognized that this marked a revolutionary departure in the history of welfare policy, reluctantly signed the bill into law on July 21, 1932. Although local governments would continue to be responsible for planning and administering welfare and work-relief programs, the federal government would henceforth be the primary source of those funds; in the first quarter of 1933, for instance, 94 percent of the public unemployment relief funds spent in Utah came from the federal government. The number of Utahns receiving public assistance also rose dramatically, from 29,206 in August 1932 to 171,357 in March 1933, due to the severity of the Depression and the huge influx of federal funds. Between September 1932 and March 1933, Utah received five dollars per capita in relief money from the Reconstruction Finance Corporation, making it the second-highest state in the nation in per capita relief. For the balance of the decade, federal relief dollars pouring into the state would alter the state's infrastructure, produce an army of relief laborers, and generate widespread, impassioned debate over the proper mix of local and national involvement in the economic welfare of the state's residents.[96]

12

UTAH ENCOUNTERS THE NEW DEAL

DEMOCRATIC LANDSLIDE, 1932

For a time prior to the 1932 election it seemed that Utah might select Republican president Herbert Hoover over his Democratic challenger, Franklin D. Roosevelt. Some devotees of Prohibition, such as Provo resident Belle Berry, were determined "not to vote for the Democrats because of the big push to get liquor legalized." Other Utahns felt that Roosevelt, a wealthy New Yorker, did not understand the West's needs and interests: no one who knew the region well, they reasoned, would have chosen railroad problems as the focus for his keynote speech in Salt Lake City while overlooking more salient local issues, including silver, public roads and lands, and reclamation. Many admired Hoover's integrity and distrusted Roosevelt, whose campaign speeches were often contradictory and vague. On November 3 LDS Church president Heber J. Grant publicly declared his "staunch support" as a "private citizen" for Hoover. Still, Hoover's reluctance to send revenue to the states to relieve unemployment rankled many. One critic quipped, "If you put a rose in Hoover's hand it would wilt." On Election Day Roosevelt garnered 57.8 percent of the nation's vote; Utahns were only slightly more conservative, awarding Roosevelt 56.5 percent of their votes. In all but seven rural counties, more people voted for Roosevelt than Hoover.[1]

Not only Hoover but his party took a beating in 1932 because of the Depression. Utahns elected Democrat Henry H. Blood as their new governor and replaced Republican incumbents in Congress Don B. Colton and Frederick C. Loofbourow with Democrats Abe Murdock and J. Will Robinson. Utah's state representatives and senators did not stand for election in 1932, but the handwriting was on the wall; in 1933 Democrats captured 86 percent of the seats in Utah's house and nearly 57 percent in the senate.[2]

In a stunning upset, Mormon apostle Reed Smoot, who had represented the Beehive State in the US Senate since 1903 and been named Utah's most distinguished citizen in a *Salt Lake Telegram* poll in 1930, was beaten by University of Utah political science professor Elbert D. Thomas, who obtained nearly 58 percent of the votes cast. Smoot had been in the Senate longer than any other person then serving, and Utah Republicans had touted his experience as indispensable. A November 1 advertisement declared, "Utah will want a man in the Senate who 'knows the ropes.'" Democrats countered that Smoot's seniority would matter little when Democrats took control on Capitol Hill. "Who will have the better opportunity to 'keep Utah on the map'—an 'old guard' stand-pat Republican, out of harmony with the administration and congress? Or—a progressive, forward-looking, versatile member of the majority party? The next administration will be Democrat!" proclaimed a Thomas advertisement. Democrats astutely blamed part of the nation's economic malaise upon the ill-advised Smoot-Hawley tariff of 1930 that discouraged international trade with the highest protective tariff on imports in the country's history. Warwick Lamoreaux, a university student who had previously identified as a liberal Republican, "had never equated the depression with the political process" until he heard Democratic senator William King blaming Smoot's policies for it. King's speech "penetrated my most inner feelings," Lamoreaux recalled, as King argued that "the Smoot-Hawley tariff was hurting us domestically and internationally." When Lamoreaux "realized the economic mess could be the responsibility of one of our own Utahns," he decided to vote for Smoot's opponent.[3]

Smoot was deeply embittered by his defeat. Attempting to console him, church president Heber J. Grant confided, "I know of nothing that has been more disappointing to me than the failure of our people to return you to the Senate." But Grant's condolences did not erase the fact that the church had not endorsed Smoot's candidacy, due partly to the objections of ardent Democrat and fellow apostle Anthony W. Ivins. Smoot bitterly complained, "The members of my Church were my principal opponents, some of them in high places." Privately, he reportedly groused, "Bro. Ivins had me defeated all over Utah before I knew a thing about it."[4]

PORTENTS OF REFORM: REGULATING BANKS
AND REPEALING PROHIBITION

A pressing problem facing the nation was the precarious situation of banks. In order to prevent depositors from withdrawing funds and inciting financial panic, Governor Blood temporarily closed all banks in the state on March 3, following a course taken by adjoining states. Banking commissioner John Malia examined the accounts of each state bank, and by March 14 all state and national banks had reopened. In June Congress would enact legislation ensuring bank deposits up to twenty-five hundred dollars.[5]

Roosevelt had come out in favor of repealing Prohibition, largely as a bid for popular support but also as a means of generating tax revenue and creating jobs in the liquor industry. After Congress approved a repeal amendment, the battle moved to the states, where ratification was to occur in state conventions rather than legislatures. Utah lawmakers in 1933 called a constitutional convention to vote on the repeal amendment. Voters would choose a slate of either wet or dry candidates for the convention. In a special session called by Governor Blood in July 1933, legislators also approved a ballot measure that would allow Utahns to vote on whether to remove Prohibition from the state constitution. Evangelicals and Mormon leaders, including Rev. Rollin Ayers and John F. Bowman, banded together to prevent repeal, while an assortment of Democratic Party and other civic leaders, including Clarence Bamberger and Margaret Keyser, lobbied for repeal. In November 101,600 Utahns voted to repeal the Eighteenth Amendment, while only 67,200 voted to retain it. By a majority of 37,506, Utahns voted to scrap the state constitution's Prohibition mandate. By deliberately scheduling its repeal convention for December 5, after thirty-five other states had repealed the Eighteenth Amendment, Utahns secured the distinction of being the state that tipped the national balance in favor of the Twenty-First Amendment.[6]

NEW DEAL RELIEF PROGRAMS

The Democratic landslide of 1932 opened the floodgates to new levels of federal involvement and investment. Roosevelt's domestic programs came to be known collectively as the New Deal, a casual phrase from Roosevelt's speech at the Democratic National Convention in Chicago that journalists extracted and enshrined in the public consciousness. Utah's economic plight, the federal government's ownership of more than half the land in the state, the lobbying abilities and connections of former governor George Dern who was serving in Roosevelt's cabinet, and the ability of state and county officials to tap into well-organized church networks for identifying economic need helped to make Utah a prime recipient of federal largesse. As financial ties to the federal government multiplied, so did Utah's incorporation under the centralizing administrative apparatus of the New Deal.[7]

The Civilian Conservation Corps, a nationwide employment relief agency created in April 1933, funneled more nonrepayable funds to New Deal projects in Utah than any other federal agency. Between April 1933 and June 1942, the agency spent roughly $52,756,183 on projects in the state. It operated 116 camps where young men between ages seventeen and twenty-five worked on conservation and development programs, including forest culture and protection, erosion and flood control, reclamation, road building, range development, wildlife protection, and development of recreational facilities. More than 85 percent of the young laborers on Utah projects came from out of state, although their supervisors and foremen were generally local men. Still, between 1933 and 1938 the CCC employed 15,165 Utahns as young enlistees and 3,358 more as supervisory or service personnel.[8]

The prospect of hosting a large number of young, single outsiders nearby initially concerned many Utahns, who worried about the camps' effects on community morals. Taylor C. Nuttall, one of 24 Utah boys employed with 190 New Yorkers in a camp north of Bryce Canyon, characterized the New Yorkers as "an awfully scummy crew." In Delta, one woman recalled, many residents initially treated CCC boys "like an epidemic of smallpox. Anyone who professed to be moral practically refused to walk on the same side of the street with any of the CCC boys. The Church preached against it, parents were alarmed, and stories were circulated to scare the young girls." As time passed, though, attitudes changed, and the insularity of small communities was breached. Joseph Bernini, a CCC laborer from New York, explained, "At first people were apprehensive, but soon we were very welcome and invited into homes and public functions."[9]

At community dances CCC crews and local youth became acquainted. CCC boys working near Zion Park often attended dances in Springdale until the admission price was raised. The boys organized a boycott and loitered outside the hall while the girls inside danced with each other. When two of the boys violated the boycott and sauntered inside, their peers stormed the hall, hauled them out, stripped them naked, and left them to make their way back to camp. Downriver at Hurricane folks decided to introduce some friendly competition and charge only half as much as Springdale for their dances. Finally, Springdale reinstated the original admission fee.[10]

CCC crews terraced steep slopes along the Wasatch Range to check erosion in places such as Willard Basin by digging ditches two or three feet deep and six feet wide on steep hillsides. Crews also built check dams at the bases of canyons and rivulets. In Utah County, for instance, 225 young men in a camp near Springville built small dams and retention basins near the mouths of Rock, Slate, and Little Rock Canyons to contain runoff and prevent damage to farms and homes in the valley. Between 1933 and 1941 CCC crews built more than 400 impounding and diversion dams statewide and developed 792 springs, water holes, and small reservoirs. The CCC also improved thousands of miles of roads through national forests.

CCC crews also helped build larger dams, including Pine View east of Ogden; built recreational facilities, such as the Aspen Grove and Mutual Dell amphitheaters on Mount Timpanogos; developed picnic facilities in many places; and fought forest fires. They also planted 3.2 million trees. As historian Beth R. Olsen observed in 1994, "Most of the forest, range, and wildlife improvements used by the Utah populace during the past fifty-plus years were built by the CCC."[11]

Utahns praised CCC crews for their service. In Garfield County the Henrieville camp, supervised by Lionel Chidester, saved sheep herds from starvation following fierce winter storms in 1937. One rancher wrote:

> I have lived here for forty-seven years, during that time I have never seen as cold a spell [as] from December 27th to January 28th, 1937. There was not a break in the weather, ranging from ten to thirty-eight below zero, snow from two to four feet deep and drifted badly. This camp, with the superintendent in the lead, saved several herds of sheep by breaking trails, hauling feed, supplies, etc....The towns of Cannonville, Henrieville, and Tropic would have been snow bound if it had not been for...superintendent Chidester and his men.[12]

As historian Kenneth Baldridge observed, Utahns eventually liked the CCC not only because of the improvements made and services rendered by the corps but also because of the money that the program brought into the state. The government invested an average of $20,000 in constructing a camp, and camp residents and administrators spent an additional $5,000 a month in local stores. Young Utahns in the CCC earned $30 a month, although nearly three-fourths of their earnings were sent to their parents.[13]

The CCC experience dramatically affected many Utahns, who traveled to new places, met new people, and learned new skills thereby. One worker, Taylor C. Nuttall, wrote, "These camps are wonderful places for young men....It is the most wonderful thing in the world for the conditioning of young men and boys both mentally and physically, not to mention morally." Looking back on his experiences thirty years after the Depression, another enrollee commented, "It made a man of me....I learned how to take orders and give them in a way that could be understood.... [I]t was the most rewarding experience that I have ever had in my life." Some young workers mastered skills in the camps that enabled them to provide for themselves throughout life, from masonry to heavy equipment operation. Others, such as Jay Neeley, met their future spouses in the CCC: after graduating from West High in Salt Lake, Neeley was stationed at camps in the Uinta Basin, where he met his future wife, Renee Mickelson.[14]

While the CCC invested heavily in Utah, the New Deal agency that hired more Utahns than any other was the Works Progress Administration, which spent

$28,381,996 in the state between its creation in 1935 and June 30, 1939—most of it in wages. An average of 12,000 Utahns per month received paychecks from the WPA, with the peak employment being 15,061 in March 1936. The mean duration of employment for men was 9.2 months, compared to 11.6 for women.[15]

Between 1935 and the end of 1940, WPA workers built 773 bridges and viaducts and developed nearly 4,200 miles of road, including mileage up Little Cottonwood Canyon to a new winter recreation area at Alta. They built 272 new buildings, including two college dormitories; three libraries; two hospitals; an art museum in Springville; a Stadium House at the State Agricultural College; armories in Logan, American Fork, Nephi, Mount Pleasant, Fillmore, and Cedar City; nine new schools; and a courthouse in Wayne County. WPA workers built 26,821 privies for farmhouses, installed 363 miles of water line, and laid 241 miles of storm and sewer line. They also built or improved recreational facilities, including 35 new stadiums, 15 new parks, 8 new playgrounds, 80 new tennis courts, 11 new swimming pools, and 4 new outdoor theaters. WPA crews also began work on an Army Air depot at Ogden. Musicians on WPA payrolls gave 954 concerts, and 5 of them (2 clarinetists, 1 violinist, 1 pianist, and 1 drummer) formed the Works Progress Orchestra in December 1935, which grew into a 45-member orchestra that became the forerunner of the Utah Symphony. Meanwhile, artists displayed works and taught classes in WPA art centers and painted murals in Kingsbury Hall at the University of Utah, the federal building in Provo, and Price's city hall. Scholars, librarians, teachers, and others wrote local histories, a state guidebook, and inventories of historical records in public buildings. Women working for the WPA sewed more than 800,000 articles of clothing, canned millions of quarts of food, prepared nearly 10 million school lunches, and operated 16 nursery schools.[16]

Critics joked that the acronym WPA stood for "We Piddle Around," observing that some projects seemed to progress at a snail's pace. Mormon president Heber J. Grant cautioned, "Workers for the WPA must be workers by the job and not by the day: that is, they must work with energy to get each job well done as soon as possible, and not merely put in time, or 'kill' time while drawing pay. There is a WPA project being carried on near my own home, and I know from personal observation that a great many of the workers are not putting their hearts into the job. In fact, they are going just about as slowly as they possibly can." Others maintained that the stereotypical image of lazy shovel leaners did not fit the WPA at all. Afton Larsen, a pipe layer for the WPA in Ephraim, explained, "That WPA, that was work, not just a handout.... Digging trenches when the ground was frozen about one and a half feet down, well that was work."[17]

While WPA workers did not grow wealthy, their wages enabled them to subsist. Pay varied depending upon the worker's skills and the local cost of living. Professionals employed by the WPA in Salt Lake County earned as much as $94 a month, while unskilled laborers there earned $55. In counties with fewer than 5,000 residents and lower prevailing wages, unskilled laborers were paid $40 a month. Frances Wilde recalled that the money her brother made as a WPA worker on road crews "was quite a boon to our family." Prices were cheap, and even $40 a month was money that "we didn't have before then."[18]

The Federal Emergency Relief Administration, a predecessor of the WPA, ranked third among New Deal agencies in the amount of money granted to Utah. Between its creation in 1933 and its termination in 1935, FERA funneled $20,343,968 to the state. States used FERA funds for both direct cash welfare payments and work-relief projects. Relief dollars were distributed by the state emergency relief administration and, initially, by private organizations, including the LDS Church, Jewish Relief, Catholic Welfare, and the Red Cross.[19]

Like the WPA, FERA employed some Utah men and women on public works projects, including a new hospital in Carbon County and an amphitheater for the State Agricultural College in Logan. In 1934 alone relief workers graded 892 miles and graveled 485 miles of road, built 205 bridges, constructed nearly 44,000 feet of curbs and gutters, laid 452,569 feet of water pipe, cleaned and repaired 910,984 feet of ditches, laid 127,118 feet of sewer line, constructed 33 public buildings, built 11 swimming pools, controlled weeds on 792 acres, cleared 100 canyon campsites, canned 194,549 cans of fruit and vegetables, made 24,639 articles of clothing, and cleaned and repaired 31,910 library books. One of the more creative projects was designed by Juanita Brooks, the dean of women at Dixie College, in order to benefit "widows with families, or other unemployed women." These women interviewed elderly residents, compiling their life histories. FERA funds were used to hire teachers for adult education classes and preschools and college students for on-campus work. At the suggestion of Nels Anderson, a former Utahn working as a FERA administrator in Washington, DC, students and others at Dixie College collected and typed historical documents for $30 a month.[20]

Although FERA funded work-relief projects, more than half of its beneficiaries received direct cash payments, or the dole. FERA also loaned money to marginal farmers to enable them to improve their farms or develop new ones under its Rural Rehabilitation Division and enabled states to care for the homeless through its Transient Relief Service. The Transient Service offered medical care, temporary housing, vocational training, and recreational activities for the homeless. Utahns, along with residents of adjacent states, relied far more heavily upon FERA than did most states. During the fiscal year 1934–35, the percentage of Utah's population on general or special relief was the fifth highest in the nation.[21]

In part, Utah's heavy reliance upon FERA that year stemmed from its receipt of $1.2 million earmarked for drought-relief projects, including construction of water-storage facilities, improvement of irrigation systems, and grants to hard-pressed farmers for purchasing feed for livestock. Only Texas, Missouri, and South Dakota received more drought-relief funds that year.²² One especially ambitious project in 1934 helped residents of Uintah County. Faced with severe water shortages, farmers in communities such as Davis Ward knew that they had "no hope whatever of maturing any grain crops or cutting hay." There was so little water running in the Green River that adults could ford it in some places without getting their knees wet. In May 1934 Uintah County's drought-relief committee proposed that emergency relief funds be used to purchase irrigation pumps and fuel so that farmers could lease, temporarily plant, and irrigate 1,800 acres of river bottomland near Leota. Erastus Peterson, former extension agent for the county, became project supervisor. Ultimately, 185 households participated. The leased land along the river was divided into family-sized tracts averaging 9 acres. Although some farmers commuted between the project and their regular homes, others camped out along the river in tents, log cabins, and brush huts. Ida Jenkins lived with her nine children in a typical makeshift "lean-to...lined with cardboard boxes on the inside... [with] a dirt floor and a dirt roof." The families cooked over open fires and washed their clothes in river water. Coupons furnished by FERA enabled participants to procure food. Although the muggy heat, mosquitoes, blow snakes, and brackish water made life onerous at times, the campers enjoyed fishing, swimming, visiting, and playing games in their spare time. Enoch Lewis even erected a makeshift dance pavilion. Partly because the project did not get under way until late May and early June and because temperatures dipped below freezing for several consecutive nights early in September, participants harvested only 6,004 tons of corn, 225 tons of hay, 1,915 bushels of potatoes, and 65 tons of squash, as well as some garden produce. The total harvest was valued at $288 per family. Although the harvest was small, it was critical. "I don't believe we would have ever gotten by that winter with our stock if we hadn't had that," commented one participant.²³

Two other New Deal relief agencies, the Civil Works Administration (CWA) and the Public Works Administration (PWA), also funneled millions of dollars westward from Washington, DC, to Utah. The CWA was created late in November 1933 to provide work for unemployed Americans during the coming winter. During its brief lifetime (November 1933–March 1934), the CWA spent $5.2 million in Utah on 1,437 projects. Employment on CWA projects peaked at 20,451 in mid-January. Workers earned between 50 cents and $1.20 an hour, depending upon their skills. Nearly half of CWA funds spent in the state were used on street and road projects. CWA crews also developed water supplies and built public buildings. They constructed sewer systems in Brigham and Cedar City; swimming pools in Duchesne, Scipio, and Tooele; rifle ranges in Brigham City and Antimony; and tennis courts in four communities.²⁴

Unlike the WPA, which lavished funds on the state, the PWA, headed by Harold Ickes, was more niggardly. When Governor Blood visited Washington in 1933 to seek PWA funding for buildings and reclamation projects, Ickes complained in his diary, "A delegation from Utah, headed by Secretary Dern, and including Governor Blood...came in to nag again about some reclamation projects for their state. This group has been hanging about Washington for more than three weeks....They seem to be proceeding on the theory that they can just wear down our resistance and get what they want." Despite the lobbying, Utah ranked only thirty-fourth in its receipt of PWA funds on a per capita basis. Still, the agency spent more than $10 million in Utah during the 1930s and facilitated valuable projects, including Pineview Dam, which provided irrigation water for Weber and Box Elder Counties. The PWA also helped to build 9 other water projects, 43 agricultural projects, well over 20 public schools, a home economics building and student commons at Utah State University, a library at the University of Utah, dormitories, and 140 roads.[25]

Another work-relief agency, the National Youth Administration, invested $3,889,104 between 1935 and 1943. The NYA employed high school– and college-age youth on a variety of projects, many of which were designed to improve facilities or provide services (or both) at more than 100 secondary schools and 11 colleges and universities. At Payson High School, for instance, four mechanically minded students with an interest in physics built a reflecting telescope for the school. At Carbon College, more than one hundred students were hired to build an addition for the vocational training building. The NYA's student work projects received the most publicity, but nearly two-thirds of the NYA money spent in Utah went to nonstudent youth who worked on projects, including weed control and pipelines.[26]

The Rocky Mountain region, including Utah, leaned more heavily upon New Deal relief programs than any other region in the nation. Within the region Utah and New Mexico benefited disproportionately; near the end of the decade, 7.7 percent of Utah's labor force was employed on public emergency work—a percentage that was exceeded only by Oklahoma (7.9) and New Mexico (9.1).[27]

Although it did not provide as much money for the state during the 1930s as did relief agencies, the Social Security Administration, established as the Social Security Board in 1935, ultimately affected more Utahns directly than any other New Deal welfare initiative. The Social Security Act of 1935 established an old-age and survivors insurance program for workers over the age of sixty-four. Payments were contingent upon retirement and were determined based upon wages earned between December 31, 1936, and the recipient's sixty-fifth birthday; the maximum monthly benefit was set at $85. The act also provided federal funds to the states for unemployment benefits and matching federal funds for welfare to indigent senior citizens, visually handicapped residents, and female-headed families with children. Utah ranked second per capita in the nation in Social Security funds disbursed during the 1930s. By June 1938, 10,996 senior citizens, 218 blind people, and parents of 6,864 children in 2,799 families were receiving assistance under the Social

Security Act. Although some have speculated that Social Security expenditures in the state were high because of the greater longevity of Utah's residents, Utah actually had a smaller percentage of its population over the age of sixty-four (5.5 percent in 1940) than did the nation at large (6.9 percent).[28]

REMAKING RURAL UTAH: NEW DEAL AGRICULTURAL PROGRAMS

Initially, farmers were excluded from the old-age insurance provisions of the Social Security Act. However, a separate package of New Deal programs attempted to boost farmers' income. Monetarily, the most important New Deal agricultural agency, the Agricultural Adjustment Administration, paid farmers to take land out of production in order to reduce commodity surpluses and boost prices. In Utah the AAA spent more than $10.7 million. Local committees, assisted by county extension agents, established quotas for the number of acres to be planted in key crops—most notably wheat and sugar beets. Farmers then contracted to limit their production of those crops in return for federal payments. Between 1933 and 1937 Utah farmers signed 4,752 AAA corn contracts, 18,378 wheat contracts, and 18,639 sugar beet contracts.[29]

The AAA also sought to boost livestock prices by culling herds. In 1934 the Agricultural Adjustment Administration began buying emaciated livestock from Utahns who could not feed their animals because of the drought. Ranchers received close to $1.8 million under this program. They sold 126,370 beef cattle and 206,504 sheep to the government at average prices of $13.89 per cow and $2 per sheep. The government bought one-fourth of the cattle in the Uinta Basin under this program. The best animals were either distributed by the Rural Rehabilitation Division as subsistence cattle or butchered; owners were permitted to take whatever meat they could eat, and the rest was canned and distributed by the Federal Surplus Relief Corporation. Animals unfit for consumption were slaughtered and buried in mass graves or burned. In Utah 27.5 percent of the cattle and more than half of the sheep purchased were condemned as unfit for food. Ranchers resented the low prices paid for their animals but recognized it was the best option available. Still, memory of the program rankled many of them. Nearly fifty years after the incident, Uintah County rancher Merrill Lisonbee could not forget the day when the government bought and slaughtered thirty-six cows in his corral. The animals were too thin to be used for meat, so Lisonbee dragged the carcasses to a nearby ravine, piled brush on them, and burned them. Thinking of the waste and loss still brought tears to his eyes.[30]

Government payments to farmers boosted their income only slightly. According to Department of Agriculture reports, federal payments to Utah's farmers, totaling $10,955,000 between 1933 and 1939, accounted for only 3.8 percent of farmers' cash income. However, AAA programs also indirectly boosted commodity prices and income by reducing surpluses. For instance, while the government's buyout of livestock was painful to ranchers contemplating what they might have made in better times, it helped to increase the value of their remaining animals. Ranchers' income from cattle and sheep sales, exclusive of government payments, rose 47.9 percent between 1932 and 1935.[31]

In 1936 the Supreme Court ruled that the AAA's source for subsidies for farmers—a tax on the food-processing industry—was unconstitutional. Subsequently, Congress identified alternate sources of funding and enacted the Soil Conservation and Domestic Allotment Act of 1936, providing for continued payments to farmers. The law paid farmers for soil-conservation practices, such as rotating crops and devoting portions of their farms to soil-conserving grasses rather than soil-depleting cash crops. Nearly fifteen thousand farmers participated in this program in 1937 and received payments of $929,000 that year. By mid-1938 46,794 acres formerly devoted to soil-depleting crops had been removed from production and soil-building practices had been implemented on 247,000 acres of farmland.[32]

To correct loopholes in the 1936 act, Congress passed a second Agricultural Adjustment Act in 1938 that made payments for soil-conservation practices contingent upon removing land from cultivation and authorized the secretary of agriculture to establish acreage quotas for key commodities and pay growers of those crops when prices dipped below target levels. Utah farmers received $624,000 under this program in 1938.[33]

While the principal objective of AAA and its successor programs was to boost farm income, some New Deal agencies aimed at more fundamental reforms. The Soil Erosion Service (1933) and its successor in the Department of Agriculture, the Soil Conservation Service (1935), educated farmers regarding soil-conservation practices, established demonstration projects to illustrate the techniques and advantages of conservation, and supervised the rehabilitation of eroded and depleted soils on public lands. To complement federal demonstration projects, President Roosevelt in 1937 encouraged the states to establish and empower local soil-conservation districts to enact land-use regulations. Utah was the fifth state to pass enabling legislation providing for the formation of such districts to take advantage of the benefits of the 1936 act. By 1945 thirty-three districts covering more than two-thirds of the state's landmass had been created. SCS expenditures in Utah to 1939 totaled $984,850. By 1945 the SCS had replanted more than 50,000 acres in the state to control erosion, had built 702 water-storage structures, and had initiated soil-conserving practices such as contour plowing and cultivation on more than 32,000 acres. The service and its predecessor agencies had also purchased more than 69,000 acres of submarginal land that were being managed by the Forest Service and the SCS.[34]

Unlike the AAA, which mainly benefited large growers, the Resettlement Administration (RA) and its successor, the Farm Security Administration, targeted low-income farmers. These agencies invested nearly $6 million in Utah, mainly in the form of subsistence grants and low-interest loans for seed, livestock, and equipment. By the middle of 1939, more than seventy-four hundred Utah farm families had received money from the agencies.[35]

The RA also tried to reform rural land use by identifying poor farmland that should never have been plowed—a consequence of decades of laissez-faire federal land policy—and then buying, restoring, and managing it. RA administrator Rexford Tugwell described the program as a "simultaneous attack on the wastage of people and the inefficient use of resources." Land-use planners pinpointed thirty-five areas in the state for land-use adjustment, including 5,280 farms, many of which had already been abandoned. This ambitious proposal largely fell by the wayside. By the end of the Depression, the government had purchased only 69,110 acres, located at only two sites: nearly 30,000 acres in Johns Valley in the vicinity of Widtsoe, a community about forty miles north of Bryce Canyon, and more than 40,000 acres in Rush Valley, between Benmore and Tintic Junction. Most of the land in Johns Valley was subsequently managed by the Forest Service, while the SCS managed the lands in Tooele County as grazing land.[36]

Farmers occupying the land that was purchased were desperately poor. In 1934 Orson Adair, a resident of Johns Valley, described the situation there: "It is fall...and the people have milk cows, some horses, chickens, pigs and in some cases a few sheep to feed this winter, and nothing to feed them....Will you please picture a community in a locality where practically no income is available other than forty dollars a month [in relief payments]? That is the very limit to our earnings. We have no gardens, no fruit trees, no pastures." Residents in Rush Valley were equally destitute: Joe and Jane Oborn had raised a good grain crop in 1927, but thereafter spiraled downward because of severe drought and falling farm prices. By the mid-1930s, encumbered with more than $4,000 in debt and a family to support, they desperately wanted to sell or trade their farm, but no one was interested in a place where rain rarely fell and the wind stirred up the dry soil and blew it away.[37]

To accommodate capable farmers stranded on submarginal land, the RA and affiliated agencies identified more than 80,000 acres statewide that were either already developed or could be developed to accommodate as many as twelve to thirteen hundred families. Although agency employees carefully studied many sites for prospective farming communities, the RA developed none in Utah. Instead, the government purchased and improved existing farms across the state to accommodate thirty-three Utah families whose submarginal lands had been purchased by the agency. The families received long-term low-interest loans from the government to enable them to buy their new farms from the government.[38]

Although most who sold their land to the government in Johns Valley missed their tight-knit community after their resettlement turned Widtsoe into a ghost town, most fared better economically on their new farms. Typical was Ray Hoffman, who relocated on a sugar beet farm in Draper with "good soil and good water rights." Looking back on the experience after nearly fifty years, Hoffman believed resettlement to have been "the best thing to do" and something that had "helped a lot." A minority, though, like Reed Beebe, who relocated on a farm in Piute County, failed on their new farm and bitterly denounced the resettlement program as a hornet's nest of corruption and fraud. By 1965 two-thirds of those who had relocated with federal assistance remained on the farms they had obtained with the government's help, and by 1989, more than fifty years after relocation, 39 percent of the relocatees or their descendants retained at least some of the property they had acquired as a result of resettlement.[39]

Residents of some of the state's most isolated rural regions also benefited from the reformist efforts of another New Deal agency, the Rural Electrification Administration, which was created in 1935. The REA spent only $18,548 in Utah between 1935 and 1939—partly because Utah already ranked third in the nation in the percentage of its farm homes with electric lights (58.1 percent). Nevertheless, the REA still brought electricity to hundreds of homes and farms in Duchesne, Garfield, and Kane Counties during the 1930s. Originally designed as a public works program to provide work relief to the unemployed, rural electrification failed on this count because few unemployed workers possessed the requisite technical and electrical skills. But the idea of improving rural lifestyles through federal loans to rural cooperatives was sufficiently appealing on its own to persuade Congress to appropriate funds for "generating plants, electric transmission and distribution lines, or systems for the furnishing of electric energy to persons in rural areas who are not receiving central station service."[40]

During the 1930s two newly organized rural cooperatives, Garkane Power Association in Garfield and Kane Counties and Moon Lake Electric in Duchesne County, borrowed money from the REA for electrical systems. In 1939 power lines began to deliver electricity on both projects. As historian William Leuchtenburg has observed, "The REA revolutionized rural life." Lamar LeFevre, a resident of Wayne County, recalled the magical moment when electric lights first illuminated his home. "We're sitting here. The coal oil lamps were on. There was eight of us. And all at once this bright light come on. It was almost like I guess resurrection day will be." Electricity simplified many tasks. In Duchesne County Harvey and Fontella Taylor eagerly swapped an electric iron for their six- or seven-pound sad irons that had to be heated on the stove. "I tell you, it saved a lot of work," reflected Fontella. Women commonly averred that appliances such as electric water pumps, vacuums, irons, refrigerators, stoves, water heaters, and washing machines reduced their workload by half. Electricity also made it easier to accomplish tasks after dark. Even milking cows was more pleasant. Who could be nostalgic, as Lamar LeFevre reflected, about "crap clear up to the top of your shoes and no light" in the barn? Residents of Tridell were so eager to part with their old kerosene lamps that they planned a funeral for them, complete with a casket.[41]

PROPPING UP THE ECONOMY

Many Utahns applied for crop loans from another New Deal entity, the Commodity Credit Corporation. Thousands more refinanced home and farm mortgages or borrowed money for crop production or livestock enterprises through the Farm Credit Administration, a New Deal agency created in 1933 through a merger of existing government lending agencies. Institutions affiliated with the FCA loaned $41.8 million to Utahns from 1933 to 1939. At the end of 1939, 43 percent of the farm mortgage debt in Utah was supervised by the FCA-affiliated Federal Land Bank of Berkeley and the Land Bank commissioner. Meanwhile, the Home Owners' Loan Corporation refinanced mortgages for more than 10,700 Utah home owners who were on average two years delinquent in their principal and interest payments and nearly three years delinquent in their taxes. Because it possessed the highest level of resident home ownership in the nation, Utah received more assistance per capita from HOLC than any other state. Close to 40 percent of the mortgages on nonfarm dwellings in Utah in 1940 had been refinanced by the agency.[42]

During the 1930s another New Deal agency, the Federal Housing Administration, insured nearly four thousand private loans for home purchase and more than ten thousand additional loans for property improvement, such as remodeling, home repairs, and construction of sheds and garages. Close to 12 percent of the new homes built in the state between 1935 and 1940 were financed with FHA-insured loans.[43]

In addition to New Deal programs, federal agencies that predated the New Deal, including the Bureau of Public Roads, the Veterans Administration, the Bureau of Reclamation, and the Forest Service, spent millions of dollars in the state during the 1930s on projects that employed Utahns. For instance, the Bureau of Reclamation began work on major projects including Hyrum Lake, Moon Lake, the Ogden River project, and the Provo River project. Collectively, these four agencies spent more than $41 million in Utah.[44]

Over the Depression decade, the state and federal governments increased their outlays. In addition to assuming part of the cost of most public works projects under federal cost-sharing provisions, Utahns through their state taxes supported unemployable individuals who did not qualify for federal assistance under the terms of the Social Security Act. The number of Utahns receiving welfare checks from the state rose steadily following passage of the Social Security Act. By February 1938 more than thirteen thousand Utahns drew upon the state welfare apparatus, and by 1940 welfare payments consumed one-third of the state's budget.[45]

CONSERVATIVE OPPOSITION TO THE NEW DEAL

Conservatives nationwide cynically decried what they perceived to be an avalanche of alphabet agencies buying votes with borrowed money and co-opting and incorporating state and local governments as vassals of a federal lord. Utah conservatives shared the same concerns as New Deal opponents elsewhere. Franklin S. Harris, leader of the state Republican ticket in 1938, expressed these views succinctly. "The Democratic party, which so long championed local self government and economy, has completely abandoned these principles and has thrown the nation into dangerous centralization of authority and an unheard of spree of spending." J. Reuben Clark, de facto leader of the state's Republicans, complained about having to compete with Democratic subsidies to voters in the form of New Deal programs—what he called the "largesse of the Emperor."[46]

The impotence of Utah conservatives in the mid-1930s is understandable, given Utahns' dependence upon New Deal programs, but it is nevertheless more remarkable than the powerlessness of conservatives elsewhere, because seven in ten Utahns belonged at least nominally to the LDS Church, an entity whose governing council, the First Presidency, vigorously attacked the New Deal and opposed Roosevelt's reelection in 1936. Skepticism of some leaders toward the New Deal had been evident in the church's General Conferences as early as October 1933, when Apostle J. Reuben Clark expressed fears that dependence upon the government for relief would "debauch us." This was balanced, though, by Apostle Stephen L. Richards's statement in the same conference, urging Mormons to "give our government our united support."[47]

As time passed, though, criticism of the New Deal became more common in the church's conferences; twelve months after he had admonished Mormons to support the government, Richards expressed serious reservations about the "regrettable tendency to 'sponge' on the government." By the summer of 1936 Republican leaders in the state were using church president Heber J. Grant's criticism of the New Deal to drum up support for the party. Grant's dislike for the New Deal was palpable in his opening address at the church's October 1936 General Conference. Although he admitted that some work-relief projects were constructive, he warned that the dole could "ruin" the nation, advised farmers not to participate in New Deal crop-reduction schemes, and criticized the inefficiency of a work-relief project near his home.[48]

On October 31, 1936, the church-owned *Deseret News* printed an unequivocal front-page editorial castigating the incumbent and endorsing his opponent without naming either one. Written by J. Reuben Clark of the First Presidency and published on the front page at the insistence of President Heber J. Grant, the editorial appealed to Mormon scripture to establish the Constitution's divine origins and then proceeded to outline Roosevelt's attitudes toward the document.[49] The *News* alleged that the president had "characterized the Constitution as of 'horse and buggy days,'" referring to a favorite whipping boy of conservatives: Roosevelt's spontaneous comment in a press conference on May 31, 1935, four days after the Supreme Court had ruled against the National Recovery Act, a key piece of New Deal legislation. In its decision the Court had narrowly interpreted the interstate commerce clause in the Constitution, ruling that the clause conferred upon the federal government only the right to regulate the actual shipment of goods between states. Roosevelt complained, "The country was in the horse-and-buggy age when that clause was written." Now, in an era when the nation's economic and political life was far more integrated and when a broad interpretation of that clause was needed in order to permit the federal government to "administer laws that have a bearing on, and general control over, national economic problems and national social problems," Roosevelt had lamented, "We have been relegated to the horse-and-buggy definition of interstate commerce."[50]

Although Roosevelt had singled out a clause in the Constitution rather than the entire document, and although the phrase, as Thomas Alexander has observed, correctly characterized modes of travel in the eighteenth century, conservatives like Clark argued that the statement revealed not only Roosevelt's perception of the document as outmoded but also his desire to broaden presidential power at the states' expense in a "tyrannical" fashion.[51]

The editorial offered additional evidence of Roosevelt's attitudes toward the Constitution, mentioning that he had "advised members of Congress to join in enacting laws irrespective of the belief of the Congressmen as to the constitutionality of such laws." Here Clark referred to a letter written by Roosevelt to Samuel Hill of the House Committee on Ways and Means on July 6, 1935, in which Roosevelt had advised, "I hope your committee will not permit doubts as to constitutionality, however reasonable, to block the suggested legislation [the Guffey-Snyder Coal Bill]." The editorial noted that the president who had made these statements was sworn to "preserve, protect, and defend the Constitution." In earlier drafts of the editorial, Clark had also reiterated common charges that Roosevelt was a Communist, noting that even some Democrats had "publicly accuse[d] him of sympathy or affiliation with Communism," but this allegation was removed before the editorial was printed.[52]

Having castigated the incumbent without mentioning his name, the editorial praised Republican Alf Landon as "the other candidate" because he had "declared he stands for the Constitution and for the American system of government which it sets up." Noting the church's affinity for "constitutional government," the editorial concluded, "Church members, who believe the revelations and the words of the Prophet, must stand for the Constitution. Every patriot, loving his country and its institutions, should feel in duty bound to vote to protect it."[53]

The editorial, showcased on the front page and opposing not specific policies but the personification of the entire New Deal, was far more strident and controversial than the paper's previous Depression-era editorials. O. N. Malmquist, political columnist for the *Tribune* in the 1930s, believed that it was "doubtful that the church leadership had ever taken a stronger stand against one candidate and for another, either publicly or within organization ranks, than in the 1936 election."[54]

Predictably, therefore, the editorial raised a "rumpus." Its tone was less strident than that of an editorial appearing the following morning in the *Salt Lake Tribune* that criticized Roosevelt even more heavily, accused his administration of sympathizing with communism, and argued that "the election of Governor Landon...is the quickest and surest way back to constitutional government and the American tradition." Nevertheless, the *News*'s statement attracted more attention because of the paper's ties to the LDS Church. Republicans hailed the editorial, along with the *Tribune*'s endorsement of Landon, as "courageous" and attempted to capitalize upon the constitutional arguments, billing their candidates as defenders of the Constitution in last-minute campaigning in Utah. "Only in the Republican party platform can a citizen feel certain that his constitutional rights will continue to be enjoyed," declared national committeeman George W. Snyder the day before the election.[55]

Some Democrats were amused by the editorial: A. S. Brown, national Democratic committeeman for Utah, reportedly quipped, "If the *Deseret News* and the Mormon church can carry the state of Utah for Alf Landon, I'll join the church because I'll have seen a miracle." Most Utah Democrats were shocked or embittered rather than amused, though. Taking no chances, Democratic politicians disputed the editorial, billing Roosevelt as a defender and savior of the Constitution. At a rally in Bingham the night before the election, state Democratic chairman Calvin W. Rawlings, an active Mormon, labeled the attacks on Roosevelt "false and unwarranted" and claimed that "President Roosevelt saved the Constitution and our democracy against the only threat of their destruction in my lifetime or yours." Pointing out that great presidents including Jefferson, Jackson, and Lincoln had acted beyond the scope of the Constitution in "champion[ing] the cause of the common people," Rawlings reminded his audience that Roosevelt's "horse and buggy" remark had been a spontaneous reaction to the Supreme Court's decision.[56]

In full-page ads in Utah newspapers Democrats proclaimed that "Roosevelt Saved the Constitution" by "restoring peace and prosperity." Quoting Roosevelt that "the flag and the Constitution stand for democracy, not tyranny; for freedom, not subjection, and against a dictatorship of mob rule and the OVERPRIVILEGED alike," the ads criticized the church for violating Utah's constitutional prohibition against religious domination of politics and encouraged Mormons, "Have no fear of frightening cries of Republican reactionaries who would inject church influence in this campaign. American people resent church interference. Latter Day Saints will not be swayed by such attempts. They have a safe guide in their own Doctrine and Covenants which says, 'We do not believe it just to mingle religious influence with civil government.'"[57]

In a front-page editorial on November 2, the *Logan Herald-Journal*, one of the state's most liberal city papers, rebutted the stance taken by the *Deseret News* and *Salt Lake Tribune*, labeling both papers part of "Utah's capitalistic press." The Logan paper particularly criticized the *Deseret News*, though. Referring to prominent Republicans in the church hierarchy, including former senator Reed Smoot and J. Reuben Clark, the *Herald-Journal* averred that the stance taken by the *Deseret News* had been "inspired by the political bitterness of those who sat in high places and who were confidants of those who ruled before the present administration." Dismissing the argument that Roosevelt had jeopardized the Constitution as "so absurd and far-fetched as to be ridiculous," the paper praised the New Deal for improving economic conditions and thereby reducing the likelihood of revolution. Whereas the *Deseret News* had enlisted religion in support of Landon, the *Herald-Journal* linked Roosevelt's program to deity. "In our humble opinion, Destiny produced the man who successfully was to lead us through a period of calamity.... [W]ell may the American people thank God for giving us a fearless, daring pilot."[58]

On Election Day, in a state where nearly seven in ten residents were LDS, 69.3 percent of Utah's voters endorsed Franklin D. Roosevelt at the polls. Only Kane County registered more votes for Landon than for Roosevelt. "Obviously the people have not learned their lesson," Clark ruefully remarked. If anything, support for Roosevelt had solidified following the editorial. Only 66.6 percent of the respondents polled by the *Tribune* in the last two weeks of October indicated that they would vote for Roosevelt at the polls, but 69.3 percent of Utah's voters did so—a higher percentage than in any of the installments of the *Tribune*'s two-month poll. Roosevelt in 1936 received a higher percentage of the vote than any previous presidential candidate in Utah, aside from William Jennings Bryan in 1896. Not until Richard Nixon's landslide reelection in 1972 would a candidate for president again receive as high a percentage of the votes as Roosevelt did that year.[59]

Again in 1938 LDS Church leaders attempted to undercut the New Deal and recapture one of Utah's two seats in the Senate for the Republicans by strongly urging Franklin S. Harris, president of Brigham Young University, to contest New Dealer Elbert Thomas's seat. Thomas, as a strong supporter of President Roosevelt, had advertised his commitment to a "continuation of the New Deal." Harris, one of the state's most prominent residents, had for several weeks resisted the overtures of

Republican leaders asking him to run for office. When these efforts failed, J. Reuben Clark met with Harris briefly on August 8. Clark, who had previously been invited by Republicans to join the race and declined, informed Harris that "the First Presidency wished me to run" and asked him to travel to Salt Lake to meet with the entire presidency the next day. At that meeting the First Presidency "told me they would like me to make the senate race." The next day Harris filed the necessary forms to run for office. On August 11 he wrote to his brother Sterling that his candidacy was "not a matter of personal choice" and told his brother Emer that "those whose instructions I never disobey asked me to go forward in the race." He informed his children, "I suppose that for the self respect of the family we shall have to put up as good a fight as possible."[60]

Harris focused in his campaign on "the huge national debt which has accumulated under the excessive spending of the New Deal" and maintained that federal relief efforts were harming "the rugged virtues of thrift, industry, frugality, and reliability." Campaigning on the New Deal record and the benefits of federal funds for Utah, Democrats countered, "In the next Congress Dr. Harris would fare/Like a dog in Alaska without any hair." In an effort to mobilize church resources, Harris sent a letter to LDS bishops in Utah on October 10, requesting their support as bishops and community leaders. The letter criticized the "Santa Claus Era" with its "unheard-of spree of spending" and alleged that many welfare recipients were "more willing to receive help from the public than to earn what they get by their own efforts." It warned of the "dangerous centralization of authority" accompanying the New Deal. Gordon Hyde, bishop of the Ensign Ward in Salt Lake City, responded with a letter to Harris that he also mailed to fellow bishops in Utah. A staunch supporter of the New Deal, Hyde maintained that "as a bishop in one of the largest wards of the Church...I have never found a case where the head of a family has not been willing to work for what he has received." Hyde enumerated the monetary benefits to Utahns of New Deal programs, including the NYA, PWA, and WPA, and pointed out, "It is my opinion, and that of many other Bishops, that without the aid of the present government relief projects it would be impossible to care for the unemployed members of our Church." Democrats also circulated a letter, signed by "A Bishop," accusing Harris of attempting to mix church and state and arguing that such mixture was "destructive of the Church...and would destroy the foundation of our Constitution and democracy. Members of the Church are capable of making up their own minds on political matters and will vote as their judgment and interests dictate."[61]

To the extent that the First Presidency hoped to be able to oust Thomas, they were disappointed. Although Harris polled a higher percentage of votes than Reed Smoot had garnered in his race against Thomas in 1932, Thomas nevertheless secured 55 percent of the vote, including many LDS leaders such as Samuel E.

Bringhurst, president of the Cottonwood Stake, who was convinced that the state was "fortunate" to be represented by Thomas. Harris did carry eleven counties in the state, though, and evaluated, "I did not really expect to be elected" but believed that "I may have made some contribution to the ultimate recovery of the party." Clark expressed satisfaction that Harris's candidacy had enabled the Republicans to smooth over factional differences and to "cut down the lead of two years ago."[62]

THE CHURCH SECURITY PROGRAM

In addition to their efforts to roll back the New Deal through direct political interference, the LDS First Presidency endeavored to wean their members from direct relief and to restore a measure of self-sufficiency by instituting a mammoth program of church-sponsored relief, the Church Security Program, renamed the Welfare Plan in 1938. To a greater extent than any other indigenous antidote to the Depression, this program focused national media attention upon Utah. The program drew inspiration from earlier relief efforts undertaken by local wards and stakes and from nineteenth-century Mormon attempts to cut Utah's ties to the corporate national economy. But the most important factors in persuading church leaders to centralize their approach to church welfare included their concern for the poor who might be left without support because of changes in federal welfare policy, their opposition to the dole, and their conviction that neighbors and churches rather than federal agencies should provide for the poor. In March 1935 J. Reuben Clark had pressed President Grant to "announce to the people [in the April conference] that we intend to intensify our efforts to take care of our own poor and unemployed without resorting to the Government." But Grant demurred. Instead, leaders gathered additional data regarding the extent of Mormon reliance on federal payments. In the fall of 1935, a survey of 495,000 Mormons, roughly three-fourths of whom lived in Utah, revealed that 19.9 percent were on relief and that nine-tenths of these were receiving government rather than church assistance. Shortly before the survey had been undertaken, Apostle Melvin J. Ballard counseled church members, "Get off relief just as soon as you can. If you don't you will be thrown off and it will be a sorry day when that time comes." Six months later federal officials announced that direct relief payments would cease on July 1. The First Presidency seized upon the announcement as an opportune pretext for initiating the long-contemplated Church Security Program to assume responsibility for all church members who were receiving direct relief.[63]

On April 7, 1936, the church-owned *Deseret News* printed a First Presidency message roughly outlining the new program. Leaders of congregations were asked to supervise the preservation of food and the procurement of clothing, bedding, and fuel for the coming winter. Many congregations had already been involved in these tasks. But the announcement broke new ground in committing the general church "to assist to the utmost extent possible in providing work on its own properties for its unemployed members, as also in providing other work in wisely rehabilitating ranches, farms, gardens, and orchards that may be used to furnish foodstuffs for those in need." Reflecting church leaders' conviction that work relief was preferable to handouts, local leaders were advised that "relief is not to be normally given as charity" but that it was "to be distributed for work or service rendered." For the time being, "pending further developments in working out the Church plan," church members employed on federal work-relief projects were instructed to "endeavor to retain their positions." But the announcement hinted that the church might "fully" care for all needy Latter-day Saints if church members enthusiastically supported the program. An official statement printed two months later confirmed that the church's "ultimate objective" was indeed "eventually to take care of all of its people exclusive of government relief."[64]

The *Deseret News* indicated, "The curtailment of Federal aid which is now forecast makes it imperative that the church shall, so far as it is able, meet this emergency." Meeting with President Roosevelt the following month, Melvin J. Ballard explained that the church was "anxious to be in full cooperation with the government" and indicated that "we are not criticizing or fighting the government." Nevertheless, some, including Clark, the chief architect of the plan, viewed the security program as an alternative to the New Deal. In an interview reported by the *New York Times* in May 1936, Clark indicated that the church intended "to take Mormons off home relief first with those on work relief to be taken care of later." Clark explained, "The president of the church feels that it is time we got back to first principles and cared for our own." He estimated that the church would spend less than half what it cost the government for relief because the program would rely upon volunteer labor. Welfare, the First Presidency explained several years later, was "essentially a neighbor to neighbor obligation" and "not a function of civil government." The federal government had overreached its proper bounds. The First Presidency's initial announcement of the plan corroborated Clark's statement. "If each Church member meets fully his duty and grasps his full opportunity for blessing, full necessary relief will be extended to all needy Church members."[65]

Within a few weeks the Church Welfare Committee had grouped Mormon congregations in the American West into thirteen regions for welfare purposes. Congregations in each region were to jointly purchase or construct a storehouse where surplus commodities, donations, and produce from church work-relief projects would be preserved, stored, and distributed. Each region's immediate goal was to accumulate by October 1 enough food, clothing, and fuel "to provide for every needy family through the winter" and in the process to generate work for all "employable" recipients of church assistance.[66]

Church relief efforts expanded as the decade progressed. As a continuation of the work-relief programs undertaken in 1936, some members were employed on church projects, including landscaping church property and remodeling or constructing church buildings. By 1939 the church was sponsoring projects ranging from farms to mines and canneries designed to furnish food, clothing, fuel, other commodities, and employment to needy individuals. In some cases the crops and commodities produced were marketed commercially, while in other cases they were shipped to storehouses. Through the network of storehouses, goods produced in one area were made available for distribution to members elsewhere. For instance, unemployed members in central Utah leased a mine, extracted coal, shipped most of it to a storehouse, and in return obtained food and clothing produced on other work-relief projects from the storehouse.

In 1936 the Church Relief Committee had expressed its desire to assist members "in placing themselves on a financially independent basis." Few of the make-work programs undertaken that year were intended to provide long-term stability for recipients. By 1939, though, progress had been made in this regard. With church assistance some young members had secured apprenticeships in plumbing, carpentry, and masonry, while others had received loans for college tuition. Would-be farmers had received help in obtaining more than one hundred thousand acres of land. To promote self-sufficiency the church had also furnished funds for rural development. In eastern Utah, for instance, hundreds of members used church funds to construct three small reservoirs.[67]

In 1938 the church established Deseret Industries, a thrift store patterned after Goodwill Industries. Members were encouraged to donate used furniture, clothing, and other manufactured items to Deseret Industries, where they were cleaned, restored, or repaired by individuals "who might find it difficult to qualify for employment in private industry." The refurbished goods were then made available for nominal purchase or for free distribution to needy families who had been referred by their local ecclesiastical leaders.[68]

By 1939 more than 155,400 members were receiving some assistance from the program; total cash assistance rendered averaged only $9.59 per person, but this figure excluded the value of commodities, which constituted the bulk of welfare assistance. Roughly 50 percent of the church's 746,384 members lived in Utah, and church welfare expenditures had always been greater in Utah and particularly the Salt Lake Valley than elsewhere, so it seems reasonable that at least 80,000 Utahns in that year received some assistance.[69]

Conservative and liberal journalists described the Church Security Program as an alternative to or even a substitute for the New Deal in articles appearing in nationally prominent magazines, including the *Nation*, *Cosmopolitan*, and the *Saturday Evening Post*. *Reader's Digest* claimed that within a year and a half of the announcement of the Church Security Program, every Mormon who had been a recipient of direct relief had been "removed from government relief rolls." Richard Neuberger, who visited a welfare cannery in Salt Lake City late in the 1930s, labeled the program "America's most unique attempt to answer the grim question of unemployment and relief."[70]

APPRAISING THE NEW DEAL'S SIGNIFICANCE

Despite the Church Security Program's impressive achievements, such rhetoric exaggerated the importance of church welfare by ignoring the fact that the number of Utahns, including Mormons, receiving assistance from the federal government remained exceptionally high. Utah ranked fifth in the nation in the amount of direct relief expended by the government on a per capita basis in 1937 and 1938. The state and federal governments, which had issued payments to 34,948 individuals in December of 1935, prior to the creation of the Welfare Program, issued payments to nearly the same number of recipients, 34,900, the following year. While payments dropped in December 1937 to 32,199, largely because of spending cuts nationwide, close to 41,500 Utahns received welfare checks from the government in December 1938 and again in December 1939. Given average household size, close to 163,897 Utahns likely lived in households where public assistance was received in the last month of the decade, nearly four years after the Welfare Program's inception. A study conducted by University of Chicago sociologist Louis Wirth in 1939 concluded that Mormons were disproportionately represented on welfare rolls; according to Wirth, around 71 percent of Utah's population was LDS, but 79.3 percent of the state's welfare recipients and 83 percent of the WPA laborers were Mormons.[71]

The fruits of full-fledged incorporation within the New Deal network were rich. Between 1933 and 1939, federal agencies in Utah, excluding the military, spent $289,301,781, the equivalent of about $4.8 billion in 2014. Federal expenditures accounted for about 20 percent of Utahns' personal income during those years. Utah ranked twelfth in the nation on a per capita basis in nonrepayable expenditures by the federal government and ninth per capita in total expenditures, including loans and insurance, during these years.[72]

Although the New Deal did not eradicate the state's economic woes or rescue the state entirely from the Great Depression, to a much greater degree than was the case in the nation at large, federal largesse stimulated economic recovery, perhaps because it was so heavy. The extent of recovery was remarkable. Unemployment, which had greatly exceeded the national average in 1933, had dropped by 1940 to 9.6 percent, considerably below the national rate of 14.6 percent at the time. Gross farm income had rebounded to 77 percent of its 1929 level by 1940, up from 43 percent.

Economic recovery was also reflected in rising salaries. Per capita income rose nearly 75 percent between 1933 and 1940. By the latter year it amounted to $480, or 89 percent of the pre-Depression 1929 figure. In light of the heightened purchasing power of the dollar—the dollar in 1940 possessed 1.2 times the purchasing power of the dollar in 1929—Utahns' real wages in 1940 were greater than they had been immediately prior to the Depression.[73]

Utahns' purchase of new automobiles and homes in the latter half of the 1930s likewise bespoke consumer confidence and recovery. In 1940 Utahns owned 117,463 passenger cars—21,802 more than in 1929. Home construction had also picked up. Between 1935 and 1940 an average of 255 new homes were completed each month, a rate that actually exceeded construction rates in the 1910s (247 per month) and the 1920s (246 per month).[74]

The ambitious and effective response of the Democratic Party to the Great Depression made the party the dominant one in the state from 1932 to the latter part of the 1940s. The state legislature, which passed enabling legislation to facilitate New Deal programs in Utah, was overwhelmingly Democratic during the 1930s. Although he opposed many New Deal programs, conservative Democrat William King overcame challenges within his own party and held on to his seat in the Senate by beating Republican Don Colton in 1934. But in an intense primary election six years later, King lost to Abe Murdock, a pro–New Deal liberal, who defeated Republican Philo T. Farnsworth in the general election. Utah Democrats retained both seats in the US Senate and both seats in the US House until 1946, the governorship until 1948, and a majority in the state house and senate until 1947.[75]

In addition to priming the pump, helping to revitalize the economy, and shoring up the Democrats' political prospects in Utah, the New Deal vastly expanded the state's infrastructure by building roads and bridges, installing water and sewer lines, developing recreational facilities, building large and small reservoirs, and constructing public buildings such as schools and courthouses. An orchestra had been created, art galleries had been established, and public buildings had been beautified with murals. Electricity had been brought to some of the state's most isolated rural regions. And the state's financial institutions had been shored up through federal regulation as well as insurance of bank deposits.

Federal assistance had permitted hundreds to obtain university training while working part-time on campuses across the state. Under federal protection union membership had soared, and workers' wages had risen.[76] The risks of farming had been limited somewhat, while farmers' dependence upon the federal government had risen because of price supports for key commodities and payments for acreage restriction. And Utahns, along with other Americans, had been introduced to an incipient welfare state, including pensions for the elderly and unemployment insurance, federal assistance to the handicapped, and aid to single mothers with dependent children. Such programs had smoothed the rougher edges of laissez-faire capitalism, while preserving the system itself: lawmakers had stopped short of guaranteeing employment or minimum subsistence to every family, providing comprehensive health insurance, nationalizing industry, or radically redistributing wealth.

Work relief, public works, rural electrification, payments to farmers, and other New Deal programs that created a safety net for Utahns and improved the standard of living came at a price: during the 1920s the state had allotted an average of 0.15 percent of its annual revenue for public welfare; between 1934 and 1940 it devoted 27.9 percent of its revenue for welfare. As a result of increased demands upon the government and reduced revenues at existing tax rates, the legislature raised taxes. In 1933 lawmakers instituted a graduated tax on individual income and a corporate tax. Taxes were also levied in Utah on beer beginning in 1934, and in 1935 a new law increased inheritance taxes. A new 2 percent sales tax, instituted by the state legislature in 1933 in order to meet federal requirements for matching welfare funds, affected all consumers and provided more than $4 million in state revenue in 1940. Federal income taxes, which had been raised substantially over their 1929 level under the Revenue Act of 1932—the largest percentage increase in peacetime in American history for the top income bracket—fell slightly for lower income groups later in the decade but continued to rise for those in the highest income brackets. Still, fewer than 5 percent of Americans made enough money to pay federal income taxes at the end of the decade. Federal, state, and local tax collections in Utah totaled $47,327,041 in 1940, compared to $28,707,824 in 1929—an increase of nearly two-thirds.[77]

The New Deal, along with the Reconstruction Finance Corporation established under Hoover, also contributed to the nation's debt, which rose from $16,185,310,000 in 1930 to $42,967,531,000 in 1940. Having borrowed funds to fight the American Revolution and having borrowed periodically over its history for purposes such as waging war, purchasing land, buying gold, and funding internal improvements, the nation had historically been in debt. The New Deal raised that debt to unprecedented levels, though, shattering the previous all-time high of $25,484,506,000 following World War I. Nevertheless, the national debt in 1940 paled alongside the whopping debt of $258,682,187,000 at the conclusion of World War II. At the same time that the federal debt was rising during the 1930s, the state's debt was being repaid, thanks to increased tax revenues. In 1938 Utah's debt reached its lowest level in twenty years.[78]

While conservatives' fears that generous welfare programs would turn many welfare recipients into long-term wards of the government were exaggerated, they were not entirely unfounded. Most Utahns who relied at times upon federal or state welfare during the Depression permanently vacated relief rolls as the economy improved. By December 1946 only 4.5 percent of the state's population was receiving general public assistance, compared to 5.8 percent of the nation's population that year and more than 20 percent of the state's households in 1934. But a higher percentage of Utah's senior citizens and households headed by single parents remained on welfare beyond the Second World War than did Americans generally. At the end of 1946, Utah had the fifth-highest welfare rate for senior citizens in the nation, or 36.9 percent compared to a national average of 21.3 percent. In that same year, the state tied for twelfth place in the nation in the proportion of its families receiving aid to dependent children.[79]

Whether the benefits of the New Deal for Utah outweighed the costs or not, the program transformed the state in many important ways. Even more sweeping and enduring transformations than those wrought by the Great Depression and New Deal would occur in Utah, though, between 1941 and 1945 as a result of the Second World War.

13

SIMPLY REVOLUTIONARY
Utahns Confront the Second World War

SURPRISE ATTACK

December 7, 1941, began like any other Sunday in Utah. The weather was typical for early December: cloudy to partly cloudy skies prevailed over much of the state, with no precipitation expected. In Salt Lake City temperatures were forecast to rise from the midtwenties in the early morning to the midforties by afternoon.[1] By the time that Japanese bombers began their work of destruction in faraway Hawaii, crippling much of America's Pacific fleet, it was late morning in the Intermountain West. For a time, many Utahns continued their Sunday routine, oblivious to the destruction occurring thousands of miles away and its implications for them.

Relations between the United States and Japan had been severely strained for months and had gone from bad to worse in late November and early December. Under these conditions top-level military strategists and diplomats knew that the Japanese might attack American forces somewhere in the Pacific and had taken precautionary measures. Few considered Pearl Harbor a likely target, though. It was simply too remote from Japan. The audacity and stunning success of the Japanese bombers in their air attack shocked even top-level diplomats and military commanders.[2]

The average Utahn, of course, knew far less than the nation's power brokers about relations with Japan. Although news of the attack flashed across the airwaves, reaching Utahns far more quickly than it would have done in preradio days, at least some residents whose lives would be forever altered by the war enjoyed a few more hours of blissful ignorance that Sunday afternoon. Such was the case for Marie and Pete Grange, newlyweds in Carbon County. After church the Granges drove out into the foothills with two other couples for an afternoon of joyriding and target shooting. That evening when they returned to town, Pete ran over to his parents' home to borrow a deck of cards and some board games. Nearly a half century later, Marie remembered what happened next: "He wasn't gone very long, and he came running in and he said, 'Hey, hey, turn on the radio,' and we said, 'Why?' and he said, 'We are at war, we are at war!' We said, 'Yeah, yeah, you are just telling us another story.' He said, 'No, really. The Japs bombed Pearl Harbor.' Everybody said, 'Where's Pearl Harbor?'"[3]

WAR'S IMPACT ON SOLDIERS AND THEIR FAMILIES

"Where's Pearl Harbor?" Many Utahns were asking the same question that Sunday. The Cowleys and other Utahns would become painfully aware of that distant base's significance in the ensuing months and years. In the wake of the Japanese attack and American declaration of war, thousands would be sent overseas to fight in a conflict with globalizing ramifications for the state. Their service in distant lands revealed Utah's incorporation within the international geopolitical arena. Close to 71,000 Utahns served in the armed forces during the Second World War, including hundreds of women, who constituted roughly 2 percent of all Utahns in the military. Approximately 41 percent of those who served enlisted—an exceptionally high rate. Nearly half of the state's households bid farewell to someone entering the armed forces during the war. Rachel Elison, who frequented train stations because her boyfriend was an engineer on a military train, witnessed hundreds of goodbyes. "It was a very traumatic thing," she recalled, "to go down in the station and see mothers and little kids telling their dads goodbye or watching whole families see their son off who was going overseas." Parting was doubly difficult for Roy Hammond, a young medical doctor from Provo: after bidding his wife, Anita, farewell at the Kearns Army Air Base, he rode with other recruits to the train station downtown. There, as they awaited their train, Hammond and some of his traveling companions walked to the Hotel Utah for supper. Coincidentally, Anita and some of her relatives happened to be in the dining room when they arrived, "so we had to say good-bye all over again."[4]

As they parted, everyone knew that they might not see one another again. Death's specter seemed to haunt neighborhoods. Dan Gardner of Salt Lake City remembered, "You could go up and down the streets and I could tell you the kids who used to live here and went out and were fly boys or whatever and never came back. . . . We saw a lot of our neighbors and friends would go out and get themselves killed." More than 3,600 of those who served—roughly 1 in 20—did not make it home alive, including 1,450 who were killed in action. Utah's death rate of 5.1 percent was more than twice that of American soldiers generally—2.5 percent. Perhaps the difference was attributable in part to Utahns' patriotic willingness to take risks for their country—after all, a much greater percentage of Utahns enlisted rather than waiting to be drafted. Nevertheless, Utah's rate of combat fatalities, 2 percent, was only slightly higher than the national rate of 1.8 percent.[5]

Utahns who lost a loved one forever carried the bitter memory of how they learned the news and their struggles to come to terms with it. Telegrams communicating the death of a soldier were marked so that messengers would know to "use compassion in delivering them." Lorene Rasmussen, whose brother James was killed in Italy, recalled, "I had never seen Dad so devastated. That was the hardest thing I think that he ever had to endure." Some, like Marie Grange, "went to pieces" and had to be "put out" with a tranquilizer. Thereafter, she was haunted by the question of how her husband had died. One night she dreamed she saw her husband and asked him where he had been wounded. "He put both hands over his stomach." Subsequently, a nightmarish vision unfolded of a suit her husband had worn to the junior prom. In the dream it "came home from the service and had blood on the front of the pants. I knew then where he had been wounded."[6]

Some, whose relatives were reported missing in action, endured months of agonizing uncertainty before learning that their loved ones were dead. When one of Viola Eschler's three sons was reported missing in action, she was terrified. "No one can describe the feeling of not knowing what had happened," she explained. Eventually, a letter arrived from her son's friend, but a note attached to the letter asked her not to open it "until I heard from the government." Convinced that the letter contained the details of her son's demise, but not wanting to betray the young man's trust, Eschler kept the letter in her drawer for a year. "When the time came that I could open that letter, I found out that there were only a few marines and solders that were there to meet a whole army of Japanese people. All but two of them were killed."[7]

The wartime experiences of Utahns in the service varied from those who saw little if any combat—only about 34 percent of men mobilized into the army nationwide saw combat—to those like George Wahlen, who endured extreme risks in battle and survived, distinguishing themselves and earning prestigious medals for their valor on the battlefield. A native of Ogden, Wahlen entered the Naval Reserve in June 1943, and after training as a medical corpsman in San Diego he was assigned to the Fifth Marine Division, which participated in the landing on Iwo Jima. There on February 25 he sustained a painful wound. Ignoring his own pain, he pushed beyond the front line to rescue an immobilized marine. With bullets whizzing about him, he carried the young man back for medical attention. His commanding officers reported that he later again "defied the continuous pounding of heavy mortars and the deadly fire of enemy rifles to care for the wounded, working rapidly in an area swept by constant fire and treating fourteen casualties." During this rescue episode he was bloodily wounded and nearly knocked unconscious by a grenade blast and painfully wounded by pieces of shrapnel in the buttocks and legs. Five days later Wahlen was again wounded but "gallantly refused evacuation, moving out with his company the following day in a furious assault across six hundred yards of open terrain and repeatedly rendering medical aid while exposed to the blasting fire of powerful Japanese guns." After a large artillery shell knocked him to the ground and broke his leg, he "resolutely crawled fifty yards to administer first aid to still another fallen fighter." For his valor he received a Purple Heart and a Congressional Medal of Honor.[8]

Despite their severity, Wahlen's physical wounds healed. Others lost more, dragging the wreckage of permanently maimed bodies for the rest of their lives. Although they did not necessarily receive medals for their valor, their struggles were Herculean. Woolas Macey of northern Utah was one of more than three thousand amputees from around the country at Bushnell Hospital in Brigham City. There he learned to walk, dance, and climb stairs with an artificial limb. Macey joined a one-legged bowling team that "travelled all over the state," bowling as a rehabilitative strategy to "make us forget." Macey jauntily responded to inquiries about his lost leg with the rejoinder, "No, I didn't lose it. I know where it is but I can't get it." To others who had lost limbs he would preach, "You lose a leg, so what? You make a go of it." After returning home from Bushnell, he still "couldn't do a lot of things that [he] wanted to do," but he "tried anyway." He married a neighbor within a year of returning home, and together they reared five children.[9]

Despite their invisibility, psychological wounds for some veterans were as daunting as physical ones, although they were not as carefully recorded. Nationwide, more than one million soldiers—about 6 percent of those who served—struggled with debilitating psychiatric problems, and Utah's veterans had their share of such troubles. "How many people that war affected mentally!" reflected Frances Wilde. In Salem, a town with fewer than seven hundred residents where she had grown up, Wilde had a cousin who "was never the same after the war." Another young veteran in town became an alcoholic, and another "was mentally disturbed and he died young." War may not have been the sole culprit in any of these cases, but it undeniably created psychological stress. Some veterans, such as David Clarke, who served on a submarine in the Pacific, sought to minimize psychological pain by refusing to think about or discuss the war. When asked in 1998 to describe his wartime experiences, he tersely responded, "No one will ever know or understand what we went through."[10]

In addition to its physical and psychological impact, the war affected the education and careers of men and women who served in the military. Caught up in patriotic hoopla, some juniors and seniors dropped out of high school in order to enlist. Largely as a result of these enlistments, the number of high school graduates in the state in 1944 was 14.3 percent smaller than the number of graduates in 1942. Joseph Haws, a student at Provo High School during the war, estimated that between his junior and senior years, "over half of my class enlisted.... Only the girls were left to go to Senior Prom the next fall." Wartime enlistments by high school boys, coupled with a lack of parental supervision in many households where both parents were at work, led to reduced school attendance in the state. Average school attendance during the war fell to 81 percent of those enrolled, compared to 86 and 87 percent in the years immediately preceding the war.[11]

Military service also reduced the civilian student body at universities. Enrollment at the University of Utah, for instance, fell by more than one-fourth between 1940–41 and 1943–44. When Melba Barker Larsen graduated from Weber College in 1945, women outnumbered men in her graduating class nine to one. To accommodate this imbalance, student body officers at Weber instituted a new ball, the Polygamist Prance, where "one fellow would have to take as many girls as asked him to the dance."[12]

Although many youth deferred their education because of the war, wartime service also opened new educational opportunities to many, giving them firsthand experience with exotic places and foreign cultures and transforming some of them into world citizens. Bill McGinnis of Salt Lake City, who served in the navy in the South Pacific and Japan, became increasingly fascinated with foreign lands due to his travels during the war and subsequently pursued a career in the foreign service and international banking, living in China, Iraq, and Japan. For others, wartime service provided occupational training and experience, opening doors for careers in fields, including auto mechanics, air transportation, the military, and medicine. It also developed leadership, communications skills, and character. Alvin Barlow, for instance, believed that the gains of military service outweighed the liabilities. Despite a wartime injury to his shoulder, his experience in the service laid the foundations for his role as a community leader. It "gave me a good background for when I came home from the war." By opening some soldiers' eyes to the immensity of human suffering and poverty abroad, wartime service nurtured character traits such as compassion and a commitment to reducing suffering. Boyd Packer, who served four years in the military during and after the Second World War, could never forget the "common" sight in postwar Japan of "starving children" attempting to sleep in train stations under "a newspaper or a few old rags." The image of one particularly pathetic child begging for help, "holding [a] rusty tin can, with [a] dirty rag around his swollen jaw," was particularly emblazoned upon Packer's mind.

"Perhaps I was scarred by that experience. If so, it is a battle scar, a worthy one, for which I bear no shame. It reminds me of my duty!" he reflected thirty-eight years after his return home.[13]

By enacting the GI Bill in 1944, Congress proffered full-tuition benefits and stipends to veterans for education at any level, enabling many who otherwise would not have pursued postsecondary schooling to do so. Lois Langford of Riverton, who served in the army during the war, enrolled in LDS Business College after the war, thanks to her veteran benefits. The student population skyrocketed at all of the state's institutions of higher learning. At the University of Utah, during the 1946–47 academic year, 9,859 students enrolled, up from 3,693 in 1944–45.[14]

Veterans also benefited economically from military service. Chief among those benefits was the privilege of purchasing a home, with the Veterans Administration guaranteeing half the amount of veterans' home loans. Shortly after his return from the war, David Clarke and his new bride, Dorothy Anderson, purchased a home under the GI Bill. By cashing war savings bonds as they matured and applying the money toward their mortgage, the couple paid for their entire home in thirteen years.[15]

Service in the Second World War had especially far-reaching cultural consequences for Utah's Indians, incorporating them within mainstream political, cultural, and economic currents. Many of them moved away from the reservation at least temporarily because of the war effort. Reactions to the draft in 1940 and 1941, prior to the bombing of Pearl Harbor, were mixed. The Navajo Nation Tribal Council passed a resolution in 1940 pledging to "aid and defend our government and its institutions against all subversive and armed conflict." On some reservations, Indians opposed the draft, arguing that it violated tribal sovereignty and that the war was a white man's conflict. One leader on the Uintah and Uncompahgre Reservation stated, "We don't want our boys to go to war. Long time ago we buried the tomahawk with the white man, put it way underground. Now we don't want to take it up again and break our promise. We aren't making this trouble with other countries— it is you white people who are doing that. We don't want war." In Wells, Nevada, at a protest meeting in October 1940, George Paharagosam from Washakie joined with others in opposing the draft, arguing that the Shoshones had signed peace treaties with the United States in the 1860s and should therefore be exempt from military service. A delegation including Paharagosam traveled to Salt Lake and presented their arguments to the press, the governor's office, and officials at Fort Douglas, who forwarded their petition to the Bureau of Indian Affairs. However, officials in the bureau dismissed the petition, alleging that the protesters were a "small" group operating on the fringe of Shoshone society.[16]

After a federal court ruled that tribal status did not exempt Indians from military service, thousands were drafted. Even more enlisted, especially among the Navajo; nationwide, at least twenty-five thousand American Indians served in the military during the war, including more than one hundred Utes, close to four thousand Navajos, dozens of Western Shoshones and Goshutes from Nevada and Utah, and a "small number" of Paiutes. Prior to leaving the reservation, some Navajo soldiers underwent a "Going to War ceremony." Maurice Knee explained, "The blessing that they gave me was supposed to put a shield around me, an invisible shield, that the bullet would come right for my nose and hit that shield and go away. And it worked." Seth Bigman recalled, "The medicine man prayed for me when I'm going over and coming back....He prayed that I'll be coming home safe....So I did, I came home safe."[17]

As historian James Rawls notes, "Perhaps the most distinctive contribution of Native Americans in World War II was their service in a Marine Corps signal unit known as the 'code talkers.'" Close to four hundred Navajos were involved in this effort, which entailed devising a code for military communications based upon the Navajo language. In this code the Navajo words were assigned alternate meanings; for instance, the Navajo term for *buzzard* became the code word for *bomber*. Sent in with early assault waves, the code talkers worked in pairs. One would set up a hand-cranked generator connected by a cable to a microphone and transmitter. While he cranked the generator, the other would relay messages through the microphone regarding the status of the assault, the location of enemy artillery, and the need for reinforcements. As one code talker explained, "We got information off the ship after a landing and kept those in charge of the operation informed." Major Howard M. Conner reported, "Were it not for the Navajos, the Marines would never have taken Iwo Jima....During the first forty-eight hours, while we were landing and consolidating our shore positions, I had six Navajo radio nets operating around the clock."[18]

Generally, Indians in the service were treated well by their fellow soldiers. Their experiences were a powerful catalyst for the drive for equality after the war. As Private First Class Wade Hadley, a Navajo, expressed matters in a letter:

> I am not bragging myself but I have been overseas three years now....I know I'm educated and grown-up man....I sometimes wonder...the people and the government will treat me the same way as they did before the war....As far as the Army is concern, everybody is being treated the same. Being in the service that I can vote at the election. I can drink in the public bars any time I please. Because I risk my life in the front line for it. There for I should have the privilege. This deal should continue after the war....I know the other nationality are not better human being than we are.[19]

While the Second World War directly and powerfully affected the nearly seventy-one thousand Utahns who served in the military, it also influenced the rest of the state's residents, whose experiences were confined to the home front.

Spouses of those in the service particularly felt the war's impact. Facing the possibility that they or their lovers might be killed in battle, many young Americans chose to live for the moment, marrying hastily and letting the future take care of itself. This was less true in Utah than in the nation at large, though. The state's marriage rate had historically surpassed the nation's, but during the war a smaller proportion of Utahns than Americans in general tied the knot. Indeed, Utah's marriage rate plummeted to 10.3 per 1,000 residents in 1944, the lowest level since the turn of the century.[20]

Despite gossip regarding "Allotment Annies" who married soldiers for the economic rewards of a handsome life insurance policy and a monthly government allotment check, most wives hoped and prayed that the war would end soon and that their husbands would return unimpaired. Anita Hammond, whose husband served in New Guinea, recalled, "Those were lonely times." After a month of separation from her husband, Elliott, Marjorie Reid Killpack of Price wrote of her loneliness. "This not being able to see you at night and have you cuddle me to sleep is the hardest part of our separation." Nearly two years later, she wrote, "My days are not complete, for you are gone. It's good I can't think too much as I'd spend my time trying to heal a very lonely and empty heart. I'm only half here without you, my dear, and love you more than life itself." The lyrics to a popular song played upon the stresses faced by spouses on the home front who did their best to maintain a facade of gaiety in their letters to their husbands but were consumed with worry, frustration, or exhaustion:

> *When I write to you and say*
> *everything is okay*
> *and my letters seem gay*
> *can't you read between the lines?*[21]

The stresses of wartime separation for wives on the home front were compounded by the large number of babies born in Utah during the war, many of whom were conceived shortly before their fathers departed. Not until the second half of the 1940s and the return of thousands of GIs would the nation's genuine baby boom commence, with birthrates soaring dramatically in 1946. In Utah, though, a mini–baby boom unfolded during the war itself: the state's birthrate rose from 24.3 per 1,000 residents in 1940 to 27.4 in 1942 and 29.6 in 1943 before falling to 24.7 in 1945. Not since the early 1920s had the birthrate been so high.[22]

The baby boom strained young mothers at home alone. Marjorie Thompson was a young wife in her early twenties with one son and a daughter on the way when her husband, Clark, entered the service. Although it was common for soldiers' wives to feel overwhelmed by the challenges of rearing children single-handedly, maintaining a home, and encouraging a husband serving overseas, Thompson felt ashamed of her inability to cope with these war-induced stresses. Retrospectively, she judged that she "probably took it harder than a lot of people," but her experiences illustrate how heavy the wartime burdens for spouses could be. Unable to eat because of depression, Thompson began to lose weight, bottoming out at ninety pounds. For three months she hardly slept and "had dark circles under [her] eyes." Consumed with worry about her husband, she recalled, "With every letter I got from Clark, I didn't know what to expect....I was just exhausted and worried...[and] felt like the whole weight of the world was on my shoulders. I had these two children to raise, and I wasn't feeling well." Although she loved her children and "wanted to enjoy them so much," she was unable to do so and relied upon her relatives to help care for them much of the time. The burdens of single parenting were so oppressive that she decided she never wanted to have another child and told her husband so when he returned.[23]

Absent from one another for years on end, some lonely husbands and wives longing for romance and companionship became intimately involved with another person. Marjorie Thompson saw young, pretty women from Cache Valley "stepping out on their husbands. They were coming out to Kearns Base and dating the GI's." In some cases, wives assumed their husbands were dead when they were reported missing in action, only to discover after they had begun dating someone else that their husbands were still alive; after Benjamin Gabaldon was reported missing in action in Europe and his wife heard nothing more for several months, she "took up with another fellow." After the war the Gabaldons reunited and "tried to make a go of it," but they had grown too distant. "We just couldn't get along anymore so we decided on separating," Ben explained, adding, "The same thing happened to a lot of guys." Court records confirm Gabaldon's assessment: divorce rates soared during and after the war to unprecedented levels, rising from 2.5 divorces annually per 1,000 Utahns in 1940 to 3.4 in 1943 and 1944, 4.5 in 1945, and 5.5 by 1946, an annual rate as high as peak rates of the 1980s and 1990s, when close to half of all marriages are projected to end in divorce.[24]

Even many who remained faithful to each other through their long separation struggled following the war because their lives had moved in different directions. As June Anderson, whose husband was gone for twenty-seven months, explained, "The time separated from my husband changed our lives so much and we had to make a new start and get acquainted all over again." Doris Bowers-Irons reflected similar sentiments. After her husband, Tim, shipped overseas in 1943, she moved from Nephi to Sevier County to take a job as an LDS seminary teacher. "We were, I think, torn apart a great deal....All the people I knew Tim had never heard of. My friends were totally different from any he had ever known. All of his friends were totally different from any I had ever known. We didn't seem to have a bond."

Following their return many veterans and their wives had to renegotiate roles and responsibilities since they had become more self-sufficient because of their separation. When Clark Thompson returned home, "He wanted to be the father, he wanted to be the leader, and yet I didn't want him to be.... I would get upset if he would discipline the children. It took us awhile to get adjusted in that respect," his wife, Marjorie, explained.[25]

Along with the soldiers' wives, their children were directly affected by the war. Lola Van Wagenen, a Provo girl whose father was in the Pacific theater, resembled most children in her simplistic understanding of the war. She never "really understood what the fight was all about in any sense other than the fact that these were bad people who were trying to do harm to our country." For most children, like Van Wagenen, having a father overseas who was "going to be one of those that were going to try to save our country" was a source of "honor and pride." Because of the war, children spent several years in a matriarchal household—and for some whose fathers never returned, that became a permanent reality. Sanoma Bowers-Irons's mother "never did tell her she had a father" and "didn't even have any of his pictures around where she could see them" because she did not want her daughter to face the shock that other children were enduring of "knowing that their fathers wouldn't be returning" because of death or divorce. Consequently, Sanoma "had a difficult time accepting" her father when he did return. Children whose fathers were overseas also could not develop a normal rapport with their parent. Contrasting the experiences of her children born before and after the war, Marjorie Thompson lamented that those who lived through the war "missed out" because of their father's absence and never seemed to be "as close to their father as the three youngest."[26]

PATRIOTIC FERVOR AND ITS FALLOUT

To a greater extent than any other war in the twentieth century, the Second World War affected most Utahns as a force of globalization and incorporation—even those whose loved ones were not soldiers. A strong patriotic fervor generally suffused the state and nation; although many had hoped to avoid war prior to the Japanese attack on Pearl Harbor, that attack galvanized support for fighting far more effectively than any amount of political exhortation could have done. "Patriotism was high," James Packer of North Logan recalled. Not only the threat that the Axis powers posed to national security but the fact that so many residents of every community were fighting created an ultrapatriotic environment. As Packer explained, "There was a great pride in knowing that our friends were in the service." Consequently, "everyone knew all of the armed forces songs," recalled Marjorie Dyreng. Many communities feted those who were about to depart for military service. In Mayfield residents would gather for a "big ward dinner and a program" where each departing soldier was presented with a savings bond. "It was a good send-off. It was doing something special for them," recalled Ora Petersen. Likewise, soldiers who were at home on furlough were honored at parties.[27]

Soldiers engaged in this "good war" were touted as role models by community leaders and parents. In Cedar City LDS bishop H. H. Lunt invited everyone in town to attend a special sacrament meeting in January 1943 featuring Lieutenant Roscoe Booth, who was billed by the newspaper editor as "Cedar City's No. 1 hero of World War II." Soldiers and war culture provided particularly compelling role models for impressionable children. Don Cannon, an elementary school student in Salt Lake City, spent many summer evenings with his young friends on a big front porch, mesmerized as his neighbor recounted the heroic and adventurous exploits of American soldiers around the globe. Some of the tales were so inspiring that more than fifty years later, Cannon could still vividly remember them. Saturated with wartime stories and war-related newsreels, children imitated soldiers in their play, sporting toy destroyers and machine guns. In Provo, as recruits training at BYU paraded daily from their dorms to University Hill, children from nearby neighborhoods fell in line behind them, banging on "their cans or whatever they could pound" and pretending to be just like the men in uniform.[28]

Many young women also idolized soldiers and the soldier image. "We used to stand in the mornings and see them marching by so trim and straight," recalled Melba Barker Larsen, a student a Weber College. "We looked at those handsome fellows and thought, 'I'd like to go with that one.'" Likewise, Marjorie Dyreng, a freshman at BYU, would often accompany her girlfriends to the train station to "see the fellows off to war"—a pastime she regarded as exciting and patriotic. Ed Liechty often saw his older sister and her friends standing in their yard in Springville, waving to the troops as trains rolled by bound for Salt Lake City. Scribbling their names and addresses on scraps of paper, some men tossed them out the open windows to the girls below, and Ed's sister wrote regularly to one of the men she "met" in this way until he died two years later. These young women's fascination with handsome GIs may have been at least partly hormonal, but soldiers possessed greater appeal than other men because of the wartime conviction that those in uniform were noble and gallant combatants fighting to preserve the American way.[29]

In such an emotionally charged, prowar climate where local soldiers were honored, opponents of the war and particularly conscientious objectors were shunned and even harmed. Joseph Haws, a high school student at the time in Provo, described most Utahns' contempt for such individuals. "No one could understand them, why healthy men didn't want to fight, especially those of us who couldn't go yet [because of age]. We couldn't believe it." In LaPoint residents "hung one guy with the chainhorse by the heels" for unpatriotic behavior. Even those who could not serve because of medical reasons felt ostracized. Jay Hall, a student at the State

Agricultural College who was classified by draft boards as 4-F—ineligible for military service for health reasons—felt that he and the other 4-Fs "were the outcasts of the young men." Hall was embarrassed and offended when Governor Maw in a public address on campus quipped that he felt sorry for women on campus because "all they had to go with was 4-F's."[30]

A few men who could not qualify for military service because of health or occupation, such as J. Eldon Dorman, a medical doctor in Carbon County, volunteered for the Utah Civil Air Patrol. They attended classes two nights a week, where they studied aviation and aircraft recognition, received uniforms, and participated in military drills. "We were told to fly and 'observe the country' as much as possible. We were not told anything specific to watch for, but to report anything 'unusual,'" recalled Dorman, who loved to fly over the San Rafael Swell between Price and Hanksville early in the morning before going to work at the clinic.[31]

Some Utahns tried to demonstrate their patriotism by ridiculing or persecuting first- or second-generation immigrants from Japan, Germany, and Italy as well as 4-Fs. Japanese and Japanese Americans were particularly targeted. Anti-Japanese sentiment in Utah, as elsewhere in the nation, predated the war, as reflected in the enactment of immigration-restriction legislation on the national level and laws prohibiting interracial marriage on the state level. The attack on Pearl Harbor and America's entry into the war against Japan seemed to further legitimize anti-Japanese sentiment, though, and it escalated to a fevered pitch.[32]

Anticipating that others would blame them for Pearl Harbor, Japanese Americans in Utah represented by Jun Kuramada, president of the Salt Lake chapter of the Japanese American Citizen's League, issued a statement expressing shock and outrage at the bombing. Despite such expressions of loyalty to the United States, Japanese Americans residing in the state were widely regarded as potential spies or saboteurs. Law enforcement officials confiscated radios, cameras, and large knives owned by them. Many Japanese and Japanese Americans, such as Jinzaburo Matsumiya, a section foreman for the Union Pacific Railroad, were summarily fired because of their ethnicity. Notwithstanding the urgent need for workers during the war, many Japanese Americans could "only find work at a restaurant or hotel."[33]

During the war most landlords refused to rent to Japanese Americans, and many property owners refused to sell to them. Chiyo Matsumiya "drove all over" Salt Lake County looking for a house to rent during the war but was repeatedly told that the property "wasn't for rent to a 'Jap.'" Some Japanese residents were threatened and persecuted. In Salt Lake City the Japanese cemetery was vandalized, and shots were fired at the home of a Japanese family. In Gunnison and Spanish Fork, some people seemed "ready to come out and bomb us," recalled Edythe Kaneko. Everywhere, those of Japanese ancestry were closely watched. Parking his car in Salt Lake City near a water-pumping station, University of Utah professor Edward

Hashimoto was accosted by a gun-toting, self-appointed watchman who suspected he was "trying to blow the place up." Citizens were so eager to arrest Japanese after Pearl Harbor was bombed that the *Deseret News* printed a warning that "only federal agents may arrest aliens." Treatment of the Japanese was so bad that some Chinese Americans in Ogden sported badges proclaiming "I am Chinese American" in order to protect themselves. On a societal level, then, invidious characterization of the Japanese prevailed.[34]

But on the individual level, some Caucasians openly befriended Japanese Americans. After moving to Spanish Fork during the war, Noble and Edythe Kaneko "had a lot of friends," recalled Edythe. "They didn't care about the war. They invited us to all their functions and treated us as one of them." Similarly, when Yukus Inouye moved to American Fork in 1943, W. D. Chapman risked censure from the community and sold him an eighty-acre farm. "He took me down and introduced me to everybody in the area: grocery-store owners, bank officers, other farmers. He was really impressive," recalled Inouye.[35]

Despite the hospitality of some, wartime ridicule and persecution were strong enough that some Japanese Americans became ashamed of their backgrounds. "A lot of families" burned family photographs and memorabilia "because they were fearful of the connection with Japan." Similarly, Helen Kuramada and her friends felt that "the more distance you could put between yourself and your heritage, the better off you were." One friend told her that "she forgot how to use chopsticks."[36]

Japanese and Japanese Americans may have borne the brunt of Utahns' wartime rage, but German and Italian immigrants were not entirely exempt. German immigrants were suspected of treason, "isolated" and "watched," recalled Frances Wilde. Dominick and Jenny Barber, Italian immigrants with six sons serving in the US Army, were confined to their homes after 9:00 p.m. because they were Italian citizens. "Nobody every stopped to think, 'Why would my father send six sons without raising Cain if he was not going to be a good citizen?'" recalled his son Eugene. "That upset me." Acting on a tip from a coworker, the Federal Bureau of Investigation "spied on" Italian immigrant Vito Bonacci, in Spring Glen. "I didn't think we deserved it. I told one guy, 'He's got his mother, father, brothers, and sister in Italy. He's working here and buying United States government bonds so the army can go and kill his parents you're following him around? It makes no sense,'" recalled his wife, Filomena.[37]

Patriotic fervor was used to justify and express national and racial prejudice, but it was also turned to more constructive uses as a tool in motivating Americans to sacrifice for the war effort. Thirty-five Navajos affixed their thumbprints to a letter penned by Indian trader Harry Goulding to General Dwight D. Eisenhower in 1943, pledging to dig for vanadium, a steel hardener, in a new mine near Blanding in order to "help win the war." Cecil Parrish recalled, "We went in there [the mines] to retain freedom for our people.... It was for the young men and women that we did this and also for our land." Attempting to give Americans a financial stake in the conflict and thereby "make the country war-minded," as well as to raise capital for the war, Secretary of the Treasury Henry Morgenthau Jr. encouraged Americans to buy bonds. Although they along with Americans elsewhere often failed to meet the goals or quotas for bond purchases set by the government, Utahns did invest millions in war bonds, which even became standard Christmas gifts in some homes.[38]

Patriots not only bought war bonds but also salvaged and donated resources for the war effort from chewing-gum wrappers to scrap metal. One dramatic donation, a heavy cast-iron tub, was retrieved from the third floor of the Reed Smoot family home in central Provo, using a crane. Many Utahns also "sow[ed] the seeds of victory" and raised family "victory gardens" to help reduce consumer demand for commercially grown food that was needed to feed the troops. Some children in urban areas received a reprieve from school in the springtime to help people till and rake plots for victory gardens.[39]

Authorities also counted upon Utahns' patriotism to uphold mandatory rationing of scarce commodities such as fabric, gasoline, rubber, and sugar that were integral to national defense. Gus P. Backman, rationing chairman for the state, supervised the allocation of rationed goods through local rationing boards. After more than a year of rationing, consumers could appreciate a poem printed in the *Iron County Record* in 1943:

> *And when I die, please bury me*
> *'Neath a ton of sugar, under a rubber tree*
> *Lay me to rest in a new auto machine*
> *And water my grave with good gasoline.*

Although Utahns complained widely about rationing and many obtained more than their fair share by means such as hoarding and using the ration books of deceased relatives or family members in the service, they endured rationing. Such forbearance on the part of consumers, says Dan Gardner, a grocer, would be inconceivable today: "It just set up a way of life that I don't think would be swallowed today."[40]

As historian Jessie Embry has concluded, rationing in Utah led to "inconvenience, not sacrifice, and shortages, not real privation." Even with rationing, historian John M. Blum has observed, the lifestyle of Americans "was better than that of any other people in the world, and better, too, than it had been only a few years" earlier during the Depression. Restaurateurs like Ted Speros of Lamb's Cafe in Salt Lake City had to "tailor [their] menu" because some foods were unavailable, but they never closed for lack of food. Many homemakers disliked using substitute sweeteners such as honey in place of sugar, but the substitutes were widely available and the government made large stocks of sugar available for home canning. One of the least-popular substitutes—oleo margarine in place of butter—may have seemed "gross" and "greasy looking" to many Utahns, including Lola Van Wagenen, but eventually some cooks and consumers decided they preferred it to butter in certain situations. Because of rationing, some motorists took extreme measures to conserve gasoline—after work at Fort Douglas Donna Fifield and her friend would coast down Fifth South to Ninth East in Salt Lake before turning over the engine. But they managed to get to work and back every day. People who needed fuel for their work such as policemen, clergymen, farmers, medical personnel, workers in defense plants, or those who had to commute for their jobs had ample fuel, and there was enough wiggle room in the system, combined with a black market, to ensure that even many who wanted to take long trips could do so. Donna Fifield summed up the level of sacrifice that rationing required when she stated, "I think we missed hosiery more than anything else."[41]

ECONOMIC GROWTH AND PROSPERITY

To many Utahns, rationing was particularly annoying because it prolonged the Depression-era habits of scrimping and doing without in an era when the economy was actually booming. To a degree unprecedented in the state's history, Utah's economy surged forward during the war, bringing prosperity to many Utahns. Indeed, the war probably touched more Utahns economically than in any other way. Coal production, which had amounted to only 3.6 million tons in 1940, topped 6 million tons in 1942 and rose to nearly 6.8 million tons in 1945. In 1940 Utah's mines had produced 463 million pounds of copper—a record up to that point in time—but three years later Utah's copper mines produced 748 million pounds. Output from the state's iron mines rose even more dramatically, from 262,087 long tons of ore in 1939 to 1.9 million in 1945.[42]

Farming boomed, too, in response to government incentives and high demand. In Utah farm acreage rose by 41 percent between 1940 and 1945. In order to ensure an adequate food supply for the troops and the civilian population, the government deferred military service for agricultural workers. Government propagandists instructed farm boys that as far as Uncle Sam was concerned, their bib overalls and work clothes were every bit as much a "uniform" as any soldier's regalia. Thanks to government contracts, prices for farm products were high, and gross farm income roughly doubled between 1941 and 1945. For the first time in their lives, young farmers such as Francis and Ora Petersen truly had money to spend. The Petersens, who had lived in a two-room cabin in Sanpete County without running water or electric appliances since their marriage in 1938, were finally "able to do things" thanks to wartime prices for farm products. The couple drilled a well and installed a pump to bring water to their home and their turkey sheds in 1943. Soon after, they bought an electric washing machine and installed an indoor toilet. With money they had saved during the war, the Petersens built a modern three-bedroom home when building materials were released for private construction following the war.[43]

In addition to invigorating traditional centerpieces of Utah's economy such as mining and agriculture, the war promoted economic growth by enormously expanding the number of government jobs in defense installations. Northern Utah seemed an ideal location; it was far enough inland to preclude Japanese attack; it was crisscrossed by transcontinental highways and railroads; it possessed a generally clear, dry climate that facilitated travel and storage; it boasted a fairly large population as well as a relative abundance of open land; and it was roughly equidistant from major port cities on the Pacific Coast. Two federal defense installations that predated the war, Fort Douglas and Ogden Arsenal, were expanded between 1941 and 1945. By the time that the United States entered the war, construction was also under way at three other facilities—Wendover Army Air Base, Ogden Air Depot (Hill Field), and Utah General Depot—that had been approved as part of America's defense buildup in the years immediately preceding American entry into the war. Within a year of America's declaration of war, six other defense installations—Kearns Army Air Base, Clearfield Naval Supply Depot, Tooele Ordnance Depot, Deseret Chemical Depot, Dugway Proving Ground, and Bushnell Military Hospital—were announced. Between 1941 and 1943 defense spending created approximately 49,500 new jobs in Utah.[44]

Utah's construction industry boomed as a result of generous contracts for building wartime installations at breakneck speed. In the final quarter of 1942, 34,591 construction workers were employed in Utah, compared to 13,386 in the final quarter of 1941 and 5,184 in the last quarter of 1940. With monthly wages for workers late in 1942 averaging $249—43.5 percent higher than the average Utah wage—the construction industry was the best-paying sector of the economy. Not surprisingly, under these conditions many Utahns such as Vern Richins became temporary construction workers. Richins and his wife, Wilma, left their home in Draper and moved into a one-room cabin in Wendover. There Vern earned excellent wages helping to build Wendover Air Force Base twelve to sixteen hours a day.[45]

Fort Douglas, located on the east bench of Salt Lake City since 1862, became the regional headquarters for the Army Ninth Service Command after coastal areas were deemed too vulnerable to sabotage or attack by the Japanese. From January 1942 to March 1946 officers at the fort supervised the army's operations in the Rocky Mountain and Pacific states. The fort also served as an induction center for processing draftees and recruits from Utah and surrounding states and as a separation center where men were mustered out of the service. Personnel at the fort also managed the financial affairs of all army installations in Utah, repaired military vehicles, and remade weapons and instruments.[46]

At Wendover nearly 1.9 million acres were set aside for an air base, despite protests from stockmen who had been using the desert rangeland. Near the end of 1943, 17,500 military personnel were working at the base, along with 2,000 civilians. Byron Dussler, an Illinoisan stationed in Wendover, characterized the populace in 1944 as a "motley crowd of soldiers, civilians, wives, girlfriends, all stranded at Wendover." Aside from beer busts, sleep, the weather, and the State Line Casino, which had "a spirit and color that makes one feel the pep and tang of mischief," Dussler disliked the base. Its worst aspects were "no sheets, Chow, 6:15 rising, 10:00 bed check, double bunks, [and] everything else." During the war crews of B-17, B-24, and B-29 bombers trained at the base's ranges, where they practiced bombing a mock city made of salt from the salt flats. In 1945 the crew who would drop atomic bombs on Hiroshima and Nagasaki, including Colonel Paul W. Tibbets Jr. and bombardier T. W. Ferebee, trained at Wendover.[47]

In the spring of 1942, Kearns Army Air Base was built on 5,450 acres of farmland southwest of Salt Lake City at a cost of approximately seventeen million dollars. The base, which contained 926 tar-paper buildings, 1.7 million square feet of warehouse space, recreational facilities, sixteen mess halls, a hospital, four chapels, a library, a post office, a bank, and a telegraph office, became Utah's third-largest city during the war, housing more than 40,000 soldiers and employing more than 1,000 civilians. At the base army airmen learned to use grenades, bayonets, gas, and rifles and trained in camouflage and airdrome maneuvers. Following the war the government auctioned off the base, and the site became a fast-growing suburb.[48]

Tooele Ordnance Depot was developed in 1942–43 on 25,000 acres of open land four miles south of Tooele as a reserve ammunition depot for Ogden Arsenal, which had run out of room. The depot included 902 igloos—storage facilities for explosives with convex or domed roofs; 43 warehouses, including a dozen designed for small arms ammunition; repair shops for tanks, artillery equipment and trucks; 29 barracks; a hospital; and 1,080 homes and apartments. As a major storage and shipping facility for the Army Ordnance Corps, the depot received and shipped 1.6 million tons of matériel during the war. Workers at the depot also salvaged or rebuilt 896 tanks, 997 automobiles and trucks, and 1,347 major artillery pieces. At its wartime peak, the base employed 2,000 civilians, 1,500 servicemen, and nearly 1,400 prisoners of war (POWs). Nearby Tooele's population nearly tripled during the war, including 380 Japanese American families who were recruited from relocation centers in Arizona and Wyoming to assist with the work at the depot.[49]

Dugway Proving Ground began when 126,720 acres in the Great Salt Lake Desert were transferred from the public domain to the Chemical Warfare Service in January 1942. Eventually, the Dugway Proving Ground would encompass 850,000 acres. Warehouses covering more than 49,000 square feet were constructed for storing chemical weapons, explosives, and other equipment. Target areas were established, including mock villages and bomb shelters, and personnel at the base experimented with chemical munitions such as the highly effective M-2 and M-4 chemical mortars and with protective equipment, flame throwers, incendiary bombs, and fuel thickeners. Following the war the facility closed but reopened during the Korean War.[50]

Deseret Chemical Depot, built in 1942–43 in Rush Valley at a cost of fifteen million dollars, stored chemical and biological weapons. The storage depot was remote enough that the military built housing, stores, recreational facilities, and restaurants to accommodate 750 workers. Despite the employment and income generated by these facilities and the impetus given to scientific research at universities, the depot and proving ground also facilitated the release of lethal concentrations of chemicals into Utah's atmosphere, particularly in the Cold War era, and prevailing winds carried the chemicals toward major population centers.[51]

Fifteen miles south of Ogden and two miles from Ogden Air Depot on more than 800 acres of rich farmland in Clearfield, the navy established the Clearfield Naval Supply Depot in 1942–43 at a cost of thirty-seven million dollars. Facilities at the depot included a headquarters building and nearly 200 acres of warehouse space as well as outside storage pads. Employment at the facility peaked at 7,624 in 1944. Operating twenty-four hours a day, the facility received, stored, and shipped an immense variety of naval goods, including war matériel, clothing, electronics, musical instruments, spare parts, beds, and tools.[52]

Ogden Air Depot (Hill Field), the largest wartime employer of civilians in Utah, was constructed between 1938 and 1942 in Davis County. In the spring of 1943, wartime employment at the facility peaked, with 6,000 military employees and 15,780 civilian workers. During the war, the base's principal responsibilities included repairing and maintaining aircraft engines, parachutes, and radios for the Army Air Corps and storing supplies. As the war wound down, the depot became an important storage facility for surplus airplanes, but the number of employees dropped to 8,543 by July 1945.[53]

Utah General Depot, also known for a time during the war as Utah Quartermaster Depot and Utah Army Service Forces Depot, employed an estimated 12,000 civilian and military workers at its peak in 1944. The facility was constructed on 1,679 acres of prime farmland in Weber County that had been expropriated by the federal government in 1940. By the end of the war twenty-eight brick warehouses containing more than 5 million square feet of storage space had been built. The depot received, stored, maintained, and shipped supplies for the army to northern California and Nevada, Oregon, Washington, Utah, Idaho, and Montana, including chemical weapons and protective clothing, heavy equipment and tools, medical supplies, clothing, bedding, and general supplies such as utensils, razor blades, office supplies, and nonperishable foods. Workers at the depot also repaired heavy equipment for the army and printed and shipped many army publications.[54]

Ten miles southwest of Ogden in Sunset, the old Ogden Arsenal, an ordnance depot for ammunition built in the 1920s, was refurbished and expanded. The facility was used for industrial operations such as "linking 30 and 50 caliber cartridges into machine-gun belts" in 1942 and 1943. After manufacturing at the arsenal ended late in 1943 and the facility became mainly a storage and shipping point, civilian employment fell from 6,000 to 2,000.[55]

In Brigham City Bushnell Military Hospital was completed in 1942 at a cost of nine million dollars. The facility was located on lands donated by the city and included sixty buildings. During the war 13,000 soldiers were treated at Bushnell, including those with neurological and neuropsychiatric conditions. Amputees were fitted with artificial limbs and trained to use them there. Douglas Kershaw, an Army Air Corps cadet from Salt Lake City who spent six months at Bushnell because of illness, recalled that there he "saw the horror of people being shot up." Particularly unforgettable was the "big morgue.... [T]here were just so many boys that didn't make it and they sent them out in boxes."[56]

Utah's military installations also included POW base camps at Clearfield, Fort Douglas, Hill Field, Deseret Chemical Depot, Tooele Ordnance Depot, and Utah General Depot and branch camps at Bushnell Hospital and Dugway Proving Ground as well as in Logan, Orem, Salina, and Tremonton, where close to 20,000 Germans and Italians were held. Thousands of prisoners of war were housed in barracks and tents behind wire fences. Those held at base camps assisted with war work, including repairing vehicles, driving trucks, caring for grounds, and stacking equipment. Under contract arrangements between local farmers and the military, prisoners were also employed as farm laborers, and growers reimbursed the government at minimum wage for the prisoners' work. Don Cannon, an elementary school student, would occasionally accompany his grandfather, a Provo fruit grower, to the Orem camp to pick up prisoners. Cannon would "ride in the back with the prisoners and talk to them and they'd look at my watch and they'd talk, the best they could, in English." Cannon enjoyed the experience until a prison guard reprimanded his grandfather and prohibited him from permitting a young boy to fraternize with the enemy. Prisoners generally worked eight to ten hours per day and a minimum of six days per week. Although the POWs were usually well treated in the camps and in the community, armed guards did physically and verbally harass or abuse some of them, and the meals became increasingly skimpy as the war wound down. Thirty-three prisoners of war who died in Utah are buried at Fort Douglas, including nine who were shot by a mentally deranged guard in Salina in the summer of 1945.[57]

Finding an adequate number of civilian employees to staff defense installations, particularly in Davis and Weber Counties where they were so heavily concentrated, was difficult. Defense installations created close to 50,000 jobs in Utah, including 35,486 jobs in Davis and Weber Counties alone. Utah's workforce had to expand substantially in order to staff these facilities adequately. Defense installations offered high pay and other incentives to make work there appealing. Armed with the promise of high salaries, recruiters for defense installations focused heavily upon women, the handicapped, senior citizens, and students. As Antonette Chambers Noble has observed, recruiters appealed to Utahns' patriotism, mixed in some cases with "scare tactics, guilt and fear." One call for 3,500 workers at Tooele Ordnance Depot proclaimed, "It is your patriotic duty to work if you are not bedfast at the present time." Clearfield Naval Supply Depot's elderly employees included one ninety-nine-year-old worker. High school and college students were also recruited to work after school, on weekends, and over vacations. Administrators and professors at the State Agricultural College organized a "special labor project" in Cache Valley, transporting more than 600 high school and college students to Ogden on weekends to work in defense installations for $6.50 a day. Installations also obtained workers by relaxing entry-level skill requirements; recruiting Native Americans, Mexican Americans, Puerto Ricans, and African Americans; and employing prisoners of war and Japanese civilian internees. Jobs abounded, even for racial minorities. "I never worried about jobs. During the war, the jobs came looking for you," recalled William Tang, who moved to Salt Lake City in 1942. Still, as Nathan "Woody" Wright, an African American machinist from Connecticut who sought work at Hill Air Force Base in 1942, learned, some supervisors would hire only whites.[58]

A small number of Southern Paiutes moved to the Wasatch Front to obtain work in wartime industries, while others made their way to Los Angeles. Hundreds of Navajos left their reservation to work at defense installations, including Fort Wingate. Their wages helped to shift the reservation economy from barter to a cash system. Among those who moved from southern Utah was Arvilla Benson. Writing back home to Cedar City, she told a friend that it was "about the frist [sic] time" she had been to Salt Lake. "It was Big City," she wrote. "I am planting [planning] on working over there." With the skills they had acquired through National Youth Administration sewing programs during the Depression, some young women from Kanosh and the Shivwits Reservation qualified for jobs in factories manufacturing parachutes and military uniforms. By 1943 a goodly proportion of the members of the Shivwits Tribal Council were working outside southern Utah.[59]

Representatives of defense installations and wartime factories particularly sought to recruit Utah's women. Articles and advertisements in newspapers and magazines attempted to harmonize traditional feminine ideals with war work, pointing to similarities between housework and factory labor, stressing "natural" feminine traits such as manual dexterity and patience that qualified women for industrial work, or maintaining that working women were expressing a "truly feminine" ideal in "stand[ing] by their men." Close to 24,000 women took jobs in defense installations and war industries—at Ogden Arsenal more than half the employees were women. Women's share of the labor force rose from 18 percent in 1940 to 37 percent in 1944, a much more dramatic rise than the corresponding national increase of 28 to 36 percent. Unlike earlier generations of female workers, most of the women entering the workforce during World War II were married. Some were hired to operate heavy equipment and work in heavy industry: women played significant roles in all of the state's major economic sectors except for mining, where the law barred them.[60]

Notwithstanding recruiters' appeals to women's patriotism and femininity, economic need and the promise of decent wages were the primary reasons women entered the workforce. But war work was also a means of supporting the troops and expressing patriotism, and some who worked sacrificed greatly to do so. Marjorie Dyreng of Manti worked at Standard Parachute Company, sewing parachutes for eight hours a day and patriotically investing her salary in savings bonds. For Dyreng, who was allergic to the fabric used in the parachutes, the work entailed some sacrifice for the troops overseas. Dorothy Lemmon, an employee at Remington Arms Plant and Tooele Army Depot, entered the workforce so that she could "make a little bit" of money, but altruism also entered into the equation. Holding a job and still having a family to care for in the evenings was not "too easy for me," she explained, and she did it partly because "they took a lot of the men into the service and they needed help."[61]

More than 600 women worked at Geneva Steel in Orem between January 1944 and September 1945, including close to 200 who labored on the production floor. Eighty percent of them were married. Many, like Elizabeth Talbot, had worked before the war and applied at Geneva because they could earn more there. Josephine Cooper, reportedly the first woman to be hired at the plant, worked initially as a custodian but soon became a crane operator. Cooper, who worked for more than twenty years at Geneva until her retirement in 1967, was exceptional. Geneva's 600 female wartime employees worked an average of only four months.[62]

Such high turnover rates are surprising, particularly since 75 percent of the women surveyed in a national poll in 1945 said they hoped to keep their jobs when the war ended. Opposition from LDS Church leaders to mothers' employment outside the home may have contributed to exceptionally high turnover rates at places like Geneva with predominantly Mormon workers. As early as October 1942, the LDS First Presidency had warned mothers that their responsibilities "may not be passed to others. Nurses cannot do it; public nurseries cannot do it; hired help cannot do it—only mother, aided as much as may be by the loving hands of father, brothers and sisters." Not only mothers who took work "for gold [or] fame" but those who did so in the name of "civic service" were singled out for reprimand. "Remember that 'a child left to himself bringeth his mother to shame,' (Prov. 29:15)," the First Presidency warned. Eighteen months later Apostle Steven L. Richards reiterated that "war does not change our obligations and responsibilities concerning our children." Other authorities speaking in LDS General Conferences partially attributed rising divorce rates and increased juvenile delinquency to working mothers' absence from the home. However, when church leader Adam S. Bennion visited the Standard Parachute Plant in 1943, he praised the stamina of women who "work a full shift at the plant and then hurry home to take care of their own household duties and some of them are good enough to look after the children of other mothers who then replace them on a second shift."[63]

When in the 1980s historian Antonette Chambers Noble asked Utah women about "conflict between their church and the[ir] decision to work" during the war, "no one indicated any problems." Noble's study suggests that perhaps church leaders' rhetoric played little if any role in high wartime turnover rates among Utah women workers. On the other hand, the results may simply show that no one wanted to talk about the problems four decades later or that they had forgotten them.[64]

Of equal if not greater importance in explaining women's departure from the workforce during the war are other factors, including the difficulty of juggling home and work responsibilities and lack of support from husbands. As Amanda Borneman discovered in her study of women workers at Standard Parachute in Manti, "The pressure to stay home with their children and the weight of multiple burdens could be heavy." A survey of 337 married working women in Salt Lake in 1939 showed that nearly 23 percent of them were responsible for all housework in their homes and that working mothers also played key roles in caring for their children after work. If anything, these trends accelerated during the war, with longer workdays and military service for many husbands.[65]

The paucity of day-care centers also made it difficult for young mothers to work for extended periods of time. Using grants from the Federal Works Agency, school districts in places with wartime industries and defense installations did establish day-care facilities for preschoolers between the ages of two and five and hired personnel for after-school supervision of elementary and junior high students whose parents worked. In 1944 nineteen day-care centers and fourteen extended-care facilities were operating in Utah. Since each center could accommodate only 50 to 70 children, though, they met the needs of only a few hundred of the thousands of families with working mothers.[66]

After studying women workers in Manti's Standard Parachute factory, historian Amanda Borneman concluded that the women's wartime work experiences were "central to their lives." The women Borneman studied developed confidence and independence as a result of their work experiences, made new friends, contributed significantly to the economic well-being of their households, and passed a positive view of women's participation in the labor force on to their children.[67]

Although the construction and staffing of defense installations such as Tooele Army Depot and Ogden Arsenal offered high-paying jobs to many Utahns, most of those jobs faded with the end of the war. Between 1944 and 1947, Utah lost 70 percent of the 49,500 jobs that had been created directly by defense spending during the war. Nevertheless, wartime defense had created an infrastructure, including offices, warehouses, loading docks, railroads, and landing fields, that would act as a powerful magnet, drawing defense dollars to the state during the Cold War, the Korean conflict, and the Vietnam War. Indeed, as Thomas G. Alexander has observed, defense installations that were established or expanded during the war became "the keystone of Utah's postwar prosperity," especially in the northern part of the state. Defense installations also created a multiplier effect because of local goods from manufactured items to foodstuffs and services such as electricity bought by those installations. For every job created at the defense installations themselves, an estimated 0.8 jobs were created in surrounding communities.[68]

Aside from the capital flowing into the state because of federal defense installations, the federal government allocated $284 million in public funds for constructing industrial plants in Utah between 1940 and 1945. Utah secured close to 38 percent of the federal government's appropriations for wartime industrial plants in the Rocky Mountain states and more than 2.8 times the national per capita investment in new factories. Industrial plants built with federal funds during the war included Geneva Steel in Orem, built at a cost of $203 million; the Remington Small Arms plant in Salt Lake County, built with an investment of $19 million for buildings and $11 million for machinery; the Eitel McCullough Radio Tube Plant in Salt Lake, which employed 15,000 workers at its wartime peak; Lehi Refractory, a manufacturer of silica bricks; the Kalunite mill, where low-grade aluminum ore was processed; a tungsten plant operated by Union Carbide in Salt Lake; a plant for the Vanadium Corporation of America at Monticello; and a vanadium mine in Blanding. Utah Oil Refinery in Salt Lake City was enlarged at a cost of $15 million by the government during the war because of demand for aviation gasoline.[69]

Although federal funds underwrote 91 percent of Utah's industrial expansion during the war, other enterprises were constructed or significantly enlarged with private capital. The Standard Parachute Company, a California corporation, constructed a plant in Manti 1942 where parachutes were manufactured. After the plant's closure in the summer of 1944, it was purchased and converted into a military clothing factory by Reliance Manufacturing. All told, the number of manufacturing facilities in Utah rose by more than 40 percent between 1939, when there were 549 facilities, and 1947, when there were 772 facilities.[70]

The state's Department of Publicity and Industrial Development, which was established in 1941, played a key role in attracting war-related industry to Utah. Additionally, Governor Herbert Maw and Utah's senators and representatives sought industrial investment. For instance, Maw and Senator Abe Murdock masterfully lobbied in the Washington pork barrel to secure a small-arms plant for Utah. Their experiences illustrate the importance of personality and partisanship in explaining Utah's success in attracting federal funds during the 1940s.[71]

In the spring of 1941, after reading that the War Department intended to build three small-arms plants, Maw traveled to Washington to lobby on Utah's behalf. Working closely with Murdock, who had recently replaced William King in the Senate, Maw obtained an audience with President Roosevelt. The president launched into a monologue, lauding the state of Utah and its Mormon pioneer heritage and attempting, Maw believed, to wile away the appointment in small talk and prevent Maw from lobbying. About fifteen minutes into the monologue, Maw butted in shrewdly with a joke: "Mr. President, I've done something that you'll never be able to do.... I'm a Maw and a Pa at the same time." As the president chuckled, Maw continued, "I've come to request a defense plant to provide employment for the descendants of those noble pioneers you've been talking about." When Roosevelt demurred, Maw seized upon a new strategy, claiming that conservative Democrat and former senator William King, an inveterate opponent of Roosevelt and the New Deal, had allied with Republicans in the state to defeat New Dealers Elbert Thomas and Abe Murdock when they came up for reelection in 1944 and 1946. If New Deal supporters like Thomas and Murdock were given credit for bringing a huge number of jobs to Utah, their prospects for reelection would be substantially improved. Decades later, Maw recalled Roosevelt's response. "'Do you mean to tell me that that rat King is lining up the Republicans to defeat my friend Thomas?' He studied it for a minute and he realized and took a pencil out of his pocket and wrote a little note on a pad in front of us and said, 'You know, Governor, I feel Utah can get one of those plants.' And that's how we got it."[72]

The real story was actually more complex. Roosevelt did tell Maw twice in the course of his interview, "I think you should get the plant." But Maw still had to meet with military officials, and he had to work to persuade Thomas to call in his political chips by lobbying Roosevelt and military officers for the plant. Murdock, meanwhile, pursued the plant more assiduously. "It would mean more to you personally than anything that could be done," Maw wrote Thomas on May 2.

> The people out here know that you are the first ranking member on the Military Affairs Committee of the Senate and take it for granted that you have authority to get that industry started here through the army if you want it. They are assuming that you have a lot more authority than I know that you

do have in the matter so far as the placing of the various industries are concerned. If the plant comes you will get the credit. If the plant doesn't come a lot of your enemies will blame you. You of course know how people react on any matter that comes near to their hearts.

Maw concluded, "I hope that you will not think that I am presuming too much when I urge you to see [Roosevelt] and try to get him behind our state." Thomas took the hint and replied to the governor, "I cannot begin to say how much I appreciate everything you said in your letter. I am deeply grateful for your personal feelings and I hope we shall always be able to continue such a relationship." Two months later after several additional conferences, Utah's officials on Capitol Hill in Washington triumphantly informed Utahns that the War Department would probably build one of its small-arms plants in their state. Four days later, on June 11, the War Department formally confirmed that the plant would be built. Rejoicing in the way that the announcement had shored up the fortunes of New Deal Democrats in Utah, Maw publicly stated, "To Senators Thomas and Murdock and to Representatives Robinson and Granger, we Utahns are indebted for their fine teamwork in helping to bring this plum to our state."[73]

Constructed on five thousand acres in the western Salt Lake Valley between Ninth and Twenty-First South, the 211-building small-arms plant was operated under contract from the War Department by the Remington Arms Company. Employment at the plant exceeded 10,000 between July 1942 and November 1943—a gigantic number in light of the fact that Salt Lake's entire prewar labor force in 1940 had been 57,260. From its opening in 1941 until the end of 1943, the plant produced .30- and .50-caliber ammunition for M-1 and Browning automatic rifles and .50-caliber machine guns. In January 1944 ammunition manufacturing ceased, and the plant was converted for reclaiming used war matériel, a function that it performed until early 1946. As Leonard Arrington and Thomas Alexander have noted, the plant not only increased wages in northern Utah and generated business for local firms but also "create[d] a reservoir of goods, industrial plants, and skills upon which the people of Utah could draw after the war."[74]

In the same conference with Roosevelt where Maw lobbied for construction of a small-arms plant, the president raised the possibility that a pig-iron plant might be built in the state. Several months later the Office of Production Management announced plans to construct an integrated steel plant on land near the old Geneva resort, west of Orem. In addition to its remoteness from vulnerable areas along the Pacific Seaboard, the site was desirable because of the availability of water, the proximity to railroads and highways, the work ethic and relatively high educational level of the local population, and the site's proximity of deposits of raw materials such as coal, iron ore, limestone, and dolomite. In the long run, Geneva Steel was the Utah's most important wartime industrial development, attracting roughly two-thirds of the public funds available to Utah for industrial development during the war. Between 1942 and 1944 three blast furnaces with a daily capacity of 1,120 tons each, nine open-hearth furnaces, a plate mill, a structural mill, a slabbing and blooming mill, and coke ovens were built by Columbia Steel Company and nearly one hundred subcontractors. In addition to production facilities, the company built a 312-acre water reservoir and laid seventy-six miles of railroad track. Close to ten thousand men worked on the project, and the population of Orem and surrounding communities temporarily swelled with the influx of out-of-state construction workers. The plant opened in 1944 with fifteen hundred employees. Within a year, employment nearly tripled, rising to forty-two hundred by early 1945, including hundreds of local farmers who took jobs at the plant and operated their farms after hours. Demand for raw materials led to expanded mining of iron ore, coal, limestone, and dolomite. By the war's end, the plant had produced 643,000 tons of steel plate and 144,280 tons of structured shaped steel. In addition to pig iron and hot-rolled steel products, the plant produced by-products, including sulfate of ammonia, benzol, toluol, xylol, solvent naphtha, coal tar, and naphthalene. Following the war, production virtually ceased for ten months before United States Steel outbid six competitors to purchase the facility from the War Assets Administration for $47.5 million, less than one-fourth of its cost to the government.[75]

The effects of the steel mill upon Utah County's economy were phenomenal. Wages provided thousands of county residents who had formerly relied upon odd jobs and farmwork with a steady income. By 1950 more than one-third of the workforce in the county was employed in manufacturing—more than twice the percentage for Salt Lake County and by far the highest percentage of any county in the state. Frances Wilde, whose brother-in-law obtained work at Geneva, explained the allure of industrial work: "Just imagine never having had a check and then all of sudden you've got a job with a check every two weeks. It would be a big check, $100 or more." After the war with earnings from Geneva "for the first time," workers like Wilde's brother-in-law "could buy a car, they could go on a vacation and do things that they had never done before." Wage work at Geneva boosted business at stores, gas stations, restaurants, and other establishments. Retail sales in Utah County exceeded $27 million in 1945, compared to $15 million in 1940. The plant further developed the local economy by attracting other related firms to the area because of the availability of steel and other by-products from the plant. By 1947 the county boasted seventy-six manufacturing establishments compared to fifty-eight in 1940. Detracting from the economic benefits were the increased industrial pollution. Following the war farmers and stockmen sought compensation for losses they attributed to fluorine gas from Geneva.[76]

Much as wartime spending made residents of Utah County prosperous, federal and private investment in defense installations and factories elsewhere, coupled with generally high wartime prices for Utah's agricultural and mineral products, brought greater prosperity to Utahns statewide. Federal spending in Utah during the 1930s, totaling $289.3 million, had substantially reduced the Depression's severity. Far heavier spending during the war catapulted Utahns into genuine prosperity: the federal government spent roughly $628 million on buildings at military installations, $280 on construction of factories, and hundreds of millions more on civilian wages. Total direct federal spending amounted to at least $1.1 billion and may have been as high as $1.36 billion.[77]

Such heavy spending helped to boost per capita personal income by nearly 125 percent. Thanks to high-paying jobs, many Utahns were able to put money aside in the bank. Total assets in Utah's insured banks rose from $199 million in 1940 to $586 million by the war's end. Many residents also used wartime wages to reduce debt. Farm mortgage debt shrank by 45 percent between 1941 and 1945. Rising prices partially offset gains in income, though. Retail food prices in Salt Lake at the end of the war were one-third higher than in 1941. Nationwide, consumer prices generally were 22 percent greater in 1945 than in 1940.[78]

Although the state's economy boomed throughout the war, especially in comparison to the 1930s, this was particularly so in 1942 and 1943. Particularly in manufacturing and construction and to a lesser extent in mining, jobs were much more plentiful in 1942 and 1943 than in the following two years, despite the opening of Geneva Steel in 1944. Per capita income likewise rose most dramatically between 1941 and 1942, increasing by 35 percent in that one year. The highest per capita income figures for the entire war era were for 1943. Indeed, 1942 and 1943 were the only years during the war when the state's per capita income actually exceeded the national figure.[79]

WARTIME MIGRATION

At the same time that the war was invigorating Utah's economy, it was also radically altering the state's population profile and social structure, particularly in areas that attracted defense dollars and government installations. Thousands of young soldiers converged upon northern Utah as they trained or labored at the state's military installations. Ted Speros, a restaurateur in Salt Lake City, remembered that the soldiers' presence "changed the face and look of downtown Salt Lake City and changed our lives." Business boomed as "soldiers from Kearns, Hill Air Force Base, and Dugway came into the city. They went to shows, dances, restaurants, and crowded the streets and all the establishments. All they wanted was to be entertained and well fed." Speros and his employees served more than seven hundred meals a day, many of them to GIs.[80]

Few of the soldiers training in Utah were native to the state. Their presence boosted religious and ethnic diversity. Hundreds of Jewish soldiers from the East temporarily swelled the ranks of the state's tiny Jewish community. Many Jews in Salt Lake City eagerly tried to accommodate the soldiers, renting a room where they could socialize, arranging for religious services on bases, making and serving meals, hosting dances, and arranging celebrations for religious holidays. Rose Arnowitz made "five gallons of horseradish for a seder when there were so many Jewish soldiers here; the only place big enough to have it was in the South High School cafeteria." Margaret Herbert, who moved to Salt Lake City after graduating from Pleasant Grove High School in 1941, encountered "people from all over the United States and with such diverse backgrounds and regional accents." It was a heady time for a young girl to be in such an exciting, cosmopolitan setting. It also marked in her mind "the end of innocence for Utah."[81]

Utah became more diverse not only religiously and ethnically but also racially. Roughly 1 million African Americans served in the military during the war—by 1944 they constituted 10 percent of America's troops—and consequently "a lot of black soldiers" passed through Utah. Militant black soldiers who "were going overseas to kill for freedom" and were determined "to have some freedom here before they went" pushed back the color line in at least some places. In Ogden black GIs "literally [tore] up" cafés and theaters whose proprietors refused equal service to them. Woody Wright, who experienced the color line firsthand in Ogden, believed that the soldiers were "the reason Twenty-fifth Street got desegregated."[82]

Some old-stock Utahns warned their children not to associate closely with the soldiers. "Our mothers were concerned about racial problems because there were a lot of black soldiers," Margaret Herbert recalls. But race was not the only concern for many Mormon parents, who feared that their children might fall in love and marry a GI who did not share their faith. Notwithstanding parental objections, some did exactly that. Rachel Elison, a twenty-year-old Mormon from southern Idaho, moved to Salt Lake City to work in the office of an oil refinery in 1942. Despite parental objections, she sought out soldiers' company. One weekend she went to a dance at the Coconut Grove dance hall, and "there were just tons of soldiers there...out to get dates." She felt like a fish out of water among those who drank, but eventually, she met and fell in love with Frances Ham, a teetotaling master sergeant in the air force from Tennessee. She believed Ham was better behaved than most Mormon men his age and pleaded with her parents to stop lecturing her and to accept him as he was. In 1943 she and her beau traveled to Tennessee to marry.[83]

In addition to the soldiers, civilians from out of state moved to Utah during the war. As James L. Clayton has indicated, "A statistically accurate method of estimating state migration is wanting." Nevertheless, it appears that much of the state's wartime population growth was temporary, owing partly to a huge influx of construction workers in 1942 and 1943. After accounting for natural increase, Clayton estimated a net in-migration of 13,027 in 1942 and 43,893 in 1943, followed by a net outward migration of 37,223 in 1944 and 24,821 in 1945. According to these estimates, excluding those who had been born in Utah during the war, Utah's civilian population at the end of 1945 was smaller by 5,124 than when Pearl Harbor was attacked in December 1941. One reason for the decrease was the departure of thousands of Utah natives, including Dick Jackson, the son of a Rich County stockman, who sought jobs in the aircraft plants and other wartime industries on the West Coast. At Northrup Aircraft in Southern California, Jackson earned far more money than he had ever made in Utah. An even bigger reason, though, was the temporary absence of tens of thousands of Utahns serving in the military, who apparently took their time returning home after the war. Postwar migration, coupled with births and the return home of thousands of soldiers following the war, boosted the state's population to 638,000 by mid-1946, compared to 551,000 in July 1941, a net gain, excluding natural increase, of more than 28,000.[84]

The influx of civilians to Utah during the war included thousands of members of racial minorities. The war drew African American civilians westward in record numbers. While most of them went to the coast—340,000 southern blacks migrated to California alone—several thousand came to Utah, where they found work, often in defense installations. More than 2,400 African American workers were recruited in the South by personnel directors at Clearfield for employment at Clearfield Naval Supply Depot alone. Most of these wartime workers left after the war. Nevertheless, some remained: by 1950 about 2,729 African Americans lived in Utah, more than twice the number (1,235) who had inhabited the state ten years earlier.[85]

Mexican Americans and American Indians also migrated to Utah—especially from northern New Mexico and southern Colorado—because of wartime economic opportunities and the recruiting efforts of mines, factories, and defense installations. Many of these workers apparently left the state after the war, for the number of Mexicans residing Utah in 1950 was only 1,396—just 327 more than in 1940. Utah's temporary Hispanic migrants also included hundreds of Mexican nationals recruited under the Bracero Program, which was instituted under joint agreement of the United States and Mexico in 1942.[86]

As Utah's population grew, severe housing shortages developed, particularly in Weber, Davis, and Tooele Counties, where federal installations were concentrated. To help alleviate the shortage, the federal government constructed seven housing projects, including Grandview Acres in Ogden, and also developed trailer parks. Ultimately, the federal government built six thousand new homes and apartments, while private developers constructed eight thousand new units to accommodate the wartime demand.[87]

Old-timers expressed alarm at the crowded conditions in schools, in stores, and on highways and disapproved of the lifestyles of some newcomers, particularly single, footloose construction workers. Two journalists who visited Provo in 1944 found that some old-timers "were unhappy about the tremendously increased business the beer parlors in Provo were doing," while others "objected to the sudden overcrowding of everything from stores to homes."[88]

Many longtime residents of Utah linked the wartime influx of outsiders to increased crime, illegitimacy, and social disorder. Although rumors of gang activity in federally developed housing projects may have been exaggerated, Thomas Alexander has shown that rates of auto theft, larceny, burglary, and particularly aggravated assault increased in Utah during the war. Government agencies also reported increases in sex crimes, juvenile crime, and the number of unwed mothers applying for welfare. Factors such as inadequate supervision of youth at home, lack of community and social obligations among the fluid and rootless migrant population, long-term separation of husbands and wives, and inadequate housing were often blamed for these developments.[89]

JAPANESE AMERICAN RELOCATION AND INCARCERATION

Whereas most civilian migrants to Utah during the war came because of economic opportunity, restrictive national policies drove thousands of West Coast Japanese Americans to the state. In December 1941 Utah's Japanese American population stood at 2,210. The number of ethnic Japanese in Utah increased dramatically in 1942. On March 2 Japanese and Japanese Americans residing in portions of California, Oregon, Washington, and Arizona were encouraged by John L. DeWitt of the Western Defense Command to relocate voluntarily for national security reasons. Acting upon DeWitt's recommendation, 519 West Coast Japanese moved voluntarily to Utah. Most of them settled in downtown Salt Lake's Japanese district. Jun Kurumada, president of the local chapter of the Japanese American Citizens League, opened an information bureau in Salt Lake, where relocatees from the Pacific Coast could obtain information regarding jobs and housing in Utah. "I got to hear some really heart-wringing stories then," recalled his wife, Helen.[90]

The "largest single group to resettle [voluntarily] anywhere outside of the West Coast"—130 people—moved onto a thirty-five-hundred-acre tract at Keetley, between Heber and Park City. Fred Isamu Wada, a successful produce dealer from Oakland, California, leased the land from Keetley's mayor, George Fisher, and recruited Japanese workers. Moving into abandoned buildings, the migrants repaired them, grubbed sagebrush, removed rocks, and planted truck crops, including lettuce, strawberries, rutabagas, and onions. The Japanese farmers eventually overcame the hostility of many of their Anglo neighbors and recovered their investments. Their experiences at Keetley were sufficiently positive that following the war, roughly one-third of them chose to remain in Utah rather than return to California.[91]

The voluntary relocation of several hundred ethnic Japanese, including the Keetley colony, was followed later in 1942 by a massive influx of involuntary relocatees.

Ultimately, 11,212 West Coast Japanese, mainly from the San Francisco Bay Area, were held behind barbed wire in the Central Utah Relocation Center, more commonly known as Topaz, an internment camp constructed by the federal government on a nineteen-thousand-acre tract fifteen miles northwest of Delta. Forced to walk away from their homes and businesses in California, many suffered catastrophic economic losses as well as psychological trauma. As one of the internees, Miné Okubo, explained, "There were untold hardships, sadness, and misery." The first contingent arrived in September while the camp was still under construction. Yoshiko Uchida recalled, "When we stepped into our room it contained nothing but four army cots without mattresses. No inner sheetrock walls or ceilings had yet been installed, nor had the black pot-bellied stove that stood outside our door. Cracks were visible everywhere in the siding and around the windows." When it was completed, Topaz consisted of thirty-four residential blocks containing hastily constructed 20-by-120-foot pine barracks covered with tar paper and heated with potbellied stoves. Each barrack was divided into six apartments. Each block of barracks had its own restrooms, laundry, and dining hall. The community also contained a gymnasium, schools, libraries, churches, a post office, and a fire station.[92]

Nearly fifty years after relocation, few surviving internees had good things to say about the physical facilities at Topaz. Ronald Yutaka Yoshida characterized living conditions there as "horrible" because the barracks were "ill-constructed" and offered "no privacy." To make matters worse, there was no plumbing in the barracks; residents had to "go outside [the barracks] to go to the latrines." John Hada remembered how cold the buildings were without insulation, and Joe Suyemoto remembered how "crowded" his apartment seemed. Most of all, people remembered the white alkaline dust that filtered between the boards of the rudely constructed barracks. "There was so much dust in the rooms that we swept up two buckets of dust from each of the rooms before we could move in.... There were many nights we went to sleep with a damp handkerchief placed over our mouth and nose to keep from inhaling the dust," recalled one Nisei internee.[93]

Amid such unpleasant surroundings, many adults coped, recalls Joe Mori, by drawing upon traditional concepts such as "'gaman' [to endure] and 'shikataganai' [can't help it]." Others, such as Yukari Uchida, vented their frustration in poetry. "Banished to this Desert land, I cherish the Blessing of the sky," she wrote. On another occasion, she lamented, "Grown old so soon in a foreign land, What do they think, these people eating in lonely silence?"[94]

Walled in by barbed-wire fences and armed guards who patrolled the camp, the internees, most of whom were American-born US citizens, were prisoners, a fact that was driven home forcefully when James Hatsuaki Wakasa was shot by an armed guard on April 11, 1943, forty to sixty-five inches inside the barbed-wire fence that ringed the perimeter of the camp. The guard who fired the shots claimed that Wakasa, who had raised his arms after the guard called to him, looked like he was planning to crawl through the fence. The shooting accentuated divisions in the camp between those who countenanced submission and those who advocated protest. "A small group of pro-Japan agitators became increasingly threatening. These men, tough, arrogant, and belligerent, blatantly fashioned knives and other weapons from scrap metal and sat sharpening them in front of their barracks.... All were angry, and focused their resentment primarily on those Issei who worked in positions of responsibility and leadership requiring close contact with the white administrative staff," recalled Yoshiko Uchida. The divisions in the camp at large were replicated in microcosm in individual households, where "the concept of family life was rapidly breaking down." Uchida remembered, "Many children drifted away from their parents, rarely bothering to spend time in their own barracks, even eating all their meals with friends at other mess halls."[95]

Within a month of their arrival, some young internees left Topaz and other relocation centers elsewhere in the West to study at colleges, including the University of Utah and BYU; the State Agricultural College barred them from enrollment. Most of their professors and fellow students were cordial, but many of the students were ostracized and persecuted in the larger community; they were denied employment, harassed on the streets, and denied admission to some church services because of wartime hysteria.[96]

Another 1,000 internees were allowed to leave the camp that fall to work on farms or in businesses such as canneries and restaurants. Early in 1943, after returning to the camp, those who had worked outside completed a survey regarding the treatment they had received. Close to 85 percent reported that their treatment had been "good," 12 percent rated their treatment by whites as "fair," and 3 percent reported a "poor" reception.[97]

Internment affected Japanese American teenagers socially in a variety of ways. Miye Yoshida likened internment to "a three-year summer camp" because she had "never had so many Japanese American friends." Similarly, Takuzo Handa "had a wonderful time," partly because she fell in love. Her time in the camp "enable[d] me to overcome the nagging feeling that mankind is doomed." Meanwhile, John Juji Hada "felt a vast loneliness," and Jim Noda "felt like a prisoner."[98]

Eventually, under a loyalty-oath program announced in February 1943, the government permitted more than 3,000 of those incarcerated to leave Topaz for employment in Utah or other areas away from the West Coast after forswearing allegiance to the Japanese emperor and pledging allegiance to the United States. As part of the loyalty oath, draft-age men were questioned regarding their willingness to fight anywhere in the world for the United States. After their release from camps under the loyalty-oath program, 300 Japanese American families, principally from camps outside of Utah, settled in Tooele, where they worked at Tooele Army

Depot. Meanwhile, 451 internees from Topaz fought in the US Army. Thousands of others remained in the camp until it closed. An additional 560, who were embittered by their experiences at Topaz, refused to pledge unqualified allegiance to the United States and were therefore transferred along with their family members from Topaz to Tule Lake in northeastern California. Of them, 447 requested expatriation or repatriation to Japan.[99]

Although most internees at Topaz left Utah following their release from the camp, many of them returning to the San Francisco Bay Area once the war had ended, some chose to remain. One estimate places the number that chose to settle at least temporarily in the state at 5,000. By 1950 the number of Japanese and Japanese American residents of Utah stood at 3,060, an increase of nearly 1,200 over the 1940 population.[100]

In addition to the internment of more than 10,000 people of Japanese descent at Topaz, more than 50 Japanese Americans were incarcerated at Dalton Wells, a former Civilian Conservation Corps camp that was renamed the Moab Isolation Center. These prisoners, who had been branded by authorities as troublemakers at other internment camps for their vigorous protests of Japanese internment, were held in barracks under military guard without trial, isolated from family, and prohibited at one point from even visiting inmates in adjacent buildings unless accompanied by a guard. Eight of the protesters proved troublesome enough that authorities transferred them to the county jail in Moab. In April 1943 the men were transported to a former Indian school in Leupp, Arizona. Five of them made the trip caged in the bed of a pickup truck in a box with only one hole for ventilation.[101]

A MIXED LEGACY

Evidence regarding Japanese internment camps, increases in juvenile delinquency and assault, rising divorce rates, increased air pollution, and physical and psychological casualties of wartime service serve as reminders that even the legacy of Utah's full-fledged incorporation within the "good war," as World War II has often been called, was mixed. The war's legacy was mixed in another way, too, that historians have sometimes overlooked. Undoubtedly, World War II brought burgeoning population growth, created new jobs, and revitalized the economies of Weber, Davis, Salt Lake, Tooele, Utah, and to a lesser extent Box Elder Counties. Provo's population grew by a phenomenal 43.6 percent between 1940 and 1947. Economically, wartime installations brought new jobs and boosted the construction industry on a much smaller scale in Manti, Monticello, Blanding, and Delta. Moreover, prosperity blanketed the state, thanks to heavy demand and high war-induced prices for products from the state's farms, ranches, and mines. Still, the effects were uneven.

Whereas New Deal largesse had been spread across the state, with significant investments in each county, wartime spending was different: defense spending accentuated the urbanization and industrialization of the Wasatch Front region, increasing that region's economic and political power, while actually bleeding the outlying counties of population and increasing their economic and political marginality. Concentration of population and wealth along the Wasatch Front resulted naturally from the Beehive State's increased incorporation within America's evolving urban-industrial order. Thousands of Utahns relocated to be near defense installations. As Margaret Herbert of Pleasant Grove recalled, "I came to Salt Lake because all of my friends were coming to Salt Lake to work in the military efforts." The out-migration was particularly pronounced from rural regions, as people like Jack Barton's family, who operated a ranch in the Uinta Basin, moved to the Wasatch Front because they "thought they could get a little ahead" due to the wartime boom.[102]

The Census Bureau estimated that by November 1943, twenty-two of the state's twenty-nine counties had fewer residents than in 1940; partly, this reflected the temporary absence of residents serving in the military, but it also reflected civilian migration. Even with Utah's phenomenally high birthrate, only Carbon, Davis, Millard, Salt Lake, Tooele, Utah, and Weber Counties had a larger civilian population in November 1943 than before the war. By 1950, long after soldiers had returned home, seventeen of the state's twenty-nine counties still had fewer residents than in 1940. The massive population gains over the decade had occurred largely in places impacted by heavy government spending and wartime demand for Utah products such as copper and coal: Davis (96 percent population growth), Tooele (60 percent), Weber (47 percent), Utah (42 percent), Carbon (34 percent), and Salt Lake Counties (30 percent). Meanwhile, nine counties experienced double-digit percentage declines in population over the decade, led by Daggett (35.5 percent), Summit (22.6 percent), and Garfield (21.0 percent). Naturally, economic vigor, reflected in housing values, was greatest in Salt Lake, Davis, Utah, and Weber Counties. It was lowest in Summit, Piute, Emery, and Garfield Counties.[103]

The war also abetted a trend that had been apparent since 1932: despite the LDS Church Security Program's quest for self-sufficiency, Utah had been incorporated within America's drive for national security, making the state dependent upon federal investment for its economic prosperity. Total direct federal spending during the war in Utah amounted to at least $1.1 billion and may have been as high as $1.36 billion. Thus, federal investment approximated the combined gross farm income ($587,388,000) and value of gold, silver, copper, lead, and zinc produced in the state ($623,553,000) in the six-year period 1940–45. Whereas agriculture, mining, and the processing of mineral and agricultural products had been the leading sectors of Utah's economy prior to World War II, the war made defense its foremost source of revenue. For a time this seemed to be a temporary aberration; federal defense spending dwindled between 1946 and 1950, jobs declined, and more people moved out of the state than into the region. The presence of wartime defense installations in Utah served as a magnet for additional defense contracts and military spending during the Korean War and Cold War, though. Thus, the economic legacies of World War II endured for decades. Twenty years after the end of the war, defense spending remained "the major source of Utah's income."[104]

CONCLUSION

Many historians have investigated facets of Utah's coming of age. They have sought to pinpoint the pivotal era when Utah became modern, along with the episodes and currents that brought about the change. Many followed the eminent American historian Frederick Jackson Turner in highlighting critical transitional events clustered near the end of the nineteenth century similar to Turner's 1890 closing of the frontier. They did so with good reason: that era was momentous.

In his classic *Great Basin Kingdom*, Leonard Arrington charted the "great capitulation," by which he meant the LDS Church's abandonment of both economic communitarianism and self-sufficiency and its wholesale embrace of individualistic capitalism in the final years of the nineteenth century. "Faith became increasingly separated from community policy, and religion from society. Individualism, speculation, and inequality—once thought to be characteristics of Babylon—were woven into the fabric of Mormon life," he wrote. Arrington pinpointed the 1890s as the crucial decade that marked the "transition from Utah, the Mormon Commonwealth, to Utah, a State in the national commonwealth."[1]

Viewing the same transitional era through the lens of politics, historian Gustive Larson applied the term *Americanization* to Utah's evolution from Mormon theocracy to American state. Larson traced the legislative and judicial crusade against Mormon theocracy and polygamy in the 1870s and 1880s, culminating in the abandonment of religiously based political parties and polygamy in the early 1890s. In Larson's narrative, statehood marked the triumphal conclusion of the transitional era.[2]

As subsequent scholars of Utah and Mormonism scrutinized interpretations of the 1890s as a watershed era, they identified developments beyond the 1890s in the Progressive Era that seemed equally pivotal. Ethan Yorgason situated the "transformation" of Mormonism and the Americanization of the Mormon culture region between 1880 and 1920, arguing that Mormons and non-Mormons united behind economic development and white racial superiority and set the state on a trajectory toward social and economic conservatism in those years. Kathleen Flake identified the critical divide for Mormons with the Reed Smoot hearings of 1904–7 and the resultant Second Manifesto that made plural marriage an excommunicable offense. In *Mormonism in Transition*, Thomas Alexander viewed Wilford Woodruff's 1890s Manifesto as the entry to a "second...phase of Mormon history." Charting the impact of bureaucratization, standardization, modernization, and Progressive reform over the next four decades, he identified the era 1890–1930 as one of "transition" and argued that the revolution in Mormonism "had largely been completed" by 1930.[3]

In his centennial history of Utah, Alexander surveyed the rough outlines of a change that began in the territorial era and culminated following World War I: "From a Mormon kingdom," he wrote, "Utah became a colony of American capitalism" in which raw materials, including agricultural and mineral products, were produced and shipped out of state to be manufactured into finished products. As early as the 1870s Utah had manifested some of these colonial characteristics, but by 1921 Utah might well have been called "an economic colony of Wall Street."[4]

Historians have focused less attention upon the Great Depression and World War II as critical agents of modernization in Utah, although they have acknowledged the importance of those eras in their surveys of the state. Alexander observed, "Utah's economy shifted into a new phase" as Utah moved from being "a colony of Wall Street to a colony of Washington" under the influence of New Deal spending and World War II.[5]

Each of these historians has highlighted elements of a transformation that is synthesized and more broadly interpreted in this volume under the framework of incorporation and globalization: the entire half century was actually a critical, unique period of modernization, incorporation within the nation, and globalization. The thirties and forties, which witnessed an unprecedented infusion of federal funds and carried Utahns around the world, were as crucial to these developments as the previous decades.

The years prior to 1946 set Utahns upon a path to globalization, a process that would accelerate in subsequent decades. Powerful events that reverberated across the world during the first fifty years of statehood, including the Spanish-American War, the Philippine-American War, a deadly influenza epidemic, two world wars, and the worst depression of the century, reached Utahns in their mountain retreats and profoundly influenced their lives. Service in the military carried tens of thousands of Utahns overseas and altered their outlook and worldview. Meanwhile, thousands of southern and eastern Europeans and Japanese and Mexican immigrants entered the state to work in the state's railroads, mines, and smelters. Their migration, impelled partly by events abroad, facilitated Utah's industrialization by providing a cheap, mobile workforce and diversified Utah's population ethnically and religiously. The migrants became part of transnational communities, retaining social, familial, economic, and cultural ties to their homelands while becoming enmeshed in new networks as residents and workers in the Beehive State. The linkages between Utah and distant lands would multiply over the rest of the twentieth century and beyond, but precedents and patterns for globalization were established in the state's adolescent years.

Although Utah's history from the 1760s onward can be loosely understood and interpreted within the context of the centralizing and integrating impact of incorporation and imperialism (a frontier-era variant of incorporation), incorporation especially lends itself as an interpretive framework to developments in Utah's awkward, adolescent years, the first half century of statehood.[6] The scale and scope of resource extraction and economic investment in the decades following 1896 dwarfed enterprises in the pioneer era. Wage labor, corporate procedures, and corporate institutions from railroads to large smelters emerged as the ascendant catalysts of production and distribution. Those early decades of the century witnessed the rise of commercial copper mining and smelting; the spread of commercially oriented agriculture, including dryland farming and capital-intensive irrigation projects; and the development of food-processing industries, from sugar factories to canneries.

Powerful national currents in government and politics, including progressivism, socialism, and the New Deal, altered Utahns' relationship to and incorporation within the nation in the first half century of statehood. Utahns participated in national political crusades and lobbying efforts for Prohibition, reclamation, 100 percent Americanism, and free silver. Affiliation with the national Democratic, Republican, and Socialist Parties crosscut the Mormon and non-Mormon communities, undermining internal loyalties and identities. Much of the political distrust and animus between Mormons and non-Mormons dissipated. Movements that fed upon that animus, including the American Party and the Order of Sevens, collapsed in this era, and Mormon majorities helped to elect non-Mormon governors in 1916, 1924, and 1928. The LDS Church's ability early in the century to sway election results, seen at the polls in 1912 after President Joseph F. Smith publicly endorsed President Taft's candidacy, was compromised by the increased independence of Mormon voters, as reflected in the First Presidency's unsuccessful campaigns in the 1930s to defeat President Roosevelt and Senator Thomas.

Utah's Indian populations reached their nadir and then began to rise in this era. Incorporation was a contested process for Utah's Indians. Militant resistance flared briefly in San Juan County, and hundreds of aggrieved Utes trekked to South Dakota, seeking an alliance with the Sioux against the United States. Goshutes resisted the draft in World War I, and Navajos rejected elements of the Indian New Deal. Although new reservations were established for the Paiutes and Goshutes and the Navajo reservation was expanded, the Utes lost much of their land base due to the federal policy of allotment. The Indian Citizenship Act of 1924 confirmed the US citizenship of all Indians, and hundreds of them fought for the United States in World War II. Indians in this era rode the federal policy pendulum as it swung between assimilation and cultural retention, a pendulum that would continue to shift as the century progressed.

Incorporation extended to cultural values and beliefs, including materialism. Utah's Mormon and Gentile business elites found common ground in economic boosterism and the quest for commercial prosperity. They defined progress in terms of productivity, profit, and state-sanctioned private property. A struggle for the soul of the state unfolded, as the corporate system met the human dimensions of production and as corporate mines, smelters, railroads, and other businesses sought to socialize and incorporate workers within the new order. Part of that socialization was accomplished through civic religion and patriotism, which provided common ground for many laborers and owners. The prospect of upward economic mobility and intergenerational economic mobility also played a role. The agents of mass culture, including radio, cinema, and mass marketing, fostered shared knowledge and identity. Finally, federal arbitration and the legislative guarantee of workers' right to unionize defused class-based tension.

Utahns expected that incorporation within the Union would bring greater self-government, including the ability to acquire and manage the state's land, water, timber, and minerals. But Americans in this urban-industrial era increasingly valued the West's public lands for their recreational, spiritual, and aesthetic value. Thus, the federal government began to reserve valuable timbered lands in the late 1890s in order to conserve them. National parks and monuments were set aside as preserves. Many Utahns endorsed these policies, but federal control placed stockmen and lumber companies at the mercy of federal managers who regulated and restricted their access to national forests, monuments, and parks. Then in the 1930s the remaining public domain was closed to settlement. To a significant degree Utah tended to be divided against itself regarding the propriety of government control. Questions of property, equity, morality, and the balance of power between the state and the nation that were first raised in this era as a result of shifts in public lands management would persist and remain profoundly important for Utah into the twenty-first century.

The economic benefits of incorporation were immense. In mining, agriculture, industry, and business, jobs were created and fortunes were built. Incorporation within the nation opened the floodgates to federal largesse that flowed into the state at the expense of more heavily populated and industrialized states. Congress funded the construction of highways and superbly engineered dams and water systems that the state by itself could not afford to build. The creation of national forests and parks generated additional jobs and appropriations. The economic benefits of incorporation within the Union became fully apparent in the 1930s and 1940s. Beginning with the Reconstruction Finance Corporation and extending through the New Deal era, federal dollars for economic recovery and development poured into the state. Then defense spending during the 1940s expanded Utah's industrial base, generated thousands of jobs at defense installations, and transformed Utah into an economic satellite of Washington, DC.

But the economic legacy of incorporation was mixed. The transformation of society from the land-based, traditional culture of the past to corporate modernism entailed industrial strife and a systematic repression of wageworkers only less destructive than the subjugation of American Indians and other minorities. Handicapped by marginal resources, a shortage of water, and distance from markets, the state at large never attained widespread prosperity. Even the flush times of World War II graced the state unevenly; most of the state's rural counties lost population in the face of job opportunities and economic growth along the Wasatch Front. While the New Deal created temporary jobs, conserved natural resources, and enhanced infrastructure statewide, the concentration of wartime defense installations and factories in a handful of counties along with military service were powerful centripetal forces that marginalized rural Utah and caused the state's outlying counties to hemorrhage as their residents flocked to new opportunities along the Wasatch Front.

The Depression marked a critical juncture in the process of incorporation. LDS Church leaders warned of the perils of dependency and by introducing the Church Security Program or Welfare Plan sought to reenthrone Utah's traditional economic models based upon thrift and self-sufficiency. The finality with which Utahns in the 1930s and 1940s rejected models of self-sufficiency, modest economic attainment, and local control and embraced centralized authority and an economy dependent upon federal largesse marked the true end of economic ideals and aspirations dating to the pioneer era. Utah had entered modern times.

NOTES

ABBREVIATIONS

BYU Brigham Young University
CCF Central Classified Files
DN Deseret News
HBLL Harold B. Lee Library, Brigham Young University, Provo, UT
NA National Archives, College Park, MD
RG Record Group
SLH Salt Lake Herald
SLT Salt Lake Tribune

INTRODUCTION

1. Denise A. Edwards, "Life Spans Oxen, Airplanes," *DN*, July 22, 1972, Church News Section, 7.
2. Alan Trachtenberg, *The Incorporation of America: Culture and Society in the Gilded Age*; Richard Maxwell Brown, *No Duty to Retreat: Violence and Values in American History and Society*; R. Brown, "Western Violence: Structure, Values, Myth." Without using Trachtenberg's terminology, Nancy J. Taniguchi explores several features of Utah's incorporation during the Progressive Era, including integration within national and regional economic networks, the decline in the power of old elites, and the increased importance of federal regulation. See Taniguchi, *Necessary Fraud: Progressive Reform and Utah Coal*, 249–52.

I. POLITICS AT THE TURN OF THE CENTURY

1. *DN*, January 6, 1896.
2. A speech by Orlando W. Powers quoted in his biographical sketch serves as an example of such statements. Orson F. Whitney, *History of Utah*, 4:537.
3. For excellent studies, see B. Carmon Hardy, *Solemn Covenant: The Mormon Polygamous Passage*, 58; Henry Wolfinger, "An Irrepressible Conflict," 124; Edward Leo Lyman, *Political Deliverance: The Mormon Quest for Utah Statehood*, 180–81; and Sarah Barringer Gordon, *The Mormon Question: Polygamy and Constitutional Conflict in Nineteenth-Century America*.

4. George Q. Cannon, *Collected Discourses Delivered by President Wilford Woodruff, His Two Counselors, the Twelve Apostles, and Others*, 2:276.

5. On the territories as empire and the process of federal growth, see especially Walter Nugent, "Frontiers and Empires in the Late Nineteenth Century." See also J. E. Eblen, *The First and Second United States Empires: Governors and Territorial Government, 1874–1912*; Arthur Bestor, "Constitutionalism and the Settlement of the West: The Attainment of Consensus, 1754–1784"; Robert F. Berkhofer Jr., "The Northwest Ordinance and the Principle of Territorial Evolution"; Berkhofer, "Jefferson, the Ordinance of 1784 and the Origins of the American Territorial System"; and Howard R. Lamar, *The Far Southwest, 1845–1912: A Territorial History*, 305–414.

6. Trachtenberg, *Incorporation of America*; R. Brown, *No Duty to Retreat*; R. Brown, "Western Violence"; Carlos A. Schwantes, "The Concept of the Wageworkers' Frontier: A Framework for Future Research"; John Walton, *Western Times and Water Wars: State, Culture, and Rebellion in California*. Of these we depend most heavily upon Trachtenberg and Brown.

7. Trachtenberg, *Incorporation of America*, 3–6.

8. Thomas Cochran quoted in ibid., 7.

9. Lyman, *Political Deliverance*, demonstrates this point nicely but asks few questions about what the corporate involvement of the church and its political connection imply about changes in Mormon culture. The relationship between corporate involvement and culture is explored in Ethan R. Yorgason, *Transformation of the Mormon Culture Region*.

10. Richard W. Peterson, *Bonanza Rich: Lifestyles of the Western Mining Entrepreneurs*.

11. Leonard J. Arrington, *Great Basin Kingdom: An Economic History of the Latter-day Saints, 1830–1900*, 64–65, 196–205, 235–65; Horace Greeley, *An Overland Journey from New York to San Francisco in the Summer of 1859*, quoted in William Mulder and Russell Mortensen, eds., *Among the Mormons: Historic Accounts by Contemporary Observers*, 324–28.

12. Isaac Russell to National Board of Censorship, January 24, 1912, Box 4, Folder 16, Scott Kenney Collection. For a good statement on how young Utahns began to coalesce into a conscious force, see Gene A. Sessions, ed., *Mormon Democrat: The Religious and Political Memoirs of James Henry Moyle*, esp. 157–236. On the experiences of young Mormons in eastern educational institutions, see Thomas W. Simpson, "Mormons Study 'Abroad': Latter-day Saints in American Higher Education, 1870–1940."

13. G. Sessions, *Henry J. Moyle*, 28.

14. Arrington, *Great Basin Kingdom*, 380–412.

15. On Rawlins, see Joseph L. Rawlins, "Autobiography," typescript copy, Marriott Library, University of Utah; *"The Unfavored Few": The Autobiography of Joseph L. Rawlins*; and Joan Ray Harrow, "Joseph L. Rawlins, Father of Utah Statehood." For Frank J. Cannon, see Cannon and Harvey J. O'Higgins, *Under the Prophet in Utah: The National Menace of a Political Priestcraft*; and Kenneth M. Godfrey, "Frank J. Cannon: Declension in the Mormon Kingdom."

16. Stanley S. Ivins, "A Constitution for Utah"; Jean Bickmore White, "The Making of the Convention President: The Political Education of John Henry Smith."

17. Quoted in Mulder and Mortensen, *Among the Mormons*, 418–19.

18. G. Sessions, *James H. Moyle*, 183.

19. Anthony W. Ivins, a young Utah Democrat from St. George, was apparently high on the list of gubernatorial possibilities. On learning he had accepted a mission to Mexico for the church, party workers then approached Heber J. Grant, businessman apostle, to whom a "majority of" convention votes were "already pledged." Ruled an inappropriate candidate

by Wilford Woodruff because he was a polygamist, and perhaps because church policy at the moment did not favor strengthening the Democratic Party, Grant was also unavailable. Much later he admitted how appealing the offer had been; he asked a General Conference crowd in 1934, "Do you think I would not like to have been the first governor of the State of Utah, where I was born? If you do, you are mistaken. I do not know of anything that I should have liked better than that at that particular time." See Grant to Katharine Ivins, March 11, 1938, Grant Papers; and *Conference Report* (October 1934): 126, both cited in L. F. Aydelotte, "The Political Thought and Activity of Heber J. Grant, Seventh President of the Church of Jesus Christ of Latter-day Saints," 18–19.

20. For a good treatment of this election, see Jean Bickmore White, "Utah State Elections, 1895–1900," 56–61, 81–95.

21. Edward Leo Lyman, "Heber M. Wells and the Beginnings of Utah's Statehood," 42–43; Gustive O. Larson, "An Industrial Home for Polygamous Wives."

22. Lyman, "Heber M. Wells," 60–67; *Report of the Coal Mine Inspector for the State of Utah from April 6th to December 31st, 1896*, 47.

23. See J. White, "Utah State Elections," 95–108; Lyman, *Political Deliverance*, 264–85; F. Cannon and O'Higgins, *Under the Prophet in Utah*, 144–69. White and Lyman depend heavily upon newspaper accounts and the journal of Abraham H. Cannon, apostle son of George Q. Cannon and brother of Frank. Frank Cannon and O'Higgins presented the former's reminiscence written after he was a Denver newspaperman and no longer associated with the church. It was given something of a muckraking spin by O'Higgins. For the bitter relationship between Cannon and Brown, see Cannon and O'Higgins, *Under the Prophet*, 220–25. In the senatorial election of 1898, Brown's wife and his mistress, Anna M. Bradley, forgot their bitter differences long enough to publicly indict Cannon's private morals. As Cannon recalled, this show of unity "passed in the miseries that overtook them…Mrs. Brown" dying "of the scandal" and Bradley killing Brown in a Washington, DC, hotel (ibid., 224). See also Linda Thatcher, "'The Gentile Polygamist': Arthur Brown, Ex-Senator from Utah."

24. Davis Bitton, "The B. H. Roberts Case of 1898–1900"; Truman G. Madsen, *Defender of the Faith: The B. H. Roberts Story.*

25. Edward Leo Lyman, "The Alienation of an Apostle from His Quorum: The Moses Thatcher Case," 68, cites Abraham H. Cannon Journal, August 20, 1886.

26. Material is voluminous. Important are Calvin Reasoner, *The Late Manifesto in Politics: Practical Working of "Counsel" in Relation to Civil and Religious Liberty in Utah*; Stanley S. Ivins, *The Moses Thatcher Case*; Ivins, "A Constitution for Utah," 100–116; C. W. Penrose, *The Thatcher Episode: A Concise Statement in the Case*; Lyman, "Alienation of an Apostle"; and M. A. Miller, "Thatcher Resilenced."

27. James R. Clark, comp., *Messages of the First Presidency of the Church of Jesus Christ of Latter-day Saints, 1822–1964*, 3:271–77.

28. J. White, "Utah State Elections," 112.

29. Ibid., 115–16; John P. Hatch, ed., *Danish Apostle: The Diaries of Anthon H. Lund, 1890–1921*, 81.

30. J. White, "Utah State Elections," 110–29; Harold U. Faulkner, *American Economic History.*

31. J. White, "Utah State Elections," 126, 146.

32. Ibid., 157–59; J. White, "Gentle Persuaders"; Elizabeth C. McCrimmon, "Dr. Martha Hughes Cannon: First Woman State Senator in America," unpublished manuscript, Utah State Historical Society.

33. *SLT*, November 1, 1896, cited in J. White, "Gentle Persuaders," 33.

34. J. White, "Gentle Persuaders," 38–39; S. A. Kenner, *Utah as It Is with a Comprehensive Statement of Utah as It Was*, 450–51.

35. J. White, "Gentle Persuaders," 42–49; Stewart L. Grow, "Utah's Senatorial Election of 1899: The Election That Failed."

36. Raye Price, "Utah's Leading Ladies of the Arts," 82–83; Kenner, *Utah as It Is*, 112, 439–40; Andrew Jenson, *Latter-day Saint Biographical Encyclopedia*, 4:186.

37. J. White, "Utah State Elections," 159–60.

38. Ronald Gerald Coleman, "A History of Blacks in Utah, 1825–1910," 97–103, 188–210.

39. *SLT*, November 15, 1896; *DN*, November 17, 18, 19, 1896, cited in J. White, "Utah State Elections," 160–63.

40. *SLT*, Feb. 5, 1897, cited in J. White, "Utah State Elections," 171.

41. Paragraphs on the resurgence of polygamy depend heavily upon Hardy, *Solemn Covenant*, especially on chapters 4–7 and appendix 1; and D. Michael Quinn's monograph-length article "LDS Church Authority and New Plural Marriages, 1890–1904." The Utah Commission, or Board of Registration and Election in the Territory of Utah, was established by Congress under the Edmunds Act of 1882 and functioned until 1896, when Utah became a state. Among its duties, the commission identified and disfranchised polygamists. See Stewart L. Grow, "A Study of the Utah Commission."

42. Carmon Hardy discusses Roberts's domestic situation at length and concludes that his marriage to Dr. Margaret Curtis Shipp took place after the Manifesto, perhaps as late as 1894, as claimed by antipolygamy activist Charles Mostyn Owen. For Hardy's careful documentation, see *Solemn Covenant*, 246–47, 270–71nn. See also Martha Sonntag Bradley, *Kidnapped from That Land: The Government Raids on the Short Creek Polygamists*, 18–39.

43. *SLT*, September 15, November 3, 1898, cited in J. White, "Utah State Elections," 202, 211.

44. Bitton, "B. H. Roberts Case," 32–33; Craig Mikkelsen, "The Politics of B. H. Roberts," 34–35.

45. See *SLH*, November 5, 6, 1898; and *SLT*, November 7, 1898, all cited in J. White, "Utah State Elections," 212–16. The "whip" statement is from a Joseph F. Smith interview in the *Salt Lake Tribune*, January 9, 1899, cited in Hardy, *Solemn Covenant*, 246, 270.

46. Bitton, "B. H. Roberts Case," 35.

47. Jean Bickmore White, ed., *Church, State, and Politics: The Diaries of John Henry Smith*, entries for September 6, 1898, and February 2, 1899, on 406, 438.

48. For accounts of the election, see F. Cannon and O'Higgins, *Under the Prophet in Utah*, 222–34; J. White, "Utah State Elections," 218–36; Grow, "Utah's Senatorial Election of 1899"; and B. H. Roberts, *A Comprehensive History of the Church of Jesus Christ of Latter-day Saints*, 6:344–45.

49. *DN*, February 2, 1897, cited in Harrow, "Joseph L. Rawlins," 120.

50. Other states where state elections failed included Wyoming and California in the West and Delaware and Pennsylvania in the East. Late in 1900 Pennsylvania launched a reform movement that culminated in the Seventeenth Amendment to the Constitution in 1913. See Noble Warrum, *Utah since Statehood: Historical and Biographical*, 1:122.

51. On the war and Utah in overview, see Richard I. Reeves, "Utah and the Spanish American War"; and Richard C. Roberts, "History of the Utah National Guard, 1894–1954," 74–112. Contemporary accounts include A. Prentiss, ed., *The History of the Utah Volunteers in the Spanish American War and in the Philippine Islands*; and Charles R. Mabey, *The Utah Batteries: A History*. For an intimate sense of crisis church leaders felt in the late 1890s, see Scott G. Kenney, ed., *Wilford Woodruff's Journal, 1833–1898*, 9:443–563; J. White, *Church,*

State, and Politics, 365–471; Seymour B. Young Diary for 1896 to 1900, microfilm; and especially Brigham Young Jr., Diaries 1897–1898, microfilm, LDS Church History Library. On Mormon pacifism, see D. Michael Quinn, "The Mormon Church and the Spanish-American War: An End to Selective Pacifism."

52. *Conference Report* (Salt Lake City: Church of Jesus Christ of Latter-day Saints, 1898), 2–9, 25–28, 31–32, 39–40, 56–60, 81–88.

53. M. R. Merrill, *Reed Smoot: Apostle in Politics*, 98.

54. Coleman, "History of Blacks in Utah," 166–70. Leaving only a skeleton force of 16 at Fort Douglas, the 486 men of the Twenty-Fourth fought in Cuba and returned to a gigantic welcome in Salt Lake City on September 30.

55. Susa Young Gates, "Fashions," quoted in R. Paul Cracroft, "Susa Young Gates: Her Life and Literary Work," 23–24.

56. Brigham Young Jr., Diaries 1896–1898, entries for April 24–28, 1898; D. Quinn, "Mormon Church and the Spanish-American War," 28; R. Roberts, "History of the Utah National Guard." American secretary of state John Hay referred to the conflict as the "splendid little war."

57. *SLH*, April 26, 1898; and *SLT*, April 26, 1898, both cited in R. Roberts, "History of the Utah National Guard," 78–79.

58. R. Roberts, "History of the Utah National Guard," chap. 4; Mabey, *Utah Batteries*; Prentiss, *History of the Utah Volunteers*.

59. Milton R. Merrill, *Reed Smoot: Utah Politician*, 52; Eugene Young, "Revival of the Mormon Problem"; Eugene Young, "Polygamy Is Reviving," *New York Herald*, February 5, 1899.

60. See James David Giullilan, *Thomas Corwin Iliff: Apostle of Home Missions in the Rocky Mountains*, 65–97; Hardy, *Solemn Covenant*, 248, 297; and John M. Whitaker Diary, August 23, 1896, Whitaker Collection.

61. Bitton, "B. H. Roberts Case," 36–46; Hardy, *Solemn Covenant*, 244–50; Gary J. Bergera, *The Autobiography of B. H. Roberts*, chaps. 22–23; B. Roberts, *Comprehensive History of the Church*, 6:363–74.

62. See M. R. Merrill, *Apostle in Politics*, 16.

63. *SLT*, January 10, 1900; *SLH*, January 13, 1900.

64. *DN*, February 3, 1900; *SLH*, April 25, 1900; *SLT*, February 9, 18, 1900; *SLH*, February 20, 1900; M. C. Merrill, *Utah Pioneer and Apostle: Marriner Wood Merrill and His Family*, 248–50; Harrow, "Joseph L. Rawlins," 116–69.

65. Biographical material on these four men is from M. R. Merrill, *Apostle in Politics*; M. R. Merrill, *Reed Smoot: Utah Politician*; O. N. Malmquist, *The First 100 Years: A History of the "Salt Lake Tribune," 1871–1971*, chaps. 15–20; Kent S. Larsen, *The Life of Thomas Kearns*; J. F. Paschal, *Mr. Justice Sutherland: A Man against the State*; J. White, "Utah State Elections"; and Lyman, "Heber M. Wells."

66. Abraham Owen Smoot was among Mormondom's financial leaders and had been mayor of Salt Lake City for a decade, mayor of Provo for a similar period, and president of Utah Stake for twenty years. For a cogent and convincing study of family in Mormon leadership during this period, see D. Michael Quinn, "The Mormon Hierarchy, 1832–1932: An American Elite" and *The Mormon Hierarchy: Origins of Power*.

67. See the Wells clipping file from *SLH*, January 1900, Special Collections, Marriott Library, University of Utah, for the included material.

68. *SLT*, March 20, 27, April 25, 1900; *DN*, March 23, 1900; *SLH*, April 3, 25, 1900.

69. Larsen, *Life of Thomas Kearns*, 44–50.

70. Hatch, *Danish Apostle*, 101. Malmquist, *First 100 Years*, 186–87, 190–91, 196, 198–99, discusses Snow's deal with Kearns at length; and 226 cites a *Salt Lake Tribune* article dated January 12, 1903, reporting the alleged conversation between Smoot and McKinley. See also R. J. Snow, "The American Party in Utah: A Study of Political Party Struggles during the Early Years of Statehood," 26–30. Snow cites Smoot's account of Lorenzo Snow's instructions to him not to run (57).

71. Hatch, *Danish Apostle*, 107.

72. The day after Snow's death, former senator Arthur Brown is said to have announced to the crowd assembled at a Salt Lake bar that "Tom Kearns died last night." As historian Malmquist put it, Snow's death was "another ebb" in what had been a "tide, rising slowly … toward … accommodation" (*First 100 Years*, 191).

73. Paschal, *Mr. Justice Sutherland*, 45–53, esp. 50, 51; M. R. Merrill, *Apostle in Politics*, 21, 26, 28, 32, 113.

74. M. R. Merrill, *Apostle in Politics*, 20.

75. *SLH*, March 12,1900.

76. Kathleen Flake, *The Politics of American Religious Identity: The Seating of Senator Reed Smoot, Mormon Apostle*; Michael H. Paulos, "Under the Gun at the Smoot Hearings: Joseph F. Smith's Testimony."

2. POLITICS IN THE PROGRESSIVE ERA

1.   R. Snow, "American Party in Utah," 62–63. This treatment of the American Party depends upon Snow but also utilizes M. R. Merrill, *Apostle in Politics*; Thomas G. Alexander and James Allen, *Mormons and Gentiles: A History of Salt Lake City*; and John S. McCormick, "Red Lights in Zion: Salt Lake City's Stockade, 1908–11."

2.   Callister to Smoot, March 10, 1903, quoted in M. R. Merrill, *Apostle in Politics*, 180.

3.   Ibid.

4.   The best source on this subject is Craig W. Fuller's excellent "Land Rush in Zion: Opening of the Uncompahgre and Uintah Indian Reservations." See also Newell C. Remington, "A History of the Gilsonite Industry"; and Wesley C. Calef, "Land Associations and Occupance Problems in the Uinta Country."

5.   *SLT*, July 3, 1905; *Box Elder News*, June 29, 1905.

6.   *SLT* for July, August, September 1905, esp. July 9, 17, and August 2.

7.   *DN*, September 23, 28, 1908.

8.   Frank C. Robertson, *A Ram in the Thicket: The Story of a Roaming Homesteader Family on the Mormon Frontier*, 218–20.

9.   *DN*, August 23, 1908, is among the sources of information on Belle London's role.

10. See J. McCormick, "Red Lights in Zion"; Jeffrey Nichols, *Polygamy and Prostitution: Comparative Morality in Salt Lake City, 1847–1911*, 135–67; R. Snow, "American Party in Utah," esp. 172–96, 206–7; and Alexander and Allen, *Mormons and Gentiles*, 147–51.

11. *DN*, September 23, 1908; Alexander and Allen, *Mormons and Gentiles*, 148–50.

12. *DN*, December 14, 1908.

13. R. Snow, "American Party in Utah," 172–95, esp. 179–84.

14. *DN*, September 15, 1908.

15. M. R. Merrill, *Reed Smoot: Utah Politician*, 10–15. See also *SLH*, July 11, 1908, cited in William L. Roper and Leonard J. Arrington, *William Spry: Man of Firmness, Governor of Utah*, 71.

16. *Inter-Mountain Republican*, December 9, 1908, cited in R. Snow, "American Party in Utah," 192.

17. R. Snow, "American Party in Utah," 226.

18. Topham's conviction was based as much upon hearsay and prejudice as upon solid evidence. See Nichols, *Polygamy and Prostitution*, 158–61, 165, 186.

19. Thomas G. Alexander, "Political Patterns of Early Statehood, 1896–1919," 418–23; Thomas G. Alexander, *Utah, the Right Place*, 262–63.

20. Thomas G. Alexander, *Mormonism in Transition: A History of the Latter-day Saints, 1890–1930*, 258–71; Paul H. Peterson, *An Historical Analysis of the Word of Wisdom*.

21. M. R. Merrill, *Apostle in Politics*, 189.

22. *SLT*, January 15, 16, 18, 30, 31, February 3, 18, 1903; and *SLH*, January 18, 1903, all quoted in F. T. Morn, "Simon Bamberger: A Jew in a Mormon Commonwealth" 79–82.

23. M. R. Merrill, *Apostle in Politics*, 190; Bruce Dyer, "A Study of the Forces Leading to the Adoption of Prohibition in Utah in 1917," 9. As Dyer points out, the *Inter-Mountain Republican* devoted a large space on its "front page to anti-liquor propaganda." Under the heading "Shall Utah Have Prohibition?" were "run the opinions of those who favored either state-wide prohibition or tightly controlled local option." For information on Callister's role as Smoot's field marshal and church liaison, see Ellen Gunnell Callister, "The Political Career of Edward Henry Callister, 1885–1916."

24. *Inter-Mountain Republican*, March 18, 1908, quoted in Dyer, "Forces Leading to the Adoption," 12.

25. *Conference Report* (April 1908): 23, 27, 64–65, 69.

26. *SLT*, April 6, 1908.

27. Kiesel to Smoot, May 28, 1908, quoted in M. R. Merrill, *Apostle in Politics*, 190.

28. Ibid.; Kenneth G. Stauffer, "Utah Politics, 1912–1918," 106.

29. Dyer, "Forces Leading to the Adoption," 19.

30. W. Roper and Arrington, *William Spry*.

31. Joseph Howell has not been the object of much attention biographically. From Wellsville, Howell was elected to Congress for seven terms (1902–14). Well liked throughout the state, he was sometimes criticized for his loyalty to the Smoot machine and for being so long in office that he had distanced himself from the voters. M. R. Merrill lauds his contributions to the Smoot machine and intelligent contributions as a party man. See *Apostle in Politics*, chap. 4. Also see the Herschel Bullen Papers.

32. *Conference Report* (October 1908): 64–65. See also Dyer, "Forces Leading to the Adoption," 20–23; and M. R. Merrill, *Apostle in Politics*, 189.

33. Dyer, "Forces Leading to the Adoption," 21–22.

34. M. R. Merrill, *Apostle in Politics*, 191.

35. Ibid., 196.

36. Ibid.

37. Reed Smoot to Joseph F. Smith, January 21, 1909, quoted in ibid., 193.

38. Smoot to Smith, February 15, 1909; Smith to Smoot, February 15, 1909; E. H. Callister, Thos. Hull, and James H. Anderson to Smith, February 15, 1909; and Smith to Callister, Hull, and Anderson, February 16, 1909, cited in ibid., 194–95.

39. W. Roper and Arrington, *William Spry*, 82–83; Dyer, "Forces Leading to the Adoption," 42–47.

40. Reed Smoot Diary, September 29, 1910, in *In the World: The Diaries of Reed Smoot*, edited by Harvard S. Heath, 69–70; Nephi L. Morris to Francis M. Lyman, March 20, 1912, cited in Stauffer, "Utah Politics, 1912–1918," 106.

41. For the outcome of the June election, see *DN*, June 27, 1911. See also Brent G. Thompson, "'Standing between Two Fires': Mormons and Prohibition, 1908–1917," 43–44.

42. *Conference Report* (October 1911): 128.

43. Alexander, *Mormonism in Transition*, 74–91, 119–24.

44. *SLT*, September 7, 1912.

45. *SLT*, September 7, 1912; Smoot Diary, September 24, 1912, in *In the World*, edited by Heath, 162; Brian Q. Cannon, "'Taft Has Made a Good President': Mormons and Presidential Politics in the Election of 1912."

46. *Conference Report* (October 1912): 66–68, 126. Joseph F. Smith told of "a man, high in authority in the nation," who "damned" the Constitution, arguing that "'the popular sentiment of the people is the constitution!'" That, declared Smith, "is the sentiment of anarchism that . . . is spreading over 'the land of liberty and home of the brave.' We do not tolerate it. Latter-day Saints cannot tolerate such a spirit as this. It is anarchy. It means destruction. It is the spirit of mobocracy. . . . [W]e cannot afford to yield to that spirit or contribute to it in the least degree" (ibid., 10–11).

47. B. Cannon, "'Taft Has Made a Good President'"; C. Austin Wahlquist, "The 1912 Presidential Election," 95; Stauffer, "Utah Politics, 1912–1918," 20–92.

48. *DN*, July 20, 1916, cited in Dyer, "Forces Leading to the Adoption," 62.

49. M. R. Merrill, *Apostle in Politics*, 207–11; John M. Whitaker, Daily Journal 1881–1949, January 18, 1914, Whitaker Collection.

50. See Whitaker, Daily Journal, Whitaker Collection; and Lyman Clarence Pedersen, "John Mills Whitaker: Diarist, Educator, Churchman," 183–93.

51. Whitaker journal entries during March, April, and May 1914, Whitaker Collection. This was not the first time that Mormons and Evangelicals had cooperated in working toward Prohibition. Heber J. Grant had previously become an officer in the Anti-Saloon League of Utah, and in 1908 Rev. Louis S. Fuller, the league's superintendent in Utah, met several times with Grant and other LDS general authorities. See Alexander, *Mormonism in Transition*, 262–63.

52. *DN*, October 13, 1914.

53. Whitaker, Daily Journal, October 22, 1914, Whitaker Collection.

54. Smoot Diary, November 13, 1914, March 10, 1915, in *In the World*, edited by Heath, 247–48, 263; Nephi Morris to Smoot, February 18, 1915; Smoot to Morris, March 9, 1915, cited in Stauffer, "Utah Politics, 1912–1918," 147.

55. Under a heading of January 1915 in his diary, John H. Whitaker records two conversations with Father W. K. Ryan during the legislative debate.

56. *Progressive*, February 1916 [no day listed], quoted in Stauffer, "Utah Politics, 1912–1918," 146.

57. *Goodwin's Weekly*, January 9, 27, 1915, quoted in Stauffer, "Utah Politics, 1912–1918," 146.

58. Bruce Dyer interview with Anna Startup, Provo, UT, March 25, 1958, referenced in Dyer, "Forces Leading to the Adoption," 98. With reference to Startup's combative approach to the legislative process, see John M. Whitaker's Daily Journal, January 1–March 15, 1915, Whitaker Collection. Whitaker tells of trying to get Startup to moderate his approach while he stayed at Whitaker's home during the legislative session.

59. Whitaker, Daily Journal, January 1–March 18, 1915, Whitaker Collection; *DN*, March 19, 1915.

60. Whitaker Journals, n.d., 199, Whitaker Collection.

61. J. Cecil Alter, *Early Utah Journalism: A Half Century of Forensic Warfare, Waged by the West's Most Militant Press*, 94.

62. Thompson, "'Standing between Two Fires,'" 47.

63. *Kane County News*, April 1, 1915; *DN*, April 2, 1915; Dyer, "Forces Leading to the Adoption," 102.

64. *Conference Report* (April 1915): 66, 139–40; Dyer, "Forces Leading to the Adoption," 100–105 (emphasis added).

65. Dyer, "Forces Leading to the Adoption," 104. Charles Peterson commuted from BYU with Dyer during 1957 and 1958 while both were working on master's degrees and listened in for hours while Dyer conversed with Preston Nibley and John H. Whitaker about classified records and personal experiences.

66. See Whitaker, Daily Journal, March 17–26, 1916, Whitaker Collection.

67. E. H. Callister to Reed Smoot, August 8, 1916, cited in M. R. Merrill, *Apostle in Politics*, 213. See also Brad Hainsworth, "Utah State Elections, 1916–1924," 39.

68. Thompson, "'Standing between Two Fires,'" 50.

69. Morn, "Simon Bamberger," 111–15; Stauffer, "Utah Politics, 1912–1918," 163–64; Dyer, "Forces Leading to the Adoption," 117.

70. On Wilson and the campaign of 1916, see Stauffer, "Utah Politics, 1912–1918," 180–91; and *Salt Lake Herald-Republican*, November 10, 1916, as cited in Stauffer, "Utah Politics, 1912–1918," 191. See also David Sarasohn, "The Election of 1916: Realigning the Rockies," which shows Mormons in states neighboring Utah voting heavily for Wilson in 1912 and all mountain states going Democratic in 1916 in a movement that, while not revolutionary in character, aligned them with the Democrats in a way that persisted through World War II.

71. John R. Sillito, "Parley P. Christensen: A Political Biography, 1869–1954," 122.

72. Ibid. On Anthony W. Ivins's role, see *SLT*, September 9, January 20, 1916, quoted in Stauffer, "Utah Politics, 1912–1918," 187–90.

73. For most of this development, we have depended on Stauffer, "Utah Politics, 1912–1918," 144–91, but have drawn also from M. R. Merrill, *Apostle in Politics*, 177–239; Dyer, "Forces Leading to the Adoption," 108–25; Morn, "Simon Bamberger," 111–43; and Callister, "Political Career of Edward Henry Callister," 141–68.

74. B. H. Roberts, *Proceedings of the Democratic State Convention*, 21; Stauffer, "Utah Politics, 1912–1918," 165–66.

75. Stauffer, "Utah Politics, 1912–1918," 184.

76. *SLT*, November 9, 14, 1916, cited in Stauffer, "Utah Politics, 1912–1918," 190; see also 184. There was some substance in the charge that Sutherland was a "tool of the interests," if not in the Senate, then professionally as a lawyer when he and his firm had represented the Rio Grande Western Railway. See Taniguchi, *Necessary Fraud*.

77. Stauffer, "Utah Politics, 1912–1918," 186.

78. Statistics are taken from Stauffer, "Utah Politics, 1912–1918," 189. Hainsworth, "Utah State Elections," presents a slightly different set of figures, perhaps because Stauffer counted fusionist votes with the Democratic vote. Stauffer and Bruce Dyer both refer to the election of 1916 as a revolution, and indeed so it seemed to be. Stauffer, "Utah Politics, 1912–1918," 189; Dyer, "Factors Leading to the Adoption," 113–21.

79. Stauffer, "Utah Politics, 1912–1918," 191.

80. *SLT*, March 11, 1917. On progressive legislation, see Hainsworth, "Utah State Elections," 43–45; and Stauffer, "Utah Politics, 1912–1918," 193–97. On Thurman, see John R. Alley Jr., "Utah State Supreme Court Justice Samuel R. Thurman."

81. Malmquist, *First 100 Years*, 292–301.

82. *SLT*, November 4, 1918, quoted in W. Roper and Arrington, *William Spry*, 292–93.

83. For information on the election of 1918, we depended on Stauffer, "Utah Politics, 1912–1918," 192–200; and Hainsworth, "Utah State Elections," 46–61.

84. Richard C. Roberts, "The Utah National Guard in the Great War, 1917–18," 312–16; Brandon Johnson, "'A Perfect Hell': Utah Doughboys in the Meuse-Argonne Offensive," 338–42; Noble Warrum, *Utah in the World War*, 165–442; Helen Z. Papanikolas, "Immigrants, Minorities, and the Great War," 354, 361; John D. Barton, *A History of Duchesne County*, 225; Allan Kent Powell, "Our Cradles Were in Germany: Utah's German American Community and World War I," 377–78.

85. Papanikolas, "Immigrants, Minorities, and the Great War," 349, 354, 357, 367, 385; A. Powell, "Our Cradles Were in Germany," 380.

86.   R. Roberts, "Utah National Guard in the Great War," 318; Johnson, "'Perfect Hell,'" 341.

87.   R. Roberts, "Utah National Guard in the Great War," 324–29; Warrum, *Utah in the World War*, 56–59.

88. Warrum, *Utah in the World War*, 56–59; Johnson, "'Perfect Hell,'" 344, 350; R. Roberts, "Utah National Guard in the Great War," 327; Allan Kent Powell, "World War I in Utah."

89. Warrum, *Utah in the World War*, 66–69; Miriam B. Murphy, "'If Only I Shall Have the Right Stuff': Utah Women in World War I."

90. Warrum, *Utah in the World War*, 103, 127; Albert C. T. Antrei, *A History of Sanpete County*, 256; Janet Burton Seegmiller, *A History of Iron County: Community above Self*, 103.

91. Warrum, *Utah in the World War*, 105–6; A. Powell, "Our Cradles Were in Germany," 385–86.

92. Warrum, *Utah in the World War*, 121–24, 131; Pearl D. Wilson, *A History of Juab County*, 164.

93. Frederick M. Huchel, *A History of Box Elder County*, 235; Linda King Newell, *A History of Piute County*, 234; Newell, *A History of Garfield County*, 254; Jessie L. Embry, *A History of Wasatch County*, 116; Ronald G. Watt, *A History of Carbon County*, 79, 170. Potash was needed to recycle aluminum. Antimony was used as an alloy in lead and tin products. Ozokerite was used in manufacturing rubber, insulating electric wires, and increasing heat resistance in candles.

94.   F. Ross Peterson, *A History of Cache County*, 152; Richard Neitzel Holzapfel, *A History of Utah County*, 171.

95.   R. Roberts, "Utah National Guard in the Great War," 329; *Ogden Standard*, November 12, 1918, quoted in Leonard J. Arrington, "The Influenza Epidemic of 1918–19 in Utah," 170–71; Embry, *History of Wasatch County*, 122.

96. Arrington, "Influenza Epidemic," 176; McPherson, "Influenza Epidemic of 1918," 191–200.

97. Arrington, "Influenza Epidemic"; Jeffrey K. Taubenberger and David M. Morens, "1918 Influenza: The Mother of All Pandemics"; "Scientists Find Earliest Known Evidence of 1918 Influenza Pandemic."

98. *Goodwin's Weekly*, August 11, 1917, quoted in Stauffer, "Utah Politics, 1912–1918," 200; John S. McCormick, "Hornets in the Hive: Socialists in Early Twentieth-Century Utah."

99. For Howell's response to him, see Bullen Papers.

100. The best source on Christensen is John Sillito's excellent work "Parley P. Christensen"; for material in these two paragraphs, we have depended on p. 86. The quote is from the *Park Record*, August 27, 1910. See also Gaylon L. Caldwell, "Utah's First Presidential Candidate: Parley P. Christensen."

101. *Goodwin's Weekly*, January 23, 1915, termed him a "man without a party" and charged that he had bolted only "because he couldn't hog the whole show." Quoted in Sillito, "Parley P. Christensen," 106–7.
102. Sillito, "Parley P. Christensen," 170; *DN*, July 23, 1920.
103. Sillito, "Parley P. Christensen," 121–98.
104. Ibid., 171.

3. AGRICULTURE IN THE NEW STATE

1. Leonard J. Arrington and Thomas G. Alexander, *A Dependent Commonwealth: Utah's Economy from Statehood to the Great Depression*, 35–36; E. B. Brossard, *Important Factors in the Operation of Irrigated Utah Farms*, 26.
2. Jill Thorley Warnick, "Women Homesteaders in Utah, 1869–1934," 47.
3. See Stanford J. Layton, *"To No Privileged Class": The Rationalization of Homesteading and Rural Life in the Early Twentieth-Century American West*, esp. 22–23; Robert Alan Goldberg, *Back to the Soil: The Jewish Farmers of Clarion, Utah, and Their World*; and William L. Bowers, *The Country Life Movement in America, 1900–1920*.
4. The best single volume on land policy during these years is Paul W. Gates, *History of Public Land Law Development*.
5. Among the best-known publications were *Irrigation Age*, a periodical with regional and national aspirations that was published in Salt Lake City for several years during the 1890s under the editorship of William E. Smythe, and Smythe's *The Conquest of Arid America*, which extols Mormon irrigation and Utah development. Clesson S. Kinney, *A Treatise on the Law of Irrigation*, was a learned and comprehensive lexicon of water law worldwide produced by an unflagging Salt Lake City irrigation lawyer; still relevant is the superb work of George Thomas, *The Development of Institutions under Irrigation: With Special Reference to Early Utah Conditions*. Equally a classic of Utah irrigation is Elwood Mead, *Report of Irrigation Investigations in Utah*.
6. *Report of the State Bureau of Immigration, Labor and Statistics for the Years 1913–1914*, 24–29. For an effective treatment of how William H. Smart, president of the Wasatch Stake, interpreted his call to lead Mormon settlers into the Uinta Basin, see William B. Smart, *Mormonism's Last Colonizer: The Life and Times of William H. Smart*.
7. In Woolf's defense it should be said that after promoting a project by raising a pampered crop near Green River, Utah, he blew the whistle on a Nevada project that rested on very shaky water prospects. See *The Autobiography of William L. Woolf*, 32–35, 41–65, copy in L. Tom Perry Special Collections, HBLL.
8. Charles H. Brough, *Irrigation in Utah*, 88; Leonard J. Arrington, *Beet Sugar in the West: A History of the Utah-Idaho Sugar Company, 1891–1966*, 20–21.
9. Typescript titled "Historical Information, La Sal National Forest," 133–34, Supervisor's Office, Manti–La Sal National Forest, Price, UT; Goldberg, *Back to the Soil*, 55–85, 126; Everett L. Cooley, "Clarion, Utah: Jewish Colony in 'Zion'"; Sarah Yates, "From Dust to Dust: A Russian Sojourn."
10. See *SLT*, issues for August and September 1905, esp. August 1, 1905; *New York Times*, August 2, 1905; "Journal History of the Church of Jesus Christ of Latter-day Saints," August 11, 1905, a scrapbook of letters, newspaper clippings, and other documents compiled by the LDS Church Historian's Office, microfilm copy available at the Harold B. Lee Library at BYU, digitized copy available from the electronic catalog of the LDS Church History Library, http://churchhistorycatalog.lds.org/; Craig Fuller, Gregory D. Kendrick, and

Robert W. Righter, *Beyond the Wasatch: The History of Irrigation in the Uinta Basin and Upper Provo River Area of Utah*, 15–58; and Fuller, "Land Rush in Zion: Opening of the Uncompahgre and Uintah Indian Reservations," esp. chaps. 3–6.

11.   On William Smart, see Smart, *Mormonism's Last Colonizer*; and Fuller, "Land Rush in Zion," 171–75, 209–33. For population data, see the *Vernal Express*, February 16, December 13, 1907. For settlement data generally, see Fuller, Kendrick, and Righter, *Beyond the Wasatch*, chaps. 1–2; and Remington, "History of the Gilsonite Industry." Knight's role is revealed in the Knight Construction Company Papers. For the Dry Gulch Irrigation Company's role, see *Autobiography of William L. Woolf*, 71–102.

12.   York F. Jones and Evelyn K. Jones, *Lehi Willard Jones, 1854–1947*, 148–62; *Iron County Record*, March 14, 1913.

13.   For data on West Millard developments, see *Millard County Chronicle*; George T. Blanch, "A Farm Organization and Management Study in Western Millard County, Utah"; Merrill K. Ridd, "The Influences of Soil and Water Conditions on Agricultural Development in the Delta Area, Utah"; and various reports in the *Utah Agricultural Experiment Station Bulletin*. See especially the papers and reminiscences of LaVell Johnson on file at the Utah State Historical Society in Salt Lake City and Dudley Crafts, *History of the Sevier Bridge Reservoir*, which traces the filings, company organizations, and especially the court cases and decrees.

14.   A. F. Bracken, "State Report on Land-Use Study for Utah" ([Logan, UT]: Resettlement Administration, 1935), 124–37, copy in Charles S. Peterson Papers, Box 122, Utah State Historical Society; J. Howard Maughan, "The Extent of Desirable Major Land-Use Adjustments and Areas Suitable for Settlement" (Logan, UT: Resettlement Administration, 1936), 6–8, copy in authors' possession; Brian Cannon, "Remaking the Agrarian Dream: The New Deal's Rural Resettlement Program in Utah," 177–78; Marshall E. Bowen, "Crops, Critters, and Calamity: The Failure of Dry Farming in Utah's Escalante Desert, 1913–1918."

15.   David Lavender, *One Man's West*, 143–51; Charles S. Peterson, *Look to the Mountains: Southeastern Utah and the La Sal National Forest*, 156–78; Peterson, "San Juan: A Hundred Years of Cattle, Sheep, and Dry Farms." For memories of La Sal town, see Oscar Jameson Oral History and G. Milton Jameson Oral History, Charles Redd Center Oral History Project 1974, Perry Special Collections, HBLL.

16.   See John A. Widtsoe, *Dry-Farming: A System of Agriculture for Counties under a Low Rainfall*; John Lamborn, "A History of the Development of Dry-Farming in Utah and Southern Idaho"; Norah E. Zink, "Dry Farming Adjustments in Utah"; and numerous reports by Widtsoe and others in the *Utah Agricultural Experiment Station Bulletin*. For dry farming in a neighboring state, see Annie Pike Greenwood, *We Sagebrush Folks*. Vardis Fisher, *Toilers in the Hills*, reveals the underside of the dry-farm experience. Barbara Allen, *Homesteading the High Desert*, reflects an upbeat picture based primarily upon reminiscences. Bleaker portraits are Marshall E. Bowen, *Utah People in the Nevada Desert: Homestead and Community on a Twentieth Century Farmers' Frontier*; M. Bowen, "Crops, Critters, and Calamity"; and Craig L. Torbenson, "The Promontory-Curlew Land Company: Promoting Dry Farming in Utah." Pierce Hardman Oral Interview by Charles S. Peterson, copy in Peterson's possession, is a lengthy remembrance of a Mendon, Utah, native who homesteaded near the Utah-Idaho border, made it pay, and as roads improved and educational needs required lived in Logan and commuted.

17.   Juanita Brooks, *Uncle Will Tells His Own Story*, 134–37; Earl Halls, "Incidents in the Life of Earl Halls," 9–13, typescript in Peterson's possession; *San Juan County: Basic Data*

of Economic Activities and Resources; M. Bowen, "Crops, Critters, and Calamity," 1; Torbenson, "Promontory-Curlew Land Company," 25.

18. *Biennial Report of the State Board of Horticulture, 1897–98*; *Utah Church & Farm: A Journal Devoted to the Religious, Domestic, Farming and Manufacturing Interests* 1 (August 25, 1894): 58.

19. *Biennial Report of the State Board of Horticulture*; C. Brough, *Irrigation in Utah*, 91.

20. C. Brough, *Irrigation in Utah*, 85–95; Arvil L. Stark, "History of Growing Fruit in Utah"; Charles S. Peterson, "The 'Americanization' of Utah's Agriculture."

21. See Journal of William T. Tew, September 7, 1906, July 13, 1907, April 9, 1909, original and typescript in Peterson's possession, photocopy of holograph, Utah State Historical Society; and Walter Paul Reeve, "'A Little Oasis in the Desert': Community Building in Hurricane, Utah, 1860–1930," 120–23.

22. Stark, "History of Growing Fruit in Utah," 113; Don Strack, "Utah's Canning Industry: List of Canneries and Canning Companies"; Leonard J. Arrington, "Transition to the Modern Era, 1890–1910"; A. J. Simmonds, *On the Big Range: A Centennial History of Cornish and Trenton...1870–1970*, 65–76. See also R. Clayton Brough, *Mosida, Utah: Past, Present, & Future*.

23. US Census Bureau, *Report on the Statistics of Agriculture in the United States at the Eleventh Census, 1890*, 310.

24. Paul R. Willie, "History of Dairying in Cache Valley"; William W. Owens, "Status of the Dairy Industry in Utah," typescript, 1924, copy in Peterson's possession; Andrew M. Israelsen, *Utah Pioneering: An Autobiography*, 166–209; Y. Jones and E. Jones, *Lehi Willard Jones*, 93–96; Warnick, "Women Homesteaders"; Charles Lambert Diary, entries June 1878 to 1895, Utah State Historical Society, Salt Lake City; David L. Goudelock and Gertrude Goudelock, Desert Land Entry, U-Adjustment Folder, Denver Branch Federal Records Center, Lakewood, CO; Diary of Albert F. Potter, July 1 to November 22, 1902, typescript, esp. 18–19, 40–43, Special Collections, Merrill-Cazier Library, and http://forestry.usu.edu/htm/rural-forests/forest-history/the-potter-diaries/; Charles S. Peterson, "Albert F. Potter's Wasatch Survey, 1902: A Beginning for Public Management of Natural Resources in Utah"; C. Peterson, *Look to the Mountains*, 166–67.

25. W. E. Carroll, *Report of the Richmond-Lewiston Cow Testing Association*; Lyman H. Rich, *Dairy Production on Utah Farms*, 1–10; *Utah Agricultural Statistics and Utah Department of Agriculture Annual Report*, 58–63; William W. Owens, "Status of the Dairy Industry in Utah, 1924," 3, George B. Caine Papers; F. R. Linfield, "The Condition and Progress of Dairying in Utah for the Year 1899," 124; T. E. Woodward, *The Outlook of the Dairy Industry in Utah*, 11.

26. Various references to these developments appear in what were apparently manuscripts of papers read by George B. Caine in a collection under his name in Special Collections at the Utah State University Merrill-Cazier Library. These manuscripts are dated as early as 1917 and run through the late 1930s. In addition, see *Utah Farmer*, May 16, 1960; *Logan Herald Journal*, July 23, 1967; and Willie, "History of Dairying in Cache Valley."

27. "History of Lorenzo Hansen," *Logan Herald Journal*, August 13, 1937.

28. *Third Annual Report of the Utah Farmers' Institutes, 1899*; Owens, "Status of the Dairy Industry in Utah," 1–3.

29. Willie, "History of Dairying in Cache Valley," 52–57; Owens, "Status of the Dairy Industry in Utah," 1–3; "History of Lorenzo Hansen."

30. *Deseret Farmer*, February 20, 1909.

31. Watt, *History of Carbon County*, 46–47, 57–58.

32. Union Pacific System, "Resources of Utah," March 1910, Caine Papers.

33. F. B. Linfield, "Report of the Condition and Progress of the Dairy Industry of Utah for 1897–98," 100–107; F. R. Linfield, "Condition and Progress," 113–24.

34. Arrington, *Beet Sugar in the West*, 132–34.

35. Published sources on Utah's sugar industry include Matthew C. Godfrey, *Religion, Politics, and Sugar: The Mormon Church, the Federal Government, and the Utah-Idaho Sugar Company, 1907–1921*; Arrington, *Beet Sugar in the West*; Leonard J. Arrington, *David Eccles: Pioneer Western Industrialist*; J. R. Bachman, *Story of the Amalgamated Sugar Company, 1897–1961*; Fred G. Taylor, "Notes on the Development of the Beet Sugar Industry in Utah"; Taylor, *A Saga of Sugar, Being a Story of the Romance and Development of Beet Sugar in the Rocky Mountain West*; and Charles L. Schmalz, "Sugar Beets in Cache Valley: An Amalgamation of Agriculture and Industry." We have used all of these but have followed Arrington's *Beet Sugar in the West* closely.

36. Arrington, *Beet Sugar in the West*, 40–53; C. Brough, *Irrigation in Utah*, esp. chaps. 5–9; Alexander Toponce, *Reminiscences of Alexander Toponce: Pioneer, 1839–1923*, 185–94; G. Thomas, *Development of Institutions under Irrigation*, 208–14, 245.

37. M. Godfrey, *Religion, Politics, and Sugar*, 56–68; Arrington, *Beet Sugar in the West*, 47–53; Yamato Ichihashi, *Japanese in the United States: A Critical Study of the Problems of the Japanese Immigrants and Their Children*, 171; Neila C. Seshachari, "Asian Indian," 2.

38. Arrington, *Beet Sugar in the West*, 54–56.

39. Ibid., 56–76; M. Godfrey, *Religion, Politics, and Sugar*, 94–126.

40. In addition to M. Godfrey, *Religion, Politics, and Sugar*, 94–95, and Arrington, *Beet Sugar in the West*, this section depends upon Arrington, *David Eccles*; Schmalz, "Sugar Beets in Cache Valley"; F. Taylor, "Development of the Beet Sugar Industry"; and Simmonds, *On the Big Range*, 65–75.

41. John D. Nash, "The Tribulations of an Early Idaho Irrigation District," 10–14, n. 15; Schmalz, "Sugar Beets in Cache Valley."

42. Arrington, *Beet Sugar in the West*, 79–100, 182–99; F. Taylor, "Development of the Beet Sugar Industry," 937–40. On Carbon and Emery Counties, see Ray Branch, "History of Sugar Beet Industry in Carbon County"; and Watt, *History of Carbon County*, 46–70.

43. On the multiple-plot village farming pattern, see G. Lowry Nelson, *The Mormon Village: A Pattern and Technique of Land Settlement*; Charles S. Peterson, *Changing Times: A View from Cache Valley, 1890–1915*, 19–20; and Ray Stannard Baker, "The Vitality of Mormonism," 171.

44. Journal of William T. Tew, original and typescript in Peterson's possession.

45. Ibid.

46. M. Godfrey, *Religion, Politics, and Sugar*, 14; Branch, "History of Sugar Beet Industry in Carbon County"; *A Country Printer: The Autobiography of Elisha W. Warner*. Warner's social point of view is developed throughout his memoir, but see especially chap. 8, "Encountering the World."

47. C. Peterson, *Look to the Mountains*, chap. 5; Peterson, "San Juan in Controversy: American Livestock Frontier vs. Mormon Cattle Pool"; Peterson, "Small Holding Land Patterns in Utah and the Problem of Forest Watershed Management"; Peterson, "Grazing in Utah: A Historical Perspective."

48. In the nineteenth century, the town-pool herding system placed sharp limits on the number of people who actually cowboyed. With the establishment early in the twentieth

century of a grazing permit system based on farms adjacent to national forests, the Forest Service sounded the death knell of the town pool and individualized the village-based range experience. In the long run, this led thousands who might otherwise have identified only with the farm ethos to see themselves in the range-cattle tradition. A natural result was the merging of the pioneer and cowboy myths, making them a single strand, more than in most western subcultures. C. Peterson, "Small Holding Land Patterns."

49. Compiled from US Bureau of the Census, Agricultural Censuses for 1890, 1900, 1909, 1910, and 1920.

50. This oversimplifies the situation somewhat, as even village grazing invited roundups, summer camps, corrals, and milk ranches. Even a few bona fide ranches were established within or close to the village core. Examples are the Ireland Company, with forty thousand acres of public land under fence south of Salina Canyon, and the McIntyres, import Texans who ranched near Lyndell in Millard County.

51. C. Peterson, *Look to the Mountains*, 79–106; Stena Scorup, *J. A. Scorup: A Utah Cattleman*; B. W. Allred, interview by Charles Peterson, June 2, 1973, MSS OH 1, Perry Special Collections, HBLL; Veda B. S. N. Williams, interview by Gregory P. Maynard, July 14, 17, 1973, MSS OH 352, Perry Special Collections, HBLL; Milton H. Williams, interview by Gregory P. Maynard, June 13, July 7, August 8, 1973, MSS OH 345, Perry Special Collections, HBLL; Leonard J. Arrington, *Utah's Audacious Stockman, Charlie Redd.* For a revisionist view of the departure of the large cattle companies, see Clyde L. Denis, "Departure of the Late Nineteenth-Century Cattle Companies from Southeastern Utah: A Reappraisal."

52. Scorup, *J. A. Scorup*, 38–46; Peterson, "Hundred Years of Cattle." As an employee of Redd Ranches from 1953 to 1956, Charles Peterson heard references to many burnings that were suspected arson and a few for which evidence was good.

53. Pearl Baker, *Robbers Roost Recollections*, esp. chap. 1.

54. Nutter had started his bidding at $100 for the entire 675,000 acres in comparison to James Clyde's bid of $250 on behalf of Heber City cattlemen. The Indian commissioner responded in anger that bidding would have to begin at $7,000. A round of bidding and maneuvering then ensued, with the lease going to the Strawberry Cattle Company for $7,100. In addition, $2,300 was collected for trailing sheep across the reservation and trespass. See Fuller, "Land Rush in Zion," 91–97.

55. Diary of Albert Potter, August 8, 1902, Special Collections, Merrill-Cazier Library, electronic copy available at http://forestry.usu.edu/htm/rural-forests/forest-history/the-potter-diaries/http://forestry.usu.edu/htm/rural-forests/forest-history/the-potter-diaries; Virginia N. Price and John T. Darby, "Preston Nutter: Utah Cattleman, 1886–1936"; Fuller, "Land Rush in Zion," 87–137. Frank Liddell, interview by Charles Peterson, July 22, 1973, transcript in Perry Special Collections, HBLL, focuses entirely on Liddell's experience as a young cowboy and later foreman at Nutter's Nine Mile Ranch.

56. William L. Tennent, "The John Jarvie Ranch: A Case Study in Historic Site Development and Interpretation," 39–46; John Rolfe Burroughs, *Where the Old West Stayed Young*, 67, 207, 316; "The J. S. Hoy Manuscript," Colorado State University Library, Fort Collins, 103, 216, cited in Tennent, "John Jarvie Ranch"; Dick Dunham and Vivian Dunham, *Flaming Gorge Country*, 178–79.

57. See Bullen Papers.

58. On the McIntyres, see William H. McIntyre, "The Mormons in Canada: The McIntyre Ranch."

59. Price and Darby, "Preston Nutter," 242–45; Nellie I. Cox, *The Arizona Strip: A Harsh Land and Proud*, 187–200; Liddell interview, 11–15.

60. Richard C. Roberts and Richard W. Sadler, *A History of Weber County*, 278–79; Wain Sutton, ed., *Utah: A Centennial History*, 3:391–93; *Ogden Standard*, December 2, 1909.

61. Most Census counts exclude lambs. The 1900 Census, however, reported all sheep, reckoning lambs at one-third of the total. In our count we have added a factor of one-third in other Census years. See US Bureau of the Census, Agricultural Censuses, 1890–1925. On factories and wool, see E. N. Wentworth, *America's Sheep Trails: History, Personalities*, 234–36; and E. H. Mecham, "The History of the Sheep Industry in Utah," 23.

62. Developed from Bureau of Agricultural Economics compilations prepared by the Salt Lake office of the Grazing Service. "History of Grazing," chap. 1, table 2, Federal Writers' Project Collection.

63. US Bureau of the Census, Manuscript Population Schedule for Draper Precinct and other Wasatch Front precincts for 1900.

64. Hamilton Gardner, *History of Lehi*, 187, 199; Diary of Albert F. Potter, July 1902–November 1902, 1–2; J. C. Dowdle Journal 1844–1908, entries for 1900–1902, Joel E. Ricks Collection; Harry Lunn interview by Craig Fuller, October 25, 1974, 31–52, 61–72, typescript, Special Collections, Merrill-Cazier Library.

65. James R. Moss, "The Deseret Live Stock Company, 1891–1933"; Jean Ann McMurrin, "The Deseret Live Stock Company: The First Fifty Years, 1890–1940."

66. M. G. Seeley, "A History of the Rambouillet Breed of Sheep in Utah"; Paul H. Roberts, *Hoof Prints on Forest Ranges: The Early Years of National Forest Range Administration*, 42; Pearl M. Olsen, *Nickels from a Sheep's Back: Biography of John K. Madsen*.

67. Alma C. Esplin, "Sheep," in *Utah: A Centennial History*, edited by Sutton, 1:163–67.

68. Agricultural incomes in Utah compared unfavorably with farm income nationwide. See Arrington and Alexander, *Dependent Commonwealth*, 8–10. It seems that Utah's farmers were unable to compete in the national marketplace and as a consequence extended the subsistence economy of pioneer times.

4. INDUSTRIAL DEVELOPMENT IN THE PROGRESSIVE ERA

1. Arrington and Alexander, *Dependent Commonwealth*, 4.

2. On the effort of the western city to establish a tributary region, see Gilbert Stelter, "The City and Westward Expansion: A Western Case Study."

3. Richard Poll et al., eds., *Utah's History*, 690.

4. Researchers in the 1930s pegged Mormon population statewide at 60 percent, with the eastern-tier counties running from 32.3 percent in Grand County to 50 percent in Daggett. Historical Records Survey, *Inventory of the Church Archives of Utah*, 1:49–50; Lowry Nelson and T. David Hettig, "Some Changes in the Population of Utah as Indicated by the Annual L.D.S. Church Census, 1929–1933," 117.

5. US Bureau of the Census, *Population, 1920: Composition and Character of the Population by States*, 1034.

6. R. Peterson, *Bonanza Rich*, considers several of Salt Lake's wealthy mining magnates. Arrington and Alexander, *Dependent Commonwealth*, 20, lists 1896 as the year the Mining Exchange was established. Writing in 1909, William H. Tibbals quoted transactions made in 1891 and referred to "the Old Exchange" first organized in 1865, in *Salt Lake Mining Review*, November 30, 1909, 23.

7. Don Maguire, "The Mines of Tintic, Utah," 155; V. C. Heikes, "History of Mining and Metallurgy in the Tintic District," 106–7; Philip F. Notarianni, "Tale of Two Towns: The Social Dynamics of Eureka and Helper, Utah," 37–40.

8. We have depended on Philip F. Notarianni, *Faith, Hope and Prosperity: The Tintic Mining District*; and Notarianni, "Tale of Two Towns."

9. On Tintic Standard and the town of Dividend, see Raymond D. Steele, *Goshen Valley History*, 207–16; and Notarianni, *Faith, Hope and Prosperity*, 108–9.

10. J. William Knight, *The Jesse Knight Family: Jesse Knight, His Forebears and Family*; Gary Fuller Reese, "'Uncle Jesse': The Story of Jesse Knight, Miner, Industrialist, Philanthropist," 24–25, 30; Notarianni, *Faith, Hope and Prosperity*, 42–63, 92–97; Notarianni, "Tale of Two Towns"; Richard H. Peterson, "Jesse Knight, Utah's Mormon Mining Mogul"; Will C. Higgins, "Some of the Mines of Tintic District," *Salt Lake Mining Review*, November 15, 1907, 19–20.

11. Unattributed newspaper clipping from late 1916 in David Keith Scrapbook.

12. B. S. Butler et al., *The Ore Deposits of Utah*, quoted in *Salt Lake Mining Review*, July 30, 1920.

13. *DN*, December 16, 1916; "List of Utah Dividend-Paying Stocks," *Salt Lake Mining Review*, September 30, 1910. The San Francisco district's Horn Silver mine (an eight-mile vein controlled in much of the early-twentieth-century period by Samuel Newhouse) paid high dividends in the early days and continued to pay small dividends throughout the World War I period. According to the above sources, the Horn Silver's cumulative dividends were $5,672,000 in 1916. A 1920 government source reported that by 1913, it "had yielded metals" valuing $20,768,471 and had paid $6,892,000 in dividends (Butler et al., *Ore Deposits of Utah*, 504). See also "The Great Horn Silver Vein, in Beaver County," "Valuation of Utah Mines," "Utah Mines Increase Wages," and "Midyear Conditions in Utah," *Salt Lake Mining Review*, June 15, July 30, and August 15, 1919.

14. "About Historical Park City" in "Silver King Coalition Mines Company" clipping, December 1910, Keith Scrapbook; Butler et al., *Ore Deposits of Utah*, 286.

15. Malmquist, *First 100 Years*, 180–82; *DN*, February 12, 1916; Hal Compton and David Hampshire, "Park City," 321–22; Larsen, *Life of Thomas Kearns*, 9–14.

16. State law had long mandated eight-hour days underground. Newspaper clipping dated April 22, 1911, Keith Scrapbook; *Salt Lake Mining Review* July 30, 1919, 38; and "Silver King's Annual Report," clipping under the date May 30, 1920, Keith Scrapbook.

17. Will C. Higgins, "Park City Mining District, Utah," clipping in Keith Scrapbook.

18. Because panning and other practical extraction methods showed no color at Mercur, an early assayer who found substantial amounts of gold was "pronounced an 'Ananias,'" and it is said that more than one assayer was forced to go out of business in Salt Lake City because his record had become tainted with trickery and jobbery in giving good returns on this apparently worthless rock" (*Report of the Utah State Conservation Commission, 1911–1912*, 157).

19. Butler et al., *Ore Deposits of Utah*, 382–87; Arrington and Alexander, *Dependent Commonwealth*, 21; Douglas D. Alder, "The Ghost of Mercur."

20. Butler et al., *Ore Deposits of Utah*.

21. T. A. Rickard, *A History of American Mining*, 191; Toponce, *Reminiscences of Alexander Toponce*, 56–58; Mark Pendleton, "Memories of Silver Reef"; and esp. G. W. Barrett, "Colonel E. A. Wall: Mines, Miners, and Mormons"; and Barrett, "Enos Andrew Wall: Mine Superintendent and Inventor."

22.   J. M. Boutwell, *Economic Geology of the Bingham Mining District, Utah*, 281; Warrum, *History of Utah since Statehood*, 3:733–34; Lafayette Hanchett, "He Sold Aladdin's Lamp," in *"The Old Sheriff," and Other True Tales*, 132; Leonard J. Arrington and Gary B. Hansen, *"The Richest Hole on Earth": A History of the Bingham Copper Mine*, 17–28.

23.   John A. Widtsoe, *The Relation of Smelter Smoke to Utah Agriculture*; Gary B. Hansen, "Industry of Destiny: Copper in Utah"; *The Federal Reporter*; John E. Lamborn and Charles S. Peterson, "The Substance of the Land: Agriculture v. Industry in the Smelter Cases of 1904 and 1906"; Arrington and Hansen, *"Richest Hole on Earth,"* 18–19.

24.   Butler et al., *Ore Deposits of Utah*, 340–82; A. B. Parsons, *The Porphyry Coppers*, chaps. 2–4; T. A. Rickard, *The Utah Copper Enterprise*; Rickard, *History of American Mining*; Harvey O'Connor, *The Guggenheims: The Making of an American Dynasty*; Arrington and Hansen, *"Richest Hole on Earth."*

25.   Arrington and Hansen, *"Richest Hole on Earth."*

26.   Ibid., 54–56; *Salt Lake Mining Review*, February 28, 1901, April 15, February 28, 1910; Will C. Higgins, "Inspection of Electric Railroads and Power Plants," *Salt Lake Mining Review*, December 15, 1910; Higgins, "Description of Bingham & Garfield R.R.," *Salt Lake Mining Review*, May 15, 1911.

27.   O'Connor, *Guggenheims*, 290, as cited in Arrington and Hansen, *"Richest Hole on Earth,"* 8.

28.   Arrington and Hansen, *"Richest Hole on Earth,"* 90; Hanchett, "He Sold Aladdin's Lamp," 140.

29.   H. T. Haines, *Facts and Figures Pertaining to Utah*, 10; Sutton, *Utah: A Centennial History*, 2:848–49.

30.   Robert Athearn, *Rebel of the Rockies: A History of the Denver and Rio Grande Western Railroad*; Athearn, *Union Pacific Country*; William John Gilbert Gould, *My Life on Mountain Railroads*.

31.   *DN*, December 16, 1916; "List of Utah Dividend-Paying Stocks"; "Valuation of Utah Mines"; "Utah Mines Increase Wages"; "Midyear Conditions in Utah"; Butler et al., *Ore Deposits of Utah*, 504.

32.   Taniguchi, *Necessary Fraud*, 10–20, 41–45; Thomas G. Andrews, *Killing for Coal: America's Deadliest Labor War*, 48–49; Nancy J. Taniguchi, *Castle Valley America: Hard Land, Hard-Won Home*.

33.   Taniguchi, *Necessary Fraud*, 3–4, 7, 71–72, 110, 131–32.

34.   *Eastern Utah Advocate*, April 22, 1909, cited in Taniguchi, *Necessary Fraud*, 99, 107, 124, 137–40.

35.   Taniguchi, *Necessary Fraud*, 109, 137, 155, 170.

36.   Ibid., 120–21.

37.   Charles Nettleton Strevell, *As I Recall Them*, 196–204; Will C. Higgins, "The Independent Coal and Coke Company," *Salt Lake Mining Review*, September 30, 1910; Higgins, "Success of the Consolidated Fuel Co.," *Salt Lake Mining Review*, April 15, 1911; Higgins, "The Castle Valley Coal Company," *Salt Lake Mining Review*, June 30, 1911.

38.   "New Railroads for Eastern Utah Coal Fields," *Salt Lake Mining Review*, March 15, 1912; "Railroad to St. George," *Salt Lake Mining Review*, March 30, 1910; "Important Railroad Work," *Salt Lake Mining Review*, December 15, 1910. Talk of building railroads through Emery County to the south and to the Uinta Basin in the north was almost endless. Among proposed undertakings were D&RG lines from Meeker, Colorado, to Dragon in the gilsonite fields in 1913 and from Thistle Junction to the Uinta Basin in 1915. *Vernal Express*,

June 20, 1913, December 10, 1915, cited in H. E. Bender Jr., *Uintah Railway: The Gilsonite Route*, 111.

39. Knight, *Jesse Knight Family*, 70–72.

40. *Report of the State Coal Mine Inspector of the State of Utah, 1915–1916*, 152–58.

41. Taniguchi, *Necessary Fraud*, 179; Nancy J. Taniguchi, "No Proper Job for a Stranger: The Political Reign of Mark Braffet," 153.

42. Taniguchi, *Necessary Fraud*, 209–17.

43. Tracing this in careful detail is Fuller, "Land Rush in Zion," 138–63.

44. Good sources include the *Vernal Express*, which reflects a local point of view, and the *Grand Junction Daily Sentinel*, whose viewpoint favors the West Slope of Colorado. Studies include Fuller, "Land Rush in Zion"; Remington, "History of the Gilsonite Industry"; and Bender, *Uintah Railway*.

45. Bender, *Uintah Railway*, 23–62; Remington, "History of the Gilsonite Industry," 222–81.

46. Remington, "History of the Gilsonite Industry," 222–81.

47. Robert S. McPherson, *Comb Ridge and Its People: The Ethnohistory of a Rock*, 136–37; Osmond L. Harline, "Utah's Black Gold: The Petroleum Industry," 293; "The San Juan Oil Field," *Salt Lake Mining Record*, December 15, 1909; Charles Goodman, "History of the Oil Fields in San Juan County, Utah," *Salt Lake Mining Record*, April 15, 1910.

48. Harline, "Utah's Black Gold"; "Much Interest Manifested in Oil Discoveries," *Salt Lake Mining Review*, March 15, 1901; "Oil Review," *Salt Lake Mining Review*, May 30, 1901; Marcus E. Jones, "Utah Oil Fields," *Salt Lake Mining Review*, June 16, 1901; "The San Rafael Oil Company's Operations," *Salt Lake Mining Review*, December 30, 1901; George H. Hansen and Mendell M. Bell, comps., *Oil and Gas Possibilities of Utah*. Also see "Utah Light and Traction Company: History of Origin and Development," report prepared at the request of the Federal Power Commission, May 11, 1937, 106, Utah State Historical Society.

49. "Progress Made by the Pittsburg–Salt Lake Oil Co.," *Salt Lake Mining Review*, May 30, 1907; "Wayne and Garfield Counties," quoted from *Richfield Reaper* in *Salt Lake Mining Review*, August 30, 1907; "Excitement at Escalante," quoted from *SLH* in *Salt Lake Mining Review*, August 30, 1907; "Wayne County Excited," special to *SLT* cited in *Salt Lake Mining Review*, August 30, 1907; "Juab County Oil Fields," quoted from the *Inter-Mountain Republican* in *Salt Lake Mining Review*, November 30, 1907.

50. McPherson, *Comb Ridge*, 135–37, 142–43; Charles Goodman, "History of the Oil Fields in San Juan County, Utah," *Salt Lake Mining Review*, April 15, 1910; Paul Young, *Back Trail of an Old Cowboy*, 34–40.

51. "Interest in Virgin City Oil," *Salt Lake Mining Review*, August 15, 1907; "Clean-Up by Cedar City People," *Salt Lake Mining Review*, August 30, 1907; *First Biennial Report of the Utah Conservation Commission*, 163–65.

52. *Salt Lake Mining Review*, September 15, 30, October 15, 1907.

53. Ibid.; Y. Jones and E. Jones, *Lehi Willard Jones*, 231; Amasa Jay Redd, *Lemuel Hardison Redd, Jr., 1856–1923: Pioneer-Leader-Builder*, 138. George Middleton's summary of his career as a wildcatter is relevant: "The previous year oil had been struck in the Virgin Valley.... Fired by enthusiasm I went into the oil field, bought options on oil land and organized the Star Crescent Oil Company. In a few days we sold ten thousand dollars' worth of the stock. We bought a fine drilling outfit and employed an expert driller. We drilled four wells and got oil each time, but the quantity of oil in the field was not sufficient to make the wells commercially profitable. We wound up with a big loss instead of any gain. I decided that

oil was not my game, paid up my score, wiped the oil all off me and quit" (*Memoirs of a Pioneer Surgeon*, 172).

54. "The San Juan Oil Field," *Salt Lake Mining Review*, December 15, 1909; C. W. Hayes, "The Leasing of Public Oil Lands," *Salt Lake Mining Review*, December 30, 1909; P. Gates, *History of Public Land Law Development*, 731–45.

55. Harline, "Utah's Black Gold," 296; C. Gregory Crampton, *Standing Up Country: The Canyon Lands of Utah and Arizona*, 144; W. E. Calvert, "Oil Possibilities of the Rio Virgin Anticline," *Salt Lake Mining Review*, March 30, 1919; "Oil Prospects in Washington County, Utah," *Salt Lake Mining Review*, November 15, 1919; "Getting Under Way in Uinta Basin," *Salt Lake Mining Review*, May 15, 1920; "Utah on Brink of Big Oil Boom," *Salt Lake Mining Review*, January 15, 1921; B. J. Silliman, "Oil Possibilities of the Southeastern Utah Field," *Salt Lake Mining Review*, February 15, 1921.

56. Gas had monopolized Salt Lake City and Ogden municipal lighting from 1872 to 1883. During the first years of statehood, it was manufactured from coal or pumped from Davis County gas wells.

57. "Utah Light and Traction Company," 34–46.

58. Ibid., 114–15.

59. Ibid., 111.

60. Ibid., 132.

61. Ibid., 135–36.

62. Boyd L. Dastrup, "Electrification of Utah, 1880 to 1915," 33–54; H. Gardner, *History of Lehi*, 282–83.

63. Dastrup, "Electrification of Utah," 50–52; Y. Jones and E. Jones, *Lehi Willard Jones*, 163–74; E. K. Jones and Y. F. Jones, *Mayors of Cedar City and Histories of Cedar City, Utah*, 139.

64. Dastrup, "Electrification of Utah," 41–46; Hugh T. Lovin, "Lucien Nunn, Provo Entrepreneur, and His Hydropower Realm in Utah and Idaho."

65. Dastrup, "Electrification of Utah," 90–91. For a list of hydro and steam plants taken over by Utah Power & Light, including Knight Power Company's system, see *Second Biennial Report of the State Bureau of Immigration, Labor and Statistics, 1913–1914*, 190–92.

66. The principal source for the Logan conflict is Leon Fonnesbeck, *The Logan City Light Plant*. E. Jones and Y. Jones, *Mayors of Cedar City*, 275–84, quotes minutes of the Cedar City Council discussing the role of Cedar City, Logan, Hyrum, Brigham City, and Murray in a way that lends credence to the point of view that independent city systems were indeed beleaguered.

67. Roland Stucki, *Commercial Banking in Utah, 1847–1960*, chap. 2–3; reports of the secretary of state from 1896 to 1912 and of the state bank commissioner after 1913 when a state law creating the agency and defining its duties went into effect. Particularly see *Report of the Bank Commissioner, 1913–1914*; Warrum, *History of Utah since Statehood*, 1:306–23; and Sutton, *Utah: A Centennial History*, 2:946–47.

68. Data for this section are derived from the American Bankers' Directory for January 1919 as abstracted in Warrum, *History of Utah since Statehood*, 1:311–23; and *Report of the Bank Commissioner, 1913–1914*.

69. Interestingly, the Provo Commercial & Savings Bank was the only state bank that listed a "special deposit," leading one to wonder if a bank among whose leaders the senator sat was of special use for campaign purposes. See *Report of the Bank Commissioner, 1913–1914*, 74.

70. Arrington, *David Eccles*, 256–62.

71. L. W. Macfarlane, *Dr. Mac: The Man, His Land, and His People*, 191–95.

72. Thomas G. Alexander, "Generating Wealth from the Earth, 1847–2000," 40; Industrial Workers of the World, *Coal Mine Workers and Their Industry: An Industrial Handbook.*

5. THE FORMATION OF THE WAGEWORKERS' FRONTIER

1. Trachtenberg, *Incorporation of America*, 77; C. Vann Woodward, *Reunion and Reaction: The Compromise of 1877 and the End of Reconstruction*, 246.
2. Trachtenberg, *Incorporation of America*, 21–26, 41–48, 74–75, quote on 74–75.
3. S. B. Pawar, "An Environmental Study of the Development of the Utah Labor Movement, 1860–1935," 53–57, 90–146.
4. Ibid., 140–44.
5. Utah, *Constitution* (Salt Lake City, 1895), Article XVI, Section 1, and Article XII, Section 16; Pawar, "Environmental Study," 150–55.
6. *SLT*, February 26, June 14, 1896, quoted in Pawar, "Environmental Study," 173.
7. *DN*, May 8, 1899, quoted in Pawar, "Environmental Study," 177.
8. Shearing crews sometimes waged spontaneous strikes, convinced sheep owners were hedging on contracted prices, which were often fixed to reflect wool's selling price. Openly favoring strikers was the *Manti Messenger*, May 15, 1897, which described a strike against A. J. Augured, "heaviest sheep owner and director of sheepmen's opinions." By contrast, the *Ephraim Enterprise*, May 5, 1904, printed a veiled threat that owners or civil authorities would need to bring in the militia to deal with similar unrest.
9. Hundreds of memoirs and oral histories tell of city-bred youngsters and off-season students working farm and cowboy jobs.
10. *SLT*, August 6, 1899, cited in Pawar, "Environmental Study."
11. The following paragraphs on railroading depend heavily on Gould, *My Life on Mountain Railroads*. The foregoing passages about Gould's background depend especially on William Richard Gould's foreword, vii–xiii.
12. *Second Biennial Report of the State Bureau of Immigration, Labor and Statistics*, 323; *Third Report of the State Bureau of Immigration, Labor and Statistics, 1913–1914*, 28.
13. Gould, *My Life on Mountain Railroads*, 168–69.
14. See Athearn, *Rebel of the Rockies*, 195–96, 215.
15. Gould, *My Life on Mountain Railroads*.
16. Schwantes, "Concept of the Wageworkers' Frontier"; *SLT*, November 9, 1903, cited in Frederick S. Buchanan, *A Good Time Coming: Mormon Letters to Scotland*, 290–91.
17. *The Statistics of the Population of the United States…from the Original Returns of the Ninth Census*, 338; 1900 Manuscript Census cited in Notarianni, "Tale of Two Towns," 129.
18. Pamela S. Perlich, *Utah Minorities: The Story Told by 150 Years of Census Data*, 13; Don C. Conley, "The Pioneer Chinese of Utah"; Conley, "The Chinese in Utah"; *Utah Guide*, 362; US Bureau of the Census, *Thirteenth Census of the United States Taken in the Year 1910: Abstract of the Census*, 581; US Bureau of the Census, *Fourteenth Census of the United States Taken in the Year 1920: Population, 1920*, 31; Eric Yuan-Chin Cheng, "Chinese," 52; Clara Ruggeri interview, by Philip Notarianni and Kent Powell, August 27, 1975, MSS A2787, Utah State Historical Society; George Kraus, "Chinese Laborers and the Construction of the Central Pacific," indicates Chinese workers moved to other jobs, returned to China, or moved to the Pacific Coast.
19. Leslie G. Kelen and Eileen Hallet Stone, *Missing Stories: An Oral History of Ethnic and Minority Groups in Utah*, 215; Howard Stevens, interview, May 25, 1976, Charles Redd Center Interviews, MSS OH 375, Perry Special Collections, HBLL. With some

variation, A. C. Watts also told the story in his "Opening First Commercial Coal Mine Described," 37. Watts attaches the episode to opening the first commercial mine and indicates the Chinese were the first work crew. This would have been in 1882 or before. Other scattered references tie it to 1899. In either case, men of American and British background would have been the earliest workers there, and the Chinese would have come in as a new element in the labor scene.

20. Notarianni, "Tale of Two Towns," 115.

21. Ibid., 178, explains that "perhaps to impair union solidarity," coal operators "fostered divisiveness by segregating groups in coal camps" and then cites the location of Castle Gate Italians at "Willow Creek canyon away from the main area" as evidence.

22. *Second Biennial Report of the State Bureau of Immigration, Labor and Statistics*, 333; Lillie Erkkila Wools[e]y, interview by Madge Tomsic and Alene Kirkwood, July 10, 1993, recording at Helper Museum, Helper, UT.

23. Wools[e]y interview; Craig Fuller, "Finnish Americans," 188–90; Alan Kent Powell, *The Next Time We Strike: Labor in Utah's Coal Fields*, 34–35.

24. On the "Coal Combine," see *DN*, July 18, 1895, October 19, 1898; and James W. Dilley, *History of the Scofield Mine Disaster*, 109.

25. *Report of the Coal Mine Inspector for the State of Utah for the Years 1897 and 1898*; *Report of the Coal Mine Inspector for the State of Utah for the Years 1899 and 1900*.

26. *DN*, August 3, 1895; *Report of the Coal Mine Inspector . . . 1899 and 1900*, 80.

27. *Report of the Coal Mine Inspector . . . 1899 and 1900*, 61–115; A. Powell, *Next Time We Strike*, 27–37; Dilley, *History of the Scofield Mine Disaster*.

28. Dilley, *History of the Scofield Mine Disaster*, 95.

29. Ibid. credits John Erickson with doing "heroic work among his fellow countrymen" in a photo caption on page 8 but on page 54 offers the following comment: "The Finlanders, who have been quite numerous about the mines, have sixty-one of their number among the dead. Notwithstanding this not a single Finlander, except Nestor Uro, who has labored incessantly, volunteered to aid in the rescue and the bodies of the Finns have been recovered by miners of other nationalities.

    "Some of the miners say that it is on account of their superstition, and they are not surprised or angry at their refusing to join them."

30. The state mine inspector's account of the recovery attempt is solid and factual. See *Report of the State Coal Mine Inspector for . . . 1899 and 1900*. Dilley, *History of the Scofield Mine Disaster*, provides an eyewitness account of events outside the mine and firsthand accounts from the participants. Thomas switches positions on the question of Finnish culpability within the body of his 1900 report, first accusing Macki and then exonerating him. Thomas cites a suggestive statement by William Coulthard, a twenty-three-year veteran of coal mines, that apparently reflected widely held opinion. "The Finlanders were very careless," said Coulthard. "They would fire from three to four shots one after another. I have seen, after they have fired a large shot, a blaze shoot across the face, I should think for several yards back, be blazing clear across the face. I never felt comfortable when it was that way, and I have often told them, but you might as well talk to nothing as those fellows" (77–78).

31. Journal of Seymour B. Young, May 1, 2, 1900; and Journal of William T. Tew, May 1, 1900, both at the Utah State Historical Society. Newspapers cited are from Dilley, *History of the Scofield Mine Disaster*, 178–82.

32. Heber M. Wells, *Message of the Governor of Utah to the Fourth Session of the State Legislature of Utah*, 22–24.

33. Most of the information on the character of the community is drawn from Dilley, *History of the Scofield Mine Disaster*. See especially page 133 and chapters 5, 6, and 7, which reference a number of uncited newspaper accounts and a number of internally cited reports and documents. See also *Report of the State Coal Mine Inspector for . . . 1899 and 1900*; A. Powell, *Next Time We Strike*, chap. 2; and Seymour B. Young diary, May 4–6, 1900.

34. Dilley, *History of the Scofield Mine Disaster*. Chapters 6–8 deal most directly with the benevolent societies, but references and biographies appear throughout.

35. Wells, *Message of the Governor of Utah to the Fourth Session*, 22–24.

36. Ibid., 23; Dilley, *History of the Scofield Mine Disaster*, 292.

37. *Report of the State Coal Mine Inspector for . . . 1899 and 1900*, 62; Dilley, *History of the Scofield Mine Disaster*, 284–86, 292.

38. *Second Biennial Report of the State Bureau of Immigration, Labor and Statistics*, 333.

39. Philip F. Notarianni, "Italianita in Utah: The Immigrant Experience," 308.

40. Ibid., 307–9; Notarianni, *Faith, Hope and Prosperity*, 92.

41. G. W. Kramer in the *Eastern Utah Advocate*, December 12, 1903, quoted in Notarianni, "Italianita in Utah," 310; Kelen and Stone, *Missing Stories*, 275.

42. US Census Bureau, *Thirteenth Census of the United States Taken in the Year 1910*, 581; *Second Biennial Report of the State Bureau of Immigration, Labor and Statistics*, 333.

43. *Ninth Biennial Report of the State Mine Inspector for the State of Utah for the Years 1911–1912*, 94; A. Powell, *Next Time We Strike*, 96; Notarianni, "Tale of Two Towns"; Notarianni, "Italianita in Utah."

44. Notarianni, "Tale of Two Towns," 127–28; Helen Z. Papanikolas, "Utah's Coal Lands: A Vital Example of How America Became a Great Nation," 121.

45. See Notarianni, "Tale of Two Towns," 130. See also Notarianni, "Italianita in Utah."

46. Notarianni, "Tale of Two Towns," 130.

47. A. Powell, *Next Time We Strike*, chap. 3, is the only in-depth treatment of the 1901 strike, although other labor historians make reference to it. For Scanlon's comments, see ibid., 37; *Intermountain Catholic*, May 5, 1900; and Dilley, *History of the Scofield Mine Disaster*, 203.

48. *DN*, February 9, 1901; *SLH*, February 16, 1901, cited in A. Powell, *Next Time We Strike*, 47; *SLT*, January 30, 1904; Pawar, "Environmental Study," 241–42.

49. *SLT*, February 8, 1901, reported that Italians "would be with the strikers to a man," but they dared not. Quoted in A. Powell, *Next Time We Strike*, 45, 234.

50. A. Powell, *Next Time We Strike*, chap. 3.

51. On the strike of 1903–4, we have depended primarily upon ibid., chap. 4; Allan Kent Powell, "The 'Foreign Element' and the 1903–4 Carbon County Coal Miners' Strike"; Notarianni, "Tale of Two Towns," 89–98, 127–48, 176–219, 235–52; and R. Roberts, "History of the Utah National Guard," 58–72. When not otherwise noted, quotes are from A. Powell, *Next Time We Strike*, chap. 4.

52. *Report of the State Coal Mine Inspector for the Years 1903 and 1904*, 66.

53. Ibid.

54. *Nephi Record*, December 11, 1903, cited in A. Powell, *Next Time We Strike*, 56.

55. Samuel A. King, "Statement and Brief Concerning the Campaign of the Coal Operators in Utah against Organized Labor and the Unionizing of the Utah Coal Fields," photocopy, Utah State Historical Society, 3; A. Powell, *Next Time We Strike*, 67; *Report of the State Coal Mine Inspector . . . 1903 and 1904*, 73.

56. *United Mine Workers Journal*, January 21, 1924, quoted in A. Powell, *Next Time We Strike*, 69; Notarianni, "Tale of Two Towns," 204–6.

57. A. Powell, *Next Time We Strike*, 71.
58. Ibid., 78; Richard Raspa, "Exotic Foods among Italian-Americans in Mormon Utah: Food as Nostalgic Enactment of Identity," 187.
59. Melba Tew Hayes, interview by Charles Peterson, January 30, 1995, copy in Peterson's possession.
60. A. Powell, *Next Time We Strike*, 80.
61. Employment figures are calculated from a 1903 press release by G. W. Kramer, Pleasant Valley Coal Company vice president, and the 1905 report of the state mine inspector. See *Eastern Utah Advocate*, December 3, 1903, quoted in Notarianni, "Italianita In Utah," 310; and *Report of the State Coal Mine Inspector for the Years 1904 and 1905*, 21.

6. THE TORTUROUS MATURATION OF AN INDUSTRIAL WORKFORCE

1. All by Helen Z. Papanikolas: "Bootlegging in Zion: Making and Selling the 'Good Stuff,'" 89; *Emilia—Yoryis, Emily—George*; "The Greeks of Carbon County"; "Growing Up Greek in Helper, Utah"; "Life and Labor among the Immigrants of Bingham Canyon"; "Magerou, the Greek Midwife"; *The Peoples of Utah; Toil and Rage in a New Land: The Greek Immigrants in Utah*; "Toil and Rage in a New Land: The Greeks in a New Land"; "Unionism, Communism, and the Great Depression: The Carbon County Coal Strike of 1933"; "Utah's Coal Lands"; "Utah's Ethnic Legacy"; and "Wrestling with Death: Greek Immigrant Funeral Customs in Utah."
2. This depends directly upon Papanikolas, *Toil and Rage*, 100–105. Much the same material may be found in personal detail in Papanikolas, *Emilia—Yoryis, Emily—George*, a biography of her parents with autobiographical chapters on the years of her life when she lived with them. Peter Condas's account is printed in Kelen and Stone, *Missing Stories*, 377–78.
3. In *Toil and Rage in a New Land*, 112, Helen Papanikolas indicates two Greeks may have been killed in the Scofield disaster. If so, the fact that no name identifiable as Greek appears on the roster of victims suggests that they were among the large number of new immigrants who were assigned Anglo names in connection with their employment. See also *Second Biennial Report of the State Bureau of Immigration, Labor and Statistics*, 33; and *Thirteen Census of the United States Taken in the Year 1910*, 581.
4. Papanikolas, *Toil and Rage*, 110, 122; *First Report of the State Bureau of Immigration, Labor and Statistics, 1911–1912*, 31; Pawar, "Environment Study," 301.
5. Kelen and Stone, *Missing Stories*, 378. For an excellent, detailed discussion of Greek labor recruitment, see Gunther Peck, *Reinventing Free Labor: Padrones and Immigrant Workers in the North American West, 1880–1930*.
6. Papanikolas, *Toil and Rage*, esp. 100–120.
7. Ibid., 143.
8. James P. Heaton, interview by Charles S. Peterson, February 1, 1995, copy in Peterson's possession.
9. Papanikolas, *Toil and Rage*, 136–51.
10. A superb account of Greek wageworkers is Papanikolas, *Emilia—Yoryis, Emily—George*, esp. 133–68, 185–243.
11. John H. Yang, ed., *Asian Americans in Utah: A Living History*, 154–55. Good descriptions of Skliris's operation are found in G. Peck, *Reinventing Free Labor*; Papanikolas, *Toil and Rage*, 121–31; and Papanikolas, "Life and Labor." On Demeter's death and the Skliris shooting, see A. Powell, *Next Time We Strike*, 88–89.

12. With "only about fifty or sixty Mormon men, women, and children" of a total of 1,881 at Bingham in 1900, Mormons played "only a peripheral role" in labor affairs in the copper industry of that period. Gunther Peck, "Padrones and Protest: 'Old' Radicals and 'New' Immigrants in Bingham, Utah, 1905–1912," 162.

13. Quoted in the *Third Report of the State Bureau of Immigration, Labor and Statistics*, 15–16. See also Papanikolas, *Toil and Rage*, 122; Pawar, "Environmental Study," 301; and *DN*, September 20, 1912.

14. For a discussion of the interaction of race, ethnicity, and class upon the Americanizing influences of Utah labor relations, see G. Peck, "Padrones and Protest," 157–78.

15. A. Powell, *Next Time We Strike*, 91–93; George Jackson, interview by Charles Peterson, notes in Peterson's possession. Independent Coal and Coke owner and general manager Strevell, *As I Recall Them*, 200, granted that an "insurrection" took place in which "one of our men was killed" and claimed the "reason…was never explained." He reported rumors that "several bodies [Greeks] were found." In 1911 the Carbon County government was in complete control of the Utah Fuel Company, and Strevell's conclusion that "no action was ever taken by the peace officials" seems probable.

16. G. Peck, *Reinventing Free Labor*; Papanikolas, *Toil and Rage*; and Papanikolas, "Life and Labor," remain the basic sources for the Bingham strike. For more specific data used here, see G. Peck, "Padrones and Protest," 165.

17. G. Peck, "Padrones and Protest," 167.

18. Karl A. Elling, "The History of Organized Labor in Utah, 1910–1920," 101; Pawar, "Environmental Study," 297; Papanikolas, *Toil and Rage*, 123.

19. Papanikolas, *Toil and Rage*, 122–24; G. Peck, "Padrones and Protest," 168–69. Although Papanikolas and Peck agree on the quick growth of the Bingham WFM local during the late summer of 1912, there is evidence the union picked up momentum during 1910 and in 1911. Bingham unionist E. G. Locke reported that 1,000 miners from Bingham alone attended the union's annual outing at Wandamere. Elling, "History of Organized Labor," 31.

20. Papanikolas, *Toil and Rage*, 124–26.

21. *New York Call*, October 3, 1912; *DN*, September 20, 1912, cited in G. Peck, "Padrones and Protest," 157, 169; *Salt Lake Herald-Republican*, September 20, 1912, as cited in Papanikolas, *Toil and Rage*, 126.

22. G. Peck, "Padrones and Protest," 171.

23. Papanikolas, *Toil and Rage*, 124–31; G. Peck, "Padrones and Protest," 170–76.

24. Papanikolas, *Toil and Rage*, 133.

25. G. Peck, "Padrones and Protest," 175.

26. Italians numbering 495 and 171 South Slavs are reported as leaving Utah the same years. See *Second Biennial Report of the State Bureau of Immigration, Labor and Statistics*, 316; and *Third Report of the State Bureau of Immigration, Labor and Statistics*, 33.

27. William H. González and Genaro M. Padilla, "Monticello, the Hispanic Cultural Gateway to Utah," 9–11; Kelen and Stone, *Missing Stories*, 450; Jorge Iber, *Hispanics in the Mormon Zion, 1912–1999*, 4–12; Wallace Stegner, *Mormon Country*, 269.

28. Kelen and Stone, *Missing Stories*, 491; Iber, *Hispanics in the Mormon Zion*, 10–13; Armando Solorzano, Lisa M. Ralph, and J. Lynn England, "Community and Ethnicity: Hispanic Women in Utah's Carbon County," 61–62, 66.

29. Iber, *Hispanics in the Mormon Zion*, 14–17; Jorge Iber, "'El diablo nos está llevando': Utah Hispanics and the Great Depression," 160–67, 170–71; Jerald H. Merrill, "Fifty Years with a Future: Salt Lake's Guadalupe Mission and Parish," 246–51.

30. A good source on IWW organization and early development is Patrick Renshaw, *The Wobblies: The Story of Syndicalism in the United States.*

31. Selig Perlman and Philip Taft, *Labor Movements*; *SLT*, June 20, 1910, March 1, 1915, March 8, 1925; Pawar, "Environmental Study," 303–5; Elling, "History of Organized Labor," 35–36, 51–52. On the IWW's struggle for free-speech rights in Salt Lake, see John S. McCormick and John R. Sillito, "'We Are Not Seeking Trouble and So Will Just Go Along Quietly': The IWW's Free Speech Fight in Salt Lake City."

32. Joseph H. Peck, *What Next, Doctor Peck?* On the Utah Construction Company, see Sterling D. Sessions and Gene A. Sessions, *History of Utah International: From Construction to Mining.*

33. J. Peck, *What Next, Doctor Peck?*

34. A. Powell, *Next Time We Strike*, 97–101; Pawar, "Environmental Study," 305–12.

35. Excellent treatments of the Soldier Summit strike and the free-speech riots are found in McCormick and Sillito, "'We Are Not Seeking Trouble'"; and Gibbs M. Smith, *Joe Hill*, 118–22. See also *DN*, August 16, 1913, cited in Pawar, "Environmental Study," 311; and Elling, "History of Organized Labor," 44.

36. Elizabeth Gurley Flynn in *Solidarity*, May 22, 1915, quoted in G. Smith, *Joe Hill*, 126. For a revisionist interpretation and new evidence on the lovers' quarrel, see William M. Adler, *The Man Who Never Died: The Life, Times, and Legacy of Joe Hill, American Labor Icon.*

37. *Salt Lake Herald-Republican*, November 2, 6, 9, 20, 1915, cited in G. Smith, *Joe Hill*, 128–29.

38. We have drawn upon sections on the Industrial Workers of the World and Joe Hill in Pawar, "Environmental Study"; Elling, "History of Organized Labor"; W. Roper and Arrington, *William Spry*, chaps. 19–28, which was commissioned by Spry's son-in-law and takes a position only slightly modified from Spry's own; Wallace Stegner, *Joe Hill: A Biographical Novel*, first published as *The Preacher and the Slave* (New York: Doubleday, 1950); Philip S. Foner, *The Case of Joe Hill*; and G. Smith, *Joe Hill*, which we have depended upon much more than the others, including all of the quoted material.

39. Renshaw, *Wobblies*, 159; G. Smith, *Joe Hill*, 208.

40. John Farnsworth Lund, "The Night before Doomsday," 156–57; Population Schedule, Pleasant View Precinct, 1920 Census, http://search.ancestry.com/Browse/view.aspx?dbid=6061&path=Utah.Utah.Pleasant+View.204.15.

41. Papanikolas, *Toil and Rage*, 152–56. Historian Theodore Saloutos concluded that because of the "patriotic exuberance of the Greek-Americans and their preponderantly male members, the figure 60,000 or even 70,000 would be a reasonable estimate" (*The Greeks in the United States*, 167–68).

42. Papanikolas, *Toil and Rage*, 152–58.

43. *Logan Journal*, January 18, 1917.

44. C. Peterson, *Look to the Mountains*, 138, 142–43; "Historical Information, La Sal National Forest," Manti–La Sal National Forest History Files; *Grand Valley Times*, January 13, August 30, September 6, 20, 1918.

45. Papanikolas, *Emilia—Yoryis, Emily—George*, 273; Clara Ruggeri, interview by Philip Notarianni and Alan Kent Powell, August 27, 1975, MSS A 2787, Utah State Historical Society.

46. R. K. Cunningham Jr., "Internment, 1917–1920: A History of the Prison Camp at Fort Douglas, Utah, and the Treatment of Enemy Aliens in the Western United States"; Jeorg A. Nagler, "Enemy Aliens and Internment in World War I: Alvo von Alvensleben in Fort

Douglas, Utah, a Case Study"; A. Powell, "Our Cradles Were in Germany"; Papanikolas, "Immigrants, Minorities, and the Great War."

47. Cunningham, "Internment, 1917–1920," 92–93, 134–37, 169.

48. Ibid. is particularly strong on the press's role.

49. Ibid.; Nagler, "Enemy Aliens and Internment"; A. Powell, "Our Cradles Were in Germany."

50. Heath, *In the World*, 413; *SLT*, March 29, 1919, cited in Nagler, "Enemy Aliens and Internment," 403.

51. *DN*, December 28, 1918, September 16, 1919. Material for these paragraphs comes from Papanikolas, *Toil and Rage*, 155–60; Leroy Eugene Cowles, "The Utah Educational Program of 1919 and Factors Conditioning Its Operation," esp. the abstract, chap. 4, and appendixes 4 and 9. See also many issues of the *Utah Educational Review* from 1918 to 1925 in which aspects of the Utah Educational Program are discussed.

52. Cowles, "Utah Educational Program of 1919," esp. 110–38; Philip F. Notarianni, "Italian Fraternal Organizations in Utah, 1897–1934," 179.

53. Cowles, "Utah Educational Program of 1919," 55–66. Cowles used destination data from arriving immigrants to calculate a net gain of 6,374 aliens for the state between 1920 and 1925. In 1921–22 the Census count of 22,004 aliens was merely broken down to fit the state's forty school districts. In Salt Lake County aliens numbered 10,952 for almost half the state total. Carbon County was second, its 2,980 aliens representing 19.23 percent of its population, while Weber County's 2,189 was the third-largest alien group.

54. Papanikolas, *Emilia—Yoryis, Emily—George*, 273.

55. Cowles, "Utah Educational Program of 1919," appendix 9.

56. Ibid., 61, appendix 9; Philip F. Notarianni, "Utah's Ellis Island: The Difficult Americanization of Carbon County," 190–92.

57. Papanikolas, *Toil and Rage*, 161–65; Walker Lowry, *Wallace Lowry*, 165–67, 185–88.

58. Renshaw, *Wobblies*, 172–73; A. Powell, *Next Time We Strike*, 115.

59. Steven Bligh McNutt, "Utah's Reaction to the 1919–1920 Red Scare," 39; Andrew Hunt, "Beyond the Spotlight: The Red Scare in Utah," 360–61.

60. Pawar, "Environmental Study," 333–59; Elling, "History of Organized Labor," 33–35, 50, 103, 114–15; Hunt, "Beyond the Spotlight."

61. This section depends entirely on A. Powell, *Next Time We Strike*, 105–20.

62. Ibid., 121–28; Allan Kent Powell, "Utah and the Nationwide Coal Miners' Strike of 1922."

63. Accounts of this incident, favorable to the operators and claiming positive identification of strikers seen at a distance from a moving train, appeared in the local and state press and in an operators' brief prepared for the US Coal Commission. The strikers' point of view presented in attorney Samuel King's opposing brief for the Coal Commission blamed the operators with opening fire and denied that strikers charged with Webb's murder had anything to do with it, a position that appears to have been generally sustained by the outcome of the trial and pardons process. See A. Powell, *Next Time We Strike*, 130–40; A. Powell, "Utah and the Nationwide Coal Miners' Strike," 147–49; R. Roberts, "History of the Utah National Guard," 223–27; State of Utah, *Biennial Report of the Adjutant General, Utah National Guard, 1921–1922*, 17–19, Utah State Historical Society; and Samuel A. King, "Statement and Brief Concerning the Campaign of the Coal Operators in Utah against Organized Labor and the Unionizing of the Utah Coal Fields," July 1923, photocopy, 28–39, 45–48, Utah State Historical Society.

64. King, "Statement and Brief," 45; A. Powell, *Next Time We Strike*, 121–40; *DN*, June 17, 1922; Kelen and Stone, *Missing Stories*, 271.

65. A. Powell, *Next Time We Strike*, 136–38.

66. King, "Statement and Brief," 28–39, 45–48; A. Powell, *Next Time We Strike*, 136–40.

67. On the other hand, urban labor leaders like R. G. Sleater of the Salt Lake Typographers' Union put together lasting central organizations in Salt Lake City and Ogden. Others, like the onetime socialist and radical labor leader William M. Knerr, joined the "enemy," continuing as a moderating influence for labor and as a longtime friend in court on the Utah Industrial Commission. But they too failed to create any kind of umbrella structure from which the beleaguered mine workers could seek state-level coordination.

68. *Report of the Industrial Commission of Utah: July 1, 1920 to June 20, 1922*, 378. These statistics raise problems that are not sustained by other data in the same report. See listing by name of fatalities, 926–30, some of which may involve partial years. Nationwide, coal mines averaged 3.71 accidental deaths per million tons, while Colorado, New Mexico, and Wyoming averaged 7.97, 6.16, and 4.82 deaths per million tons, respectively.

69. Ibid.

70. A. Powell, *Next Time We Strike*, 141–52; Papanikolas, *Toil and Rage*, 176–82; Saline Hardee Fraser, "One Long Day That Went on Forever"; Michael Katsanevas Jr., "The Emerging Social Worker and the Distribution of the Castle Gate Relief Fund"; Janeen Arnold Costa, "A Struggle for Survival and Identity: Families in the Aftermath of the Castle Gate Mine Disaster."

71. Fraser, "One Long Day That Went on Forever," 384; Kelen and Stone, *Missing Stories*, 381.

72. Ibid.; A. Powell, *Next Time We Strike*, 146–47; Dilley, *History of the Scofield Mine Disaster*, 93–94.

73. A. Powell, *Next Time We Strike*, 147–49.

74. Ibid., 143; Philip F. Notarianni, "Hetacomb at Castle Gate, Utah, March 8, 1924," 63, 65, 66, 69, 71; Katsanevas, "Emerging Social Worker," 242.

75. Between 1941 and 1945, 140 men died in coal mines, 55 more than died at war. The year 1945 was particularly tough, with 7 dying in a Kenilworth electrical accident and 23 in a Sunnyside gas explosion. A. Powell, *Next Time We Strike*, 197.

76. Although Helen Papanikolas and Philip Notarianni have touched on the role of the Klan, Larry Gerlach's fine *Blazing Crosses in Zion: The Ku Klux Klan in Utah* is the only effective source for understanding its development. Unless otherwise indicated, quotes are drawn from it.

77. Gerlach, *Blazing Crosses in Zion*, 31–32.

78. Ibid., 41–53.

79. Ibid., 55–69.

80. Ibid., 69–75.

81. Ibid., 75–80; Kelen and Stone, *Missing Stories*, 175.

82. Gerlach, *Blazing Crosses in Zion*, 75–88, esp. 82, 140–41.

83. Ruggeri interview; Gerlach, *Blazing Crosses in Zion*, 88–101.

84. Gerlach, *Blazing Crosses in Zion*, 88–101.

85. Ibid.; Yiorges Anagnostou, "Helen Papanikolas, Folklorist of Ethnicity," 71.

86. Ronald W. Walker, "A Gauge of the Times: Ensign Peak in the Twentieth Century," 20–21.

87. Larry R. Gerlach, "Justice Denied: The Lynching of Robert Marshall," 356–59, 361.

88. Joseph Stipanovich, "Falcons in Flight: The Yugoslavs"; Stipanovich, "South Slav Settlements in Utah, 1890–1934"; Stipanovich, *The South Slavs in Utah: A Social History*.

89. Stipanovich, *South Slavs in Utah*, 41; *Second Biennial Report of the State Bureau of Immigration, Labor and Statistics*, 333; George Prpic, *Croatian Immigrants in America*,

392. Less rigorously arrived at than figures used by historians of other ethnic groups, Stipanovich's count suggests that other ethnic groups may have been undercounted in the census, too.

90. Stipanovich, *South Slavs in Utah*, 47–55, 71–83. See also David L. Shirer, "Murray, Utah, Families in Transition, 1890–1920," 342–45.

91. Stipanovich, *South Slavs in Utah*, 61–62, 81–89.

92. Ibid., 62–66; L. Nelson and Hettig, "Some Changes in the Population," 107–11.

93. Gerlach, *Blazing Crosses in Zion*, 139.

94. *Wyoming Labor Journal*, October 16, 1923, cited in A. Powell, *Next Time We Strike*, 153–54.

95. Coal company papers and union records dealing with this period are cited in A. Powell, *Next Time We Strike*, 153–64.

96. *Typographical Journal* 71 (December 1927): 613–14; Salt Lake Typographical Union Local no. 115, "Minutes," November 27, 1927, 2, as cited in Pawar, "Environmental Study," 389–406.

97. A. Powell, *Next Time We Strike*, 165–94; Papanikolas, "Unionism, Communism, and the Great Depression"; Pawar, "Environmental Study," 405–33; Rollo West, "Statement on the Carbon County Strike of 1933," copies at Marriott Library at the University of Utah and the Utah State Historical Society.

98. See Papanikolas, "Unionism, Communism, and the Great Depression," 272–73.

99. Ibid., 167–77; Pawar, "Environmental Study," 428–32.

100. West, "Statement on the Carbon County Strike of 1933," 39.

101. Papanikolas, "Unionism, Communism, and the Great Depression," 269–70; West, "Statement on the Carbon County Strike of 1933," 70, 140, 160.

102. Helen Z. Papanikolas, who interviewed many strikers and read the oral histories of many more, reported that "nearly three hundred men" were deputized. Rolla West admits that more than the hundred suggested by Governor Blood's emissary "joined" up, but neglects to say how many more. Papanikolas, "Unionism, Communism, and the Great Depression," 279; West, "Statement on the Carbon County Strike of 1933," 63–65.

103. Independent to the last, Roberts died shortly, still running counter to the sympathies of top Mormon leaders on this as he had on other important political issues.

104. Frank Bonacci to John L. Lewis, December 6, 1934, United Mine Workers of America Records, District 22 Correspondence, 1935, cited in A. Powell, *Next Time We Strike*, 188, 190–92.

105. Douglas Hileman, superintendent of Spring Canyon Mine, interview by Charles Peterson, September 22, 1969, notes in Peterson's possession.

7. AT THE WHIPLASH END OF PLURALISM: INDIANS IN THE NEW STATE

1. Ronald L. Holt, *Beneath These Red Cliffs: An Ethnohistory of the Utah Paiutes*, 40.

2. Martha C. Knack, *Boundaries Between: The Southern Paiutes, 1775–1995*, 48–129.

3. Angus M. Woodbury, "A History of Southern Utah and Its National Parks," 122; Holt, *Beneath These Red Cliffs*, 34; Gary Tom and Ronald Holt, "The Paiute Tribe of Utah," 131; John Alton Peterson, *Utah's Black Hawk War*, 81–82. Subagent Thomas W. Sale estimated in 1865 that there were nearly three thousand Paiutes in the Southwest. See W. Paul Reeve, *Making Space on the Western Frontier: Mormons, Miners and Southern Paiutes*, 53.

4. Knack, *Boundaries Between*, 131–45; Holt, *Beneath These Red Cliffs*, 40–41, 57–60, 104–6; Tom and Holt, "Paiute Tribe of Utah," 139–41.

5. Charles S. Peterson conversation with Rev. John Mahon of the Good Shepherd Presbyterian Church in St. George, who apparently drew from Craton Rice, *Ambassador to the Saints.*

6. Tom and Holt, "Paiute Tribe of Utah," 139–44.

7. A. F. Farrow, "The Kaibab Indians"; Tom and Holt, "Paiute Tribe of Utah," 145.

8. For a comprehensive history of these people, see Robert S. McPherson, *As If the Land Owned Us: An Ethnohistory of the White Mesa Utes.* See also Robert S. McPherson and Mary Jane Yazzie, "The White Mesa Utes," 250–53; and McPherson, "Paiute Posey and the Last White Uprising," 250.

9. McPherson, "Paiute Posey"; Robert S. McPherson, "Canyons, Cows and Conflict: A Native American History of Montezuma Canyon, 1874–1933," 251–52; McPherson and Yazzie, "The White Mesa Utes," 254–57. Dated but still useful is Forbes Parkhill, *The Last of the Indian Wars.* See also C. Peterson, *Look to the Mountains,* 55–77, 155–56. On the Mormon point of view toward Indians and a youthful response to Paiute unrest from 1913 to 1924, see Alma Uriah Jones, interview by Gary L. Shumway, August 4–7, 1981, 49–78, MSS OH 498, Perry Special Collections, HBLL. On the Paiute Strip, see Harve Williams, interview by Gregory Maynard, June 13, 1973, 26–34, MSS OH 345, Perry Special Collections, HBLL. For a lawman's memory of his role in the Posey War, see Fred W. Keller, interview by Michael Hurst and Charles Peterson, July 22, 1973, MSS OH 250, Perry Special Collections, HBLL.

10. Knack, *Boundaries Between,* 142–45; Nathella Griffin Woolsey, *The Escalante Story, 1875–1964,* 381–86.

11. Holt, *Beneath These Red Cliffs,* 37; Robert J. Franklin and Pamela A. Bunte, *The Paiute,* 61–62, 76–78; Knack, *Boundaries Between,* 138–39.

12. Brigham Johnson, interview by Charles Peterson, April 1, 1995, copy in Peterson's possession.

13. Moccasin Ward Minutes, October 13, 1955, copy in Brigham Johnson's possession, St. George, UT; Juanita Brooks, "Indian Relations on the Mormon Frontier," 47; James Hayes to Miss K. C. McBeth, December 12, 1907, Idaho State Historical Society Collections; Bonnie Sue Lewis to Chas Peterson, November 16, 1994, in Peterson's possession.

14. Ralph Thompson, interview by Charles Peterson, March 25, 1971, copy in Peterson's possession.

15. Farrow, "The Kaibab Indians," 57–59; Brooks, "Indian Relations on the Mormon Frontier," 40.

16. Moccasin Ward Minutes, 1955.

17. *MX/Native American Cultural and Socio-economic Studies—Draft,* 3.274.

18. Steven J. Crum, *The Road on Which We Came: A History of the Western Shoshone*; Dennis R. Defa, "The Goshute Indians of Utah"; Defa, "A History of the Gosiute Indians to 1900"; Carling Malouf, *Shoshone Indians*; Steven J. Crum, "The Skull Valley Band of the Goshute Tribe: Deeply Attached to Their Native Homeland"; David L. Wood, "Gosiute-Shoshone Draft Resistance, 1917–18."

19. Information on acreage and reservation development is taken largely from *MX/Native American Studies,* 3.246–51, 3.276–81; Crum, "Skull Valley Band of the Goshute Tribe"; Defa, "Goshute Indians of Utah," 113; and Ronald R. Bateman, *Deep Creek Reflections: 125 Years of Settlement at Ibapah, Utah, 1859–1984,* 158–77, 243–45, 279–98, 366–463, and esp. 487–90.

20. Crum, "Skull Valley Band of the Goshute Tribe"; Bateman, *Deep Creek Reflections*; J. Peck, *What Next, Doctor Peck?,* 154–205.

21. Wood, "Gosiute-Shoshone Draft Resistance."

22. Mae Parry, "The Northwestern Shoshone," 33–58; Wood, "Gosiute-Shoshone Draft Resistance"; Defa, "Goshute Indians of Utah," 114–15; J. Peck, *What Next, Doctor Peck?*, 189–205; Bateman, *Deep Creek Reflections*, 366–70; Matthew E. Kreitzer, "Willie Ottogary: Northwestern Shoshone Journalist, 1906–1929," chaps. 2–3. Ottogary's "Washakie Reports" in the *Logan Journal* have been edited and reprinted in Matthew Kreitzer, ed., *The Washakie Letters of Willie Ottogary: Northwestern Shoshone Journalist and Leader, 1906–1929*.

23. Defa, "Goshute Indians of Utah," 116.

24. In addition to Kreitzer, "Willie Ottogary"; Scott R. Christensen, *Sagwitch: Shoshoni Chieftain, Mormon Elder, 1822–1884*; and Charles E. Dibble, "The Mormon Mission to the Shoshoni Indians, Part Three," are good sources on the Washakie mission. No study of the larger Indian mission movement of the late 1870s and 1880s has been written. This would include the northern Utah missions (Deep Creek, Skull Valley, Indianola, and Washakie) that emerged in the late 1870s and early 1880s.

25. *Logan Journal*, May 29, 1909, March 19, 1910, September 23, 1912.

26. Reference to the athletic events picks up in the 1920s. See *Logan Journal*, June 13, 1925; August 7, 21, October 30, 1926; and July 23, 1927, for baseball. Ottogary's sons were most active as prizefighters in the years after 1925. See the *Logan Journal*, February 27, March 6, 13, April 17, May 1, June 19, September 2, 18, 1926; January 8, 1927; January 28, November 10, 1928. They often fought by arrangement of Seth Pubigee, who also raced horses and with Ottogary's help maintained a training camp for the Ottogary boys and two or three other Shoshone boxers.

27. Rabbits were by all odds the most important game. Ottogary fails to mention whether they were a source of food, but they were hunted during winter months by boys and young men apparently as a sport rather than by the family gathering groups or work details that foraged otherwise. Some winters thousands of "bunnies," as Ottogary often called them, were killed, and on a few occasions he mentions that ears brought a five-cent bounty and that skins could be sold.

28. For a fine statement on Indian homesteading in Box Elder County, see Kenneth Dean Hunsaker, "Feeding the Indians of Northern Utah," term paper in Peterson's possession.

29. On annuities, see *Logan Journal*, February 10, May 12, 1923; December 6, 1924; February 21, 1925. On school support from the agency, see June 29, 1925; September 2, October 23, November 27, 1926. On Ottogary's son's graduation, see January 23, 1925. For Charlie Broom, see March 13, April 16, December 30, 1912, and May 29, 1920, which notes Broom's death to small pox.

30. In addition to the *Logan Journal* in which Ottogary items appeared from 1909 to 1929, his columns appeared in the *Box Elder News* (1911–23), the *Box Elder Journal* (1925), the *Tremonton Times* (1906–7), and the *Oneida County Enterprise* (1924).

31. Brigham D. Madsen, *The Northern Shoshoni*, 99–104, provides a brief summary of the Washakie experience. More complete treatment is found in the works of Matt Kreitzer and Scott Christiansen, cited above.

32. Clifford Duncan, "The Northern Utes of Utah," 191–97.

33. David Rich Lewis, *Neither Wolf nor Dog: American Indians, Environment, and Agrarian Change*, 34–45.

34. Duncan, "Northern Utes," 201–2; Fuller, "Land Rush in Zion," 29–87.

35. Ibid., 87–111.

36. Ibid., 103; Thomas G. Alexander, *The Rise of Multiple-Use Management in the Intermountain West: A History of Region 4 of the Forest Service*, 18–19; and Fred A. Conetah, *A History of the Northern Ute People*, 123–26, discuss the 1905 opening of the reservation. For an excellent cartographic presentation of how the forest reserve intruded on the Indian reserve, see p. 124.

37. On the General Allotment Act, see Leonard A. Carlson, *Indians, Bureaucrats, and Land: The Dawes Act and the Decline of Indian Farming*; Delos S. Otis, *The Dawes Act and the Allotment of Indian Lands*; and Frederick E. Hoxie, *A Final Promise: The Campaign to Assimilate the Indians, 1880–1920*.

38. Short accounts of the opening are found in Conetah, *History of the Northern Ute People*; Lewis, *Neither Wolf nor Dog*, 53–62; and Duncan, "Northern Utes," 201–5. For a much more detailed account, see Fuller, "Land Rush in Zion," chaps. 3–5.

39. Duncan, "Northern Utes," 205–6; Lewis, *Neither Wolf nor Dog*, 54–59; Floyd A. O'Neil, "An Anguished Odyssey: The Flight of the Utes, 1906–1908."

40. Fuller, "Land Rush in Zion," 112–36; Craig W. Fuller, "Development of Irrigation in Wasatch County," 106–21.

41. Fuller, "Land Rush in Zion," 190–92, 200–202.

42. Duncan, "Northern Utes," 207–8; Norris Hundley Jr., "The Dark and Bloody Ground of Indian Water Rights: Confusion Elevated to Principle"; Hundley, "The *Winters* Decision and Indian Water Rights: A Mystery Reexamined"; A. H. Kneale, *Indian Agent*, 268–70; Lewis, *Neither Wolf nor Dog*, 60.

43. Lewis, *Neither Wolf nor Dog*, 61–62.

44. Ibid., 62–70.

45. Ibid., 62–63; Joseph Jorgensen, *The Sundance Religion: Power for the Powerless*, 90–91.

46. Lewis, *Neither Wolf nor Dog*, 63.

47. Jorgensen, *Sun Dance Religion*, 21–23, cites the *Denver Republic*; Frances Densmore, *Northern Ute Music*, 79–80; Karl E. Young, "Sun Dance at Whiterocks, 1919." In a 1969 centennial retracing of the Powell expedition, Charles Peterson heard George Stewart, longtime Roosevelt lawyer and white-water enthusiast, describe the "Ute Trail" by which this ceremonial traffic made its annual junkets along the west rim of Desolation Canyon.

48. K. E. Young, "Sun Dance at Whiterocks," 240–41.

49. Omer C. Stewart, *Ute Peyotism: A Study of a Cultural Complex*; Stewart, *Washo-Northern Paiute Peyotism: A Study of Acculturation*; David F. Aberle and Omer C. Stewart, "Navaho and Ute Peyotism: A Chronological and Distributional Study."

50. Kim M. Gruenwald, "American Indians and the Public School System: A Case Study of the Northern Utes," 246–49.

51. Conetah, *History of the Northern Ute People*, 134–53.

52. Ibid.; Duncan, "Northern Utes," 201–10.

53. Lewis, *Neither Wolf nor Dog*, 70.

54. For information on the Long Walk and its devastating impact, see Gerald Thompson, *The Army and the Navajo: The Bosque Redondo Reservation Experiment, 1863–1868*; and Nancy C. Maryboy and David Begay, "The Navajos of Utah," 280–84.

55. Deon C. Greer et al., *Atlas of Utah*, 110; Sheriff Willard Butt to Governor Caleb W. West, November 23, 1895, Caleb W. West Papers; C. Peterson, *Look to the Mountains*, 75; Robert S. McPherson, *The Northern Navajo Frontier, 1860–1900: Expansion through Adversity*.

56.   S. S. Patterson, report dated August 23, 1887, in *Annual Report of the Commissioner of Indian Affairs to the Secretary of the Interior for the Year 1887*, 171–77; McPherson, *Northern Navajo Frontier*, 77; Brooks, *Uncle Will Tells His Own Story*, 128–37.

57.   McPherson, *Northern Navajo Frontier*, 67.

58.   David M. Brugge, "Navajo Use and Occupation of the Area North of the San Juan River in Present-Day Utah," unpublished manuscript, 1966, 83, copy in Navajo Tribal Office, Window Rock, AZ.

59.   Ibid., 80.

60.   Ibid., 80–97.

61.   See documents cited in ibid., 108–12, 118.

62.   Correspondence quoted in ibid., 106–17.

63.   Documents cited in ibid., 119–29.

64.   For a complete account of this incident, see Robert S. McPherson, "Too Much Noise in That Bunch across the River."

65.   See reports and documents cited in J. Lee Correll, *Bai-a-lil-le: Medicine Man or Witch?*, esp. 33; and reports cited in Brugge, "Navajo Use and Occupation," 125–33. See also Robert S. McPherson, *Navajo Land, Navajo Culture: The Utah Experience in the Twentieth Century*, 53–54.

66.   Jim Joe to Shelton, November 20, 1907; E. A. Sturges to Adjutant General, August 12, 1908, quoted in Brugge, "Navajo Use and Occupation," 134, 139.

67.   Correll, *Bai-a-lil-le*, 38–39.

68.   In a final adjustment the Aneth Extension was redrawn in 1958 to include McCracken Mesa, when Indian land at Glen Canyon Dam was turned over to the government. Robert McPherson, *A History of San Juan County: In the Palm of Time*, 144. McPherson cites Garrick Bailey and Robert Glen Bailey, *A History of the Navajos: The Reservation Years*, 105.

69.   Maryboy and Begay, "The Navajos of Utah," 294–95; G. A. Boyce, *When Navajos Had Too Many Sheep: The 1940's*, 85–90; Peter Iverson, *The Navajo Nation*, chaps. 1–2.

70.   A fine example of Navajos working in concert were the twelve or fifteen families whose experience running sheep on the public domain north of Aneth was described by Mary Jelly in 1961. As part of the group's effort, Jelly and her sons built two dams, excavated several springs, and nurtured seeps along McElmo and Montezuma Creeks. Others maintained mesa-top barriers for overnight grazing, and all apparently had farms, some on the San Juan River but some also located north along the creeks running through the public domain. Sheep operations were scattered, allowing for seasonal movement, and differed dramatically in size. With upwards of a thousand sheep, and as many horses, Hastiin Sleepy was said to range over a ninety-square-mile area in Utah and Arizona. More typical were the Jellys, who had 370 sheep, and Beulah Jones, with 100, who ran north and west on McCracken Mesa. Mary Jelly Affidavits before the Indian Claims Commission, January 21, 1961, #722, Doris Duke Collection.

71.   Maryboy and Begay, "The Navajos of Utah," 297–98; McPherson, *Navajo Land, Navajo Culture*, 108.

72.   Christine A. Mitchell, "'Work and Devotion': Father Harold Baxter Liebler at St. Christopher's Mission, 1943–1962"; Boyce, *When Navajos Had Too Many Sheep*, 33, 51, 86, 93, 101–4, 119.

73.   Richard White, *The Roots of Dependency: Subsistence, Environment, and Social Change among the Choctaws, Pawnees, and Navajos*, argues persuasively that Navajos passed from underdevelopment to dependency during this period.

8. CHANGING FEDERALISM: THE OUTDOORS AND ITS MANAGEMENT

1. Solomon F. Kimball, "President Brigham Young's Excursion Party."
2. On the public domain, see E. Louise Peffer, *The Closing of the Public Domain: Disposal and Reservation Policies, 1900–50.*
3. R. L. Dewsnup to R. B. Hansen, July 23, 1979, open file labeled "Revolution in the West, 1980," State Attorney General's Office, Salt Lake City, copy in Peterson's possession.
4. On Mormons and the environment, see Thomas G. Alexander, "Stewardship and Enterprise: The LDS Church and the Wasatch Oasis Environment, 1847–1930"; Dan B. Flores, "Agriculture, Mountain Ecology, and the Land Ethic: Phases of the Environmental History of Utah"; Flores, "Islands in the Desert: An Environmental Interpretation of the Rocky Mountain Frontier"; and Donald Worster, "The Kingdom, the Power, and the Water."
5. Kimball, "President Brigham Young's Excursion Party," 415–16; Lila Duncan-Larson, "H. L. A. Culmer, Utah Artist and Man of the West, 1854–1914"; H. L. A. Culmer, "Mountain Scenery of Utah"; Culmer, "The San Rafael Swell," *SLH*, May 9, 1909.
6. Charles S. Peterson, "A Utah Moon, Juanita Brooks Lecture for 1984"; Dale L. Morgan, *The Great Salt Lake*, 325, 337–47, 375, 420–21; Alfred Lambourne, *Our Inland Sea: The Story of a Homestead*, esp. 233. See also *DN*, June 25, 1898, for the ruling of the secretary of the interior that "guano is a mineral."
7. Stanley Welsh, "Utah Plant Types—Historical Perspective, 1840–1981—Annotated List, and Bibliography," 136–37; Neil M. Judd, *Men Met along the Trail: Adventures in Archaeology*, 67–71.
8. Welsh, "Utah Plant Types," 138–42; B. A. Wetherill, *The Wetherills of the Mesa Verde: Autobiography of Benjamin Alfred Wetherill*, 195–213.
9. Welsh, "Utah Plant Types"; Walter P. Cottam, *Our Renewable Wild Lands: A Challenge*. This volume contains six of Cottam's most striking articles.
10. C. W. Lockerbie, "Our Changing World"; H. Christian Thorup, "Clarence Cottam: Conservationist, the Welder Years," 66–67; Andrew Karl Larson, *The Education of a Second Generation Swede: An Autobiography*, 325–59, esp. 350–53.
11. In the pre-Cummings era, James E. Talmage's name is often mentioned in connection with the Deseret Museum. William Derby Johnson of Kanab, who was involved in the 1872 Powell explorations, studied at "Yale College, to fit" himself to take charge of the "museum on account of the failing health of Prof. Barfoot" (Dale Morgan, ed., "The Exploration of the Colorado River and the High Plateaus of Utah in 1871–72"). See also Charlie R. Steen, "The Natural Bridges of White Canyon: A Diary of H. L. A. Culmer, 1905"; W. W. Dyar, "The Colossal Bridges of Utah: A Recent Discovery of Natural Wonders"; and "Utah to Have a National Park," *Inter-Mountain Republican*, August 11, 1907. For good accounts of 1921 and 1931 VIP tours to southeastern Utah, see Middleton, *Memoirs of a Pioneer Surgeon*, 267–80; and Judd, *Men Met along the Trail*, 17–18. Harvey Leake and Gary Topping, in "The Bernheimer Explorations in Forbidding Canyon," summarize Bernheimer's role and comment on Johnson and John Wetherill. On the proposed national park, see Ansel F. Hall, *General Report of the Rainbow Bridge–Monument Valley Expedition of 1933*; P. T. Reilly, "Norman Nevills: Whitewater Man of the West"; and Jared Farmer, *Glen Canyon Dammed: Inventing Lake Powell & the Canyon Country*, 85–87.
12. M. Edward Moseley, "The Discovery and Definition of Basketmaker, 1890–1914"; Judd, *Men Met along the Way*, 64–64; Henry Montgomery, "Prehistoric Man in Utah," 227–34,

289–306, 335–42; Frank McNitt, *Richard Wetherill: Anasazi*, 55–67; McPherson, *Comb Ridge and Its People.*

13. McNitt, *Richard Wetherill: Anasazi*, 1–5, 148–294; Judd, *Men Met along the Trail*, 3–45; Wetherill, *Wetherills of the Mesa Verde*, 269–90; McPherson, *Comb Ridge.*

14. Byron Cummings, *The Great Natural Bridges of Utah*; Cummings, *The Ancient Inhabitants of the San Juan Valley*; Walter A. Kerr, "Byron Cummings, Classic Scholar and Father of University Athletics," 145–50; Judd, *Men Met along the Trail*, chaps. 1–3; Farmer, *Glen Canyon Dammed*, 68–71; McPherson, *Comb Ridge and Its People*, 150–72. To Utah's loss, Cummings left Salt Lake for the University of Arizona in 1915 over an academic-freedom controversy.

15. F. S. Dellenbaugh, *The Romance of the Colorado River . . . with Special Reference to the Voyages of Powell . . .*; Dellenbaugh, *A Canyon Voyage . . . 1871–1872*, which provides a brief Dellenbaugh bibliography; John Riis, *Ranger Trails*; Gary Topping, "An Adventure for Adventure's Sake, Recounted by Robert B. Aird"; W. L. Rusho, *Everett Ruess: A Vagabond for Beauty.*

16. Judd, *Met Men along the Trail*, 1–45, 60–84; Neil M. Judd, "Beyond the Clay Hills: An Account of the National Geographic Society's Reconnaissance of a Previously Unexplored Section in Utah."

17. Wallace Stegner, "Notes on a Life Pecking at a Sandstone Cliff," in *Mormon Country*, 302–18; Millie Kay Haws, interview by Lynne Ames, Vernal, UT, August 21, 1983, copy in Peterson's possession; Earl Douglass, "The Glories of the Uintah Basin," *Salt Lake Mining Review* 21–22 (February–September 1920); G. E. Untermann and Billie R. Untermann, "Dinosaur Country"; Glenn Sandiford, "Bernard DeVoto and His Forgotten Contribution to Echo Park"; Mark K. Harvey, "Utah, the National Park Service, and Dinosaur National Monument, 1909–56," esp. 256; Harvey, "Battle for Dinosaur: Echo Park Dam and the Birth of the Modern Wilderness Movement."

18. Alfred Runte, *National Parks: An American Experience*; Hal K. Rothman, "'A Regular Ding-Dong Fight': Agency Culture and Evolution in the NPS-USFS Dispute, 1916–1937," 143–48; Frank Graham Jr., *The Adirondack Park: A Political History*, 52–64; P. Gates, *History of Public Land Law Development*, 564–84; Gifford Pinchot, *The Fight for Conservation*, 42–48.

19. J. M. Haymond, "History of the Manti Forest, Utah: A Case of Conservation in the West," 123–25.

20. Worster, "Kingdom, Power, and Water"; Flores, "Agriculture, Mountain Ecology, and the Land Ethic"; and Charles S. Peterson, *"Take Up Your Mission": Mormon Colonizing along the Little Colorado River, 1870–1900*, touch briefly on the negative impact of Mormon idealism on the environment. See also Alexander, "Stewardship and Enterprise."

21. Samuel Fortier, "The Beneficial Effects of Forests in Increasing Seepage Flow," 25–26. Chief of grazing Albert Potter wrote in 1902 of Utah Agricultural College's G. L. Swendsen and studies measuring "Logan River and Summit Creek showing that since deforestation and damage to range, floods have come down earlier in the spring and streams have almost gone dry later in season when water was most needed." See "Diary of Albert F. Potter's Wasatch Survey, July 1, to November 22, 1902," http://forestry.usu.edu/htm/rural-forests/forest-history/the-potter-diaries.

22. Heber M. Wells, "Governor's Message, January 12, 1897," 36–38; *DN*, September 21, 1895, January 13, 1896.

23. Heber M. Wells, "Governor's Message, January 10, 1899," 33–35. In a similar effort, Wyoming got a "state game preserve" in 1905 for elk in Jackson Hole. Runte, *National Parks*, 120.

24. Heber M. Wells, "Governor's Message, 1901," 19–20; J. W. Humphrey, "My Recollections of the Manti Forest, June, 1953," 2, Manti–La Sal National Forest Historical Files.

25. F. S. Richards, "Statement from Arid Land Reclamation Fund Commission"; Potter Diary, July 1 to November 22, 1902; C. Peterson, "Albert F. Potter's Wasatch Survey."

26. Potter Diary.

27. Sanpete and Emery County newspapers cover this in great detail. See, for example, the *Emery County Progress*, September 8, 15, 1900; November 9, 30, 1901; March 22, May 24, June 7, 14, November 15, 1902; October 24, 31, November 14, 1903.

28. P. H. Roberts, *Hoof Prints on Forest Ranges*, 42, 107.

29. Gifford Pinchot, *Breaking New Ground*; Potter Diary. In 1903 Governor Heber M. Wells warned that the "course" so far "pursued by the government in the control and management of the alleged forest reserves [has] not been such as to encourage the belief that real good will result" ("Governor's Message, 1903," 34). On District (later Region) 4, see Alexander, *Rise of Multiple-Use Management*.

30. C. Peterson, *Look to the Mountains*, 170–88; District Forester to Supervisors, March 7, 1918, G-Supervision Folder, Manti–La Sal National Forest Historical Files.

31. Seely to Smoot, January 4, 1911; Seely to Forester, January 13, 1911; Seely and N. S. Nielsen to Smoot, January 23, 1911; and Smoot to the Forester, January 21, 1911, in Records Relating to Grazing Supervision, Region 4, 1908–12; C. E. Rachford, "Memo to the Forester, November 12, 1921," G-G-Supervision 1915–1922, Region IV Papers, RG 95, NA; District Forester to Supervisors, March 7, 1918, Manti–La Sal National Forest Historical Files; C. C. Anderson, "History of Grazing," 9; Federal Writers' Project Collection; J. W. Humphrey, "Grazing on the Manti National Forest," December 7, 1928, Manti–La Sal National Forest Historical Files; C. Peterson, *Look to the Mountains*, 170–73; C. Peterson, "Small Holding Land Patterns."

32. US Department of Agriculture, *Forest and Range Resources of Utah: Their Protection and Use*, 57–60.

33. Charles S. Peterson and Linda E. Speth, *A History of the Wasatch-Cache National Forest*, 112–22; Douglas M. Bird, "A History of Timber Resource Use in the Development of Cache Valley, Utah"; Asa R. Bowthorpe, "History of Pioneer Sawmills and Local Canyons of the Salt Lake Valley" (1961), Forest History Wasatch, 2 binders, Wasatch-Cache National Forest Historical Records; Potter Diary.

34. Timber Management Folder, Manti–La Sal National Forest Historical Files. For a full treatment of the larger influences on management policies, see Alexander, *Rise of Multiple-Use Management*, 59–66.

35. Alexander, *Rise of Multiple-Use Management*, 57–72.

36. *Grand Valley Times*, November 13, 1908. Exceptions included David Eccles, Charles W. Nibley, and a handful of other wealthy northern Utah lumbermen.

37. This situation pertained to the entire southern part of the state: stumpage sales by the La Sal Forest were ahead of Dixie National Forest and not far behind the Sevier, Fishlake, or Fillmore Forests. *Cliffdwellers' Echo*, December 1912; Forest Service, *Timber Management Report, 1911*; *Grand Valley Times*, March 2, 1900, February 13, 1917; "Historical Information, La Sal National Forest," 107–8; Alexander, *Rise of Multiple-Use Management*, 61; C. Peterson, *Look to the Mountains*, 208–15.

38. Humphrey, "My Recollections of the Manti Forest," 6; *Life Story of Melvin Young*, 34–37, 40–41, 44–47, 50–55b.

39. Lyle F. Watts, "Smiths Fork, Green River Block," Timber Survey, 1915, 13; N. B. Eckbo, "East Fork and West Fork of Blacks Fork"; and F. S. Baker and A. G. Hauge, "Report on Tie Operation: Standard Timber Company, 1912–1913," all in Evanston District Historical Files; Peterson and Speth, *Wasatch-Cache National Forest*, 130–36.

40. F. S. Baker, "Memorandum for Office in Charge of Robert Price Sale Area, Meadow Creek, Cache National Forest"; and Paul A. Grossenbach, "Management Plan, Bear Lake Corking Circle, Cache National Forest, 1942," History Cache National Forest, II, both in Wasatch-Cache National Forest Historical Files; Peterson and Speth, *Wasatch-Cache National Forest*, 136–40.

41. *DN*, February 9, 1923.

42. Taniguchi, *Necessary Fraud*, examines this dilemma at length, including the various delays that ensued as different levels of government fought out the land-control question in court and as private entrepreneurs scrambled for advantage. See also Reed Smoot, "School Lands Campaign," a nine-page summary of the effort of the Utah congressional delegation and state officials between 1913 and 1927 to "vest absolute title in the States to the public school land sections named in the Enabling Act." Zion National Park Legislation, Reed Smoot Papers; Humphrey, "My Recollections of the Manti Forest," 4–5.

43. Governor William Spry, "Conservation," speech before the American Mining Congress, October 27, 1911; Spry, "Storage and Use of Flood Waters," speech before the Western Governors' Conference, August 2, 1912; Spry, "True Conservation and How to Accomplish It," speech before the Western Governors' Conference, June 6, 1913; Spry, "State Control of Natural Resources," speech delivered at the Seventh Meeting of the Governors, November 11, 1914; Spry, "Message to the Eleventh Legislature," January 18, 1915, 4–7, all in Official Documents and Addresses of William Spry, Utah State Archives; Governor Charles R. Mabey, "Message to the Fifteenth Legislature," January 10, 1923, Charles Mabey Papers; Governor George Dern, "School Land Titles in Public Land States," 19–21, speech delivered at the Governors' Conference, July 17, 1926; Dern, "Message to the Seventeenth Legislature," January 11, 1927, 18–19; Dern, "Message to the Eighteenth Legislature," 44–47; January 15, 1929, Speeches of George H. Dern, Utah State Archives.

44. *SLT*, March 17, 1921; and *DN*, March 17, 1921, both quoted in W. Roper and Arrington, *William Spry*, 207–8.

45. Runte, *National Parks*; Thomas G. Alexander, "Senator Reed Smoot and Western Land Policy, 1905–1920"; Horace M. Albright and Robert Cahn, *The Birth of the National Park Service: The Founding Years, 1913–33*.

46. Ted J. Warner, ed., *The Domínguez-Escalante Journal*, 144–45.

47. *Autobiography of Parley Parker Pratt*, 365–70; Milton R. Hunter, *Brigham Young the Colonizer*, chap. 5; Oliver R. Smith, ed., *The Journal of Jesse Nathaniel Smith: Six Decades in the Early West*, 32–35.

48. John W. Powell, *The Exploration of the Colorado River*, 137–45; Angus M. Woodbury, *A History of Southern Utah and Its National Parks*, 185–86; *DN*, August 7, 1852, cited in C. Gregory Crampton, "Mormon Colonization in Southern Utah and in Adjacent Parts of Arizona and Nevada, 1851–1900," 51–63, 84–89; J. Cecil Alter, ed., "Journal of Priddy Meeks," 187.

49.   Woodbury, *History of Southern Utah*, 187, 192; *Emery County Progress*, November 21, 1903; General Land Office, Utah Field Notes, vol. 162, September 8, 1909, 59–61, Zion National Park Historical Files.

50.   G. E. Hair to CGLO, May 9, 1914; T. E. Hunt to CGLO, July 12, 1916, Zion National Park, Box 564, Administration Superintendent, 1925–1932, pts. 1–2, Records of the National Park Service, RG 79, NA.

51.   Olive Wooley Burt, "A Kid Named Jones Had a Dream," 28. On the emergence of railroads, see Edward Leo Lyman, "From the City of Angels to the City of Saints: The Struggle to Build a Railroad from Los Angeles to Salt Lake City"; J. W. Hulse, "W. A. Clark and the Las Vegas Connection: The 'Midas of the West' and the Development of Southern Nevada"; Alfred Runte, "Promoting the Golden West: Advertising and the Railroad"; Runte, *National Parks*, 113; Woodbury, *History of Southern Utah*, 194–206; Dena S. Markoff, *The Dudes Are Always Right: The Utah Parks Company in Zion National Park, 1923–1972*.

52.   Runte, *National Parks*; Albright and Cahn, *Birth of the National Park Service*, 32–52, 99, 101; Woodbury, *History of Southern Utah*.

53.   Horace M. Albright, "Early History of ZNP," for Angus M. Woodbury, August 4, 1944, Zion National Park Historical Files; Albright and Cahn, *Birth of the National Park Service*, 34–36, 39, 49–50, 63, 84; Douglas White, "Awakening of Zion Canyon," manuscript dealing with the Salt Lake Line's role in 1917, Zion National Park Historic Foundation.

54.   Albright and Cahn, *Birth of the National Park Service*, 63, 84. For geopolitical development of the Park Service and interagency rivalry, see Runte, *National Parks*. For Reed Smoot's involvement in the creation of Zion and Bryce Canyon National Parks, see Thomas G. Alexander, "Red Rock and Gray Stone: Senator Reed Smoot, the Establishment of Zion and Bryce Canyon National Parks, and the Rebuilding of Downtown Washington, D.C." See also E. T. Scoyen, "The National Parks and Their Relation to the Future Development of Southern Utah," January 10, 1931, 4, RG 79, NA; Nick Scrattish, "The Modern Discovery, Popularization, and Early Development of Bryce Canyon, Utah"; Hal Rothman, "Shaping the Nature of a Controversy: The Park Service, the Forest Service, and the Cedar Breaks Proposal"; Rothman, "'Regular Ding-Dong Fight'"; and Greer, *Atlas of Utah*, 260–64.

55.   *SLT*, January 1, 1921; Andrew Karl Larson, "Zion National Park with Some Reminiscences Fifty Years Later," 420–25; Heath, *In the World*, 454–55, 532–41. The tendency of Mather and Albright to avoid confrontation and maintain the pleasantries of friendship is apparent throughout the Zion National Park Historical Files and especially in Albright and Cahn, *Birth of the National Park Service*.

56.   Industrial tourism was defined by Edward Abbey as "big business. It means money. It includes the motel and restaurant owners, the gasoline retailers, the oil corporations, the road-building contractors, the heavy equipment manufacturers, the state and federal engineering agencies and the sovereign, all-powerful automotive industry" (*Desert Solitaire: A Season in the Wilderness*, 56).

57.   Burt, "Kid Named Jones," 26–29; Carl A. Gray to Louis C. Crampton, January 29, 1924, Zion National Park, RG 79, NA; Markoff, *Dudes Are Always Right*, 128–49; and P. P. Patraw to Cedar City Chamber of Commerce, December 22, 1937, Box 1992, CCF 1933–1949, RG 79, NA.

58.   *SLT*, January 1, 1921.

59.   Michael Lyle Shamo, "Making the Desert Blossom: Public Works in Washington County, Utah," 101–36; Markoff, *Dudes Are Always Right*, 122; Woodbury, *History of Southern Utah*, 203–6; Burt, "Kid Named Jones"; *SLT*, July 7, 1930; "Address by Governor George H. Dern

at Dedication of Zion–Mt. Carmel Highway, July 4, 1930," and related correspondence, Zion National Park Roads, Box 560, CCF 1907–1949, RG 79, NA.

60. Ryan Paul, "Traveling the Painted Canyons: The Story of the Utah Parks Company, 1923–1970" (2006), unpublished paper in Cannon's possession; Markoff, *Dudes Are Always Right*, 149–55; Woodbury, *History of Southern Utah*, 203; A. Larson, "Zion National Park"; J. L. Crawford, interview by Charles Peterson, January 17, 1996, St. George, UT. Crawford, the son of a Springdale family, grew up while the park was developing and became a ranger after World War II.

61. Data on attendance are drawn from annual reports in the Zion National Park Historical Files, but also and especially from "Zion National Park: A Resource of the State of Utah," April 1, 1943, 12, CCF, Zion National Park, RG 79, NA; "Zion Monument Development Urged at Motor Court Meet," *SLT*, November 3. 1946; and Markoff, *Dudes Are Always Right*, 190–93.

62. Supt. E. T. Scoyen to the Director, December 12, 1929, Privileges, Grazing 1926–1932, Box 564; Superintendent P. R. Franke, May 29, 1941, Zion 501-02-503, Box 1892, CCF 1933–1949; F. A. Kittredge to the Director, December 5, 1929; E. T. Scoyen, "Justification of Estimates for River Protection Work," ca. 1929, Box 557, CCF 1907–1932, RG 79, NA; A. Larson, *Education of a Second Generation Swede*, 82.

63. Although park personnel did not concern themselves with the matter, references to floods scouring fish habitat from the stream and reluctance to resort to stocking fish appear incidentally in the Zion Park record.

64. In 1922 Albert Petty, who grew up at one of the canyon farms, reported that he and three others had been the first to go through the Narrows and that they had "Waded the Bigest Part of 16 Miles in Watter." Petty to Stephen Mather, April 23, 1922, Zion National Park Historical Files. For the Easter pageant, see H. E. Petersen to Director, July 22, 1939, Zion National Park Administration File 201, CCF 33–49, RG 79, NA. For a summary report on closing the Easter pageant, see *Washington County News*, February 27, 1941.

65. The Bridge Mountain sheep were closely monitored but had disappeared by the end of World War II. Wildlife specialists still hiked the area looking for them until at least 1949, by which time a rope through the chimney was rotted enough to turn all but the most reckless adventurers back. *SLT*, December 31, 1929; Zion National Park Press Release, January 6, 1930, Newspaper Articles 501-03, CCF 1907–1932, RG 79, NA; Crawford interview.

66. S. S. Johnson to A. B. Cammerer, June 30, 1927; E. T. Scoyen to Director, July 13, 1927; Cammerer to Ralph Graves, July 8, 1928; Scoyen to Director, April 12, July 12, 1930; Cammerer to Scoyen, July 22, 1930; Cammerer to Johnson, July 22, 1930; T. J. Allen Jr. to Director, July 28, 1931; C. J. Smith to Regional Director, August 19, 1945, Climbing 1927 to 1931, Box 2010, CCF, Records of the Office of the Secretary of the Interior, RG 48, NA.

67. On this absentee factor in Utah's tourist industry over the course of the twentieth century, see Stephen C. Sturgeon, "The Disappearance of Everett Ruess and the Discovery of Utah's Red Rock Country."

68. Scoyen to the Director, December 26, 1928, 602-1, Box 551, Zion National Park, RG 79, NA; Scoyen to the Director, January 14, 1931; Scoyen, "The National Parks and Their Relation to the Future Development of Southern Utah," Zion National Park, 601-1, Box 551, RG 79, NA; Wayne K. Hinton, "Getting Along: The Significance of Cooperation in the Development of Zion National Park," 322–23, 327–28, 330.

69. Hinton, "Getting Along"; Crawford interview.

70. Scoyen, "The National Parks and Their Relation to the Future Development of Southern Utah"; "National Parks: A Resource of the State of Utah," April 1, 1943, NPS 1933–1949, Zion National Park Box 1887, CCF, RG 79, NA.

71. G. Vanderbilt Caesar, "National or City Parks?"; Scoyen to Director, October 23, 1927; A. E. Demaray to G. H. Lorimer, November 1, 1927; Lorimer to Demaray, November 3, 1927; Publicity File #501, CCF 1907–1932, RG 79, NA.

72. Cammerer to Walter Ruesch, April 22, 1926; Demaray to R. T. Evans, August 3, 1925; A. M. Woodbury, "Educational Report, July 1928," Zion National Park 601-1, Box 551, RG 79, NA; Alexander, *Rise of Multiple-Use Management*, 68–70; Pinchot, *Breaking New Ground*, 71; Peterson and Speth, *Wasatch-Cache National Forest*, 62–63, 251–67; Ronald B. Hartzer, Edward P. Cliff, and David A. Clary, *Half a Century in Forest Conservation: A Biography and Oral History of Edward P. Cliff*, 60; *Provo Daily Herald*, editorial, January 24, 1958; H. C. Bryant to Chief, Wild Life Division, November 29, 1933; Cammerer to P. P. Patraw, December 14, 19, 1933, ZNP 619-30, Box 1897, CCF 1933–1949, RG 79, NA.

73. "Outline of Lecture Course in National Parks," June 22, 1935; "National Parks: A Resource of the State of Utah," April 1, 1943, 6, Zion National Park 1933–1949, Box 1887, CCF, RG 79, NA.

74. See *SLT*, September 22, 25, 1929, August 21, 1932; Mark Anderson to C. C. Anderson, January 6, 1941, Federal Writers' Project Grazing History Records; Layton, *"To No Privileged Class,"* 87; Peterson and Speth, *Wasatch-Cache National Forest*, 65–69; Robert W. Wells Jr., "A Political Biography of George Dern," 95. See also Minutes of Public Land States Conference, August 1929, George Dern Papers.

75. A. F. Bracken, "State Report on Land-Use Study for Utah" ([Logan, UT]: Resettlement Administration, 1935), 49–78, copy in Peterson Papers, Box 122, Utah State Historical Society.

76. James R. Skillen, *The Nation's Largest Landlord: The Bureau of Land Management in the American West*; James Muhn and H. R. Stuart, *Opportunity and Challenge: The Story of BLM*; Peffer, *Closing of the Public Domain*.

77. Mark Anderson to C. C. Anderson, January 6, 1941, Federal Writers' Project Grazing History Records; Peterson and Speth, *Wasatch-Cache National Forest*, 65–69. The 2,255,228 acres of the "proposed purchase and acquisition area" included something more than a half-million acres of private land and 1,733,390 acres of public domain. Bracken, "State Report on Land-Use Study for Utah," 67–70.

78. Jonathan S. Thow, "Capitol Reef: The Forgotten National Park," 36–38; *Richfield Reaper*, September 4, 1930, quoted in ibid., 37; C. C. Anderson, interview by Harry Reed, Moab, UT, "National Park Service vs Stockmen," Federal Writers' Project Grazing History Records; Mark Anderson to C. C. Anderson, January 6, 1941, Federal Writers' Project Grazing History Records; Scoyen to Director, November 3, 1930; C. L. Wirth to P. P. Patraw, June 10, 1935; maps of Zion "Exclusion" and Utah and Arizona "Exclusions," generally; Patraw to R. W. Toll re: "Boundaries Kolob Canyons," September 3, 1935, Zion National Park, Box 551, RG 79, NA.

79. "Minutes of the Public Meeting Held June 16, 1936, at Zion National Park Lodge [about the Kolob Extension]," Zion National Park, RG 79, NA. In addition to treating the prospects of southern Utah and its relationship to the national parks, E. T. Scoyen, "The National Parks and Their Relation to the Future Development of Southern Utah," addresses the hostility of stockmen but discounts it because they are few in number (Zion National Park, RG 79, NA).

80. "Minutes of the Public Meeting Held June 16, 1936"; Patraw to Toll, "Boundaries Kolob Canyons," 9–10.

81. "Minutes of the Public Meeting Held June 16, 1936"; D. N. Madsen to Director, June 18, 1936, Zion National Park Files, RG 79, NA; Hal K. Rothman, *Devil's Bargains: Tourism in the Twentieth-Century American West*.

82. F. C. Koziol, interview by A. R. Standing, May 3, 1965, Bountiful, UT, http://www.fs.usda.gov/Internet/FSE_DOCUMENTS/stelprdb5189938.pdf; Peterson and Speth, *Wasatch-Cache National Forest*, 267–75.

9. WATER FOR AN ARID STATE

1. *DN*, May 6, 10, 17, 1922.

2. Thomas G. Alexander, "Interdependence and Change: Mutual Irrigation Companies in Utah's Wasatch Oasis in an Age of Modernization, 1870–1930."

3. Robert G. Dunbar, *Forging New Rights in Western Waters*, 82.

4. Ibid., 17; G. Thomas, *Development of Institutions under Irrigation*, 139; Richard W. Sadler and Richard C. Roberts, *The Weber River Basin: Grass Roots Democracy and Water Development*, 106.

5. *Beaver County News*, February 16, 1917. See Governor Heber M. Wells's messages to the Utah Legislature, 1897–1907, for updating irrigation laws: "Governor's Message, January 12, 1897"; "Governor's Message, January 10, 1899"; "Governor's Message, 1901"; "Governor's Message, 1903," 34; "Governor's Message, 1905"; "Governor's Message, 1907." Summarizing the laws of 1897, 1901, and 1903 at length is R. P. Teele, "General Discussion of Irrigation in Utah." The classic treatment of water institutions, including legislation, is G. Thomas, *The Development of Institutions under Irrigation*.

6. Sadler and Roberts, *Weber River Basin*, 107–8; G. Thomas, *Development of Institutions under Irrigation*, 203–18; C. Brough, *Irrigation in Utah*.

7. Reeve, "'Little Oasis in the Desert,'" 222–45; Andrew Karl Larson, "Hurricane," in *"I Was Called to Dixie": The Virgin River Basin, Unique Experiences in Mormon Pioneering*, 382–402; Frank Adams, "Agriculture under Irrigation in the Basin of Virgin River," 220–22.

8. George A. Klipper, "The Development and Impact of East Canyon Reservoir," unpublished term paper, Weber State University, 1974, copy in Peterson's possession; Jay D. Stannard, "Irrigation in the Weber Valley," 196–97; Sadler and Roberts, *Weber River Basin*, 117–21.

9. Roger Walker, "The Delta Project: Utah's Successful Carey Act Project." On West Millard drainage, see Ridd, "Influence of Soil and Water Conditions"; and numerous bulletins published by the Utah Agricultural College Research Station.

10. "State Land Commissioner vs. Sevier River Land and Water Company," Land Commissioner Reports, Dern Papers. See also Crafts, *History of Sevier Bridge Reservoir*; Crafts, "Historical Background of the Sevier River Water Rights," paper delivered at a 1965 Millard County Water Conservancy meeting, copy in Peterson's possession; Gertrude Kendall Baker, "Cross Currents: A Family Chronicle and Delta South Tract History," transcribed by LaVell S. Johnson, March 1972, Utah State Historical Society; Johnson, "McCornick: Ghost Town," Utah State Historical Society; Zeke Johnson, "Looking Back over My Shoulder," autobiography, Johnson Papers.

11. *Beaver Weekly Press*, 1904–15; *Beaver County News*, 1907–15.

12. "State of Utah Reservoir Land Grant Fund," State Land Board folder labeled March to December 1932, Series 210, Dern Papers; "Hatch Reservoir Gone," *Panguitch Progress*, May 29, 1914; Guy Sterling, "Failure of the Dam of the Hatchtown Reservoir, Utah";

Sterling, "Analysis of the Failure of an Earth-Fill Dam"; W. M. Timmins, "The Failure of the Hatchtown Dam, 1914," 262–63; Crafts, *History of Sevier Bridge Reservoir*, 87–90; John Swensen Harvey, *A Historical Overview of the Evolutions of Institutions Dealing with Water Resource Use, and Water Resource Development in Utah—1847 through 1947*, 78–80; *Biennial Report of the Board of Land Commissioners for the Years 1919–1920*, 6–8; J. Howard Maughan, "Report for the Land Planning Section Resettlement Administration" (July 1936), 33–35, Box 1, 21 0902.2, State Engineer Papers.

13. *DN*, May 21, 25, 1928; Watt, *History of Carbon County*, 52–53.

14. Boxes 158–67, MSS 278, Jesse Knight Papers.

15. Sadler and Roberts, *Weber River Basin*, 121–25.

16. A pronounced advocate of regional planning, Doremus as Salt Lake City engineer had led a movement in the 1890s claiming Utah Lake as Salt Lake City's "proper reservoir" and exchanged its murky water for mountain streams held by Salt Lake County irrigators.

17. *Report of the Arid Land Reclamation Fund Commission, 1903–1904*; *Second Annual Report of the Reclamation Service, 1902–1903*, 451–86; Reclamation Service, *Third Annual Report of the Reclamation Service, 1903–1904*, 494–599; *Sixth Annual Report of the Reclamation Service, 1906–1907*, 214–23. The best source on the intransigence of water users in the Weber Basin counties is *Report of the State Engineer, 1905–1906*, where engineer Caleb Tanner, who had replaced the beleaguered Doremus, wrote, "It is a matter of regret that after more than fifty years of settlement any irrigation resource of the state should remain aboriginal and undeveloped; it is beyond regret, it is lamentable, if communities that have partially utilized an irrigation resource, stand stiff necked against a full utilization of that resource, if it can be had without risk or prejudice to their present interests, if the new regime of maximum benefit would mean simply a consolidation of ditch interests, individual and corporate, into one large efficient organization" (26). Tanner comes near the real point. Looking at the cost-benefit playoff in terms of their relative abundance, the Weber River people of 1906 had reason to stall. Later conditions would change.

18. John A. Widtsoe, "History and Problems of Irrigation Development in the West with Discussions Presented by Samuel Fortier, Arthur P. Davis, C. E. Grunsky, and F. H. Newell at Salt Lake City, 1925," esp. 681–95.

19. *Federal Reclamation by Irrigation*, 196; Heath, *In the World*, 211. For Mead's role, see James R. Kluger, *Turning on Water with a Shovel: The Career of Elwood Mead*, esp. 111–27. Widtsoe's ideas are developed briefly in "History and Problems of Irrigation Developments in the West" and at length in *Success on Irrigation Projects*; Eric A. Stene, *Strawberry Valley Project*, 17. See also Brian Q. Cannon, "'We Are Now Entering a New Era': Federal Reclamation and the Fact Finding Commission of 1923–24."

20. Sadler and Roberts, *Weber River Basin*, 124–34; Stephen A. Merrill, "Reclamation and the Economic Development of Northern Utah: The Weber River Project," 257–60.

21. Sadler and Roberts, *Weber River Basin*, 124–34.

22. Jay M. Bagley, "Utah's Water Development Framework," presented at a Governor's Advisory Council on Science and Technology symposium, April 1979; W. L. Rusho, "Bureau of Reclamation: State Summary for Utah," copies in Peterson's possession.

23. C. Gregory Crampton and Dwight L. Smith, eds., *The Colorado River Survey: Robert Stanton and the Denver, Colorado Canyon and Pacific Railroad*.

24. Robert Stanton, *The Hoskaninni Papers: Mining in Glen Canyon, 1897–1902*; C. Gregory Crampton, *The San Juan Canyon Historical Sites*; Crampton, *Standing Up Country*, 138–47; Crampton, *Ghosts of Glen Canyon: History beneath Lake Powell*, 80–83, 114–17.

25. Ferry information is taken from general sources. Local newspapers including the *Grand Valley Times* and the *Uintah Express* are good sources. See Judd, *Men Met along the Trail: Adventures in Archaeology*; and Steen, "Natural Bridges of White Canyon," 55–84. On Lees Ferry, see W. L. Rusho and C. Gregory Crampton, *Lee's Ferry: Desert River Crossing*; Crampton, *Ghosts of Glen Canyon*, 74–75; P. T. Reilly, "Warren Marshall Johnson, Forgotten Saint"; and Tennent, "John Jarvie Ranch," 47–82.

26. Roy Webb, *Riverman: The Story of Bus Hatch*, 30; E. L. Kolb, *Through the Grand Canyon from Wyoming to Mexico*, 95, 103–4.

27. The *Grand Valley Times* is a key source for river information during the turn-of-the-century years. See issues for November 20, December 4, 18, 1896; October 1, November 4, 1897; December 13, 1901; January 13, May 23, 1902; January 13, April 7, May 5, 19, 26, 1905; and September 17, 1909. Also *Moab Times Independent*, June 18, 1959, quoted in Richard E. Westwood, *Elwyn Blake's Colorado River Expeditions*, 10; and Kolb, *Through the Grand Canyon*, 111–16. Although Galloway is usually billed as a recluse, two letters describing his 1896 trip that survive in the *Grand Valley Times* suggest that even he worked consciously on image.

28. Data on Galloway are scarce and scattered and not always consistent. The only primary accounts are his two letters in *Grand Valley Times*, December 4, 18, 1896. The former reports a Green River stop, and the latter purports to be a letter from Galloway dated December 10 at Hite. Woodbury, "History of Southern Utah," 193, mentions a 1908 expedition in which "Nathan" Galloway taught David Rust "the Canadian method of shooting rapids" (backward) and in turn was guided onto the Markagunt Plateau "to hunt Grizzly bears." Other Galloway references are in Kolb, *Through the Grand Canyon*; R. Westwood, *Blake's Colorado River Expeditions*, xvi, 51, 75, 130; Webb, *Riverman*, 23–24; and Otis Marston, "River Runners: Fast Water Navigation," 292–94.

29. Herbert E. Gregory, *The San Juan Oil Field, Utah*, 11–25; Hugh D. Miser, *The San Juan Canyon, Southeastern Utah: A Geographic and Hydrographic Reconnaissance*, 2–3; R. Westwood, *Blake's Colorado River Expeditions*, 3–122; Webb, *Riverman*, 75.

30. Kolb, *Through the Grand Canyon*, 135–36, 335–44.

31. *Autobiography of William L. Woolf*, 45–47, 65–80.

32. Marston, "River Runners," 307; Gary Topping, "Charles Kelly's Glen Canyon Ventures and Adventures," 129–30.

33. Webb, *Riverman*; Roy Webb, "Les voyageurs sans trace: The DeColmont-DeSeyne Kayak Party of 1938"; Reilly, "Norman Nevills."

34. We have depended primarily on Norris Hundley Jr., *Water and the West: The Colorado River Compact and the Politics of Water in the American West*; papers and reports of the Utah state engineer, 1917–35; and papers, correspondence, and reports of Utah governors Simon Bamberger, George Dern, and Henry H. Blood. Also useful were Kluger, *Turning on Water with a Shovel*; Philip L. Fradkin, *A River No More: The Colorado River and the West*; Donald Worster, *Rivers of Empire: Water, Aridity, and the Growth of the American West*; and Donald J. Pisani, *To Reclaim a Divided West: Water, Law, and Public Policy, 1838–1902*.

35. Hundley, *Water and the West*, chaps. 1–2, esp. pp. 51, 54.

36. Ibid., chap. 3, pp. 44, 84–85, 126–31; *Duchesne Record*, September 28, 1918; *Biennial Report of the State Engineer to the Governor of Utah, 1917–1918*, 22; *DN*, January 18–21, 1919; *SLT*, January 18–19, 1919.

37. Hundley, *Water and the West*, 44, 84–85.

38. Ibid., 108.

39. Ibid., 146–49.

40. Ibid., chaps. 4–8; Daniel Tyler, *Silver Fox of the Rockies: Delphus E. Carpenter and Western Water Compacts.* Wide coverage was given the events of 1922 in the Salt Lake City papers—especially the January meeting, the hearings, and the November Santa Fe session that produced the compact. The river trip is chronicled in *DN*, September 25, 1922; and A. R. Mortensen, ed., "Journal of John A. Widtsoe: Colorado River Party, September 1922."

41. *Report of the State Engineer, 1921–1922*, 53–64; Hundley, *Water and the West*, 180–214.

42. Hundley, *Water and the West*, 277–80; George Dern, "Statement at the Hearings Before the Committee on Irrigation and Reclamation," US Senate, December 17, 1927, 11, bound as a pamphlet at Utah State Historical Society.

43. Hundley, *Water and the West*, 261–64, 272–80; and especially the following by George H. Dern: "The Boulder Dam"; *The Colorado River*; *Message of Governor George H. Dern to the Seventeenth Legislature of the State of Utah*; *Message of Governor George H. Dern to the Eighteenth Legislature of the State of Utah, January 15, 1929*; *Message of Governor George H. Dern to the Nineteenth Legislature of the State of Utah*; and *School Land Titles in Public Land States: Address of Governor George H. Dern before the Governors' Conference.*

44. Hundley, *Water and the West*, chaps. 8–10.

45. Joseph E. Stevens, *Hoover Dam: An American Adventure*, esp. chap. 1; S. Sessions and G. Sessions, *History of Utah International.*

46. "Citizens of Manti to Legislative Assembly," February 11, 1888, praying for "a law forbidding the herding or pasturing of sheep in any Canyon in Utah Territory where the waters of such canyon are the only source of supply for the people living below" (cited in *SLT*, February 10, 1958); G. M. Hunt to Corps of Engineers, September 20, 1938, folder labeled Flood Control Price, State Engineer's Papers; L. L. Taylor, Supplementary Data on Grand County, December 20, 1938, folder labeled Flood Control Monticello, Water Resources, State Engineer's Papers; C. L. Forsling, "Erosion on Uncultivated Lands in the Intermountain Region"; Frank C. Robertson, *A Ram in the Thicket: An Autobiography*, 175–88; Andrew M. Honker, "'Been Grazed Almost to Extinction': The Environment, Human Action, and Utah Flooding, 1900–1940," 28, 35–37, 40–41.

47. G. H. Bacon to H. H. Horton, February 21, 1930, State Engineer Folder 1929–32, Dern Papers.

48. This section depends heavily on F. S. Baker and J. H. Paul, *The Floods of 1923 in Northern Utah*; Forsling, "Erosion on Uncultivated Lands"; and *Life History of Luther M. Winsor.* For information on southern Utah flooding, see R. V. R. Reynolds, *Grazing and Floods: A Study of Conditions in the Manti National Forest, Utah*; and Walter P. Cottam, *Is Utah Sahara Bound?* See also Sylvester Q. Cannon, chairman, *Torrential Floods in Northern Utah, 1930: Report of Special Flood Commission*; Kenneth W. Baldridge, "Nine Years of Achievement: The Civilian Conservation Corps in Utah"; and Charles S. Peterson and Linda E. Speth, "A History of the Wasatch-Cache National Forest," typescript (1980), 224–44, http://www.fs.usda.gov/Internet/FSE_DOCUMENTS/stelprdb5053310.pdf.

49. Glen M. Leonard, *A History of Davis County*, 326; Honker, "'Been Grazed Almost to Extinction,'" 23–47.

50. S. Cannon, *Torrential Floods in Northern Utah*; 86-1-63 Flood Control, *Revised Statutes of Utah, 1933*; Carl Mattson, "Big Game as It Affects the Grazing of Livestock," speech delivered at the annual convention of the Utah State Woolgrowers, January 25, 1935, State Land Board Public Hearings, 1935, SE-1 22.4 1935–37, Henry E. Blood Papers.

51. Peterson and Speth, "History of Wasatch-Cache National Forest," 235–38; National Forest Reservation Commission to Governor H. H. Blood, October 27, 1936, State Land Board File, SE-1 22.4 1934–37, Blood Papers.

52. Honker, "'Been Grazed Almost to Extinction.'"

53. Peterson and Speth, "History of Wasatch-Cache National Forest," 235–38; National Forest Reservation Commission to Governor H. H. Blood, October 27, 1936, State Land Board File, SE-1 22.4 1934–37, Blood Papers.

54. Glynn Bennion, "Let's Stop Kidding Ourselves or Sow Sheep Manure—and Reap the Dust" and "Grazing History," Box 2, Federal Writers' Project Collection. See also A. F. Bracken, "State Report on Land-Use Study for Utah" ([Logan, UT]: Resettlement Administration, 1935), 134, copy in Peterson Papers, Box 122, Utah State Historical Society; J. Howard Maughan, "Continuation of Study of the Extent of Desirable Major Land-Use Adjustments and Areas Suitable for Settlement" (Logan, UT: Resettlement Administration, 1936), 40, copy in Independent Commission: Planning Board—Agriculture, 1934–41, Utah State Archives; "Grantsville Dust Bowl" (Soil Conservation Service); and H. J. Helm and G. S. Quate, "Report on the Wind Erosion and Dust Menace, Grantsville, Tooele."

55. David S. King to Warwick Lamoreaux, June 1, 1934, entered in Warwick Lamoreaux Diary, June 1, 1934, photocopy, Utah State University Archives; George Dewey Clyde, *Utah Cooperative Snow Surveys and Water Supply Forecast, 1935*; Minutes of Meeting of Water Users and Other Interested Parties on Bear River, Held Monday May 7, 1934, in the Capitol Building; Memorandum Covering the Findings and Conclusions and Arrangements of the Governor's Committee in Re: Distribution of Water on Bear River…1934, folder labeled Bear River Emergency, 1934, Blood Papers.

56. George Dewey Clyde, "Preliminary Report on the Use of Water and Benefits on Land Irrigated with Water from Bear Lake and Bear River during the Season 1934," September 15, 1934, in folder labeled Bear River Emergency, 1934–1935, Blood Papers.

57. Ibid.; and documents in folders labeled Bear River Emergency, 1934–1935, and Green River–Bear River Diversion, 1934–1937, Box 84, Blood Papers.

58. Hyrum, Porcupine, and Newton dams were developed under Bureau of Reclamation auspices in the 1930s. While in Cache Valley, the first two are at some distance from the Bear River and the latter in its immediate vicinity. See George Dewey Clyde, "History of Irrigation in Utah," 32.

59. *DN*, December 7, 1946; *Report of the State Engineer for 1938–1940*; *Report of the State Engineer for 1940–1942*; *Report of the State Engineer for 1942–1944*; *Report of the State Engineer for 1944–1946*, copies in Box 1, Series 880, Department of Natural Resources, Utah State Archives; Adam Eastman, "From Cadillac to Chevy: Environmental Concern, Compromise, and the Central Utah Project Completion Act."

10. UTAH IN THE 1920S

1. Bruce Barton, *The Man Nobody Knows: A Discovery of the Real Jesus*, last page of the preface.

2. Edward A. Geary, "A 'Visitable Past': Virginia Sorensen's Sanpete," 221–23.

3. Arrington, *Beet Sugar in the West*, 97–99; F. Taylor, *Saga of Sugar*, 112; Aydelotte, "Political Thought and Activity of Heber J. Grant," chap. 5; *Conference Report* (April 1922): 2–6.

4. *SLT*, December 31, 1930; Thomas G. Alexander, "From War to Depression," 466; J. Barton, *History of Duchesne County*, 219; *DN*, June 15, July 20, 1922.

5. *SLT*, January 2, 1927; "Measures of Economic Changes in Utah, 1847–1947," 53.

6. *SLT*, January 2, 1927; January 1, December 30, 1928; *DN*, October 23, 1928; "Measures of Economic Changes," 42; Huchel, *History of Box Elder County*, 227–28; Richard S. Van Wagoner, "The Lehi Sugar Factory—100 Years in Retrospect," 191–92, 203; Schmalz, "Sugar Beets in Cache Valley," 381, 388; M. Godfrey, *Religion, Politics, and Sugar*, 198–99; F. Taylor, "Development of the Sugar Beet Industry," 940.

7. Elmo G. Geary and Edward A. Geary, "Community Dramatics in Early Castle Valley," 130.

8. *DN*, February 3, 1923; Chad Orton, "Planting the Banner of Zion: A Brief History of the Church in Los Angeles."

9. *SLT*, December 27, 1920; J. Barton, *History of Duchesne County*, 234–36; "Measures of Economic Changes," 52; Virginia C. Parker, "Diamonds in the Dust: John W. Carlson's Alfalfa Seed Research," 399.

10. *SLT*, January 2, 1927; *DN*, October 8, 14, 1928; Leonard, *History of Davis County*, 238–40.

11. Edward A. Geary, "History Written on the Land in Emery County," 211–12; Federal Writers' Program, *Utah: A Guide to the State*, 400.

12. *Utah: A Guide to the State*, 210, 334; "Measures of Economic Changes," 52; Richard A. Firmage, *A History of Grand County*, 242.

13. William Peterson, "History of Agriculture in Utah," 227; Michael W. Johnson, Robert E. Parson, and Daniel A. Stebbins, *A History of Daggett County*, 169–71; "Measures of Economic Changes," 50–52; Don Strack, "Utah's Canning Industry," in *Utah History Encyclopedia*, edited by Allan Kent Powell; George P. Caine, "Dairying in Utah," May 7, 1927, Caine Papers.

14. Elroy Nelson, "The Mineral Industry: A Foundation of Utah's Economy," 185; *DN*, June 17, 1922.

15. *Utah: A Guide to the State*, 317.

16. E. Nelson, "Mineral Industry," 185; Philip F. Notarianni, "Tintic Mining District," 356; *DN*, August 9, 1927.

17. *SLT*, December 31, 1920; January 1, 1921; January 1, 1922.

18. Compton and Hampshire, "Park City," 332–33; *SLT*, December 31, 1922; Embry, *History of Wasatch County*, 138; Dickson H. Leavens, *Silver Money*, 145–50.

19. *SLT*, December 30, 1923; January 2, February 20, 1924; January 2, 1927; January 1, December 30, 1928; January 1, 1930; *DN*, January 14, 20, 1926.

20. *Utah: A Guide to the State*, 404; Thomas G. Alexander, "From Dearth to Deluge: Utah's Coal Industry," 241; "Measures of Economic Changes," 77; Allan Kent Powell, "Coal Industry," in *From the Ground Up*, edited by Whitley, 121–22, 129, 136; *SLT*, January 1, 5, 1930.

21. *DN*, December 14, 1925; March 15, 1934; *SLT*, January 3, 1926; Walter Jones, "Petroleum Industry"; Harline, "Utah's Black Gold," 297.

22. *SLT*, January 17, 26, February 15, 1920; January 9, 1921; *DN*, July 3, 1929.

23. Bernard DeVoto, "The West: A Plundered Province," 355, 360.

24. G. B. Hansen, "Industry of Destiny," 267–78.

25. *SLT*, March 1, 1924; *DN*, June 17, 1922; "Measures of Economic Changes," 88; *Utah: A Guide to the State*, 285, 409; Sutton, *Utah: A Centennial History*, 3:244.

26. *DN*, June 17, 30, 1922; Papanikolas, "Utah's Coal Lands," 120; Holzapfel, *History of Utah County*, 202–3; "History of Pacific States."

27. Sutton, *Utah: A Centennial History*, 3:202, 314–15.

28. Strack, "Utah's Canning Industry," in *Utah History Encyclopedia*, edited by Powell; Sutton, *Utah: A Centennial History*, 3:388; Don Strack, "Major Rail-Served Industries in Ogden."

29. "Measures of Economic Changes," 85; *R. L. Polk & Co.'s Provo City and Utah County Directory, 1929*, 317; Strack, "Major Rail-Served Industries"; R. Roberts and Sadler, *History of Weber County*, 278.

30. W. Peterson, "History of Agriculture in Utah," 166–67; Rebecca Andersen, "The Baron Woolen Mills: A Utah Legend," 122–23; "Measures of Economic Changes," 84–88; Holzapfel, *History of Utah County*, 149–50; *SLT*, January 15, 1930.

31. Thomas G. Alexander, "Ogden, a Federal Colony," 298; Alexander, "Ogden's 'Arsenal of Democracy,' 1920–1955."

32. "Measures of Economic Changes," 21; *DN*, May 25, June 24, 1922; *SLT*, February 17, 1924; Roger Roper, "Homemakers in Transition: Women in Salt Lake City Apartments, 1910–1940," 352, 357, 364–65.

33. "Measures of Economic Changes," 90; *Provo City and Utah County Directory, 1929*, 327; Sutton, *Utah: A Centennial History*, 3:150, 180, 297.

34. "Measures of Economic Changes," 41, 45, 102; Wilson, *History of Juab County*, 169, 173–74.

35. *DN*, October 2, 1928; Hainsworth, "Utah State Elections," 243. In 1924 KZN's name was changed to KFPT, and the *Salt Lake Tribune* became a co-owner of the station with the *News*. The *Tribune* sold its shares of stock in 1947. Dan E. Jones, "Utah Politics, 1926–1932," 47.

36. *Utah: A Guide to the State*, 389; Sean Dennis Cashman, *America Ascendant: From Theodore Roosevelt to FDR in the Century of American Power, 1901–1945*, 54; "Measures of Economic Changes," 35; *SLT*, February 8, 15, 20, 1920.

37. *Fifth Biennial Report: State Road Commission, 1917–1918*, 13, 23; *Sixth Biennial Report: State Road Commission, 1919–1920*, 13–14; Kimball L. Young, "Utah Public Debt History"; *SLT*, January 1, 1922; January 1, 1924; July 9, 1927; E. A. Geary, "'Visitable' Past," 224; Watt, *History of Carbon County*, 86; Jesse G. Petersen, "The Lincoln Highway and Its Changing Routes in Utah," 209, 211–12; State Senate of Utah, *Senate Journal: Eighteenth Session of the Legislature of the State of Utah*, 44.

38. Roger D. Launius, "Crossroads of the West: Aviation Comes to Utah, 1910–1940," 113–16, 119–21, 123–24.

39. Voyle L. Munson, "Lewis Leo Munson, an Entrepreneur in Escalante, Utah, 1896–1963," 138. In many respects, though, places like Escalante remained isolated. Only a poor road connected Escalante with the outside world. Munson's daughter Voyle, who was a teenager in the 1920s, recalled that "the roads discouraged travel" and "most people" lacked a car anyway. Of her five closest friends, "only one had been as far as Marysvale, the railroad terminus, some ninety miles away." Some had never even been to Panguitch, the county seat.

40. "Measures of Economic Changes," 23; *SLT*, December 30, 1928; *DN*, October 23, 1928.

41. US Bureau of the Census, *Sixteenth Census of the United States: 1940, Housing*, 2:557–60; George T. Blanch, *A Study of Farm Organization by Types of Farms in Uinta Basin, Utah*, 17–18, 65–66; LeAnn Wabel, "History of Anna R. Lemon Johnson" (n.p., 1983), copy in Peterson's possession; Kelen and Stone, *Missing Stories*, 84–85.

42. Stanford J. Layton, "Charles Rendell Mabey"; Wayne Stout, *History of Utah*, 2:452–58.

43. Stout, *History of Utah*, 2:458–64, 505; Charles R. Mabey, *Our Father's House: Joseph Thomas Mabey Family History*, 304; "Measures of Economic Changes," 28–31; R. Wells, "Political Biography of George Dern," 96.

44. Stout, *History of Utah*, 2:487; Alexander, *Utah, the Right Place*, 297–98; "Measures of Economic Changes," 28–35.

45. Loretta L. Hefner, "The National Women's Relief Society and the U.S. Sheppard-Towner Act," 256, 258–62, 265–66; David Roy Hall, "Amy Brown Lyman and Social Service Work in the Relief Society," 100–102.

46. D. Jones, "Utah Politics, 1926–1932," 42–43, 46; Hainsworth, "Utah State Elections," 158, 261, 265; Alexander, *Utah, the Right Place*, 298; Alexander and Allen, *Mormons and Gentiles*, 184; Stanford J. Layton, "Governor Charles R. Mabey and the Utah Election of 1924," 34.

47. Frank W. Fox, *J. Reuben Clark: The Public Years*, 418.

48. Hainsworth, "Utah State Elections," 171–72, 215; *DN*, October 26, 1922; Gary C. Kunz, "Provo in the Jazz Age: A Case Study"; Alexander and Allen, *Mormons and Gentiles*, 184.

49. Hainsworth, "Utah State Elections," 223–27.

50. R. Wells, "Political Biography of George Dern," 1–42; *SLT*, November 6, 1928; Hainsworth, "Utah State Elections," 284.

51. R. Wells, "Political Biography of George Dern," 46, 49; Hainsworth, "Utah State Elections," 316.

52. Hainsworth, "Utah State Elections," 314.

53. *DN*, November 6, 1924, quoted in R. Wells, "Political Biography of George Dern," 56.

54. R. Wells, "Political Biography of George Dern," 115; Poll et al., *Utah's History*, 711; Hundley, *Water and the West*, 262.

55. Alexander, "From War to Depression," 476; R. Wells, "Political Biography of George Dern," 61–71; *SLT*, January 1, 1928.

56. R. Wells, "Political Biography of George Dern," 83–84, 117; *Richfield Reaper*, November 1, 1928.

57. D. Jones, "Utah Politics, 1926–1932," 35–36.

58. R. Wells, "Political Biography of George Dern," 86, 90, 135–36.

59. D. Jones, "Utah Politics, 1926–1932," 81–84, 92–93; *SLT*, October 28, November 2, 4, 1928.

60. D. Jones, "Utah Politics, 1926–1932," 81, 112; *SLT*, November 5, 6, 1928; *DN*, January 14, 1958.

61. Poll et al., *Utah's History*, 711.

62. D. Jones, "Utah Politics, 1926–1932," 130–31, 159.

63. R. Wells, "Political Biography of George Dern," 105–13; D. Jones, "Utah Politics, 1926–1932," 139–46.

64. R. Wells, "Political Biography of George Dern," 98–100, 103–5, 122–23.

65. LDS Church Directory for 1924, LDS Church History Library; William M. Paden, *The Churches of Utah*; M. R. Rathjen, "The Distribution of Major Non-Mormon Denominations in Utah."

66. Wilson, *History of Juab County*, 181–82; Martha Sonntag Bradley, *A History of Beaver County*, 230–32; *SLT*, February 17, 1924; *Utah: A Guide to the State*, 222.

67. John R. Sillito, "'Our Tone': Tony Lazzeri's Baseball Career in Salt Lake City, 1922–1925," 345–48; Jessie L. Embry, "'The Biggest Advertisement for a Town': Provo Baseball and the Provo Timps, 1913–1958," 200–204; Jessie L. Embry and Adam Seth Darowski, "Coming Home: Community Baseball in Cache Valley, Utah," 110–11; A. Philip Cederlof, "The Peerless Coal Mines," 341.

68. Bradley, *History of Beaver County*, 225–26; Newell, *History of Garfield County*, 275–76.

69. *DN*, February 10, 1927; *SLT*, January 1, 1929; Bruce N. Westergren, "Utah's Gamble with Pari-mutuel Betting in the Early Twentieth Century," 7–12, 17, 21.

70. Richard S. Van Wagoner, "Saratoga, Utah Lake's Oldest Resort," 119; D. Robert Carter, "Provonna Beach Resort: Born of a Boom, Died of Depression," 334, 341–50; Watt, *History of Carbon County*, 324; Nancy D. McCormick and John S. McCormick, *Saltair*.

71. Huchel, *History of Box Elder County*, 212; B. Cannon, "Remaking the Agrarian Dream," 138; *Utah: A Guide to the State*, 296; J. Barton, *History of Duchesne County*, 199; *SLT*, July 11, 1927.

72. *SLT*, January 23, 1924.

73. "Erma Leona Gudmundson"; *Utah: A Guide to the State*, 420; *DN*, January 10, 1939; "Passing Events"; Carlton Culmsee, *A Modern Moses at West Tintic*.

74. Kunz, "Provo in the Jazz Age," 67.

75. *Manti Messenger*, August 28, 1925.

76. Kunz, "Provo in the Jazz Age," 69. For information on the Social Advisory Committee, see Thomas G. Alexander, "Between Revivalism and the Social Gospel: The Latter-day Saint Social Advisory Committee."

77. *DN*, May 4, 1922; "It Does Not Pay!"; L. John Nuttall, "Helps in Teacher Training."

78. *SLT*, December 31, 1922; February 26, 1924.

79. *SLT*, December 28, 1926; January 3, 1928.

80. Phil Roberts, "Wyoming's Pioneers of Prohibition: The United States Army, the U.S. District Court, and Federal Enforcement of Laws Governing Morality," 638; Papanikolas, "Bootlegging in Zion," 279–80.

81. *DN*, November 15, 1921; February 25, November 23, 1922; March 10, 1923; February 8, 1931.

82. Norman H. Clark, *Deliver Us from Evil: An Interpretation of American Prohibition*, 146–47; Kunz, "Provo in the Jazz Age," 11–12, 14, 69.

83. *SLT*, December 29, 1924; Jody Bailey and Robert S. McPherson, "'Practically Free from the Taint of the Bootlegger': A Closer Look at Prohibition in Southeastern Utah," 151.

84. Jean M. Westwood, "Richard Dallin Westwood: Sheriff and Ferryman of Early Grand County," 83–84; *SLT*, January 1, 3, 1926; *DN*, January 22, 1927.

85. Papanikolas, "Bootlegging in Zion," 268–91; J. Bailey and McPherson, "'Practically Free,'" 151–53, 155, 161–62; *SLT*, January 6, 1924.

86. Cassandra Tate, *Cigarette Wars: The Little White Slaver*, 39–57; *DN*, February 15, 1921; John S. H. Smith, "Cigarette Prohibition in Utah, 1921–23," 362, 364.

87. Hainsworth, "Utah State Elections," 227–33; *New York Times*, February 21, March 4, 1923.

88. *DN*, March 2, 1923; "Measures of Economic Changes," 28.

89. Bernard DeVoto, "Utah"; David Rich Lewis, "Bernard DeVoto's Utah," 88–97. On Beauregard, see Tom Alder, "The Art and Too-Brief Life of Donald Beauregard."

90. Bernard DeVoto to Robert C. Elliott, November 14, 1930, in "Bernard DeVoto and the Mormons: Three Letters," edited by Wallace Stegner, 41.

91. Lewis, "Bernard DeVoto's Utah," 97–103; *SLT*, February 21, 24, 26, March 14, 1924.

92. *SLT*, December 31, 1922; January 6, February 17, March 2, 1924; *DN*, October 2, 20, 1928.

93. *DN*, October 8, 28, 1928; *SLT*, March 1, 1924; Robert S. Olpin, Ann W. Orton, and Thomas F. Rugh, *Painters of the Wasatch Mountains*, 43–44.

94. *DN*, October 20, 22, 1928; Ronald W. Walker and Alexander M. Starr, "Shattering the Vase: The Razing of the Old Salt Lake Theatre," 79.

95. R. W. Walker and Starr, "Shattering the Vase," 81–82.

96. George D. Pyper, *The Romance of an Old Playhouse*, 396–403.

97. R. W. Walker and Starr, "Shattering the Vase," 83; Ila May Maughan, *Pioneer Theater in the Desert*, 153.

98. Myrtle E. Henderson, *A History of the Theatre in Salt Lake City from 1850 to 1870*, 108.

99. *Salt Lake Telegram*, October 19, 26, 1930.

100. "Measures of Economic Changes," 23; Frederick Lewis Allen, *Only Yesterday: An Informal History of the 1920's.*

11. HARD TIMES: WEATHERING THE GREAT DEPRESSION

1.   "Measures of Economic Changes," 23; State of Utah, *Messages of Governor Henry H. Blood to the Twentieth Legislature of the State of Utah and Inaugural Address, 1933,* 33–46.
2.   Kelen and Stone, *Missing Stories,* 229–35.
3.   Robert S. McElvaine, *The Great Depression: America, 1929–1941,* 75; "Measures of Economic Changes," 23; Garth L. Mangum and Bruce D. Blumell, *The Mormons' War on Poverty: A History of LDS Welfare, 1830–1990,* 96, 102.
4.   US Bureau of the Census, *Historical Statistics of the United States: Colonial Times to 1970,* 1:483; "Measures of Economic Changes," 53; Arrington and Alexander, *Dependent Commonwealth,* 63; McPherson, *History of San Juan County,* 113; F. Peterson, *History of Cache County,* 278; Douglas D. Alder and Karl F. Brooks, *A History of Washington County: From Isolation to Destination,* 238.
5.   "Measures of Economic Changes," 71, 77; Watt, *History of Carbon County,* 121–22.
6.   "Measures of Economic Changes," 80, 89, 96; John K. Bluth and Wayne K. Hinton, "The Great Depression," 483; US Bureau of the Census, *Historical Statistics of the United States,* 2:1019.
7.   Merrill Stucki, "An Economic Study of Farmers' Cooperative Business Associations in Utah," 90, 101; Brian Q. Cannon, "Struggle against Great Odds: Challenges in Utah's Marginal Agricultural Areas," 323; Bluth and Hinton, "The Great Depression," 482; Michael P. Malone and Richard W. Etulain, *The American West: A Twentieth-Century History,* 88–89. The West's dependence upon external investment capital and external markets is discussed in DeVoto, "The West."
8.   Irvin Hull, "Survey of Stranded Populations in Utah," typescript (1934), 2, Folder 1, Box 4, Lowry Nelson Collection; Federal Works Agency and Work Projects Administration, *Final Statistical Report of the Federal Emergency Relief Administration,* 248, 291.
9.   Twenty-three percent of the state's population resided on farms, and an additional 27 percent lived in nonfarm homes in rural districts. US Bureau of the Census, *Fifteenth Census of the United States, 1930: Population,* 3:1087; Bunnell, "Depression Memories," 265; Frances Wilde, interview by Brian Cannon, July 30, 1998, copy in Cannon's possession.
10. Alexander and Allen, *Mormons and Gentiles,* 199–200; Papanikolas, "Unionism, Communism, and the Great Depression," 259; Edward A. Geary, *A History of Emery County,* 289; Mary M. Oakes and Chestina B. Larsen, "Health Survey of Provo City," typescript [1933], 4–5, Provo Folder, Box 3, Nelson Collection; Alta Albrecht, interview by Kam Brian, November 1, 1996, transcript in Cannon's possession.
11. Lynn A. Sorensen, interview by Janet Peterson, quoted in the *Friend,* January 1989, 7; Kelen and Stone, *Missing Stories,* 258; Oakes and Larsen, "Health Survey," 5; Argene Vance Olsen, "Coping with the Depression, 1930–1940" (closure project, BYU Department of Independent Study, 1987), 4, Perry Special Collections, HBLL.
12. US Bureau of the Census, *Sixteenth Census: Housing,* 2:553; Belle Berry to Arthur and Stella Vance, March 1, 1932, quoted in Olsen, "Coping with the Depression," 6–7; Kelen and Stone, *Missing Stories,* 90; Laurence B. Johns, interview by Thomas G. Alexander, November 25, 1976, Charles Redd Center Oral History Project, Special Collections, HBLL.
13. Hugh McMillian to Henry H. Blood, May 23, 1933, quoted in A. Powell, *Next Time We Strike,* 164.

14. Alexander and Allen, *Mormons and Gentiles*, 200; Watt, *History of Carbon County*, 374; Kelen and Stone, *Missing Stories*, 292.

15. Weston L. Bayles, "Recent Economic Trends in Provo (to 1932)," typescript [1932], 12, Folder 2, Box 3, Nelson Collection; US Bureau of the Census, *Sixteenth Census: Housing*, 2:561. The 1930 Census did not investigate nonfarm mortgages, but in 1920 nearly 40 percent of the nonfarm, owner-occupied homes in the nation were mortgaged, and in 1940 45 percent were mortgaged.

16. Lester V. Chandler, *America's Greatest Depression, 1929–1941*, 73; "Measures of Economic Changes," 54; "Data Pertaining to the Activities of the State Land Board, State of Utah," February 5, 1935, Land Board Correspondence, 1935, Blood Papers; untitled State Land Board document, Land Board Correspondence, January–February 1932, Dern Papers.

17. Glen Gates to Governor Blood, November 21, 1934, FERA Correspondence, Blood Papers; A. F. Bracken, "State Report on Land-Use Study for Utah" ([Logan, UT]: Resettlement Administration, 1935), 102, copy in Peterson Papers, Box 122, Utah State Historical Society; Pearl Jeffrey, "Causes and Extent of Migration from Pahvant Valley," typescript (n.d.), 1–7, Folder 2, Box 5, Nelson Collection; *DN*, February 17, 1933.

18. Firmage, *History of Grand County*, 273; Clark Knowlton, "Washington County and the Depression," typescript, 29, 31, copy in Peterson's possession; J. Howard Maughan, "Continuation of Study of the Extent of Desirable Major Land-Use Adjustments and Areas Suitable for Settlement" (Logan, UT: Resettlement Administration, 1936), 36, Box 01, copy in Independent Commission: Planning Board—Agriculture, 1934–41, Utah State Archives; Russell R. Keetch, "Annual Report of Extension Work, Uintah County, 1936, 7, Special Collections, Merrill-Cazier Library; A. F. Bracken, "Utah Report on the Extent and Character of Desirable Adjustment in Rural Land-Use and Settlement Areas" (n.p., 1934), 16, Agriculture Planning Board Reports, Utah State Archives.

19. US Bureau of the Census, *Sixteenth Census: Housing*, 2:553, 555.

20. US Bureau of the Census, *Sixteenth Census of the United States: 1940, Population*, vol. 2, pt. 7, p. 17.

21. Sunshine Rae Sturt, "Through the Eyes of a Child: The Depression Years for Barbara Ann," typescript (1994), 1–10, copy in Cannon's possession.

22. Ibid., 3, 4; Kelen and Stone, *Missing Stories*, 228, 461–62.

23. Bunnell, "Depression Memories," 266; Kelen and Stone, *Missing Stories*, 405; "Measures of Economic Changes," 90.

24. Alder and Brooks, *History of Washington County*, 239; Doris K. Burton, *A History of Uintah County: Scratching the Surface*, 261.

25. Franklin S. Harris to Alice Louise Reynolds, November 16, 1932, quoted in Ernest L. Wilkinson and W. Cleon Skousen, *Brigham Young University: A School of Destiny*, 292; Ora Petersen, interview by Brian Cannon, July 28, 1998, copy in Cannon's possession.

26. US Bureau of the Census, *Sixteenth Census: Population*, vol. 4, pt. 4:638, and vol. 2, pt. 7:43–47; Jenean A. Girot, interview by Brian Cannon, August 10, 1998, copy in Cannon's possession; Watt, *History of Carbon County*, 277.

27. David F. Boone, "Missionary Work, 1900–Present," 181; Sheri L. Dew, *Go Forward with Faith: The Biography of Gordon B. Hinckley*, 55–56, 114; Kelen and Stone, *Missing Stories*, 337.

28. Elmer H. Gibson, "Annual Report of Extension Work, Sanpete County, 1939," 69, Special Collections, Merrill-Cazier Library; US Bureau of the Census, *Sixteenth Census: Population*, vol. 4, pt. 1:78, pt. 4:643.

29. Ralph V. Chamberlin, *The University of Utah: A History of Its First Hundred Years, 1850 to 1950*, 393, 442; Joel Edward Ricks, *The Utah State Agricultural College: A History of Fifty Years, 1888–1938*, 115; K. Lawrence Hale, "Cumulative Enrollment of Daytime Students," Perry Special Collections, HBLL, copy in Cannon's possession; Richard W. Sadler, ed., *Weber State College: A Centennial History*, 56, 76; Anne O. Leavitt, *Southern Utah University: A Heritage History, the First Hundred Years*, 98, 100; Edward L. Christensen, *Snow College Historical Highlights: The First 100 Years*, 41; Emil Nyman, "A Short History of Westminster College: The First Century, 1875–1975," unpublished typescript (1975), 25, copy in Perry Special Collections, HBLL; Robert J. Dwyer, "Catholic Education in Utah, 1875–1975," 374–75; Alder and Brooks, *History of Washington County*, 248; Watt, *History of Carbon County*, 292.

30. Wilkinson and Skousen, *Brigham Young University*, 291, 292; Chamberlin, *University of Utah*, 416; E. Christensen, *Snow College*, 41.

31. Olsen, "Coping with the Great Depression," 5; Wilkinson and Skousen, *Brigham Young University*, 291.

32. Sadler, *Weber State College*, 79–80; Chamberlin, *University of Utah*, 416.

33. Sadler, *Weber State College*, 66–67; Wilkinson and Skousen, *Brigham Young University*, 292; Olsen, "Coping with the Great Depression," 10; Chamberlin, *University of Utah*, 416.

34. Achsa E. Paxman and Emily C. Nielsen, "Relief and Welfare Agencies in Provo City," typescript [1933], Folder 2, Box 3, Nelson Collection; Sadler, *Weber State College*, 67; F. Peterson, *History of Cache County*, 291.

35. Chamberlin, *University of Utah*, 417–18; Wilkinson and Skousen, *Brigham Young University*, 293; Ricks, *Utah State Agricultural College*, 116; Ronald G. Watt, "National Youth Work Relief Programs, 1933 to 1966."

36. Wilkinson and Skousen, *Brigham Young University*, 291, 317; Sadler, *Weber State College*, 81.

37. Dew, *Go Forward with Faith*, 46–47; Kelen and Stone, *Missing Stories*, 180.

38. US Bureau of the Census, *Sixteenth Census: Population*, vol. 2, pt. 7:17; Bunnell, "Depression Memories," 267.

39. US Bureau of the Census, *Historical Statistics of the United States*, 1:483; Wilde interview.

40. Kurt R. Hill, "A Climatological Study of Dry Periods and a Runs Analysis of Precipitation along the Wasatch Front," 3, 4.

41. Leonard J. Arrington, "Utah's Great Drought of 1934," 247, 253; "Measures of Economic Changes," 49, 53; McPherson, *History of San Juan County*, 188.

42. "Measures of Economic Changes," 52–53; Albrecht interview; Loreen P. Wahlquist, "Memories of a Uinta Basin Farm," 169.

43. Hull, "Survey of Stranded Populations," 3; US Bureau of the Census, *Fifteenth Census of the United States, 1930: Unemployment*, 2:101–3.

44. US Bureau of the Census, *Historical Statistics of the United States*, 1:166–67; Chandler, *America's Greatest Depression*, 7.

45. A. Powell, *Next Time We Strike*, 162–63; "Measures of Economic Changes," 77; Hull, "Survey of Stranded Populations," 1–5.

46. Ora Petersen interview.

47. *Polk's Salt Lake City Directory, 1941*, 404. Not all members of the upper class were so lucky. T. N. Taylor, one of Provo's most prosperous businessmen and bankers, witnessed his bank fail in 1932 after twenty-six years in the business. "When the people started the run we simply could not get cash in fast enough to pay them off," he recalled. Taylor lost fifty thousand dollars in the bank failure, although he was able to keep his commodious

home on Fifth West in Provo. Olsen, "Coping with the Great Depression," 54–55; *Provo City Directory—1939*, 186.

48. Alexander and Allen, *Mormons and Gentiles*, 215; US Bureau of the Census, *Sixteenth Census: Population*, vol. 2, pt. 7:36; Miriam B. Murphy, "Women in the Utah Work Force from Statehood to World War II," 145, 152, 153, 155; Albrecht interview; Wilde interview; Rebecca Lindsay, "Reflections on Ephraim, Utah, during the Great Depression," typescript [1993], 10–12, copy in Cannon's possession; F. Peterson, *History of Cache County*, 290.

49. Ora Petersen interview; Kelen and Stone, *Missing Stories*, 90.

50. Wilde interview; Sturt, "Through the Eyes of a Child," 1; R. Roberts and Sadler, *History of Weber County*, 284.

51. Calvin L. Rampton, *As I Recall*, 29.

52. "Measures of Economic Changes," 90; Kelen and Stone, *Missing Stories*, 466; Barney L. Flanagan, "A Labor Inspector during the Great Depression," 240.

53. Bayles, "Recent Economic Trends," 15; E. A. Geary, *History of Emery County*, 285–86; "Measures of Economic Changes," 100, 102.

54. Olsen, "Coping with the Great Depression," 3; Girot interview.

55. *DN*, September 17, 1998; US Bureau of the Census, *Sixteenth Census: Population*, vol. 4, pt. 4:621.

56. Elmer H. Gibson, "Annual Report of Extension Work, Sanpete County, 1939," 69, Special Collections, Merrill-Cazier Library; Astrid Larsen, interview by Rebecca Lindsay, February 1993, quoted in Lindsay, "Reflections on Ephraim," 7; Ora Petersen interview.

57. US Bureau of the Census, *Sixteenth Census: Population*, vol. 2, pt. 7:17.

58. Albrecht interview; Edgel Liechty, interview by Brian Cannon, August 13, 1998, copy in Cannon's possession; Mangum and Blumell, *Mormons' War on Poverty*, 108.

59. Lowry Nelson, "The Population of Utah," typescript (n.d.), 2–3, Folder 3, Box 4, Nelson Collection; US Bureau of the Census, *Sixteenth Census: Population*, vol. 2, pt. 7:13.

60. Reed and Ileen Reynolds, interview by Brian Cannon, January 12, 1985; and JoAnn Cannon, interview by Brian Cannon, October 30, 1998, both in Cannon's possession.

61. Bunnell, "Depression Memories," 266–67; Reynolds interview; Kelen and Stone, *Missing Stories*, 405; Lyn Trinnaman, "Life in the Great Depression," typescript (1994), 6, copy in Cannon's possession; Zeke Johnson, "Zeke: A Story of Mountain and Desert" (n.d.), Folder 29, Box 11, Gary Topping Papers.

62. Bunnell, "Depression Memories," 265; Sturt, "Through the Eyes of a Child," 4; Kelen and Stone, *Missing Stories*, 90.

63. Bunnell, "Depression Memories," 266; Olsen, "Coping with the Great Depression," 4; Lila Gentry, interview by Lyn Trinnaman, February 25, 1994, quoted in Trinnaman, "Life in the Great Depression," 6–7; "Measures of Economic Changes," 90.

64. Watt, *History of Carbon County*, 7; F. Peterson, *History of Cache County*, 290; Firmage, *History of Grand County*, 280; Olsen, "Coping with the Great Depression," 6; Kelen and Stone, *Missing Stories*, 292.

65. Kelen and Stone, *Missing Stories*, 405; Rampton, *As I Recall*, 28–36.

66. A. Powell, *Next Time We Strike*, 165–94, 201–4; Roger Biles, *A New Deal for the American People*, 89–90, 128; Bluth and Hinton, "The Great Depression," 490.

67. Wilde interview; Kelen and Stone, *Missing Voices*, 337–38.

68. Watt, *History of Carbon County*, 373; Sturt, "Through the Eyes of a Child," 2–3; Kelen and Stone, *Missing Voices*, 90; Eunice Seymour McGinnis, "Life History," copy in Cannon's possession.

69. Papanikolas, "Unionism, Communism, and the Great Depression," 259; Charles S. Peterson, *Utah: A History*, 149; US Bureau of the Census, *Sixteenth Census of the United States: 1940, Population; Internal Migration, 1935 to 1940, Social Characteristics of Migrants*, 192–93, passim.

70. US Bureau of the Census, *Fifteenth Census: Population*, 3:1087; US Bureau of the Census, *Sixteenth Census: Population*, vol. 2, pt. 7:14; Richard O. Ulibarri, "Utah's Unassimilated Minorities," 636–37; Ulibarri, "Utah's Ethnic Minorities: A Survey," 223.

71. Charles A. Cannon, interview by Brian Cannon, May 24, 1998, copy in Cannon's possession; US Bureau of the Census, *Sixteenth Census: Social Characteristics of Migrants*, 192–93.

72. F. Peterson, *History of Cache County*, 290; Liechty interview.

73. US Bureau of the Census, *Historical Statistics of the United States*, 1:130–33; US Bureau of the Census, *Sixteenth Census: Population*, vol. 2, pt. 7:32, 36, 37, and vol. 3, pt. 5:655; Alexander and Allen, *Mormons and Gentiles*, 214–15; Wilde interview; Murphy, "Women in the Utah Work Force," 153, 214.

74. F. Peterson, *History of Cache County*, 289–90; Nina Moore, interview by Lyn Trinnaman, March 5, 1994, quoted in Lyn Trinnaman, "Life in the Great Depression," 4–5.

75. Wilde interview; June Crane, interview by Rebecca Lindsay, February 1993, quoted in Lindsay, "Reflections on Ephraim," 14; US Bureau of the Census, *Sixteenth Census: Population*, vol. 3, pt. 1:55.

76. Kelen and Stone, *Missing Stories*, 399, 415; Alexander and Allen, *Mormons and Gentiles*, 227.

77. Kelen and Stone, *Missing Stories*, 447; John Mills Whitaker, "Transcript Journal, Summer 1930," 16, Box 4, MS2, Whitaker Collection.

78. Alexander and Allen, *Mormons and Gentiles*, 224; E. A. Geary, *History of Emery County*, 292.

79. Joe Bagnall, interview by Lynn Trinnaman, February 25, 1994, quoted in Trinnaman, "Life in the Great Depression," 10–11; Reynolds interview.

80. McElvaine, *Great Depression*, 208; "Measures of Economic Changes," 93; US Bureau of the Census, *Sixteenth Census: Housing*, vol. 2, pt. 5:60; US Bureau of the Census, *Historical Statistics of the United States*, 2:796.

81. *Polk's Salt Lake City Directory, 1937*, 1228; *Polk's Ogden City Directory, 1936–37*, 629; *Polk's Provo City Directory, 1935–36*, 488; *Polk's Logan (Utah) City Directory, 1935–36*, 369; *Telephone Directory: Price, Green River, Helper, Huntington, Scofield*, 5–19, 21–25; Kelen and Stone, *Missing Stories*, 399; Watt, *History of Carbon County*, 344; J. Eldon Dorman, *"Confessions of a Coal Camp Doctor," and Other Stories*, 52.

82. "Measures of Economic Changes," 93; *DN*, September 17, 1998; Baldridge, "Nine Years of Achievement"; Writers Program of the Work Projects Administration, *Provo—Pioneer Mormon City*, 159.

83. Lindsay, "Reflections on Ephraim," 19; E. A. Geary, *History of Emery County*, 273.

84. Watt, *History of Carbon County*, 325; *Polk's Salt Lake City Directory, 1937*, 46, 496; Rae Rust, "A Survey of the Recreational Conditions in Kanab," 3, 7, Folder 2, Box 5, Nelson Collection; "Measures of Economic Changes," 93; *Utah State Historical Society Newsletter* 48 (June 1998): 5; Ray Hoffman, interview by Brian Cannon, August 21, 1985, copy in Cannon's possession.

85. Papanikolas, "Toil and Rage," 194; Allen and Alexander, *Mormons and Gentiles*, 253.

86. Ora Petersen interview; Hull, "Survey of Stranded Populations," 1–5.

87.   G. Lowry Nelson, *In the Direction of His Dreams: Memoirs*, 241; Paxman and Nielsen, "Relief and Welfare Agencies in Provo City"; Alexander and Allen, *Mormons and Gentiles*, 199–200.

88.   Mangum and Blumell, *Mormons' War on Poverty*, 96; *Provo Daily Herald*, March 3, 1933; S. R. DeBoer, "Uinta Basin" (n.p., 1936), in State Engineer 1935 Correspondence, Blood Papers; George Whornham, "Annual Report of Extension Work, Millard County" (n.p., 1934), 15, Special Collections, Merrill-Cazier Library; Bracken, "State Report on Land-Use Study for Utah," 118–19.

89.   Kelen and Stone, *Missing Voices*, 446–47; Whitaker, 1930 Journal, 2, Whitaker Collection; Bluth and Hinton, "The Great Depression," 484; *Provo Daily Herald*, January 30, 1933; *DN*, January 30, 1931; February 17, 1933.

90.   Paxman and Nielsen, "Relief and Welfare Agencies."

91.   E. A. Geary, *History of Emery County*, 280; F. Peterson, *History of Cache County*, 284; *Provo Daily Herald*, November 8, 1931.

92.   Watt, *History of Carbon County*, 374; Alder and Brooks, *History of Washington County*, 239; E. A. Geary, *History of Emery County*, 280; F. Peterson, *History of Cache County*, 283.

93.   Paxman and Nielsen, "Relief and Welfare Agencies"; Mangum and Blumell, *Mormons' War on Poverty*, 101–5, 110.

94.   Mangum and Blumell, *Mormons' War on Poverty*, 99–102, 280; F. Peterson, *History of Cache County*, 283; Whitaker Journal, 3:876, Whitaker Collection.

95.   Mangum and Blumell, *Mormons' War on Poverty*, 107–8.

96.   McElvaine, *Great Depression*, 69–70; Federal Emergency Relief Administration, *Index of the Monthly Reports of the Federal Emergency Relief Administration: June 1933 through December 1933*, 14; Biles, *New Deal for the American People*, 22; Alma Vernon Rasmussen, "The Government Work Relief Program in Utah, 1932–1940," 8; Mangum and Blumell, *Mormons' War on Poverty*, 111–12.

12. UTAH ENCOUNTERS THE NEW DEAL

1.   Argene Vance Olsen, "Coping with the Depression, 1930–1940" (closure project, BYU Department of Independent Study, 1987), 8, Perry Special Collections, HBLL; G. Nelson, *In the Direction of His Dreams*, 261; *SLT*, September 17, November 10, 1932; William E. Leuchtenburg, *Franklin D. Roosevelt and the New Deal, 1932–1940*, 11, 13; Stout, *History of Utah*, 3:86; Frank H. Jonas and Garth N. Jones, "Utah Presidential Elections, 1896–1952," 305.

2.   Poll et al., *Utah's History*, 711; *DN*, November 3, 1932.

3.   Poll et al., *Utah's History*, 702, 704, 707; *SLT*, November 1, 1932; John A. Widtsoe to Elbert D. Thomas, February 29, 1933, Personal File 1933–39, Corr: Latter-day Saints, Box 17, Elbert D. Thomas Papers; Chandler, *America's Greatest Depression*, 12; Warwick C. Lamoreaux interview, quoted in D. Jones, "Utah Politics, 1926–1932," 178–79.

4.   Heber J. Grant to Reed Smoot, January 4, 1933, microfilm reel 2, Folder 14, Box 49, Smoot Papers; Harvard S. Heath, "Reed Smoot: The First Modern Mormon," 1034; M. R. Merrill, *Apostle in Politics*, 9; *DN*, November 3, 7, 1932; Florence Ivins Hyde, "My Story," MSS A1874, Utah State Historical Society.

5.   Biles, *A New Deal for the American People*, 34–35, 45; R. Thomas Quinn, "Out of the Depression's Depths: Henry H. Blood's First Year as Governor," 225–26.

6.   John Kearnes, "Utah, Sexton of Prohibition."

7.   Leuchtenburg, *Roosevelt and the New Deal*, 8; Mangum and Blumell, *Mormons' War on Poverty*, 112–19. On Dern's influence, see Albert L. Warner, "The Secretary of War: A Prophet of the New Deal."

8.   Federal Works Agency and Work Projects Administration, *Final Statistical Report of the Federal Emergency Relief Administration*, 8; Office of Government Reports, "Utah: Federal Loans and Expenditures, 1933–1939," mimeograph, 1939, 2:22, Special Collections, Merrill-Cazier Library; Leonard J. Arrington, *Utah, the New Deal and the Depression of the 1930s*, 27; Beth R. Olsen, "Utah's CCC's: The Conservators' Medium for Young Men, Nature, Economy, and Freedom," 261, 262, 270; Kenneth W. Baldridge, "Reclamation Work of the Civilian Conservation Corps, 1933–1942," 284; National Emergency Council, "Utah, 1933–1938," mimeograph, 1938, Box 21, Thomas Papers. Originally called the Emergency Conservation Work program, the CCC received its new name on June 28, 1937.

9.   Baldridge, "Nine Years of Achievement," 290, 322, 327; Taylor C. "Bud" Nuttall to Elbert Thomas, July 9, 1933, folder titled "Personal Corr. N," Box 17, Thomas Papers.

10.   Baldridge, "Nine Years of Achievement," 321.

11.   Ibid., 58–59, 196; Baldridge, "Reclamation Work," 280–84; B. Olsen, "Utah's CCC's," 263–64, 271, 273.

12.   Baldridge, "Nine Years of Achievement," 351.

13.   Ibid., 327; B. Olsen, "Utah's CCC's," 262.

14.   Nuttall to Thomas, July 9, 1933; Baldridge, "Nine Years of Achievement," 359; B. Olsen, "Utah's CCC's," 273–74; Ora Petersen, interview by Brian Cannon, July 28, 1998, copy in Cannon's possession; *DN*, August 6, 1998.

15.   A. Rasmussen, "Government Work Relief," 53–54, 85; Office of Government Reports, "Utah," 35; Arrington, *Utah, the New Deal and the Depression*, 21, 27.

16.   A. Rasmussen, "Government Work Relief," 104–9, 166–67; Ricks, *Utah State Agricultural College*, 118; Alder and Brooks, *History of Washington County*, 241; Alta Albrecht, interview by Kam Brian, November 1, 1996, transcript in Cannon's possession; Ed Liechty, interview by Brian Cannon, August 13, 1998, copy in Cannon's possession; Afton Larsen, interview by Rebecca Lindsay, February 1993, quoted in Rebecca Lindsay, "Reflections on Ephraim, Utah, during the Great Depression" [1993], copy in Cannon's possession; D. Burton, *History of Uintah County*, 342; R. Roberts and Sadler, *History of Weber County*, 288; Bluth and Hinton, "The Great Depression," 500; Will South, "The Federal Art Project in Utah: Out of Oblivion or More of the Same?," 288–89, 291–93; Lavon B. Carroll, "Melba Judge Lehner and Child Care in the State of Utah"; Alex D. Smith, "The Symphony in America, Maurice Abravanel, and the Utah Symphony Orchestra: The Battle for Classical Music," 43–44.

17.   *DN*, October 2, 1936; Larsen interview.

18.   Frances Wilde, interview by Brian Cannon, July 30, 1998, copy in Cannon's possession.

19.   Federal Works Agency, *Final Statistical Report*, 5–9; Arrington, *Utah, the New Deal and the Depression*, 27; G. Nelson, *In the Direction of His Dreams*, 244.

20.   A. Rasmussen, "Government Work Relief," 22, 35–38; *The Emergency Work Relief Program of the Federal Emergency Relief Administration, April 1, 1934 to July 1, 1935*, 5; Watt, *History of Carbon County*, 314; Federal Works Agency, *Final Statistical Report*, 54; Ricks, *Utah State Agricultural College*, 118; Juanita Brooks, *Quicksand and Cactus: A Memoir of the Southern Mormon Frontier*, 331–35.

21.   Federal Works Agency, *Final Statistical Report*, 25, 45–47, 53–74, 80, 235–50.

22.   Arrington, *Utah, the New Deal and the Depression*, 13; Federal Works Agency, *Final Statistical Report*, 19, 110; A. Rasmussen, "Government Work Relief," 25–29.

23. T. David Hettig, ed., "An Economic and Sociological Report of the Green River Drought Pumping Project of 1934," typescript (1935), 3–10, 16, 22, 29–30, Perry Special Collections, HBLL; *Vernal Express*, May 17, 1934; Lowry Nelson and Howard R. Cottam, "The Green River Drought Relief Project of 1934," 119; Robert P. Cooper, *Leota: End of William H. Smart's Stewardship*, 151–52, 155; Leland Workman, interview by Brian Cannon, August 22, 1985; Merrill Lisonbee, interview by Cannon, August 22, 1985; and Frank Johnson, interview by Brian Cannon, August 22, 1985, copies in Cannon's possession.

24. Federal Works Agency, *Final Statistical Report*, 8–9; A. Rasmussen, "Government Work Relief," 11, 13–15, 17; Bluth and Hinton, "The Great Depression," 487; Arrington, *Utah, the New Deal and the Depression*, 11.

25. R. Quinn, "Out of the Depression's Depths," 236–38; R. Roberts and Sadler, *History of Weber County*, 271–72; Arrington, *Utah, the New Deal and the Depression*, 20, 27; National Emergency Council, "Utah, 1933–1938"; Bureau of Reclamation, "Final Report on Design and Construction of Hyrum Dam and Reservoir," typescript (1938), copy in Special Collections, Merrill-Cazier Library.

26. Federal Security Agency, *Final Report of the National Youth Administration, Fiscal Years 1936–1943*, 5, 242, 246; Arrington, *Utah, the New Deal and the Depression*, 17; Watt, *History of Carbon County*, 295, 375.

27. US Bureau of the Census, *Sixteenth Census of the United States*, 3:27.

28. Arrington, *Utah, the New Deal and the Depression*, 17–18; Social Security Act of 1935, http://www.ourdocuments.gov/doc.php?doc=68&page=transcript; A. Rasmussen, "Government Work Relief," 49; US Bureau of the Census, *Sixteenth Census of the United States*, 2:56–78.

29. Biles, *New Deal for the American People*, 61, Arrington, *Utah, the New Deal and the Depression*, 27; National Emergency Council, "Utah, 1933–1938."

30. Federal Works Agency, *Final Statistical Report*, 109; A. Rasmussen, "Government Work Relief," 31–39, 176; D. Burton, *History of Uintah County*, 176; Janet Poppendieck, *Breadlines Knee-Deep in Wheat: Food Assistance in the Great Depression*; Lisonbee interview.

31. "Measures of Economic Changes," 52–53; Arrington, *Utah, the New Deal and the Depression*, 27.

32. Leuchtenburg, *Roosevelt and the New Deal*, 170; Arrington, *Utah, the New Deal and the Depression*, 14; National Emergency Council, "Utah, 1933–1938."

33. Biles, *New Deal for the American People*, 70; Leuchtenburg, *Roosevelt and the New Deal*, 255; Arrington, *Utah, the New Deal and the Depression*, 14; R. Douglas Hurt, *American Agriculture: A Brief History*, 291.

34. Arrington, *Utah, the New Deal and the Depression*, 27; H. H. Bennett, *Report of the Chief of the Soil Conservation Service* (1945), 33–39; Bennett, *Report of the Chief of the Soil Conservation Service* (1937), 2.

35. Bennett, *Report of the Chief* (1945), 33–39; Bennett, *Report of the Chief* (1937), 2; Office of Government Reports, "Utah," 16–17.

36. J. Howard Maughan, "Continuation of Study of the Extent of Desirable Major Land-Use Adjustments and Areas Suitable for Settlement" (Logan, UT: Resettlement Administration, 1936), Box 01, copy in Independent Commission: Planning Board—Agriculture, 1934–41, Utah State Archives; Rexford G. Tugwell, "The Resettlement Idea," 160; *Garfield County News*, October 18, 1935; *Nephi Times-News*, October 17, 1935; H. H. Bennett, *Report of the Chief of the Soil Conservation Service, 1941*, 18; Bennett, *Report of the Chief* (1945), 39–40.

37. Orson Adair et al. to Rexford Tugwell, August 1936, Box 490, State Projects Files—Utah, RG 96, NA; Joseph Oborn, interview by Brian Cannon, November 30, 1985, copy in Cannon's possession.

38. The estimate of twelve to thirteen hundred households in need of relocation is found in A. F. Bracken, "State Report on Land-Use Study for Utah" ([Logan, UT]: Resettlement Administration, 1935), copy in Peterson Papers, Box 122, Utah State Historical Society. On the actual resettlement program in Utah, see B. Cannon, "Remaking the Agrarian Dream." Fifteen families relocated using FERA funds that were administered by the RA as part of what was labeled the Widtsoe Resettlement Project, while eighteen others relocated as part of the Sevier Valley Farms project using funds from the RA's and FSA's coffers. The distinction between the two projects was merely a means of keeping funds straight.

39. Ray Hoffman, interview by Brian Cannon, August 21, 1985; and Reed Beebe, interview by Cannon, August 10, 1985, copies in Cannon's possession. Persistence rates for relocatees were computed using real estate records filed in the courthouses of Utah, Piute, Garfield, and Sevier Counties. For information on the cost-effectiveness of resettlement in Utah, see Brian Q. Cannon, "Keeping Their Instructions Straight: Implementing the Rural Resettlement Program in the West," 264–65.

40. Arrington, *Utah, the New Deal and the Depression*, 27; US Bureau of the Census, *Fifteenth Census of the United States, 1930: Agriculture*, 2:539; Rural Electrification Act of 1936, http://www.ccrh.org/comm/moses/primary/electrif.html; D. Clayton Brown, *Electricity for Rural America: The Fight for the REA.*

41. Leuchtenburg, *Roosevelt and the New Deal*, 157–58; Lamar LeFevre, interview, n.d., Garkane Power oral history videotape; Harvey and Fontella Taylor, interview by Richard Kitchen, May 29, 1993; Medina Smith, interview by Kitchen, May 29, 1993; and Muriel Mooseman, interview by Kitchen, May 29, 1993, copies in Cannon's possession.

42. Office of Government Reports, "Utah," 15, 38; Arrington, *Utah, the New Deal and the Depression*, 23, 27; US Bureau of the Census, *Sixteenth Census of the United States*, 2:561.

43. Office of Government Reports, "Utah," 39; US Bureau of the Census, *Sixteenth Census: Housing*, 2:555.

44. Arrington, *Utah, the New Deal and the Depression*, 27; National Emergency Council, "Utah, 1933–1938."

45. A. Rasmussen, "Government Work Relief," 49; "Measures of Economic Changes," 30.

46. F. S. Harris to My Dear Bishop, October 10, 1938, Folder: General File, 1933–38: 1938 Campaign Correspondence, Box 21, Thomas Papers; J. Reuben Clark to Alfred Landon, [November 9, 1936], Folder 10, Box 347, J. Reuben Clark Papers.

47. Mangum and Blumell, *Mormons' War on Poverty*, 121, 125.

48. Ibid., 125; Margaret M. Cannon to J. Reuben Clark, July 21, 1936, Folder 1, Box 348, Clark Papers; *DN*, October 2, 1936.

49. *DN*, October 31, 1936; F. Burton Howard, *Marion G. Romney: His Life and Faith*, 109; D. Michael Quinn, *J. Reuben Clark: The Church Years*, 75; editorials found in folder labeled Editorials 1934–39, Box 208, Clark Papers. Although Clark wrote the editorial, it reflected the position of all three members of the First Presidency and was approved by each of them. Writing to David O. McKay the following year, Clark referred to the document along with two subsequent editorials as "our Deseret News editorials" (February 6, 1937, Folder 1, Box 358, Clark Papers).

50. *DN*, October 31, 1936; Samuel I. Rosenman, comp., *The Public Papers and Addresses of Franklin D. Roosevelt*, 4:200–222.

51. Alexander, *Utah, the Right Place*, 331; "Topeka Draft Mainly by JRC," Folder 9, Box 347, Clark Papers.

52. *DN*, October 31, 1936; typewritten draft of editorial titled "The Constitution," folder labeled Editorials 1934–39, Box 208, Clark Papers; James P. Warburg, "Hell-Bent for Election," *Washington Post*, September 17, 1935, copy in Folder 3, Box 88, Smoot Papers; *New York Herald Tribune*, March 23, 1935, clipping in folder titled Roosevelt, Box 314, Clark Papers. On the passage of the Guffey-Snyder Act of 1935, see Leuchtenburg, *Roosevelt and the New Deal*, 161–62.

53. *DN*, October 31, 1936.

54. Malmquist, *First 100 Years*, 331. Malmquist was correct in his remarks about opposition to one candidate, although Joseph F. Smith's endorsement of William Howard Taft in the October 1912 *Improvement Era* was crystal clear. On Smith's 1912 endorsement, see B. Cannon, "'Taft Has Made a Good President.'"

55. *SLT*, November 1–3, 1936.

56. Frank Herman Jonas, "Utah: Sagebrush Democracy," 34; Rampton, *As I Recall*, 47; *SLT*, November 3, 1936.

57. *SLT*, November 2, 1936; *DN*, November 2, 1936; *Salt Lake Telegram*, November 2, 1936.

58. *Logan Herald Journal*, November 2, 1936. Particularly Apostle Reed Smoot had been a strong supporter of the Hoover administration. Hoover campaigned for Smoot in Utah just before the election, praising his work in the Senate. See M. R. Merrill, *Apostle in Politics*, 135–37, 230, 232–33.

59. Poll et al., *Utah's History*, 700–701; J. Reuben Clark to Alfred Landon, [November 9, 1936], Folder 10, Box 347, Clark Papers; *SLT*, November 1, 5, 1936.

60. Campaign pamphlet, Box 21, Thomas Papers; Clark to Wm. R. Castle, May 9, 1938, Folder 10, Box 360, Clark Papers; *Logan Herald Journal*, August 12, 1938; Franklin S. Harris to Emer Harris, August 12, 1938, Folder H, Box 73; Franklin S. Harris to Sterling Harris, August 12, 1938, Folder H, Box 73; Franklin S. Harris to his children, August 12, 1938, Folder H, Box 73, Franklin S. Harris Papers; Franklin S. Harris, "Diary, 1937–1942," MSS 923.7 H24, typescript, 1022, Perry Special Collections, HBLL.

61. Franklin S. Harris, "Real Security"; Bluth and Hinton, "The Great Depression," 494; campaign poster, Box 21, Thomas Papers; F. S. Harris to My Dear Bishop, October 10, 1938, Box 21, Thomas Papers; A Bishop to Franklin S. Harris, n.d., Box 22, Thomas Papers; Gordon Gaylor Hyde to Franklin S. Harris, October 25, 1938, Folder H, Box 73, Harris Papers.

62. S. E. Bringhurst to Elbert D. Thomas, November 10, 1938, Box 22, Thomas Papers; Franklin S. Harris to George Lewis Harris, November 10, 1938, Folder H, Box 73, Harris Papers; J. Reuben Clark to William R. Castle, November 22, 1938, Folder 10, Box 360, Clark Papers.

63. Mangum and Blumell, *Mormons' War on Poverty*, 126–32, 135, 137, 290–21; Leonard J. Arrington and Wayne K. Hinton, "Origin of the Welfare Plan of the Church of Jesus Christ of Latter-day Saints," 212–13; J. Reuben Clark to Heber J. Grant, March 1, 1935, Folder 7, Box 353, Clark Papers.

64. *DN*, April 7, 1936; Henry A. Smith, "Church-Wide Security Program Organized," 337.

65. *DN*, April 7, June 9, 1936; *New York Times*, May 25, 1936, L20; First Presidency to William C. Fitzgibbon, October 11, 1941, Folder 19, Box 26, Dean Brimhall Papers; Mangum and Blumell, *Mormons' War on Poverty*, 132.

66. H. Smith, "Church-Wide Security Program," 336–37.

67. *What Is the "Mormon" Security Program?*; C. Orval Stott, "The Agricultural Program of the Church Welfare Program"; Albert E. Bowen, *The Church Welfare Plan*, 98–99; Harold B. Lee to Edgar B. Brossard, January 28, 1938, Folder 510, Box 843, General Administrative and Project Records, 1919–1929, RG 115, NA, Denver; Bruce D. Blumell, "The Church Welfare Program," 10–12, typescript, Joseph Fielding Smith Institute Library, BYU.

68. Mangum and Blumell, *Mormons' War on Poverty*, 48–49.

69. Ibid., 131–32, 154; Richard L. Neuberger, "Depression: 'Perhaps the Mormons Are Pointing the Way,'" 457.

70. Arrington and Hinton, "Origin of the Welfare Plan," 205; Neuberger, "Depression," 455.

71. Mangum and Blumell, *Mormons' War on Poverty*, 146; "Measures of Economic Changes," 39; Joseph F. Darowski, "The WPA versus the Utah Church," 180.

72. Arrington, *Utah, the New Deal and the Depression*, 27; Leonard J. Arrington, "The New Deal in the West: A Preliminary Statistical Inquiry," 313–14; "Measuring Worth" (Comparative Prices); US Department of Labor, CPI Inflation Calculator, http://www.bls.gov/data/inflation_calculator.htm; Bluth and Hinton, "The Great Depression," 495.

73. "Measures of Economic Changes," 23, 53, 103.

74. Ibid., 35; US Bureau of the Census, *Sixteenth Census: Housing*, 2:555, 566–72.

75. Bluth and Hinton, "The Great Depression," 492–94; Poll et al., *Utah's History*, 702–12.

76. Alexander, "From Dearth to Deluge," 242.

77. "Measures of Economic Changes," 28, 30, 33; Chandler, *America's Greatest Depression*, 125; US Bureau of the Census, *Historical Statistics of the United States*, 2:1111–12; Biles, *New Deal for the American People*, 231.

78. US Bureau of the Census, *Historical Statistics of the United States*, 1117–18; Bluth and Hinton, "The Great Depression," 494.

79. "Measures of Economic Changes," 40; Federal Works Agency and Work Projects Administration, *Final Statistical Report of the Federal Emergency Relief Administration*, 248. It might be hypothesized that a higher percentage of Utah's senior citizens were on welfare because they tended to live longer than Americans at large. (The longer they lived, the more likely that their limited savings would be depleted.) However, the difference in life expectancy between Utah men and American men in 1940 was negligible (61.7 years versus 61.6 years), and the difference between Utah and American women was also fairly small (67.0 versus 65.9 years). See Ken R. Smith and Sven E. Wilson, "Dyin' in Zion: Longevity and Mortality in Utah," 45.

13. SIMPLY REVOLUTIONARY: UTAHNS CONFRONT THE SECOND WORLD WAR

1. *SLT*, December 7, 1941.

2. Gordon W. Prange, *At Dawn We Slept: The Untold Story of Pearl Harbor*.

3. Allan Kent Powell, *Utah Remembers World War II*, 193–94.

4. Ibid., xi, xii; Alexander, *Utah, the Right Place*, 358; John E. Christensen, "The Impact of World War II," 509; Leonard J. Arrington, "Utah's Ambiguous Reception: The Relocated Japanese Americans," 94; Rachel Elison Ham, interview by Paige Dinger (1998), quoted in Dinger, "Rations, War Time, and Salt Lake City: A Personal Look at a Woman's Life in Salt Lake City during the 1940s" (1998), 4, copy in Cannon's possession; Anita Smoot Hammond, interview by Cannon Gerstner, December 7, 1998, quoted in Gerstner, "A Richly Diverse Heritage: Roy Bartlett and Anita Smoot Hammond," 11, copy in Cannon's possession.

5. Dan Gardner, interview by Alan Westenskow, September 21, 1998, copy in Cannon's possession; J. Christensen, "Impact of World War II," 509; Alexander, *Utah, the Right Place*, 358; US Bureau of the Census, *Historical Statistics of the United States*, 2:1140.

6. A. Powell, *Utah Remembers World War II*, 195–96; Lorene Myrtle Barker Rasmussen, interview by Michael Van Wagenen, October 19, 1991, MSS OH 1438, Perry Special Collections, HBLL.

7. Viola T. Eschler, interview by Michael Van Wagenen, November 23, 1991, MSS OH 1281, Perry Special Collections, HBLL.

8. John Mack Faragher et al., *Out of Many: A History of the American People*, 2:809; Navy Department Press Release, "President to Present Medal of Honor to George E. Wahlen, Pharmacist's Mate, Second Class, U.S. Naval Reserve," October 1, 1945, copy in Cannon's possession; A. Powell, *Utah Remembers World War II*, 75–80.

9. Woolas Ainley Macey, interview by Michael Van Wagenen, September 17, 1992, MSS OH 1439, Perry Special Collections, HBLL.

10. Faragher et al., *Out of Many*, 2:811; Frances Wilde, interview by Brian Cannon, July 30, 1998, copy in Cannon's possession; David H. Clarke, interview by Stacey Clarke (1998), quoted in Stacey Clarke, "Life in Utah through the Eyes of David and Dorothy Clarke, 1930–1945," 1998, 8, copy in Cannon's possession.

11. "Measures of Economic Changes," 62, 63; Joseph Wayne Haws, interview by Krista Haws, November 8, 1992, quoted in Krista Haws, "Why Did They Go to War?" (1992), 7, copy in Cannon's possession.

12. Chamberlin, *University of Utah*, 496; Melba Barker Larsen, interview by Michael Van Wagenen, October 12, 1991, 3, MSS OH 1273, Perry Special Collections, HBLL.

13. JoAnn McGinnis Cannon, interview by Brian Cannon, January 7, 1999, copy in Cannon's possession; Alvin R. Barlow, interview by Michael Van Wagenen, October 16, 1991, 6, MSS OH 1440, Perry Special Collections, HBLL; *Official Report of the One Hundred Fifty-Fourth Annual General Conference of the Church of Jesus Christ of Latter-day Saints*, 62.

14. John Morton Blum, *V Was for Victory: Politics and American Culture during World War II*, 250; A. Powell, *Utah Remembers World War II, 146*; Chamberlin, *University of Utah*, 511–12.

15. Blum, *V Was for Victory*, 250; Clarke, "Life in Utah," 10.

16. Maryboy and Begay, "The Navajos of Utah," 299; Conetah, *History of the Northern Ute People*, 140; Crum, *Road on Which We Came*, 121.

17. Maryboy and Begay, "The Navajos of Utah," 299–300; Knack, *Boundaries Between*, 243; Crum, *Road on Which We Came*, 121; Conetah, *History of the Northern Ute People*, 140.

18. James J. Rawls, *Chief Red Fox Is Dead: A History of Native Americans since 1945*, 7–9; Maryboy and Begay, "The Navajos of Utah," 299.

19. Gerald D. Nash, *World War II and the West: Reshaping the Economy*, 143.

20. "Measures of Economic Changes," 20.

21. Gerstner, "A Richly Diverse Heritage," 12; Marjorie [Reid Killpack] to "My Dearest," January 15, 1943; Marjorie to "My Dear Husband," November 1, 1944, in *Since You Went Away: World War II Letters from American Women on the Home Front*, edited by Judy Barrett Litoff and David C. Smith, 100, 102; Sammy Cahn, "Can't You Read Between the Lines?," http://lyricsplayground.com/alpha/songs/c/cantyoureadbetweenthelines.shtml.

22. "Measures of Economic Changes," 18.

23. Marjorie Watts Thompson, interview by Michael Van Wagenen, November 17, 1991, 5, 7–8, MSS OH 1489, Perry Special Collections, HBLL.

24. M. Thompson interview, 8; Benjamin Gabaldon quoted in A. Powell, *Utah Remembers World War II*, 99; "Measures of Economic Changes," 20; J. Christensen, "Impact of World War II," 512; Tim B. Heaton, Thomas A. Hirschl, and Bruce A. Chadwick, eds., *Utah in the 1990s: A Demographic Perspective*, 93. In 1980 Utah's divorce rate was 5.4 per 1,000, as was the case in 1987. By 1990 the rate had fallen to 5.2 per 1,000.

25. June Anderson quoted in Antonette Chambers Noble, "Utah's Rosies: Women in the Utah War Industries during World War II," 144; Doris Warren Bowers-Irons quoted in A. Powell, *Utah Remembers World War II*, 191–92; M. Thompson interview, 8.

26. Lola Jean Van Wagenen, interview by Michael Van Wagenen, November 19, 1991, 6, MSS OH 1486, Perry Special Collections, HBLL; A. Powell, *Utah Remembers World War II*, 191–92; M. Thompson interview, 8.

27. James Elmo Packer, interview by Michael Van Wagenen, October 19, 1991, 8, MSS OH 1283, Perry Special Collections, HBLL; Marjorie Dyreng Gagon, interview by Miriam Gunter (1998), quoted in Gunter, "Marjorie Dyreng Gagon," 1998, 5, copy in Cannon's possession; Ora Petersen, interview by Brian Cannon, July 28, 1998, copy in Cannon's possession.

28. *Iron County Record*, January 14, 1943; Donald Q. Cannon, interview by Brian Cannon, December 14, 1997, 4, transcript in Cannon's possession; Lola Van Wagenen interview, 7; Wilde interview.

29. Larsen interview, 4; Gunter, "Marjorie Dyreng Gagon," 5; Ed Liechty, interview by Brian Cannon, August 13, 1998, notes in Cannon's possession.

30. Haws, "Why Did They Go to War?," 6; Jay Markham Hall, interview by Michael Van Wagenen, September 18, 1992, 4, 10, MSS OH 1485, Perry Special Collections, HBLL.

31. Dorman, *"Confessions of a Coal Camp Doctor,"* 129.

32. Patrick Q. Mason, "The Prohibition of Interracial Marriage in Utah, 1888–1963"; Kelen and Stone, *Missing Stories*, 219, 226.

33. Helen Gim Kurumada quoted in Kelen and Stone, *Missing Stories*, 236; Chiyo Matsumiya quoted in ibid., 323.

34. Chiyo Matsumiya quoted in Kelen and Stone, ibid., 322; Edward Hashimoto quoted in ibid., 346; William W. Louie quoted in ibid., 218; *DN*, December 9, 1941; January 3, 1942.

35. Edythe Kaneko quoted in *Missing Stories*, 329, 331; Yukiyoshi "Yukus" or "Yuki" Inouye quoted in ibid., 339. See also Allan Kent Powell, "Utah and World War II," 125–26.

36. Inouye quoted in Kelen and Stone, *Missing Stories*, 339; Helen Gim Kurumada quoted in ibid., 237–38.

37. Wilde interview; Eugene Robert Barber quoted in Kelen and Stone, *Missing Stories*, 259; Filomena Fazzio Bonacci quoted in ibid., 279–80.

38. Blum, *V Was for Victory*, 17, Rose Arnovitz quoted in Kelen and Stone, *Missing Stories*, 168; McPherson, *Navajo Land, Navajo Culture*, 173; Jessie L. Embry, "Fighting the Good Fight: The Utah Home Front during World War II," 265–67; Lola Van Wagenen interview, 8; Clarence R. Silver interview by Cherilyn A. Walley, February 12, 1994, 13, MSS OH 1748, Perry Special Collections, HBLL.

39. Gerstner, "A Richly Diverse Heritage," 12; A. Powell, *Utah Remembers World War II*, 138–39.

40. Embry, "Fighting the Good Fight," 247–48; *Iron County Record*, April 22, July 8, 1943; D. Gardner interview, 4.

41. Embry, "Fighting the Good Fight," 243, 245, 246; Theros John "Ted" Speros quoted in Kelen and Stone, *Missing Stories*, 416; Lola Van Wagenen interview, 9; Donna J. Fifield, interview by Michael Van Wagenen, September 28, 1991, 5, MSS OH 1269, Perry Special Collections, HBLL; Blum, *V Was for Victory*, 94.

42. "Measures of Economic Changes," 73; E. Nelson, "Mining Industry," 184–86; Alexander, "From Dearth to Deluge," 241, 243.

43. "Measures of Economic Changes," 47, 53; Harry Isadore Smith quoted in Kelen and Stone, *Missing Voices*, 141; Rex Bevan Blake, interview by Michael Van Wagenen, October 16, 1991, 10, MSS OH 1234, Perry Special Collections, HBLL, 5; Ora Petersen interview.

44. Leonard J. Arrington and George Jensen, *The Defense Industry of Utah*, 27–28; Antonette Chambers Noble, "Utah's Defense Industries and Workers in World War II," 366; James L. Clayton, "An Unhallowed Gathering: The Impact of Defense Spending on Utah's Population Growth, 1940–1964," 230.

45. "Measures of Economic Changes," 25; Vern Richins, interview by Samuel M. Richins, November 25, 1998, quoted in Samuel M. Richins, "Poverty and War in Utah," 1998, 8, typescript in Cannon's possession.

46. Leonard J. Arrington and Thomas G. Alexander, "The U.S. Army Overlooks Salt Lake Valley: Fort Douglas, 1862–1965," 344–45.

47. Leonard J. Arrington and Thomas G. Alexander, "World's Largest Military Reserve: Wendover Air Force Base, 1941–63," 326–27, 330–31; Thomas G. Alexander, "Utah War Industry during World War II: A Human Impact Analysis," 76; Roger D. Launius, "One Man's Air Force: The Experience of Byron Dussler at Wendover Field, Utah, 1941–46," 149–50.

48. Thomas G. Alexander, "Brief Histories of Three Military Installations in Utah: Kearns Army Air Base, Hurricane Mesa and Green River Test Complex," 123–26.

49. Leonard J. Arrington and Thomas G. Alexander, "They Kept 'Em Rolling: The Tooele Army Depot, 1942–1962."

50. Leonard J. Arrington and Thomas G. Alexander, "Sentinels on the Desert: The Dugway Proving Ground (1942–1963) and Deseret Chemical Depot (1942–1955)," 32–37.

51. Arrington and Alexander, "Sentinels in the Desert," 37–38, 43; *DN*, December 15, 1993; January 27, April 10, 1994; February 28, 1998; Chip Ward, *Canaries on the Rim: Living Downwind in the West*, 98–148.

52. Leonard J. Arrington and Archer L. Durham, "Anchors Aweigh in Utah: The U.S. Naval Supply Depot at Clearfield, 1942–1962."

53. Leonard J. Arrington, Thomas G. Alexander, and Eugene A. Erb Jr., "Utah's Biggest Business: Ogden Air Materiel Area at Hill Air Force Base, 1938–1965," 12–16; John D. McConahay, "The Economic Impact of Hill Air Force Base on the Ogden Area," 70.

54. Leonard J. Arrington and Thomas G. Alexander, "Supply Hub of the West: Defense Depot Ogden, 1941–1964."

55. Alexander, "Ogden's 'Arsenal of Democracy.'"

56. Andrea Kaye Carter, "Bushnell General Military Hospital and the Community of Brigham City, Utah, during World War II," 10–26; J. Christensen, "Impact of World War II," 500; Alexander, "Utah War Industry during World War II," 77; Douglas Horrocks Kershaw, interview by Genevieve Green, October 28, 1998, quoted in Genevieve Green, "The Effects of the Great Depression and World War Two on Utah and in the Life of Douglas Horrocks Kershaw" (1998), 9, copy in Cannon's possession.

57. Ralph A. Busco and Douglas D. Alder, "German and Italian Prisoners of War in Utah and Idaho"; Allan Kent Powell, *Splinters of a Nation: German Prisoners of War in Utah*; A. Powell, *Utah Remembers World War II*, vii; interview of Donald Q. Cannon by Brian Q. Cannon, December 14, 1997, transcript in Cannon's possession; Noble, "Utah's Defense Industries," 373; Arrington and Alexander, "They Kept 'Em Rolling," 11.

58.   Clayton, "Unhallowed Gathering," 230; Arrington and Durham, "Anchors Aweigh," 114–15; Arrington and Alexander, "U.S. Army Overlooks Salt Lake Valley," 346; Alexander, "Ogden's 'Arsenal of Democracy,'" 244–45; Arrington and Alexander, "They Kept 'Em Rolling," 11–12; Arrington and Alexander, "Supply Hub of the West," 104–5; Arrington and Alexander, "Sentinel on the Desert," 38; Alexander, "Kearns Army Air Base," 125; Arrington and Alexander, "World's Largest Military Reserve," 334; Arrington, Alexander, and Erb, "Utah's Biggest Business," 13; Alexander, *Utah, the Right Place*, 351; Noble, "Utah's Defense Industries," 371–74; Kelen and Stone, *Missing Voices*, 98, 226, 440; Carmen Teresa Whalen, "Puerto Ricans," 448.

59.   Maryboy and Begay, "The Navajos of Utah," 299; Knack, *Boundaries Between*, 243.

60.   A. Powell, *Utah Remembers World War II*, 158; Noble, "Utah's Rosies," 124, 126, 127–28; US Bureau of the Census, *Historical Statistics of the United States*, 1:132.

61.   Amanda Midgley Borneman, "'Proud to Send Those Parachutes Off': Central Utah's Rosies during World War II" (article); Gunter, "Marjorie Dyreng Gagon," 4–5; Dorothy Lemmon quoted in A. Powell, *Utah Remembers World War II*, 159, 160.

62.   Ruth Ellenberg, "Women of Steel" (1992), 8, copy in Cannon's possession; Elizabeth Talbot, interview by Ruth Ellenberg, October 20, 1992, quoted in ibid., 8.

63.   Faragher et al., *Out of Many*, 2:802; *General Conference Report: October 1942*, 12; *General Conference Report: April 1944*, 47; *General Conference Report: April 1945*, 141; *General Conference Report: April 1946*, 28; Amanda Sue Midgley Borneman, "'Proud to Send Those Parachutes Off': Central Utah's Rosies during World War II" (thesis), 81–82.

64.   Noble, "Utah's Rosies," 145.

65.   Borneman, "'Proud to Send Those Parachutes Off'" (thesis), 89; US Department of Labor, *Women Workers in Their Family Environment*, 49–50, 77.

66.   L. Carroll, "Melba Judge Lehner," 52–60.

67.   Borneman, "'Proud to Send Those Parachutes Off'" (article), 136–39.

68.   Clayton, "Unhallowed Gathering," 230; Thomas G. Alexander, "The Transformation of Utah: From a Colony of Wall Street to a Colony of Washington," 21; Arrington and Jensen, *Defense Industry of Utah*, 34.

69.   Leonard J. Arrington and Anthony T. Cluff, *Federally-Financed Industrial Plants Constructed in Utah during World War II*, 10, 70–72.

70.   Ibid., 64, 66–67; Alexander, "Transformation of Utah," 16; Borneman, "'Proud to Send Those Parachutes Off'" (thesis), 28–33.

71.   Alexander and Allen, *Mormons and Gentiles*, 233.

72.   Herbert Maw quoted in A. Powell, *Utah Remembers World War II*, 155–57.

73.   Thomas G. Alexander and Leonard J. Arrington, "Utah's Small Arms Ammunition Plant during World War II," 186; Hebert B. Maw to Elbert D. Thomas, May 2, 1941; Thomas to Maw, May 9, 1941, Folder General File 1942 Utah Governor Maw, Box 39, Thomas Papers; *SLT*, June 11, 1941.

74.   Alexander and Arrington, "Utah's Small Arms Ammunition Plant"; US Bureau of the Census, *Sixteenth Census: Population*, 3:654.

75.   Alexander and Arrington, "Utah's Small Arms Ammunition Plant," 186, 194; J. Christensen, "Impact of World War II," 501–2; Alexander, *Utah, the Right Place*, 350; Charles H. Holmes, "The Economic Impact of Geneva Steel Company (United States Steel Subsidiary) on Utah County, Utah," 10–51, 77, 84, 133; Gustive O. Larson, "Bulwark of the Kingdom: Utah's Iron and Steel Industry," 258–60; E. Nelson, "Mining Industry," 186.

76.   Holmes, "Economic Impact of Geneva Steel," 79, 84, 96, 107, 134, 136; Wilde interview.

77. Leonard J. Arrington, *Utah, the New Deal and the Depression of the 1930s*, 27; Alexander and Arrington, "Utah's Small Arms Ammunition Plant," 185; Arrington and Jensen, *Defense Industry of Utah*, 13.

78. "Measures of Economic Changes," 54, 102; J. Christensen, "Impact of World War II," 505.

79. "Measures of Economic Changes," 22, 23.

80. Theros John "Ted" Speros quoted in Kelen and Stone, *Missing Voices*, 415–16.

81. Margaret Atwood Herbert quoted in A. Powell, *Utah Remembers World War II*, 171; Rose Arnowitz quoted in Kelen and Stone, *Missing Voices*, 168.

82. Faragher et al., *Out of Many*, 2:809, 812; A. Powell, *Utah Remembers World War II*, 171–72; Nathan "Woody" Wright quoted in Kelen and Stone, *Missing Voices*, 99.

83. A. Powell, *Utah Remembers World War II*, 171–72; Dinger, "Rations, Wartime, and Salt Lake City," 3–4, 7–8, 10.

84. Clayton, "Unhallowed Gathering," 235, 237; Dick Jackson, interview by Heather Jackson [1998], quoted in Heather Jackson, "Winds of Struggle: Utah in the 1930s and 1940s" (1998), 10, copy in Cannon's possession; Todd Forsyth Carney, "Utah and Mormon Migration in the Twentieth Century, 1890–1955."

85. Richard White, *"It's Your Misfortune and None of My Own": A New History of the American West*, 509; Noble, "Utah's Defense Industries," 172; Poll et al., *Utah's History*, 691.

86. Ulibarri, "Utah's Ethnic Minorities," 231–32; Noble, "Utah's Defense Industries," 372–73; Poll et al., *Utah's History*, 637; Kelen and Stone, *Missing Stories*, 440.

87. James B. Allen, "Crisis on the Home Front: The Federal Government and Utah's Defense Housing in World War II"; Alexander, "Utah War Industry during World War II," 79–80.

88. Murray Moler and Andre Fontaine, "Utah's Steel Guinea Pig"; Arrington and Cluff, *Federally-Financed Industrial Plants*, 43.

89. Alexander, "Utah War Industry during World War II," 81–85; Joseph F. Merrill in *General Conference Report: April 1946*, 28–29.

90. Sandra C. Taylor, *Jewel of the Desert: Japanese American Internment at Topaz*, 106; Arrington, "Utah's Ambiguous Reception," 94; Helen Gim Kuramada in Kelen and Stone, *Missing Stories*, 237.

91. Sandra C. Taylor, "Japanese Americans and Keetley Farms: Utah's Relocation Colony."

92. S. Taylor, *Jewel of the Desert*, 92–95, 109, 222; Miné Okubo, *Citizen 13660*, ix; Yoshiko Uchida, *Desert Exile: The Uprooting of a Japanese-American Family*, 109; Akiko J. Tohmatsu, "Japanese American Youth in Topaz Relocation Center, Utah: An Oral History," 36–37.

93. Tohmatsu, "Japanese American Youth," 36–39, 43; S. Taylor, *Jewel of the Desert*, 92–95, 109, 222.

94. Tohmatsu, "Japanese American Youth," 44; Uchida, *Desert Exile*, 121.

95. S. Taylor, *Jewel of the Desert*, 136–46; Uchida, *Desert Exile*, 123, 140.

96. R. Todd Welker, "Utah Schools and the Japanese American Student Relocation Program"; Aiji Uchiyama, telephone interview by Brian Cannon, April 12, 2000, notes in Cannon's possession.

97. Arrington, "Utah's Ambiguous Reception," 96–97; S. Taylor, *Jewel of the Desert*, 112–17.

98. Tohmatsu, "Japanese American Youth," 41–45.

99. Ulibarri, "Utah's Ethnic Minorities," 224; S. Taylor, *Jewel of the Desert*, 147–53.

100. S. Taylor, *Jewel of the Desert*, 90–97, 108–9, 112–18, 136–46, 210, 222, 272; Ulibarri, "Utah's Ethnic Minorities," 224; Arrington, "Utah's Ambiguous Reception," 96–97.

101. Firmage, *History of Grand County*, 293–94. See also Bruce D. Louthan and Lloyd M. Pierson, "Moab Japanese-American Isolation Center: The Dark Postlude in the History of Dalton Wells CCC Camp."

102. Jack Douglas Barton quoted in A. Powell, *Utah Remembers World War II*, 138; Margaret Atwood Herbert quoted in ibid., 171.

103. "Measures of Economic Changes," 10, 11; US Bureau of the Census, *Census of Population, 1950*, vol. 2, *Characteristics of the Population*, pt. 44, p. 9; US Bureau of the Census, *Census of Housing, 1950*, vol. 1, pt. 6, *General Characteristics*, 44–45. The Census did not report housing values for Daggett County.

104. "Measures of Economic Changes," 53, 69; Arrington and Jensen, *Defense Industry of Utah*, 33–37.

CONCLUSION

1. Arrington, *Great Basin Kingdom*, 380, 409.

2. Gustive O. Larson, *The "Americanization" of Utah for Statehood*. See also Edward Leo Lyman's excellent *Political Deliverance*.

3. Yorgason, *Mormon Culture Region*; Flake, *Politics of Identity*; Alexander, *Mormonism in Transition*, 3.

4. Alexander, *Utah, the Right Place*, 451, 52.

5. Ibid., 457–58. Alexander and Arrington highlighted the impact of federal spending in Utah during the 1930s and 1940s in several articles that were published in the 1960s that are cited in chapters 13 and 14 of this volume. See also Alexander, "Utah War Industry during World War II: A Human Impact Analysis."

6. For recent discussions of incorporating forces on the urban frontier as they relate to empire and imperialism, see Jay Gitlin, Barbara Berglund, and Adam Arenson, eds., *Frontier Cities: Encounters at the Crossroads of Empire*.

BIBLIOGRAPHY

ARCHIVES

Blood, Henry H. Papers. Utah State Archives, Salt Lake City.

Brimhall, Dean. Papers. Special Collections, Marriott Library. University of Utah, Salt Lake City.

Bullen, Herschel. Papers. Special Collections, Merrill-Cazier Library. Utah State University, Logan.

Bureau of Reclamation. Records. Record Group 115. National Archives, Lakewood, CO.

Caine, George B. Papers. Special Collections, Merrill-Cazier Library. Utah State University, Logan.

Clark, J. Reuben. Papers. L. Tom Perry Special Collections, Harold B. Lee Library. Brigham Young University, Provo, UT.

Dern, George. "Messages to the Legislature, 1927, 1929." Governor Messages to the Legislature, Series 182. Utah State Archives, Salt Lake City.

———. Papers. Utah State Archives. Salt Lake City.

———. Statement at the Hearings Before the Committee on Irrigation and Reclamation, US Senate, December 17, 1927. Bound in pamphlet form. Utah State Historical Society Library, Salt Lake City.

Duke, Doris. Collection. Special Collections, Marriott Library. University of Utah, Salt Lake City.

Evanston District Historical Files. Forest Service, Evanston, WY.

Farmers Home Administration. Records. Record Group 96. National Archives, College Park, MD.

Federal Writers' Project Collection. USU MSS COLL 009, Special Collections, Merrill-Cazier Library. Utah State University, Logan.

Federal Writers' Project Grazing History Records. Utah State University Library and Utah Historical Society Library, Logan and Salt Lake City.

Harris, Franklin S. Papers. L. Tom Perry Special Collections, Harold B. Lee Library. Brigham Young University, Provo, UT.

Idaho State Historical Society Collections. Boise.

Johnson, Zeke. Papers. MS O511, Special Collections. University of Utah, Salt Lake City.

Keith, David. Scrapbook. Utah State Historical Society, Salt Lake City.

Kenney, Scott. Collection. L. Tom Perry Special Collections, Harold B. Lee Library. Brigham
    Young University, Provo, UT.
Knight, Jesse. Papers. L. Tom Perry Special Collections, Harold B. Lee Library. Brigham Young
    University, Provo, UT.
Knight Construction Company. Papers. L. Tom Perry Special Collections, Harold B. Lee Library.
    Brigham Young University, Provo, UT.
L. Tom Perry Special Collections, Harold B. Lee Library. Brigham Young University, Provo, UT.
LDS Church History Library. Salt Lake City.
Mabey, Charles. Papers. Utah State Archives, Salt Lake City.
Manti–La Sal National Forest Files. Manti–La Sal National Forest, Price, UT.
National Archives. College Park, MD.
National Park Service. Records. Record Group 79. College Park, MD.
Nelson, Lowry. Collection. L. Tom Perry Special Collections, Harold B. Lee Library. Brigham
    Young University, Provo, UT.
Peterson, Charles S. Papers. Mss B. 1608. Utah State Historical Society, Salt Lake City.
Ricks, Joel E. Collection. Special Collections, Merrill-Cazier Library. Utah State University,
    Logan.
Smoot, Reed. Papers. L. Tom Perry Special Collections, Harold B. Lee Library. Brigham Young
    University, Provo, UT.
Special Collections, Merrill-Cazier Library. Utah State University, Logan.
State Engineer's Papers. Utah State Archives, Salt Lake City.
Thomas, Elbert D. Papers. Utah State Historical Society, Salt Lake City.
Topping, Gary. Papers. Utah State Historical Society, Salt Lake City.
Utah State Archives. Salt Lake City.
Utah State Historical Society. Salt Lake City.
Utah State University Archives. Logan.
Wasatch-Cache National Forest Historical Records. Uinta-Wasatch-Cache National Forest, Salt
    Lake City.
Welling, Milton H. Papers. Accession 2302, Special Collections, Marriott Library. University of
    Utah, Salt Lake City.
West, Caleb W. Papers. Utah State Archives, Salt Lake City.
Whitaker, John Mills. Collection. Special Collections, Marriott Library. University of Utah, Salt
    Lake City.
Zion National Park Historical Files. Springdale, UT.

GOVERNMENT DOCUMENTS

*Annual Report of the Commissioner of Indian Affairs to the Secretary of the Interior for the Year
    1887*. Washington, DC: GPO, 1887.
Biennial Report of the Board of Land Commissioners for the Years 1919–1920. Kaysville, UT: Board
    of Land Commissioners.
Biennial Report of the State Board of Horticulture, 1897–98. Salt Lake City: Deseret News Press,
    1899.
Biennial Report of the State Engineer to the Governor of Utah, 1917–1918. Salt Lake City: n.p., 1919.
*The Emergency Work Relief Program of the Federal Emergency Relief Administration, April 1, 1934
    to July 1, 1935*. Washington, DC: GPO, 1935.
Federal Emergency Relief Administration. *Index of the Monthly Reports of the Federal Emergency
    Relief Administration: June 1933 through December 1933*. Washington, DC: GPO, 1937.

Federal Reclamation by Irrigation. Senate Document no. 92, 68th Cong., 1st sess. Washington, DC: GPO, 1924.

The Federal Reporter. Vol. 140. St. Paul: West, 1906.

Federal Security Agency. *Final Report of the National Youth Administration, Fiscal Years 1936–1943.* Washington, DC: GPO, 1944.

Federal Works Agency and Work Projects Administration. *Final Statistical Report of the Federal Emergency Relief Administration.* Washington, DC: GPO, 1942.

Federal Writers' Program. *Utah: A Guide to the State.* New York: Hastings House, 1941.

Fifth Biennial Report: State Road Commission, 1917–1918. Salt Lake City: F. W. Gardiner, [1918].

First Biennial Report of the Utah Conservation Commission. Salt Lake City: Arrow Press, 1912.

First Report of the State Bureau of Immigration, Labor and Statistics, 1911–1912. Salt Lake City: Arrow Press, 1913.

Forest Service. *Timber Management Report, 1911.* Timber Management Folder. Manti–La Sal National Forest Files, Manti–La Sal National Forest, Price, UT.

Ninth Biennial Report of the State Mine Inspector for the State of Utah for the Years 1911–1912. Salt Lake City: Arrow Press, 1913.

Reclamation Service. *Third Annual Report of the Reclamation Service, 1903–1904.* Washington, DC: GPO, 1905.

Report of the Bank Commissioner, 1913–1914. Salt Lake City: Arrow Press, 1915.

Report of the Coal Mine Inspector for the State of Utah for the Years 1897 and 1898. Salt Lake City: Deseret News Press, 1899.

Report of the Coal Mine Inspector for the State of Utah for the Years 1899 and 1900. Salt Lake City: Deseret News Press, 1901.

Report of the Coal Mine Inspector for the State of Utah from April 6th to December 31st, 1896. Salt Lake City: Deseret News Press, 1897.

Report of the Industrial Commission of Utah: July 1, 1920 to June 20, 1922. Salt Lake City: Arrow Press, [1922].

Report of the State Bureau of Immigration, Labor and Statistics for the Years 1913–1914. Salt Lake City: Arrow Press, 1915.

Report of the State Coal Mine Inspector for the Years 1903 and 1904. Salt Lake City: Deseret News Press, 1905.

Report of the State Coal Mine Inspector for the Years 1904 and 1905. Salt Lake City: Deseret News Press, 1906.

Report of the State Coal Mine Inspector of the State of Utah, 1915–1916. Salt Lake City: Tribune Printing, 1917.

Report of the State Engineer, 1905–1906. Salt Lake City: Deseret News Press, 1907.

Report of the State Engineer, 1921–1922. Salt Lake City: Arrow Press, 1922.

Report of the Utah State Conservation Commission, 1911–1912. In *Public Documents, State of Utah,* 1:157. Salt Lake City: Arrow Press, 1913.

Reports of the State Engineer, 1938–1946. Box 1, Series 880. Division of Water Rights Biennial Reports. Department of Natural Resources, Utah State Archives, Salt Lake City.

Revised Statutes of Utah, 1933. Kaysville, UT: Inland Printing, 1933.

Second Annual Report of the Reclamation Service, 1902–1903. House Document no. 44, 58th Cong., 2nd sess. Washington, DC: GPO, 1904.

Second Biennial Report of the State Bureau of Immigration, Labor and Statistics, 1913–1914. Salt Lake City: Arrow Press, 1915.

Sixth Annual Report of the Reclamation Service, 1906–1907. Washington, DC: GPO, 1907.

Sixth Biennial Report: State Road Commission, 1919–1920. Kaysville, UT: Inland Printing, [1920].

State of Utah. *Constitution of the State of Utah as Framed by the Constitutional Convention*. Salt Lake City: Tribune Job Printing, 1895.

——— . *Messages of Governor Henry H. Blood to the Twentieth Legislature of the State of Utah and Inaugural Address, 1933*. Salt Lake City: n.p., 1933.

State Senate of Utah. *Senate Journal: Eighteenth Session of the Legislature of the State of Utah*. Salt Lake City: n.p., 1929.

The Statistics of the Population of the United States . . . from the Original Returns of the Ninth Census. Washington, DC: GPO, 1872.

Third Annual Report of the Utah Farmers' Institutes, 1899. Salt Lake City: Deseret News Press, 1899.

Third Report of the State Bureau of Immigration, Labor and Statistics, 1913–1914. Salt Lake City: Arrow Press, 1917.

US Bureau of the Census. *Census of Housing: 1950*. Vol. 1, *General Characteristics*. Washington, DC: GPO, 1953.

——— . *Census of Population: 1950*. Vol. 2, *Characteristics of the Population*. Washington, DC: GPO, 1952.

——— . *Fifteenth Census of the United States, 1930: Agriculture*. 5 vols. Washington, DC: GPO, 1932.

——— . *Fifteenth Census of the United States, 1930: Population*. 6 vols. Washington, DC: GPO, 1932.

——— . *Fifteenth Census of the United States, 1930: Unemployment*. 2 vols. Washington, DC: GPO, 1932.

——— . *Fourteenth Census of the United States Taken in the Year 1920: Population, 1920*. Washington, DC: GPO, 1921.

——— . *Historical Statistics of the United States: Colonial Times to 1970*. 2 vols. Washington, DC: GPO, 1975.

——— . *Population, 1920: Composition and Character of the Population by States*. Washington, DC: GPO, 1922.

——— . *Report on the Statistics of Agriculture in the United States at the Eleventh Census, 1890*. Washington, DC: GPO, 1895.

——— . *Sixteenth Census of the United States: 1940, Housing*. Vol. 2, *General Characteristics*. Washington, DC: GPO, 1943.

——— . *Sixteenth Census of the United States: 1940, Population*. 4 vols. Washington, DC: GPO, 1943.

——— . *Sixteenth Census of the United States: 1940, Population; Internal Migration, 1935 to 1940, Social Characteristics of Migrants*. Washington, DC: GPO, 1946.

——— . *Thirteenth Census of the United States, 1910: Population by States and Territories*. Washington, DC: GPO, 1910.

——— . *Thirteenth Census of the United States Taken in the Year 1910: Abstract of the Census*. Washington, DC: GPO, 1913.

US Department of Agriculture. *Forest and Range Resources of Utah: Their Protection and Use*. Misc. pub. no. 90. Washington, DC: GPO, 1930.

US Department of Labor. *Women Workers in Their Family Environment*. Women's Bureau Bulletin no. 183. Washington, DC: GPO, 1941.

Utah Agricultural Statistics and Utah Department of Agriculture Annual Report. Salt Lake City: Utah Department of Agriculture, 1994.

Work Projects Administration. *Final Statistical Report of the Federal Emergency Relief Administration*. Washington, DC: GPO, 1942.

Writers Program of the Work Projects Administration. *Provo—Pioneer Mormon City*. American Guide Series. Portland, OR: Binford and Mart, 1942.

NEWSPAPERS AND PERIODICALS

Beaver County News
Beaver Weekly Press
Box Elder Journal
Box Elder News
Cliffdwellers' Echo
Deseret Farmer
Deseret News
Duchesne Record
Eastern Utah Advocate
Emery County Progress
Ephraim Enterprise
Goodwin's Weekly
Grand Junction Daily Sentinel
Grand Valley Times (Moab, UT)
Intermountain Catholic (Salt Lake City)
Inter-Mountain Republican (Salt Lake City)
Iron County Record
Kane County News
Logan Herald Journal
Logan Journal
Manti Messenger
Millard County Chronicle
Moab Times Independent
Nephi Record
Nephi Times-News
New York Times
Oneida County Enterprise
Panguitch Progress
Park Record
Progressive
Provo Daily Herald
Richfield Reaper
Salt Lake Herald
Salt Lake Herald-Republican
Salt Lake Mining Review
Salt Lake Telegram
Salt Lake Tribune
Tremonton Times
Uintah Express
United Mine Workers Journal
Vernal Express

Washington County News
Wyoming Labor Journal

OTHER SOURCES

Abbey, Edward. *Desert Solitaire: A Season in the Wilderness*. New York: Ballantine Books, 1968.

Aberle, David F., and Omer C. Stewart. "Navaho and Ute Peyotism: A Chronological and Distributional Study." In *Peyotism in the West*, edited by Jesse D. Jennings and Sharon S. Arnold, 133–265. Salt Lake City: University of Utah Press, 1984.

Adams, Frank. "Agriculture under Irrigation in the Basin of Virgin River." In *Report of Irrigation Investigations in Utah*, edited by Elwood Mead, 207–65. Washington, DC: GPO, 1903.

Adler, William M. *The Man Who Never Died: The Life, Times, and Legacy of Joe Hill, American Labor Icon*. New York: Bloomsbury, 2011.

Albright, Horace M., and Robert Cahn. *The Birth of the National Park Service: The Founding Years, 1913–33*. New York: Howe Brothers, 1985.

Alder, Douglas D. "The Ghost of Mercur." *Utah Historical Quarterly* 29 (January 1961): 33–42.

Alder, Douglas D., and Karl F. Brooks. *A History of Washington County: From Isolation to Destination*. Salt Lake City: Utah State Historical Society, 1996.

Alder, Tom. "The Art and Too-Brief Life of Donald Beauregard." http://www.artistsofutah. org/15bytes/08dec/page5.html.

Alexander, Thomas G. "Between Revivalism and the Social Gospel: The Latter-day Saint Social Advisory Committee." *BYU Studies* 23 (Winter 1983): 19–39.

——— . "Brief Histories of Three Military Installations in Utah: Kearns Army Air Base, Hurricane Mesa and Green River Test Complex." *Utah Historical Quarterly* 34 (Spring 1966): 121–37.

——— . "From Dearth to Deluge: Utah's Coal Industry." *Utah Historical Quarterly* 31 (Summer 1963): 235–47.

——— . "From War to Depression." In *Utah's History*, edited by Richard D. Poll et al., 463–80. Logan: Utah State University Press, 1989.

——— . "Generating Wealth from the Earth, 1847–2000." In *From the Ground Up: The History of Mining in Utah*, edited by Colleen Whitley, 37–57. Logan: Utah State University Press, 2006.

——— . "Interdependence and Change: Mutual Irrigation Companies in Utah's Wasatch Oasis in an Age of Modernization, 1870–1930." *Utah Historical Quarterly* 71 (Fall 2003): 292–314.

——— . *Mormonism in Transition: A History of the Latter-day Saints, 1890–1930*. Urbana: University of Illinois Press, 1986.

——— . "Ogden, a Federal Colony." *Utah Historical Quarterly* 47 (Summer 1979): 291–309.

——— . "Ogden's 'Arsenal of Democracy,' 1920–1955." *Utah Historical Quarterly* 33 (Summer 1965): 237–45.

——— . "Political Patterns of Early Statehood, 1896–1919." In *Utah's History*, edited by Richard D. Poll et al., 409–28. Logan: Utah State University Press, 1989.

——— . "Red Rock and Gray Stone: Senator Reed Smoot, the Establishment of Zion and Bryce Canyon National Parks, and the Rebuilding of Downtown Washington, D.C." *Pacific Historical Review* 72 (February 2003): 12–26.

——— . *The Rise of Multiple-Use Management in the Intermountain West: A History of Region 4 of the Forest Service*. Washington, DC: US Forest Service, 1987.

——— . "Senator Reed Smoot and Western Land Policy, 1905–1920." *Journal of the Southwest* 13 (Autumn 1971): 245–64.

———. "Stewardship and Enterprise: The LDS Church and the Wasatch Oasis Environment, 1847–1930." *Western Historical Quarterly* 25 (Autumn 1994): 340–64.

———, ed. *Times of Transition, 1890–1920*. Provo, UT: Joseph F. Smith Institute for LDS History, 2003.

———. "The Transformation of Utah: From a Colony of Wall Street to a Colony of Washington." *BYU Thetean* 25 (1996).

———. *Utah, the Right Place*. 2nd ed. Salt Lake City: Gibbs Smith, 2003.

———. "Utah War Industry during World War II: A Human Impact Analysis." *Utah Historical Quarterly* 51 (Winter 1983): 72–92.

Alexander, Thomas G., and James B. Allen. *Mormons and Gentiles: A History of Salt Lake City*. Boulder: Pruett, 1984.

Alexander, Thomas G., and Leonard J. Arrington. "Utah's Small Arms Ammunition Plant during World War II." *Pacific Historical Review* 34 (May 1965): 185–96.

Allen, Barbara. *Homesteading the High Desert*. Salt Lake City: University of Utah Press, 1987.

Allen, Frederick Lewis. *Only Yesterday: An Informal History of the 1920's*. New York: Harper & Brothers, 1931.

Allen, James B. "Crisis on the Home Front: The Federal Government and Utah's Defense Housing in World War II." *Pacific Historical Review* 38 (November 1969): 407–28.

Alley, John R., Jr. "Utah State Supreme Court Justice Samuel R. Thurman." *Utah Historical Quarterly* 61 (Summer 1993): 233–48.

Alter, J. Cecil. *Early Utah Journalism: A Half Century of Forensic Warfare, Waged by the West's Most Militant Press*. Salt Lake City: Utah State Historical Society, 1938.

———, ed. "Journal of Priddy Meeks." *Utah Historical Quarterly* 10 (1942).

Anagnostou, Yiorges. "Helen Papanikolas, Folklorist of Ethnicity." In *Folklore in Utah: A History and Guide to Resources*, edited by David Stanley, 67–77. Logan: Utah State University Press, 2004.

Andersen, Rebecca. "The Baron Woolen Mills: A Utah Legend." *Utah Historical Quarterly* 75 (Spring 2007): 116–33.

Andrews, Thomas G. *Killing for Coal: America's Deadliest Labor War*. Cambridge, MA: Harvard University Press, 2008.

Antrei, Albert C. T. *A History of Sanpete County*. Salt Lake City: Utah State Historical Society and Sanpete County Commission, 1999.

Arrington, Leonard J. *Beet Sugar in the West: A History of the Utah-Idaho Sugar Company, 1891–1966*. Seattle: University of Washington Press, 1966.

———. *David Eccles: Pioneer Western Industrialist*. Logan: Utah State University Press, 1975.

———. *Great Basin Kingdom: An Economic History of the Latter-day Saints, 1830–1900*. Salt Lake City: University of Utah Press, 1993.

———. "The Influenza Epidemic of 1918–19 in Utah." *Utah Historical Quarterly* 58 (Spring 1990): 165–82.

———. "The New Deal in the West: A Preliminary Statistical Inquiry." *Pacific Historical Review* 38 (August 1969): 311–16.

———. "Transition to the Modern Era, 1890–1910." In *The History of a Valley: Cache Valley, Utah-Idaho*, edited by Joel E. Ricks and Everett L. Cooley, 205–39. Logan, UT: Cache Valley Centennial Commission, 1956.

———. *Utah, the New Deal and the Depression of the 1930s*. Ogden, UT: Weber State College Press, 1983.

———. "Utah's Ambiguous Reception: The Relocated Japanese Americans." In *Japanese Americans: From Relocation to Redress*, edited by Roger Daniels, Sandra C. Taylor, and Harry H. L. Kitano, 92–98. Rev. ed. Seattle: University of Washington Press, 1991.

———. *Utah's Audacious Stockman, Charlie Redd*. Logan: Utah State University Press, 1995.

———. "Utah's Great Drought of 1934." *Utah Historical Quarterly* 54 (Summer 1986): 245–63.

Arrington, Leonard J., and Thomas G. Alexander. *A Dependent Commonwealth: Utah's Economy from Statehood to the Great Depression*. Charles Redd Monographs in Western History no. 4. Provo, UT: Brigham Young University Press, 1974.

———. "Sentinels on the Desert: The Dugway Proving Ground (1942–1963) and Deseret Chemical Depot (1942–1955)." *Utah Historical Quarterly* 32 (Winter 1964): 32–43.

———. "Supply Hub of the West: Defense Depot Ogden, 1941–1964." *Utah Historical Quarterly* 32 (Spring 1964): 99–112.

———. "They Kept 'Em Rolling: The Tooele Army Depot, 1942–1962." *Utah Historical Quarterly* 31 (Winter 1963): 4–14.

———. "The U.S. Army Overlooks Salt Lake Valley: Fort Douglas, 1862–1965." *Utah Historical Quarterly* 33 (Fall 1965): 326–50.

———. "World's Largest Military Reserve: Wendover Air Force Base, 1941–63." *Utah Historical Quarterly* 31 (Fall 1963): 324–35.

Arrington, Leonard J., Thomas G. Alexander, and Eugene A. Erb Jr. "Utah's Biggest Business: Ogden Air Materiel Area at Hill Air Force Base, 1938–1965." *Utah Historical Quarterly* 33 (Spring 1965): 9–33.

Arrington, Leonard J., and Anthony T. Cluff. *Federally-Financed Industrial Plants Constructed in Utah during World War II*. Utah State University Monograph Series, vol. 16, no. 1. Logan: Utah State University Press, 1969.

Arrington, Leonard J., and Archer L. Durham. "Anchors Aweigh in Utah: The U.S. Naval Supply Depot at Clearfield, 1942–1962." *Utah Historical Quarterly* 31 (Spring 1963): 109–18.

Arrington, Leonard J., and Gary B. Hansen. *"The Richest Hole on Earth": A History of the Bingham Copper Mine*. Logan: Utah State University Press, 1963.

Arrington, Leonard J., and Wayne K. Hinton. "Origin of the Welfare Plan of the Church of Jesus Christ of Latter-day Saints." In *The Exodus and Beyond: Essays in Mormon History*, edited by Lyndon W. Cook and Donald Q. Cannon, 203–22. Salt Lake City: Hawkes, 1980.

Arrington, Leonard J., and George Jensen. *The Defense Industry of Utah*. Logan: Utah State University Department of Economics, 1965.

Athearn, Robert. *Rebel of the Rockies: A History of the Denver and Rio Grande Western Railroad*. New Haven, CT: Yale University Press, 1962.

———. *Union Pacific Country*. Chicago: Rand McNally, 1971.

Aydelotte, L. F. "The Political Thought and Activity of Heber J. Grant, Seventh President of the Church of Jesus Christ of Latter-day Saints." Master's thesis, Brigham Young University, 1965.

Bachman, J. R. *Story of the Amalgamated Sugar Company, 1897–1961*. Caldwell, ID: Caxton, 1962.

Bailey, Garrick, and Robert Glen Bailey. *A History of the Navajos: The Reservation Years*. Santa Fe, NM: School of American Research Press, 1986.

Bailey, Jody, and Robert S. McPherson. "'Practically Free from the Taint of the Bootlegger': A Closer Look at Prohibition in Southeastern Utah." *Utah Historical Quarterly* 57 (Spring 1989): 150–64.

Baker, F. S., and J. H. Paul. *The Floods of 1923 in Northern Utah*. Bulletin of the University of Utah no. 15. Salt Lake City: University of Utah, 1925.

Baker, Pearl. *Robbers Roost Recollections*. Logan: Utah State University Press, 1991.

Baker, Ray Stannard. "The Vitality of Mormonism." *Century*, June 1904, 165–77.

Baldridge, Kenneth W. "Nine Years of Achievement: The Civilian Conservation Corps in Utah." PhD diss., Brigham Young University, 1971.

———. "Reclamation Work of the Civilian Conservation Corps, 1933–1942." *Utah Historical Quarterly* 39 (Summer 1971): 265–85.

Barrett, G. W. "Colonel E. A. Wall: Mines, Miners, and Mormons." *Idaho Yesterdays* 14 (Summer 1970): 3–11.

———. "Enos Andrew Wall: Mine Superintendent and Inventor." *Idaho Yesterdays* 15 (Spring 1971): 24–31.

Barton, Bruce. *The Man Nobody Knows: A Discovery of the Real Jesus*. Indianapolis: Bobbs-Merrill, 1924.

Barton, John D. *A History of Duchesne County*. Salt Lake City: Utah State Historical Society and Duchesne County Commission, 1998.

Bateman, Ronald R. *Deep Creek Reflections: 125 Years of Settlement at Ibapah, Utah, 1859–1984*. Salt Lake City: privately published, 1984.

Bender, H. E., Jr. *Uintah Railway: The Gilsonite Route*. Berkeley: Howell-North Books, 1970.

Bennett, Hugh H. *Report of the Chief of the Soil Conservation Service*. Washington, DC: GPO, 1937.

———. *Report of the Chief of the Soil Conservation Service*. Washington, DC: GPO, 1945.

———. *Report of the Chief of the Soil Conservation Service, 1941*. Washington, DC: GPO, 1941.

Bergera, Gary J. *The Autobiography of B. H. Roberts*. Salt Lake City: Signature Books, 1990.

Berkhofer, Robert F., Jr. "Jefferson, the Ordinance of 1784 and the Origins of the American Territorial System." *William and Mary Quarterly* 29 (April 1972): 231–62.

———. "The Northwest Ordinance and the Principle of Territorial Evolution." In *The American Territorial System*, edited by John Porter Bloom, 45–55. Athens: Ohio University Press, 1969.

Bestor, Arthur. "Constitutionalism and the Settlement of the West: The Attainment of Consensus, 1754–1784." In *The American Territorial System*, edited by John Porter Bloom, 13–44. Athens: Ohio University Press, 1969.

Biles, Roger. *A New Deal for the American People*. DeKalb: Northern Illinois University Press, 1991.

Bird, Douglas M. "A History of Timber Resource Use in the Development of Cache Valley, Utah." Master's thesis, Utah State University, 1964.

Bitton, Davis. "The B. H. Roberts Case of 1898–1900." *Utah Historical Quarterly* 25 (January 1957): 27–46.

Blanch, George T. "A Farm Organization and Management Study in Western Millard County, Utah." Master's thesis, Utah State University, 1931.

———. *A Study of Farm Organization by Types of Farms in Uinta Basin, Utah*. Utah Agricultural Experiment Station Bulletin no. 285. Logan: Utah Agricultural Experiment Station, 1939.

Blum, John Morton. *V Was for Victory: Politics and American Culture during World War II*. New York: Harcourt Brace Jovanovich, 1976.

Bluth, John K., and Wayne K. Hinton. "The Great Depression." In *Utah's History*, edited by Richard D. Poll et al., 481–96. 1978. Reprint, Logan: Utah State University Press, 1989.

Boone, David F. "Missionary Work, 1900–Present." In *Mapping Mormonism: An Atlas of Latter-day Saint History*, edited by Brandon S. Plewe et al., 178–81. Provo, UT: Brigham Young University Press, 2012.

Borneman, Amanda Sue Midgley. "'Proud to Send Those Parachutes Off': Central Utah's Rosies during World War II." In *Utah in the Twentieth Century*, edited by Brian Q. Cannon and Jessie L. Embry, 130–35. Logan: Utah State University Press, 2009.

———. "'Proud to Send Those Parachutes Off': Central Utah's Rosies during World War II." Master's thesis, Brigham Young University, 2006.

Boutwell, J. M. *Economic Geology of the Bingham Mining District, Utah.* Washington, DC: GPO, 1905.

Bowen, Albert E. *The Church Welfare Plan.* Independence, MO: Zion's Printing, 1946.

Bowen, Marshall E. "Crops, Critters, and Calamity: The Failure of Dry Farming in Utah's Escalante Desert, 1913–1918." *Agricultural History* 73 (Winter 1999): 1–26.

———. *Utah People in the Nevada Desert: Homestead and Community on a Twentieth Century Farmers' Frontier.* Logan: Utah State University Press, 1994.

Bowers, William L. *The Country Life Movement in America, 1900–1920.* Port Washington, NY: National University, 1974.

Boyce, G. A. *When Navajos Had Too Many Sheep: The 1940's.* San Francisco: Indian Historian Press, 1974.

Bradley, Martha Sonntag. *A History of Beaver County.* Salt Lake City: Utah State Historical Society and Beaver County Commission, 1999.

———. *Kidnapped from That Land: The Government Raids on the Short Creek Polygamists.* Salt Lake City: University of Utah Press, 1996.

Branch, Ray. "History of Sugar Beet Industry in Carbon County." In *Centennial Echoes from Carbon County,* edited by Thursey Jessen Reynolds, 68–70. Price, UT: Daughters of the Utah Pioneers, 1948.

Brooks, Juanita. "Indian Relations on the Mormon Frontier." *Utah Historical Quarterly* 12 (January–April 1944): 1–48.

———. *Quicksand and Cactus: A Memoir of the Southern Mormon Frontier.* Salt Lake City: Howe Brothers, 1982.

———. *Uncle Will Tells His Own Story.* Salt Lake City: Taggart, 1970.

Brossard, E. B. *Important Factors in the Operation of Irrigated Utah Farms.* Utah Experiment Station Bulletin no. 16. Logan: Utah Agricultural College, 1917.

Brough, Charles H. *Irrigation in Utah.* Baltimore: Johns Hopkins University Press, 1899.

Brough, R. Clayton. *Mosida, Utah: Past, Present & Future.* Provo, UT: Press Publishing, 1974.

Brown, D. Clayton. *Electricity for Rural America: The Fight for the REA.* Westport, CT: Greenwood Press, 1980.

Brown, Richard Maxwell. *No Duty to Retreat: Violence and Values in American History and Society.* New York: Oxford University Press, 1991.

———. "Western Violence: Structure, Values, Myth." *Western Historical Quarterly* 24 (February 1993): 5–20.

Buchanan, Frederick S. *A Good Time Coming: Mormon Letters to Scotland.* Salt Lake City: University of Utah Press, 1988.

Bunnell, Helen E. "Depression Memories." *Utah Historical Quarterly* 54 (Summer 1986): 265–67.

Burroughs, John Rolfe. *Where the Old West Stayed Young.* New York: Bonanza Books, 1962.

Burt, Olive Wooley. "A Kid Named Jones Had a Dream." *Utah Magazine,* June 1946, 26–29.

Burton, Doris Karren. *A History of Uintah County: Scratching the Surface.* Salt Lake City: Utah State Historical Society, 1996.

Burton, Richard Francis. *The City of the Saints, and across the Rocky Mountains.* New York: Harper & Bros., 1862.

Busco, Ralph A., and Douglas D. Alder. "German and Italian Prisoners of War in Utah and Idaho." *Utah Historical Quarterly* 39 (Winter 1971): 155–72.

Butler, B. S., G. F. Loughlin, V. C. Hiekes, and George H. Girty. *The Ore Deposits of Utah*. US Geological Service Professional Paper 111. Washington, DC: GPO, 1920.

Caesar, G. Vanderbilt. "National or City Parks?" *Saturday Evening Post*, October 22, 1927, 54–56.

Caldwell, Gaylon L. "Utah's First Presidential Candidate: Parley P. Christensen." *Utah Historical Quarterly* 28 (October 1960): 327–42.

Calef, Wesley C. "Land Associations and Occupance Problems in the Uinta Country." PhD diss., University of Chicago, 1948.

Callister, Ellen Gunnell. "The Political Career of Edward Henry Callister, 1885–1916." Master's thesis, University of Utah, 1967.

Cannon, Brian Q. "Keeping Their Instructions Straight: Implementing the Rural Resettlement Program in the West." *Agricultural History* 70 (Spring 1996): 251–67.

———. "Remaking the Agrarian Dream: The New Deal's Rural Resettlement Program in Utah." Master's thesis, Utah State University, 1986.

———. "Struggle against Great Odds: Challenges in Utah's Marginal Agricultural Areas." *Utah Historical Quarterly* 54 (Fall 1986): 308–27.

———. "'Taft Has Made a Good President': Mormons and Presidential Politics in the Election of 1912." In *Times of Transition, 1890–1920*, edited by Thomas G. Alexander, 55–66. Provo, UT: Joseph Fielding Smith Institute for Latter-day Saint History, 2003.

———. "'We Are Now Entering a New Era': Federal Reclamation and the Fact Finding Commission of 1923–24." *Pacific Historical Review* 66 (May 1997): 185–211.

Cannon, Frank J., and Harvey J. O'Higgins. *Under the Prophet in Utah: The National Menace of a Political Priestcraft*. Boston: C. M. Clark, 1911.

Cannon, George Q. *Collected Discourses Delivered by President Wilford Woodruff, His Two Counselors, the Twelve Apostles, and Others*. Edited by Brian H. Stuy. 3 vols. Sandy: B. H. S., 1988.

Cannon, Sylvester Q., chairman. *Torrential Floods in Northern Utah, 1930: Report of Special Flood Commission*. Agricultural Experiment Station Circular 92. Logan: Utah State Agricultural College, 1931.

Carlson, Leonard A. *Indians, Bureaucrats, and Land: The Dawes Act and the Decline of Indian Farming*. Westport, CT: Greenwood Press, 1981.

Carney, Todd Forsyth. "Utah and Mormon Migration in the Twentieth Century, 1890–1955." Master's thesis, Utah State University, 1992.

Carroll, Lavon B. "Melba Judge Lehner and Child Care in the State of Utah." *Utah Historical Quarterly* 61 (Winter 1993): 40–62.

Carroll, W. E. *Report of the Richmond-Lewiston Cow Testing Association*. Utah Experiment Station Bulletin no. 127. Logan, UT: F. W. Gardiner Press, 1913.

Carter, Andrea Kaye. "Bushnell General Military Hospital and the Community of Brigham City, Utah, during World War II." Master's thesis, Utah State University, 2008.

Carter, D. Robert. "Provonna Beach Resort: Born of a Boom, Died of Depression." *Utah Historical Quarterly* 66 (Fall 1998): 334–54.

Cashman, Sean Dennis. *America Ascendant: From Theodore Roosevelt to FDR in the Century of American Power, 1901–1945*. New York: New York University Press, 1998.

Cederlof, A. Philip. "The Peerless Coal Mines." *Utah Historical Quarterly* 53 (Fall 1985): 336–56.

Chamberlin, Ralph V. *The University of Utah: A History of Its First Hundred Years, 1850 to 1950*. Salt Lake City: University of Utah Press, 1960.

Chandler, Lester V. *America's Greatest Depression, 1929–1941*. New York: Harper & Row, 1970.

Cheng, Eric Yuan-Chin. "Chinese." In *Asian Americans in Utah: A Living History*, edited by John H. Yang. Salt Lake City: Utah Office of Asian Affairs, 1999.

Christensen, Edward L. *Snow College Historical Highlights: The First 100 Years*. Provo, UT: Community Press, 1988.

Christensen, John E. "The Impact of World War II." In *Utah's History*, edited by Richard D. Poll et al., 497–514. Provo, UT: Brigham Young University Press, 1978.

Christensen, Scott R. *Sagwitch: Shoshoni Chieftain, Mormon Elder, 1822–1884*. Logan: Utah State University Press, 1999.

Clark, James R., comp. *Messages of the First Presidency of the Church of Jesus Christ of Latter-day Saints, 1822–1964*. Vol. 3. Salt Lake City: Bookcraft, 1966.

Clark, Norman H. *Deliver Us from Evil: An Interpretation of American Prohibition*. New York: W. W. Norton, 1976.

Clayton, James L. "An Unhallowed Gathering: The Impact of Defense Spending on Utah's Population Growth, 1940–1964." *Utah Historical Quarterly* 34 (Summer 1966): 227–42.

Clyde, George Dewey. "History of Irrigation in Utah." *Utah Historical Quarterly* 27 (January 1959): 27–36.

———. *Utah Cooperative Snow Surveys and Water Supply Forecast, 1935*. Logan: Utah State Agricultural College, 1935.

Coleman, Ronald Gerald. "A History of Blacks in Utah, 1825–1910." PhD diss., University of Utah, 1980.

Compton, Hal, and David Hampshire. "Park City." In *From the Ground Up: The History of Mining in Utah*, edited by Colleen Whitley, 318–41. Logan: Utah State University Press, 2006.

Conetah, Fred A. *A History of the Northern Ute People*. Edited by K. L. MacKay and Floyd A. O'Neil. Salt Lake City: Uintah-Ouray Tribe, 1982.

Conley, Don C. "The Chinese in Utah." In *Utah History Encyclopedia*, edited by Allan Kent Powell, 85–86. Salt Lake City: University of Utah Press, 1984.

———. "The Pioneer Chinese of Utah." In *The Peoples of Utah*, edited by Helen Z. Papanikolas, 251–77. Salt Lake City: Utah State Historical Society, 1976.

Cooley, Everett L. "Clarion, Utah: Jewish Colony in 'Zion.'" *Utah Historical Quarterly* 36 (Spring 1968): 113–31.

Cooper, Robert P. *Leota: End of William H. Smart's Stewardship*. Salt Lake City: privately published, 1979.

Correll, J. Lee. *Bai-a-lil-le: Medicine Man or Witch*. Navajo Historical Publications, Biographical Series, no. 3. Window Rock, AZ: Navajo Tribe Parks and Recreation, 1970.

Costa, Janeen Arnold. "A Struggle for Survival and Identity: Families in the Aftermath of the Castle Gate Mine Disaster." *Utah Historical Quarterly* 58 (Summer 1988): 279–92.

Cottam, Walter P. *Is Utah Sahara Bound?* Salt Lake City: University of Utah Extension Division, 1947.

———. *Our Renewable Wild Lands: A Challenge*. Salt Lake City: University of Utah Press, 1961.

Cowles, Leroy Eugene. "The Utah Educational Program of 1919 and Factors Conditioning Its Operation." PhD diss., University of California, 1926.

Cox, Nellie I. *The Arizona Strip: A Harsh Land and Proud*. Las Vegas: Cox, 1982.

Cracroft, R. Paul. "Susa Young Gates: Her Life and Literary Work." Master's thesis, University of Utah, 1951.

Crafts, Dudley. *History of the Sevier Bridge Reservoir*. Delta, UT: DuWil, 1976.

Crampton, C. Gregory. *Ghosts of Glen Canyon: History beneath Lake Powell*. St. George, UT: Publishers Place, 1986.

———. "Mormon Colonization in Southern Utah and in Adjacent Parts of Arizona and Nevada, 1851–1900." Unpublished ms., 1965.

———. *The San Juan Canyon Historical Sites.* University of Utah Anthropological Papers no. 70, Glen Canyon Series no. 22. Salt Lake City: University of Utah Press, 1964.

———. *Standing Up Country: The Canyon Lands of Utah and Arizona.* New York: Alfred A. Knopf, 1973.

Crampton, C. Gregory, and Dwight L. Smith, eds. *The Colorado River Survey: Robert Stanton and the Denver, Colorado Canyon and Pacific Railroad.* Salt Lake City: Howe Brothers, 1987.

Crum, Steven J. *The Road on Which We Came: A History of the Western Shoshone.* Salt Lake City: University of Utah Press, 1994.

———. "The Skull Valley Band of the Goshute Tribe: Deeply Attached to Their Native Homeland." *Utah Historical Quarterly* 55 (Summer 1987): 250–67.

Culmer, H. L. A. "Mountain Scenery of Utah." *Contributor*, February–March 1892, 201–7.

Culmsee, Carlton. *A Modern Moses at West Tintic.* Logan: Utah State University Press, 1967.

Cummings, Byron. *The Ancient Inhabitants of the San Juan Valley.* Bulletin of the University of Utah no. 2. Salt Lake City: University of Utah, 1910.

———. *The Great Natural Bridges of Utah.* Bulletin of the University of Utah no. 3. Salt Lake City: University of Utah, 1910.

Cunningham, R. K., Jr. "Internment, 1917–1920: A History of the Prison Camp at Fort Douglas, Utah, and the Treatment of Enemy Aliens in the Western United States." Master's thesis, University of Utah, 1976.

Darowski, Joseph F. "The WPA versus the Utah Church." In *Utah in the Twentieth Century*, edited by Brian Q. Cannon and Jessie L. Embry, 167–85. Logan: Utah State University Press, 2009.

Dastrup, Boyd L. "Electrification of Utah, 1880 to 1915." Master's thesis, Utah State University, 1976.

Defa, Dennis R. "The Goshute Indians of Utah." In *A History of Utah's American Indians*, edited by Forrest S. Cuch, 73–122. Salt Lake City: Utah State Division of Indian Affairs, Utah State Division of History, 2003.

———. "A History of the Gosiute Indians to 1900." Master's thesis, University of Utah, 1979.

Dellenbaugh, F. S. *A Canyon Voyage . . . 1871–1872.* New Haven, CT: Yale University Press, 1962.

———. *The Romance of the Colorado River . . . with Special Reference to the Voyages of Powell. . . .* New York: G. P. Putnam's Sons, 1902.

Denis, Clyde L. "Departure of the Late Nineteenth-Century Cattle Companies from Southeastern Utah: A Reappraisal." *Utah Historical Quarterly* 80 (Fall 2012): 354–73.

Densmore, Frances. *Northern Ute Music.* Bureau of Ethnology Bulletin no. 75. Washington, DC: GPO, 1922.

Dern, George. "The Boulder Dam." In *Proceedings of the Twentieth Annual Session of the Governors' Conference, New Orleans, 1928*, 121–37. Tallahassee, FL: T. J Appleyard, [1928].

———. *The Colorado River.* Colorado Springs: n.p., 1926.

———. *Message of Governor George H. Dern to the Eighteenth Legislature of the State of Utah, January 15, 1929.* Salt Lake City: n.p., 1929.

———. *Message of Governor George H. Dern to the Nineteenth Legislature of the State of Utah.* Salt Lake City: n.p., 1931.

———. *Message of Governor George H. Dern to the Seventeenth Legislature of the State of Utah.* Salt Lake City: n.p., 1927.

———. *School Land Titles in Public Land States: Address of Governor George H. Dern before the Governors' Conference.* Cheyenne, WY: n.p., 1926.

DeVoto, Bernard. "Utah." *American Mercury*, March 1926, 317–23.

———. "The West: A Plundered Province." *Harper's Monthly Magazine*, August 1934, 355–64.

Dew, Sheri L. *Go Forward with Faith: The Biography of Gordon B. Hinckley*. Salt Lake City: Deseret Book, 1996.

Dibble, Charles E. "The Mormon Mission to the Shoshoni Indians, Part Three." *Utah Humanities Review* 1 (July 1947): 279–93.

Dilley, James W. *History of the Scofield Mine Disaster*. Provo, UT: Skelton, 1900.

Dorman, J. Eldon. *"Confessions of a Coal Camp Doctor," and Other Stories*. Price, UT: Peczuh, 1995.

Dunbar, Robert G. *Forging New Rights in Western Waters*. Lincoln: University of Nebraska Press, 1983.

Duncan, Clifford. "The Northern Utes of Utah." In *A History of Utah's American Indians*, edited by Forrest S. Cuch, 167–224. Salt Lake City: Utah State Division of Indian Affairs, Utah State Division of History, 2003.

Duncan-Larson, Lila. "H. L. A. Culmer, Utah Artist and Man of the West, 1854–1914." Master's thesis, University of Utah, 1987.

Dunham, Dick, and Vivian Dunham. *Flaming Gorge Country*. Denver: Eastwood, 1977.

Dwyer, Robert J. "Catholic Education in Utah, 1875–1975." *Utah Historical Quarterly* 43 (Fall 1975): 362–78.

Dyar, W. W. "The Colossal Bridges of Utah: A Recent Discovery of Natural Wonders." *Century*, August 1904, 505–11.

Dyer, Bruce. "A Study of the Forces Leading to the Adoption of Prohibition in Utah in 1917." Master's thesis, Brigham Young University, 1958.

Eastman, Adam. "From Cadillac to Chevy: Environmental Concern, Compromise, and the Central Utah Project Completion Act." In *Utah in the Twentieth Century*, edited by Brian Q. Cannon and Jessie L. Embry, 343–66. Logan: Utah State University Press, 2009.

Eblen, J. E. *The First and Second United States Empires: Governors and Territorial Government, 1874–1912*. Pittsburgh: University of Pittsburgh Press, 1968.

Eighty-Fifth Annual Conference of the Church of Jesus Christ of Latter-day Saints. Salt Lake City: Deseret News Press, 1915.

Eighty-Second Semi-Annual Conference of the Church of Jesus Christ of Latter-day Saints. Salt Lake City: Deseret News Press, 1911.

Eighty-Third Semi-annual Conference of the Church of Jesus Christ of Latter-day Saints. Salt Lake City: Deseret News Press, 1912.

Elling, Karl A. "The History of Organized Labor in Utah, 1910–1920." Master's thesis, University of Utah, 1962.

Embry, Jessie L. "'The Biggest Advertisement for a Town': Provo Baseball and the Provo Timps, 1913–1958." *Utah Historical Quarterly* 71 (Summer 2003): 196–214.

———. "Fighting the Good Fight: The Utah Home Front during World War II." *Utah Historical Quarterly* 63 (Summer 1995): 241–67.

———. *A History of Wasatch County*. Salt Lake City: Utah State Historical Society and Wasatch County Commission, 1996.

Embry, Jessie L., and Adam Seth Darowski. "Coming Home: Community Baseball in Cache Valley, Utah." *Utah Historical Quarterly* 70 (Spring 2002): 108–22.

"Erma Leona Gudmundson." http://www.rcrookston.com/More%20Gudmundson/erma_leona_gundmundson.htm.

Faragher, John Mack, et al. *Out of Many: A History of the American People*. 2 vols. 2nd ed. Upper Saddle River, NJ: Prentice Hall, 1997.

Farmer, Jared. *Glen Canyon Dammed: Inventing Lake Powell & the Canyon Country*. Tucson: University of Arizona Press, 1999.

Farrow, A. F. "The Kaibab Indians." *Utah Historical Quarterly* 3 (April 1930): 57–58.

Faulkner, Harold U. *American Economic History*. 8th ed. New York: Harper & Row, 1960.

Firmage, Richard A. *A History of Grand County*. Salt Lake City: Utah State Historical Society and Grand County Commission, 1996.

Fisher, Vardis. *Toilers in the Hills*. Boston: Houghton Mifflin, 1928.

Flake, Kathleen. *The Politics of American Religious Identity: The Seating of Senator Reed Smoot, Mormon Apostle*. Chapel Hill: University of North Carolina Press, 2004.

Flanagan, Barney L. "A Labor Inspector during the Great Depression." *Utah Historical Quarterly* 54 (Summer 1986): 240–44.

Flores, Dan B. "Agriculture, Mountain Ecology, and the Land Ethic: Phases of the Environmental History of Utah." In *Working on the Range: Essays on the History of Western Land Management and the Environment*, edited by John R. Wunder, 157–86. Westport, CT: Greenwood Press, 1985.

———. "Islands in the Desert: An Environmental Interpretation of the Rocky Mountain Frontier." PhD diss., Texas A&M University, 1978.

Foner, Philip S. *The Case of Joe Hill*. New York: International, 1965.

Fonnesbeck, Leon. *The Logan City Light Plant*. Caldwell, ID: Caxton, 1944.

Forsling, C. L. "Erosion on Uncultivated Lands in the Intermountain Region." *Scientific Monthly* 34 (April 1932): 311–21.

Fortier, Samuel. "The Beneficial Effects of Forests in Increasing Seepage Flow." In *Preliminary Report on Seepage Water and the Underflow of Rivers*. Utah Agricultural College Bulletin no. 38. Logan: Utah Agricultural College, 1895.

Fox, Frank W. *J. Reuben Clark: The Public Years*. Provo, UT: Brigham Young University Press, 1980.

Fradkin, Philip L. *A River No More: The Colorado River and the West*. Tucson: University of Arizona Press, 1984.

Franklin, Robert J., and Pamela A. Bunte. *The Paiute*. New York: Chelsea House, 1990.

Fraser, Saline Hardee. "One Long Day That Went on Forever." *Utah Historical Quarterly* 48 (Fall 1980): 366–79.

Fuller, Craig W. "Development of Irrigation in Wasatch County." Master's thesis, Utah State University, 1973.

———. "Finnish Americans." In *Utah History Encyclopedia*, edited by Allan Kent Powell, 188–90. Salt Lake City: University of Utah Press, 1984.

———. "Land Rush in Zion: Opening of the Uncompahgre and Uintah Indian Reservations." PhD diss., Brigham Young University, 1990.

Fuller, Craig, Gregory D. Kendrick, and Robert W. Righter. *Beyond the Wasatch: The History of Irrigation in the Uinta Basin and Upper Provo River Area of Utah*. Edited by Gregory D. Kendrick. Denver: Bureau of Reclamation, 1988.

Gardner, Hamilton. *History of Lehi*. Salt Lake City: Deseret News Press, 1913.

Gates, Paul Wallace. *History of Public Land Law Development*. Washington, DC: GPO, 1968.

Gates, Susa Young. "Fashions." *Young Woman's Journal*, September 1898, 427.

Geary, Edward A. *A History of Emery County*. Salt Lake City: Utah State Historical Society and Emery County Commission, 1996.

———. "History Written on the Land in Emery County." *Utah Historical Quarterly* 66 (Summer 1998): 196–224.

———. "A 'Visitable Past': Virginia Sorensen's Sanpete." *Utah Historical Quarterly* 58 (Summer 1990): 216–31.

Geary, Elmo G., and Edward A. Geary. "Community Dramatics in Early Castle Valley." *Utah Historical Quarterly* 53 (Spring 1985): 112–30.

Gerlach, Larry R. *Blazing Crosses in Zion: The Ku Klux Klan in Utah*. Logan: Utah State University Press, 1982.

———. "Justice Denied: The Lynching of Robert Marshall." *Utah Historical Quarterly* 66 (Fall 1998): 355–64.

Gitlin, Jay, Barbara Berglund, and Adam Arenson, eds. *Frontier Cities: Encounters at the Crossroads of Empire*. Philadelphia: University of Pennsylvania Press, 2013.

Giullilan, James David. *Thomas Corwin Iliff: Apostle of Home Missions in the Rocky Mountains*. New York: Methodist Book Concern, 1919.

Godfrey, Kenneth M. "Frank J. Cannon: Declension in the Mormon Kingdom." In *Differing Visions: Dissenters in Mormon History*, edited by Roger D. Launius and Linda Thatcher, 241–61. Urbana: University of Illinois Press, 1994.

Godfrey, Matthew C. *Religion, Politics, and Sugar: The Mormon Church, the Federal Government, and the Utah-Idaho Sugar Company, 1907–1921*. Logan: Utah State University Press, 2007.

Goldberg, Robert Alan. *Back to the Soil: The Jewish Farmers of Clarion, Utah, and Their World*. Salt Lake City: University of Utah Press, 1986.

González, William H., and Genaro M. Padilla. "Monticello, the Hispanic Cultural Gateway to Utah." *Utah Historical Quarterly* 52 (Winter 1984): 9–28.

Gordon, Sarah Barringer. *The Mormon Question: Polygamy and Constitutional Conflict in Nineteenth-Century America*. Chapel Hill: University of North Carolina Press, 2002.

Gould, William John Gilbert. *My Life on Mountain Railroads*. Edited by William Richard Gould. Logan: Utah State University Press, 1995.

Graham, Frank, Jr. *The Adirondack Park: A Political History*. New York: Alfred A. Knopf, 1976.

Greeley, Horace. *An Overland Journey from New York to San Francisco in the Summer of 1859*. New York: C. M. Saxton, Barker, 1860.

Greenwood, Annie Pike. *We Sagebrush Folks*. New York: D. Appleton–Century, 1934.

Greer, Deon C., et al. *Atlas of Utah*. Provo, UT: Brigham Young University Press, 1981.

Gregory, Herbert E. *The San Juan Oil Field, Utah*. United States Geological Survey Bulletin 431. Washington, DC: GPO, 1911.

Grow, Stewart L. "A Study of the Utah Commission." PhD diss., University of Utah, 1954.

———. "Utah's Senatorial Election of 1899: The Election That Failed." *Utah Historical Quarterly* 39 (Winter 1971): 30–39.

Gruenwald, Kim M. "American Indians and the Public School System: A Case Study of the Northern Utes." *Utah Historical Quarterly* 64 (Summer 1996): 246–63.

Haines, H. T. *Facts and Figures Pertaining to Utah*. Salt Lake City: Arrow Press, 1915.

Hainsworth, Brad. "Utah State Elections, 1916–1924." PhD diss., University of Utah, 1968.

Hall, Ansel F. *General Report of the Rainbow Bridge–Monument Valley Expedition of 1933*. Berkeley: University of California Press, 1934.

Hall, David Roy. "Amy Brown Lyman and Social Service Work in the Relief Society." Master's thesis, Brigham Young University, 1992.

Hanchett, Lafayette. *The Old Sheriff, and Other True Tales*. New York: Margent Press, 1937.

Hansen, Gary B. "Industry of Destiny: Copper in Utah." *Utah Historical Quarterly* 31 (Summer 1963): 263–79.

Hansen, George H., and Mendell M. Bell, comps. *Oil and Gas Possibilities of Utah*. Salt Lake City: Utah Geological and Mineralogical Survey, 1949.

Hardy, B. Carmon. *Solemn Covenant: The Mormon Polygamous Passage*. Urbana: University of Illinois Press, 1992.

Harline, Osmond L. "Utah's Black Gold: The Petroleum Industry." *Utah Historical Quarterly* 33 (Summer 1963): 291–311.

Harris, Franklin S. "Real Security." In *Brigham Young University: A School of Destiny*, by Ernest L. Wilkinson and W. Cleon Skousen, 302–3. Provo, UT: Brigham Young University Press, 1976.

Harrow, Joan Ray. "Joseph L. Rawlins, Father of Utah Statehood." Master's thesis, University of Utah, 1973.

Hartzer, Ronald B., Edward P. Cliff, and David A. Clary. *Half a Century in Forest Conservation: A Biography and Oral History of Edward P. Cliff*. Washington, DC: History Section, Forest Service, 1981.

Harvey, John Swensen. *A Historical Overview of the Evolutions of Institutions Dealing with Water Resource Use, and Water Resource Development in Utah—1847 through 1947*. Salt Lake City: Utah Division of Water Resources, 1991.

Harvey, Mark K. "Battle for Dinosaur: Echo Park Dam and the Birth of the Modern Wilderness Movement." *Montana: The Magazine of Western History* 45 (Winter 1995): 32–45.

———. "Utah, the National Park Service, and Dinosaur National Monument, 1909–56." *Utah Historical Quarterly* 59 (Summer 1991): 243–63.

Hatch, John P., ed. *Danish Apostle: The Diaries of Anthon H. Lund, 1890–1921*. Salt Lake City: Signature Books, 2006.

Haymond, J. M. "History of the Manti Forest, Utah: A Case of Conservation in the West." PhD diss., University of Utah, 1972.

Heath, Harvard S., ed. *In the World: The Diaries of Reed Smoot*. Salt Lake City: Signature Books, 1997.

———. "Reed Smoot: The First Modern Mormon." PhD diss., Brigham Young University, 1990.

Heaton, Tim B., Thomas A. Hirschl, and Bruce A. Chadwick, eds. *Utah in the 1990s: A Demographic Perspective*. Salt Lake City: Signature Books, 1996.

Hefner, Loretta L. "The National Women's Relief Society and the U.S. Sheppard-Towner Act." *Utah Historical Quarterly* 50 (Summer 1982): 255–67.

Heikes, V. C. "History of Mining and Metallurgy in the Tintic District." In *Geology of Ore Deposits of the Tintic Mining District, Utah*, edited by Waldemar Lindgren and C. F. Loughlin, 105–17. Washington, DC: GPO, 1919.

Helm, H. J., and G. S. Quate. "Report on the Wind Erosion and Dust Menace, Grantsville, Tooele." In *Conservation History of Tooele County*, 60–76. Grantsville, UT: Grantsville and Shambip Soil Conservation Districts, [ca. 1976].

Henderson, Myrtle E. *A History of the Theatre in Salt Lake City from 1850 to 1870*. Evanston, IL: n.p., 1934.

Higgins, Will C. "Park City Mining District, Utah." *Railroad Red Book* (January 1911).

Hill, Kurt R. "A Climatological Study of Dry Periods and a Runs Analysis of Precipitation along the Wasatch Front." Master's thesis, Brigham Young University, 1991.

Hinton, Wayne K. "Getting Along: The Significance of Cooperation in the Development of Zion National Park." *Utah Historical Quarterly* 68 (Fall 2000): 313–31.

Historical Records Survey. *Inventory of the Church Archives of Utah*. Salt Lake City: Utah Historical Records Survey, 1940.

"History of Pacific States." http://www.pscipco.com/history_ps.html.

Holmes, Charles H. "The Economic Impact of Geneva Steel Company (United States Steel Subsidiary) on Utah County, Utah." Master's thesis, Utah State University, 1956.

Holt, Ronald L. *Beneath These Red Cliffs: An Ethnohistory of the Utah Paiutes.* Albuquerque: University of New Mexico Press, 1992.

Holzapfel, Richard Neitzel. *A History of Utah County.* Salt Lake City: Utah State Historical Society and Utah County Commission, 1999.

Honker, Andrew M. "'Been Grazed Almost to Extinction': The Environment, Human Action, and Utah Flooding, 1900–1940." *Utah Historical Quarterly* 67 (Winter 1999): 23–47.

Howard, F. Burton. *Marion G. Romney: His Life and Faith.* Salt Lake City: Bookcraft, 1988.

Hoxie, Frederick E. *A Final Promise: The Campaign to Assimilate the Indians, 1880–1920.* Lincoln: University of Nebraska Press, 1983.

Huchel, Frederick M. *A History of Box Elder County.* Salt Lake City: Utah State Historical Society and Box Elder County Commission, 1999.

Hulse, J. W. "W. A. Clark and the Las Vegas Connection: The 'Midas of the West' and the Development of Southern Nevada." *Montana: The Magazine of Western History* 37 (Winter 1987): 48–56.

Hundley, Norris, Jr. "The Dark and Bloody Ground of Indian Water Rights: Confusion Elevated to Principle." *Western Historical Quarterly* 9 (October 1978): 454–82.

———. *Water and the West: The Colorado River Compact and the Politics of Water in the American West.* 2nd ed. Berkeley: University of California Press, 2009.

———. "The *Winters* Decision and Indian Water Rights: A Mystery Reexamined." *Western Historical Quarterly* 13 (January 1982): 17–42.

Hunt, Andrew. "Beyond the Spotlight: The Red Scare in Utah." *Utah Historical Quarterly* 61 (Fall 1993): 357–80.

Hunter, Milton R. *Brigham Young the Colonizer.* 3rd ed. Independence, MO: Zion's, 1945.

Hurt, R. Douglas. *American Agriculture: A Brief History.* Ames: Iowa State University Press, 1994.

Iber, Jorge. "El diablo nos está llevando: Utah Hispanics and the Great Depression." *Utah Historical Quarterly* 66 (Spring 1998): 159–67.

———. *Hispanics in the Mormon Zion, 1912–1999.* College Station: Texas A&M Press, 2000.

Ichihashi, Yamato. *Japanese in the United States: A Critical Study of the Problems of the Japanese Immigrants and Their Children.* Stanford, CA: Stanford University Press, 1932.

Industrial Workers of the World. *Coal Mine Workers and Their Industry: An Industrial Handbook.* Chicago: IWW, [ca. 1921]. http://www.workerseducation.org/crutch/pamphlets/coal/coal.html.

Israelsen, Andrew M. *Utah Pioneering: An Autobiography.* Salt Lake City: Deseret News Press, 1938.

"It Does Not Pay!" *Improvement Era*, 1929. http://gospelink.com/.

Iverson, Peter. *The Navajo Nation.* Westport, CT: Greenwood Press, 1981.

Ivins, Stanley S. "A Constitution for Utah." *Utah Historical Quarterly* 25 (April 1957): 95–116.

———. *The Moses Thatcher Case.* Salt Lake City: Modern Microfilm, ca. 1960.

Jenson, Andrew. *Latter-day Saint Biographical Encyclopedia.* 4 vols. Salt Lake City: A. Jensen History, 1901.

Johnson, Brandon. "'A Perfect Hell': Utah Doughboys in the Meuse-Argonne Offensive." *Utah Historical Quarterly* 80 (Fall 2012): 334–63.

Johnson, Michael W., Robert E. Parson, and Daniel A. Stebbins. *A History of Daggett County.* Salt Lake City: Utah State Historical Society and Daggett County Commission, 1998.

Jonas, Frank Herman. "Utah: Sagebrush Democracy." In *Rocky Mountain Politics*, edited by Thomas C. Donnelly, 11–50. Albuquerque: University of New Mexico Press, 1940.

Jonas, Frank Herman, and Garth N. Jones. "Utah Presidential Elections, 1896–1952." *Utah Historical Quarterly* 24 (October 1956): 289–308.

Jones, Dan E. "Utah Politics, 1926–1932." PhD diss., University of Utah, 1968.

Jones, E. K., and Y. F. Jones. *Mayors of Cedar City and Histories of Cedar City, Utah*. Cedar City, UT: privately published, 1986.

Jones, Walter. "Petroleum Industry." In *Utah History Encyclopedia*, edited by Allan Kent Powell. http://www.media.utah.edu/UHE/w/WWI.html.

Jones, York F., and Evelyn K. Jones. *Lehi Willard Jones, 1854–1947*. Salt Lake City: Woodruff, 1972.

Jorgensen, Joseph. *The Sundance Religion: Power for the Powerless*. Chicago: University of Chicago Press, 1972.

Judd, Neil M. "Beyond the Clay Hills: An Account of the National Geographic Society's Reconnaissance of a Previously Unexplored Section in Utah." *National Geographic Magazine* 45 (March 1924): 275–302.

———. *Men Met along the Trail: Adventures in Archaeology*. Norman: University of Oklahoma Press, 1968.

Katsanevas, Michael, Jr. "The Emerging Social Worker and the Distribution of the Castle Gate Relief Fund." *Utah Historical Quarterly* 50 (Summer 1982): 241–54.

Kearnes, John. "Utah, Sexton of Prohibition." *Utah Historical Quarterly* 47 (Winter 1979): 5–21.

Kelen, Leslie G., and Eileen Hallet Stone. *Missing Stories: An Oral History of Ethnic and Minority Groups in Utah*. Salt Lake City: University of Utah Press, 1996.

Kenner, S. A. *Utah as It Is with a Comprehensive Statement of Utah as It Was*. Salt Lake City: Deseret News Press, 1904.

Kenney, Scott G., ed. *Wilford Woodruff's Journal, 1833–1898*. 9 vols. Salt Lake City: Signature Books, 1985.

Kerr, Walter A. "Byron Cummings, Classic Scholar and Father of University Athletics." *Utah Historical Quarterly* 23 (Spring 1955): 145–93.

Kimball, Solomon F. "President Brigham Young's Excursion Party." *Improvement Era*, January–March 1911, 189–201, 310–21, 414–21.

Kinney, Clesson S. *A Treatise on the Law of Irrigation*. 4 vols. 2nd ed. San Francisco: Bender-Moss, 1912.

Kluger, James R. *Turning on Water with a Shovel: The Career of Elwood Mead*. Albuquerque: University of New Mexico Press, 1992.

Knack, Martha C. *Boundaries Between: The Southern Paiutes, 1775–1995*. Lincoln: University of Nebraska Press, 2001.

Kneale, A. H. *Indian Agent*. Caldwell, ID: Caxton, 1950.

Knight, William. *The Jesse Knight Family: Jesse Knight, His Forebears and Family*. Salt Lake City: Deseret News Press, 1940.

Kolb, E. L. *Through the Grand Canyon from Wyoming to Mexico*. New York: Macmillan, 1946.

Kraus, George. "Chinese Laborers and the Construction of the Central Pacific." *Utah Historical Quarterly* 37 (Winter 1969): 41–57.

Kreitzer, Matthew E., ed. *The Washakie Letters of Willie Ottogary: Northwestern Shoshone Journalist and Leader, 1906–1929*. Logan: Utah State University Press, 2000.

———. "Willie Ottogary: Northwestern Shoshone Journalist, 1906–1929." Master's thesis, Utah State University, 1993.

Kunz, Gary C. "Provo in the Jazz Age: A Case Study." Master's thesis, Brigham Young University, 1983.

Lamar, Howard R. *The Far Southwest, 1845–1912: A Territorial History*. New Haven, CT: Yale University Press, 1966.

Lamborn, John E. "A History of the Development of Dry-Farming in Utah and Southern Idaho." Master's thesis, Utah State University, 1978.

Lamborn, John E., and Charles S. Peterson. "The Substance of the Land: Agriculture v. Industry in the Smelter Cases of 1904 and 1906." *Utah Historical Quarterly* 53 (Fall 1985): 308–25.

Lambourne, Alfred. *Our Inland Sea: The Story of a Homestead*. Salt Lake City: Deseret News Press, 1909.

Larsen, Kent S. "The Life of Thomas Kearns." Master's thesis, University of Utah, 1964.

——— . *The Life of Thomas Kearns*. New York: Nauvoo Books, 2005.

Larson, Andrew Karl. *The Education of a Second Generation Swede: An Autobiography*. St. George, UT: privately printed, 1979.

——— . *"I Was Called to Dixie": The Virgin River Basin, Unique Experiences in Mormon Pioneering*. Salt Lake City: Deseret News Press, 1961.

——— . "Zion National Park with Some Reminiscences Fifty Years Later." *Utah Historical Quarterly* 37 (Fall 1969): 408–25.

Larson, Gustive O. *The "Americanization" of Utah for Statehood*. San Marino, CA: Huntington Library, 1971.

——— . "Bulwark of the Kingdom: Utah's Iron and Steel Industry." *Utah Historical Quarterly* 31 (Summer 1963): 248–61.

——— . "An Industrial Home for Polygamous Wives." *Utah Historical Quarterly* 38 (Summer 1970): 263–75.

Launius, Roger D. "Crossroads of the West: Aviation Comes to Utah, 1910–1940." *Utah Historical Quarterly* 58 (Spring 1990): 108–30.

——— . "One Man's Air Force: The Experience of Byron Dussler at Wendover Field, Utah, 1941–46." *Utah Historical Quarterly* 54 (Spring 1986): 137–56.

Lavender, David. *One Man's West*. New York: Doubleday, 1943.

Layton, Stanford J. "Charles Rendell Mabey." In *Utah History Encyclopedia*, edited by Allan Kent Powell. http://www.media.utah.edu/UHE/w/WWI.html.

——— . "Governor Charles R. Mabey and the Utah Election of 1924." Master's thesis, University of Utah, 1969.

——— . *"To No Privileged Class": The Rationalization of Homesteading and Rural Life in the Early Twentieth-Century American West*. Provo, UT: Charles Redd Center for Western Studies, 1988.

Leake, Harvey, and Gary Topping. "The Bernheimer Explorations in Forbidding Canyon." *Utah Historical Quarterly* 55 (Spring 1987): 137–67.

Leavens, Dickson H. *Silver Money*. Bloomington, IN: Principia Press, 1939.

Leavitt, Anne O. *Southern Utah University: A Heritage History, the First Hundred Years*. Cedar City: Southern Utah University Press, 1997.

Leonard, Glen M. *A History of Davis County*. Salt Lake City: Utah State Historical Society and Davis County Commission, 1999.

Leuchtenburg, William E. *Franklin D. Roosevelt and the New Deal, 1932–1940*. New York: Harper and Row, 1963.

Lewis, David Rich. "Bernard DeVoto's Utah." In *Utah in the Twentieth Century*, edited by Brian Q. Cannon and Jessie L. Embry, 88–108. Logan: Utah State University Press, 2009.

———. *Neither Wolf nor Dog: American Indians, Environment, and Agrarian Change*. New York: Oxford University Press, 1994.

Life History of Luther M. Winsor. Murray, UT: R. Fenton Murray, 1962.

Life Story of Melvin Young. Lehi, UT: privately published, 1981.

Linfield, F. B. "Report of the Condition and Progress of the Dairy Industry of Utah for 1897–98." In *Second Annual Report of the Utah Farmers' Institutes, 1897–98*, 100–107. Salt Lake City: Deseret News Press, 1898.

Linfield, F. R. "The Condition and Progress of Dairying in Utah for the Year 1899." In *Fourth Annual Report of the Utah Farmers' Institutes*, 109–24. Salt Lake City: Tribune Job Printing, 1900.

Litoff, Judy Barrett, and David C. Smith, eds. *Since You Went Away: World War II Letters from American Women on the Home Front*. Lawrence: University Press of Kansas, 1991.

Lockerbie, C. W. "Our Changing World." *Utah Audubon News*, February–December 1949.

Long, Kelly Ann. *Helen Foster Snow: An American Woman in Revolutionary China*. Boulder: University Press of Colorado, 2006.

Louthan, Bruce D., and Lloyd M. Pierson. "Moab Japanese-American Isolation Center: The Dark Postlude in the History of Dalton Well SCCC Camp." *Canyon Legacy* 19 (Fall–Winter 1993): 28–31.

Lovin, Hugh T. "Lucien Nunn, Provo Entrepreneur, and His Hydropower Realm in Utah and Idaho." *Utah Historical Quarterly* 76 (Spring 2008): 132–47.

Lowry, Walker. *Wallace Lowry*. N.p.: privately printed, 1974.

Lund, John Farnsworth. "The Night before Doomsday." *Utah Historical Quarterly* 51 (Spring 1983): 154–61.

Lyman, Edward Leo. "The Alienation of an Apostle from His Quorum: The Moses Thatcher Case." *Dialogue: A Journal of Mormon Thought* 18 (Summer 1985): 67–91.

———. "From the City of Angels to the City of Saints: The Struggle to Build a Railroad from Los Angeles to Salt Lake City." *California History* 70 (Spring 1991): 76–93.

———. "Heber M. Wells and the Beginnings of Utah's Statehood." Master's thesis, University of Utah, 1967.

———. *Political Deliverance: The Mormon Quest for Utah Statehood*. Urbana: University of Illinois Press, 1986.

Mabey, Charles R. *Our Father's House: Joseph Thomas Mabey Family History*. Salt Lake City: Beverly Craftsman, 1947.

———. *The Utah Batteries: A History*. Salt Lake City: Daily Reporter, 1900.

Macfarlane, L. W. *Dr. Mac: The Man, His Land, and His People*. Cedar City: Southern Utah University Press, 1985.

Madsen, Brigham D. *The Northern Shoshoni*. Caldwell, ID: Caxton, 1980.

Madsen, Truman G. *Defender of the Faith: The B. H. Roberts Story*. Salt Lake City: Bookcraft, 1980.

Maguire, Don. "The Mines of Tintic, Utah." *Colliery Engineer* 19 (November 1898): 153–55.

Malmquist, O. N. *The First 100 Years: A History of the "Salt Lake Tribune," 1871–1971*. Salt Lake City: Utah State Historical Society, 1971.

Malone, Michael P., and Richard W. Etulain. *The American West: A Twentieth-Century History*. Lincoln: University of Nebraska Press, 1989.

Malouf, Carling. *Shoshone Indians*. New York: Garland, 1974.

Mangum, Garth L., and Bruce D. Blumell. *The Mormons' War on Poverty: A History of LDS Welfare, 1830–1990*. Salt Lake City: University of Utah Press, 1993.

Markoff, Dena S. *The Dudes Are Always Right: The Utah Parks Company in Zion National Park, 1923–1972*. Springdale, UT: Zion Natural History Association, 1980.

Marston, Otis. "River Runners: Fast Water Navigation." *Utah Historical Quarterly* 28 (July 1960): 281–308.

Maryboy, Nancy C., and David Begay. "The Navajos of Utah." In *A History of Utah's American Indians*, edited by Forrest S. Cuch, 265–314. Salt Lake City: Utah State Division of Indian Affairs, Utah State Division of History, 2003.

Mason, Patrick Q. "The Prohibition of Interracial Marriage in Utah, 1888–1963." *Utah Historical Quarterly* 76 (Spring 2008): 108–31.

Maughan, Ila May. *Pioneer Theater in the Desert*. Salt Lake City: Deseret Book, 1961.

May, Dean L. "Utah Writ Small: Challenge and Change in Kane County's Past." *Utah Historical Quarterly* 53 (Spring 1985): 170–83.

McConahay, John D. "The Economic Impact of Hill Air Force Base on the Ogden Area." Master's thesis, Utah State University, 1955.

McCormick, John S. "Hornets in the Hive: Socialists in Early Twentieth-Century Utah." *Utah Historical Quarterly* 50 (Summer 1982): 225–40.

———. "Red Lights in Zion: Salt Lake City's Stockade, 1908–11." *Utah Historical Quarterly* 50 (Spring 1982): 168–81.

McCormick, John S., and John R. Sillito. "'We Are Not Seeking Trouble and So Will Just Go Along Quietly': The IWW Free Speech Fight in Salt Lake City." In *Utah in the Twentieth Century*, edited by Brian Q. Cannon and Jessie L. Embry, 263–84. Logan: Utah State University Press, 2009.

McCormick, Nancy D., and John S. McCormick. *Saltair*. Salt Lake City: University of Utah Press, 1985.

McElvaine, Robert S. *The Great Depression: America, 1929–1941*. New York: Times Books, 1993.

McIntyre, William H. "The Mormons in Canada: The McIntyre Ranch." In *Treasures of Pioneer History*, edited by Kate B. Carter, 97–105. Salt Lake City: Daughters of the Utah Pioneers, 1957.

McMurrin, Jean Ann. "The Deseret Live Stock Company: The First Fifty Years, 1890–1940." Master's thesis, University of Utah, 1989.

McNitt, Frank. *Richard Wetherill: Anasazi*. Rev. ed. Albuquerque: University of New Mexico Press, 1966.

McNutt, Steven Bligh. "Utah's Reaction to the 1919–1920 Red Scare." Master's thesis, Brigham Young University, 1995.

McPherson, Robert S. *As If the Land Owned Us: An Ethnohistory of the White Mesa Utes*. Salt Lake City: University of Utah Press, 2011.

———. "Canyons, Cows and Conflict: A Native American History of Montezuma Canyon, 1874–1933." *Utah Historical Quarterly* 60 (Summer 1992): 238–58.

———. *Comb Ridge and Its People: The Ethnohistory of a Rock*. Logan: Utah State University Press, 2009.

———. *A History of San Juan County: In the Palm of Time*. Salt Lake City: Utah State Historical Society, 1995.

———. "The Influenza Epidemic of 1918: A Cultural Response." *Utah Historical Quarterly* 58 (Spring 1990): 183–215.

———. *Navajo Land, Navajo Culture: The Utah Experience in the Twentieth Century*. Norman: University of Oklahoma Press, 2001.

———. *The Northern Navajo Frontier, 1860–1900: Expansion through Adversity*. Albuquerque: University of New Mexico Press, 1990.

———. "Paiute Posey and the Last White Uprising." *Utah Historical Quarterly* 53 (Summer 1985): 248–67.

———. "Too Much Noise in That Bunch across the River." *Utah Historical Quarterly* 77 (Winter 2009): 26–51.

McPherson, Robert S., and Mary Jane Yazzie. "The White Mesa Utes." In *A History of Utah's American Indians*, edited by Forrest S. Cuch, 225–64. Salt Lake City: Utah State Division of Indian Affairs, Utah State Division of History, 2003.

Mead, Elwood. *Report of Irrigation Investigations in Utah*. USDA Bulletin 124. Washington, DC: GPO, 1903.

"Measures of Economic Changes in Utah, 1847–1947." *Utah Economic and Business Review* 7 (December 1947).

"Measuring Worth." http://www.measuringworth.com/uscompare/.

Mecham, E. H. "The History of the Sheep Industry in Utah." Master's thesis, University of Utah, 1925.

Merrill, Jerald H. "Fifty Years with a Future: Salt Lake's Guadalupe Mission and Parish." *Utah Historical Quarterly* 40 (Summer 1972): 242–64.

Merrill, M. C. *Utah Pioneer and Apostle: Marriner Wood Merrill and His Family*. N.p., 1937.

Merrill, M. R. *Reed Smoot: Apostle in Politics*. Logan: Utah State University Press, 1990.

Merrill, Milton R. *Reed Smoot: Utah Politician*. Logan: Utah State Agricultural College, 1958.

Merrill, Stephen A. "Reclamation and the Economic Development of Northern Utah: The Weber River Project." *Utah Historical Quarterly* 39 (Summer 1971): 254–64.

Middleton, G. W. *Memoirs of a Pioneer Surgeon*. Salt Lake City: Publishers Press, 1976.

Mikkelsen, Craig. "The Politics of B. H. Roberts." *Dialogue: A Journal of Mormon Thought* 9 (Summer 1974): 25–43.

Miller, M. A. "Thatcher Resilenced." *Dialogue: A Journal of Mormon Thought* 19 (Summer 1986): 4–8.

Miser, Hugh D. *The San Juan Canyon, Southeastern Utah: A Geographic and Hydrographic Reconnaissance*. United States Geological Survey Water Supply Paper 538. Washington, DC: GPO, 1924.

Mitchell, Christine A. "'Work and Devotion': Father Harold Baxter Liebler at St. Christopher's Mission, 1943–1962." Master's thesis, Utah State University, 1991.

Moler, Murray, and Andre Fontaine. "Utah's Steel Guinea Pig." *Collier's*, December 30, 1944, 11–12, 28.

Montgomery, Henry. "Prehistoric Man in Utah." *Archaeologist* 2 (1894): 227–343.

Mooney, Bernice Maher. *Salt of the Earth: The History of the Catholic Church in Utah, 1776–1987*. Salt Lake City: Catholic Diocese of Salt Lake City, 1987.

Morgan, Dale, ed. "The Exploration of the Colorado River and the High Plateaus of Utah in 1871–72." *Utah Historical Quarterly* 16–17 (1948–49): 499–503.

———. *The Great Salt Lake*. Salt Lake City: University of Utah Press, 1995.

Morn, F. T. "Simon Bamberger: A Jew in a Mormon Commonwealth." Master's thesis, Brigham Young University, 1966.

Mortensen, A. Russell, ed. "Journal of John A. Widtsoe: Colorado River Party, September 1922." *Utah Historical Quarterly* 39 (July 1955): 195–231.

Moseley, M. Edward. "The Discovery and Definition of Basketmaker, 1890–1914." *Masterkey for Indian Lore and History* 10 (October–December 1966): 140–54.

Moss, James R. "The Deseret Live Stock Company, 1891–1933." Master's thesis, Brigham Young University, 1965.

Moyle, James Henry. *Mormon Democrat: The Religious and Political Memoirs of James Henry Moyle*. Edited by Gene A. Sessions. Salt Lake City: Signature Books, 1998.

Muhn, James, and H. R. Stuart. *Opportunity and Challenge: The Story of BLM*. Washington, DC: Department of Interior, 1988.

Mulder, William, and A. Russell Mortensen. *Among the Mormons: Historic Accounts by Contemporary Observers*. Salt Lake City: Western Epics, 1994.

Munson, Voyle L. "Lewis Leo Munson, an Entrepreneur in Escalante, Utah, 1896–1963." *Utah Historical Quarterly* 64 (Spring 1996): 133–54.

Murphy, Miriam B. "'If Only I Shall Have the Right Stuff': Utah Women in World War I." *Utah Historical Quarterly* 58 (Fall 1990): 333–50.

———. "Women in the Utah Work Force from Statehood to World War II." *Utah Historical Quarterly* 50 (Spring 1982): 139–59.

MX/Native American Cultural and Socio-economic Studies—Draft. Las Vegas: Facilitators, 1980.

Nagler, Jeorg A. "Enemy Aliens and Internment in World War I: Alvo von Alvensleben in Fort Douglas, Utah, a Case Study." *Utah Historical Quarterly* 58 (Fall 1990): 388–405.

Nash, Gerald D. *World War II and the West: Reshaping the Economy*. Lincoln: University of Nebraska Press, 1990.

Nash, John D. "The Tribulations of an Early Idaho Irrigation District." http://twinlakescanalcompany.com/DocumentsTLHistory.pdf.

Nelson, Elroy. "The Mineral Industry: A Foundation of Utah's Economy." *Utah Historical Quarterly* 31 (Summer 1963): 179–91.

Nelson, G. Lowry. *In the Direction of His Dreams: Memoirs*. New York: Philosophical Library, 1985.

———. *The Mormon Village: A Pattern and Technique of Land Settlement*. Salt Lake City: University of Utah Press, 1952.

Nelson, Lowry, and Howard R. Cottam. "The Green River Drought Relief Project of 1934." *Utah Academy of Sciences, Arts and Letters* 12 (1935): 119–23.

Nelson, Lowry, and T. David Hettig. "Some Changes in the Population of Utah as Indicated by the Annual L.D.S. Church Census, 1929–1933." *Proceedings of Utah Academy of Sciences, Arts and Letters* 12 (1935): 107–18.

Nelson, Richard. "Utah Filmmakers of the Silent Screen." *Utah Historical Quarterly* 43 (Winter 1975): 10–22.

Neuberger, Richard L. "Depression: 'Perhaps the Mormons Are Pointing the Way.'" In *Among the Mormons: Historic Accounts by Contemporary Observers*, edited by William Mulder and A. Russell Mortensen, 454–58. Lincoln: University of Nebraska Press, 1958.

Newell, Linda King. *A History of Garfield County*. Salt Lake City: Utah State Historical Society and Garfield County Commission, 1999.

———. *A History of Piute County*. Salt Lake City: Utah State Historical Society and Piute County Commission, 1999.

Nichols, Jeffrey. *Polygamy and Prostitution: Comparative Morality in Salt Lake City, 1847–1911*. Urbana: University of Illinois Press, 2002.

Ninety-Second Annual Conference of the Church of Jesus Christ of Latter-day Saints. Salt Lake City: Deseret News Press, 1922.

Noble, Antonette Chambers. "Utah's Defense Industries and Workers in World War II." *Utah Historical Quarterly* 59 (Fall 1991): 365–79.

———. "Utah's Rosies: Women in the Utah War Industries during World War II." *Utah Historical Quarterly* 59 (Spring 1991).

Notarianni, Philip F. *Faith, Hope, and Prosperity: The Tintic Mining District.* Eureka, UT: Tintic Historical Society, 1992.

———. "Hetacomb at Castle Gate, Utah, March 8, 1924." *Utah Historical Quarterly* 70 (Winter 2002).

———. "Italian Fraternal Organizations in Utah, 1897–1934." *Utah Historical Quarterly* 43 (Spring 1975): 172–87.

———. "Italianita in Utah: The Immigrant Experience." In *The Peoples of Utah*, edited by Helen Z. Papanikolas, 303–31. Salt Lake City: Utah State Historical Society, 1976.

———. "Tale of Two Towns: The Social Dynamics of Eureka and Helper, Utah." PhD diss., University of Utah, 1980.

———. "Tintic Mining District." In *From the Ground Up: The History of Mining in Utah*, edited by Colleen Whitley. Logan: Utah State University Press, 2006.

———. "Utah's Ellis Island: The Difficult Americanization of Carbon County." *Utah Historical Quarterly* 47 (Spring 1979): 178–93.

Nugent, Walter. "Frontiers and Empires in the Late Nineteenth Century." *Western Historical Quarterly* 20 (November 1989): 393–408.

Nuttall, L. John. "Helps in Teacher Training." *Improvement Era*, 1923. http://gospelink.com/.

O'Connor, Harvey. *The Guggenheims: The Making of an American Dynasty.* New York: Covici Friede, 1937.

Official Report of the One Hundred Fifty-Fourth Annual General Conference of the Church of Jesus Christ of Latter-day Saints. Salt Lake City: Church of Jesus Christ of Latter-day Saints, 1984.

Okubo, Miné. *Citizen 13660.* Seattle: University of Washington Press, 1983.

Olpin, Robert S., Ann W. Orton, and Thomas F. Rugh. *Painters of the Wasatch Mountains.* Salt Lake City: Gibbs Smith, 2005.

Olsen, Beth R. "Utah's CCC's: The Conservators' Medium for Young Men, Nature, Economy, and Freedom." *Utah Historical Quarterly* 62 (Summer 1994): 261–74.

Olsen, Pearl M. *Nickels from a Sheep's Back: Biography of John K. Madsen.* N.p.: privately published, 1976.

One Hundred Fifteenth Annual Conference of the Church of Jesus Christ of Latter-day Saints. Salt Lake City: Deseret Book, 1945.

One Hundred Fourteenth Annual Conference of the Church of Jesus Christ of Latter-day Saints. Salt Lake City: Deseret Book, 1944.

One Hundred Sixteenth Annual Conference of the Church of Jesus Christ of Latter-day Saints. Salt Lake City: Deseret Book, 1946.

One Hundred Thirteenth Semi-annual Conference of the Church of Jesus Christ of Latter-day Saints. Salt Lake City: Deseret Book, 1942.

O'Neil, Floyd A. "An Anguished Odyssey: The Flight of the Utes, 1906–1908." *Utah Historical Quarterly* 36 (Fall 1968): 315–27.

Orton, Chad. "Planting the Banner of Zion: A Brief History of the Church in Los Angeles." *Ensign*, September 1992, 44–45.

Otis, Delos S. *The Dawes Act and the Allotment of Indian Lands.* Edited by Francis P. Prucha. Norman: University of Oklahoma Press, 1973.

Paden, William M. *The Churches of Utah.* [Salt Lake City]: Women's Board of Home Missions, 1923.

Papanikolas, Helen Z. "Bootlegging in Zion: Making and Selling the 'Good Stuff.'" *Utah Historical Quarterly* 53 (Summer 1985): 268–91.

———. *Emilia—Yoryis, Emily—George.* Salt Lake City: University of Utah Press, 1987.

———. "The Greeks of Carbon County." *Utah Historical Quarterly* 23 (April 1954): 143–64.

———. "Growing Up Greek in Helper, Utah." *Utah Historical Quarterly* 48 (Summer 1980): 244–60.

———. "Immigrants, Minorities, and the Great War." *Utah Historical Quarterly* 58 (Fall 1990): 351–70.

———. "Life and Labor among the Immigrants of Bingham Canyon." *Utah Historical Quarterly* 33 (Fall 1965): 289–315.

———. "Magerou, the Greek Midwife." *Utah Historical Quarterly* 38 (Winter 1970): 50–60.

———, ed. *The Peoples of Utah*. Salt Lake City: Utah State Historical Society, 1976.

———. *Toil and Rage in a New Land: The Greek Immigrants in Utah*. Salt Lake City: Utah Historical Society, 1970.

———. "Toil and Rage in a New Land: The Greeks in a New Land." *Utah Historical Quarterly* 38 (Spring 1970): 97–203.

———. "Unionism, Communism, and the Great Depression: The Carbon County Coal Strike of 1933." *Utah Historical Quarterly* 41 (Summer 1973): 254–300.

———. "Utah's Coal Lands: A Vital Example of How America Became a Great Nation." *Utah Historical Quarterly* 41 (Spring 1975): 104–24.

———. "Utah's Ethnic Legacy." *Dialogue: A Journal of Mormon Thought* 19 (Spring 1986): 41–48.

———. "Wrestling with Death: Greek Immigrant Funeral Customs in Utah." *Utah Historical Quarterly* 52 (Winter 1984): 29–49.

Parker, Virginia C. "Diamonds in the Dust: John W. Carlson's Alfalfa Seed Research." *Utah Historical Quarterly* 46 (Fall 1978): 397–414.

Parkhill, Forbes. *The Last of the Indian Wars*. New York: Crowell-Collier, 1962.

Parry, Mae. "The Northwestern Shoshone." In *A History of Utah's American Indians*, edited by Forrest S. Cuch, 25–72. Salt Lake City: Utah State Division of Indian Affairs, Utah State Division of History, 2003.

Parsons, A. B. *The Porphyry Coppers*. New York: AIME, 1933.

Paschal, J. F. *Mr. Justice Sutherland: A Man against the State*. Princeton, NJ: Princeton University Press, 1951.

"Passing Events." *Improvement Era*, May 1921, 665–70.

Paulos, Michael H. "Under the Gun at the Smoot Hearings: Joseph F. Smith's Testimony." *Journal of Mormon History* 34 (Fall 2008): 181–225.

Pawar, S. B. "An Environmental Study of the Development of the Utah Labor Movement, 1860–1935." PhD diss., University of Utah, 1968.

Peck, Gunther. "Padrones and Protest: 'Old' Radicals and 'New' Immigrants in Bingham, Utah, 1905–1912." *Western Historical Quarterly* 24 (May 1993): 157–78.

———. *Reinventing Free Labor: Padrones and Immigrant Workers in the North American West, 1880–1930*. Cambridge: Cambridge University Press, 2000.

Peck, Joseph H. *What Next, Doctor Peck?* Englewood Cliffs, NJ: Prentice Hall, 1959.

Pedersen, Lyman Clarence. "John Mills Whitaker: Diarist, Educator, Churchman." Master's thesis, University of Utah, 1960.

Peffer, E. Louise. *The Closing of the Public Domain: Disposal and Reservation Policies, 1900–50*. Stanford, CA: Stanford University Press, 1951.

Pendleton, Mark. "Memories of Silver Reef." *Utah Historical Quarterly* 3 (October 1930): 98–118.

Penrose, C. W. *The Thatcher Episode: A Concise Statement in the Case*. Salt Lake City: Deseret News Press, 1896.

Perlich, Pamela S. *Utah Minorities: The Story Told by 150 Years of Census Data*. Salt Lake City: University of Utah Bureau of Economic Research, 2002.

Perlman, Selig, and Philip Taft. *Labor Movements*. New York: Macmillan, 1935.

Petersen, Jesse G. "The Lincoln Highway and Its Changing Routes in Utah." *Utah Historical Quarterly* 69 (Summer 2001): 192–214.

Peterson, Charles S. "Albert F. Potter's Wasatch Survey, 1902: A Beginning for Public Management of Natural Resources in Utah." *Utah Historical Quarterly* 39 (Summer 1971): 238–53.

———. "The 'Americanization' of Utah's Agriculture." *Utah Historical Quarterly* 42 (Spring 1974): 108–25.

———. *Changing Times: A View from Cache Valley, 1890–1915*. 60th Faculty Honors Lecture, Utah State University. Logan: Utah State University Press, 1979.

———. "Grazing in Utah: A Historical Perspective." *Utah Historical Quarterly* 5 (Fall 1989): 300–320.

———. *Look to the Mountains: Southeastern Utah and the La Sal National Forest*. Provo, UT: Brigham Young University Press, 1975.

———. "San Juan: A Hundred Years of Cattle, Sheep, and Dry Farms." In *San Juan County, Utah: People, Resources, and History*, edited by Allen Kent Powell, 171–204. Salt Lake City: Utah State Historical Society, 1983.

———. "San Juan in Controversy: American Livestock Frontier vs. Mormon Cattle Pool." In *Essays on the American West, 1972–1973*, edited by Thomas G. Alexander, 45–68. Charles Redd Monographs in Western History no. 3. Provo, UT: Brigham Young University, 1974.

———. "Small Holding Land Patterns in Utah and the Problem of Forest Watershed Management." *Forest History* 17 (1973): 4–13.

———. *"Take Up Your Mission": Mormon Colonizing along the Little Colorado River, 1870–1900*. Tucson: University of Arizona Press, 1973.

———. *Utah: A History*. New York: W. W. Norton, 1984.

———. "A Utah Moon, Juanita Brooks Lecture for 1984." *St. George Magazine* (Summer 1986): 31–34, 91–98.

———. *A Utah Moon: Perceptions of Southern Utah*. St. George, UT: Dixie College, 1984.

Peterson, Charles S., and Linda E. Speth. *A History of the Wasatch-Cache National Forest*. Logan: Utah State University Press, 1980.

Peterson, F. Ross. *A History of Cache County*. Salt Lake City: Utah State Historical Society and Cache County Commission, 1997.

Peterson, Janet. "Friend to Friend." *Friend*, January 1989, 7.

Peterson, John Alton. *Utah's Black Hawk War*. Salt Lake City: University of Utah Press, 1998.

Peterson, Paul H. *An Historical Analysis of the Word of Wisdom*. Salt Lake City: Benchmark Books, 2005.

Peterson, Richard H. *Bonanza Rich: Lifestyles of the Western Mining Entrepreneurs*. Moscow: University of Idaho Press, 1991.

———. "Jesse Knight, Utah's Mormon Mining Mogul." *Utah Historical Quarterly* 57 (Summer 1989): 240–53.

Peterson, William. "History of Agriculture in Utah." In *Utah: A Centennial History*, edited by Wain Sutton, 1:33–242. New York: Lewis Historical, 1949.

Pinchot, Gifford. *Breaking New Ground*. New York: Harcourt Brace, 1947.

———. *The Fight for Conservation*. Seattle: University of Washington Press, 1967.

Pisani, Donald J. *To Reclaim a Divided West: Water, Law, and Public Policy, 1838–1902.* Albuquerque: University of New Mexico Press, 1992.

Polk's Logan (Utah) City Directory, 1935–36. Salt Lake City: R. L. Polk, 1935.

Polk's Ogden City Directory, 1936–37. Salt Lake City: R. L. Polk, 1936.

Polk's Provo City Directory, 1935–36. Salt Lake City: R. L. Polk, 1935.

Polk's Salt Lake City Directory, 1937. Salt Lake City: R. L. Polk, 1937.

Polk's Salt Lake City Directory, 1941. Salt Lake City: R. L. Polk, 1941.

Poll, Richard, et al., eds. *Utah's History.* Provo, UT: Brigham Young University Press, 1978.

Poppendieck, Janet. *Breadlines Knee-Deep in Wheat: Food Assistance in the Great Depression.* New Brunswick, NJ: Rutgers University Press, 1986.

Powell, Allan Kent. "The 'Foreign Element' and the 1903–4 Carbon County Coal Miners' Strike." *Utah Historical Quarterly* 43 (Spring 1975): 125–54.

———. *The Next Time We Strike: Labor in Utah's Coal Fields.* Logan: Utah State University Press, 1985.

———. "Our Cradles Were in Germany: Utah's German American Community and World War I." *Utah Historical Quarterly* 58 (Fall 1990): 371–87.

———. *Splinters of a Nation: German Prisoners of War in Utah.* Salt Lake City: University of Utah Press, 1989.

———. "Utah and the Nationwide Coal Miners' Strike of 1922." *Utah Historical Quarterly* 45 (Spring 1977): 135–41.

———. "Utah and World War II." *Utah Historical Quarterly* 73 (Spring 2005): 108–31.

———. *Utah Remembers World War II.* Logan: Utah State University Press, 1991.

———. "World War I in Utah." In *Utah History Encyclopedia,* edited by Allan Kent Powell. http://www.media.utah.edu/UHE/w/WWI.html.

Powell, John W. *The Exploration of the Colorado River.* New York: Anchor Books, 1961.

Prange, Gordon W. *At Dawn We Slept: The Untold Story of Pearl Harbor.* New York: Penguin Books, 1991.

Pratt, Parley P. *Autobiography of Parley Parker Pratt.* Salt Lake City: Deseret Book, 1938.

Prentiss, A., ed. *The History of the Utah Volunteers in the Spanish American War and in the Philippine Islands.* Salt Lake City: Tribune Job Printing, 1900.

Price, Raye. "Utah's Leading Ladies of the Arts." *Utah Historical Quarterly* 38 (Winter 1970): 65–85.

Price, Virginia N., and John T. Darby. "Preston Nutter: Utah Cattleman, 1886–1936." *Utah Historical Quarterly* 32 (Summer 1964): 232–51.

Provo City Directory—1939. Logan, UT: Directory, 1939.

Prpic, George. *Croation Immigrants in America.* New York: Philosophical Library, 1971.

Pyper, George D. *The Romance of an Old Playhouse.* Salt Lake City: Deseret News Press, 1937.

Quinn, D. Michael. *J. Reuben Clark: The Church Years.* Provo, UT: Brigham Young University Press, 1983

———. "LDS Church Authority and New Plural Marriages, 1890–1904." *Dialogue: A Journal of Mormon Thought* 18 (Summer 1985): 9–108.

———. "The Mormon Church and the Spanish-American War: An End to Selective Pacifism." *Dialogue: A Journal of Mormon Thought* 17 (Winter 1984): 11–30.

———. "The Mormon Hierarchy, 1832–1932: An American Elite." PhD diss., Yale University, 1976.

———. *The Mormon Hierarchy: Origins of Power.* Salt Lake City: Signature Books, 1994.

Quinn, R. Thomas. "Out of the Depression's Depths: Henry H. Blood's First Year as Governor." *Utah Historical Quarterly* 54 (Summer 1986): 216–39.

R. L. Polk & Co.'s Provo City and Utah County Directory, 1929. Salt Lake City: R. L. Polk, 1929.

Rampton, Calvin L. *As I Recall*. Salt Lake City: University of Utah Press, 1989.

Rasmussen, Alma Vernon. "The Government Work Relief Program in Utah, 1932–1940." Master's thesis, University of Utah, 1942.

Raspa, Richard. "Exotic Foods among Italian-Americans in Mormon Utah: Food as Nostalgic Enactment of Identity." In *Ethnic and Regional Foodways in the United States: The Performance of Group Identity*, edited by Linda Keller Brown and Kay Mussell, 185–94. Knoxville: University of Tennessee Press, 1984.

Rathjen, M. R. "The Distribution of Major Non-Mormon Denominations in Utah." Master's thesis, University of Utah, 1966.

Rawlins, Joseph L. *"The Unfavored Few": The Autobiography of Joseph L. Rawlins*. Edited by Alta Jensen. Carmel, CA: privately published, 1956.

Rawls, James J. *Chief Red Fox Is Dead: A History of Native Americans since 1945*. Fort Worth, TX: Harcourt Brace, 1996.

Reasoner, Calvin. *The Late Manifesto in Politics: Practical Working of "Counsel" in Relation to Civil and Religious Liberty in Utah*. Salt Lake City: n.p., 1896.

Redd, Amasa Jay. *Lemuel Hardison Redd, Jr., 1856–1923: Pioneer-Leader-Builder*. Salt Lake City: n.p., 1967.

Reese, Gary Fuller. "'Uncle Jesse': The Story of Jesse Knight, Miner, Industrialist, Philanthropist." Master's thesis, Brigham Young University, 1961.

Reeve, Walter Paul. "'A Little Oasis in the Desert': Community Building in Hurricane, Utah, 1860–1930." Master's thesis, Brigham Young University, 1994.

———. *Making Space on the Western Frontier: Mormons, Miners and Southern Paiutes*. Urbana: University of Illinois Press, 2006.

Reeves, Richard I. "Utah and the Spanish American War." Master's thesis, Brigham Young University, 1998.

Reilly, P. T. "Norman Nevills: Whitewater Man of the West." *Utah Historical Quarterly* 55 (Spring 1987): 181–200.

———. "Warren Marshall Johnson, Forgotten Saint." *Utah Historical Quarterly* 39 (Winter 1971): 3–22.

Remington, Newell C. "A History of the Gilsonite Industry." Master's thesis, University of Utah, 1959.

Renshaw, Patrick. *The Wobblies: The Story of Syndicalism in the United States*. New York: Doubleday, 1967.

Report of the Arid Land Reclamation Fund Commission, 1903–1904. Salt Lake City: Star, 1905.

Reynolds, R. V. R. *Grazing and Floods: A Study of Conditions in the Manti National Forest, Utah*. US Forest Service Bulletin no. 91. Washington, DC: GPO, 1911.

Rice, Craton. *Ambassador to the Saints*. Boston: Christopher, 1965.

Rich, Lyman H. *Dairy Production on Utah Farms*. Utah State Agricultural College Experiment Station, n.s., 147. Logan: Utah State Agricultural College, 1947.

Richards, F. S. "Statement from Arid Land Reclamation Fund Commission." In *Second Annual Report of Reclamation Service, 1902–3*. House Document no. 44, 58th Cong., 2nd sess., 470–71. Washington, DC: GPO, 1902.

Rickard, T. A. *A History of American Mining*. New York: McGraw-Hill, 1932.

———. *The Utah Copper Enterprise*. San Francisco: Mining and Scientific Press, 1919.

Ricks, Joel Edward. *The Utah State Agricultural College: A History of Fifty Years, 1888–1938*. Salt Lake City: Deseret News Press, 1938.

Ridd, Merrill K. "The Influences of Soil and Water Conditions on Agricultural Development in the Delta Area, Utah." PhD diss., Northwestern University, 1963.

Riis, John. *Ranger Trails*. Richmond, VA: Dietz Press, 1937.

Roberts, B. H. *A Comprehensive History of the Church of Jesus Christ of Latter-day Saints*. 6 vols. Salt Lake City: Deseret News Press, 1930.

———. *Proceedings of the Democratic State Convention*. Ogden, UT: Democratic State Committee, 1916.

Roberts, Paul H. *Hoof Prints on Forest Ranges: The Early Years of National Forest Range Administration*. San Antonio: Naylor, 1966.

Roberts, Phil. "Wyoming's Pioneers of Prohibition: The United States Army, the U.S. District Court, and Federal Enforcement of Laws Governing Morality." *Wyoming Law Review* 1 (2001): 633–45.

Roberts, Richard C. "History of the Utah National Guard, 1894–1954." 2 vols. PhD diss., University of Utah, 1973.

———. "The Utah National Guard in the Great War, 1917–18." *Utah Historical Quarterly* 58 (Fall 1990): 312–33.

Roberts, Richard C., and Richard W. Sadler. *A History of Weber County*. Salt Lake City: Utah State Historical Society, 1997.

Robertson, Frank C. *A Ram in the Thicket: An Autobiography*. New York: Abelard Press, 1950.

———. *A Ram in the Thicket: The Story of a Roaming Homesteader Family on the Mormon Frontier*. New York: Hastings House, 1959.

Roper, Roger. "Homemakers in Transition: Women in Salt Lake City Apartments, 1910–1940." *Utah Historical Quarterly* 67 (Fall 1999): 349–66.

Roper, William L., and Leonard J. Arrington. *William Spry: Man of Firmness, Governor of Utah*. Salt Lake City: University of Utah Press, 1971.

Rosenman, Samuel I., comp. *The Public Papers and Addresses of Franklin D. Roosevelt*. 13 vols. New York: Random House, 1938–50.

Rothman, Hal K. *Devil's Bargains: Tourism in the Twentieth-Century American West*. Lawrence: University Press of Kansas, 2000.

———. "'A Regular Ding-Dong Fight': Agency Culture and Evolution in the NPS-USFS Dispute, 1916–1937." *Western Historical Quarterly* 20 (May 1989): 141–61.

———. "Shaping the Nature of a Controversy: The Park Service, the Forest Service, and the Cedar Breaks Proposal." *Utah Historical Quarterly* 55 (Summer 1987): 213–35.

Runte, Alfred. *National Parks: An American Experience*. 2nd ed. Lincoln: University of Nebraska Press, 1987.

———. "Promoting the Golden West: Advertising and the Railroad." *California History* 70 (Spring 1991): 63–75.

Rusho, W. L. *Everett Ruess: A Vagabond for Beauty*. Salt Lake City: Peregrine Smith Books, 1983.

Rusho, W. L., and C. Gregory Crampton. *Lee's Ferry: Desert River Crossing*. Rev. ed. Salt Lake City: Cricket, 1992.

Sadler, Richard W., ed. *Weber State College: A Centennial History*. Salt Lake City: Publishers Press, 1988.

Sadler, Richard W., and Richard C. Roberts. *The Weber River Basin: Grass Roots Democracy and Water Development*. Logan: Utah State University Press, 1994.

Saloutos, Theodore. *The Greeks in the United States*. Cambridge, MA: Harvard University Press, 1964.

Sandiford, Glenn. "Bernard DeVoto and His Forgotten Contribution to Echo Park." *Utah Historical Quarterly* 59 (Winter 1991): 72–86.

San Juan County: Basic Data of Economic Activities and Resources. Salt Lake City: Utah State Planning Board, 1940.

Sarasohn, David. "The Election of 1916: Realigning the Rockies." *Western Historical Quarterly* 11 (July 1980): 285–308.

Schmalz, Charles L. "Sugar Beets in Cache Valley: An Amalgamation of Agriculture and Industry." *Utah Historical Quarterly* 57 (Fall 1989): 370–88.

Schwantes, Carlos A. "The Concept of the Wageworkers' Frontier: A Framework for Future Research." *Western Historical Quarterly* 18 (January 1987): 39–55.

"Scientists Find Earliest Known Evidence of 1918 Influenza Pandemic." *Science Daily*, September 19, 2011. http://www.sciencedaily.com/releases/2011/09/110919151326.htm.

Scorup, Stena. *J. A. Scorup: A Utah Cattleman.* N.p.: privately published, 1944.

Scrattish, Nick. "The Modern Discovery, Popularization, and Early Development of Bryce Canyon, Utah." *Utah Historical Quarterly* 49 (Fall 1981): 358–62.

Seegmiller, Janet Burton. *A History of Iron County: Community above Self.* Salt Lake City: Utah State Historical Society and Iron County Commission, 1998.

Seeley, M. G. "A History of the Rambouillet Breed of Sheep in Utah." Master's thesis, Utah State University, 1956.

Seshachari, Neila C. "Asian Indian." In *Asian Americans in Utah: A Living History*, edited by John H. Yang. Salt Lake City: Utah Office of Asian Affairs, 1999.

Sessions, Gene A., ed. *Mormon Democrat: The Religious and Political Memoirs of James Henry Moyle.* Salt Lake City: Historical Department of the Church of Jesus Christ of Latter-day Saints, 1975.

Sessions, Sterling D., and Gene A. Sessions. *A History of Utah International: From Construction to Mining.* Salt Lake City: University of Utah Press, 2005.

Seventy-Ninth Semi-annual Conference of the Church of Jesus Christ of Latter-day Saints. Salt Lake City: Deseret News Press, 1908.

Shamo, Michael Lyle. "Making the Desert Blossom: Public Works in Washington County, Utah." Master's thesis, Brigham Young University, 2010.

Shirer, David L. "Murray, Utah, Families in Transition, 1890–1920." *Utah Historical Quarterly* 61 (Fall 1993): 339–56.

Sillito, John R. "'Our Tone': Tony Lazzeri's Baseball Career in Salt Lake City, 1922–1925." *Utah Historical Quarterly* 72 (Fall 2004): 343–57.

———. "Parley P. Christensen: A Political Biography, 1869–1954." Master's thesis, University of Utah, 1977.

Simmonds, A. J. *On the Big Range: A Centennial History of Cornish and Trenton . . . 1870–1970.* Logan: Utah State University Press, 1970.

Simpson, Thomas W. "Mormons Study 'Abroad': Latter-day Saints in American Higher Education, 1870–1940." PhD diss., University of Virginia, 2005.

Skillen, James R. *The Nation's Largest Landlord: The Bureau of Land Management in the American West.* Lawrence: University Press of Kansas, 2009.

Smart, William B. *Mormonism's Last Colonizer: The Life and Times of William H. Smart.* Logan: Utah State University Press, 2008.

Smith, Alex D. "The Symphony in America, Maurice Abravanel, and the Utah Symphony Orchestra: The Battle for Classical Music." Master's thesis, Brigham Young University, 2002.

Smith, Gibbs M. *Joe Hill.* Salt Lake City: University of Utah Press, 1969.

Smith, Henry A. "Church-Wide Security Program Organized." *Improvement Era*, June 1936, 333–38.

Smith, John S. H. "Cigarette Prohibition in Utah, 1921–23." *Utah Historical Quarterly* 41 (Fall 1973): 358–72.

Smith, Ken R., and Sven E. Wilson. "Dyin' in Zion: Longevity and Mortality in Utah." In *Utah at the Beginning of the New Millennium: A Demographic Perspective*, edited by Kathleen D. Zick and Ken R. Smith, 44–55. Salt Lake City: University of Utah Press, 2006.

Smith, Oliver R., ed. *The Journal of Jesse Nathaniel Smith: Six Decades in the Early West*. Provo, UT: Jesse N. Smith Family Association, 1970.

Smythe, William E. *The Conquest of Arid America*. New York: Harper and Bros., 1899.

Snow, Helen Foster. *My China Years: A Memoir*. Beijing: Foreign Languages Press, 2004.

Snow, R. J. "The American Party in Utah: A Study of Political Party Struggles during the Early Years of Statehood." Master's thesis, University of Utah, 1964.

Solorzano, Armando, Lisa M. Ralph, and J. Lynn England. "Community and Ethnicity: Hispanic Women in Utah's Carbon County." *Utah Historical Quarterly* 78 (Winter 2010): 58–75.

South, Will. "The Federal Art Project in Utah: Out of Oblivion or More of the Same?" *Utah Historical Quarterly* 58 (Summer 1990): 277–94.

Stannard, Jay D. "Irrigation in the Weber Valley." In *Report of Irrigation Investigations in Utah*, edited by Elwood Mead, 196–97. Washington, DC: GPO, 1903.

Stanton, Robert. *The Hoskaninni Papers: Mining in Glen Canyon, 1897–1902*. Edited by C. Gregory Crampton and Dwight L. Smith. University of Utah Anthropological Papers no. 54, Glen Canyon Series no. 15. Salt Lake City: University of Utah Press, 1961.

Stark, Arvil L. "History of Growing Fruit in Utah." In *Utah: A Centennial History*, edited by Wain Sutton, 1:108–18. New York: Lewis Historical, 1949.

Stauffer, Kenneth G. "Utah Politics, 1912–1918." Master's thesis, University of Utah, 1972.

Steele, Raymond D. *Goshen Valley History*. N.p., 1960.

Steen, Charlie R. "The Natural Bridges of White Canyon: A Diary of H. L. A. Culmer, 1905." *Utah Historical Quarterly* 40 (Winter 1972): 55–87.

Stegner, Wallace Stegner, ed. "Bernard DeVoto and the Mormons: Three Letters." *Dialogue: A Journal of Mormon Thought* 6 (Fall–Winter 1971): 39–47.

———. *Joe Hill: A Biographical Novel*. First published as *The Preacher and the Slave*. New York: Doubleday, 1950.

———. *Mormon Country*. New York City: Duell, Sloan, and Pearce, 1942.

Stelter, Gilbert. "The City and Westward Expansion: A Western Case Study." *Western Historical Quarterly* 4 (April 1973): 187–202.

Stene, Eric A. *Strawberry Valley Project*. Bureau of Reclamation Project History (1995). http://www.usbr.gov/projects//ImageServer?imgName=Doc_1305643405083.pdf.

Sterling, Guy. "Analysis of the Failure of an Earth-Fill Dam." *Engineering News* (January 13, 1916): 56–61.

———. "Failure of the Dam of the Hatchtown Reservoir, Utah." *Engineering News* (June 4, 1914): 1274–75.

Stevens, Joseph E. *Hoover Dam: An American Adventure*. Norman: University of Oklahoma Press, 1988.

Stewart, Omer C. *Ute Peyotism: A Study of a Cultural Complex*. Boulder: University Press of Colorado, 1948.

———. *Washo-Northern Paiute Peyotism: A Study of Acculturation*. University of California Publications in Archaeology and Ethnology. Berkeley: University of California Press, 1944.

Stipanovich, Joseph. "Falcons in Flight: The Yugoslavs." In *The Peoples of Utah*, edited by Helen Z. Papanikolas, 363–84. Salt Lake City: Utah State Historical Society, 1976.

———. "South Slav Settlements in Utah, 1890–1934." *Utah Historical Quarterly* 43 (Spring 1975): 155–72.

———. *The South Slavs in Utah: A Social History.* San Francisco: R and E Research Associates, 1975.

Stott, C. Orval. "The Agricultural Program of the Church Welfare Program." *Improvement Era,* October 1939, 586–87.

Stout, Wayne. *History of Utah.* 3 vols. Salt Lake City: privately published, 1968.

Strack, Don. "Major Rail-Served Industries in Ogden" (updated 2010). http://utahrails.net/ogden/ogden-industry.php.

———. "Utah's Canning Industry." In *Utah History Encyclopedia* (1994), edited by Allan Kent Powell. http://www.media.utah.edu/UHE/UHEindex.html.

———. "Utah's Canning Industry: List of Canneries and Canning Companies." http://utahrails.net/industries/canning-list.php.

Strevell, Charles Nettleton. *As I Recall Them.* N.p., [post-1943].

Stucki, Merrill. "An Economic Study of Farmers' Cooperative Business Associations in Utah." Master's thesis, University of Utah, 1935.

Stucki, Roland. *Commercial Banking in Utah, 1847–1960.* Salt Lake City: Bureau of Economic and Business Research, 1967.

Sturgeon, Stephen C. "The Disappearance of Everett Ruess and the Discovery of Utah's Red Rock Country." In *Utah in the Twentieth Century,* edited by Brian Q. Cannon and Jessie L. Embry, 37–40. Logan: Utah State University Press, 2009.

Sutton, Wain, ed. *Utah: A Centennial History.* 3 vols. New York: Lewis Historical, 1949.

Taniguchi, Nancy J. *Castle Valley America: Hard Land, Hard-Won Home.* Logan: Utah State University Press, 2004.

———. *Necessary Fraud: Progressive Reform and Utah Coal.* Norman: University of Oklahoma Press, 1996.

———. "No Proper Job for a Stranger: The Political Reign of Mark Braffet." *Utah Historical Quarterly* 58 (Spring 1990): 145–64.

Tate, Cassandra. *Cigarette Wars: The Little White Slaver.* New York: Oxford University Press, 1999.

Taubenberger, Jeffrey K., and David M. Morens. "1918 Influenza: The Mother of All Pandemics." *Emerging Infectious Diseases* 12 (January 2006): 15–20.

Taylor, Fred G. "Notes on the Development of the Beet Sugar Industry in Utah." In *Utah: A Centennial History,* edited by Wain Sutton, 2:917–45. New York: Lewis Historical, 1949.

———. *A Saga of Sugar, Being a Story of the Romance and Development of Beet Sugar in the Rocky Mountain West.* Salt Lake City: Utah-Idaho Sugar, 1944.

Taylor, Sandra C. "Japanese Americans and Keetley Farms: Utah's Relocation Colony." *Utah Historical Quarterly* 54 (Fall 1986): 328–44.

———. *Jewel of the Desert: Japanese American Internment at Topaz.* Berkeley: University of California Press, 1993.

Teele, R. P. "General Discussion of Irrigation in Utah." In *Report of Irrigation Investigations in Utah,* edited by Elwood Mead, 19–37. Washington, DC: GPO, 1903.

Telephone Directory: Price, Green River, Helper, Huntington, Scofield. Provo, UT: Mountain States Telephone and Telegraph, 1944.

Tennent, William L. "The John Jarvie Ranch: A Case Study in Historic Site Development and Interpretation." Master's thesis, Utah State University, 1980.

Thatcher, Linda. "'The Gentile Polygamist': Arthur Brown, Ex-Senator from Utah." *Utah Historical Quarterly* 52 (Summer 1984): 231–44.

Thomas, George. *The Development of Institutions under Irrigation: With Special Reference to Early Utah Conditions*. New York: Macmillan, 1920.

Thompson, Brent G. "'Standing between Two Fires': Mormons and Prohibition, 1908–1917." *Journal of Mormon History* 10 (1983): 35–52.

Thompson, Gerald. *The Army and the Navajo: The Bosque Redondo Reservation Experiment, 1863–1868*. Tucson: University of Arizona Press, 1976.

Thorup, H. Christian. "Clarence Cottam: Conservationist, the Welder Years." PhD diss., Brigham Young University, 1983.

Thow, Jonathan S. "Capitol Reef: The Forgotten National Park." Master's thesis, Utah State University, 1986.

Timmins, W. M. "The Failure of the Hatchtown Dam, 1914." *Utah Historical Quarterly* 36 (Summer 1968): 263–73.

Tohmatsu, Akiko J. "Japanese American Youth in Topaz Relocation Center, Utah: An Oral History." Master's thesis, Utah State University, 1994.

Tom, Gary, and Ronald Holt. "The Paiute Tribe of Utah." In *A History of Utah's American Indians*, edited by Forrest S. Cuch, 123–66. Salt Lake City: Utah State Division of Indian Affairs, Utah State Division of History, 2003.

Toponce, Alexander. *Reminiscences of Alexander Toponce: Pioneer, 1839–1923*. Norman: University of Oklahoma Press, 1971.

Topping, Gary. "An Adventure for Adventure's Sake, Recounted by Robert B. Aird." *Utah Historical Quarterly* 62 (Summer 1994): 275–88.

———. "Charles Kelly's Glen Canyon Ventures and Adventures." *Utah Historical Quarterly* 55 (Spring 1987): 120–36.

Torbenson, Craig L. "The Promontory-Curlew Land Company: Promoting Dry Farming in Utah." *Utah Historical Quarterly* 66 (Winter 1998): 4–25.

Trachtenberg, Alan. *The Incorporation of America: Culture and Society in the Gilded Age*. 25th anniversary ed. New York: Farrar, Straus, and Giroux, 2007.

Tugwell, Rexford G. "The Resettlement Idea." *Agricultural History* 33 (October 1959): 159–64.

Tyler, Daniel. *Silver Fox of the Rockies: Delphus E. Carpenter and Western Water Compacts*. Norman: University of Oklahoma Press, 2008.

Uchida, Yoshiko. *Desert Exile: The Uprooting of a Japanese-American Family*. Seattle: University of Washington Press, 1982.

Ulibarri, Richard O. "Utah's Ethnic Minorities: A Survey." *Utah Historical Quarterly* 40 (Summer 1972): 210–32.

———. "Utah's Unassimilated Minorities." In *Utah's History*, edited by Richard D. Poll et al., 629–49. Logan: Utah State University Press, 1989.

Untermann, G. E., and Billie R. Untermann. "Dinosaur Country." *Utah Historical Quarterly* 26 (July 1958): 248–56.

Utah Guide. New York: Hastings House, 1942.

Van Wagoner, Richard S. "The Lehi Sugar Factory—100 Years in Retrospect." *Utah Historical Quarterly* 59 (Spring 1991): 184–204.

———. "Saratoga, Utah Lake's Oldest Resort." *Utah Historical Quarterly* 57 (Spring 1989): 108–24.

Wahlquist, C. Austin. "The 1912 Presidential Election." Master's thesis, Brigham Young University, 1962.

Wahlquist, Loreen P. "Memories of a Uinta Basin Farm." *Utah Historical Quarterly* 42 (Spring 1974): 165–77.

Walker, Roger. "The Delta Project: Utah's Successful Carey Act Project." http://www.waterhistory. org/histories/delta/delta.pdf.

Walker, Ronald W. "A Gauge of the Times: Ensign Peak in the Twentieth Century." *Utah Historical Quarterly* 62 (Winter 1994): 4–25.

Walker, Ronald W., and Alexander M. Starr. "Shattering the Vase: The Razing of the Old Salt Lake Theatre." *Utah Historical Quarterly* 57 (Winter 1989): 64–88.

Walton, John. *Western Times and Water Wars: State, Culture, and Rebellion in California.* Berkeley: University of California Press, 1992.

Ward, Chip. *Canaries on the Rim: Living Downwind in the West.* New York: Verso, 1999.

Warner, Albert L. "The Secretary of War: A Prophet of the New Deal." *Literary Digest*, March 10, 1934, 9, 39.

Warner, Elisha. *A Country Printer: The Autobiography of Elisha W. Warner.* Spanish Fork, UT: privately published, 1972.

Warner, Ted J., ed. *The Domínguez-Escalante Journal.* Salt Lake City: University of Utah Press, 1995.

Warnick, Jill Thorley. "Women Homesteaders in Utah, 1869–1934." Master's thesis, Brigham Young University, 1985.

Warrum, Noble. *Utah in the World War.* Salt Lake City: Utah State Council of Defense, 1924.

——. *Utah since Statehood: Historical and Biographical.* 3 vols. Chicago: S. J. Clarke, 1919.

Watt, Ronald G. *A History of Carbon County.* Salt Lake City: Utah State Historical Society and Carbon County Commission, 1997.

——. "National Youth Work Relief Programs, 1933 to 1966." Master's thesis, Utah State University, 1966.

Watts, A. C. "Opening First Commercial Coal Mine Described." In *Centennial Echoes from Carbon County*, edited by Thursey Jessen Reynolds. Price, UT: Daughters of the Utah Pioneers, 1948.

Webb, Roy. *Riverman: The Story of Bus Hatch.* Rock Springs, WY: Labyrinth, 1989.

——. "Les voyageurs sans trace: The DeColmont-DeSeyne Kayak Party of 1938." *Utah Historical Quarterly* 55 (Spring 1987): 167–80.

Welker, R. Todd. "Utah Schools and the Japanese American Student Relocation Program." *Utah Historical Quarterly* 70 (Winter 2002): 4–20.

Wells, Heber M. "Governor's Message, January 12, 1897." In *Journal of the House of Representatives: Second Session of the Legislature of the State of Utah.* Salt Lake City: Tribune Job Printing, 1897.

——. "Governor's Message, January 10, 1899." In *House Journal of the Third Session of the Legislature of the State of Utah.* Salt Lake City: Tribune Job Printing, 1899.

——. "Governor's Message, 1901." In *Senate Journal: Fourth Session of the Legislature of the State of Utah.* Salt Lake City: Star, 1901.

——. "Governor's Message, 1903." In *House Journal of the Fifth Session of the Legislature of the State of Utah.* Salt Lake City: Deseret News Press, 1903.

——. "Governor's Message, 1905." In *House Journal of the Sixth Session of the Legislature of the State of Utah.* Salt Lake City: Deseret News Press, 1905.

——. "Governor's Message, 1907." In *House Journal of the Seventh Session of the Legislature of the State of Utah.* Salt Lake City: Century, 1907.

——. *Message of the Governor of Utah to the Fourth Session of the State Legislature of Utah.* Salt Lake City: Deseret News Press, 1901.

Wells, Robert W., Jr. "A Political Biography of George Dern." Master's thesis, Brigham Young
    University, 1971.

Welsh, Stanley. "Utah Plant Types—Historical Perspective, 1840–1981—Annotated List, and
    Bibliography." *Great Basin Naturalist* 42 (June 1962): 129–95.

Wentworth, E. N. *America's Sheep Trails: History, Personalities.* Ames: Iowa State College Press,
    1948.

Westergren, Bruce N. "Utah's Gamble with Pari-mutuel Betting in the Early Twentieth Century."
    Utah Historical Quarterly 57 (Winter 1989): 4–23.

Westwood, Jean M. "Richard Dallin Westwood: Sheriff and Ferryman of Early Grand County."
    Utah Historical Quarterly 55 (Winter 1987): 66–86.

Westwood, Richard E. *Elwyn Blake's Colorado River Expeditions.* Reno: University of Nevada
    Press, 1992.

Wetherill, B. A. *The Wetherills of the Mesa Verde: Autobiography of Benjamin Alfred Wetherill.*
    Edited by Maurine S. Fletcher. Lincoln: University of Nebraska Press, 1987.

Whalen, Carmen Teresa. "Puerto Ricans." In *A Nation of Peoples: A Sourcebook on America's
    Multicultural Heritage,* edited by Elliott Robert Barkan, 446–63. Westport, CT: Greenwood
    Press, 1999.

What Is the "Mormon" Security Program? Independence, MO: Zion's Printing, n.d.

White, Jean Bickmore, ed. *Church, State, and Politics: The Diaries of John Henry Smith.* Salt Lake
    City: Signature Books, 1990.

———. "Gentle Persuaders: Utah's First Women Legislators." *Utah Historical Quarterly* 38
    (Winter 1970): 31–49.

———. "The Making of the Convention President: The Political Education of John Henry Smith."
    Utah Historical Quarterly 39 (Fall 1979): 350–69.

———. "Utah State Elections, 1895–1900." PhD diss., University of Utah, 1968.

White, Richard. *"It's Your Misfortune and None of My Own": A New History of the American West.*
    Norman: University of Oklahoma Press, 1991.

———. *The Roots of Dependency: Subsistence, Environment, and Social Change among the
    Choctaws, Pawnees, and Navajos.* Lincoln: University of Nebraska Press, 1983.

Whitney, Orson F. *History of Utah.* 4 vols. Salt Lake City: G. Q. Cannon, 1892.

Widtsoe, John A. *Dry-Farming: A System of Agriculture for Counties under a Low Rainfall.* New
    York: Macmillan, 1911.

———. "History and Problems of Irrigation Development in the West with Discussions
    Presented by Samuel Fortier, Arthur P. Davis, C. E. Grunsky, and F. H. Newell at Salt Lake
    City, 1925." Paper no. 1607. *Transactions of the American Society of Civil Engineers* (March
    1926).

———. *The Relation of Smelter Smoke to Utah Agriculture.* Utah State Agricultural College
    Experiment Station Bulletin no. 88. Logan: Utah State Agricultural College, 1903.

———. *Success on Irrigation Projects.* New York: John Wiley & Sons, 1928.

Wilkinson, Ernest L., and W. Cleon Skousen. *Brigham Young University: A School of Destiny.*
    Provo, UT: Brigham Young University Press, 1976.

Willie, Paul R. "History of Dairying in Cache Valley." In *Cache Valley: Essays on Her Past and
    People,* edited by Douglas D. Alder, 45–63. Logan: Utah State University Press, 1976.

Wilson, Pearl D. *A History of Juab County.* Salt Lake City: Utah State Historical Society and Juab
    County Commission, 1999.

Wolfinger, Henry. "An Irrepressible Conflict." *Dialogue: A Journal of Mormon Thought* 6
    (Autumn–Winter 1971): 124–32.

Wood, David L. "Gosiute-Shoshone Draft Resistance, 1917–18." *Utah Historical Quarterly* 49 (Spring 1981): 173–88.

Woodbury, Angus M. "A History of Southern Utah and Its National Parks." *Utah Historical Quarterly* 12 (July–October 1944): 111–222.

———. *A History of Southern Utah and Its National Parks.* Salt Lake City: Utah State Historical Society, 1950.

Woodward, C. Vann. *Reunion and Reaction: The Compromise of 1877 and the End of Reconstruction.* Boston: Little, Brown, 1951.

Woodward, T. E. *The Outlook of the Dairy Industry in Utah.* Utah State Farmers' Institute, 1907–8, no. 11. Logan: Utah Agricultural College, 1908.

Woolf, William L. *The Autobiography of William L. Woolf.* N.p.: privately published, 1979.

Woolsey, Nathella Griffin. *The Escalante Story, 1875–1964.* Springville, UT: Art City, 1964.

Worster, Donald. "The Kingdom, the Power, and the Water." In *Great Basin Kingdom Revisited: Contemporary Perspectives*, edited by T. G. Alexander, 21–38. Logan: Utah State University Press, 1991.

———. *Rivers of Empire: Water, Aridity, and the Growth of the American West.* New York: Pantheon Books, 1985.

Yang, John H., ed. *Asian Americans in Utah: A Living History.* Salt Lake City: Utah Office of Asian Affairs, 1999.

Yates, Sarah. "From Dust to Dust: A Russian Sojourn." *Beehive History* 25 (1999): 14–17.

Yorgason, Ethan R. *Transformation of the Mormon Culture Region.* Urbana: University of Illinois Press, 2003.

Young, Eugene. "Revival of the Mormon Problem." *North American Review* 168 (April 1899): 476–89.

Young, Karl E. "Sun Dance at Whiterocks, 1919." *Utah Historical Quarterly* 40 (Summer 1972): 233–41.

Young, Kimball L. "Utah Public Debt History." *Utah Historical Quarterly* 75 (Winter 2007): 2–13.

Young, Paul. *Back Trail of an Old Cowboy.* Edited by Nellie Snyder Yost. Lincoln: University of Nebraska Press, 1983.

Zink, Norah E. "Dry Farming Adjustments in Utah." PhD diss., University of Chicago, 1937.

INDEX